Jaguar &
12 Cylinder Owners Workshop Manual

Peter G Strasman

Models covered

Jaguar XJ12 and XJS, Daimler and Vanden Plas Double Six.
All Series 1, 2 and 3 models with 5343 cc V12 engines

Does not cover E type

ISBN 0 85696 478 6

ABCDE
FGHIJ
KLM

Printed in England

HAYNES PUBLISHING GROUP
SPARKFORD YEOVIL SOMERSET ENGLAND

distributed in the USA by

HAYNES PUBLICATIONS INC
861 LAWRENCE DRIVE
NEWBURY PARK
CALIFORNIA 91320
USA

Acknowledgements

Thanks are due to Jaguar Cars for the provision of technical information and for the use of certain illustrations. The Champion Sparking Plug Company supplied the illustrations showing the various spark plug conditions. The bodywork repair photographs used in this manual were provided by Holt Loyd Limited who supply 'Turtle Wax'. 'Dupli-Color Holts' and other Holts range products. Castrol Limited supplied the lubrication data.

Thanks are also due to all of those people at Sparkford who helped in the production of this manual, particularly Brian Horsfall and Tony Stedman who carried out the mechanical work and took the photographs respectively, Lee Saunders who planned the layout of each page and Matthew Minter who edited the text.

About this manual

Its aim

The aim of this manual is to help you get the best value from your car. It can do so in several ways. It can help you decide what work must be done (even should you choose to get it done by a garage), provide information on routine maintenance and servicing, and give a logical course of action and diagnosis when random faults occur. However, it is hoped that you will use the manual by tackling the work yourself. On simpler jobs it may even be quicker than booking the car into a garage and going there twice to leave and collect it. Perhaps most important, a lot of money can be saved by avoiding the costs the garage must charge to cover its labour and overheads.

The manual has drawings and descriptions to show the function of the various components so that their layout can be understood. Then the tasks are described and photographed in a step-by-step sequence so that even a novice can do the work.

Its arrangement

The manual is divided into twelve Chapters, each covering a logical sub-division of the vehicle. The Chapters are each divided into Sections, numbered with single figures, eg 5; and the Sections into paragraphs (or sub-sections), with decimal numbers following on from the Section they are in, eg 5.1, 5.2, 5.3 etc.

It is freely illustrated, especially in those parts where there is a detailed sequence of operations to be carried out. There are two forms of illustration: figures and photographs. The figures are numbered in sequence with decimal numbers, according to their position in the Chapter – eg Fig. 6.4 is the fourth drawing/illustration in Chapter 6. Photographs carry the same number (either individually or in related groups) as the Section or sub-section to which they relate.

There is an alphabetical index at the back of the manual as well as a contents list at the front. Each Chapter is also preceded by its own individual contents list.

References to the 'left' or 'right' of the vehicle are in the sense of a person in the driver's seat facing forwards.

Unless otherwise stated, nuts and bolts are removed by turning anti-clockwise, and tightened by turning clockwise.

Whilst every care is taken to ensure that the information in this manual is correct, no liability can be accepted by the authors or publishers for loss, damage or injury caused by any errors in, or omissions from the information given.

Introduction to the V12

Without a doubt, these cars are designed for the connoisseur and enthusiast, and the maintenance and repair of them will require rather more than a basic knowledge of 'do it yourself' techniques.

The cars are conventional in every respect but due to their sheer size, and high standard of specification, most operations will require more time to carry out than would be the case with a more moderately sized vehicle. The inclusion of automatic transmission and power steering as standard on all models (manual transmission option on XJS only) increases the complication of major overhaul.

On the credit side, the fact that many mechanical and body parts are common to the XJ6/Sovereign range increases the chances of obtaining good secondhand components.

These cars have a certain something which gives a pride of ownership rarely found in other makes. Provided maintenance and tuning are meticulously carried out, the vehicles will not exhibit temperamental behaviour or unreliability in operation but will provide exhilarating performance as economically as their engine capacity allows.

The following production dates will prove useful if contemplating a used model.

Jaguar XJ12

July 1972	Introduced, automatic transmission and power-assisted steering standard
October 1972	Long wheelbase four-door saloon available
September 1973	Series 2 long wheelbase saloon and new 2-door Coupe launched. Coupe has air conditioning as standard
April 1975	Fuel injection supersedes carburettor fuel system on all models
November 1977	Coupe discontinued
March 1979	Series 3 saloon introduced. GM400 automatic transmission supersedes Borg Warner type

Daimler Double Six

The production dates follow very closely those for the Jaguar XJ12 except that in September 1972, the Vanden Plas version was introduced.

Jaguar XJS

September 1975	Introduced with Coupe styling. Fuel injection, automatic transmission and air conditioning standard. Four-speed manual gearbox optionally available.
March 1979	GM400 automatic transmission supersedes Borg Warner type

Contents

Daimler Double Six Vanden Plas Series 2 saloon

Jaguar XJ12 Series 3 saloon

Jaguar XJ12 saloon – N. American specification

Jaguar XJS Coupé

General dimensions, weights and capacities

Overall dimensions

Jaguar XJ12/Daimler Double Six (excluding N America)

4-door models (Series 1 and 2)

Length	194.7 in (494.5 cm)
Width	69.7 in (177.0 cm)
Height	54.1 in (137.4 cm)
Wheelbase	113.1 in (287.3 cm)
Track (front)	58.0 in (147.3 cm)
Track (rear)	58.6 in (148.8 cm)
Ground clearance	7.0 in (17.8 cm)

4-door models (Series 3)

Length	195.3 in (496.1 cm)
Width	69.7 in (177.0 cm)
Height	54.1 in (137.4 cm)
Wheelbase	112.8 in (286.5 cm)
Track (front)	58.3 in (148.0 cm)
Track (rear)	58.9 in (149.6 cm)
Ground clearance	7.0 in (17.8 cm)

2-door models (1973 to 1977)

Length	190.7 in (484.4 cm)
Width	69.7 in (177.0 cm)
Height	54.1 in (137.4 cm)
Wheelbase	109.1 in (277.1 cm)
Track (front)	58.0 in (147. 3 cm)
Track (rear)	58.6 in (148.8 cm)
Ground clearance	7.0 in (17.8 cm)

Jaguar XJ12 (N America)

4-door models (1972)

Length	189.5 in (481.3 cm)
Width	69.7 in (177.0 cm)
Height	56.8 in (144.3 cm)
Wheelbase	108.8 in (276.4 cm)
Track (front)	58.0 in (147.3 cm)
Track (rear)	58.3 in (148.0 cm)
Ground clearance	6.0 in (15.2 cm)

4-door models (1973 to 1978)

Length	194.7 in (494.5 cm)
Width	69.7 in (177.0 cm)
Height	54.1 in (137.4 cm)
Wheelbase	112.8 in (286.5 cm)
Track (front)	58.0 in (147.3 cm)
Track (rear)	58.6 in (148.8 cm)
Ground clearance	6.0 in (15.2 cm)

4-door models (1979 on)

Length	200.5 in (509.3 cm)
Width	69.7 in (177.0 cm)
Height	54.1 in (137.4 cm)
Wheelbase	112.8 in (286.5 cm)
Track (front)	58.0 in (147.3 cm)
Track (rear)	58.6 in (148.8 cm)
Ground clearance	6.0 in (15.2 cm)

2-door models (1973 to 1977)

Length	195.0 in (495.3 cm)
Width	69.7 in (177.0 cm)
Height	54.1 in (137.4 cm)
Wheelbase	108.8 in (276.4 cm)
Track (front)	58.0 in (147.3 cm)
Track (rear)	58.6 in (148.8 cm)
Ground clearance	6.0 in (15.2 cm)

Jaguar XJS
1975 to 1978

Length	190.5 in (483.9 cm)
Width	70.6 in (179.3 cm)
Height	49.0 in (124.5 cm)
Wheelbase	102.0 in (259.1 cm)
Track (front)	58.0 in (147.3 cm)
Track (rear)	58.6 in (148.8 cm)
Ground clearance	5.5 in (14.0 cm)

1978 on
As for earlier models except:

Length (except N America)	191.7 in (486.9 cm)
Length (N America)	192.3 in (488.4 cm)
Height	49.6 in (126.0 cm)

Kerb weights (approx) (Fuel tanks full, car equipped with automatic transmission and air conditioning)

Jaguar XJ12/Daimler Double Six
4-door models

1972 (excluding N America)	3947 lb (1791 kg)
1972 (N America)	4000 lb (1816 kg)
1973 to 1978 (excluding N America)	4123 lb (1872 kg)
1973 to 1978 (N America)	4179 lb (1897 kg)
1979 on (excluding N America)	4246 lb (1928 kg)
1979 on (N America)	4300 lb (1952 kg)

2-door models

1973 to 1975 (excluding N America)	4045 lb (1836 kg)
1976 to 1977 (excluding N America)	4100 lb (1861 kg)
N America (all models) and others 1978 on	4270 lb (1939 kg)

*Jaguar XJS**

All except N America	3795 lb (1723 kg)
N America (1975 to 1977)	4085 lb (1855 kg)
N America (1978 on)	4656 lb (2114 kg)

**For versions with manual transmission, deduct 106 lb (48 kg) from the kerb weights shown*

Capacities

	Imp	US	Metric
Engine oil (including filter change)			
XJ12, Double Six:			
Series 1	16 pints	19.2 pints	9.1 litres
Series 2 on	19 pints	23.0 pints	10.7 litres
XJS	20 pints	24.0 pints	11.4 litres
Cooling systems (all models)	37 pints	44.4 pints	21.0 litres
Fuel			
XJ12, Double Six (carburettor models):			
Except N America (each tank)	12 gals	–	54.6 litres
N America (each tank)	10 gals	12 gals	45.5 litres
XJ12, Double Six (fuel injection models, each tank)	10.5 gals	12.6 gals	47.75 litres
XJS	20 gals	24.0 gals	90.0 litres
Transmission			
Manual transmission (XJS)	3.0 pints	3.6 pints	1.7 litres
Type 12 automatic transmission:			
Service drain and refill	11 pints	13.2 pints	6.3 litres
Refill from dry	16 pints	19.2 pints	9.1 litres
GM400 automatic transmission:			
Service drain and refill	16.5 pints	19.8 pints	9.4 litres
Refill from dry	22.5 pints	27.0 pints	12.75 litres
Final drive (all models)	2.75 pints	3.3 pints	1.6 litres

Use of English

As this book has been written in England, it uses the appropriate English component names, phrases, and spelling. Some of these differ from those used in America. Normally, these cause no difficulty, but to make sure, a glossary is printed below. In ordering spare parts remember the parts list will probably use these words:

English	American	English	American
Aerial	Antenna	Layshaft (of gearbox)	Countershaft
Accelerator	Gas pedal	Leading shoe (of brake)	Primary shoe
Alternator	Generator (AC)	Locks	Latches
Anti-roll bar	Stabiliser or sway bar	Motorway	Freeway, turnpike etc
Battery	Energizer	Number plate	License plate
Bodywork	Sheet metal	Paraffin	Kerosene
Bonnet (engine cover)	Hood	Petrol	Gasoline
Boot lid	Trunk lid	Petrol tank	Gas tank
Boot (luggage compartment)	Trunk	'Pinking'	'Pinging'
Bottom gear	1st gear	Propeller shaft	Driveshaft
Bulkhead	Firewall	Quarter light	Quarter window
Cam follower or tappet	Valve lifter or tappet	Retread	Recap
Carburettor	Carburetor	Reverse	Back-up
Catch	Latch	Rocker cover	Valve cover
Choke/venturi	Barrel	Roof rack	Car-top carrier
Circlip	Snap-ring	Saloon	Sedan
Clearance	Lash	Seized	Frozen
Crownwheel	Ring gear (of differential)	Side indicator lights	Side marker lights
Disc (brake)	Rotor/disk	Side light	Parking light
Drop arm	Pitman arm	Silencer	Muffler
Drop head coupe	Convertible	Spanner	Wrench
Dynamo	Generator (DC)	Sill panel (beneath doors)	Rocker panel
Earth (electrical)	Ground	Split cotter (for valve spring cap)	Lock (for valve spring retainer)
Engineer's blue	Prussian blue	Split pin	Cotter pin
Estate car	Station wagon	Steering arm	Spindle arm
Exhaust manifold	Header	Sump	Oil pan
Fast back (Coupe)	Hard top	Tab washer	Tang; lock
Fault finding/diagnosis	Trouble shooting	Tailgate	Liftgate
Float chamber	Float bowl	Tappet	Valve lifter
Free-play	Lash	Thrust bearing	Throw-out bearing
Freewheel	Coast	Top gear	High
Gudgeon pin	Piston pin or wrist pin	Trackrod (of steering)	Tie-rod (or connecting rod)
Gearchange	Shift	Trailing shoe (of brake)	Secondary shoe
Gearbox	Transmission	Transmission	Whole drive line
Halfshaft	Axleshaft	Tyre	Tire
Handbrake	Parking brake	Van	Panel wagon/van
Hood	Soft top	Vice	Vise
Hot spot	Heat riser	Wheel nut	Lug nut
Indicator	Turn signal	Windscreen	Windshield
Interior light	Dome lamp	Wing/mudguard	Fender

Miscellaneous points

An 'oil seal' is fitted to components lubricated by grease!

A 'damper' is a 'shock absorber', it damps out bouncing, and absorbs shocks of bump impact. Both names are correct, and both are used haphazardly.

Note that British drum brakes are different from the Bendix type that is common in America, so different descriptive names result. The shoe end furthest from the hydraulic wheel cylinder is on a pivot; interconnection between the shoes as on Bendix brakes is most uncommon. Therefore the phrase 'Primary' or 'Secondary' shoe does not apply. A shoe is said to be 'Leading' or 'Trailing'. A 'Leading' shoe is one on which a point on the drum, as it rotates forward, reaches the shoe at the end worked by the hydraulic cylinder before the anchor end. The opposite is a 'Trailing' shoe, and this one has no self servo from the wrapping effect of the rotating drum.

Buying spare parts and vehicle identification numbers

Buying spare parts

Spare parts are available from many sources, for example: BL garages, other garages and accessory shops, and motor factors. Our advice regarding spare parts is as follows:

Officially appointed BL garages – This is the best source of parts which are peculiar to your car and otherwise not generally available (eg complete cylinder heads, internal gearbox components, badges, interior trim etc). It is also the only place at which you should buy parts if your car is still under warranty; non-BL components may invalidate the warranty. To be sure of obtaining the correct parts it will always be necessary to give the storeman your car's engine and chassis number, and if possible, to take the old part along for positive identification. Remember that many parts are available on a factory exchange scheme – any parts returned should always be clean! It obviously makes good sense to go to the specialists on your car for this type of part for they are best equipped to supply you.

Other garages and accessory shops – These are often very good places to buy material and components needed for the maintenance of your car (eg oil filters, spark plugs, bulbs, fan belts, oils and grease, touch-up paint, filler paste etc). They also sell general accessories, usually have convenient opening hours, charge lower prices and can often be found not far from home.

Motor factors – Good factors will stock all of the more important components which wear out relatively quickly (eg clutch components, pistons, valves, exhaust systems, brake cylinders/pipes/hoses/seals/shoes and pads etc). Motor factors will often provide new or reconditioned components on a part exchange basis – this can save a considerable amount of money.

Vehicle identification numbers

When buying spare parts, always quote the car model, chassis or engine number, as necessary, to the partsman. This will ensure that the correctly fitting item is supplied for your particular car.

The chassis number is stamped on the right-hand tie-bar bracket on top of the wing valance and is repeated on the plate within the engine compartment. On XJS models, a suffix BW to the chassis number indicates automatic transmission. After 1979 this suffix is changed to GM.

The engine number is stamped on the rear of the cylinder block (photo) and on the commission plate within the engine compartment. Suffix L to engine number indicates low compression. Suffix S to engine number indicates standard compression.

The gearbox number is stamped on a label attached to the left-hand side of the gearbox and on the commission plate.

North American vehicles bear additional identification as described below.

Federal Safety Standard Plate. Attached to the driver's door pillar, this plate contains the date of manufacture and the vehicle identification number.

Tyre recommendation plate. Attached to the glovebox lid beneath the vanity mirror, it shows weight, seating capacity, seating distribution, specified tyre pressures and specified tyre size.

Timing label. Fitted under the bonnet lid, this gives basic adjustment data such as spark plug gaps and ignition timing.

Unleaded fuel label. Located on the dash panel, this warns against the use of any other type of fuel.

Location of engine number

Tools and working facilities

Introduction

A selection of good tools is a fundamental requirement for anyone contemplating the maintenance and repair of a motor vehicle. For the owner who does not possess any, their purchase will prove a considerable expense, offsetting some of the savings made by doing-it-yourself. However, provided that the tools purchased are of good quality, they will last for many years and prove an extremely worthwhile investment.

To help the average owner to decide which tools are needed to carry out the various tasks detailed in this manual, we have compiled three lists of tools under the following headings: *Maintenance and minor repair, Repair and overhaul,* and *Special.* The newcomer to practical mechanics should start off with the *Maintenance and minor repair* tool kit and confine himself to the simpler jobs around the vehicle. Then, as his confidence and experience grow, he can undertake more difficult tasks, buying extra tools as, and when, they are needed. In this way, a *Maintenance and minor repair* tool kit can be built-up into a *Repair and overhaul* tool kit over a considerable period of time without any major cash outlays. The experienced do-it-yourselfer will have a tool kit good enough for most repair and overhaul procedures and will add tools from the *Special* category when he feels the expense is justified by the amount of use these tools will be put to.

It is obviously not possible to cover the subject of tools fully here. For those who wish to learn more about tools and their use there is a book entitled *How to Choose and Use Car Tools* available from the publishers of this manual.

Threads

The majority of bolts and nuts used in the cars covered by this manual are to UNF standards. A few metric sizes may be encountered however on certain proprietary components.

Partial metrication of the brake hydraulic system has been carried out and in the interest of safety reference should be made to Chapter 9, Section 2 for location and thread compatability of hydraulic components.

Hydraulic fittings on the power-assisted steering circuit are to UNF standards.

Maintenance and minor repair tool kit

The tools given in this list should be considered as a minimum requirement if routine maintenance, servicing and minor repair operations are to be undertaken. We recommend the purchase of combination spanners (ring one end, open-ended the other); although more expensive than open-ended ones, they do give the advantages of both types of spanner.

Combination spanners to cover the range $\frac{7}{16}$ in to 1 in AF
Adjustable wrench - 9 inch
Spark plug spanner (with rubber insert)
Spark plug gap adjustment tool
Set of feeler gauges
Brake bleed nipple spanner
Screwdriver - 4 in long x $\frac{1}{4}$ in dia (flat blade)
Screwdriver - 4 in long x $\frac{1}{4}$ in dia (cross blade)
Combination pliers - 6 inch
Hacksaw, (junior)
Tyre pump
Tyre pressure gauge
Grease gun
Oil can
Fine emery cloth (1 sheet)
Wire brush (small)
Funnel (medium size)

Repair and overhaul tool kit

These tools are virtually essential for anyone undertaking any major repairs to a motor vehicle, and are additional to those given in the *Maintenance and minor repair* list. Included in this list is a comprehensive set of sockets. Although these are expensive they will be found invaluable as they are so versatile - particularly if various drives are included in the set. We recommend the $\frac{1}{2}$ in square-drive type, as this can be used with most proprietary torque wrenches. If you cannot afford a socket set, even bought piecemeal, then inexpensive tubular box spanners are a useful alternative.

The tools in this list will occasionally need to be supplemented by tools from the *Special* list.

Care and maintenance of tools

Having purchased a reasonable tool kit, it is necessary to keep the tools in a clean serviceable condition. After use, always wipe off any dirt, grease and metal particles using a clean, dry cloth, before putting the tools away. Never leave them lying around after they have been used. A simple tool rack on the garage or workshop wall, for items such as screwdrivers and pliers is a good idea. Store all normal spanners and sockets in a metal box. Any measuring instruments, gauges, meters, etc, must be carefully stored where they cannot be damaged or become rusty.

Take a little care when tools are used. Hammer heads inevitably become marked and screwdrivers lose the keen edge on their blades from time to time. A little timely attention with emery cloth or a file will soon restore items like this to a good serviceable finish.

Working facilities

Not to be forgotten when discussing tools, is the workshop itself. If anything more than routine maintenance is to be carried out, some form of suitable working area becomes essential.

It is appreciated that many an owner mechanic is forced by circumstances to remove an engine or similar item, without the benefit of a garage or workshop. Having done this, any repairs should always be done under the cover of a roof.

Wherever possible, any dismantling should be done on a clean flat workbench or table at a suitable working height.

Any workbench needs a vice: one with a jaw opening of 4 in (100 mm) is suitable for most jobs. As mentioned previously, some clean dry storage space is also required for tools, as well as for lubricants, cleaning fluids, touch-up paints and so on which become necessary.

Another item which may be required, and which has a much more general usage, is an electric drill with a chuck capacity of at least $\frac{5}{16}$ in (8 mm). This, together with a good range of twist drills, is virtually essential for fitting accessories such as wing mirrors and reversing lights.

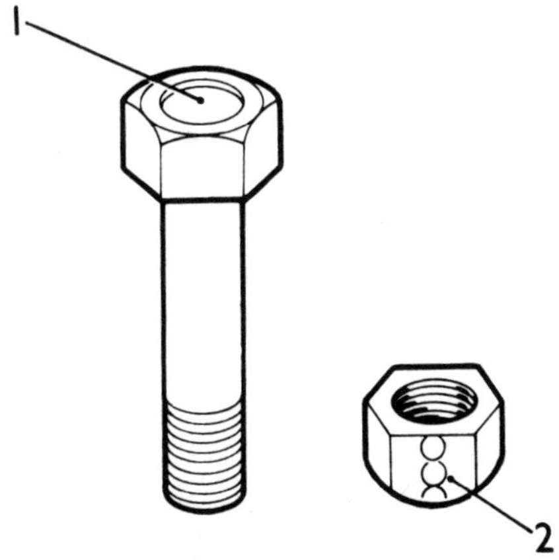

UNF bolt and nut identification

1 Recess in bolt head
2 Circles stamped onto flat of nut

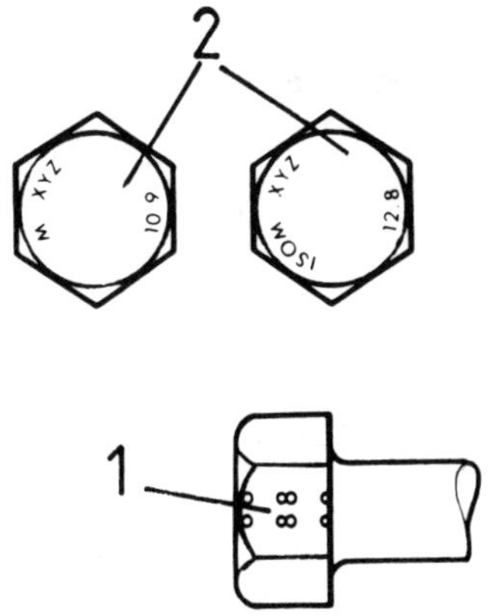

Metric bolt identification

1 Strength grade on flat of bolt head
2 Alternative markings on top of bolt head

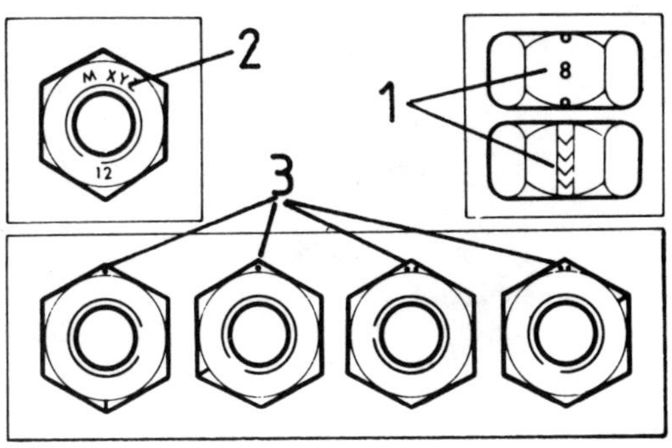

Metric nut identification

1 Strength grade on flat of nut
2 Top face marking with strength indicated numerically
3 Top face marking with dots (clock face system) used to indicate strength

Last, but not least, always keep a supply of old newspapers and clean, lint-free rags available, and try to keep any working area as clean as possible.

Sockets (or box spanners) to cover range in previous list
Reversible ratchet drive (for use with sockets)
Extension piece, 10 inch (for use with sockets)
Universal joint (for use with sockets)
Torque wrench (for use with sockets)
'Mole' wrench - 8 inch
Ball pein hammer
Soft-faced hammer, plastic or rubber
Screwdriver - 6 in long x $\frac{5}{16}$ in dia (flat blade)
Screwdriver - 2 in long x $\frac{5}{16}$ in square (flat blade)
Screwdriver - $1\frac{1}{2}$ in long x $\frac{1}{4}$ in dia (cross blade)
Screwdriver - 3 in long x $\frac{1}{8}$ in dia (electricians)
Pliers - electricians side cutters
Pliers - needle nosed
Pliers - circlip (internal and external)
Cold chisel - $\frac{1}{2}$ inch
Scriber
Scraper
Centre punch
Pin punch
Hacksaw
Valve grinding tool
Steel rule/straight edge
Allen keys
Selection of files
Wire brush (large)
Axle-stands
Jack (strong scissor or hydraulic type)

Special tools

The tools in this list are those which are not used regularly, are expensive to buy, or which need to be used in accordance with their manufacturers' instructions. Unless relatively difficult mechanical jobs are undertaken frequently, it will not be economic to buy many of these tools. Where this is the case, you could consider clubbing together with friends (or a motorists' club) to make a joint purchase, or borrowing the tools against a deposit from a local garage or tool hire specialist.

The following list contains only those tools and instruments freely available to the public, and not those special tools produced by the vehicle manufacturer specifically for its dealer network. You will find occasional references to these manufacturers' special tools in the text of this manual. Generally, an alternative method of doing the job without the vehicle manufacturers' special tool is given. However, sometimes, there is no alternative to using them. Where this is the case and the relevant tool cannot be bought or borrowed you will have to entrust the work to a franchised garage.

Valve spring compressor
Piston ring compressor
Balljoint separator
Universal hub/bearing puller
Impact screwdriver
Micrometer and/or vernier gauge
Dial gauge
Stroboscopic timing light
Dwell angle meter/tachometer
Universal electrical multi-meter
Cylinder compression gauge
Lifting tackle (photo)
Trolley jack
Light with extension lead

Buying tools

For practically all tools, a tool factor is the best source since he will have a very comprehensive range compared with the average garage or accessory shop. Having said that, accessory shops often offer excellent quality tools at discount prices, so it pays to shop around.

Remember, you don't have to buy the most expensive items on the

A Haltrac hoist and gantry in use during a typical engine removal sequence

shelf, but it is always advisable to steer clear of the very cheap tools. There are plenty of good tools around at reasonable prices, so ask the proprietor or manager of the shop for advice before making a purchase.

Spanner jaw gap comparison table

Jaw gap (in)	Spanner size
0.250	$\frac{1}{4}$ in AF
0.275	7 mm
0.313	$\frac{5}{16}$ in AF
0.315	8 mm
0.344	$\frac{11}{32}$ in AF; $\frac{1}{8}$ in Whitworth
0.354	9 mm
0.375	$\frac{3}{8}$ in AF
0.394	10 mm
0.433	11 mm
0.438	$\frac{7}{16}$ in AF
0.445	$\frac{3}{16}$ in Whitworth; $\frac{1}{4}$ in BSF
0.472	12 mm
0.500	$\frac{1}{2}$ in AF
0.512	13 mm
0.525	$\frac{1}{4}$ in Whitworth; $\frac{5}{16}$ in BSF
0.551	14 mm
0.562	$\frac{9}{16}$ in AF
0.590	15 mm
0.600	$\frac{5}{16}$ in Whitworth; $\frac{3}{8}$ in BSF
0.625	$\frac{5}{8}$ in AF
0.629	16 mm
0.669	17 mm
0.687	$\frac{11}{16}$ in AF
0.708	18 mm
0.710	$\frac{3}{8}$ in Whitworth, $\frac{7}{16}$ in BSF
0.748	19 mm
0.750	$\frac{3}{4}$ in AF
0.812	$\frac{13}{16}$ in AF
0.820	$\frac{7}{16}$ in Whitworth; $\frac{1}{2}$ in BSF
0.866	22 mm
0.875	$\frac{7}{8}$ in AF
0.920	$\frac{1}{2}$ in Whitworth; $\frac{9}{16}$ in BSF
0.937	$\frac{15}{16}$ in AF
0.944	24 mm
1.000	1 in AF
1.010	$\frac{9}{16}$ in Whitworth; $\frac{5}{8}$ in BSF
1.023	26 mm
1.062	$1\frac{1}{16}$ in AF, 27 mm
1.100	$\frac{5}{8}$ in Whitworth; $\frac{11}{16}$ in BSF
1.125	$1\frac{1}{8}$ in AF
1.181	30 mm
1.200	$\frac{11}{16}$ in Whitworth; $\frac{3}{4}$ in BSF
1.250	$1\frac{1}{4}$ in AF
1.259	32 mm
1.300	$\frac{3}{4}$ in Whitworth; $\frac{7}{8}$ in BSF
1.312	$1\frac{5}{16}$ in AF
1.390	$\frac{13}{16}$ in Whitworth; $\frac{15}{16}$ in BSF
1.417	36 mm
1.437	$1\frac{7}{16}$ in AF
1.480	$\frac{7}{8}$ in Whitworth; 1 in BSF
1.500	$1\frac{1}{2}$ in AF
1.574	40 mm; $\frac{15}{16}$ in Whitworth
1.614	41 mm
1.625	$1\frac{5}{8}$ in AF
1.670	1 in Whitworth; $1\frac{1}{8}$ in BSF
1.687	$1\frac{11}{16}$ in AF
1.811	46 mm
1.812	163 in AF
1.860	$1\frac{1}{8}$ in Whitworth; $1\frac{1}{4}$ in BSF
1.875	$1\frac{7}{8}$ in AF
1.968	50 mm
2.000	2 in AF
2.050	$1\frac{1}{4}$ in Whitworth; $1\frac{3}{8}$ in BSF
2.165	55 mm
2.362	60 mm

Jacking and towing

Jacking

Use the jack supplied with the car only for wheel changing during roadside emergencies. The jack engages with spigots situated below the body side members.

To remove a roadwheel, release the wheel nuts but do not remove them before raising the car. Fully tighten the wheel nuts after the car has been lowered to the ground.

For under-car repair or maintenance, use a hydraulic or screw jack, preferably of the trolley type. Place the jack as indicated in the following paragraphs and always supplement it with axle stands before working under the car.

To raise one front wheel, place the jack under the spring lower support pan.

To raise one rear wheel place the jack under the outer fork of the suspension wishbone. Avoid damage to the alloy hub carrier and grease nipple.

To raise both front wheels, position the jack centrally under the front suspension crossmember. Use a block of wood as an insulator on the jack head.

To raise both rear wheels, position the jack under the tie plate immediately below the differential unit. Cut a piece of wood to shape as shown and use it as an insulator to avoid the head of the jack applying pressure to the lips of the tie plate.

Towing

The car may be towed by means of the two hooks located under the front bumper. The two hooks at the rear of the car are for lashing down the vehicle during transportation and must *not* be used to tow another vehicle.

As is usual with all vehicles equipped with automatic transmission, special precautions must be observed when being towed. Add 3.6 pints (2 litres) of extra automatic transmission fluid and position the speed selector lever in 'N'. Do not tow the car for more than 30 miles (48 km) and restrict the speed to 30 mph (48 kph).

On all models, when being towed, make sure that the ignition key is in the ACC position so that the steering column will be unlocked.

With automatic transmission vehicles, remember to reduce the fluid level again before resuming normal operation. As a drain plug is not fitted, the oil pan will have to be unbolted and lowered or the union nut at the base of the fluid filler/dipstick guide tube released and sufficient fluid allowed to drain out.

Wheel changing jack

Spare wheel and anchor bolt

Front towing hook

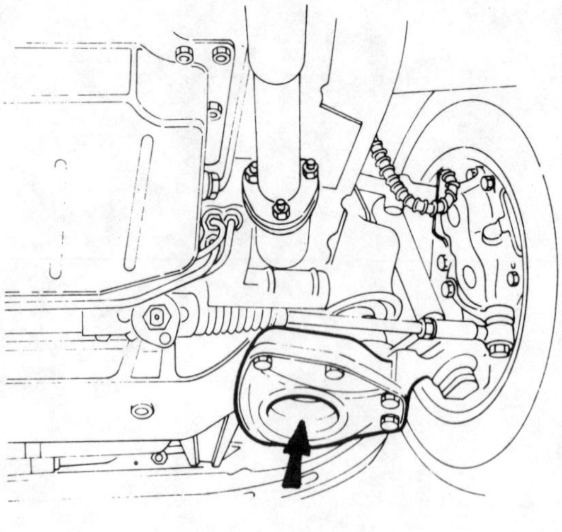

Front wheel jacking point

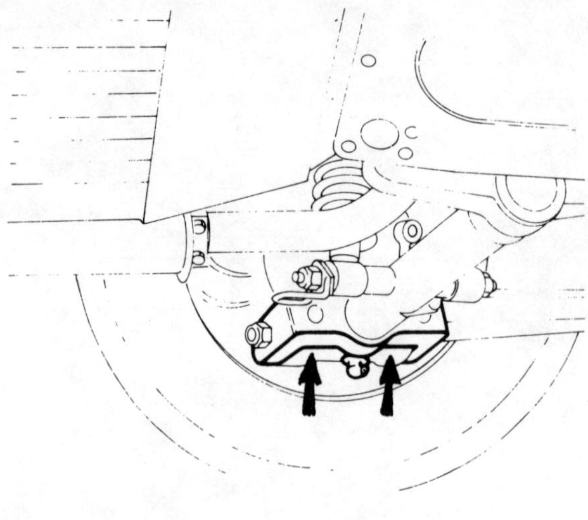

Rear wheel jacking point

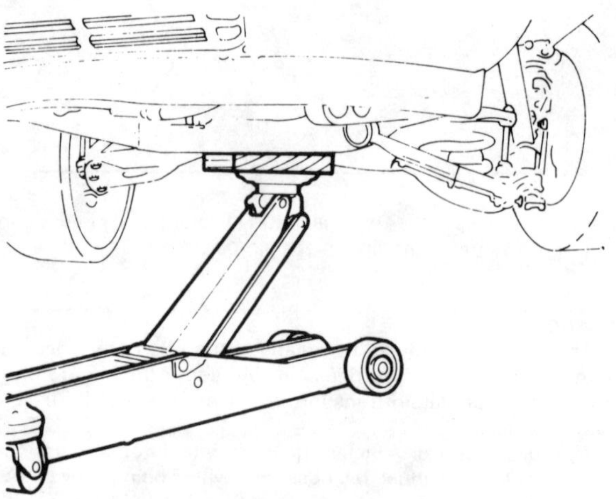

Front end (both wheels) jacking point

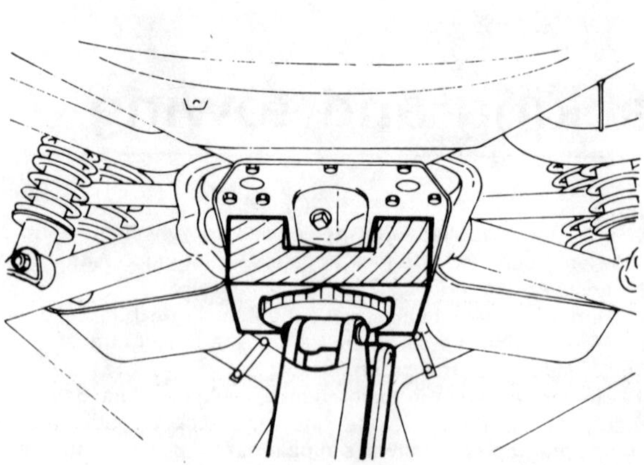

Rear end (both wheels) jacking point – note shaped block of wood

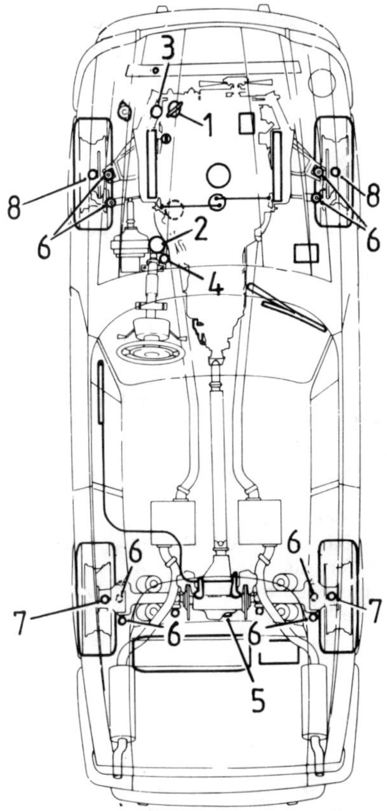

XJS (left-hand drive shown, right-hand similar)

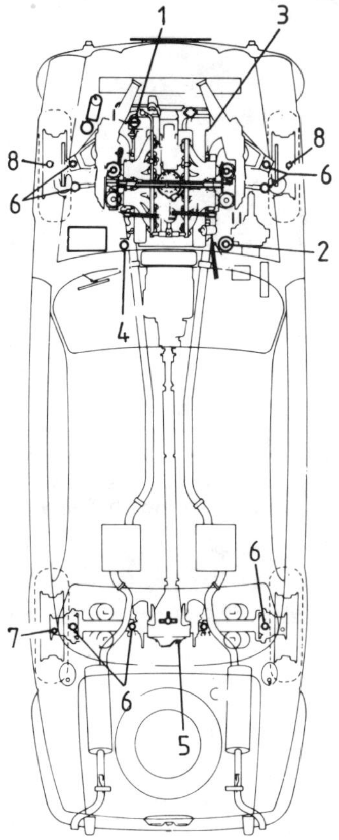

XJ12 and Double Six (right-hand drive shown, left-hand similar)

Recommended lubricants and fluids

Component or system	Lubricants type or specification	Castrol product
1 Engine	Mutligrade engine oil to MIL-L-2104B, API SE or BLS OL 02, viscosity depending on temperature	Castrol GTX
2 Brake hydraulic system	Hydraulic fluid to SAE J1703E	Castrol Girling Universal Brake and Clutch Fluid
3 Power-assisted steering	Automatic transmission fluid (same type as used in transmission)	Castrol TQF or Dexron II
4 Automatic transmission (Borg Warner Type 12)	Automatic transmission fluid type F to M2C 35F	Castrol TQF
4 Automatic transmission (GM400)	Automatic transmission fluid type Dexron 2D	Castrol TQ Dexron II
Manual gearbox (XJS)	EP90 hypoid gear oil to MIL-L-2105B	Castrol Hypoy
5 Final drive	EP90 (top up only) Special limited slip differential oil for refill	Castrol Hypoy Castrol Hypoy LS
6 Grease nipples	Multi-purpose lithium based grease to NLG1-2	Castrol LM grease
7 Rear hubs	Multi-purpose grease	Castrol LM grease
8 Front hubs	Multi-purpose grease	Castrol LM grease
Cooling system	Ethylene glycol antifreeze	Castrol Anti-freeze

Safety first!

Professional motor mechanics are trained in safe working procedures. However enthusiastic you may be about getting on with the job in hand, do take the time to ensure that your safety is not put at risk. A moment's lack of attention can result in an accident, as can failure to observe certain elementary precautions.

There will always be new ways of having accidents, and the following points do not pretend to be a comprehensive list of all dangers; they are intended rather to make you aware of the risks and to encourage a safety-conscious approach to all work you carry out on your vehicle.

Essential DOs and DON'Ts

DON'T start the engine without first ascertaining that the transmission is in neutral.
DON'T suddenly remove the filler cap from a hot cooling system – cover it with a cloth and release the pressure gradually first, or you may get scalded by escaping coolant.
DON'T attempt to drain oil until you are sure it has cooled sufficiently to avoid scalding you.
DON'T grasp any part of the engine, exhaust or silencer without first ascertaining that it is sufficiently cool to avoid burning you.
DON'T syphon toxic liquids such as fuel, brake fluid or antifreeze by mouth, or allow them to remain on your skin.
DON'T inhale brake lining dust – it is injurious to health.
DON'T allow any spilt oil or grease to remain on the floor – wipe it up straight away, before someone slips on it.
DON'T use ill-fitting spanners or other tools which may slip and cause injury.
DON'T attempt to lift a heavy component which may be beyond your capability – get assistance.
DON'T rush to finish a job, or take unverified short cuts.
DON'T allow children or animals in or around an unattended vehicle.
DON'T inflate a tyre to a pressure above the recommended maximum. Apart from overstressing the carcase and wheel rim, in extreme cases the tyre may blow off forcibly.
DO ensure that the machine is supported securely at all times. This is especially important when the machine is blocked up to aid wheel or fork removal.
DO take care when attempting to slacken a stubborn nut or bolt. It is generally better to pull on a spanner, rather than push, so that if slippage occurs you fall away from the machine rather than on to it.
DO wear eye protection when using power tools such as drill, sander, bench grinder etc.
DO use a barrier cream on your hands prior to undertaking dirty jobs – it will protect your skin from infection as well as making the dirt easier to remove afterwards. Before starting the job ensure that the cream has dried and your hands are not slippery.
DO keep loose clothing (cuffs, tie etc) and long hair well out of the way of moving mechanical parts, and always remove your watch and any rings before starting work.
DO work tidily, keeping the floor space uncluttered by removed components and tools; there is less likelihood of tripping over if this approach is adopted.
DO exercise caution when compressing springs for removal or installation. Ensure that the tension is applied and released in a controlled manner, using suitable tools which preclude the possibility of the spring escaping violently.
DO ensure that any lifting tackle used has a safe working load rating adequate for the job.
DO get someone to check periodically that all is well, when working alone on the vehicle.
DO carry out work in a logical sequence and check that everything is correctly assembled and tighten afterwards.
DO remember that your vehicle's safety affects that of yourself and others. If in doubt on any point, get specialist advice.

IF, in spite of following these precautions, you are unfortunate enough to injure yourself, seek medical attention as soon as possible.

Fire

Remember at all times that petrol (gasoline) is highly flammable. Never smoke, or have any kind of naked flame around, when working on the vehicle. But the risk does not end there – a spark caused by an electrical short-circuit, by two metal surfaces contacting each other, or even by static electricity built up in your body under certain conditions, can ignite petrol vapour, which in a confined space is highly explosive.

Always disconnect the battery earth (ground) terminal before working on any part of the fuel system, and never risk spilling fuel on to a hot engine or exhaust.

It is recommended that a fire extinguisher of a type suitable for fuel and electrical fires is kept handy in the garage or workplace at all times. Never try to extinguish a fuel or electrical fire with water.

Fumes

Certain fumes are highly toxic and can quickly cause unconsciousness and even death if inhaled to any extent. Petrol (gasoline) vapour comes into this category, as do the vapours from certain solvents such as trichlorethylene. Any draining or pouring of such volatile fluids should be done in a well ventilated area.

When using cleaning fluids and solvents, read the instructions carefully. Never use materials from unmarked containers – they may give off poisonous vapours.

Never run the engine of a motor vehicle in an enclosed space such as a garage. Exhaust fumes contain carbon monoxide which is extremely poisonous; if you need to run the engine, always do so in the open air or at least have the rear of the vehicle outside the workplace.

If you are fortunate enough to have the use of an inspection pit, never drain or pour petrol over it; the fumes, being heavier than air, will concentrate in the pit with possibly lethal results.

The battery

Never cause a spark, or allow a naked light, near the vehicle's battery. It will normally be giving off a certain amount of hydrogen gas, which is highly explosive.

Always disconnect the battery earth (ground) terminal before working on the fuel or electrical systems.

If possible, loosen the filler plugs or cover when charging the battery from an external source. Do not charge at an excessive rate or the battery may burst.

Take care when topping up and when carrying the battery. The acid electrolyte, even when diluted, is very corrosive and should not be allowed to contact the eyes or skin.

If you ever need to prepare electrolyte yourself, always add the acid slowly to the water, and never the other way round. Protect against splashes by wearing rubber gloves and goggles.

Mains electricity

When using an electric power tool, inspection light etc which works from the mains, always ensure that the appliance is correctly connected to its plug and that, where necessary, it is properly earthed (grounded). Do not use such appliances in damp conditions and, again, beware of creating a spark or applying excessive heat in the vicinity of fuel or fuel vapour.

Ignition HT voltage

A severe electric shock can result from touching certain parts of the ignition system, such as the HT leads, when the engine is running or being cranked, paticularly if components are damp or the insulation is defective. Where an electronic ignition system is fitted, the HT voltage is much higher and could prove fatal.

Routine maintenance

Maintenance is essential for ensuring safety and desirable for the purpose of getting the best in terms of performance and economy from the car. Over the years the need for periodic lubrication – oiling, greasing and so on – has been drastically reduced if not totally eliminated. This has unfortunately tended to lead some owners to think that because no such action is required the items either no longer exist or will last for ever. This is a serious delusion. It follows therefore that the largest initial element of maintenance is visual examination. This may lead to repairs or renewals.

Special note

Spark plug leads, fuel injector leads and certain other components will have identification sleeves fitted to them. The letter and number shown will conform to the following arrangement:

A – right-hand cylinder bank.

B – left-hand cylinder bank.

No 1 cylinder is nearest the crankshaft pulley/damper end of the engine; left and right-hand are as viewed from the driver's seat.

The identity sleeves may become discoloured or obliterated over a period of time. If confusion is to be avoided when disconnecting electrical leads, also vacuum, coolant or fuel pipes, always mark the ends before disconnection. The simplest way to do this is to use a piece of masking tape on each end with matching numbers or letters written on the tape with a ballpoint pen.

Every 250 miles (400 km) or weekly, whichever comes first

Brakes

Check reservoir fluid level

Check foot and handbrake movement for increased travel or falling off in efficiency

Engine

Check oil level and top up if necessary (photos)

Check coolant level

Check battery electrolyte level

Lights

Check for operation

Clean lenses

Steering

Check tyres for pressure and wear characteristics

General

Clean windscreen

Top up washer reservoir

Every 3000 miles (4800 km) or three months, whichever comes first

Engine

Check security of all hoses

Check fuel system for leaks

Check exhaust system for corrosion or leaks

Steering

Check power steering fluid level and top up if necessary (photos)

Transmission

Check oil level in final drive unit

Check fluid level in automatic transmission (photo) or oil level in manual gearbox (XJS option)

Braking system

Check disc pads for wear

Every 6000 miles (9600 km) or six months, whichever comes first

Engine

Check ignition timing

Clean and gap spark plugs

Renew engine oil and filter (photo)

Check operation of ignition retard control valve

Check idle speed

Check exhaust CO content

Check choke and fast idle setting (carburettors)

Top up piston dampers (carburettors)

Steering/suspension

Check for wear in all steering joints and condition of gaiters, then lubricate all nipples including steering housing (photos)

Adjust front hub bearings

Braking system

Check condition of all hydraulic hoses and pipes

Check and adjust handbrake

Engine oil dipstick markings

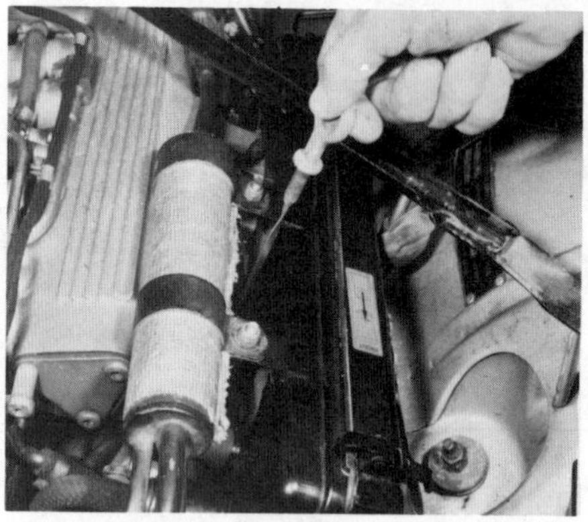

Withdrawing engine oil dipstick

Topping up engine oil

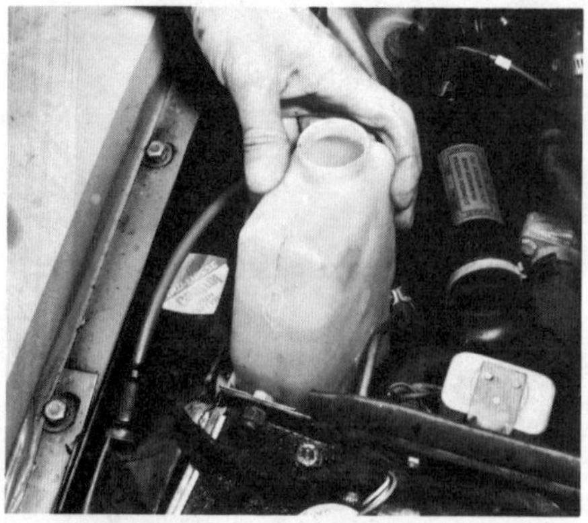

Windscreen washer fluid reservoir

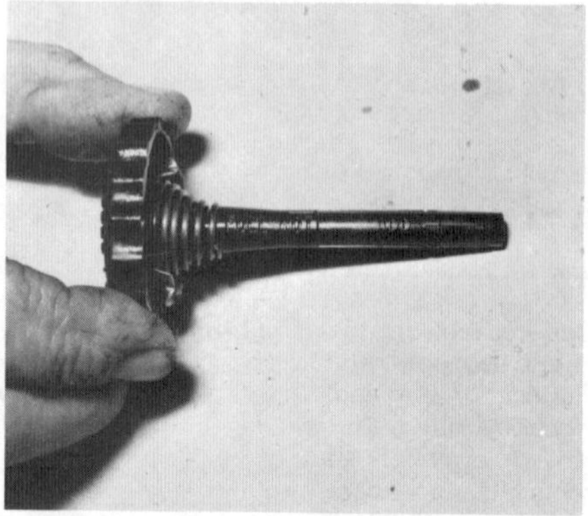

Power steering fluid dipstick

Topping up the power steering fluid reservoir

Final drive unit oil level/filler plug (arrowed)

Withdrawing the automatic transmission fluid dipstick

Topping up the automatic transmission fluid

Engine sump drain plug (arrowed)

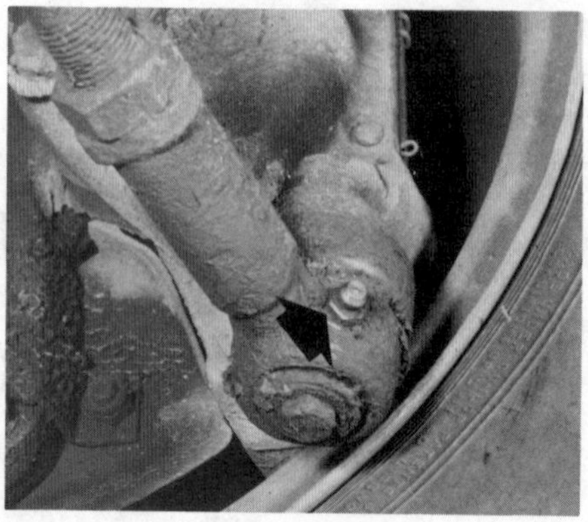

Tie-rod grease nipple (arrowed)

Front suspension upper balljoint grease nipple

Front suspension lower balljoint grease nipple

Rear suspension lower wishbone outboard grease nipple

Rear suspension lower wishbone inboard grease nipple

Steering rack grease nipple (arrowed)

Rear hub grease nipple

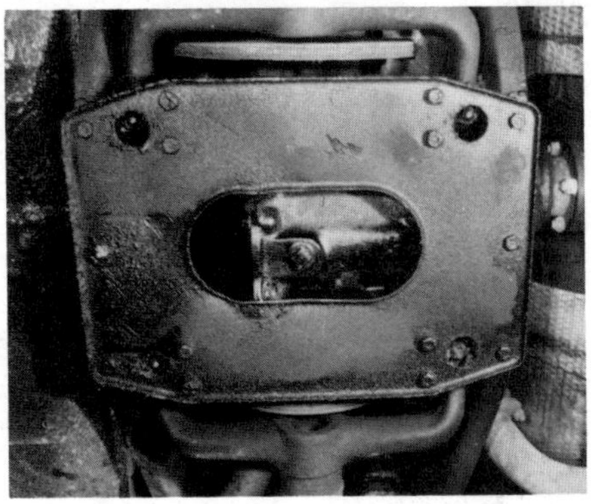

Final drive oil drain plug

General

Lubricate all controls

Every 12 000 miles (19 300 km) or twelve months, whichever comes first

---

Engine

Check operation of EGR valve (emission control)
Clean throttle housing bore
Clean crankcase breather pipes and filter
Renew air cleaner elements, test air intake valve
Test operation of diverter and check valves and gulp valve (emission control)
Renew fuel filter
Check security of all vacuum pipes
Clean and inspect ignition HT leads
Check distributor cap for cracks and lubricate distributor
Renew spark plugs
Check ignition timing
Check idle speed
Check exhaust CO content at idle speed
Check tension of drivebelts, renew where necessary

Steering and suspension

Check front wheel alignment
Lubricate rear wheel hubs

Cooling system

Drain coolant and renew with fresh antifreeze mixture (annually, regardless of mileage)

Transmission

Drain and refill final drive unit (photo)

General

Check rubber seal in fuel filler cap

Every 24 000 miles (38 600 km) or two years, whichever comes first

---

Engine

Clean EGR valve (emission control)
Renew all drivebelts
Renew charcoal canister (fuel evaporative emission control)

Braking system

Bleed out hydraulic fluid and refill with fresh

Transmission

Adjust rear brake band on Borg Warner Type 12 automatic transmission
Drain and refill the automatic transmission if operating under particularly arduous conditions giving rise to discoloration of the fluid. (Under normal operating conditions, renewal of the automatic transmission fluid is not specified as a routine service operation)

General

Inspect the windscreen wiper blades and renew if necessary

Every 48 000 miles (77 200 km) or four years, whichever comes first

---

Engine

Renew EGR valve (emission control)
Renew catalytic converters (emission control)

Suspension and steering

Check the shock absorbers and renew if necessary

Braking system

Renew all hydraulic system seals

Chapter 1 Engine

Contents

Specifications

Engine – general

No of cylinders	12
Bore	3.543 in (90.0 mm)
Stroke	2.756 in (70.0 mm)
Cubic capacity	326.0 cu in (5343 cc) 5.3 litre
Compression ratio	9:1 (S), 7.8:1 (L)
Firing order	1A, 6B, 5A, 2B, 3A, 4B, 6A, 1B, 2A, 5B, 4A, 3B (A – right bank, B – left bank, No 1 at front)
Maximum power (DIN)	284 hp at 5750 rpm
Maximum torque (DIN)	294 lbf ft at 4500 rpm

Cylinder block

Material	Aluminium alloy
Cylinder angle	60° vee
Liners	Wet, cast iron
Outside diameter of liners	3.858 in +0.001 in (97.99 mm +0.02 mm)

Cylinder heads

Material	Aluminium alloy
Valve seat angle	$44\frac{1}{2}$°

Crankshaft

No of main bearings	7
Journal diameter	3.0007 to 3.0012 in (76.218 to 76.231 mm)
Journal length:	
Front	1.170 to 1.180 in (29.72 to 29.97 mm)
Centre and rear	1.425 to 1.426 in (36.21 to 36.22 mm)
Intermediate	1.198 to 1.202 in (30.43 to 30.53 mm)
Endfloat control	Centre bearing thrust washers
Thrust washer thickness	0.010 in (0.25 mm), 0.020 in (0.51 mm)
Endfloat	0.004 to 0.006 in (0.10 to 0.15 mm)
Main bearing widths:	
Front and intermediate	0.963 to 0.973 in (24.40 to 24.65 mm)
Centre and rear	1.190 to 1.200 in (30.2 to 30.5 mm)
Running clearance	0.0015 to 0.003 in (0.04 to 0.07 mm)
Crankpin diameter	2.2994 to 2.3000 in (58.40 to 58.42 mm)
Crankpin length	1.699 to 1.701 in (43.15 to 43.20 mm)
*Regrind undersizes	0.010 in (0.25 mm), 0.020 in (0.51 mm), 0.030 in (0.76 mm), 0.040 in (1.02 mm)

**Due to the extreme hardness of the crankshaft material, regrinding is not possible on normal grinding equipment*

Connecting rods

Big-end bearing width	0.720 to 0.730 in (18.3 to 18.5 mm)
Running clearance	0.0015 to 0.0034 in (0.04 to 0.09 mm)
Big-end side clearance	0.007 to 0.013 in (0.17 to 0.33 mm)
Small-end bush width	1.03 to 1.05 in (26.2 to 26.7 mm)
Small-end bush bore	0.9375 to 0.9377 in (23.813 to 23.818 mm)

Pistons

Skirt clearance	0.0012 to 0.0017 in (0.03 to 0.04 mm)

Piston rings

Number	2 compression, 1 oil control (self-expanding, 2 rails)
Compression ring width	0.150 to 0.160 in (3.81 to 4.06 mm)
Compression ring thickness:	
Top	0.062 to 0.063 in (1.58 to 1.60 mm)
Second	0.077 to 0.078 in (1.96 to 1.98 mm)
Compression ring clearance in groove:	
Top	0.0029 in (0.07 mm)
Second	0.0034 in (0.09 mm)
Oil control ring clearance in groove	0.0055 to 0.0065 in (0.14 to 0.17 mm)
Piston ring end gap:	
Top compression	0.014 to 0.020 in (0.36 to 0.51 mm)
Second compression	0.010 to 0.015 in (0.25 to 0.38 mm)
Oil control rails	0.015 to 0.045 in (0.38 to 1.14 mm)

Gudgeon pins

Type	Fully floating
Length	3.120 to 3.125 in (79.25 to 79.38 mm)
Outside diameter:	
Red (Grade A)	0.9375 in (23.81 mm)
Green (Grade B)	0.9373 in (23.76 mm)

Camshafts

No of journals	7 on each shaft
No of bearings	7 on each shaft (machined direct in caps)
Journal diameter	1.0615 in + 0.0005 in (26.95 mm + 0.013 mm)
Running clearance	0.001 to 0.003 in (0.03 to 0.07 mm)
Thrust	Taken on front ends of shaft

Jackshaft

No of bearings	3
Running clearance	0.0005 to 0.003 in (0.013 to 0.076 mm)
Thrust	Taken on front end of shaft
Endfloat	0.005 in (0.13 mm)

Valve timing

Inlet valve opens	17° BTDC
Inlet valve closes	59° ABDC
Exhaust valve opens	59° BBDC
Exhaust valve closes	17° ATDC

Valves and valve springs

Valve clearance (inlet and exhaust, cold)	0.012 to 0.014 in (0.305 to 0.356 mm)

Inlet valve head diameter:	
XJ12 and Double Six	1.623 to 1.627 in (41.22 to 41.32 mm)
XJS models	1.620 to 1.630 in (41.15 to 41.40 mm)
Exhaust valve head diameter:	
XJ12 and Double Six	1.358 to 1.362 in (34.5 to 34.6 mm)
XJS models	1.355 to 1.365 in (34.42 to 34.67 mm)
Valve stem diameter	0.3092 to 0.3093 in (7.854 to 7.866 mm)
Valve lift	0.375 in (9.5 mm)
Valve spring free length:	
Outer	2.103 in (53.4 mm)
Inner	1.734 in (44.0 mm)

Valve guides and seats

Valve guide length:	
Inlet	1.910 in (48.5 mm)
Exhaust	2.125 in (54.0 mm)
Valve guide outside diameter:	
Standard	0.502 to 0.501 in (12.75 to 12.72 mm)
1st oversize (2 grooves)	0.507 to 0.506 in (12.88 to 12.85 mm)
2nd oversize (3 grooves)	0.512 to 0.511 in (13.01 to 12.98 mm)
Valve guide finished bore	0.311 to 0.312 in (7.90 to 7.92 mm)
Minimum clearance, valve stem to guide	0.0020 to 0.0023 in (0.05 to 0.06 mm)
Interference fit in head	0.002 to 0.006 in (0.05 to 0.15 mm)

Tappets

Outside diameter	1.373 to 1.374 in (34.87 to 34.90 mm)
Running clearance	0.001 to 0.002 in (0.02 to 0.04 mm)

Timing gear

Chain	Duplex endless
Pitch	0.375 in (9.5 mm)
No of pitches	180
Camshaft sprocket teeth	42
Crankshaft sprocket teeth	21
Jackshaft sprocket teeth	21

Lubrication system

Oil pump type	Epicyclic gear
Gear clearances:	
Driving gear to housing	0.005 to 0.012 in (0.127 to 0.305 mm)
Driving gear to crescent	0.0025 to 0.006 in (0.065 to 0.152 mm)
Driven gear to housing	0.007 to 0.010 in (0.178 to 0.254 mm)
Driven gear to crescent	0.011 to 0.018 in (0.28 to 0.46 mm)
Driving and driven gear endfloat	0.0045 to 0.0065 in (0.115 to 0.165 mm)
Oil filter type	Full flow, externally mounted. Early models – renewable element; later models – disposable cartridge
Engine oil capacity (including filter change)	
XJ12, Double Six:	
Series 1	16 Imp pts (19.2 US pts, 9.1 litres)
Series 2 on	19 Imp pts (23.0 US pts, 10.7 litres)
XJS	20 Imp pts (24.0 US pts, 11.4 litres)

Torque wrench settings

	lbf ft	Nm
Cylinder head nuts ($\frac{7}{16}$ in):		
Stage 1	25	34
Stage 2	40	54
Stage 3	52	71
Cylinder head nuts ($\frac{3}{8}$ in):		
Stage 1	20	27
Stage 2	28	38
Main bearing nuts ($\frac{3}{8}$ in)	28	38
Main bearing nuts ($\frac{1}{2}$ in)	62	84
Big-end nuts	37	50
Flywheel bolts	66	90
Crankshaft pulley bolt	150	204
Camshaft bearing cap nuts	9	12
Camshaft cover screws	8	11
Driveplate to torque converter bolts	35	48
Oil filter centre bolt	20	27
Rear mounting to bodyframe bolts ($\frac{5}{16}$ in)	18	25
Rear mounting to bodyframe bolts ($\frac{3}{8}$ in)	32	44
Front mounting to crossmember	18	25
Rear mounting to engine	30	41
Flexible mounting nuts	30	41
Exhaust manifolds to downpipes	25	34

1 General description

1 The engine fitted to all models is of twelve cylinder V type with a single overhead camshaft on each bank of cylinders.
2 The crankshaft runs in seven main bearings and from a sprocket mounted on its front end drives the camshafts and a centrally mounted jackshaft by means of a self-adjusting endless duplex chain.
3 The jackshaft drives the distributor.
4 The cylinder block is of light alloy construction with wet liners.
5 Aluminium alloy pistons are used with shallow combustion chamber depressions in their heads.
6 Two compression piston rings and one oil control ring are fitted to each piston. The gudgeon pins are of the fully floating type, retained by circlips.
7 The cylinder heads are also of light alloy construction, incorporating the valves with double valve springs.
8 The camshafts run directly in bores machined in the tappet blocks, which can be detached separately from the cylinder heads. A complete cylinder head and tappet block can be removed from its cylinder block without the need to disturb the valve timing.
9 The lubrication system comprises a crankshaft driven oil pump, an externally mounted oil filter and a bypass oil cooler (connected to the cooling system).
10 Earlier models use carburettor fuel systems (with emission control for N America). Later versions are equipped with a fuel injection system.
11 The ignition system is of Lucas Opus electronic type and incorporates a magnetic impulse type distributor which does away with the conventional mechanical contact breaker.

2 Major operations possible with engine in car

1 The following components or assemblies can be removed and refitted without removing the engine from the car:

Ancillaries:
- *Alternator (Chapter 10)*
- *Distributor (Chapter 4)*
- *Manifolds (Chapter 3)*
- *Fuel injection system components (Chapter 3)*
- *Carburettors (Chapter 3)*

Covered in later Sections of this Chapter:
- *Camshaft covers (Section 8 or 9)*
- *Camshaft (Section 10)*
- *Tappet block (Section 11)*
- *Crankshaft front oil seal (Section 12)*
- *Sandwich plate (Section 14)*
- *Oil pressure relief valve (Section 15)*

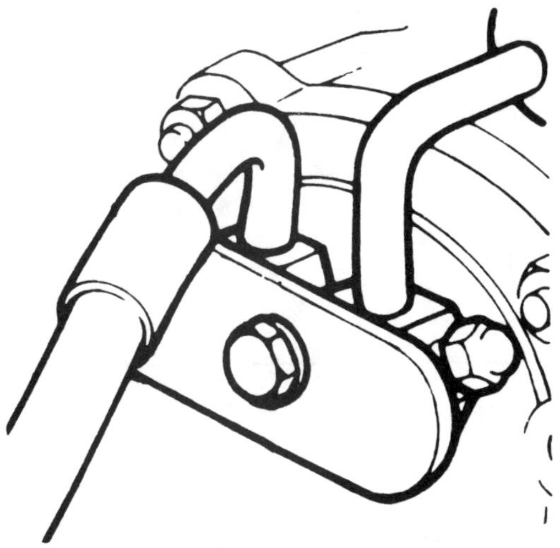

Fig. 1.1 Suction and pressure hose connections to air conditioner compressor (Sec 3)

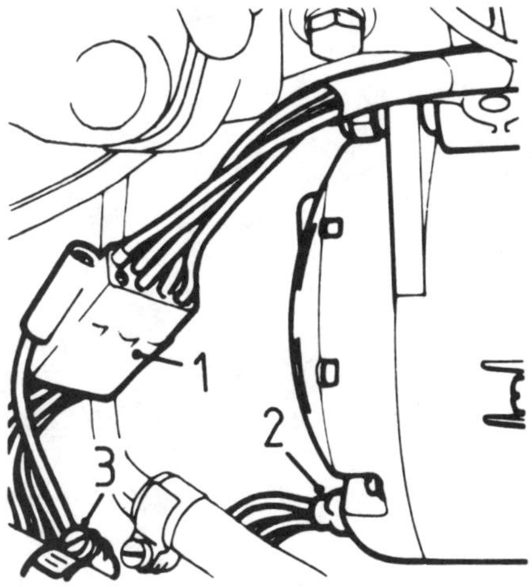

Fig. 1.2 Engine harness connector plug (1), alternator connector (2) and brake servo pipe (3) (Sec 3)

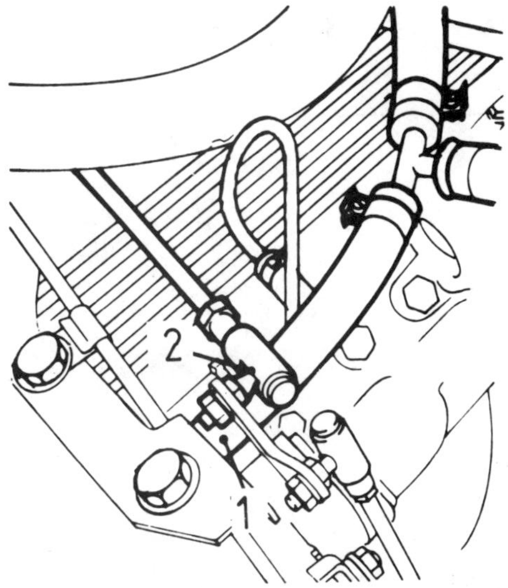

Fig. 1.3 Heater system vacuum pipe (1) and throttle cross-rod (2) (Sec 3)

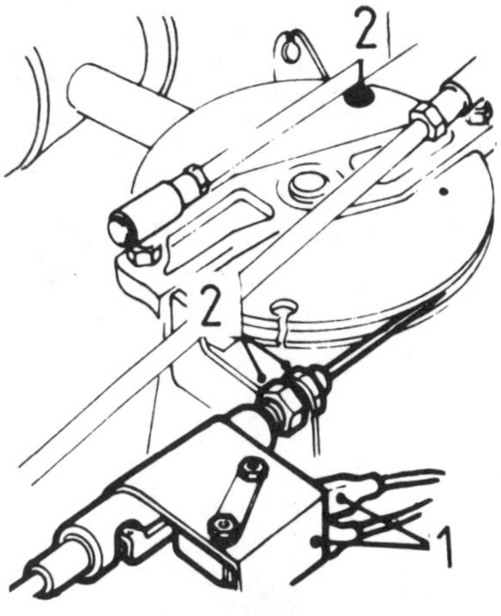

Fig. 1.4 Kickdown switch electrical connector (1) and throttle cables (2) (Sec 3)

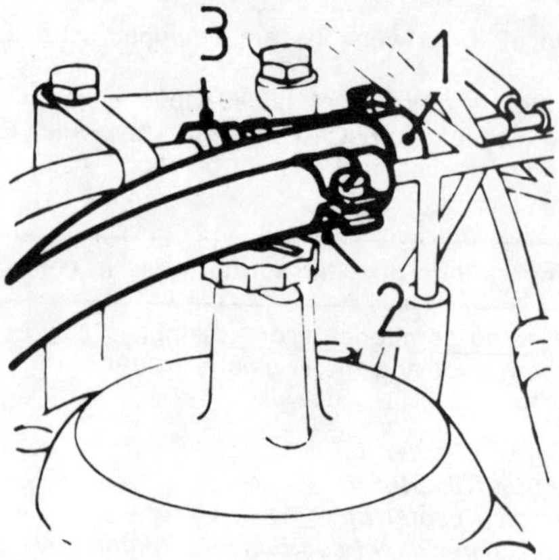

Fig. 1.5 Hose to carburettor balance pipe (1), float chamber breather balance pipe (2) and petrol feed pipe (3) (Sec 3)

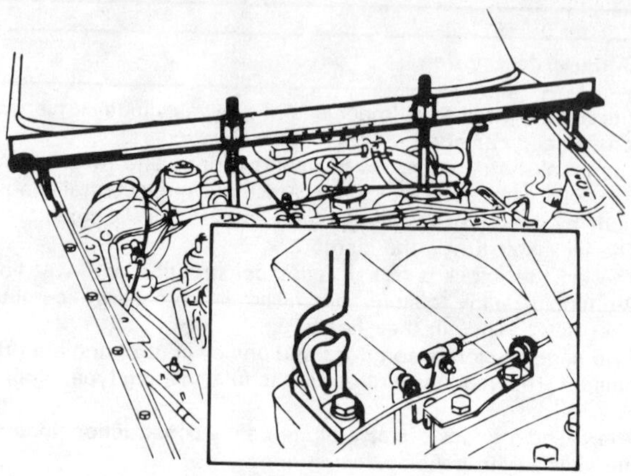

Fig. 1.6 Typical engine support crossbar (Sec 3)

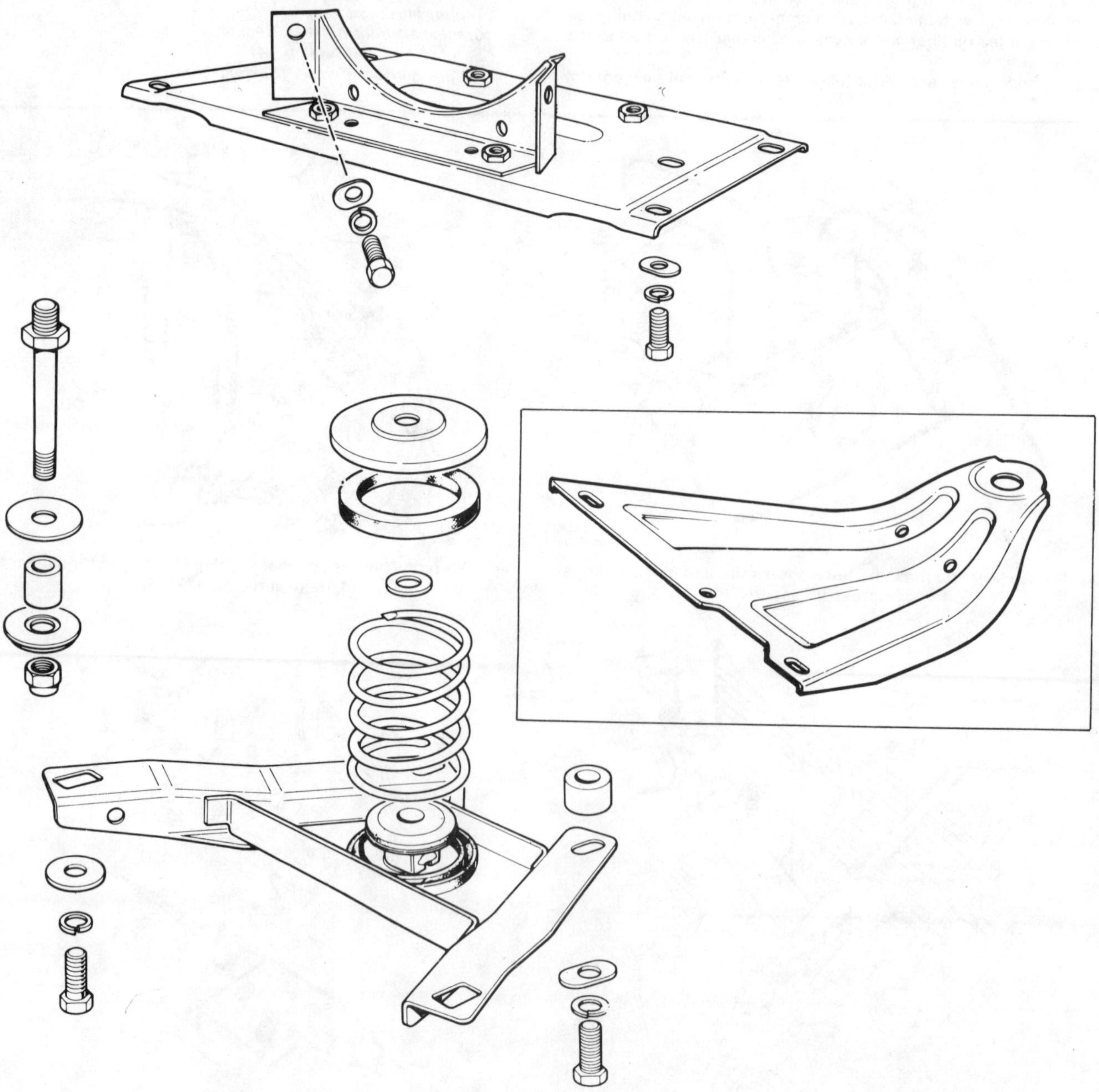

Fig. 1.7 Engine/transmission rear mounting components (Sec 3) Inset shows collision plate used on XJS automatic

3.9A Disconnecting the refrigerant pipe ahead of the condenser

3.9B Disconnecting the refrigerant pipe at the right-hand side of the engine compartment

3.11 Air conditioning compressor removed to the side of the engine compartment

3.15A Power steering pump pipe connection (arrowed)

3.15B Power steering fluid cooler

3.27 Starter motor cable bulkhead terminal (arrowed)

3.28A Engine front shield

3.28B Engine front shield bolt and bracket

3.33 Speedometer drive cable connection to transmission

3.34 Front end attachment of speed selector cable

3.35 Transmission-to-body earth strap

Oil pick up strainer (Section 16)
Engine oil cooler (Section 17)
Cylinder heads (Section 18, 19 or 20)
Crankshaft main bearing shells (Section 22)
Big-end bearing shells (Section 23)
Engine mountings (Section 24, 25 or 26)
Oil filter (Section 27 or 29)

2 For all other major overhaul operations, the engine/transmission should be removed and the transmission then separated from the engine.
3 Remember that most of the engine castings are of light alloy construction. Do not lever against them or strike them with a heavy hammer or they may distort or fracture.

3 Engine/transmission (XJ12 and Double Six with carburettors) – removal

Cars equipped with air conditioning

1 Have the system discharged by your dealer or a professional refrigeration engineer. *On no account release any of the refrigerated circuit pipe unions before discharging the system,* otherwise dangerous refrigerant gas will escape.

All cars

2 Position the car over an inspection pit or place it on ramps to give working space under the engine/transmission.
3 Mark the bonnet hinge and restraining link positions and with the help of an assistant, unbolt and remove the bonnet. Store it in a safe place where it will not get scratched.
4 Disconnect and remove the battery. If the car is to be left outside whilst the overhaul takes place, remember to raise the power-operated windows before removing the battery.
5 Unbolt and remove the wing valance stays (angled corners nearest the engine compartment rear bulkhead).
6 Drain the cooling system, retaining the antifreeze if it is suitable for further use.
7 Remove the air cleaners (Chapter 3).
8 Remove the radiator and engine oil cooler as described in Chapter 2. As the radiator top rail is unbolted, disconnect the minimum number of electrical relay connections and swing the top rail onto the top of the right-hand front wing.

Cars with air conditioning

9 Disconnect the air conditioner (system previously discharged) by releasing the union nut at the flexible-to-rigid pipe connection located just before the condenser (photo). Disconnect the remaining hose from the condenser (photo). Tap or cap all refrigerant circuit openings immediately to prevent the entry of moist air. Unbolt and remove the condenser.
10 Unbolt the amplifier from the forward end of the jackshaft cover plate located between the two cylinder banks. Lift the amplifier and unbolt the compressor rear mounting. Unbolt the compressor and release the hoses from the right-hand wing valance stay. Slacken the compressor drivebelt idler pulley adjuster and slip the belt from the compressor pulley.
11 Unbolt the compressor front mounting and having disconnected the electrical leads, lift the compressor from the engine and secure it on the left-hand wing upper surface (photo).

All cars

12 Identify and disconnect the coolant expansion tank hoses at the engine end.
13 Reaching down on either side of the engine, remove the nuts which hold the engine mountings to their brackets.
14 Drain the fluid from the power-assisted steering pump reservoir and cooler (see Chapter 11).
15 Disconnect the fluid supply and return pipes from the power steering pump. Move the pipes complete with cooling fins (photos).
16 Disconnect the leads from the rear of the alternator and separate the engine harness connector plug.
17 Disconnect the brake servo vacuum hose.
18 Disconnect the fuel supply pipe at the crossover pipe stub (see Fig.

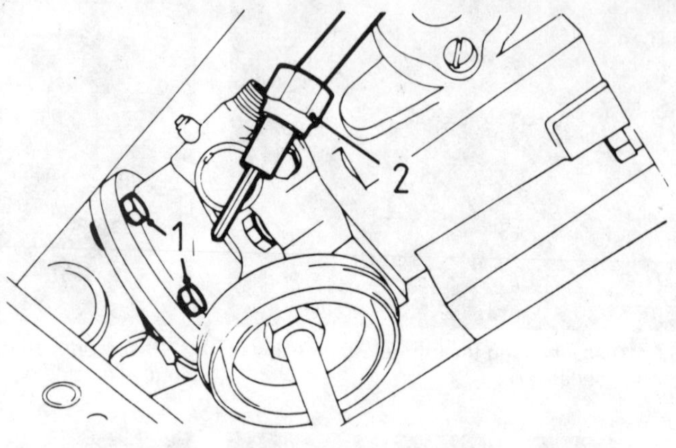

Fig. 1.8 Propeller shaft front flange bolts (1) and speedometer drive cable (2) (Sec 3)

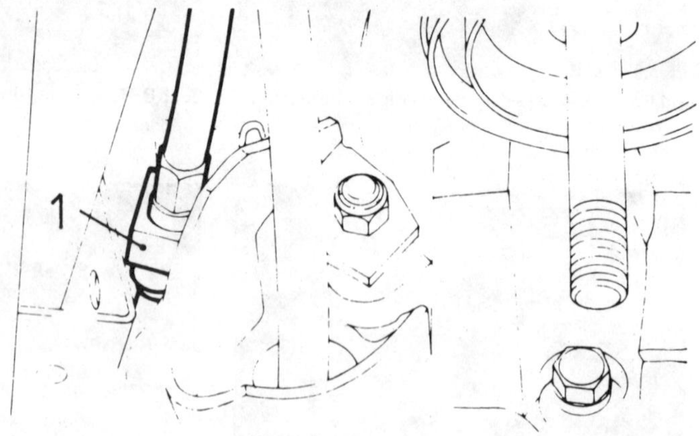

Fig. 1.9 Gearshift selector abutment (1) (Sec 3)

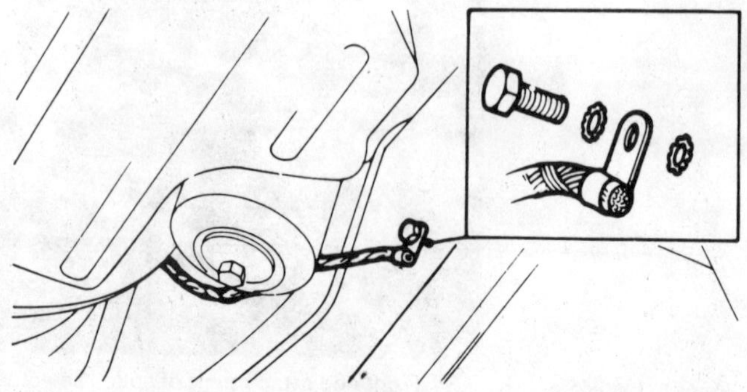

Fig. 1.10 Earth strap to side frame (Sec 3)

1.5), then disconnect the return pipe at the flexible hose which runs to the non-return valve. Tie the pipe and hose back out of the way.
19 Disconnect the heater system vacuum pipe at its manifold stub.
20 Disconnect the heater system coolant valve feed pipe, also the return pipe from the coolant rail at the bulkhead union.
21 Remove the ignition coil and ballast resistor.
22 Disconnect the throttle cross-rod at the left-hand bellcrank and swing it forward so that it rests on the engine.
23 Where fitted, disconnect the choke operating cables from the carburettors.
24 Pull the electrical connectors from the kickdown switch.
25 Disconnect the throttle cables from the pedestal plate and platform. On right-hand drive models, remove the throttle cable grommet bracket from the manifold bolt.

Cars with fuel emission control

26 Pull the pipe (carbon canister connecting) from the carburettor balance pipe, also the one from the carburettor float chamber breather balance pipe.

All models

27 Disconnect the starter motor supply cable from the bulkhead terminal (photo).
28 A crossbar engine support fitted with a hook will now be required similar to the one shown in Fig. 1.6. It should engage in the drip channel on either side of the engine compartment and be positioned directly above the engine rear lifting eyes. Rotate the raising or lowering screws on the support bar to take the weight of the engine off its mountings. At this stage, it is recommended that the engine front shield is removed to provide better access to the underside of the engine (photos).
29 Disconnect the exhaust pipes from the manifold flanges. The nuts can be reached from below using a long socket extension.
30 Remove the exhaust front pipe flanges which connect with the intermediate pipes and withdraw the pipe that is not obstructed by the steering pinion housing. On right-hand drive cars, the obstructed pipe can be removed if full right steering lock is applied and the handbrake pulled on fully. Take care not to damage the steering rack gaiter as the pipe is withdrawn.
31 Unbolt the heat shield on both sides of the engine rear mounting, then unbolt the engine rear mounting plate. Support the spring-loaded mounting plate with a jack and a block of wood and release the centre nut on the mounting plate. Unbolt the stengthening plate where one is fitted (later models). Lower the jack and withdraw the engine mounting plate.
32 Unbolt and remove the plate which covers the propeller shaft front flange. The two setscrews above the plate, which are accessible from the forward edge, should not be overlooked. Mark the relative alignment of the propeller shaft and transmission output flanges and unbolt them.
33 Disconnect the speedometer drive cable from the transmission (photo).
34 Disconnect the front end of the speed selector cable from the transmission and then release the outer cable pinch-bolt at the cable trunnion bracket on the side of the transmission casing. If the centre console is now removed (see Chapter 12), the speed selector cable assembly can be withdrawn towards the rear of the car by gripping the cable loop adjacent to the speed selector quadrant on the transmission tunnel. The cables will then be drawn out of the trunnion bracket and disconnected from the transmission (photo).
35 Disconnect the earth strap from the side subframe by unscrewing the setscrew (photo).
36 Support the transmission oil pan on a trolley jack using a block of wood as an insulator. Once the weight is taken on the jack, remove the engine crossbar support and lifting hooks.
37 A substantial hoist will now be required to be able to lift out the engine/transmission. Make sure that the chains attached to the engine lifting eyes meet the following length requirements:

Front engine lifting eyes to hook of hoist – 34.5 in (876 mm)
Rear engine lifting eyes to hook of hoist – 41.0 in (1041 mm)

38 Take the weight of the engine on the hoist, at the same time raising the trolley jack to keep the engine level. Raise 2 to 3 in (50 to 70 mm) initially, then commence sideways pressure on the engine to keep it clear of the steering pinion housing and power steering gear pipework. Continue to lift, keeping the engine/transmission level so that damage does not occur to the air conditioner expansion valve or the evaporator unions.
39 Hoist the engine/transmission from the engine compartment, increasing its tilt angle until the transmission output flange clears the bulkhead.

4 Engine/transmission (XJ12 and Double Six with fuel injection) – removal

1 The operations are very similar to those described in Section 3 for carburettor engines, except that all reference to carburettor and fuel system operations should be ignored and the following work substituted.
2 With the air conditioning system discharged, depressurise the fuel system as described in Chapter 3 and then remove the fuel cooler. Plug all open hoses.
3 Disconnect the leads from the ambient and coolant temperature sensors.
4 Release the cold start relay wiring harness from its relay.
5 Disconnect the cable from the throttle switch and trigger unit (photo).

4.5 The throttle switch

4.10 The modulator (GM400 automatic transmission)

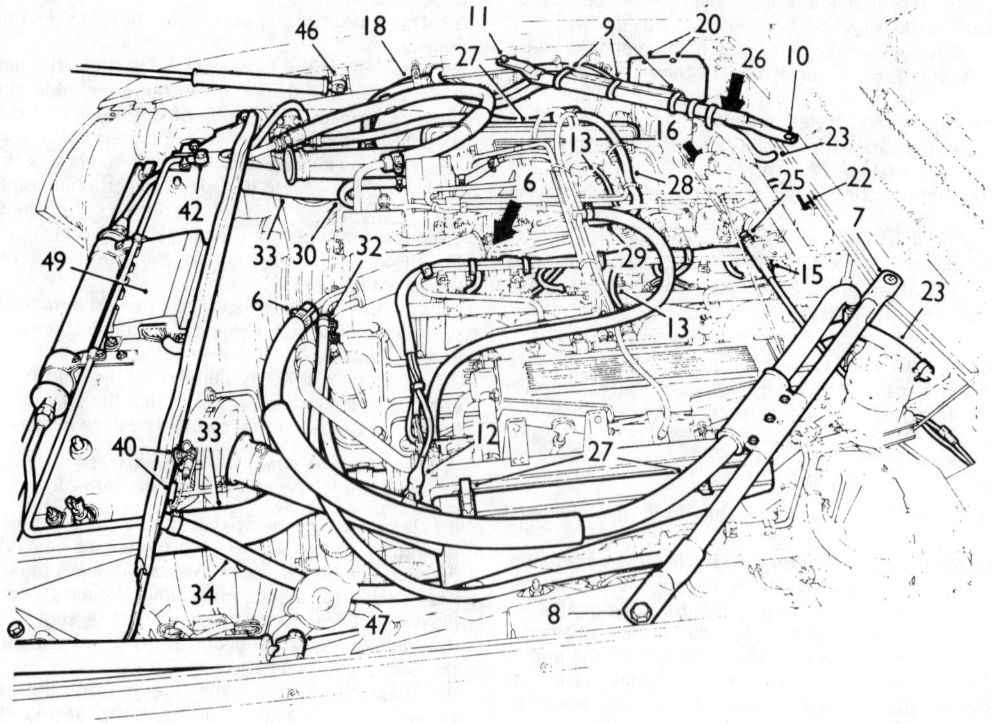

Fig. 1.11 XJS engine disconnection points (Sec 5)

6 Fuel cooler refrigerant pipe
7 Wing valance stay screw
8 Wing valance stay bolt
9 Wiring harness clips
10 Right-hand stay screw
11 Right-hand stay bolt
12 Temperature sensors
13 Cold start relay wiring harness
15 Kickdown switch wires
16 Earth leads to induction manifold
18 Engine main harness
20 Cold start relay cover screws
22 Coolant rail to heater valve connection
23 Brake servo pipe
25 Throttle cable at pedestal
26 Starter leads at bulkhead connector
27 Air cleaners
28 Fuel pressure sensor feed pipe
29 Fuel pressure sensor feed pipe tee piece
30 Fuel pipes to filter
32 Fuel pipe to fuel cooler
33 Hose connections to thermostat housing
34 Expansion tank hose
40 Fan motor fuse clips
42 Radiator expansion pipe banjo connector
46 Bonnet stay bracket
47 Bonnet stay bracket
49 Radiator top rail assembly

6 Remove (two screws) the cover from the cold start relay. Refer to Chapter 3 for details of the relay. Note the positions of the connecting wires, disconnect them and manoeuvre them through the valance bracket.
7 Remove the air cleaner covers and elements.
8 Release the clips which secure the pressure sensor feed pipe, then disconnect the pipe from the T-piece and plug all open connections.
9 Disconnect the lead from the low coolant sensor on the right-hand side of the radiator.
10 On cars which are equipped with GM400 automatic transmission (1978 on), disconnect the kickdown solenoid supply wire and unclip the wire from the transmission. Disconnect the vacuum tube from the modulator capsule (photo). Unbolt the modulator and withdraw it, but make sure that a suitably large container is placed underneath to catch the transmission fluid which will drain out. Discard the O-ring seal.

5 Engine/transmission (XJS with manual or automatic transmission) – removal

Cars with air conditioning

1 Have the air conditioning system discharged by your dealer or a qualified refrigeration engineer. *Do not disconnect any part of the system yourself* or dangerous refrigerant gas may escape.

All cars

2 Place the car over an inspection pit or on ramps to provide adequate working clearance underneath.
3 Remove the bonnet with the help of an assistant and then the radiator lower grille. Store them in a safe place.
4 Disconnect the battery.
5 Drain the cooling system (Chapter 2).
6 Depressurise the fuel system (Chapter 3).

Cars with air conditioning

7 Disconnect and remove the fuel hoses from the fuel cooler. Plug all open hoses. Unclip the condenser pipe from the radiator top rail.
8 Disconnect the outlet pipe from the receiver dryer.

All cars

9 Remove the left-hand wing valance stay, releasing the wiring harness or hose from it as it is withdrawn.
10 Disconnect the wires from the air temperature and coolant temperature sensors (fuel injection system).
11 Release the cold start relay wiring harness from the left-hand fuel rail and crossover pipe.
12 Disconnect the operating cable from the throttle switch and trigger unit (fuel injection system).
13 Disconnect the earth leads from the right-hand induction manifold, and the cables from the kickdown switch (automatic transmission).
14 Unclip the engine main wiring harness and swing it clear, then uncouple the harness multi-plug connector.
15 Remove the cover from the cold start relay on the right-hand wing valance. Mark the wiring connections, disconnect them from the relay and pull the harness through the valance bracket.
16 Disconnect the right-hand coolant rail feed pipe from the heater valve.

17 Disconnect the brake vacuum servo hoses from the left and right induction manifolds and the heater vacuum pipe from the right-hand induction manifold.
18 Disconnect the throttle cable from the throttle bracket.
19 Disconnect the starter motor and solenoid cables from their bulkhead connector.
20 Remove the air cleaner covers and filter elements.
21 Release the pressure sensor pipe securing clips (fuel injection system). Disconnect the pipe from the T-piece and plug all openings.
22 Release and disconnect the fuel pipes from the fuel filter and plug all openings. Also disconnect the fuel pipe from the cooler.
23 Disconnect the radiator top hoses from the thermostat housings.
24 Disconnect the hose from the remote expansion tank, also the heater return hose from the T-piece.

Cars with automatic transmission

25 Disconnect the transmission oil cooler flexible hoses from the rigid pipes. Plug the pipes.

All cars

26 Disconnect the alternator wiring harness at the snap connectors.
27 Disconnect the thermostatic switch two pin connector, then release the harness clips.
28 Remove and disconnect the fan motor line fuse.
29 Disconnect the smaller of the two block connectors at the front end of the right-hand wing valance.
30 Disconnect the expansion pipe (banjo union) from the radiator.
31 Unbolt the radiator top rail, noting the positions of the earth lead and wiring harness clip.
32 Unbolt the fan cowl from the radiator top rail.

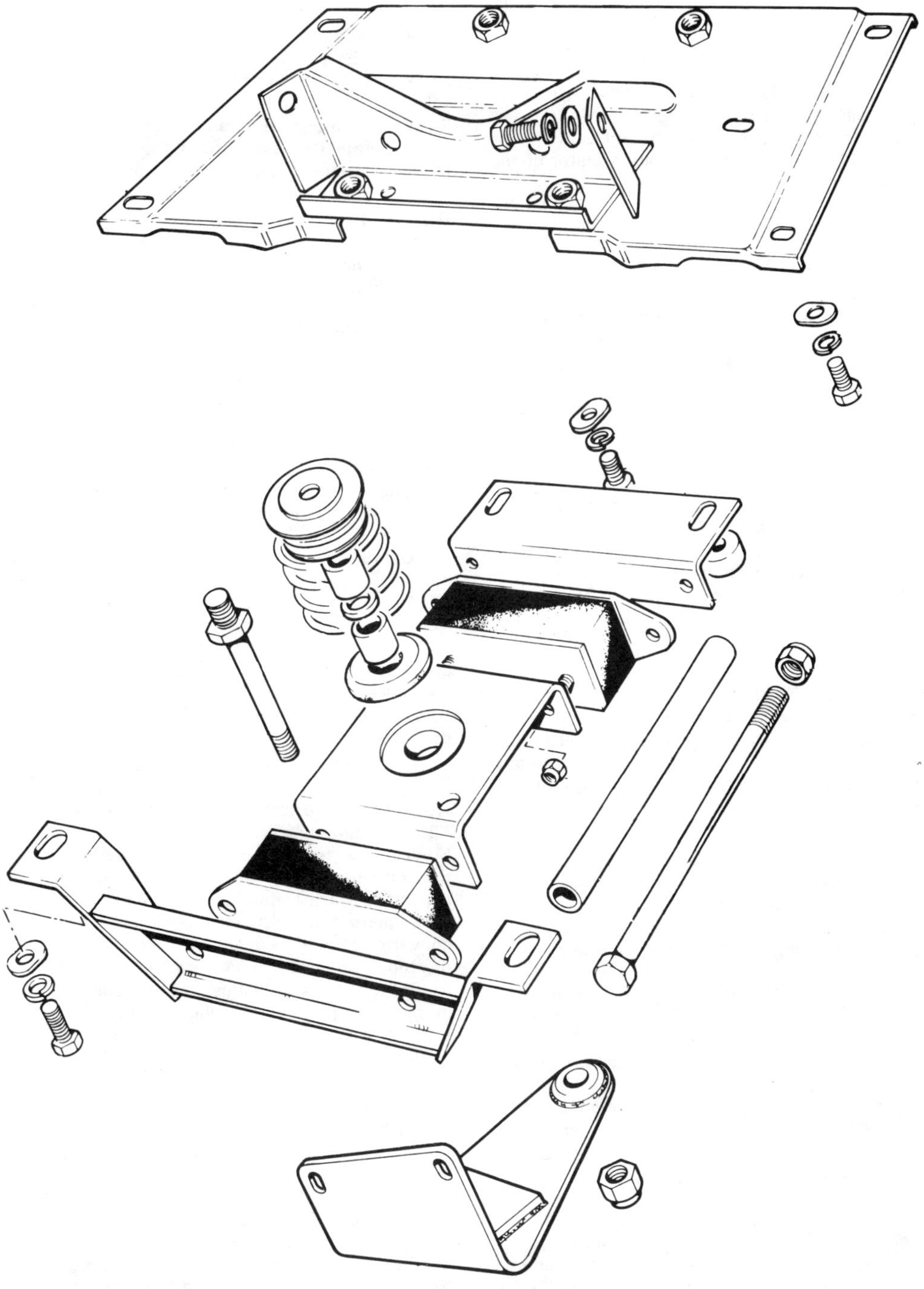

Fig. 1.12 XJS engine/transmission rear mounting (manual gearbox) (Sec 5)

33 Unbolt the stays from the left and right-hand brackets.
34 Remove the radiator top rail (complete with evaporator and receiver dryer on air conditioned cars). Note the copper washers and spacer located over the tapped hole into which the expansion pipe banjo bolt screws.
35 An engine support crossbar should now be fitted to engage in the drip channel on either side of the engine compartment. Position it directly over the engine rear lifting eyes, connect the lifting hooks and adjust to take the weight of the engine.
36 Disconnect the wire from the low coolant sensor which is located in the right-hand side of the radiator.
37 Unbolt the fan cowl from the bottom of the radiator.
38 Disconnect the radiator bottom hose and then lift the radiator enough to be able to disconnect the oil cooler pipes from the base (engine oil cooler) and the right-hand side (automatic transmission fluid cooler). Always use two spanners to disconnect the unions, otherwise the seat may tear out of the radiator coolant tank. Plug all openings.
39 Lift the radiator, fan cowl and electric fan out of the engine compartment.
40 Disconnect the exhaust intermediate pipes from the downpipes.
41 Disconnect the front, rear and intermediate heat shields.
42 Unbolt the collision plate from the transmission unit.
43 Position a trolley jack with a block of wood as an insulator under the engine rear mounting plate.
44 Remove the single remaining self-locking nut which holds the collision plate to the engine rear mounting plate stud. Remove the collision plate.
45 Unbolt the engine rear mounting plate, noting the position of any spacers and the location of the different sized bolts. The rear mounting components are of different design on manual gearbox versions.
46 Lower the jack, remove the mounting plate, the seating plate and allied components. Remove the propeller shaft cover plate after reference to Section 3, Paragraph 32.
47 Disconnect the propeller shaft from the transmission output flange, marking the flanges for correct reassembly.

Cars with manual gearbox

48 Unscrew and remove the gear lever knob, then extract the retaining screws and withdraw the gasket and gaiter from the centre console.
49 Move the gear lever to first gear position.
50 Unbolt the clutch slave cylinder from the bellhousing. Release the pushrod from the end of the release lever and push the cylinder aside. There is no need to disconnect the hydraulic pipes.

Cars with automatic transmission

51 Disconnect the gearshift selector cable from its trunnion block, remove the self-locking nut and slide the speed selector lever on the side of the transmission from its shaft. Where GM400 automatic transmission is fitted, repeat the operations given in paragraphs 24 and 34 of Section 3.

All cars

52 Disconnect the speedometer cable from the transmission and tie it back to the side of the transmission tunnel.
53 Disconnect the earth strap from the transmission bellhousing.
54 Unbolt and remove the steering gear gaiter heat shields, then remove the heat shield from the left-hand exhaust manifold.
55 Unbolt the left-hand exhaust downpipes from the manifolds, remove the downpipes and the sealing rings. Where an emission control exhaust gas recirculation (EGR) system is fitted, it will be necessary to disconnect the EGR pipes from the exhaust downpipes before removal.
56 Unbolt the right-hand exhaust downpipe from the manifold, turn the downpipes through 180° and remove them. Discard the sealing rings.
57 Unbolt the power steering fluid cooler and swing it on its bracket away from the engine.
58 Unbolt the power steering pump, release its drivebelt and tie the pump away from the engine in its normal upright attitude.
59 Support the transmission with a trolley jack. If the car is over a pit or on ramps, a strong cross support will have to be laid under the car on which the jack can be rested. Where possible it is to be preferred if the car can be pushed from the ramps or pit to provide a solid base for the jack. On cars with automatic transmission, place the jack under the rear extension housing, *not* the oil pan.
60 Remove the engine support crossbar (see paragraph 35) and attach lifting chains to the engine lifting eyes. The rear chains should be 6.0 in (154 mm) longer than the front ones. Use a hoist of adequate lifting capacity.
61 Lift the engine/transmission carefully from the car (photo). Adjust the jack under the transmission as necessary so that the engine/transmission finally takes on a steeply inclined angle as it is withdrawn from the engine compartment. On cars with manual gearbox, take care that the gear control lever is below the console and transmission tunnel during removal. Ensure that the steering gear and hydraulic pipework are not damaged during engine removal.

6 Engine – initial dismantling of transmission and ancillaries

All models

1 With the engine/transmission removed from the car, clean away all external dirt using either paraffin and a stiff brush or a water-soluble solvent.
2 Drain the engine oil and discard it.
3 Separate the engine from the transmission by carrying out the following operations according to type of transmission fitted.

Automatic transmission (Borg Warner Model 12)

4 Disconnect the oil cooler pipes and plug the unions on the transmission housing.
5 Withdraw the breather pipe, withdraw the dipstick and uncouple the dipstick guide/filler tube from the oil pan. Drain the transmission fluid by taking off the oil pan.
6 Remove the vacuum pipe from the vacuum unit.
7 Support the transmission, preferably on a trolley jack. Unscrew and remove the four nuts which hold the transmission casing to the torque converter bellhousing. Withdraw the transmission in a straight line, without allowing the weight of the transmission to hang upon the input shaft.
8 Unbolt and remove the starter motor.
9 Unbolt and remove the front cover plate from the torque converter housing.
10 Unbolt the torque converter housing from the engine cylinder block.
11 Remove the engine oil filter and the plug from the rear left-hand side of the crankcase.
12 Turn the crankshaft until the first of the driveplate-to-torque converter screws comes into view. Flatten the tabs on the lockplate and extract the screw. Continue to rotate the crankshaft until all the setscrews have been removed. Mark the relative position of the driveplate to the converter using quick-drying paint. Withdraw the converter and be prepared for some loss of fluid.

Automatic transmission (General Motors Type 400)

13 The operations are very similar to those just described for the BW Model 12, except that the torque converter housing is integral with the transmission casing and the transmission complete with torque converter will therefore be removed from the engine, once the front cover plate has been removed (photo) and the driveplate-to-torque converter bolts have been withdrawn. These bolts are accessible after the rubber plug has been extracted. A clamping bar should be bolted to the front of the bellhousing to hold the torque converter rearwards in full engagement with the oil pump drive tangs. Do this before separating the transmission from the engine, also disconnect the fluid cooler pipes (photos).

Manual transmission

14 Unbolt the flywheel housing cover plate.
15 Remove the starter motor.
16 Disconnect the gearbox breather pipe.
17 Unscrew the bolts which hold the clutch bellhousing to the cylinder block. Note the positions of the long and short bolts.
18 With the gearbox supported on a trolley jack, withdraw the gearbox from the engine. Do not allow the weight of the gearbox to hang on the input shaft whilst the latter is still engaged in the clutch driven plate.
19 Mark the relative position of the clutch cover plate to the flywheel.

5.61 Removing the engine/transmission

6.13A Front plate (GM400 transmission)

6.13B Side view of engine and GM400 automatic transmission

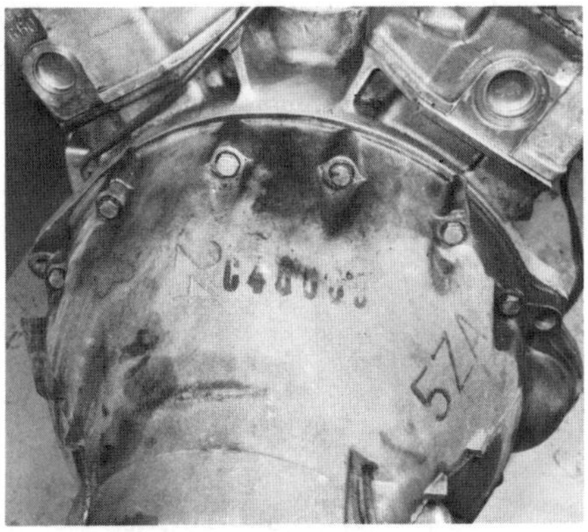
6.13C Torque converter housing upper bolts (GM 400)

6.13D Removing the driveplate bolt access plug (GM 400)

6.13E Unscrewing a driveplate/converter bolt (GM 400)

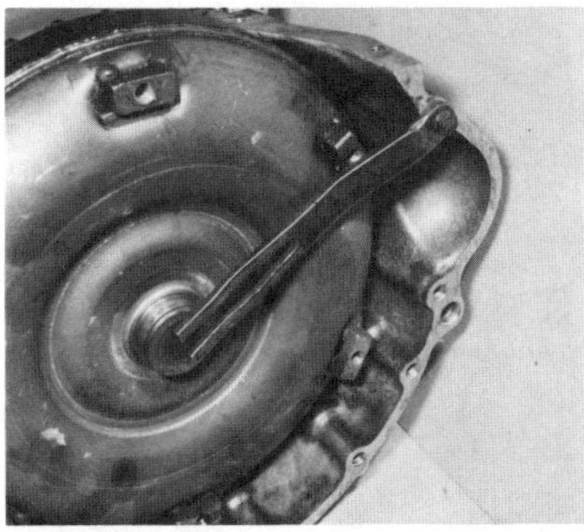
6.13F Torque converter temporary clamp

6.24 Idler assembly (fanbelt and fan removed)

7.3 Crankshaft front pulley fixing

7.4 Crankshaft front pulley/damper and centre bolt

7.5 Crankshaft damper cone

7.8A Coolant transfer pipe (arrowed)

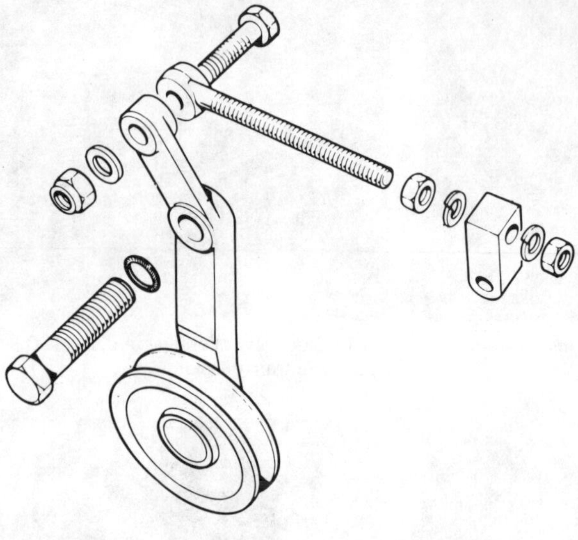

Fig. 1.13 Fanbelt idler (jockey) pulley assembly (Sec 6)

Fig. 1.14 Crankshaft damper and pulley (Sec 7)

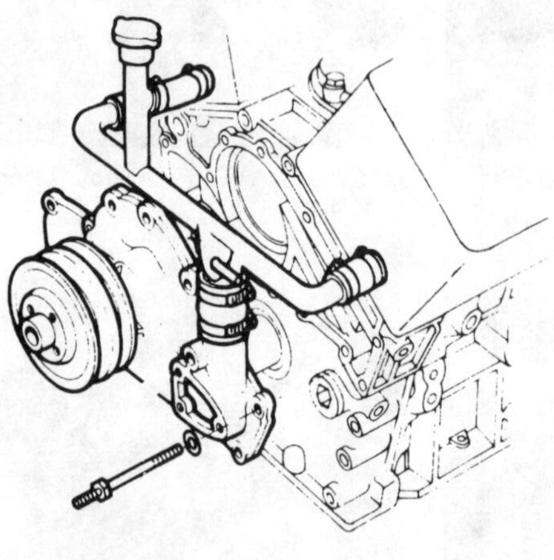

Fig. 1.15 Removing the water pump (Sec 7)

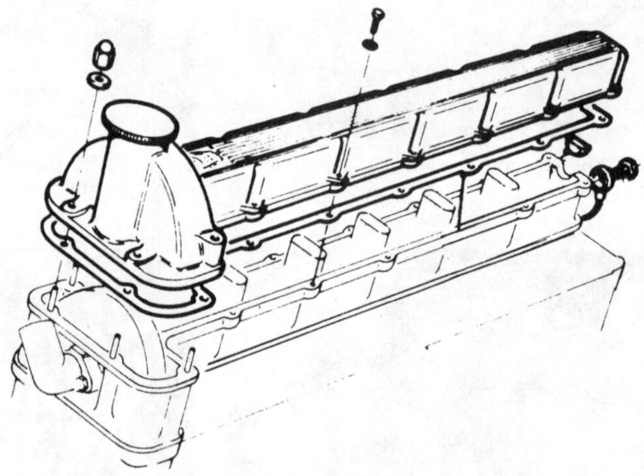

Fig. 1.16 Removing the camshaft cover (Sec 7)

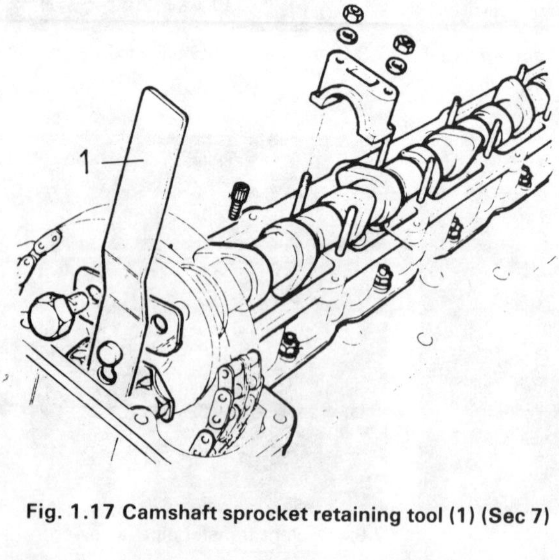

Fig. 1.17 Camshaft sprocket retaining tool (1) (Sec 7)

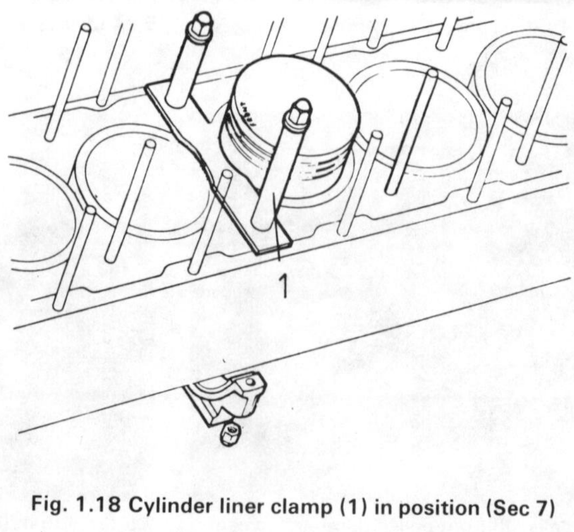

Fig. 1.18 Cylinder liner clamp (1) in position (Sec 7)

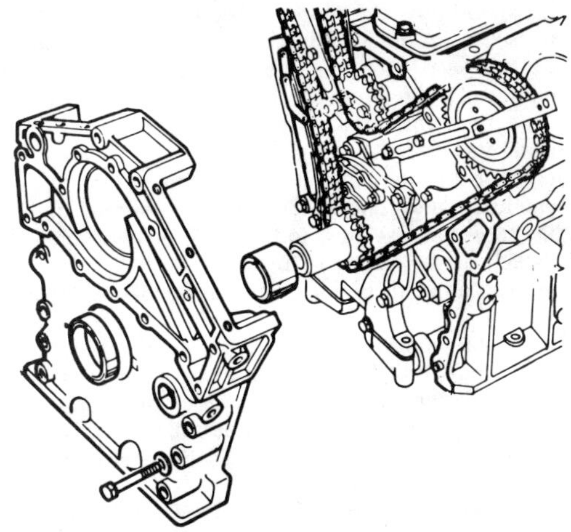

Fig. 1.19 Timing cover removed (Sec 7)

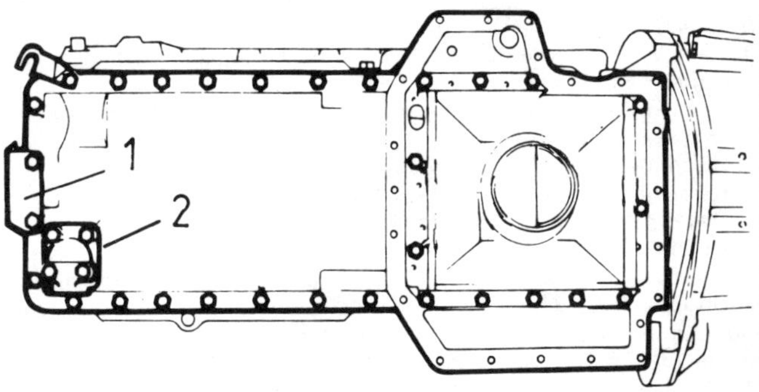

Fig. 1.20 Sandwich plate and baffle screws (Sec 7)

1 Timing scale *2 Suction union*

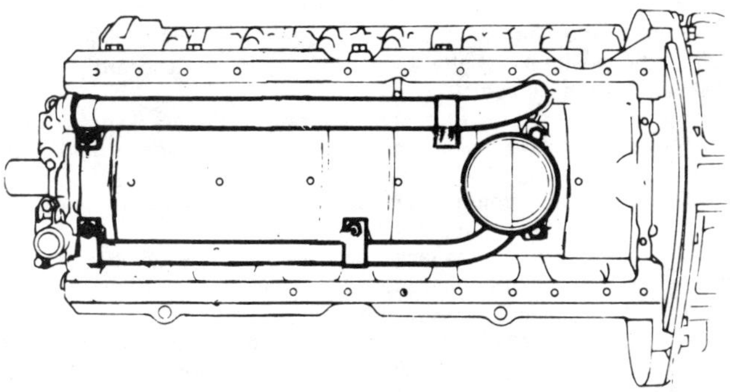

Fig. 1.21 Crankshaft undershield and delivery pipe clips (Sec 7)

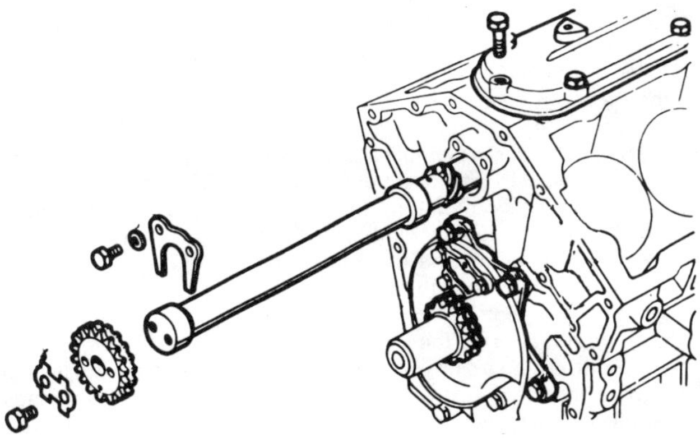

Fig. 1.22 Removing the jackshaft (Sec 7)

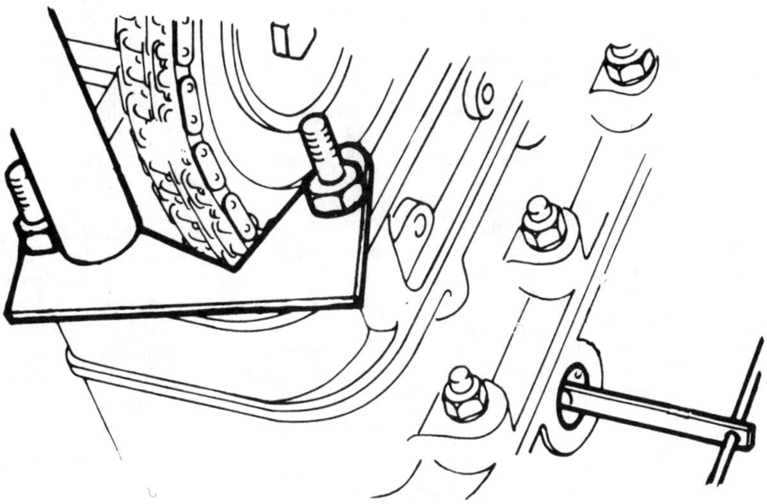

Fig. 1.23 Timing chain tensioner tools installed (XJ12 and Double Six) (Sec 7)

Unscrew the clutch cover bolts progressively until the clutch diaphragm spring pressure is relieved and then remove the cover and driven plate.

All models

20 Remove the carburettors or fuel injection equipment and manifolds after reference to Chapter 3.
21 Remove the oil pressure relief valve bleed pipe from the top of the sandwich plate.
22 Disconnect the oil cooler feed pipe.
23 Remove the engine oil filter (if not already removed).
24 Slacken the fanbelt and remove the idler pulley assembly (photo).
25 Unbolt and remove the power steering pump.
26 Remove the power steering pump bracket and adjustment link.
27 On cars fitted with air conditioning, remove the compressor. The mounting bolts are accessible only after prior withdrawal of the ignition system amplifier unit.
28 Unbolt the air pump (if so equipped – emission control system).
29 Remove the transmission fluid cooler pipes from the engine clips.
30 Unbolt and remove the alternator (see Chapter 10).

7 Engine – complete dismantling

1 This Section covers complete dismantling of the engine after it has been removed from the car and separated from the transmission, and after ancillary components have been detached. Obviously dismantling will be limited in many cases to gain access only to those parts or assemblies which require attention or renewal.
2 Where certain dismantling is to be carried out without removing the engine from the car (refer to Section 2) in order to gain access to some components and assemblies and subsequently to remove them, it will be appreciated that where necessary before in situ work is undertaken, the cooling system must be drained, the fuel system depressurised, the air conditioning system discharged (by your dealer), the battery disconnected and the bonnet removed.
3 Unbolt the pulley from the crankshaft damper and tap the pulley from the damper (photo).
4 Unscrew and remove the damper centre bolt (photo). To prevent the crankshaft turning as the centre bolt is unscrewed, jam the flyheel or driveplate starter ring gear. If the flywheel/driveplate has already been removed, insert two bolts into the crankshaft rear flange and use a long screwdriver as a lever.
5 Strike the damper sharply with a hide or plastic-faced mallet. Remove the damper, Woodruff key, the damper cover and the second Woodruff key (photo).
6 Unbolt and remove the spout from the coolant pump.
7 Unbolt and remove the coolant pump complete with backplate, cross-pipe and vent pipe (early models).
8 Unbolt and remove the coolant transfer pipe from above the right-hand exhaust manifold. Remove the distributor and the amplifier unit (Chapter 4) (photos).
9 Unscrew and remove the banjo bolts which hold the oil feed pipes to the rear of the tappet blocks and the oil gallery. The oil pressure sender unit and the oil pressure warning switch can also be removed at the same time (photos).
10 Remove the throttle pedestal bracket, the amplifier bracket and the heater return pipe.
11 Unscrew the domed nuts and setscrews and lift off the camshaft covers. Retrieve the copper washers, but discard the gaskets and neoprene plugs.
12 Flatten the camshaft sprocket lockplate tabs and remove two bolts from each sprocket.
13 The timing chain tensioner must now be retracted to its fullest extent in order to slacken the chain. (A chain tensioner is fitted to the right-hand chain run only). To do this, special tools are available, one part consisting of a hooked retractor and the other part a cranked screwdriver (tool numbers JD42/2 and JD44 for XJ12 and Double Six engines, and JD50 for XJS). Substitute tools can easily be made from a length of rod having a hook at one end and a standard screwdriver. Remove the rubber plug from the front face of the right-hand cylinder head (photo). Insert the screwdriver into the hole so that it engages in the elongated hole in the tensioner slipper (photo). Twist the screwdriver in an anti-clockwise direction and then engage the hooked rod in the hole near the top of the slipper. Pull the rod and slipper upwards. This will require considerable force. At the same time, keep the screwdriver twisted until the slipper guide tube is felt to click onto the shoulder of its central guide rod (photo). Remove the tools.
14 Turn the crankshaft by means of the flywheel or driveplate until the remaining camshaft sprocket bolts are accessible and remove them. Fit a camshaft sprocket retaining tool (JD44) to hold the sprocket to its bracket.
15 Unbolt and secure the opposite camshaft sprocket to its bracket in a similar way using a second special tool. A tool may be easily made up from thin steel flat having a forked end, or two holes of different diameters which break into each other (photo).
16 Slacken the camshaft bearing cap nuts, working from the centre outwards.
17 Lift out the camshafts.
18 Remove the nuts and Allen screws which hold the tappet block to the cylinder head. Remove the tappet block and tappets. Keep the tappets in their originally fitted order (photo).
19 Lift out the valve clearance adjusting shims, keeping them in exact order of fitting.
20 Slacken the cylinder head nuts progressively, working from the centre outwards.
21 Lift off each cylinder head and discard the gaskets.
22 Cylinder liner retainers must be fitted before the crankshaft is turned even fractionally. Obtain the official tools (JD41) or devise your own clamps which can be bolted to the cylinder block to exert downward pressure on the liners, yet will still permit the piston/rod assemblies to be withdrawn through the top of the block. Any movement of the pistons will cause the cylinder liner bottom sealing to break.
23 Unbolt and remove the timing cover from the cylinder block, noting the positions of the long and short bolts. Discard the cover gaskets and the oil seal.
24 Remove the spacer from the front end of the crankshaft.
25 Move the chain tensioner clear of its locating bracket and slide it from its dowel pin.
26 Disengage the timing chain from its sprockets and remove it. Do not disturb the chain dampers (see Section 42).
27 Unbolt and remove the jackshaft cover from the cylinder block. On cars without air conditioning, note the location of any long bolts and spacers on the jackshaft cover (photo).
28 Unbolt and remove the engine mounting brackets (photo).
29 Turn the engine upside down and unbolt the sump. Note the location of the oil cooler pipe clip.
30 Remove the bolts which secure the sandwich plate baffle and plate itself and take off the timing indicator scale.
31 Remove the union elbow from the sandwich plate. Clean away all the old gasket.
32 Unscrew the four setscrews which hold the suction pipe clips and bracket. Draw the suction pipe from the O-ring at the elbow.
33 Remove the crankshaft undershield and oil delivery pipe clips.
34 Unbolt the oil delivery pipe from the oil pump, remove the pipe from the crankcase and discard the gasket.
35 From the front end of the crankshaft, draw off the sprocket and lift out the Woodruff key.
36 Unbolt the oil pump from the cylinder block and remove it with drivegear and the Woodruff key.
37 Unbolt the sprocket from the jackshaft and remove it.
38 Unbolt the jackshaft locking plate from the cylinder block. Withdraw the plate and then pull the jackshaft from the engine (photo).
39 Check that the connecting rod big-end bearing caps are marked with identifying numbers (either 1 to 12 or 1A to 6B, see Specifications). If they are not, dot punch them taking care to locate the marks so as to indicate also which way round the cap is fitted.
40 Rotate the crankshaft by means of the flywheel or driveplate until two big-end bearing caps are at their lowest points. Unscrew the nuts and remove the bearing caps and shells. If the shells are to be refitted, tape them to their respective caps. If they are not, they may be discarded.
41 Carefully scrape the carbon ring from the top of the cylinder bore and push the piston/connecting rod assembly out of the top of the bore. Mark the piston or rod with its cylinder number and if the shell bearing is to be used again, tape it to the connecting rod.
42 Repeat the removal operations on the remaining pistons/connecting rods.
43 Unbolt and remove the flywheel (manual gearbox) or driveplate (automatic transmission) from the crankshaft rear flange.

7.8B Distributor and ignition system amplifier

7.9A Oil feed banjo bolt (upper)

7.9B Oil feed banjo bolt (lower)

7.9C Oil pressure sender unit (1) and warning switch (2)

7.13A Chain tensioner access plug

7.13B Elongated hole in chain tensioner slipper

7.13C Chain tensioner retracted onto shoulder of guide rod (arrowed)

7.15 Camshaft sprocket retaining tool in position

7.18 Tappets (cam followers) installed in the tappet block

7.27 Removing a jackshaft cover plate screw

7.28 Engine right-hand mounting bracket

7.38 Jackshaft showing distributor drivegear

44 Check that the main bearing caps are clearly identified as to position and which way round they are fitted. If not, mark them.
45 Unbolt the caps, starting with the centre one. First unscrew the small nuts and then the pillar and larger nuts. If necessary, mark the position of the pillar nuts so that there will be no confusion at reassembly.
46 Lift off the main bearing caps and slide out the rear main bearing casting. If the bearing shells are to be used again, tape them to their caps. Discard the oil seals.
47 Lift the crankshaft from the crankcase and then withdraw the upper bearing half shells, keeping them in their original order if they are to be used again.
48 The cylinder liners can only be removed upwards after the clamping tools have been removed. If the liners are to be used again, mark their positions in the block and put alignment marks on their rims and the block so that on refitting they will resume their original orientation. Press them from the block.

8 Camshaft covers – removal and refitting (engine in car, XJ12 and Double Six

1 Disconnect the throttle linkage.
2 Remove the front and rear inlet manifolds as described in Chapter 3.
3 Unscrew and remove the domed head nuts and washers and lift off the cover.
4 Refitting is a reversal of removal. Use a new gasket and neoprene sealing plug. Tighten the nuts to the specified torque.

9 Camshaft covers – removal and refitting (engine in car, XJS)

Left-hand cover

1 Remove the left-hand induction manifold (see Chapter 3).
2 Disconnect the wire from the coolant temperature sensor.
3 Move the wiring harness clear of the camshaft cover.
4 Disconnect the cross-pipe hose from the auxiliary air valve.
5 Unbolt the camshaft cover, remove it and discard the gasket and neoprene sealing plug.

Right-hand cover

6 Have the air conditioning system depressurised by your dealer.
7 Remove the right-hand induction manifold (Chapter 3).
8 Unbolt the compressor silencer and then slacken the bolt which clamps the silencer union to the compressor. Withdraw the union. Discard the sealing ring and plug the openings.
9 Unbolt and remove the camshaft cover, discarding the gasket and neoprene plug.
10 Refitting of both covers is a reversal of removal. Use new gaskets and seals. If the right-hand cover was removed, have the air conditioning system recharged by your dealer.

10 Camshaft – removal and refitting (engine in car, all models

1 Remove the appropriate camshaft cover as previously described.
2 Remove the right-hand air cleaner.
3 Extract the rubber grommet from the timing cover.
4 A special tool will now be required (JD42/2 and JD44 for engines except XJS). Insert the cranked screwdrive blade of the special tool into the hole in the front face of the engine and release the locking catch on the timing chain tensioner slipper by turning the screwdriver anti-clockwise.
5 Now use the special tool to retract the timing chain tensioner to its full extent (refer to Section 7, paragraph 13). Once the slipper guide rod has locked on its step, remove the tools.
6 Flatten the camshaft sprocket lockplate tabs and remove two of the securing bolts (photo).
7 Turn the crankshaft by means of a socket on the damper/pulley bolt until the camshaft alignment gauge (C.3993) can be inserted in the slot in the camshaft which is to be removed (photo).
8 Extract the two remaining camshaft sprocket securing bolts and fit a sprocket retaining tool (JD40) or make one up (see Section 7, paragraph 14).

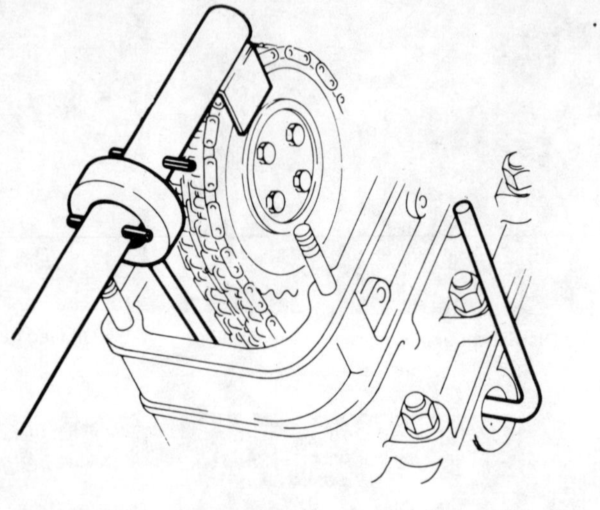

Fig. 1.24 Timing chain tensioner tools installed (XJS) (Sec 10)

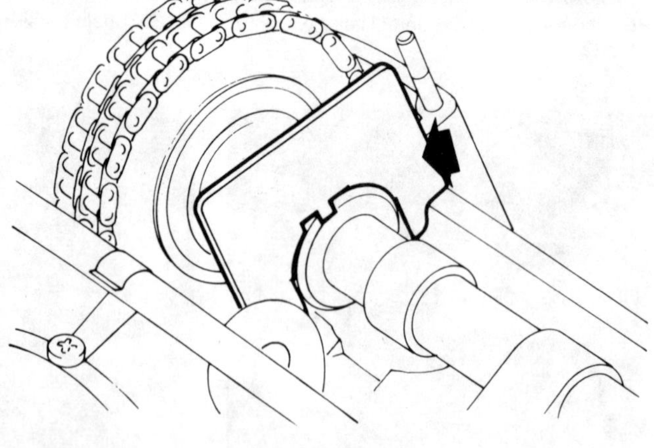

Fig. 1.25 Camshaft setting tool (arrowed) in position (Sec 10)

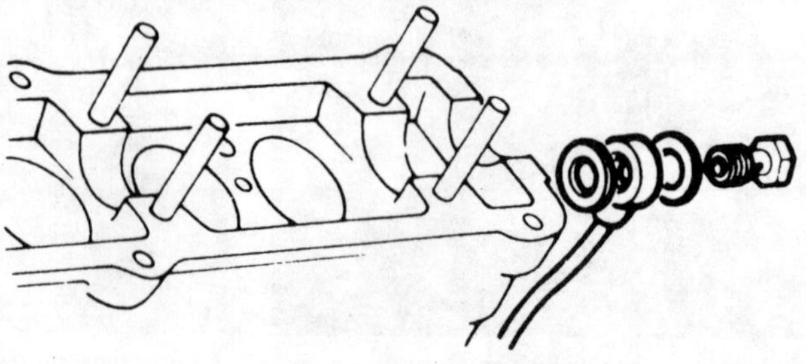

Fig. 1.26 Tappet block oil supply pipe (Sec 11)

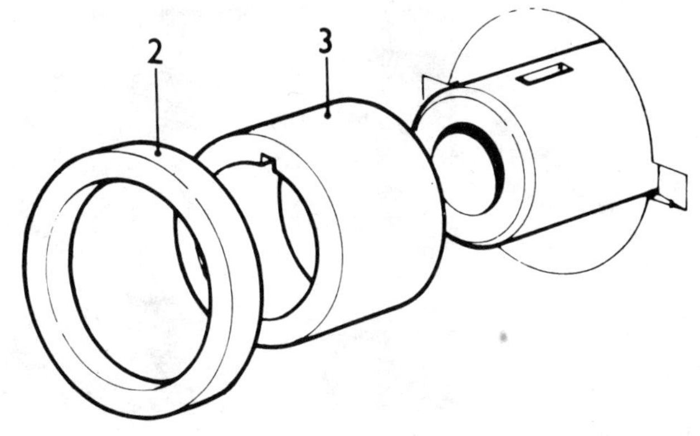

Fig. 1.27 Crankshaft front oil seal (2) and spacer (3) (Sec 12)

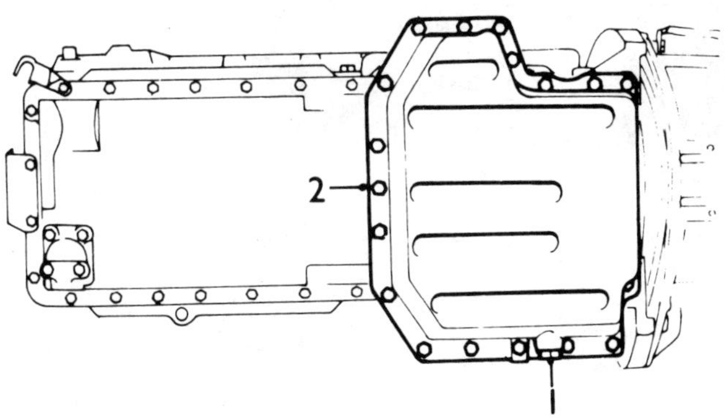

Fig. 1.28 Oil sump pan (Sec 13)

1 Oil drain plug *2 Sump pan*

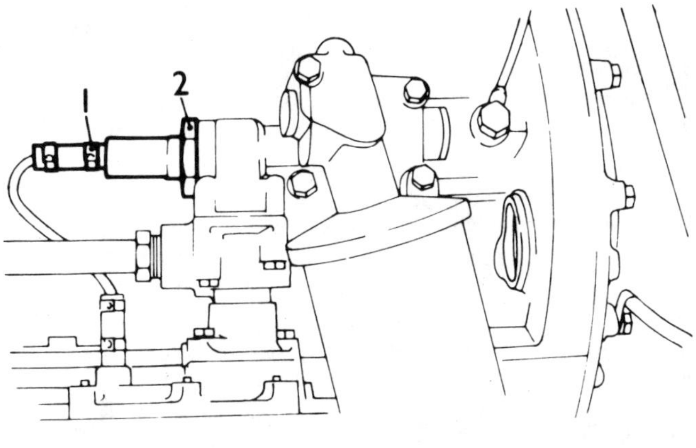

Fig. 1.29 Oil pressure relief valve (Sec 15)

1 Bleed hose *2 Relief valve body*

9 Do not rotate the crankshaft once the camshaft sprocket has been disconnected.
10 Unscrew the camshaft bearing cap nuts starting with the centre one and working towards each end.
11 Lift the camshaft from the tappet block.
12 To refit the camshaft, first oil the journals and tappets. Lower the camshaft into position and turn it until the setting gauge (C.3993) can be inserted into the slot in the camshaft.
13 Fit the bearing caps and tighten the retaining nuts to the specified torque.
14 Check that the camshaft setting gauge is still correctly aligned and engage the camshaft sprocket with the camshaft. Use a new lockplate and screw in one bolt. Bend up the lockplate tabs on this bolt.
15 Remove the setting gauge and turn the crankshaft as necessary to be able to insert and lock the remaining sprocket bolts.
16 Insert the screwdriver part of the special tool through the timing cover hole and trip the chain tensioner locking catch. Refit the rubber grommet.
17 Refit the camshaft cover.
18 Repeat the operations where necessary for the removal and refitting of the other camshaft.
19 Refit the air cleaner.

11 Tappet block – removal and refitting (engine in car, all models)

1 Disconnect the throttle linkage and remove the camshaft as previously described.
2 Unscrew and remove the banjo bolt which holds the oil supply pipe to the tappet block.
3 Disconnect the breather pipe (left-hand block only).
4 Slacken the tappet block securing nuts working them from the centre ones towards each end.
5 Lift off the tappet block and extract the tappets with their adjusting shims, keeping them in strict order as originally fitted.
6 Clean the mating surfaces of the cylinder head and tappet block thoroughly before refitting. Smear both surfaces with jointing compound and fit the tappet block, checking that the dowels are correctly located.
7 Tighten the securing nuts in a diagonal manner working from the centre out.
8 Refit the tappets and their shims in their original order having first smeared them with clean engine oil.
9 Refit the breather pipe, the banjo bolt, the camshaft and the throttle linkage.
10 If either tappet block is renewed, then the valve clearances must be checked as described in Section 50.

12 Crankshaft front oil seal – renewal (engine in car)

1 Remove the crankshaft pulley and damper as described in Section 7, paragraphs 3 to 5. Remove the starter motor if necessary in order to jam the flywheel/driveplate ring gear.
2 Prise the oil seal out of the timing cover and discard it. Withdraw the spacer.
3 Wipe out the oil seal recess and drive the new seal into position using a piece of tubing. Refit the distance piece, pulley and damper.

13 Oil sump pan – removal and refitting (engine in car)

1 The oil sump pan can be unbolted and removed provided the engine oil has first been drained into a suitable container.
2 When refitting, use a new gasket smeared on both sides with jointing compound.

14 Sandwich plate – removal and refitting (engine in car)

1 Remove the front suspension assembly as described in Chapter 11.
2 Unbolt and remove the oil sump pan as described in Section 13.
3 Disconnect the oil cooler pipes, remove them and then unbolt and remove the suction elbow first from the sandwich plate.

10.6 Camshaft sprocket bolts and lockplates

10.7 Camshaft alignment gauge in position

17.3A Engine oil cooler right-hand union

17.3B Engine oil cooler left-hand union

17.11 Air conditioning condenser must be removed for access to oil cooler

4 Release the delivery pipe and vent pipe from the sandwich plate.
5 Unbolt the sandwich plate and take off the timing indicator. Note the locations of the differing length sandwich plate screws.
6 Unbolt the baffle plate (four setscrews) and the bypass valve housing (three setscrews).
7 Clean all mating faces and renew the O-ring seals at the bypass valve housing and spigot.
8 Refitting is a reversal of removal. Use new gaskets and apply oil to the bypass valve spigot O-ring.

15 Oil pressure relief valve – removal and refitting (engine in car)

1 On cars with a catalytic converter, remove the exhaust downpipe for access to the relief valve.
2 Cut the clip from the oil pressure relief valve bleed hose and pull off the hose.
3 Unscrew the relief valve from the oil filter base.
4 Refitting is a reversal of removal, but use a new sealing washer and hose clip.

16 Oil pick-up strainer – removal and refitting (engine in car)

1 Remove the sandwich plate as described in Section 14.
2 Unscrew the four setscrews which hold the suction pipe clips and bracket. Withdaw the suction pipe from the elbow. Clean the strainer and dry it.
3 Refitting is a reversal of removal, but renew the elbow O-ring seals.

17 Engine oil cooler – removal and refitting (engine in car) – XJ12 and Double Six

1 Remove the bonnet and the two screws which hold the radiator lower grille. These are self-tapping screws located one at each end of the top edge of the grille.

XJS model

2 Extract the screws which hold the lower splash shield.

All models

3 Disconnect the pipes from the engine oil cooler, using two spanners so that the stub does not tear out of the cooler casing. Alternatively, disconnect the pipes at the unions below the crankshaft pulley (photos).
4 Extract the screws from the cooler support brackets. To reach these, the rubber plugs must first be prised from the lower front panel. Remove the cooler with any spacers.

Cars with air conditioning

5 On these vehicles, before the oil cooler can be removed, the following additional work must be carried out.
6 Unbolt the radiator top rail.
7 Extract the screws which hold the headlamp relay.
8 Disconnect the rubber couplings which connect the air intake ram pipes and the air cleaners.
9 Unbolt the fan cowls, noting location of the wiring harness clips. Ease the cowls from the radiator top rail.
10 Tie the air conditioning condenser securely to the radiator top rail and air intake ram pipes. Pass the securing cord under the lower corners of the condenser. Do not strain the condenser hoses or connections.
11 Lift the condenser just enough to clear the spigots from the oil cooler grommets. Support the condenser on blocks of wood if necessary whilst the oil cooler is removed (photo).

All models

12 Refitting on all models is a reversal of removal. On completion, run the engine, check for oil leaks and after the engine has been switched off, check the oil level and top up as necessary.

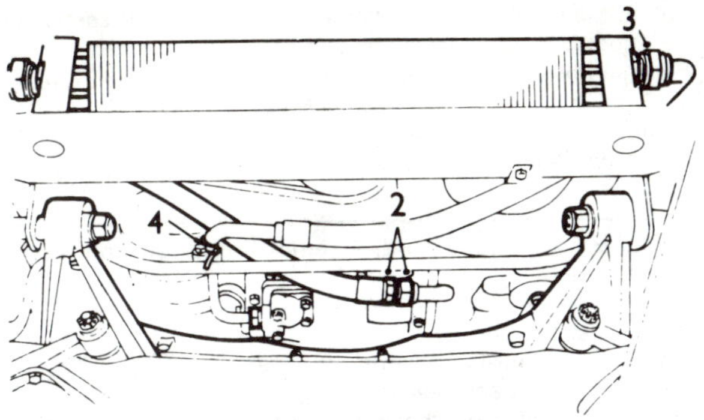

Fig. 1.30 Engine oil cooler connections (Sec 17)

2 Supply hose union
3 Oil cooler pipe union
4 Retaining strap for hose

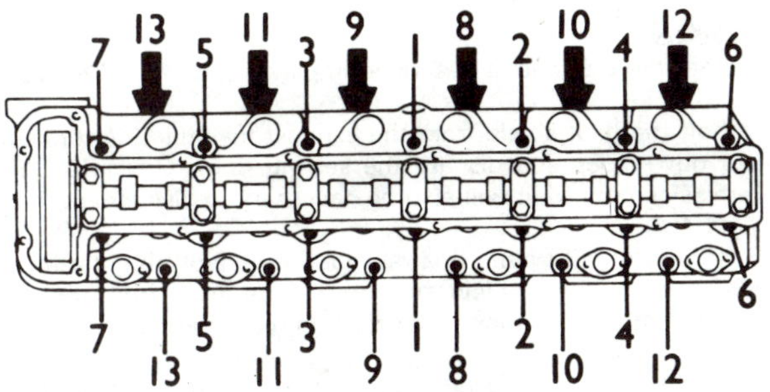

Fig. 1.31 Cylinder head nut tightening sequence (Sec 18)

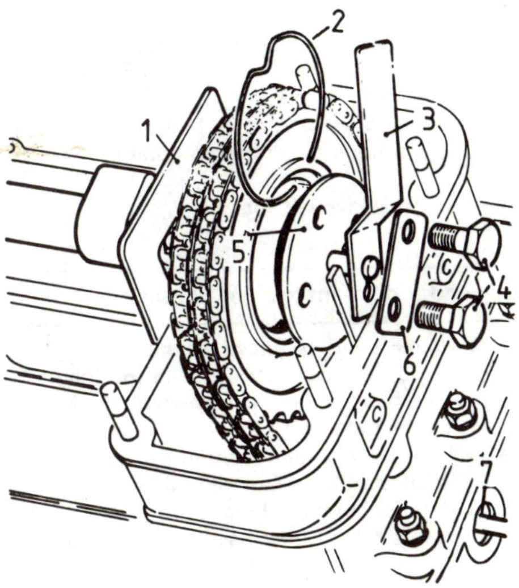

Fig. 1.32 Camshaft sprocket coupling details (Sec 18)

1 Camshaft setting tool
2 Circlip
3 Sprocket retaining tool
4 Sprocket bolts
5 Coupling
6 Lockplate
7 Chain tensioner tool

18 Cylinder head – removal and refitting (engine in car), XJ12 and Double Six)

1 Disconnect the battery and drain the cooling system.
2 According to whether the left-hand or right-hand cylinder head is being removed, remove the induction manifold from the appropriate side as described in Chapter 3. On carburettor engines, remove the manifold complete with induction housing and the carburettors.
3 Remove the respective camshaft cover as described in Section 8.
4 If the cylinder head next to the battery is being removed, then remove the battery from the engine compartment.
5 Turn the crankshaft by means of the pulley centre bolt until the camshaft setting gauge (see Section 10) can be engaged in the camshaft front flange. If both cylinder heads are going to be removed, align the right-hand camshaft with the tool.
6 Carry out the operations described in Section 10, paragraphs 3 to 6 and 8 and 9.
7 If the right-hand cylinder head is being removed, remove the starter solenoid heat shield.
8 Remove the exhaust manifold heat shield.
9 Disconnect the exhaust downpipes from the manifold and from the intermediate pipes.
10 Slacken the heater return pipe clip and ease the cross-pipe forward.
11 Unclip the coolant bleed pipe from the front of the cylinder head.
12 Unscrew the camshaft oil feed banjo bolt.
13 Remove the three nuts which hold the front of the cylinder head to the timing cover. Detach the cable clips from the studs.
14 Unscrew the cylinder head nuts, working from the centre ones outwards.
15 Remove the cylinder head and stand it on blocks of wood placed one at each end to prevent damage to the projecting valve heads.
16 *Do not rotate the crankshaft from this point on* unless cylinder liner clamps are fitted.
17 Discard the cylinder head gasket.
18 Remove the left-hand cylinder head, where required, in a similar way.
19 Clean the mating faces of the cylinder heads and the block. If the sole purpose of cylinder head removal is to renew the cylinder head gasket and neither the crankshaft nor the camshaft have been rotated since the cylinder head was removed, the refitting operations can commence as described in paragraph 25 and onwards. Where either shaft has been moved, either inadvertently or for purposes of piston decarbonising, then carry out the preliminary operations as follows.

Both cylinder heads or right-hand one only

20 Remove the distributor cover. Fit cylinder liner clamps if this has not already been done.
21 Apply a socket spanner to the crankshaft pulley nut and rotate the crankshaft until No 1 piston on the right-hand bank is at TDC, verified by the alignment of the distributor rotor with No 1 segment in the distributor cap. (The distributor rotor will not be directly in alignment with the pick-up module but will be about 5° from coincidence).
22 Turn the camshaft in the right-hand cylinder head until the setting gauge can be fitted into the slot in the camshaft front flange.
23 Repeat the operation described in the last paragraph on the left-hand cylinder head.
24 Unbolt and remove the cylinder liner clamps from the right-hand cylinder block.
25 Recheck the cleanliness of the cylinder block and head mating surfaces.
26 Fit a new cylinder head gasket ('TOP' uppermost) to the cylinder block. Do not apply any grease or jointing compound.
27 Fit the cylinder head and tighten the nuts in stages to the specified torque in the sequence shown.
28 Tighten the timing cover nuts to the specified torque.
29 Remove the camshaft sprocket retaining tool and check the alignment of the sprocket bolt holes. If they are not in alignment, extract the circlip which retains the camshaft coupling to the sprocket. Disengage the coupling from the splines and press the sprocket onto the camshaft shoulder. Now rotate the coupling until alignment of the bolt holes is achieved. Bolt the coupling to the camshaft, refit the circlip and then withdraw the setting tool.
30 If the left-hand cylinder head has been removed, repeat the operations described in paragraphs 25 to 29.

31 Turn the crankshaft until all the remaining camshaft sprocket retaining bolts can be fitted and their lockplate tabs turned up.
32 Refit the coolant pipes to the front of the cylinder head and the camshaft oil supply banjo bolt.
33 Trip the timing chain tensioner locking catch as described in Section 10. Refit the rubber plug to the hole in the timing cover.
34 Reconnect the exhaust pipes and heat shields.
35 Refit the camshaft covers and induction manifolds.
36 Refit and reconnect the battery.
37 Refill the cooling system.
38 Check the ignition timing (Chapter 4).

Left-hand cylinder head – refitting

39 Where only this cylinder head was removed, refit it in the following way.
40 Fit cylinder liner clamps (if not already done) and turn the crankshaft until the setting gauge can be inserted into the slot in the front flange of the right-hand camshaft.
41 Rotate the camshaft in the (removed) left-hand cylinder head until the setting gauge can be fitted into its flange slot.
42 Remove the cylinder liner clamps.
43 Carry out the operations described in paragraphs 25 to 29 and 31 to 38.

19 Cylinder head (left-hand) – removal and refitting (engine in car, XJS)

1 Disconnect the battery.
2 Remove both camshaft covers as previously described.
3 Slacken the hose clips on the thermostat housing and the coolant crossover pipe.
4 Extract the bolts which hold the thermostat housing, auxiliary air valve and the engine lifting eyes to the cylinder head.
5 Move the housing away from the cylinder head and discard the gaskets.
6 Unbolt the fan and fluid coupling unit from their shaft.
7 Turn the crankshaft using a socket on the pulley centre bolt, until the camshaft setting gauge (see Section 10) can be engaged in the slot in the front flange of the right-hand camshaft.
8 Remove the rubber plug from the timing cover and using the special tools, release and retract the timing chain tensioner as described in Section 10.
9 Disconnect the camshaft sprocket and fit the retaining tool also as described in Section 10.
10 Remove the heat shields from the steering rack gaiter and the exhaust downpipe.
11 Disconnect the exhaust downpipe from the left-hand manifold. Discard the sealing ring. On cars fitted with emission control, it will be necessary to disconnect the EGR pipe at the same time as the exhaust downpipe is unbolted.
12 Remove the heat shields from the exhaust manifolds.
13 Unbolt the rear exhaust manifold from the cylinder head. Remove the manifold and discard the gasket.

Cars with automatic transmission only

14 Unbolt the fluid dipstick tube and swing it away from the engine.

All models

15 Disconnect the fuel hoses from the fuel cooler (see Chapter 3). Make sure that you are not disconnecting the refrigerant hoses by mistake or dangerous refrigerant gases will be released.
16 Unbolt the amplifier unit (fuel injection system) and move it away from the cylinder head.
17 Disconnect the camshaft oil feed banjo bolt.
18 Remove the three nuts which hold the cylinder head to the timing cover.
19 Unscrew the cylinder head nuts progressively, working from the centre ones towards each end.
20 Remove the cylinder head and place it on blocks of wood to prevent damage to projecting valve heads.
21 Do not remove the camshaft setting gauge from the right-hand camshaft.
22 Commence refitting by setting the camshaft in the (removed) left-hand cylinder head with the setting gauge.
23 Carry out the operations described in Section 18, paragraphs 25 to 29 inclusive.
24 Rotate the crankshaft until the remaining camshaft sprocket bolts can be fitted. Use new lockplates and bend up the locking tabs.
25 Reverse the operations described in paragraphs 1 to 6, 8 and 10 to 17 of this Section. Use all new seals and gaskets.
26 Adjust the fanbelt tension.
27 Check the ignition timing.

20 Cylinder head (right-hand) – removal and refitting (engine in car, XJS)

1 Disconnect the battery.
2 Remove the right-hand camshaft cover.
3 Remove the fan and fluid coupling.
4 Slacken the clips on the hoses to the thermostat housing and coolant crossover pipe.
5 Unbolt the thermostat housing, the engine lifting eyes and the auxiliary air valve from the cylinder head. Move the components away from the cylinder head and discard the gaskets.
6 Release the air pump/auxiliary pulley adjusting bolt and unbolt the adjuster bracket from the cylinder head.

Cars with air conditioning

7 Remove the compressor mounting bolts, disengage the drivebelt from the compressor pulley and move the compressor away from the right-hand cylinder head.

All models

8 Repeat the operations described in paragraphs 7 to 9 inclusive of Section 19.
9 Unbolt the heat shield from the exhaust manifold, disconnect the exhaust downpipes and discard the sealing rings. On cars equipped with emission control, it will also be necessary to disconnect the EGR pipe.
10 Remove the right-hand heat shield, then unbolt the starter motor and starter motor heat shield and move them away from the engine.
11 Repeat the operations described in paragraphs 17 to 20 of Section 19.
12 *Do not turn the crankshaft from this point on* unless cylinder liner clamps are fitted.
13 If the cylinder head was removed only to renew a faulty gasket, and neither the camshaft nor the crankshaft have been disturbed, then refit it by following the work described in paragraphs 25 to 29 inclusive of Section 18.
14 Where either the camshaft or crankshaft have been moved, either inadvertently or for the purpose of piston crown decarbonising, then carry out the preliminary operations described in paragraphs 20 to 22 inclusive of Section 18.
15 Remove the cylinder liner clamps, if fitted.
16 Refit the cylinder head as described in paragraphs 25 to 29 of Section 18.
17 Reconnect the camshaft oil supply banjo bolt.
18 Reverse the operations described in paragraphs 1 to 10 of this Section.
19 Adjust the fan and drivebelt tension.

21 Cylinder head – dismantling and reassembly

1 With the cylinder head removed as described above, and the tappet block removed, remove each valve in the following way.
2 With the cylinder head placed face down on the bench on wooden blocks, remove the tappets and shims (if not already removed) and keep them exactly in their originally fitted order.
3 Using a piece of suitable diameter tubing, placed on the valve spring retaining plate, strike the tubing sharply with a hammer to ease any valve components which may have become seized by ridging or heat.
4 Using a suitable valve spring compressor, depress the first valve spring retainer until the split collets can be withdrawn. Carefully release the compressor and take off the retainer, the double valve springs and the spring lower seat. Withdraw the valve (photos).
5 Keep all components in their originally fitted order together with their respective tappets and shims. The best way to do this is to make up two trays or boxes, each subdivided into twelve compartments. Mark one tray 'right-hand cylinder head' and the other 'left-hand

cylinder head' and number the compartments 1 to 12, number 1 being at the timing chain end of the cylinder head.
6 Repeat the operations on all remaining valves.
7 Remove and discard the valve stem oil seals which are fitted to the inlet valve guides.
8 Identification of the valves is no problem as the inlet valve heads are larger than the exhaust (photo).
9 Refer to Section 43 for cylinder head examination and renovation procedures.
10 Reassembly is a reversal of dismantling. Smear each valve stem with clean engine oil before fitting and fit new valve stem oil seals. Make sure that all components are returned to their original positions. If new components have been fitted or the valves have been ground in (see Section 38) then the valve clearances will require checking and adjusting as described in Section 50.

22 Crankshaft main bearing shells – renewal (engine in car)

1 Renewal of the main bearing shells is possible without removing the engine, but it is unlikely to be required unless it is positively known that main bearing failure alone has occurred as the result of high mileage or a lubrication fault. Normally, the crankshaft will also have worn and will be renewed at the same time as the bearings during major overhaul.
2 To obtain access to the main bearings, first remove the sandwich plate as described in Section 14.
3 Unbolt and withdraw the suction pipe from the O-ring at the elbow.
4 Unbolt the crankshaft undershield and draw it clear.
5 Unbolt and remove the oil delivery pipe elbow from the oil pump casting. Leave the bolt at the outboard hole in the oil pump casting. If it must be removed, make sure that it is refitted in its original position. Note also the position of the pillar nuts.
6 Unbolt and remove the front main bearing cap. Renew the cap shell bearing and the upper shell from the crankcase web. The upper shells can often be pushed out using a probe, if not, insert a split pin into the oil hole in the crankshaft journal and slowly turn the crankshaft so that the head of the split pin pushes the shell around and out of its seat. Fit the new shell in a similar manner.
7 Oil the journal and refit the cap, tightening the nuts to the specified torque.
8 Renew the remaining main bearing shells in a similar way, but only release one bearing cap at a time. Note that the rear main bearing shell incorporates an oil groove whilst the centre shell is plain.
9 Clean the suction pipe strainer and renew all O-ring seals before refitting the dismantled components.

23 Connecting rod big-end bearings – renewal (engine in car)

1 Refer to Section 22, paragraphs 1 to 5, which apply equally to the big-end bearings.
2 Turn the crankshaft until two crankpins are at the lowest position.
3 Unbolt and remove the big-end bearing caps. Do not mix them up. Do not rotate the crankshaft with the caps off.
4 Renew the bearing shells. The piston/rod may be pushed up the bore just enough to provide access to the rod shell but do not push it further than necessary.
5 Oil the crankpins, fit the caps and tighten the nuts to the specified torque.
6 Rotate the crankshaft until two more crankpins are at their lowest point and renew the shells.
7 Repeat the foregoing operations until all big-end shell bearings have been renewed.

24 Engine front mountings – removal and refitting (engine in car, XJ12 and Double Six)

1 Disconnect the battery.
2 Remove the wing valance stays and the air cleaners.
3 Remove the horn from the engine left-hand mounting bracket.

21.4A Using a valve spring compressor

21.4B Removing valve springs

21.4C Valve stem oil seal and spring lower seat

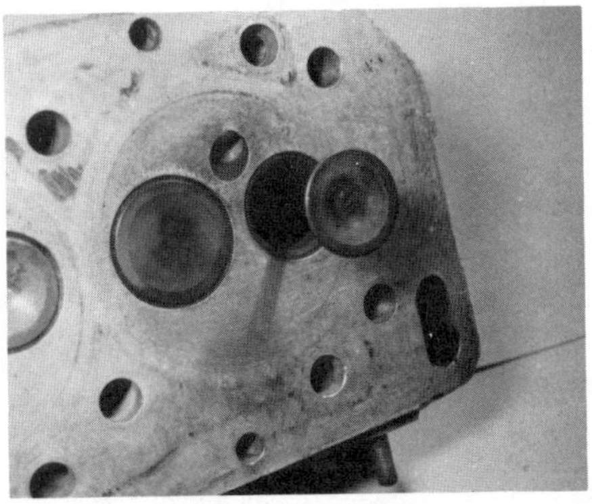

21.8 Inlet and exhaust valve heads. The exhaust valve is the smaller

29.2 Cartridge type oil filter viewed from below

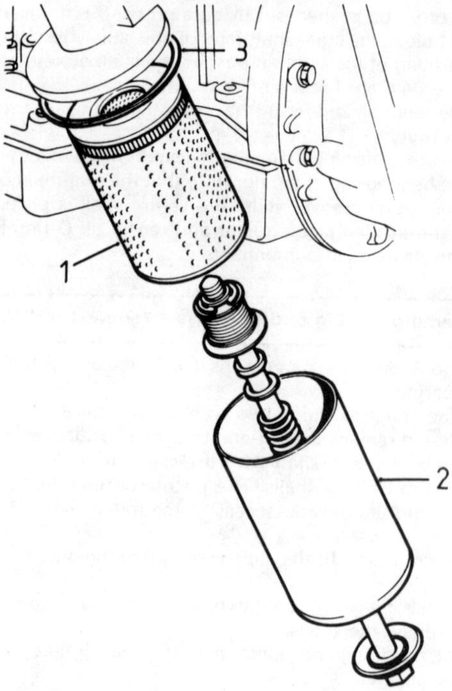

Fig. 1.33 Early type engine oil filter (Sec 27)

1 *Renewable element*
2 *Filter casing*
3 *Sealing ring*

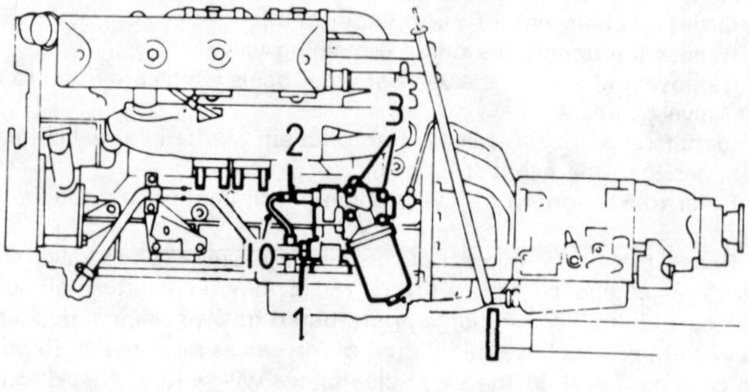

Fig. 1.34 Oil filter assembly connections (early models) (Sec 28)

1 *Oil cooler supply pipe*
2 *Pressure relief valve vent hose*
3 *Oil filter head retaining bolts*

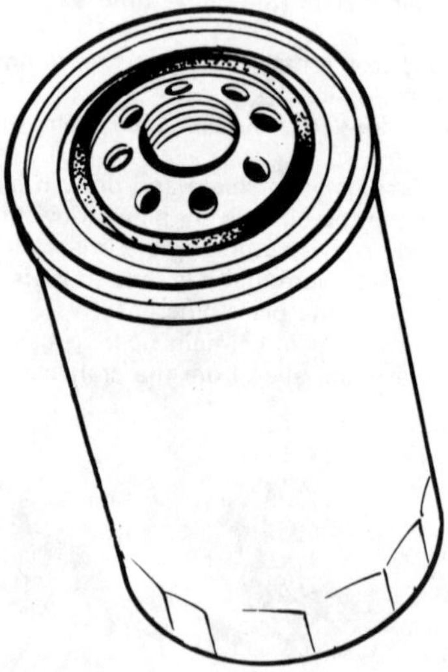

Fig. 1.35 Cartridge type oil filter (Sec 29)

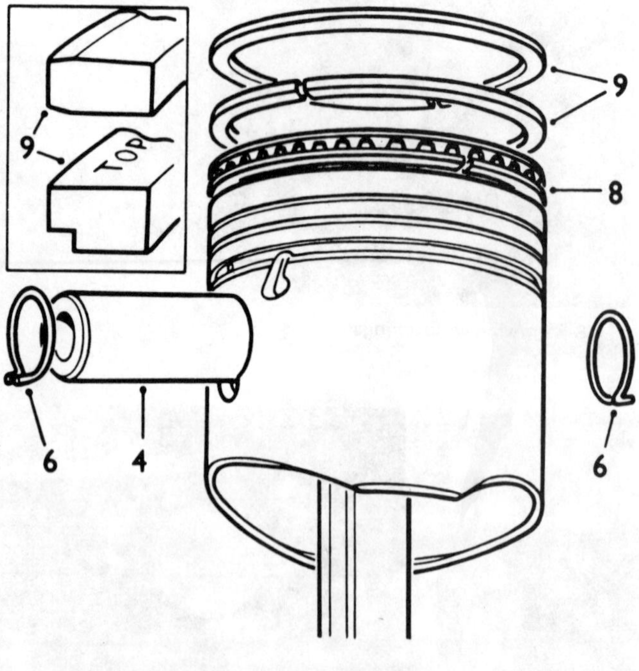

Fig. 1.36 Piston/connecting rod assembly (Sec 32)

4 *Gudgeon pin*
6 *Circlips*
8 *Oil control piston ring*
9 *Compression rings – inset shows details*

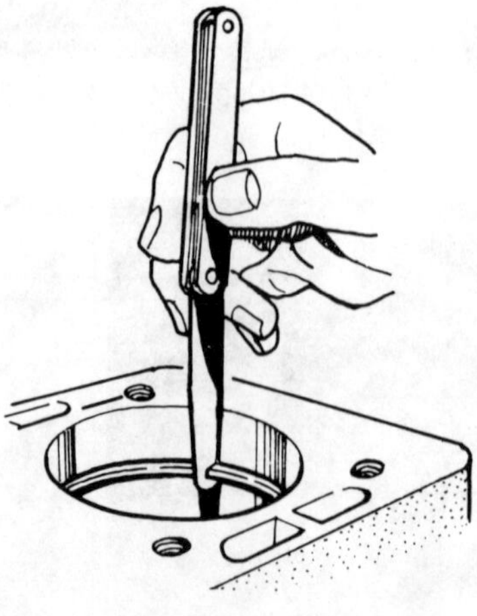

Fig. 1.37 Checking a piston ring end gap (Sec 32)

Cars with air conditioning

4 Unbolt the fan and fluid coupling unit and rest it carefully against the radiator.

Cars without air conditioning

5 Release the fan relay from the radiator top rail.
6 Unbolt and remove the fan shield.

All cars

7 Unscrew and remove the nuts from the tops and the bottoms of both engine mountings.
8 Using a suitable hoist and chains, raise the engine just enough to be able to free the front mountings. Take care not to damage the expansion valve on air conditioned cars. Do not lose the fibre washers.
9 Fit the new engine mountings so that the fibre washer is on top of the front suspension crossmember brackets.
10 Fit the plain nut and washer to hold each mounting to its crossmember bracket.
11 Lower the engine gently to locate it on its mountings. Fit the nuts to secure the engine to its mountings.
12 Remove the chains and hoist and refit all the remaining components.

25 Engine front mountings – removal and refitting (engine in car, XJS)

1 For access to the engine mountings, remove the air cleaners.
2 The removal and refitting operations are then as described in Section 24.

26 Engine rear mounting – removal and refitting (engine in car)

1 The operations are as described in earlier Sections of this Chapter. (XJ12 and Double Six – Section 3, paragraphs 28 to 31; XJS – Section 5, paragraphs 35 and 40 to 46).

27 Oil filter (renewable element type, early cars) – renewal

1 The oil filter is accessible from under the car and should be renewed at the same time as the engine oil.
2 Drain the engine oil (hot).
3 Unscrew the centre bolt from the oil filter canister. Withdraw the canister complete with bolt, sealing ring and the filter element. It will be full of oil so try not to spill it.
4 Discard the filter element and the sealing ring. If the sealing ring is still in the groove in the filter head, pick it out with a sharply pointed tool.
5 Clean out the canister and wash the filter bypass valve in clean petrol.
6 Press the new canister sealing ring into its groove, fit the new filter element and offer up the canister to the sealing ring.
7 Keep pressure applied to the canister and tighten the centre bolt to the specified torque only – no tighter.
8 Having refilled the engine with clean oil, start the engine and run for a few minutes at a fast idle. Check for leaks from the filter.
9 The new filter element will absorb about a pint of oil and the oil level should be checked on the dipstick and topped up as necessary after the engine has been switched off for a few minutes.

28 Oil filter head (renewable element type, early cars) – removal and refitting

1 Remove the left-hand air cleaner.
2 Unbolt the left-hand exhaust downpipe from the manifold and from the intermediate pipe. Remove the downpipe. On left-hand drive cars, full left steering lock must be applied before the pipe can be removed.
3 Disconnect the union on the oil cooler supply pipe.
4 Cut off the clip from the pressure relief vent hose at the nearest point to the valve.
5 Remove the oil filter canister and element.
6 Unbolt and remove the left-hand front heat shield.
7 Extract the four setscrews which secure the filter head.
8 Tap the filter head carefully to break the gasket seal and push the head upwards until the bypass valve stub pipe clears the housing.
9 Separate the vent pipe from the relief valve and withdraw the filter head assembly.
10 Refitting is a reversal of removal, but renew the O-ring seal on the bypass valve stub pipe and fit a new filter head-to-block gasket.

29 Oil filter (cartridge type) – renewal

1 Drain the engine oil (hot).
2 Use a chain, strap or special oil filter wrench to unscrew the oil filter, which is accessible from under the car (photo).
3 The new filter will be supplied with captive sealing ring.
4 Wipe the sealing surface of the filter head clean and then smear the filter cartridge seal with a little engine oil or light grease.
5 Screw the new filter into position as tightly as possible *using hand pressure only.*
6 With the engine filled with fresh oil, start it and run at a fast idle. Check the filter for leaks.
7 The new filter will absorb about one pint of oil so check and top up the engine oil after the engine is switched off.

30 Examination and renovation – general

1 With the engine stripped, all components should be thoroughly cleaned and examined for wear, as described in the following Sections. Where a high mileage has been covered, consideration should be given to renewing an assembly on an exchange basis rather than renewing an individual component in a well worn unit.

31 Crankshaft and bearings – examination and renovation

1 Examine the surfaces of the crankshaft journals and crankpins. If there is evidence of scoring, then the crankshaft will have to be renewed as the material is so hard that the regrinding facilities to be found locally will not be suitable.
2 If the bearing surfaces are good, always take the opportunity of renewing the shell bearings as a matter of routine.
3 On XJS manual gearbox models, examine the pilot bush which is installed in the centre of the crankshaft rear flange onto which the flywheel is mounted. If it is worn, it must be renewed. To do this, either tap a thread into it and screw in a bolt to extract the bush or fill the bush with grease and drive in a close fitting mandrel. The hydraulic pressure created by the latter method will eject the bush. The new bush should be soaked in engine oil for 24 hours before pressing it into position.
4 Clean out the crankshaft oil passages with wire and blow them out with compressed air if available.
5 The thrust washers which fit either side of the centre main bearing should normally be renewed at the time of major overhaul. However, when the crankshaft is installed, its endfloat must be checked, as described in Section 47, and new thrust washers of different thicknesses may be required to bring the endfloat within the specified tolerance.

32 Pistons and connecting rods – examination and renovation

1 New pistons and gudgeon pins are supplied as matched sets.
2 Worn pistons can be removed from the connecting rod simply by extracting the circlips and pushing the gudgeon pin from the piston and small end bush. The ambient temperature should not be less than 68°F (20°C) when doing this work.
3 Each piston has three rings, two upper compression and a lower oil control. Remove the rings by sliding two or three old feeler blades behind the top ring and locating the blades at equidistant points. Slide the ring upwards and off using a twisting motion.
4 Repeat the removal operations on the remaining rings.

5 If the connecting rod small-end bush is worn, exchange the rod for a factory reconditioned one as it is not possible to renew the bushes without special equipment.
6 When connecting a piston to its connecting rod, make sure that with the word 'FRONT' on the piston crown towards the timing cover end of the engine, the chamfer on the big-end rod eye is adjacent to the radius which is to be found at one end of each crankpin.
7 Use new circlips to retain the gudgeon pin.
8 Fit the new piston rings into their respective cylinder bores one at a time, push each ring half way down the bore and check the ring end gap. Any slight variation from that specified may be corrected by grinding the end squarely.
9 Test each ring in its piston groove for side clearance, which should be as specified. It is unlikely that the clearance will be incorrect if new pistons and rings are being fitted. Use a feeler blade for checking.
10 Fit the piston rings to the pistons. Start with the oil control ring assembly, making sure that the expander ends do not overlap.
11 Fit the second compression ring, which has the word 'TOP' stamped on its upper face.
12 Fit the top compression ring, which has a chromium plated periphery and is coated red. The ring may be fitted either way up. Do not remove the red coating.

33 Cylinder liners – examination and renovation

1 The cylinder bores must be examined for taper, ovality, scoring and scratches. Start by carefully examining the top of the cylinder bores. If they are at all worn a very slight ridge will be found on the thrust side. This marks the top of the piston ring travel. The owner will have a good indication of the bore wear prior to dismantling the engine, or removing the cylinder head. Excessive oil consumption accompanied by blue smoke from the exhaust is a sure sign of worn cylinder bores and piston rings.
2 Measure the bore diameter just under the ridge with a micrometer and compare it with the diameter at the bottom of the bore, which is not subject to wear. If the difference between the two measurements is more than 0.006 in (0.15 mm) then it will be necessary to fit special pistons and rings or to have the cylinder liners renewed.
3 Sometimes specially designed proprietary piston rings can be fitted to overcome bore wear for a further mileage but in the long term, new liners and pistons are the only effective cure.
4 When fitting new liners, apply jointing compound to their lower shoulders before pushing them into the cylinder block. Remove excess sealant and immediately fit retaining clamps (Tool JD41).

34 Crankshaft pulley and damper – examination and renovation

1 Check that the rubber of the damper has not deteriorated; if it has, renew the damper.
2 The drivebelt should not bottom in the Vee of the pulley; if it does, try renewing the belt but if this new belt still bottoms, then the pulley will have to be renewed as well.

35 Flywheel and starter ring gear (XJS with manual gearbox) – examination and renovation

1 If the starter ring gear is worn or the teeth are chipped, then the flywheel should be renewed complete.
2 If the surface of the flywheel is badly scored or small cracks are visible, it should be renewed; machining or surface grinding is not recommended.
3 The flywheel and clutch are balanced and if a new flywheel is fitted, then before installation, have the components re-balanced by your Jaguar dealer.

36 Driveplate – examination and renovation

1 *On cars equipped with automatic transmission,* examine the bolt holes of the driveplate for cracks and the starter ring gear for wear. If these conditions are evident, renew the driveplate complete.

37 Camshafts and bearings – examination and renovation

1 Check the camshaft bearing surfaces and lobes of the cams for wear, scoring or corrosion.
2 Check the bearing caps and the bearing surfaces on the tappet blocks in the same way.
3 If the inspection brings to light such conditions the camshaft and the tappet block must be renewed as the camshaft runs directly in the tappet block without the use of separate bearing shells.

38 Valves and seats – examination and renovation

1 Examine the heads of the valves for pitting and burning, especially the exhaust valves.
2 If the valves appear serviceable, scrape all the carbon away and carefully clean the stem of the valve. Clean the valve guide in the cylinder head and fit the valve to its guide.
3 With the valve about threequarters of its way in the guide, check it for sideways movement. If the movement appears to be excessive, remove the valve and measure the diameter of the stem, this should be not less than specified. If the stem diameter is satisfactory it means that the valve guide is worn and remedial action as indicated in Section 40 will have to be taken.
4 If no wear is present, check the valve stem for distortion by moving the valve up and down in its guide and at the same time rotating it, no restriction to movement should be felt.
5 Grinding the valves to their seats is easily carried out. First place the cylinder head upside down on the bench resting on a block of wood at each end to give clearance for the valve stems.
6 Smear a trace of course carborundum paste on the seat face and apply a suction grinding tool to the head of the valve. With a semi-rotary action, grind the valve to its seat, lifting the valve occasionally to re-distribute the paste. When a continuous ring of dull matt even finish is produced on both the valve seat and the valve, then wipe off the coarse paste and repeat the process with a fine paste, lifting and turning the valve as before. A light spring placed under the head of the valve will assist in the lifting operation. When a smooth unbroken ring of light grey matt is produced on both valve and valve seat faces, the grinding operation is complete. Be very careful during the grinding operation not to get the abrasive paste on the stem of the valve, do not handle the valve stem once you have started to use the paste because it will be transferred from the fingers to the stem and the result will be rapid wear of the valve guide. Trouble is often experienced with the suction tool not gripping the valve head, this can be overcome if the valve head and the tool are kept free of oil and grease at all times.
7 When grinding is completed, thoroughly clean the cylinder head to remove any trace of carborundum paste as this can cause a lot of damage after first start up of the engine.
8 If a valve seat is too badly burned to be renovated by grinding, it should be re-cut or renewed by your dealer.

39 Valve springs – examination and renewal

1 The valve springs should be renewed as a matter of course if they have been in use for 25 000 miles (40 000 km) or more.
2 If they have been in use for a shorter period, check their free lengths against Specification. If they have been compressed excessively when compared with a new spring, renew them.

40 Valve guides – renewal

1 If the valve guides are found to be worn as a result of the checks carried out in Section 38, first immerse the cylinder head in boiling water for half an hour.
2 Using a suitably stepped drift, drive the valve guide from the cylinder head. Attack the guide from the combustion chamber side.
3 Ream the guide bore in the head to the correct oversize (see below).
4 Coat the new valve guide with graphite grease and fit the circlip.
5 Bring the cylinder head back to temperature in boiling water and drive the guide into position until the circlip seats.

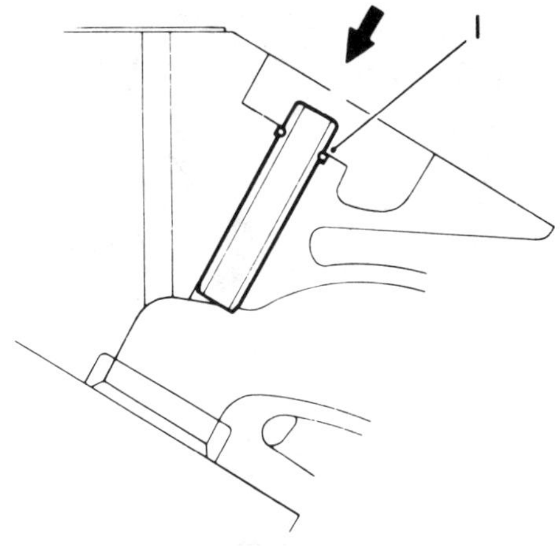

Fig. 1.38 Valve guide installation (Sec 40)

1 Circlip

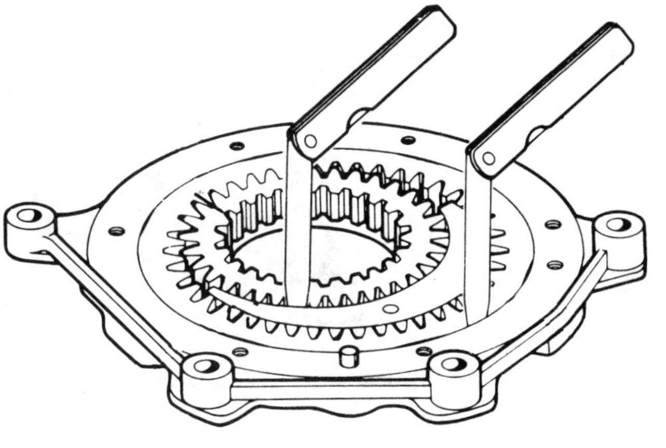

Fig. 1.39 Checking the oil pump gear radial clearance (Sec 45)

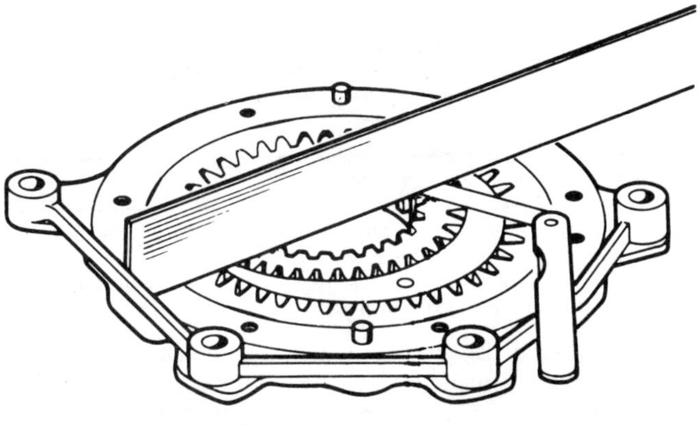

Fig. 1.40 Checking the oil pump gear endfloat (Sec 45)

6 Replacement valve guides are available in two oversizes as given in the Specifications.
7 When fitting new guides always fit one which is one oversize larger than the original. The valve guide bores in the cylinder head will require reaming to accept the oversize guides as follows:

1st oversize (2 grooves) – ream to
0.505 in (12.83 mm) + 0.0005 in (0.012 mm) – 0.0002 in (0.005 mm)
2nd oversize (3 grooves) – ream to
0.510 in (12.95 mm) + 0.0005 in (0.012 mm) – 0.0002 in (0.005 mm)

41 Tappet and shims – examination and renovation

1 Examine the bearing surface of the tappet on which the camshaft bears. Any indentation on this surface or any cracks indicate serious wear and the tappet must be renewed.
2 It is unlikely that the sides of the tappet will be worn, but if the tappet can be rocked in its guide in the tappet block it should be established by measurement which item is at fault; details of dimensions are given under Specifications at the beginning of this Chapter.
3 The tappet should also be checked to see that it moves freely in its guide, the most likely cause of restriction is dirt but rectify as necessary.
4 Clean and examine the valve adjusting shims. After a considerable mileage the valve stem will probably have made an indentation on the shim face. In this case the shim should be renewed but where the valves have been ground in, shims of alternative thickness will probably be required (refer to Section 50).

42 Timing gear and chain – examination and renovation

1 Clean the sprockets and chain in a paraffin bath and dry them on a non-fluffy rag.
2 Examine the teeth of the sprockets for wear. Each tooth forms an inverted 'V' with the periphery of the sprocket and, if worn, the side of the tooth under tension will be slightly concave in shape when compared with the other side of the tooth. If any wear is present the sprocket should be renewed.
3 Examine the links of the chain for side slackness and renew the chain if any slackness is noticeable when compared to a new chain. It is sensible to replace the chain if the engine is stripped for overhaul and when the cylinder heads are removed for decarbonisation or some other purpose, if it is known that the chain has been in use for a considerable time.
4 The chain tension slipper and the rubbing surfaces of the dampers should be examined for grooves or deterioration and renewed, if necessary.
5 If the dampers must be removed or renewed, first mark the exact positions of the camshaft sprocket hangers and the chain dampers before unbolting them. Do this using quick-drying paint or by scribing their outline on the front face of the cylinder block. If the dampers are disturbed without having marked their position then a special damper setting jig will be required as described in Section 47, paragraph 50.
6 Check the teeth of the jackshaft sprocket for wear. If there is any rocking movement when the sprocket is gripped, this is probably due to worn jackshaft bearings in the cylinder block. Closer inspection can be had by removing the top cover. Once the top cover screws are extracted do not try to tap the cover sideways if it is stuck as it is located to the block by hollow dowel pins.
7 Renewal of the jackshaft bearings is best left to your dealer unless the appropriate removal and refitting tools are available.

43 Cylinder head – decarbonising and examination

1 With the cylinder head removed, use a blunt scraper to remove all trace of carbon and deposits from the combustion spaces and ports. Remember that the cylinder head is made of aluminium alloy and can be damaged easily during the decarbonising operations. Scrape the cylinder head free from scale or old pieces of gasket or jointing compound. Clean the cylinder head by washing it in paraffin and take

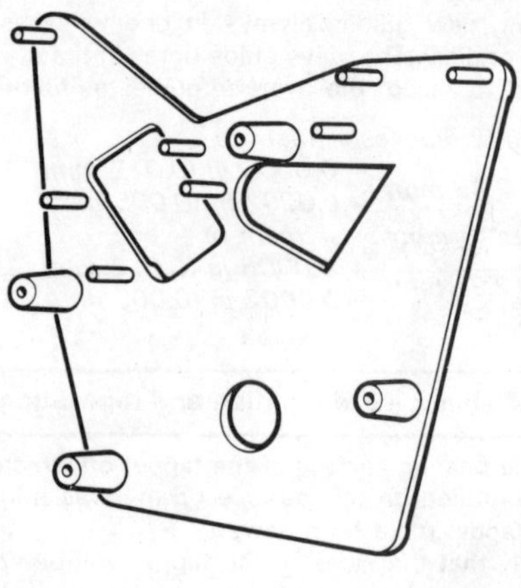

Fig. 1.41 Timing chain damper setting jig (JD38) (Sec 47)

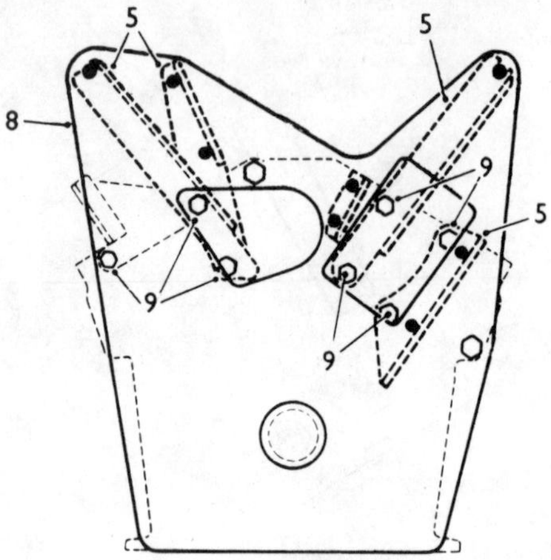

Fig. 1.42 Timing chain damper setting diagram (Sec 47)

5 Camshaft sprocket hangers
8 Setting jig
9 Damper/hanger securing bolts

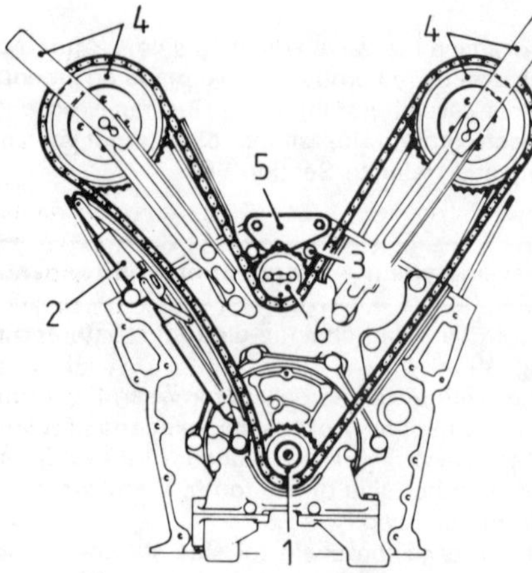

Fig. 1.43 Timing chain and gears (Sec 47)

1 Camshaft sprocket
2 Timing chain tensioner
3 Jackshaft locking plate
4 Camshaft sprockets and retaining tools
5 Jackshaft sprocket locking tool
6 Jackshaft sprocket

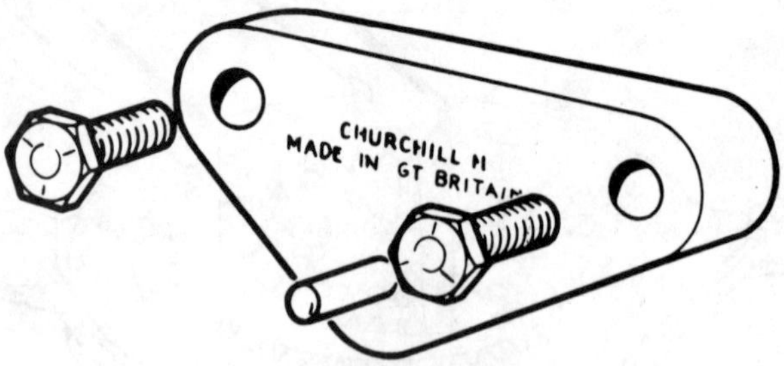

Fig. 1.44 Jackshaft sprocket locking tool (Sec 47)

particular care to pull a piece of rag through the ports and cylinder head bolt holes. Any dirt remaining in these recesses may well drop onto the gasket or cylinder block mating surface as the cylinder head is lowered into position and could lead to a gasket leak after reassembly is complete.

2 With the cylinder head clean, test for distortion if a history of coolant leakage has been apparent. Carry out this test using a straight-edge and feeler gauges or a piece of plate glass. If the surface shows any warping in excess of 0.0039 in (0.1015 mm) then the cylinder head will have to be resurfaced which is a job for a specialist engineering company.

3 Clean the pistons and top of the cylinder bores. If the pistons are still in the block then it is essential that great care is taken to ensure that no carbon gets into the cylinder bores as this could scratch the cylinder walls or cause damage to the piston and rings. To ensure this does not happen, first clamp the liners and turn the crankshaft so that two of the pistons are at the top of their bores. Stuff rag into the other four bores or seal them off with paper and masking tape to prevent particles of carbon entering the cooling system and damaging the water pump.

4 Rotate the crankshaft and repeat the carbon removal operations on the remaining pistons and cylinder bores.

5 Thoroughly clean all particles of carbon from the bores and then inject a little light oil round the edges of the pistons to lubricate the piston rings.

6 Stripped spark plug threads can be reinstated by having inserts fitted or Helicoil spring threads wound in. Either of these jobs is best left to your dealer or to a suitably equipped engineering works.

44 Oil seals – renewal

1 At time of major overhaul always renew engine oil seals even if they appear in good condition.

2 Renew the crankshaft front and rear oil seals and the O-rings on the oil pump suction and return pipes.

45 Oil pump – overhaul

1 With the oil pump removed as described in Section 7, unbolt the pump cover from the gear housing.

2 Mark the gear faces to ensure that they will be returned to their original positions on reassembly.
3 Remove both gears and wash all parts in clean fuel.
4 Check the gear teeth for wear or damage. If they are in good condition, refit the driven gear and check the clearance between the gear and the oil pump housing using feeler blades. Do not make the checks at the six flats on the gear.
5 Refit the drive gear and check the clearance between the gear and the crescent.
6 Now check the endfloat of both gears by placing a straight-edge across the oil pump housing joint face and inserting feeler blades between the straight-edge and the gears.
7 All the measurements taken should conform to the clearances given in the Specifications. If they do not, the oil pump will have to be renewed.

46 Engine – preparation for reassembly

1 To ensure maximum life with reliability from a rebuilt engine, not only must everything be correctly assembled but all components must be spotlessly clean and the correct spring or plain washers used where originally located. Always lubricate bearing and working surfaces with clean engine oil during reassembly of engine parts.
2 Before reassembly commences, renew any bolts or studs the threads of which are damaged or corroded.
3 As well as your normal tool kit, gather together clean rags, oil can, a torque wrench and a complete (overhaul) set of gaskets and oil seals.

47 Engine – reassembly

1 To reassemble the engine after complete dismantling first check that the cylinder liners are correctly seated with clamps fitted. If new liners are to be installed, smear their lower shoulders with jointing compound before pressing them into position. If the original liners are being used again but have been removed, then again use jointing compound and align the marks made prior to removal (see Section 7, paragraph 48).
2 Fit new sealing strips into the grooves in the rear main bearing casting.
3 Fit new crankshaft rear oil seal halves. Place a single drop of jointing compound in each groove before fitting the seals.
4 Fit the rear main bearing casting to the cylinder block and tighten the nuts. The oil seal should now be pre-sized by passing a piece of tubing into it of similar outside dimension to the rear journal diameter of the crankshaft. With this done, remove the main bearing casting and apply colloidal graphite to the seal.
5 Wipe out all the crankcase bearing shell recesses, fit the seven shells and oil them. Do not confuse the centre and rear main bearing shells. The rear shell incorporates a groove, the centre one does not.
6 Lower the crankshaft into position.
7 Fit the main bearing caps complete with shells having oiled the journals ready to accept them.
8 Refit the pillar nuts to their original positions.
9 Tighten all the nuts to the specified torque.
10 Now check the crankshaft endfloat using feeler blades, prising it first one way and then the other. The endfloat will be excessive as no thrust washers have yet been fitted. Select thrust washers of sufficient thickness to reduce the endfloat to that specified.
11 Remove the centre main bearing cap and slide the selected thrust washer halves into the grooves on either side of the crankcase web. Note that the oil grooves must face outwards.
12 Refit the centre main bearing cap, then tighten all cap bolts and check the crankshaft for ease of rotation.
13 Smear the bore of number 1A cylinder liner (RH front) with engine oil. Also oil the piston rings of the appropriate piston/connecting rod assembly.
14 Check that the piston ring end gaps are located at equidistant points around the piston in order to prevent gas blow-by.
15 Fix a piston ring compressor to the piston rings and compress them fully.
16 Enter the connecting rod into the cylinder bore so that the 'FRONT' mark on the piston crown is towards the timing cover end of the engine. Let the piston rest squarely on the surface of the cylinder block.
17 Place the end of a wooden handle of a hammer on the centre of the piston crown and give the head of the hammer a sharp blow with the palm of the hand. This will drive the piston assembly into the cylinder. Remove the compressor.
18 Draw the connecting rod down without scratching the bore and fit the rod bearing shell.
19 Set the crankpin to its lowest point and then draw the connecting rod big-end onto it.
20 Fit the bearing shell to the cap, making sure that the locktabs are correctly engaged.
21 Squirt oil onto the crankpin and fit the big-end cap.
22 Tighten the nuts to the specified torque.
23 Repeat the installation and reassembly operations on all the remaining piston/connecting rods. Make sure that the assemblies are returned to their correct cylinders and that the piston crown marks are all facing the front of the engine.
24 Check that the crankshaft can be rotated freely using a lever between two bolts inserted into the crankshaft rear flange.
25 Fit the oil pump to its drivegear on the front end of the crankshaft.
26 Fit new O-ring seals at both ends of the oil delivery pipe, then fit the crankshaft undershield on its pillar nuts and install the oil delivery pipe. Loosely secure the undershield and oil delivery pipe with two setscrews.
27 Fit the suction pipe using a new O-ring seal at the suction elbow. Fix the suction pipe clips and bracket using four setscrews and then tighten all six setscrews to secure the undershield.
28 Refit the flywheel (manual gearbox) or driveplate (automatic transmission) to the rear end of the crankshaft. Use new lockplates, tighten the bolts to the specified torque and bend up the lockplate tabs.
29 Fit the sprocket to the front end of the crankshaft, together with the Woodruff key.
30 If a timing chain damper has been removed or renewed, then it must be refitted in its original position (see Section 42, paragraph 5), otherwise a special setting jig will be required and the following resetting work carried out. Fit the camshaft sprocket hangers and timing chain dampers to the cylinder block, but with all bolts only finger-tight. Install the damper setting jig on the front of the cylinder block and lightly tighten the fixing bolts. Position the camshaft sprocket hangers and timing chain dampers so that they make even contact with the jig locating dowels. Tighten the hanger and damper bolts. Remove the jig.
31 Fit the timing chain tensioner, making sure that it is fully retracted.
32 Fit the jackshaft, having first oiled its journals, then install the jackshaft locking plate.
33 Fit the camshaft sprockets and retain them with the special tools (JD40) or equivalent.
34 Engage the timing chain with the teeth of the camshaft and crankshaft sprockets. Now engage the jackshaft sprocket with the chain and temporarily bolt the sprocket to the jackshaft.
35 Turn the crankshaft until No 1 piston on the right-hand (A) bank is at TDC. Check this by temporarily refitting the crankshaft pulley so that it engages with its key and observing that the 'A' mark is aligned with the 'O' mark on the timing scale (photo).
36 Check that the punch marks on the jackshaft and the jackshaft sprocket are at 180° to each other with the jackshaft mark at its highest point. If this is not so, unbolt and reposition the sprocket without moving the crankshaft.
37 In order that the jackshaft sprocket bolts can be tightened fully, the sprocket must be locked to prevent it rotating. A special tool is available for this purpose (JD39) but a rod passed between two sprocket teeth and locked in position will usually prove a good substitute. Bend up the lockplate tab.
38 Remove the sprocket locking tool but do not disturb the position of the crankshaft until the camshaft sprockets have been coupled to their respective camshafts, see paragraphs 50 to 55.
39 Fit the timing cover using a new oil seal and gaskets. Tighten the bolts in a diagonal pattern.
40 Fit the spacer to the front end of the crankshaft.
41 Fit the crankcase sandwich plate using a new gasket and remembering to secure the timing scale at the front end.
42 Fit the baffle plate to the sandwich plate.
43 Fit the sump, returning the oil cooler pipe bracket to its originally marked position.
44 Connect the suction union elbow to the sandwich plate using a new seal.

47.35 'A' mark aligns with 'O' mark when No 1A piston is at TDC

47.45 Cylinder liner top rims burnished

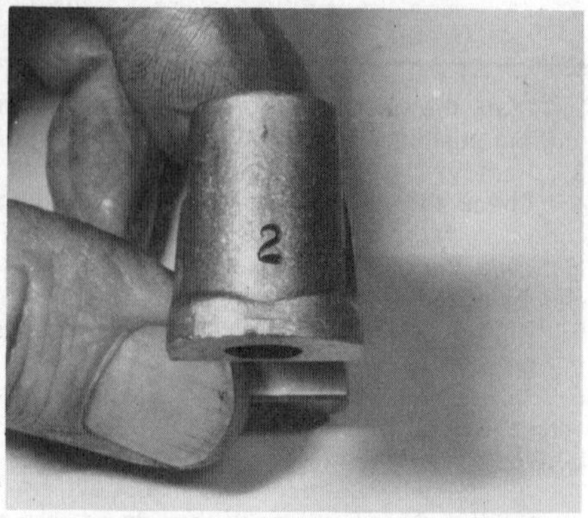

47.48 Camshaft bearing cap number

47.50 Cylinder head gasket in position

47.51 Camshaft setting gauge

47.52 Using a crowfoot wrench to tighten the cylinder head nuts

47.53A Installing a cylinder head without the tappet block

47.53B Tightening a cylinder head nut without the tappet block fitted

47.54A Fitting a tappet block

47.54B Tightening a tappet block socket headed screw

47.54C Installing the tappet blocks and shims

47.56 Tightening a camshaft bearing cap

47.60A Camshaft coupling circlip

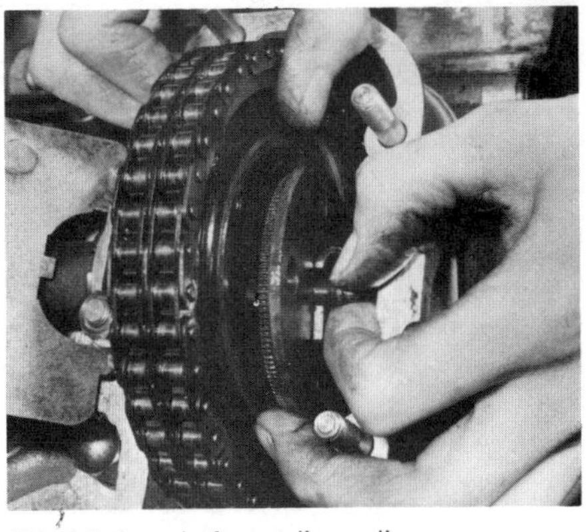

47.60B Camshaft coupling splines

47.65A Fitting a plug to the tappet block

47.65B Camshaft cover gasket in position

47.67 Coolant pump and mounting bolts 1 – Studs with nuts; 2 – Long bolts. All remaining bolts are of the same standard length

49.2A One of four engine lifting hooks (arrowed)

49.2B Installing engine over front mountings

49.5A Aluminium spigot bolted to transmission

49.5B Rear mounting plates, spigot and collision plate

49.5C Transmission lowered onto mounting plate

49.5D Collision plate and spigot self-locking nut being fitted

49.6A Right-hand exhaust heat shields

49.6B Right-hand steering gaiter heat shield

49.6C Left-hand steering gaiter heat shield

49.6D Starter solenoid heat shield

49.8 Exhaust downpipe sealing rings

49.9 Tightening the left-hand exhaust manifold flange nuts

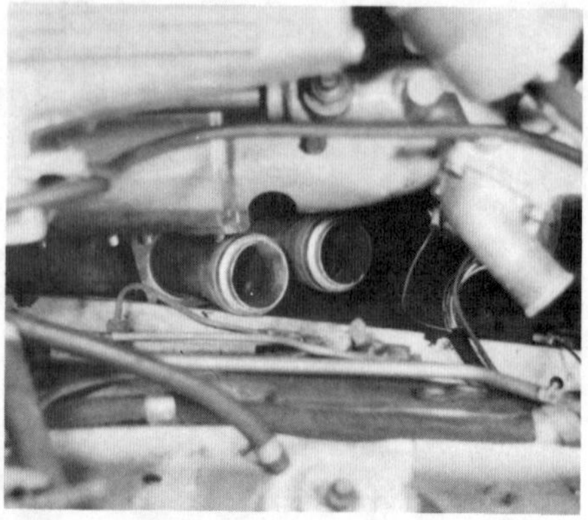
49.10A Installing the right-hand exhaust downpipe

49.10B Right-hand exhaust downpipe in position

49.12A Fitting the fluid coupling centre bolt

49.12B Using two spanners to tighten the fluid coupling bolt

49.13 Cowl/electric fan assembly

49.14 Radiator being installed

49.15A Radiator hose connections

45 Remove the cylinder liner retaining tools and clean all rust and corrosion from the top rims of the liners (photo).
46 If a crowfoot type wrench is available to reach the domed cylinder head nuts, carry out the operations in paragraphs up to 52. If such a tool is not available, move onto paragraph 53.
47 Fit the tappet blocks to their respective cylinder heads, having first smeared jointing compound to their mating faces. Tighten the socket headed screws and then the nuts to the specified torque, working from the centre towards each end. Fit the shims and tappets (cam followers) in their originally installed sequence.
48 Refit the camshafts, tightening the bearing caps (from the centre towards each end) to the specified torque. The bearing caps are numbered (photo).
49 Adjust the valve clearances as described in Section 50.
50 Locate a new cylinder head gasket, with the word 'TOP' uppermost, on scrupulously clean block surfaces without the use of jointing compound or grease (photo).
51 Rotate each camshaft until a setting gauge (C.3993, photo) can be engaged in the camshaft front flange slots.
52 Refit the cylinder heads and tighten the securing nuts in the sequence shown in Fig. 1.31 to the specified torque and in the specified stages (photo). Now proceed from paragraph 58.
53 Where a crowfoot type wrench is not available to reach the cylinder head domed nuts, fit the cylinder heads without their tappet blocks and tighten the nuts (in stages and in sequence) to the specified torque (photo).
54 Fit the tappet blocks, having smeared their cylinder head face with jointing compound. Screw in the socket headed securing screws, then the nuts. Fit the shims and the tappets in their originally fitted order (photos).
55 Before fitting the camshafts, check that the crankshaft has not moved from its TDC alignment.
56 Oil the camshaft bearing caps. Install them in their correct positions from the front of the engine onto the camshafts. The camshafts must be set as near as possible so that the notches in their front flanges are vertical and at the highest point. Some of the cam lobes will depress the valve springs as they are bolted down, so tighten the bearing caps in a very even and progressive manner to avoid distortion of the camshafts (photo).
57 Rotate each camshaft fractionally so that a setting gauge can be fitted and engaged in the front flange notches.
58 Reconnect the camshaft oil feed pipe, pressure sender and warning switch.
59 Remove the camshaft sprocket retaining tools.
60 Extract the circlip which retains the camshaft sprocket couplings. Press the sprocket onto the camshaft shoulder and then turn the coupling until the sprocket bolt holes align with those in the camshaft (photos).
61 Reconnect the couplings to the camshaft sprockets, refit the circlips and then withdraw the setting tools. Bolt the couplings to the camshafts and bend up the lockwasher tabs, using two bolts.
62 Insert the screwdriver member of the chain tensioner tool into the hole in the timing cover and release the chain tensioner locking catch. Refit the rubber plug to the hole.
63 Turn the crankshaft until the camshaft sprocket takes up a position suitable to be able to insert the remaining two bolts and lockplate. Fit and tighten the bolts and bend up the lockplate tabs.
64 Check the valve clearances (Section 50) if this was not done at paragraph 49.
65 Refit the camshaft covers, using new gaskets and neoprene plugs. The left-hand cover has the oil filler at the front (photos).
66 Refit the jackshaft cover, noting that the throttle pedestal and ignition coil mounting bracket is to the rear.
67 Reverse the dismantling operations described in paragraphs 3 to 10 inclusive of Section 7. Note the location of the coolant pump mounting bolts identified in the photograph (photo).

48 Engine – reconnecting transmission and refitting ancillaries

1 The work is a reversal of the removal operations described in Section 6. If the car is fitted with a manual gearbox then the clutch must be centralised as described in Chapter 5 before attempting to reconnect the gearbox to the engine.
2 When reconnecting the GM 400 automatic transmission to the engine, it is imperative that just before it is mated, the holes in the driveplate are aligned with the tapped holes in the torque converter. This is achieved by aligning the torque converter/driveplate paint spots. Failure to carry out this alignment before mating prevents insertion of the bolts as the rivet heads on the driveplate prevent rotation of the plate in relation to the torque converter once they are closely coupled.
3 Tension the drivebelts as described in Section 51.

49 Engine – refitting

1 The engine/transmission is refitted by reversing the removal operations described in either Section 3, 4 or 5 according to model. The following special points must however be noted.
2 Have the engine/transmission supported on the hoist so that the rear end is inclined slightly downward. As it is lowered into position, watch that components on the sides of the engine compartment are not damaged and that the engine sump drain plug does not foul the engine front mounting studs as the unit is lowered into position (photos).
3 Lower the engine/transmission until the front mounting brackets engage with the studs on the flexible mountings. Screw the nuts onto the studs.
4 Raise the rear of the transmission using a jack and a block of wood as an insulator.
5 Fit the rear mounting components according to model and type of transmission. With XJ12 or Double Six versions, the sequence is as follows:

- (a) *Fit the longer plate to the underside of the floor pan. Note the two internal securing bolts*
- (b) *Bolt the cast aluminium spigot to the transmission casing (photo)*
- (c) *Bolt the smaller plate to the underside of the floor pan. Note the spacers between this plate and the previously fitted larger one, also the coil spring and damper rings (photo)*
- (d) *Lower the transmission gently when the spigot will project through the hole in the lower plate (photo)*
- (e) *Screw on the self-locking nut complete with the collision plate. Note the spacers on the collision plate and the two other self-locking nuts (photo)*
- (f) *Tighten all nuts and bolts and remove the jack*

6 Fit the exhaust heat shields (photos).
7 Connect the speedometer cable to the transmission.
8 Cut off the sealing rings from the tops of the exhaust downpipes. Wire brush the ring seats to remove rust and corrosion. Tap new sealing rings into position, except for the front ring on the right-hand downpipe which should be fitted later (photo).
9 Fit the left-hand exhaust downpipe from below, using new securing nuts. These nuts can be tightened using a socket spanner and a long extension operated from below the car (photo).
10 Fit the right-hand exhaust downpipe from above (photos). An assistant moving the steering wheel slightly from one lock to another will facilitate the passage of this downpipe. Once the front rim of the downpipe has cleared the forward mounting stud on the manifold, tap the remaining sealing ring (paragraph 8) into position. Fit the securing nuts and tighten evenly. Refit the downpipes to the intermediate pipes.
11 Once the engine is securely mounted, locate the engine oil cooler in position and tighten the connecting pipe unions.
12 Fit the belt-driven fan to its hub, making sure that the roll pin engages in its hole. Restrain the fan by using a backing spanner on the flats of the fan shaft (photos).
13 Fit the cowl with electric fan (photo).
14 Fit the radiator by engaging its lower spigots in their cut-outs. Position the engine oil cooler on the brackets at the base of the radiator (photo).
15 Pull the top of the radiator forward, together with the fan cowl assembly, so that the hoses on the left-hand side of the radiator can be connected and the transmission fluid cooler hoses connected to the right-hand side of the radiator (photos).
16 Secure the engine oil cooler by inserting the mounting bracket bolts upwards through the holes in the lower front panel (photo). Once they are tight, fit the rubber plugs into the holes.
17 Locate the radiator top rail and the upper and lower cowl brackets, but do not fix them at this stage.
18 When refitting the air conditioner compressor, tighten the bolts on

49.15B Tightening a radiator hose clip

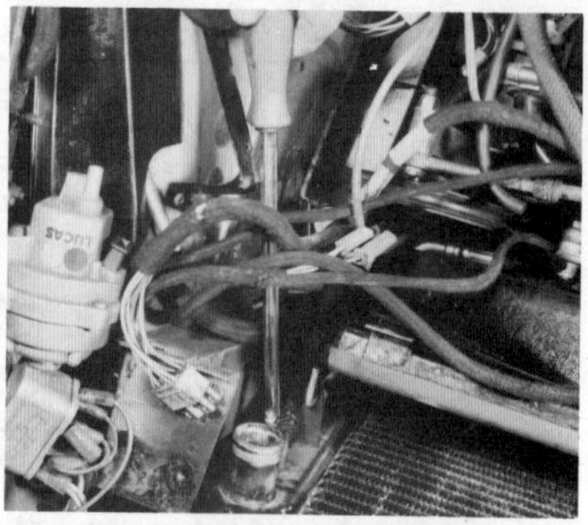

49.15C Tightening a transmission fluid cooler hose on the right-hand side of the radiator

49.16 Tightening the engine oil cooler mounting bolts

49.18A Compressor rear mounting bracket

49.18B Compressor front mounting bracket (1) and coolant cross-pipe (2)

49.19 Ignition amplifier bracket

50.4 Checking a valve clearance

50.7A Thickness mark engraved on valve clearance shim

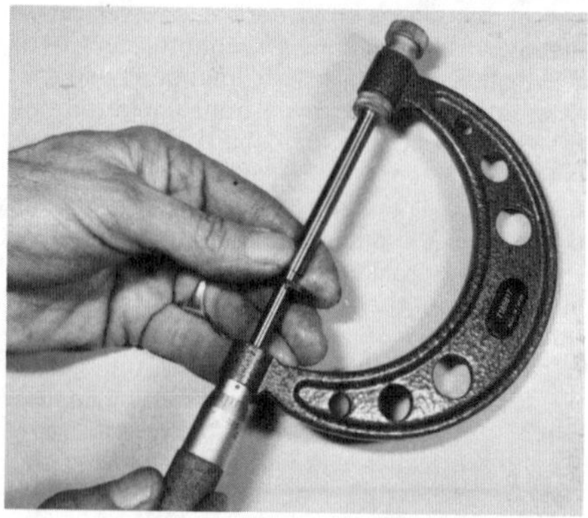

50.7B Checking the thickness of a valve clearance shim

51.3 The alternator drivebelt adjuster is accessible from below

the front mounting bracket but leave the ones on the rear bracket loose. Fit the compressor tight against the rear face of the front mounting bracket and then slide the rear bracket forward until it touches the rear mounting plate on the compressor. Lift the compressor away again and tighten the rear bracket bolts. Fit the compressor and drivebelt (photos).
19 When fitting the amplifier, note the spacers located under the bolt holes to prevent fracture of the baseplate when tightening the mounting nuts (photo).
20 The air conditioning condenser should be offered into position before bolting down the radiator top rail as the two connecting pipe stubs at the right-hand top corner must pass under the top rail.
21 Note that the brake servo hose to the induction manifolds runs (together with the air conditioner hose) at the rear quarter of the engine compartment.

Cars with automatic transmission

22 Adjust the kickdown switch and the speed selector cable as described in Chapter 6.

Cars with manual transmission

23 Bleed the clutch hydraulic system as described in Chapter 5.

Cars with air conditioning

24 Reconnect all system pipes and components.

All models

25 Refill the cooling system, refill and bleed the power steering system and refill the engine with oil.
26 Check and top up the transmission oil level. (In the case of automatic transmission, the level must be checked again when the fluid is hot – see Chapter 6.)

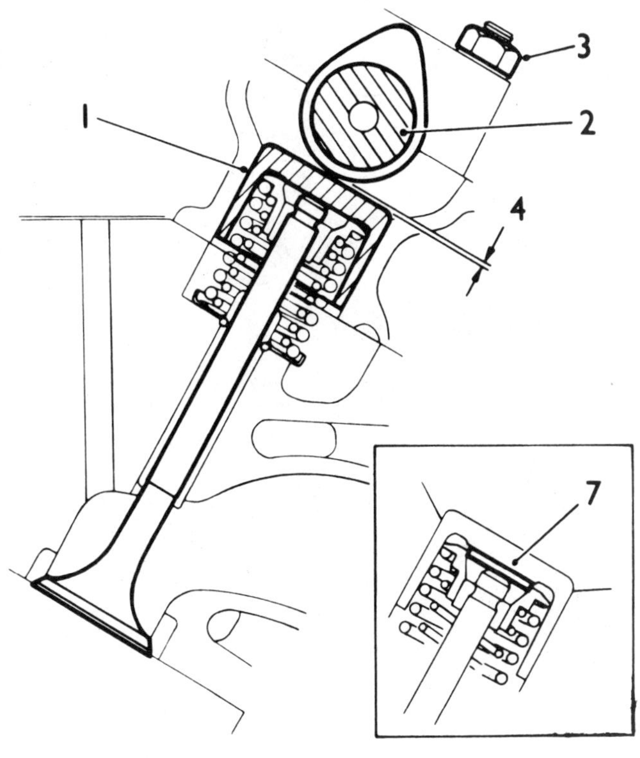

Fig. 1.45 Sectional view of valve and cam (Sec 50)

1 Tappet
2 Cam
3 Camshaft bearing cap nut
4 Clearance
7 Adjustment shim

50 Valve clearance – adjustment

1 This work can be carried out at the time of engine overhaul or as a maintenance operation at the specified service intervals. The valve clearances are measured with the engine cold.
2 *If the engine is in the car,* remove the camshaft covers (Section 8 or 9) and turn the crankshaft (by means of a socket spanner applied to the crankshaft damper centre bolt) until the first tappet is opposite the heel of the cam.
3 *If the cylinder head or tappet block is away from the engine,* the camshaft should be rotated carefully by its front flange to achieve the correct cam heel to tappet block relationship.
4 Using feeler blades, measure and record the clearance between the heel of the cam and the surface of the tappet (photo).
5 Turn the crankshaft or camshaft until each clearance on the remaining 23 tappets has been checked and recorded. Record the clearances separately for the two cylinder heads and count from the timing cover end.
6 The correct valve clearance is given in the Specifications. Where the recorded clearance differs from that specified, then by simple subtraction, establish the difference in thickness of the tappet shim required to reduce or increase the clearance as the case may be.
7 Shims are available in increments of 0.001 in (0.03 mm) from a thickness of 0.085 in to 0.110 in (2.16 to 2.79 mm). The shims are etched with a letter of the alphabet to indicate thickness, A indicating the thinnest and each succeeding letter denoting an increase in thickness of 0.001 in (0.03 mm). Obviously the possession of a micrometer will make life easier, particularly if the etched letters are indistinct or have worn off in service. In many cases, some of the original shims can be interchanged to achieve the correct clearances and it is worthwhile calculating whether this can be done before purchasing new shims (photos).
8 The shims can be changed after removing the camshafts, lifting out the tappets and extracting the shims from the tappet interiors.
9 With the camshafts refitted, recheck the valve clearances before refitting the camshaft covers.

51 Drivebelts – adjustment or renewal

1 The drivebelt configuration depends upon the equipment fitted.
2 The deflection of all drivebelts, measured under firm thumb pressure at the centre point of the longest run of the belt, should be $\frac{5}{32}$ in (4.0 mm), except for the air pump/compressor belt which should have a deflection of $\frac{1}{4}$ in (6.4 mm).
3 All drivebelts can be adjusted from above except the one for the alternator which is accessible from underneath the car (photo).
4 Adjustment is made in all cases by first releasing the jockey pulley or accessory mounting bolt and then releasing the locknut on the threaded adjuster link trunnion and turning the adjusting nut in or out to vary the effective length of the link.
5 A drivebelt may be renewed by releasing the accessory mounting bolts and by turning the adjuster nut. Move the accessory as far as possible until the belt can be slipped off the driving and driven pulleys. Never use a lever to remove or fit a belt.
6 Renewal of any but the front belt will necessitate the removal of the belts in front of it in all drivebelt arrangements.
7 Recheck the tension of a new drivebelt after the first hundred miles or so.

52 Initial start-up after major overhaul

1 Double check all hoses, wiring and battery connections. Check also that engine and cooling system drain plugs have been refitted tightly with the correct quantities of oil and coolant poured in.
2 Make sure that the battery is fully charged and that all lubricants and fuels are replenished.
3 Switch on the ignition and allow the petrol pump time to fill the carburettor float chambers or to pressurise the fuel injection system.
4 Start the engine; as soon as it fires and runs, keep it going at a fast tickover only (no faster). Watch the oil pressure gauge, after a very short wait, whilst the oil filter is being filled, it should register around 40 lbf/in^2. If, after 30 seconds, no oil pressure is registered, switch off

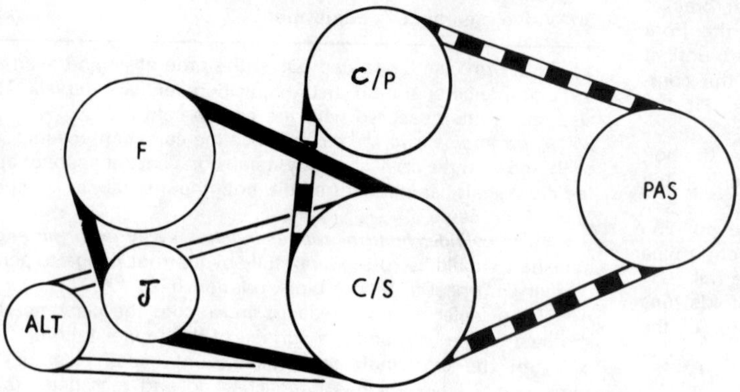

Fig. 1.46 Drivebelt arrangement – all models without exhaust emission control or air conditioning (Sec 51)

Alt	*Alternator*
C/S	*Crankshaft*
F	*Fan*
PAS	*Power-assisted steering*
C/P	*Coolant pump*
J	*Jockey pulley*

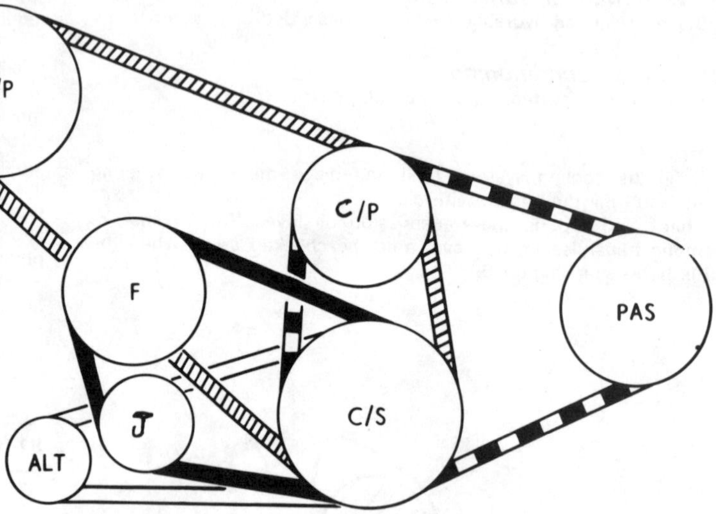

Fig. 1.47 Drivebelt arrangement – all models with exhaust emission control but without air conditioning (Sec 51)

Key as Fig. 1.46 plus:
A/P *Air pump*

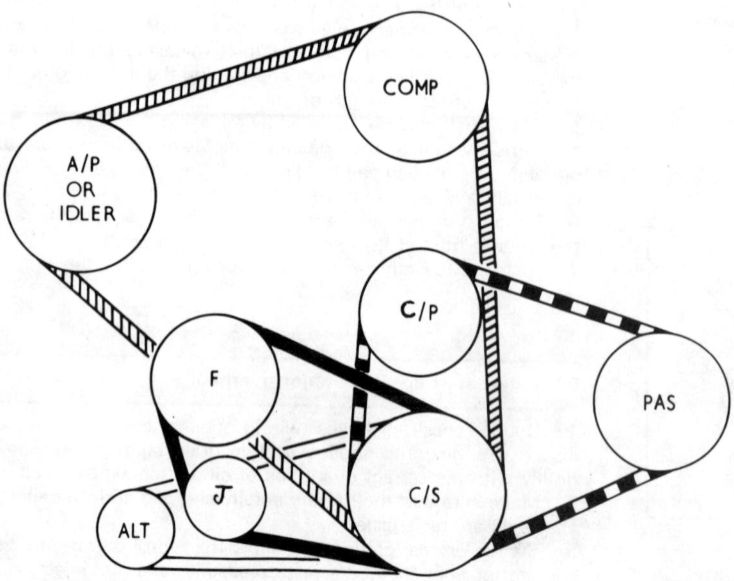

Fig. 1.48 Drivebelt arrangement – all models with exhaust emission and air conditioning (Sec 51)

Key as Figs. 1.46 and 1.47

the engine and investigate the cause; it may be that you have not fully tightened a union or the filter canister is not correctly seated on the rubber sealing ring in the head of the filter.
5 Bring the engine up to its normal working temperature. As it warms up there will be odd smells and some smoke from parts getting hot and burning off oil deposits. Look round carefully for water and oil leaks.
6 When the engine running temperature has been reached, adjust the fuel injection system or carburettors as described in Chapter 3.
7 Stop the engine and wait a few minutes to see if there are any water or oil leaks.
8 Before road testing the car it is advisable to have an assistant listening to the brake servo, run the engine for a few minutes and then operate the footbrake. If the brake servo connections are satisfactory the exhaust from the servo will be plainly heard.
9 Road test the car to check that the timing is correct and is giving the necessary smoothness and power. Do not race the engine. If new bearings or pistons or rings have been fitted, it should be treated as a new engine and run in at reduced revolutions for the first 500 miles (800 km).
10 When you are satisfied that the overhaul is completely successful, have the air conditioning system recharged by your dealer.

53 Fault diagnosis – engine

Symptom	Reason(s)
Engine fails to turn over when starter switch operated	Flat or defective battery Loose battery leads Defective starter solenoid or switch or broken wiring Engine earth strap disconnected Defective starter motor
Engine turns over but will not start	Ignition system damp or wet Ignition leads to spark plugs loose Shorted or disconnected low tension leads Disconnected or faulty component in electronic ignition system No petrol in petrol tank Vapour lock in fuel line (in hot conditions or at high altitude) Fuel pump filter blocked Faulty fuel pump Carburettor or fuel injection system fault
Engine stalls and will not start	Ignition failure No petrol in petrol tank Petrol tank breather choked Sudden obstruction in carburettors or fuel injection system Water in fuel system Ignition leads loose Battery leads loose on terminals Battery earth strap loose on body of attachment point
Engine misfired or idles unevenly	Engine earth lead loose Low tension leads loose Dirty or incorrectly gapped plugs Tracking across inside of distributor cover Ignition too retarded Faulty electronic ignition component Mixture too weak Air leak at inlet manifold Incorrect valve clearances Burnt out exhaust valves Sticking or leaking valves Weak or broken valve springs Worn valve guides or stems Worn pistons and piston rings
Lack of power	Burnt out exhaust valves Sticking or leaking valves Worn valve guides and stems Weak or broken valve springs Blown cylinder head gasket (accompanied by increase in noise) Worn pistons and piston rings Worn or scored cylinder bores Ignition timing wrongly set Incorrect valve clearances Incorrectly set spark plugs Mixture too rich or too weak Fuel filters blocked causing fuel starvation Distributor automatic balance weights or vacuum advance and retard mechanisms not functioning correctly Faulty fuel pump giving top end fuel starvation
Excessive oil consumption	Badly worn, perished or missing inlet valve stem oil seals Excessively worn valve stems and valve guides

Symptom	Reason(s)
	Worn piston rings Worn pistons and cylinder bores Excessive piston ring gap allowing blow-by Piston oil return holes choked Leaking oil filter gasket Leaking camshaft cover gasket Leaking timing case gasket Leaking sump gasket Loose sump plug Worn crankshaft oil seals Leaking external oil pipes or union O-ring seals
Unusual noises from engine	Worn valve gear (noisy tapping from top cover) Worn big-end bearing (regular heavy knocking) Worn main bearings (rumbling) Worn camshaft chain

Chapter 2 Cooling system

Contents

Specifications

System type
Thermo-syphon with front mounted radiator, expansion tank and coolant pump. Two cooling fans, one belt-driven and one electric

Thermostat

Starts to open:	
Early cars	174° to 181°F (79° to 83°C)
Later cars	190°F (88°C)
Fully open	200° to 205°F (93° to 96°C)

Pressure cap rating

XJ12 and Double Six	13 lbf/in² (0.91 kgf/cm²)
XJS	15 lbf/in² (1.05 kgf/cm²)

System capacity
37 Imp pints (44.4 US pints, 21.0 litre)

Torque wrench settings

	lbf ft	Nm
Radiator to front crossmember	25	34
Fan cowl nuts and bolts	7	10
Fan motor to mounting bracket	7	10
Engine oil cooler pipe unions	50	68
Expansion tank mounting bolts	18	25

1 General description

1 The cooling system comprises a radiator, a belt-driven coolant pump and a remotely sited expansion tank. Two thermostatic valves are incorporated to assist in rapid warm-up. The radiator is cooled by an electric fan, thermostatically controlled from the coolant pump inlet, a belt-driven fan incorporating a fluid coupling.

2 The heating system is connected into the engine cooling system.

3 Bleeding of the system after drain and refill is automatic by means of induction housing bleed tubes.

4 A cooler for the automatic transmission fluid is built into the tank at the radiator right-hand end.

5 There are certain differences between the cooling systems used on cars with carburettor fuel systems and those with fuel injection systems, as shown in the illustrations.

6 On cars with fuel injection, the thermotime switch, the coolant temperature sensor and the auxiliary air valve (see Chapter 3) function as an automatic choke during cold start conditions.

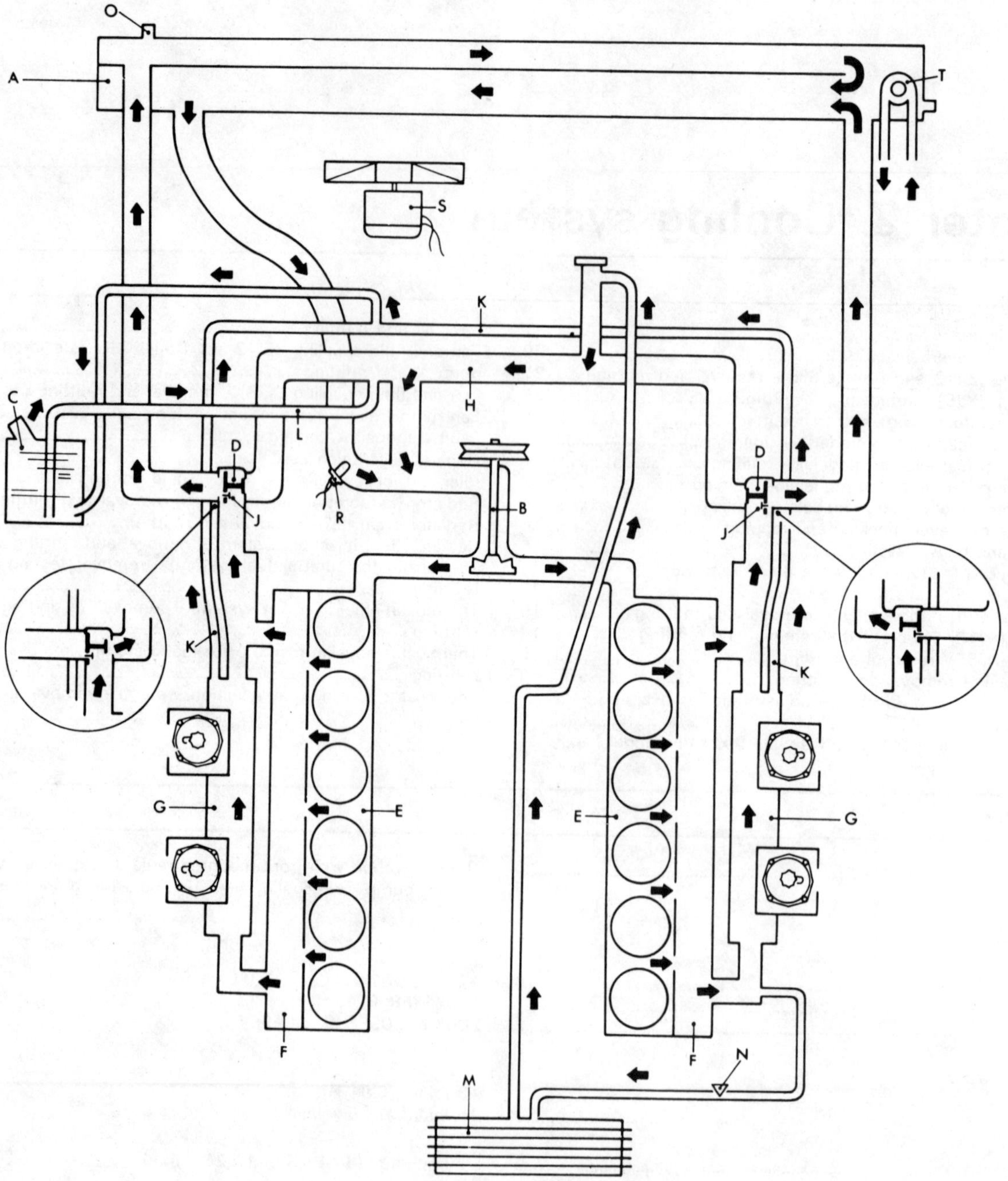

Fig. 2.1 Cooling system (carburettor engines) (Sec 1)

A	*Radiator*	*K*	*Bleed pipes*
B	*Coolant pump*	*L*	*Coolant supply pipe*
C	*Expansion tank*	*M*	*Heater matrix*
D	*Thermostats (insets show cold positions)*	*N*	*Heater coolant control valve*
E	*Cylinder block*	*O*	*Radiator bleed tap*
F	*Cylinder head*	*R*	*Electric fan thermostatic switch*
G	*Induction housing*	*S*	*Electric fan*
H	*Engine cross-pipe*	*T*	*Transmission fluid cooler*
J	*Thermostat jiggle pins*		

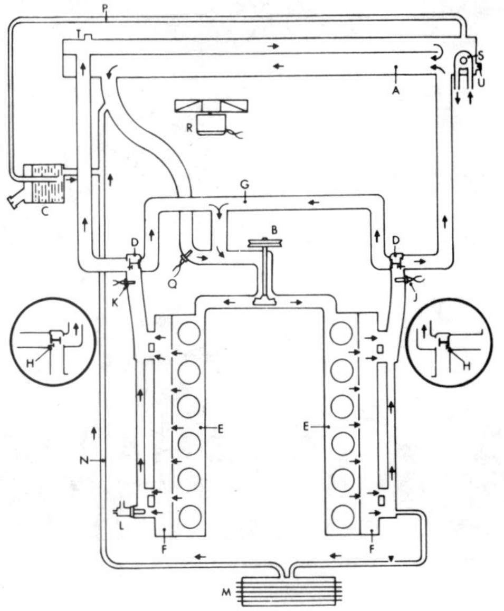

Fig. 2.2 Cooling system (fuel injection engines) (Sec 1)

A Radiator
B Coolant pump
C Expansion tank
D Thermostats
E Cylinder block
F Cylinder head
G Engine cross-pipe
H Thermostat jiggle pins (thermostats in cold position)
J Thermotime switch
K Coolant temperature sensor
L Auxiliary air valve
M Heater matrix
N Purge pipe
P Purge pipe
Q Electric fan thermostatic switch
R Electric cooling fan
S Automatic transmission fluid cooler
T Bleed tap
U Radiator drain tap

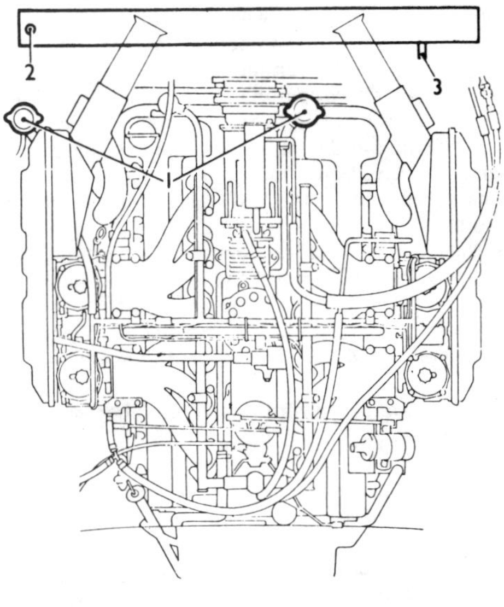

Fig. 2.3 Coolant system pressure caps (1) (carburettor engines) (Sec 2)

2 Bleed tap *3 Drain tap*

2 Cooling system (carburettor models) – draining

1 With the engine cold, remove the pressure caps from the remote expansion tank and the engine cross-pipe.
2 Open the bleed tap on the left-hand side of the radiator top rail.
3 Place a container of adequate capacity under the radiator and open the drain tap. If the coolant is less than a year old and in good condition it can be saved for re-use.
4 The expansion tank can be drained by releasing the clip and pulling the pipe from the lower stub connection.
5 If the coolant appears rusty or dark in colour, insert a hose in the expansion tank and flush the system until clear water emerges from the drain tap. If the contamination is severe it may be necessary to remove the radiator and reverse flush it.

3 Cooling system (fuel injection models) – draining

1 The operations are similar to those described in Section 2 except that there is only one cap which can be removed, the one from the expansion tank (photo).

4 Cooling system (carburettor models) – refilling

1 Make sure that both pressure caps are removed and the radiator bleed tap is open.
2 Move the right-hand heater control to 'DEF', or 'HI' on models without air conditioning.
3 Using the correct coolant mixture (see Section 7), pour it slowly into the filler neck on the engine cross-pipe until the expansion tank is full and then fit the cap to the expansion tank. Make sure that the correct cap is being refitted and that its rubber seal is in good condition.
4 Now observe the radiator bleed tap. As soon as a continuous flow of coolant runs from it, close the tap.
5 Continue to pour coolant into the cross-pipe filler until the level is within 2 in (51 mm) of the rim. Fit the cap.
6 Start the engine and run at idling speed for about three minutes. Switch off and wait for one minute, then open the radiator bleed tap and remove the cross-pipe pressure cap.
7 Add more coolant slowly into the cross-pipe filler neck until coolant again flows from the bleed tap. Close the tap.
8 Continue to pour in coolant until the level is again within 2 in (51 mm) of the top of the cross-pipe filler. Refit the pressure cap.
9 This somewhat laborious refilling method must not be shortened as air pockets remaining in the cooling system may cause local hotspots with consequent engine damage.

5 Cooling system (fuel injection models) – refilling

1 Close the radiator drain tap and then check that the pressure cap is removed from the expansion tank and the radiator bleed tap is open (photo).
2 Slowly fill the expansion tank to the brim with correct coolant (see Section 7). Wait for one or two minutes and if the level has dropped, add more coolant.
3 Close the bleed tap and fit the pressure cap to the expansion tank, having made sure that the sealing ring is in good order.
4 On cars equipped with air conditioning, set the controls to '80' and 'DEF'.
5 Start the engine and let it idle (1000 rpm approx) for about three minutes, then switch off.
6 Open the bleed tap and wait until a continuous flow of coolant is seen to be ejected, then close the tap.
7 Remove the pressure cap from the expansion tank and slowly pour in more coolant until it is full to the brim. Refit the cap.
8 This somewhat laborious refilling method must not be shortened as air pockets remaining in the cooling system may cause local hotspots with consequent engine damage.

6 Cooling system – level checking and topping up

1 Coolant level checking should be carried out regularly as described

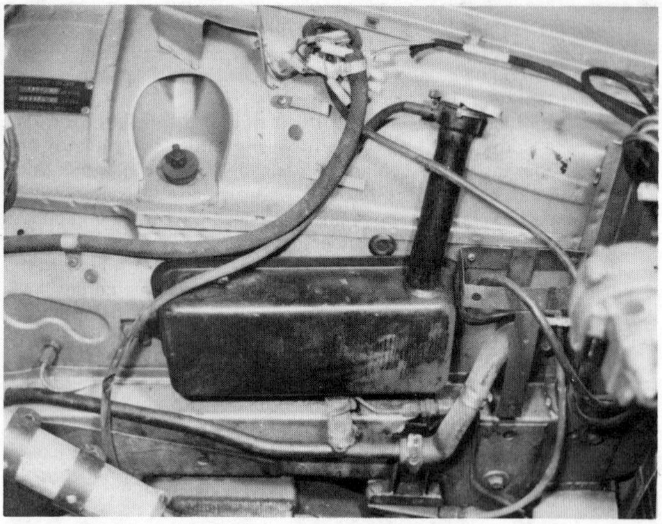

3.1 The expansion tank (fuel injection models)

5.1 The radiator bleed tap

in Routine Maintenance. If topping up is required frequently, then a leak in the system should be suspected.

2 To check the coolant level on carburettor models, make sure that the engine is cold and remove the pressure cap from the engine cross-pipe. If the coolant level is within 2 in (51 mm) of the rim, the system does not require topping up. If the level is lower, open the radiator bleed tap and pour coolant into the cross-pipe filler neck until coolant flows from the bleed tap. Close the tap and refit the pressure cap.

3 To check the coolant level on fuel injection models, make sure that the engine is cold and remove the expansion tank cap. If no more coolant can be added the system evidently does not require topping up and the cap can be refitted. If coolant is needed, fill the tank to the brim and then refit the cap.

7 Antifreeze mixture

1 Plain water should never be used in the cooling system as apart from not providing protection against adverse climatic conditions, the internal metal surfaces of the water passages will also corrode. The inhibitors found in good quality antifreeze mixtures protect iron and aluminium against corrosion for periods not exceeding twelve months.

2 In climatic conditions where antifreeze is not required make sure that a suitable corrosion inhibitor is used in the coolant.

3 The following table gives a guide to the proportion of antifreeze required for various levels of protection:

Antifreeze volume	Protection to
25%	*-15°F (-26°C)*
35%	*-38°F (-39°C)*
40%	*-42°F (-41°C)*
50%	*-53°F (-47°C)*

4 When carrying out routine topping up of the cooling system, always use coolant which has been mixed in the same proportion as the original coolant.

8 Expansion tank – removal and refitting

1 Remove the left-hand air cleaner.

2 Unclip and disconnect the pipe on the top of the expansion tank and tie it up as high as possible.

3 Disconnect and tie the pipe at the base of the expansion tank in a similar way. Drain the tank and then pull the vent pipe from the filler neck.

4 Turn the steering to full left-hand lock.

5 Working under the front left-hand wheel arch, unbolt the tank and lift it clear.

6 Refit the tank by reversing the removal operations and then refill with coolant, referring to Section 4 or 5 as applicable.

9 Fan and coolant pump drivebelt – adjustment, removal and refitting

1 The procedure for all belt configurations is covered in Chapter 1, Section 51.

10 Electric fan cowl (XJ12 and Double Six) – removal and refitting

1 Disconnect the battery and drain the cooling system.

2 *On cars equipped with air conditioning*, remove the fan and the fluid coupling unit as described in Section 12, also the right-hand air intake ram tube. Unbolt the relays from the radiator top rail and lay them with their wiring harness across the engine.

3 *On all models*, remove the left-hand air intake ram tube.

4 Detach the headlamp relay.

5 Remove the four self-locking nuts from the rear of the top rail, noting the location of the clips, washers and connectors.

6 Disconnect the lead from the coolant pump suction pipe and the cooling fan red leads at the connectors.

7 *On cars without air conditioning*, slacken the fan relay securing nuts and detach the fan shield from the studs. Unclip (one screw) the float chamber breather and vent pipe (carburettor models) and pull the pipe through the top rail grommet.

8 *On all cars*, disconnect the radiator top hose and the fan cowl lower brackets.

9 Unbolt the radiator top rail and without straining the wiring harness, ease the top rail forward to clear the fan cowl. Remove the cowl.

10 On some air conditioned models, the electric fan cowl is attached to the belt-driven cowl by self-tapping screws which must be extracted.

11 Refitting is a reversal of removal. Remember to refill the cooling system on completion.

11 Fan and fluid coupling (XJ12 and Double Six, early models) – removal and refitting

1 Slacken the fan drivebelt.

2 Unscrew and remove the four nuts which hold the fan to the fluid coupling.

3 Unscrew and remove the four nuts which hold the fluid coupling to the pulley.

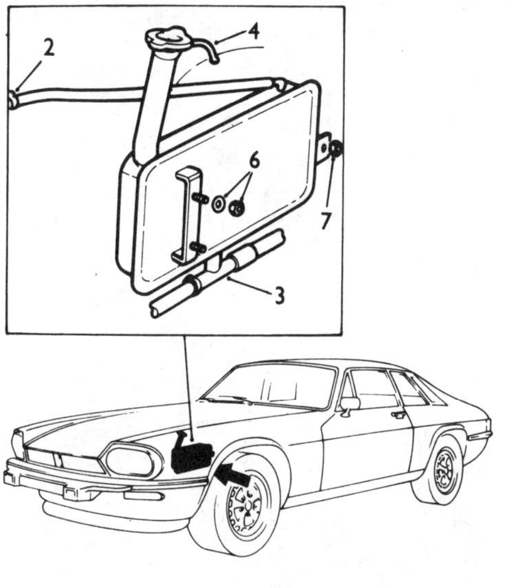

Fig. 2.4 Expansion tank fixing details (Sec 8)

2 Hose clip
3 Base pipe
4 Vent pipe
6 Mounting nut and washer
7 Mounting nut

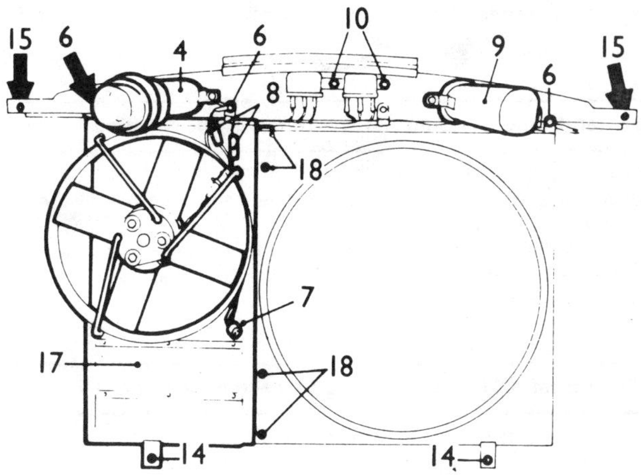

Fig. 2.5 Electric fan cowl (XJ12, Double Six) removal (Sec 10)

4 Left-hand intake ram tube
6 Top rail nuts
7 Thermostatic switch
8 Fan wires
9 Right-hand intake ram tube (air conditioned models)
10 Relay mounting screws (air conditioned models)
14 Fan cowl bracket screws
15 Top rail securing screws
17 Fan cowl
18 Screws (electric fan cowl to belt-driven fan cowl)

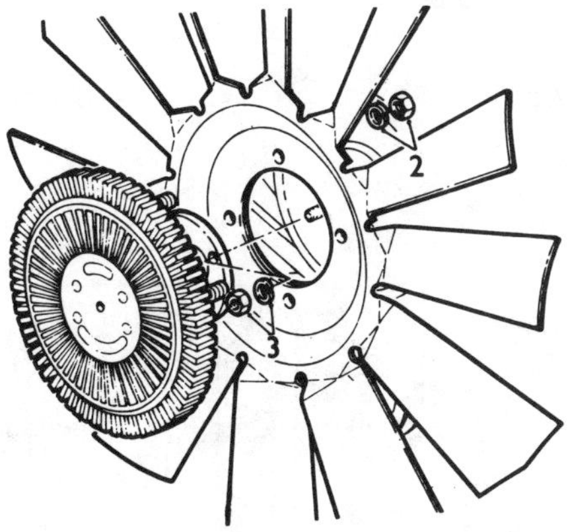

Fig. 2.6 Fan and fluid coupling (XJ12 and Double Six, early models, and XJS) (Sec 11)

2 Fan to fluid coupling nuts
3 Fluid coupling to coolant pump nuts

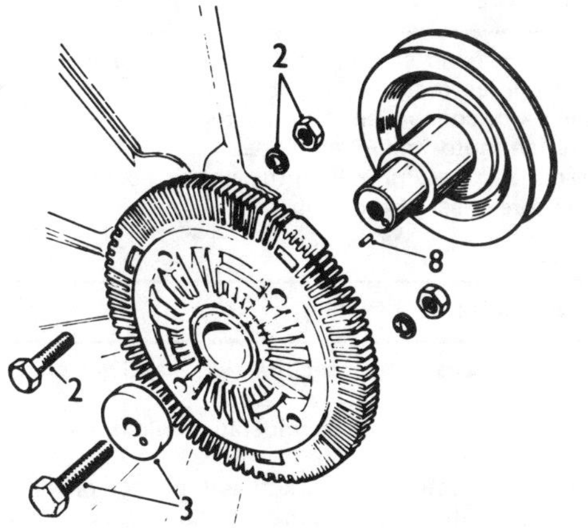

Fig. 2.7 Fan and fluid coupling (XJ12 and Double Six, later models) (Sec 12)

2 Fan to fluid coupling nuts and bolts
3 Fluid coupling centre bolt and special washer
8 Locating pin

4 Remove the fan and fluid coupling.
5 Refitting is a reversal of removal.

12 Fan and fluid coupling (XJ12 and Double Six, later models) – removal and refitting

1 Unscrew and remove the setscrews which hold the top section of the fan cowl.
2 Unbolt the fan from the fluid coupling.
3 Hold the pulley against rotation (flats are provided on the shaft for this purpose) and then unscrew the fluid coupling centre bolt. Do not lose the special washer.
4 Using a plastic faced mallet, gently tap the fluid coupling from the pulley spigot.
5 Remove the fan from the cowl.
6 To refit, first locate the four bolts in the fluid coupling and then place the fan over the pulley spindle.
7 Check that the locating pin is in position in the pulley spigot and smear the spigot with grease.
8 Position the fluid coupling on the pulley and then fit the coupling with the special bolt and washer. Ensure that the special washer engages correctly with the pin in the pulley spigot before tightening the bolt. Hold the shaft flats with an open-ended spanner.
9 Bolt the fan to the fluid coupling and refit the upper section of the cowl.

13 Fan and fluid coupling (XJS) – removal and refitting

1 Slacken the fan drivebelt.
2 Unbolt the fluid coupling from the pulley and then unbolt the fan from the fluid coupling.
3 Ease the fluid coupling away followed by the fan blade assembly.
4 Refitting is a reversal of removal. Make sure that the fan blades are fitted the correct way round.

14 Electric fan (XJ12 and Double Six) – removal and refitting

1 Remove the fan cowl as described in Section 10.
2 Unscrew and remove the three mounting nuts and lift the fan/motor assembly from the engine compartment.
3 Refitting is a reversal of removal.

15 Electric fan (XJS) – removal and refitting

1 Remove the left-hand air cleaner cover and filter element.
2 Disconnect the fan motor supply cable at its snap connector.
3 Unbolt the earth connection from the top rail.
4 Unbolt the fan motor mounting plate.
5 Lift the fan/motor assembly from the engine compartment.
6 Refitting is a reversal of removal.

16 Electric fan and relay – testing

1 If air conditioning is fitted, set the right-hand air conditioning switch to 'OFF'.
2 Pull the plug from the fan thermostatic switch, switch on the ignition but do not start the engine.
3 Bridge the disconnected plug sockets wth a piece of wire. A click should be heard from the relay and the fan motor should rotate.
4 Remove the bridge wire, switch off the ignition and reconnect the plug.

Cars with air conditioning

5 Again switch on the ignition and set the left-hand air conditioning control to '65' and the right-hand one to 'AUTO'. The air conditioner relay should be heard to operate, the cooling fan should start and the compressor clutch should engage.
6 Switch off the ignition and set the right-hand air conditioning system control to the 'OFF' position.

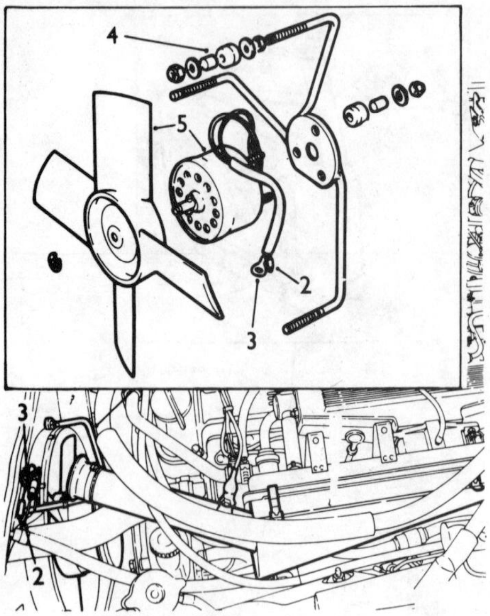

Fig. 2.8 Electrican fan (XJS) (Sec 15)

2 Motor supply wire
3 Earth lead
4 Motor mounting plate nuts
5 Fan/motor

Fig. 2.9 Fan motor relay (XJ12, Double Six) – rectangular type (Sec 17)

1 Electrical connection
2 Relay mounting nuts

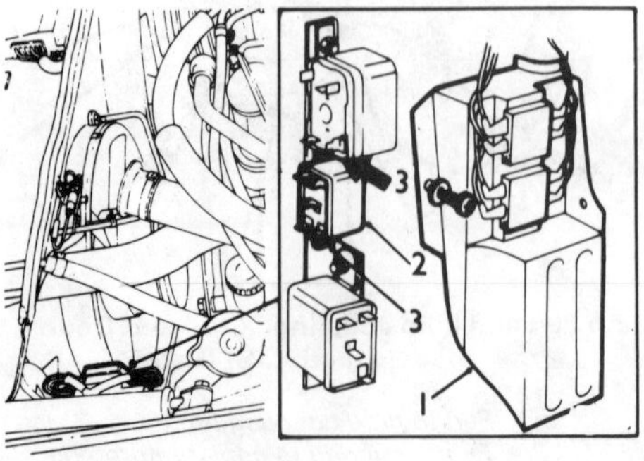

Fig. 2.10 Fan motor relay (XJS) (Sec 17)

1 Cover
2 Relay
3 Mounting nuts

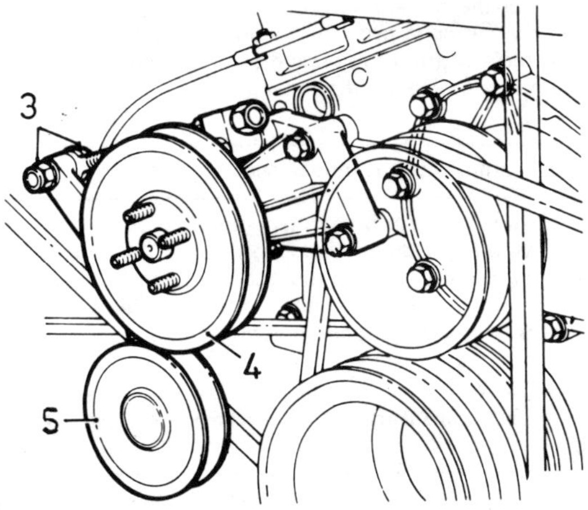

Fig. 2.11 Idler and jockey pulleys (Sec 18)

3 Adjuster bolt securing nut
4 Idler pulley
5 Jockey pulley

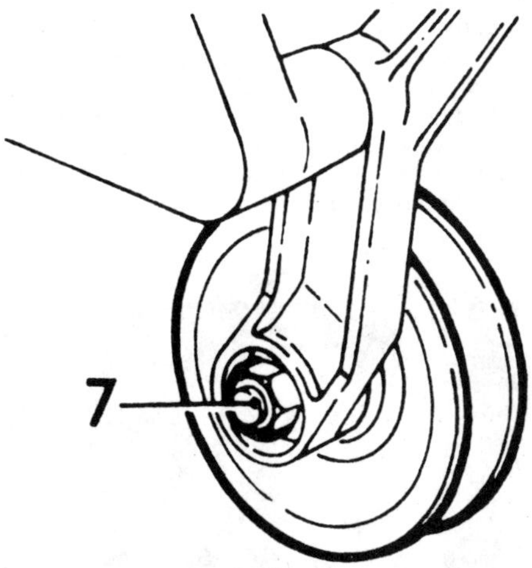

Fig. 2.12 Jockey pulley retaining nut (7) (Sec 18)

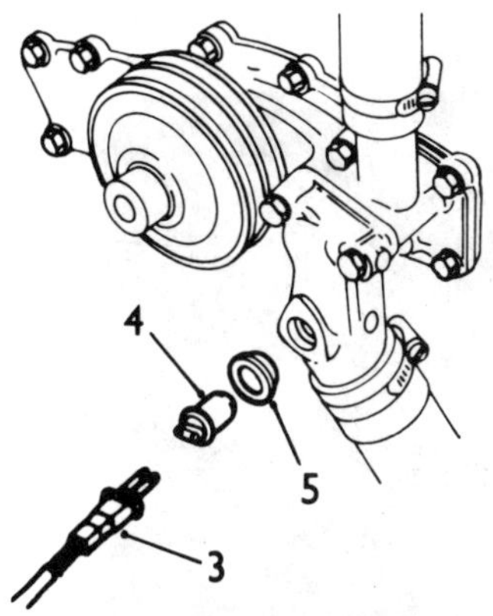

Fig. 2.13 Electric fan thermostatic switch (4), seal (5) and connector (3) (Sec 19)

17 Fan motor relay – removal and refitting

1 *On XJ12 and Double Six models,* the relay (see Chapter 10) is mounted on the right-hand side of the radiator top rail. It may be of round or rectangular design, according to model.
2 *On XJS models* the relay is mounted on a block on the left-hand side of the engine compartment.
3 Identify the connecting leads to their terminals, disconnect them and then unbolt and remove the relay.
4 Refitting is a reversal of removal.

18 Idler and jockey pulleys – removal and refitting

1 To remove the idler pulley, first take off the drivebelt and remove the fan and fluid coupling.
2 Remove the bolt which holds the adjuster bolt eye to the pulley arm.
3 Unbolt the idler pulley housing from the engine and remove it complete with jockey pulley.
4 To remove the jockey pulley from the engine independently, first withdraw the right-hand air cleaner.
5 Screw back the locknut on the fanbelt adjustment bolt and then slacken the locknut on the adjuster bolt trunnion.
6 Slacken the jockey pulley arm pivot bolt and then remove the bolt which holds the adjustment bolt eye to the pulley arm.
7 On early XJ12, Double Six and all XJS models, unscrew the nut and special washer which hold the jockey pulley spindle in the arm.
8 Refitting is a reversal of removal.

19 Electric fan thermostatic switch – removal and refitting

1 Disconnect the battery and drain the cooling system.
2 Disconnect the electrical plug from the thermostatic switch (photo).
3 Grip the switch with a pair of pliers and pull it from its rubber seal in the coolant pump bottom connector (photo).
4 Prise the rubber seal from its housing.
5 Always use a new seal when fitting the switch.
6 Fit the new seal to the housing. **Do not** apply any grease or lubricant to the seal.
7 Press the switch into the seal.
8 Reconnect the switch plug and the battery and refill the cooling system. Check the switch and seal for coolant leaks when the engine is first run.

20 Radiator (carburettor fuel system) – removal and refitting

1 Disconnect the battery, drain the cooling system and remove the bonnet.
2 Remove the left-hand air intake ram tube.
3 Disconnect the leads and remove the headlamp relay.
4 Identify the leads and pull them from the headlamp fuse boxes. Pull the leads through the radiator top rail grommet.
5 Unscrew and remove the self-locking nuts from the rear of the top rail noting the location of clips and connectors.
6 Disconnect the lead from the thermostatic switch.
7 Disconnect the fan supply cable (red) at the snap connector.
8 Unbolt the fan relay from the top rail.
9 Unbolt the top rail.
10 *On cars equipped with air conditioning,* lift up the top rail complete with receiver/drier and condenser, and lay the assembly across the top of the engine. **Do not** disconnect any of the air conditioning system hoses, but move the components as far as the flexible connecting hoses will permit.
11 *On cars without air conditioning,* remove the top rail.
12 Disconnect the top hoses from the radiator.
13 Disconnect the automatic transmission oil cooler lines from the radiator and plug all openings.
14 Remove (two self-tapping screws) the radiator lower grille.
15 Using two spanners to avoid tearing the stubs out, disconnect the hoses from the oil cooler.
16 Unbolt the oil cooler from its brackets and remove it, noting the spacers between the oil cooler and the brackets.

17 Working underneath the car, disconnect the bottom hose from the radiator.
18 Withdraw the radiator from the engine compartment.
19 Refitting is a reversal of removal. Renew any damaged grommets.

21 Radiator (fuel injection system) – removal and refitting

1 If the car is equipped with air conditioning, have the system discharged by your dealer.
2 Disconnect the battery, remove the bonnet and drain the cooling system.
3 On XJS and early XJ12 models, remove the lower grille.
4 Detach relays and sensors (but do not disconnect the leads) from the radiator assembly.
5 Disconnect the amplifier block connector (see Chapter 3).
6 Unbolt the fan cowl from the radiator top rail, noting the locations of the earth lead and the line fuse.
7 Disconnect the expansion pipe (banjo bolt) from the radiator.
8 Unbolt the radiator top rail and disconnect the earth leads from the left and right-hand harnesses.
9 Unbolt the right-hand front stay.
10 Unbolt the left-hand wing valance stay.
11 On cars equipped with air conditioning, disconnect and plug the hoses from the receiver/drier. Unclip the condenser hose from the right-hand wing valance.
12 Remove the radiator top rail (complete with receiver/drier on air conditioned models).
13 Disconnect the lead from the low coolant level sensor.
14 Disconnect the radiator right-hand top hose.
15 On cars fitted with automatic transmission, disconnect the hoses from the transmission oil cooler and plug the openings.
16 Disconnect the left-hand top hose from the radiator, also the hose from the expansion tank T-piece.
17 Disconnect the hoses from the engine oil cooler. Use two spanners to avoid tearing the stub out of the cooler.
18 Disconnect the radiator bottom hose.
19 Unbolt the fan cowl from the mounting brackets.
20 Lift the radiator from the engine compartment.
21 Refitting is the reverse of removal.

22 Radiator drain tap – removal and refitting

1 The radiator drain tap is remotely operated by a rod.
2 To remove the tap, drain the cooling system, pull the split pin from the lower end of the operating rod and unscrew the tap.
3 Refitting is a reversal of removal. Use new seals and smear the threads of the tap with jointing compound.

23 Thermostat (carburettor fuel system) – removal, testing and refitting

1 Partially drain the cooling system and remove the air cleaner to obtain access to a thermostat.
2 Disconnect the hose from the thermostat housing cover.
3 Unbolt and remove the thermostat housing cover.
4 Lift out the thermostat. If it is stuck in its seat, cut round it with a sharp knife.
5 Clean the thermostat and ensure that the small hole on the valve is clear. If the valve is open it indicates that the thermostat is unserviceable and should be renewed with one of similar operating temperature, this figure will be seen on the top side of the thermostat.
6 If correct operation of the thermostat is in doubt test it by immersing it together with a 0 to 212°F (0-100°C) thermometer in a container of cold water. Heat the water, keeping it stirred, and observe if the operation of the valve is in close agreement to the temperature marked on the body of the thermostat. Allow the water to cool down and check that the valve closes correctly.
7 Refitting is a reversal of removal. Use a new gasket, and make sure that a new thermostat (if fitted) is of the correct type.

19.2 Fan thermostatic switch connecting plug (arrowed)

19.3 Fan thermostatic switch removed

24.1A Thermostat housing

24.1B Removing the thermostat from the right-hand side of the engine

24.1C Thermostat removed

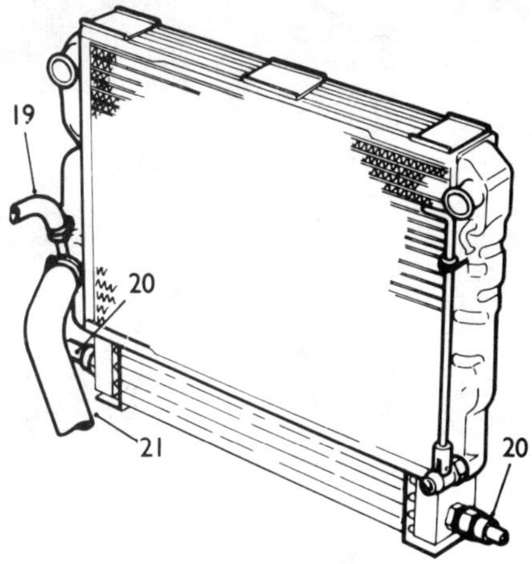

Fig. 2.14 Radiator connections (Sec 21)

19 Expansion tank T-piece hose
20 Engine oil cooler hose connections
21 Radiator bottom hose

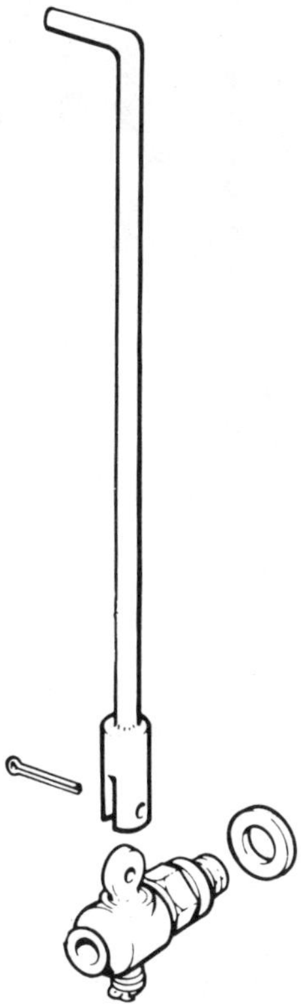

Fig. 2.15 Radiator drain tap (Sec 22)

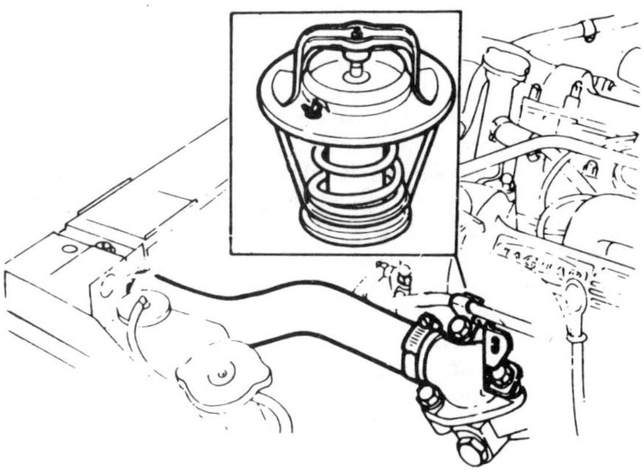

Fig. 2.16 Left-hand thermostat and housing (carburettor engines) (Sec 23)

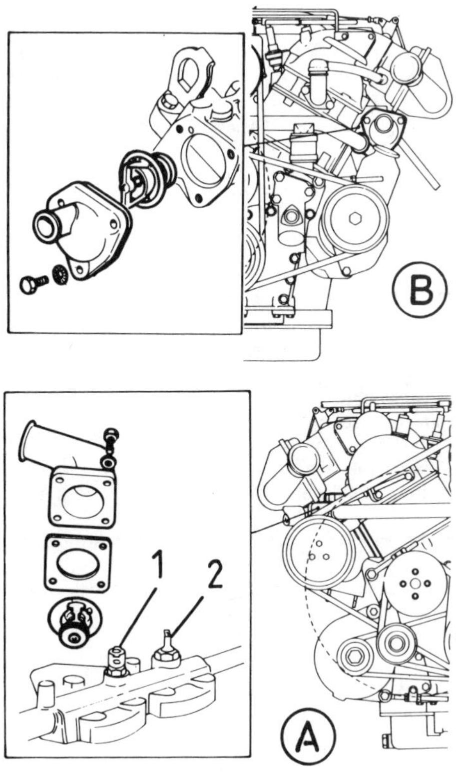

Fig. 2.18 Thermostats (fuel injection engines) (Sec 24)

A Right-hand
B Left-hand
1 Thermotime switch
2 Coolant temperature switch

Fig. 2.17 Removing the coolant pump pulley (Sec 29)

27.10 Removing the thermostatic switch housing from the coolant pump

27.14 Removing the coolant pump

27.15 Coolant pump gasket in position

24 Thermostat (fuel injection system) – removal, testing and refitting

1 The operations are similar to those described in Section 23 except that it is not necessary to remove the air cleaner for access to the thermostat (photos).

25 Thermostat housing (carburettor fuel system) – removal and refitting

1 Partially drain the cooling system and remove the air cleaner.
2 Release the clips from the three hoses attached to the thermostat housing.
3 From the right-hand thermostat housing (if it is to be removed) disconnect the lead from the coolant temperature transmitter.
4 On emission control cars, disconnect the lead from the thermal override switch on the left-hand thermostat housing (if it is to be removed).
5 Unbolt the thermostat housing and engine lifting eye from the cylinder head.
6 Disengage the induction housing bleed pipe from its clip. Lift off the thermostat housing and discard the gaskets.
7 Refitting is a reversal of removal, but use new gaskets.

26 Thermostat housing (fuel injection system) – removal and refitting

Left-hand housing

1 Remove the air cleaner.
2 Partially drain the cooling system.
3 Disconnect leads from the sensors.
4 Disconnect the crankcase breather tube from its elbow.
5 Disconnect the crankcase breather valve pipe from the coolant pipe.
6 Disconnect the radiator top hose from the thermostat housing cover.
7 Disconnect the cross-pipe hose from the thermostat housing.
8 Unbolt the thermostat housing and disconnect the housing from the coolant rail. Discard the gasket and the coolant rail sealing ring.

Right-hand housing

9 Repeat the operations described in paragraphs 2, 3, 6, 7 and 8.

Both housings

10 Refitting of both housings is a reversal of removal. Use new gaskets and coolant rail sealing rings.

27 Coolant pump (XJ12 and Double Six) – removal and refitting

1 Remove the radiator as described earlier in this Chapter.
2 Unbolt the radiator cowl lower brackets and move the cowl to one side.
3 Remove the fan and fluid coupling.
4 Remove the fanbelt.
5 Remove the fanbelt adjuster trunnion bolt and unbolt the idler pulley housing.
6 Extract the two studs so that the power steering pump belt can be removed.
7 On emission control cars, remove the air pump belt.
8 On cars with air conditioning, remove the compressor pump drivebelt.
9 Slacken the steering pump mounting bolts until the adjuster bolt can be withdrawn from its special stud. Remove the stud.
10 Unbolt the thermostatic switch housing. Remove the housing complete with bottom hose (photo).
11 Unscrew and remove the crankshaft pulley centre bolt using a socket spanner. In order to prevent the crankshaft rotating as the bolt is unscrewed try engaging gear with the handbrake fully on (manual transmission) or jam the starter ring gear (automatic transmission).
12 Tap off the damper and retrieve the cone and Woodruff key.
13 Slacken the upper clip on the engine cross-pipe hose.
14 Unbolt the coolant pump and draw it away from the cylinder block in a downward direction (photo).
15 Refitting is a reversal of removal but use all new gaskets (photo) and tighten the bolts to the specified torque. (For bolt locations, refer to Chapter 1, photo 47.86).

28 Coolant pump (XJS) – removal and refitting

1 The operations do not require prior removal of the radiator and disconnection of cowl brackets, otherwise they are as described in Section 27, paragraphs 2 to 15.

29 Coolant pump – overhaul

1 It is recommended that when a fault develops in the coolant pump, the pump is renewed or exchanged for a factory rebuilt unit.
2 Where overhaul of the original unit is preferred and the necessary repair kit is available, carry out the following operations.
3 With the coolant pump removed from the engine, clean away external dirt.
4 Using a puller with two $\frac{5}{16}$ in UNF x 2 in long bolts screwed into the tapped holes provided, draw off the pulley.
5 Using the same tool and bolts, draw off the impeller.
6 Release the locknut and using an Allen key, extract the screw from the water pump body.
7 Support the pump body and press out the bearing/shaft assembly, applying pressure at the impeller end.
8 Tap the seal assembly from the pump body.
9 Support the coolant pump sandwich plate front face and tap the pump body through the impeller orifice. On no account prise the coolant pump body and sandwich apart.

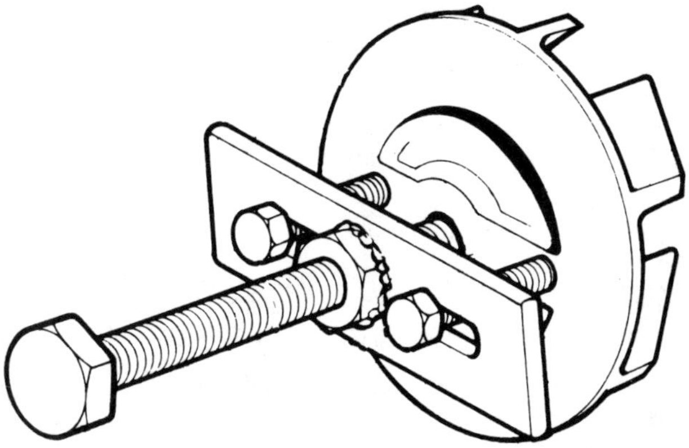

Fig. 2.19 Removing the coolant pump impeller (Sec 29)

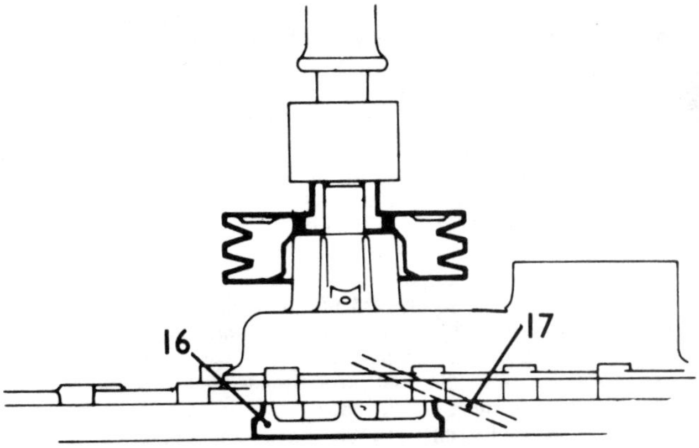

Fig. 2.20 Coolant pump impeller clearance (Sec 29)

16 Impeller *17 Clearance (impeller to sandwich)*

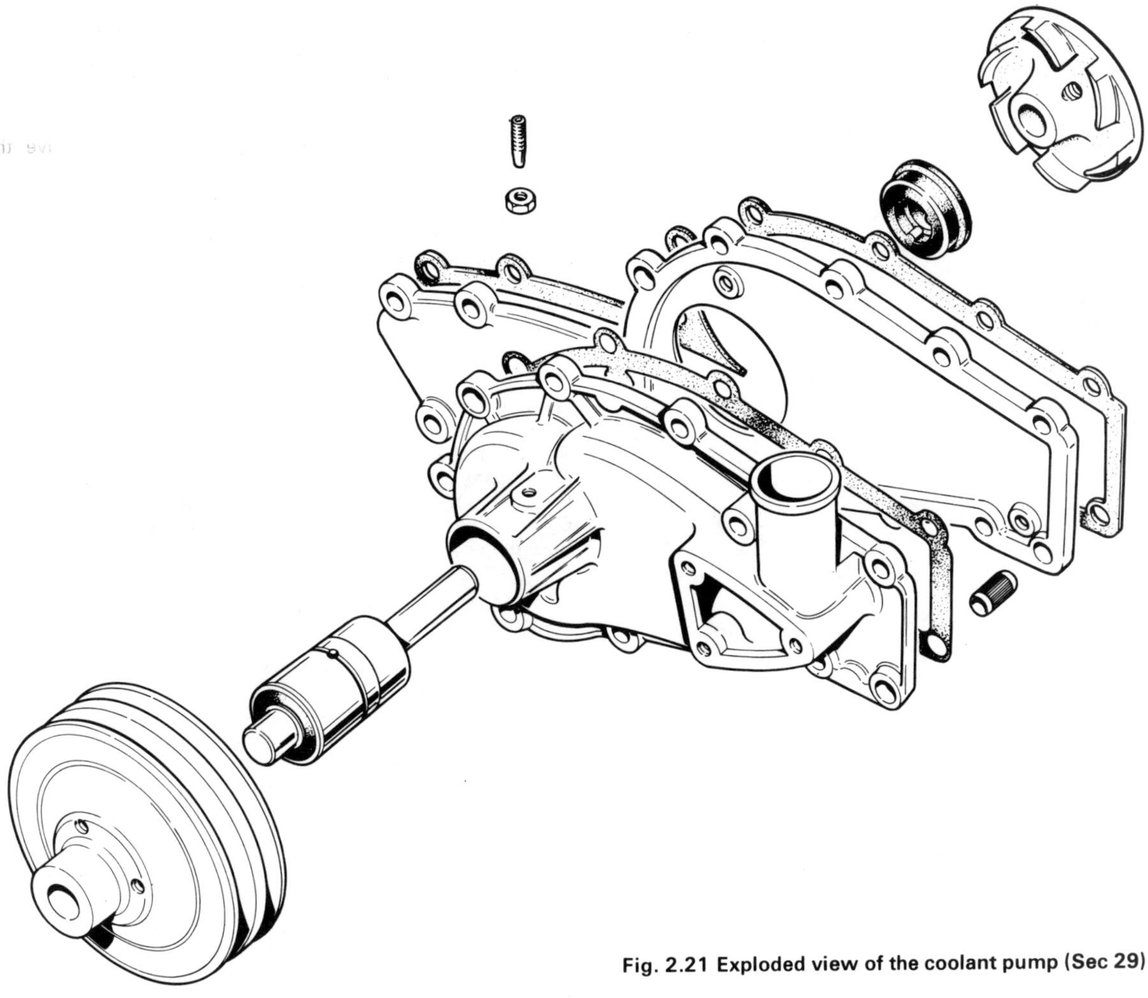

Fig. 2.21 Exploded view of the coolant pump (Sec 29)

10 Clean out the coolant pump body and scrape away old gasket from the mating flanges.
11 To reassemble the pump, place the front face of the body upwards and enter the shaft/bearing assembly (smaller shaft diameter leading) into the body. Make sure that the location holes in the body and bearing are in alignment.
12 Press the bearing into the pump body until the holes are in alignment. Apply pressure to the bearing case.
13 Insert the Allen screw and tighten the locknut.
14 Fit the seal over the impeller end of the shaft and drive it squarely into position to seat on the body shoulder.
15 Locate a new gasket (dry) over the ring dowels, assemble the sandwich and press firmly together.
16 Place the impeller, blades upward, on the press bed, insert the end of the shaft into the impeller and press on the pulley end of the shaft until the shaft fully enters the impeller.
17 Press the pulley onto the shaft in a similar way until the pulley boss is flush with the end of the shaft.
18 A clearance should exist between the impeller blades and the sandwich face of 0.025 in (0.635 mm). If this clearance is incorrect, use the press or the puller as necessary to adjust it.

30 Coolant temperature gauge and transmitter

1 The coolant temperature gauge operates on the thermal principle using a bi-metal strip surrounded by a heater winding.
2 The transmitter unit is mounted adjacent to the thermostat housing.
3 Failure of the gauge to register correctly may be due to a loose connection or faulty wiring insulation.
4 Testing of the gauge or transmitter cannot be undertaken without special equipment.
5 Removal of the gauge can be carried out, as described in Chapter 10.
6 If the fuel contents gauge and the coolant temperature gauge both become faulty at the same time, then the instrument voltage stabilizer may be the cause.

31 Fault diagnosis – cooling system

Symptom	Reason(s)
Overheating	Insufficient coolant in cooling system Fanbelt slipping Radiator core blocked or radiator grille obstructed Thermostat not opening properly Ignition timing incorrecty set (accompanied by loss of power and perhaps misfiring) Incorrect fuel/air mixture Exhaust system partially blocked Oil level in sump too low Blown cylinder head gasket (water/steam being forced down the radiator expansion pipe under pressure) Engine not yet run-in Brakes binding
Engine running cold	Thermostat jammed open Incorrect grade of thermostat fitted Thermostat missing
Leaks in system	Loose clips on coolant hoses Top or bottom coolant hoses perished Radiator leaking Thermostat gasket leaking Pressure cap spring worn or seal ineffective Cylinder liner or head cracked or joint leaking Core plug corroded

Chapter 3 Fuel, exhaust and emission control systems

Contents

Specifications

Carburettor systems

Fuel pumps

Make and type	Electric, SU AUF 411 (two twin assemblies)

Carburettors

Make and number	Zenith Stromberg, two on each cylinder head
Type:	
1972/73 (all models)	175 CD25E
1973/74 (except N America):	
RH	3551 A1 and A2
LH	3552 B1 and B2
1973/74 (N America):	
RH	3656 A1 and A2
LH	3657 B1 and B2
Needle:	
Except N America	BICE
N America 1972/73	BICF
N America 1973/74	BICK
Spring colour (all models)	Red
Idle speed (all models)	640 to 750 rpm
Fast idle speed	1600 to 1700 rpm
Exhaust CO content:	
Without emission control	4 to 6%
With emission control	3 to 4.5%

Fuel tanks

Number and situation	Two, rear mounted
Capacity (each tank):	
Except N America	12 Imp gals (54.6 litres)
N America	12 US gals (45.5 litres)

Fuel Injection Systems

System type	Bosch-Lucas electronic (D-Jetronic)

Fuel pump

Type	Lucas electric
System pressure (regulated)	28.5 to 31.3 lbf/in^2 (2.0 to 2.2 kgf/cm^2)

Exhaust CO content	1 to 2%

Fuel tanks

Number and situation:	
XJ12 and Double Six	Two, rear mounted
XJS	One, rear mounted
Capacity (each tank):	
XJ12 and Double Six	10.5 Imp gals (12.6 US gals, 47.75 litres)
XJS	20.0 Imp gals (24.0 US gals, 90.0 litres)

Fuel octane requirement

S compression engines	97 octane (UK 4-star)
L compression engines	94 octane (UK 3-star)
N American with catalytic converter	91 RON (unleaded)

Torque wrench settings

	lbf ft	Nm
Fuel tank mounting bolts	18	25
Fuel tank drain plug (small)	26	35
Fuel tank drain plug (large)	28	38
Fuel pipe unions	14	19
Fuel pipe banjo union bolts	25	34
Exhaust manifolds to downpipes	25	34
Exhaust mounting ring to crossmember	18	25
Exhaust tailpipe to body	18	25

1 General description

1 Cars built up until 1974/75 were equipped with twin carburettors on each cylinder bank.

2 Duel rear mounted fuel tanks and two (twin unit) electrically-operated fuel pumps were fitted.

3 From 1974/75 on, all models including the newly introduced XJS were equipped with the Jetronic 'D', Bosch-Lucas electronic fuel injection system.

4 XJS models have a single rear mounted fuel tank.
5 All models are equipped with some emission control devices, but the complexity and design of the system depends upon the particular model, date of production and intended operating territory.

PART A – CARBURETTOR, FUEL AND EMISSION CONTROL SYSTEMS

2 Air cleaner element – renewal

1 Open the bonnet and remove the special bolts which hold the air cleaner cover to the backplate.
2 Release the air cleaner toggle clips and remove the cover.
3 Extract the air cleaner element.
4 Wipe out the casings and fit the new element with its rectangular openings facing inward. Engage the bottom lugs of the cover, prise the top edge together and fit the toggle clips.

3 Air cleaner – removal and refitting

Left-hand

1 Disconnect the battery.
2 Unbolt the air cleaner cover from the backplate, release the clips and extract the filter element.
3 Disconnect the gulp valve inlet pipe from the air cleaner backplate.
4 Disconnect the float chamber vent pipe from the air cleaner backplate.
5 *On N American vehicles,* disconnect the canister purge pipe from the plenum chamber.
6 Disconnect the flexible air pipe from the air cleaner backplate.
7 Unbolt the backplate (five setscrews) and disconnect the vacuum pipe which runs between the manifold and temperature sensor.
8 Remove the backplate from the ram pipe flexible hose. Discard the gaskets.

Right-hand

9 The operations are similar to those described for the left-hand air cleaner except that reference to the gulp valve inlet pipe should be ignored.

Both sides

10 Refitting is a reversal of removal. Use new gaskets between the air cleaner and carburettors.

4 Air cleaner – overhaul

1 The temperature sensor unit on the air cleaner can be renewed if the retaining tabs are prised up.
2 When fitting the new sensor, use new seals.
3 The air flap vacuum motor cannot be renewed and in the event of a fault developing, the backplate must be renewed complete.

5 Ram tube – removal and refitting

1 Unbolt the ram tube brackets from the radiator top rail.
2 Disengage the flexible sleeve and withdraw the ram tube through the top rail.
3 Refit by reversing the removal operations.

6 Fuel supply system – description

1 The fuel supply system is of the full recirculation type and comprises the fuel tanks, two fuel pumps, two solenoid valves, a fuel filter and a non-return valve.
2 An instrument panel switch selects the particular tank from which fuel is to be drawn.
3 Later models have a slightly modified layout in that the system solenoid valves are normally open instead of closed as in earlier arrangements. This means that the valve adjacent to a pump operates to close the fuel return line not required instead of the opposite valve opening to provide a fuel return line to the tank. This later system prevents float chamber flooding.

7 Fuel pressure limiting (non-return) valve – removal and refitting

1 Disconnect the battery.
2 Release the clips and remove the valve from the fuel pipeline.
3 Unscrew the two sections of the valve and withdraw the ball and spring.
4 Clean the components and reassemble.
5 Refitting is a reversal of removal, but make sure that the arrow points away from the cross-pipe.

8 Fuel solenoid valve – removal and refitting

1 Disconnect the battery, remove the spare wheel and unscrew the cover from over the fuel pump. Do not extract the screw from the centre of the edge of the cover.

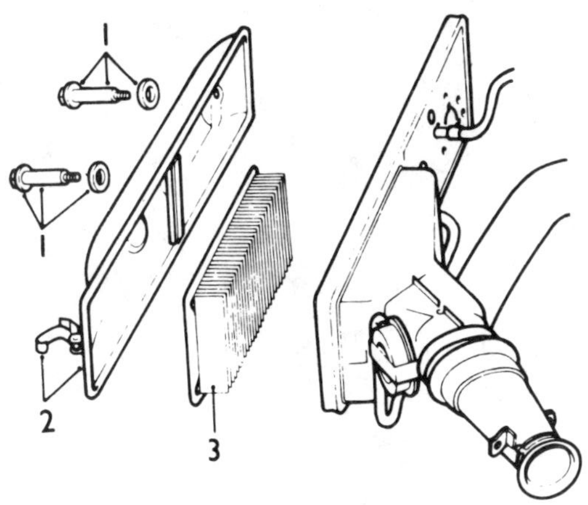

Fig. 3.1 The air cleaner (Sec 1)

1 Cover bolts
2 Toggle clips and cover
3 Filter element

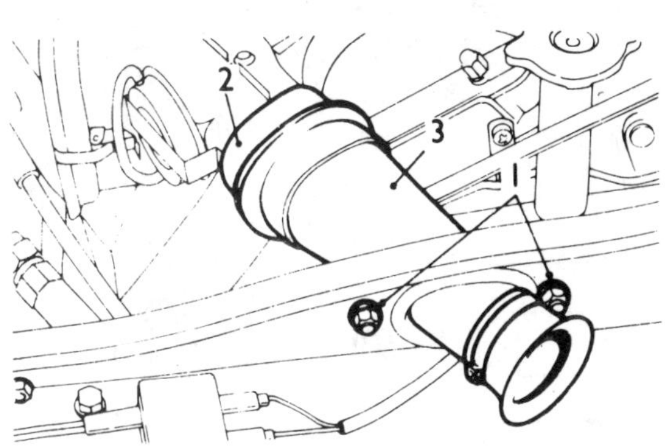

Fig.3.2 The air ram tube (Sec 5)

1 Securing bolts
2 Rubber sleeve
3 Ram tube

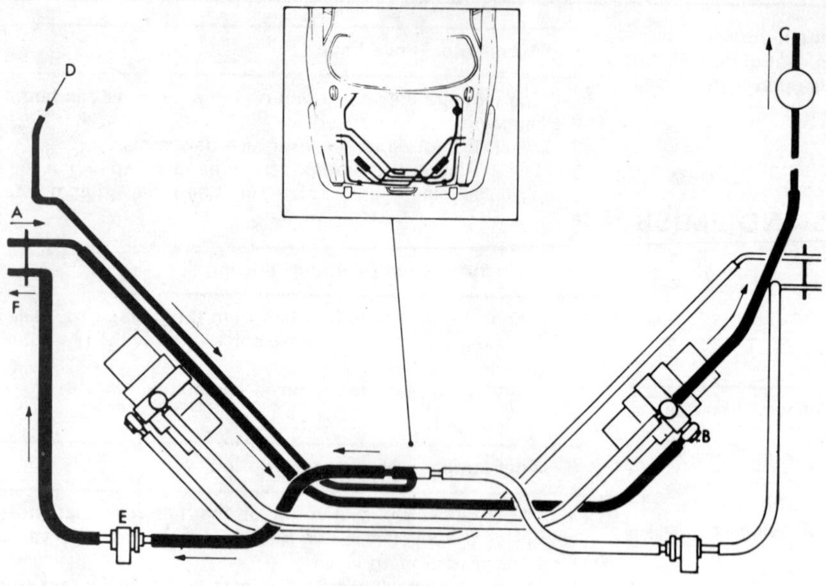

Fig. 3.3 Fuel supply system (early cars) (Sec 6)

A *Tank union*
B *Fuel pump*
C *Bulkhead connector*
D *Bulkhead union*
E *Solenoid valve*
F *Tank union*

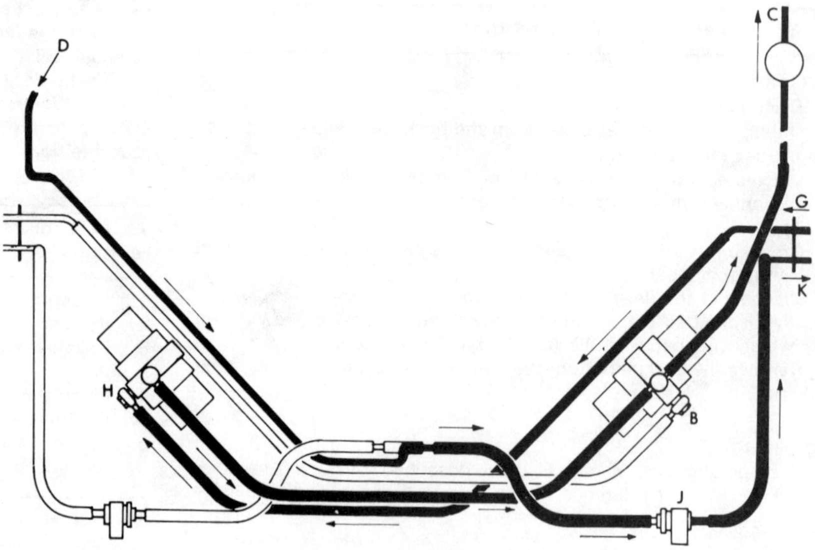

Fig. 3.4 Fuel supply system (later cars) (Sec 6)

B *Fuel pump*
C *Bulkhead connector*
D *Bulkhead union*
G *Tank union*
H *Fuel pump*
J *Solenoid valve*
K *Tank union*

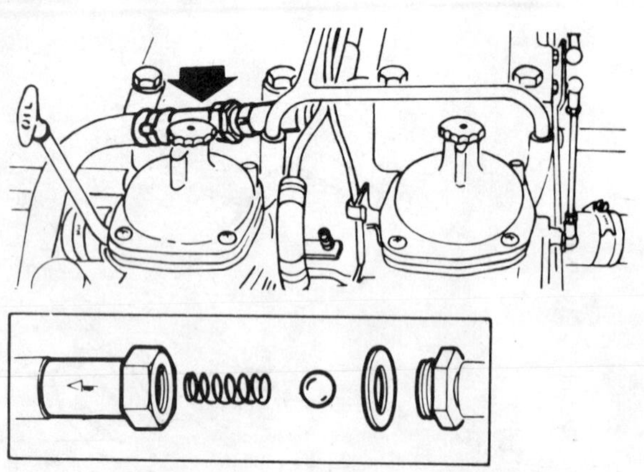

Fig. 3.5 Fuel pressure limiting valve – inset shows component parts (Sec 7)

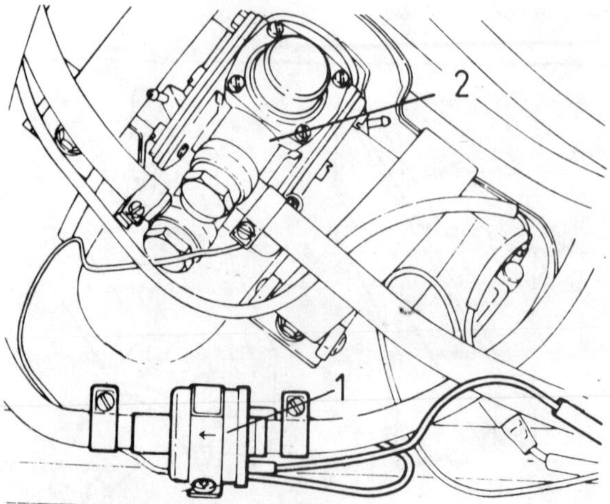

Fig. 3.6 Location of a solenoid valve (Sec 8)

1 *Solenoid valve* 2 *Fuel pump*

2 Clamp the inlet and outlet hoses to the valve to prevent loss of fuel.
3 Disconnect the hoses and separate the electrical connector.
4 Extract the securing screws and withdraw the valve.
5 The valve on earlier models can be tested after removal by connecting a 12V supply across it when it should be observed to open.
6 On later models when this test is carried out, the valve will be observed to close.
7 Refitting is a reversal of removal but make sure that the arrow on the valve points away from the centre line of the car.
8 Check that the earth leads from the valve and the fuel pump are secured beneath the lower fixing screw.

9 Fuel filter – renewal of element

1 Disconnect the battery and remove the spare wheel.
2 Clamp the fuel filter inlet hose to prevent loss of fuel.
3 Place a small container under the fuel filter bowl and unscrew and remove the centre bolt.
4 Extract and discard the filter element.
5 Clean out the filter bowl, fit the new element with the larger hole at the top and use the new seals supplied.
6 Do not overtighten the centre bolt.
7 Remove the hose clamp and the container and reconnect the battery.
8 Start the engine and check for leaks.
9 Refit the spare wheel.

10 Fuel filter – removal and refitting

1 Repeat the operations described in Section 9, paragraphs 1 and 2.
2 Disconnect both fuel pipes from the filter body and then unbolt the filter bracket.
3 Refitting is a reversal of removal.

11 Fuel cut-off inertia switch – removal and refitting

1 As an aid to safety in the event of a collision, an inertia fuel cut-off switch is located under the instrument panel on the passenger side of later models (photo).
2 To remove the switch, first disconnect the battery. Unscrew the switch cover, disconnect the leads and pull the switch from its securing clips.
3 Refit the switch so that the terminals are at the bottom and the moulded ribs towards the rear of the car. Push the switch upwards until it abuts the bracket.
4 Reconnect the lead, polarity being unimportant.
5 If a new switch is being fitted, or if the switch fitted has been tripped, depress the plunger to reset it.
6 Fit the switch cover and reconnect the battery.

12 Fuel pumps – removal and refitting

1 Before removing either fuel pump, first disconnect the battery. Remove the spare wheel and the fuel pump cover from both pump assemblies.
2 Clamp the fuel inlet hoses at both pumps to prevent loss of fuel.
3 On the pump which is being removed, disconnect the two banjo bolts.
4 Disconnect the pump mounting strap from the anchor hooks.
5 Remove the pump after identifying the leads and disconnecting them.
6 Disconnect the earth lead.
7 Refitting is a reversal of removal, but renew the banjo bolt seals where necessary.

13 Fuel pump – overhaul

1 With the fuel pump removed, note the location of the wiring harness and then clean away all external dirt.
2 Mark the relationship of the coil housing to the pump body.
3 Extract the flange screws and withdraw the coil housing from the pump body. Discard the gasket.
4 Unwind the sealing tape and remove the ring from the cover.
5 Remove the polythene sleeve from the terminal stud on the cover.
6 Remove the terminal nut, tag and lockwasher and lift off the cover.
7 Release the diaphram assembly and withdraw the coil housing. Do not separate the diaphragm/spindle as they are a combined assembly.
8 Remove the spring and rubber washer from the spindle.
9 Remove the nylon centralising guide.
10 Extract the screw which holds the terminals and contact blade to the pedestal and remove the contact blade.
11 Extract the screw which holds the condenser and earth terminals and the pedestal to the coil housing.
12 Extract the remaining screw and lift the pedestal away from the coil housing. Unless the pedestal is being renewed, do not remove the terminal from its stud.
13 Withdraw the rocker pivot pin, then the rocker assembly.
14 Extract the screws and remove the valve clamping plate from the body.
15 Note which way the valves face and then remove the valve caps and withdraw the valves. Discard the neoprene sealing rings.
16 Extract the filter gauze from the inlet valve seat and discard the neoprene sealing ring.
17 Repeat the foregoing operations on the twin section of the pump assembly.
18 Unbolt the air bottle cover from the pump body and discard the cork seal.
19 Extract the screws and remove the cover from the flow smoothing valve. Discard the O-ring.
20 Remove the diaphragm and discard the sealing washer.
21 With the pump assembly completely dismantled, clean and inspect all components. Obtain a repair kit.
22 Check that each valve lift is approximately 0.062 in (1.6 mm). If not, bend the valve cage tongues to achieve this.
23 Check the diaphragm of the flow smoothing valve and renew if necessary.
24 Check the contact breaker points for burning or pitting. If necessary, renew the rocker assembly and contact blade.
25 Make sure that the ball in the non-return vent is free to move.
26 Check the pedestal for cracks, also the ridge on which the contact blade rests. If this is damaged, renew the pedestal.
27 Commence reassembling by fitting a new sealing washer in the pump body. Observe absolute cleanliness during the following operations.
28 Fit the diaphragm to the body, concave side facing inwards.
29 Fit the flow smoothing valve cover with a new O-ring. Tighten the securing screws diagonally and evenly.
30 Fit the air bottle cover with a new cork seal, do not overtighten the centre bolt.

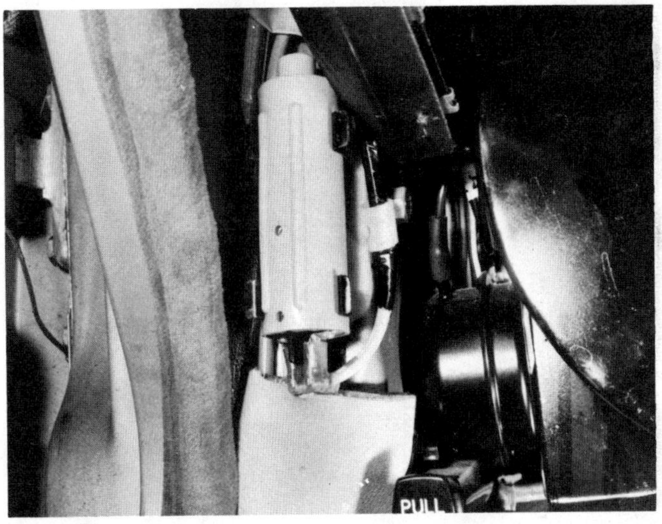

11.1 Fuel cut-off switch

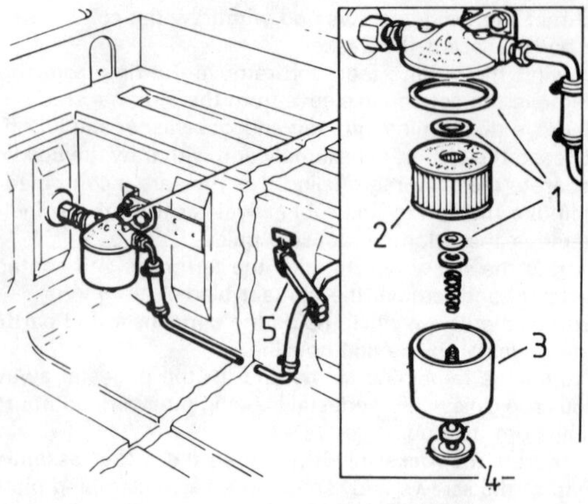

Fig. 3.7 The fuel filter (Sec 9)

1 *Seals*
2 *Element*
3 *Bowl*
4 *Centre bolt*
5 *Fuel pipe clamp*

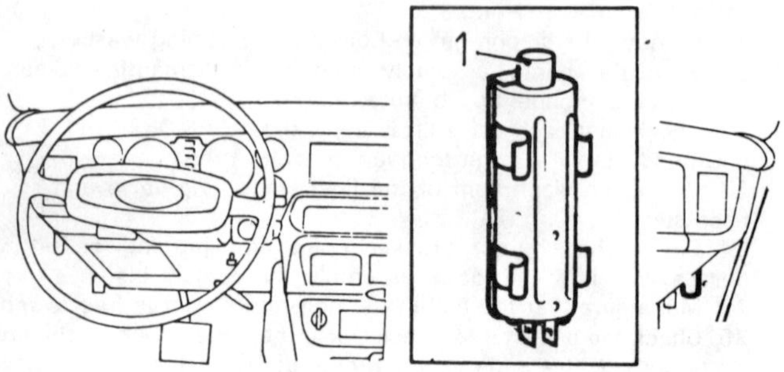

Fig. 3.8 Fuel cut-off inertia switch (Sec 11)

1 *Plunger*

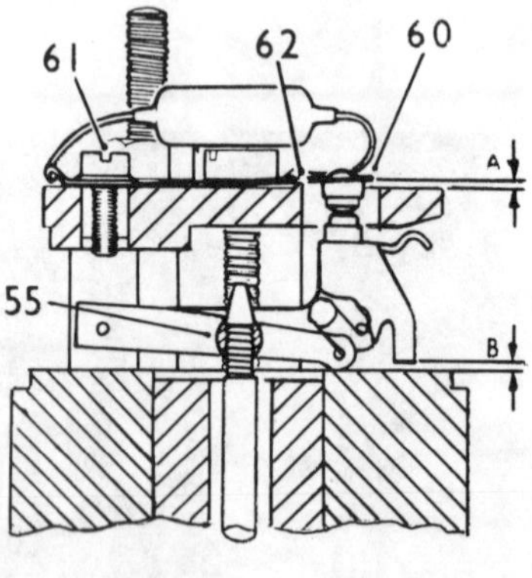

Fig. 3.10 Fuel pump contact points adjusting diagram (Sec 13)

55 *Spindle/rocker trunnion*
60 *Securing screw for contact blade and condenser and coil leads*
61 *Blade securing screw*
62 *Pedestal ridge*
A = 0.035 in (0.9 mm)
B = 0.070 in (1.8 mm)

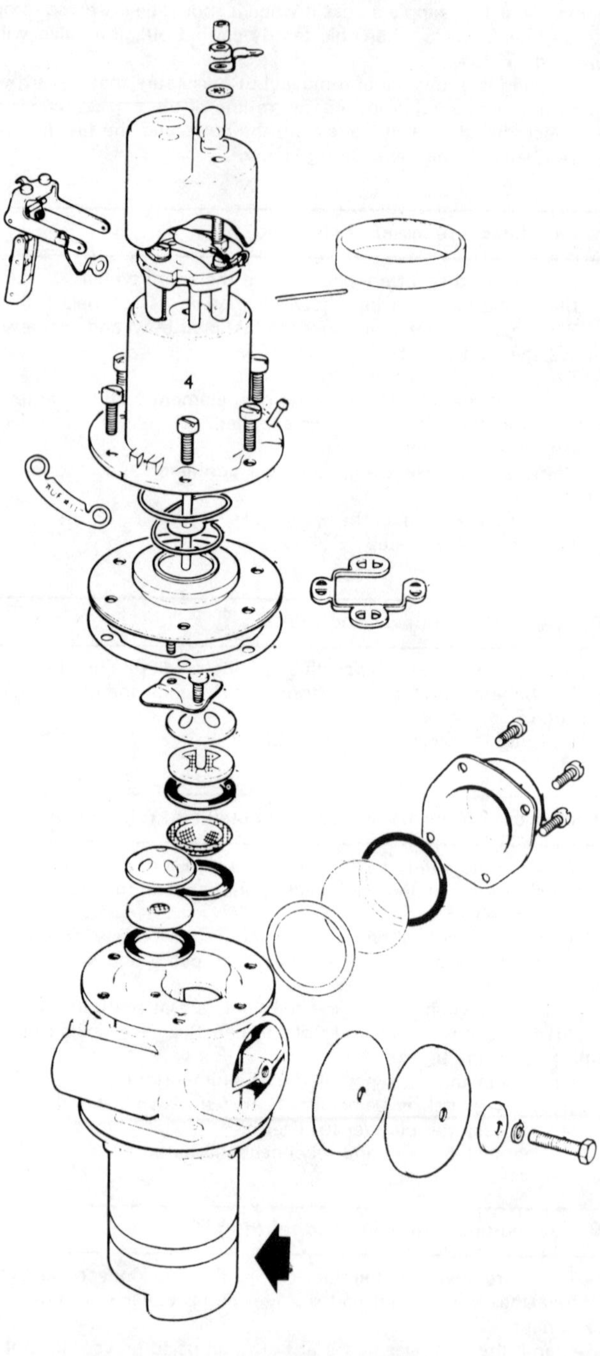

Fig. 3.9 Exploded view of a fuel pump. Twin section is arrowed (Sec 13)

31 Fit new neoprene seals into the valve recesses.
32 Fit the inlet valve filter gauze, the inlet and outlet valves and the valve caps. Fit the valve clamp plate without overtightening the screws.
33 Refit the rocker and pivot pin to the pedestal.
34 Locate the pedestal on the coil housing. Fit the screw and lockwasher finger-tight only.
35 Use the remaining pedestal screw to hold the condenser and earth terminals and then tighten both pedestal screws fully.
36 Fit the nylon centralising guide to the diaphragm assembly, followed by the rubber washer and spring.
37 Insert the spindle in the coil housing and then screw the threaded end of the spindle into the rocker assembly trunnion. Now screw in the diaphragm until the rocker no longer throws over. Unscrew the diaphragm until the rocker just throws over. Continue unscrewing until the holes are aligned, then unscrew a further $\frac{2}{3}$rds of a turn.
38 Locate a new gasket on the body flange and fit the coil housing to the body so that the marks made before dismantling are in alignment. Tighten the securing screws evenly and in diagonal sequence.
39 Fit the contact blade and the condenser and coil leads to their screw, finger-tight only.
40 Move the contact blade until the points on the blade and rocker are in alignment. Tighten the screw.
41 Make sure that with the contact points open, the contact blade rests on the narrow ridge on the pedestal. The blade may be bent slightly to achieve this.
42 Close the points with the finger and use a feeler blade to check that gap A (Fig. 3.10) is 0.035 in (0.9 mm). Bend the stop finger on the rocker assembly if necessary to obtain this dimension.
43 With the rocker assembly stop finger resting on the coil housing, check that gap B is 0.070 in (1.8 mm). If necessary, bend the stop finger to obtain this gap.
44 Fit the end cover, lockwashers, terminal tag and the nut.
45 Fit the polythene sleeve to the stud, refit the sealing ring and the sealing tape.
46 Reassemble the twin section of the pump assembly in a similar way.

14 Fuel tank – removal and refitting

1 Open the fuel tank filler cap and place a container under the fuel tank drain plug. (Do not carry out this operation when the car is over an inspection pit as fuel vapour is heavier than air and will fill the pit).
2 Remove the drain plug and drain the fuel. Refit the plug and also seal the container into which the fuel has been drained.
3 Disconnect the battery.
4 Unbolt and remove the side section of the rear bumper.
5 Remove the rear quarter fuel tank cover panel.
6 Extract the screws from the front end of the luggage boot side casing and remove the casing.
7 Extract the screws which secure the fuel tank filler cap mounting flange. Prise off the flange, taking great care not to damage the paintwork.
8 Pull the vent pipe (emission control) from its stub.
9 Remove the gasket and O-ring seal.
10 Unscrew the bolt from the luggage boot side panel.
11 Disconnect the two fuel pipes from the base of the tank. Detach the pipe connectors and push the pipes inward until their ends are flush with the panel. Support the base of the tank on a jack or blocks.
12 Unscrew the two bolts which are located in the silencer tunnel and recover the wedges.
13 Release the self-locking nut from the hanger bolt.
14 Lower the fuel tank, identify the electrical leads and disconnect them from the fuel level sender unit.
15 Disconnect the vent pipe (emission control).
16 Refitting is a reversal of removal. Remember to refit the wedges between the fuel tank and the side panel.

15 Carburettors – idle adjustment

1 Make sure that the valve clearances are correct and that the spark plug electrode gaps and the ignition timing are set to specification.
2 Have the engine at normal operating temperature with the carburettor dampers topped up with oil.

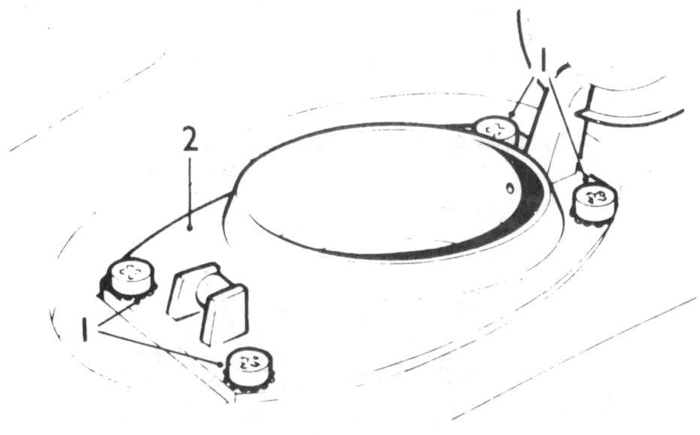

Fig. 3.12 Fuel tank filler cap flange (Sec 14)

1 Mounting screws *2 Flange*

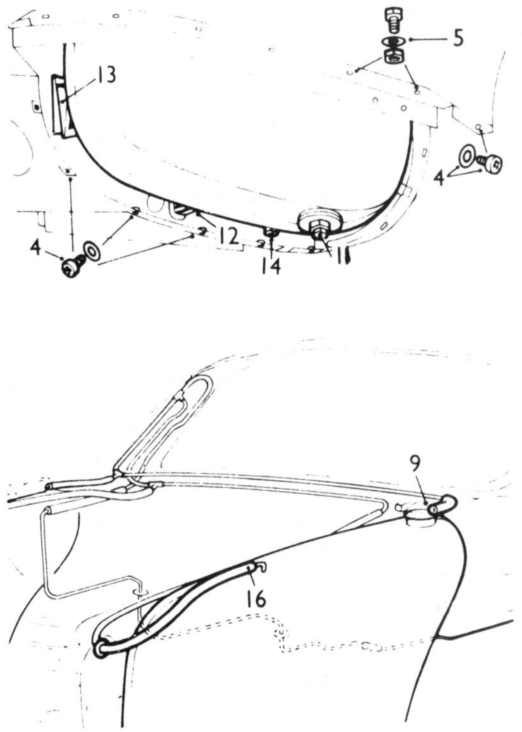

Fig. 3.11 Fuel tank mountings and connections (Sec 14)

4 Rear quarter panel screws
5 Rear quarter panel setscrews
9 Vent pipe stub
11 Drain plug
12 Fuel pipe connections
13 Wedges
14 Hanger bolt nyloc nut
16 Vent pipe

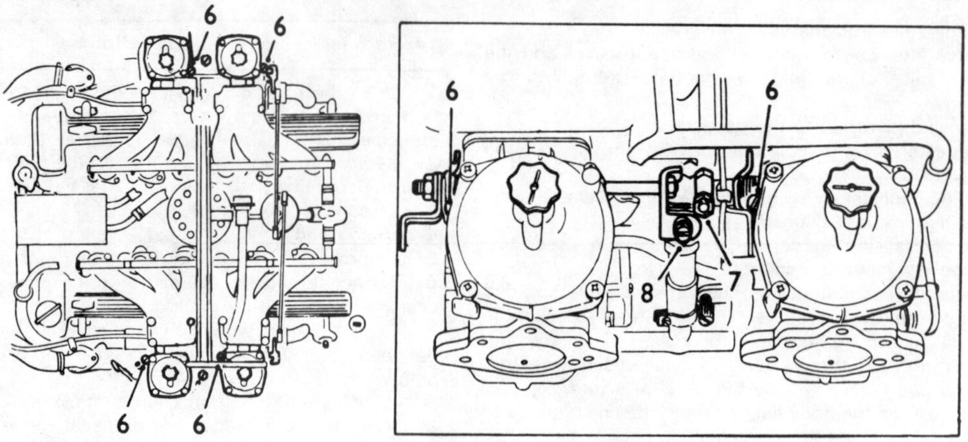

Fig. 3.13 Carburettor idle adjustment screws (Sec 15)

6 Idle trim screw
7 Throttle spindle clamp bolts
8 Throttle balancing screws

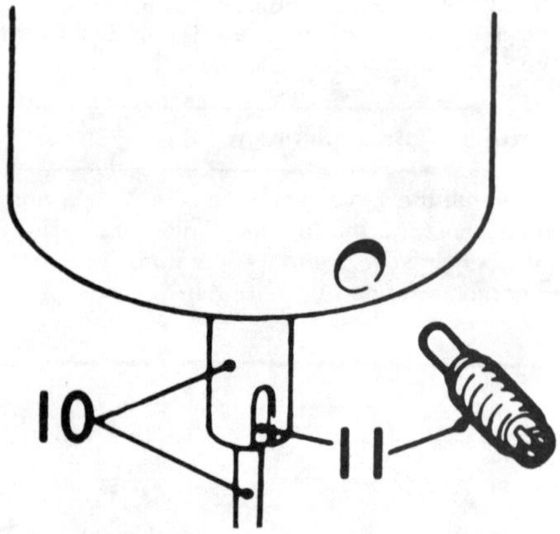

Fig. 3.14 Air piston needle and grub screw (Sec 16)

10 Needle
11 Screw and groove

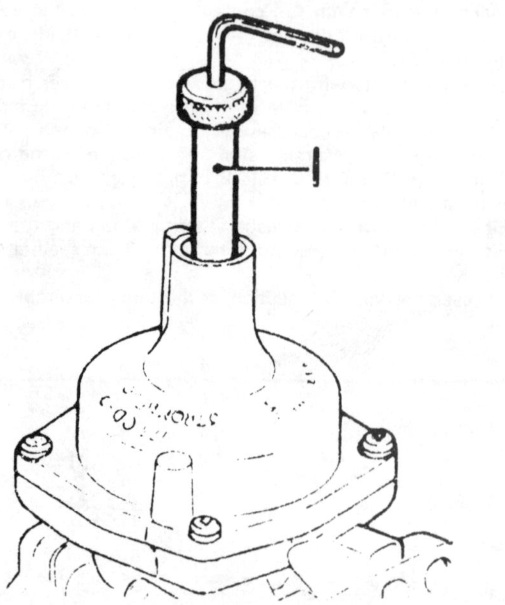

Fig. 3.15 Carburettor needle adjusting tool (1) (Sec 16)

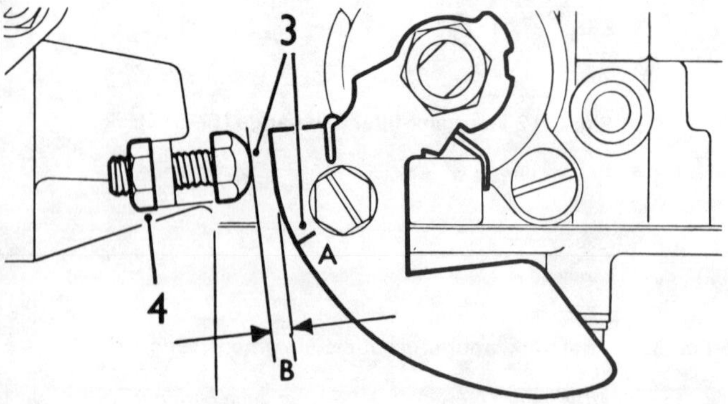

Fig. 3.16 Fast idle adjustment (Sec 17)

3 Cam and domed screw
4 Locknut
A Cam alignment mark
B Clearance

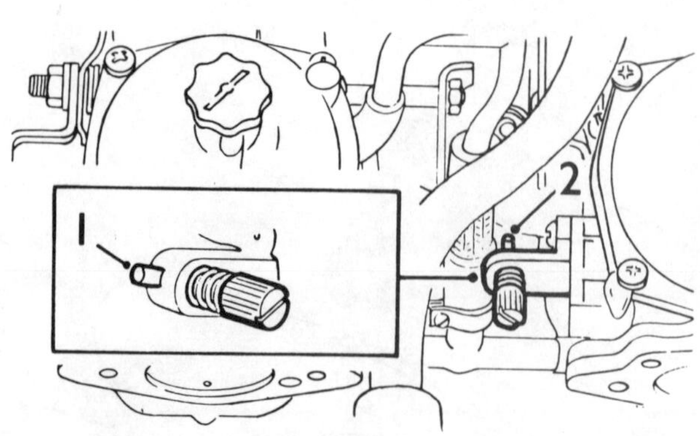

Fig. 3.17 Choke stop crosspin setting (Sec 17)

1 Crosspin in Winter setting
2 Crosspin in Summer setting

3 Remove the air cleaners and disconnect the throttle linkage.
4 Check that the choke control is fully off.
5 Slacken the idle trim screw on each carburettor (Fig. 3.13) until the screws no longer touch the throttle levers.
6 Slacken the throttle spindle clamp bolts. Make sure that the throttles are fully closed.
7 Adjust the throttle balancing screws until the tongue of the lever is central in the jaws. Tighten the clamp bolts.
8 Screw in the idle trim screws on the right-hand rear and left-hand front carburettors until they just contact the throttle levers, then give them a further $1\frac{1}{2}$ turns.
9 Start the engine and adjust the idle trim screw on the right-hand rear and left-hand front carburettors until the idling speed is within the specified limits.
10 Compare the intake hiss on the right-hand rear and left-hand front carburettors and adjust the idle trim screws on these carburettors until the hiss is identical. A length of tubing is useful when making this comparison, or better still, use a balancing flow meter.
11 Now screw in the right-hand throttle balancing screw until the intake hiss on the front right-hand carburettor matches that of the rear.
12 Screw in the left-hand throttle balancing screw until the intake hiss on the rear left-hand carburettor matches that of the front.
13 Screw in the idle trim screw on the right-hand front and left-hand rear carburettors until the screws just contact the throttle levers.
14 Reconnect the throttle linkage. The vertical link should connect with the throttle lever without having to move the lever. If this is not the case, adjust the length of the link before connecting it.
15 Refit the air cleaners.

16 Carburettors – mixture adjustment

1 Mixture adjustment is set during production and the needle setting should not normally be tampered with.
2 If adjustment must be made due to the fitting of new carburettor components, then a special carburettor adjusting tool (S.353) will be required.
3 If an air injection system (emission control) is fitted, first disconnect the pipe from the air pump side of the non-return valve. Plug the valve opening.
4 Remove the damper, then extract the screws from the cover. Before removing the cover, note the location of the projection on the damper housing which points towards the air cleaner mounting flange.
5 Lift off the cover and remove the piston return spring.
6 Withdraw the piston/damper assembly. Check that the Delrin disc on the needle is flush with the needle housing guide tube. If it is not, engage the inner tool in the needle housing and turn the housing until it is.
7 Repeat this basic needle setting operation on the needles of the three other carburettors. Carry out the work to each carburettor in turn then refit the cover. Do not interchange components between the carburettors.
8 With the engine idling ar normal operating temperature, insert the complete needle adjusting tool into the first carburettor until the inner member engages in the needle adjuster plug and the outer member in the lugs on the air valve.
9 By holding the outer member quite still to prevent the flexible diaphragm in the carburettor twisting, the inner member can be turned either clockwise (viewed from above) to enrich the mixture or anti-clockwise to weaken it. Do not exceed $\frac{3}{4}$ of a turn in either direction from the previously set position.
10 The needle adjustment must be carried out to each carburettor in conjunction with an exhaust gas analyser connected in accordance with the manufacturer's instructions. The CO content for a correctly adjusted carburettor assembly is given in the Specifications.
11 In territories where regulations permit, good results can be achieved using a proprietary combustion flame colour evaluator.
12 When using the carburettor adjusting tool, the engine may stall unless the tool is inserted slowly. Also, if the inner member of the tool is turned too far, it is possible for the needle adjuster plug to become disconnected from the air valve. If this happens, dismantle the carburettor and press the needle housing/adjuster plug into the air valve, at the same time rotating the tool inner member (inserted into the needle adjuster plug) until engagement of the plug to the air valve takes place.
13 Once the correct mixture setting has been obtained, remove the tool, replenish the damper using SAE 20 engine oil and fit the damper piston.
14 Reconnect the air delivery pipe (emission controlled cars).

17 Carburettors – fast idle adjustment

1 With the engine at normal operating temperature, remove the air cleaners.
2 Operate the choke (cold start) control until the A mark (Fig. 3.16) on the choke cam of the front right-hand carburettor is in alignment with the centre of the domed head screw.
3 Start the engine and slacken the domed head screw locknut. Turn the screw until the engine is running at the specified fast idle speed. Tighten the screw locknut.
4 Push the choke (cold start) control fully off and measure the gap (B) between the edge of the cam and the domed head screw. This must be identical on all carburettors.
5 Repeat the adjustment on the left-hand rear carburettor.
6 In extremely cold conditions, the choke stop crosspin can be rotated through 90° to lie in the slot in the casting. This is a winter setting. For all normal operating conditions, depress the spring-loaded crosspin from its slot and turn it through 90° to its summer setting.

18 Carburettors – removal and refitting

1 Disconnect the battery.
2 Remove the air cleaner.
3 Disconnect the carburettor balance pipe.

Left-hand carburettor pair

4 On cars equipped with emission control, disconnect the bypass valve inhibitor pipes from the carburettor, then disconnect the carbon canister hose from the balance pipe. Disconnect the gulp valve inlet pipe.
5 Disconnect the fuel inlet pipe from the T-piece and plug the openings.
6 Disconnect the choke cable from the rear carburettor.
7 Disconnect the throttle linkage.
8 On cars equipped with emission control, release the nut which holds the EGR pipe to the T-piece. Hold the adaptor and slacken the union nut on the EGR pipe. Disconnect the pipe from the throttle edge tapping.
9 Unscrew the nuts and washers which hold the front carburettor to the induction housing. Then release the rear carburettor.
10 Slide the carburettors from their mounting studs.
11 Discard the old gaskets.
12 Refitting is a reversal of removal. Use new gaskets and make sure that the blanking cap is fitted to the throttle edge tapping on the rear carburettor (cars without emission control).
13 After refitting, tune as previously described and check the emission control settings.

Right-hand carburettor pair

14 Repeat the operations as for the left-hand pair, ignoring reference to the carbon canister and gulp valve in paragraph 4.

19 Carburettors (complete with induction housing and manifold) – removal and refitting

1 Remove the air cleaner.
2 Drain the cooling system (Chapter 2).
3 Unbolt and remove the valance stay.

Right-hand

4 On cars with air conditioning, unclip the hoses from the condenser – do not disconnect them!
5 Disconnect the right-hand fuel pipe from the inlet and T-piece hoses. Plug the inlet hose.
6 Disconnect the brake servo vacuum hose from the manifold valve.
7 Pull off the carburettor balance branch pipe. Unclip the balance pipe and lay it across the front of the engine.
8 Release the float chamber pipe from its clip.

Fig. 3.18 Exploded view of typical Stromberg carburettor (Sec 20)

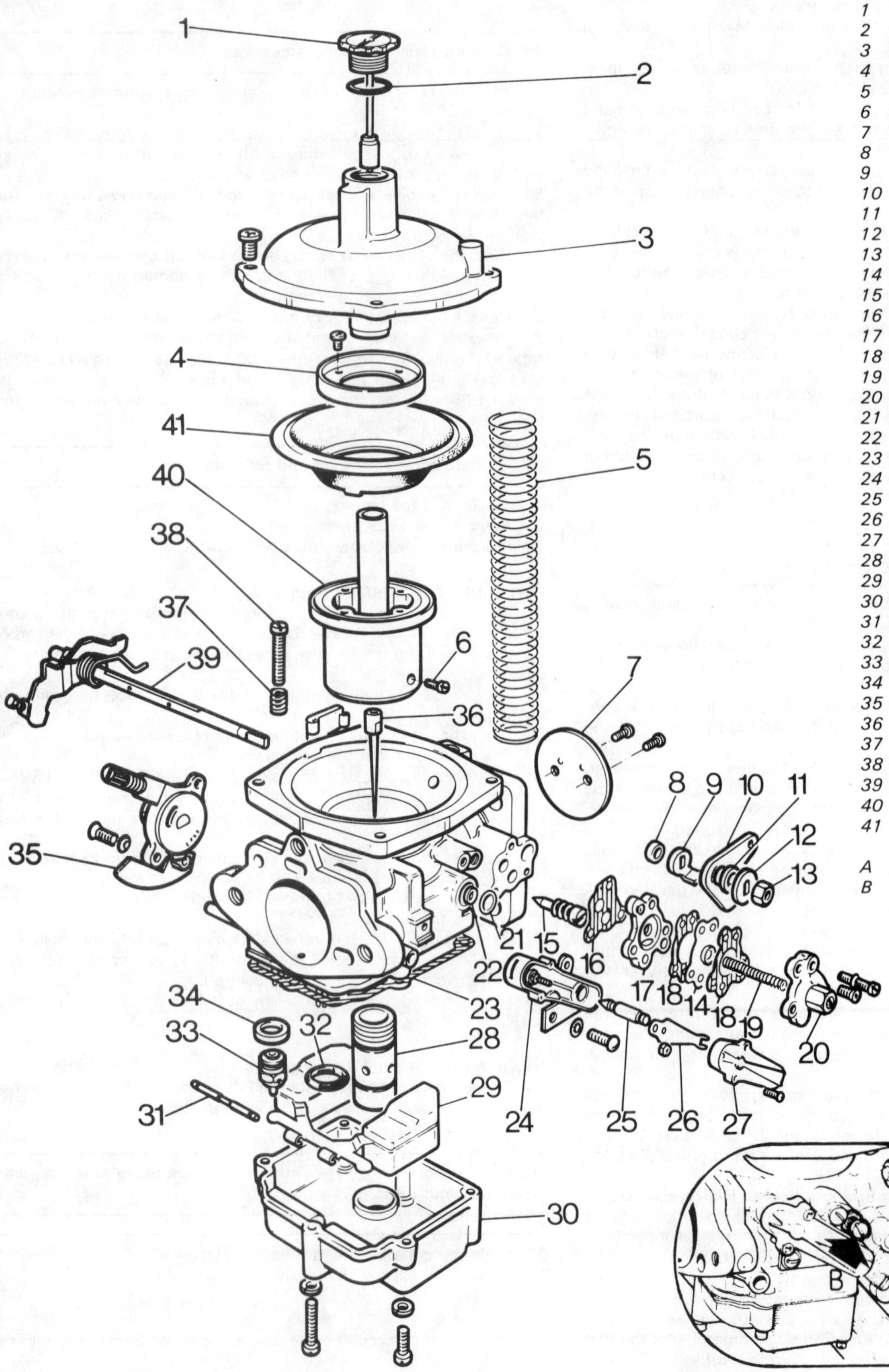

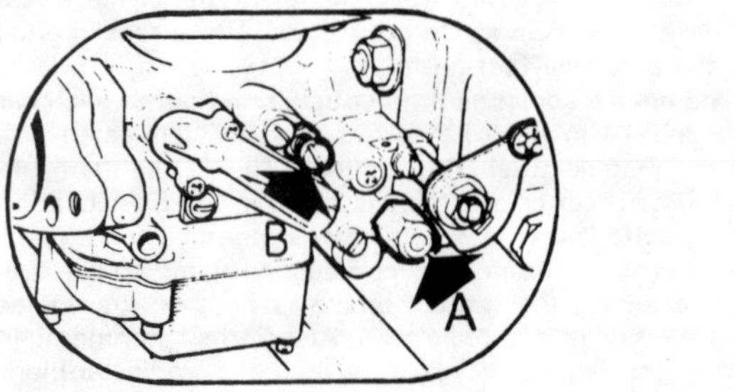

1 Damper
2 Seal
3 Cover
4 Diaphragm retaining ring
5 Piston return spring
6 Needle securing screw
7 Butterfly valve plate
8 Bush
9 Pick-up lever
10 Floating lever
11 Washer
12 Lockwasher
13 Nut
14 Diaphragm
15 Idle trim screw
16 Gasket
17 By-pass valve
18 Gasket
19 Spring
20 Cover
21 Seal
22 Seal
23 Gasket
24 Temperature compensator
25 Tapered plug
26 Bi-metallic strip
27 Cover
28 Jet assembly
29 Float
30 Float chamber
31 Float pivot
32 'O' ring
33 Fuel inlet needle valve
34 Washer
35 Choke assembly
36 Needle
37 Spring
38 Throttle stop screw
39 Throttle spindle
40 Piston
41 Diaphragm

A Throttle bypass valve
B Idle trim screw

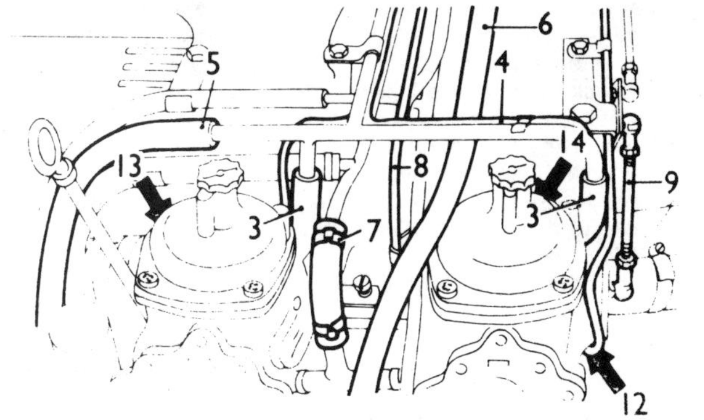

Fig. 3.19 Carburettor pipe connections (left-hand) on emission control cars (Sec 18)

3	*Balance pipe*	8	*Choke cable (rear carburettor)*
4	*By-pass valve inhibitor pipes*	9	*Throttle linkage*
5	*Carbon canister pipe*	12	*Throttle edge tapping*
6	*Gulp valve inlet pipe*	13	*Carburettor mounting nuts*
7	*Fuel inlet pipe*		

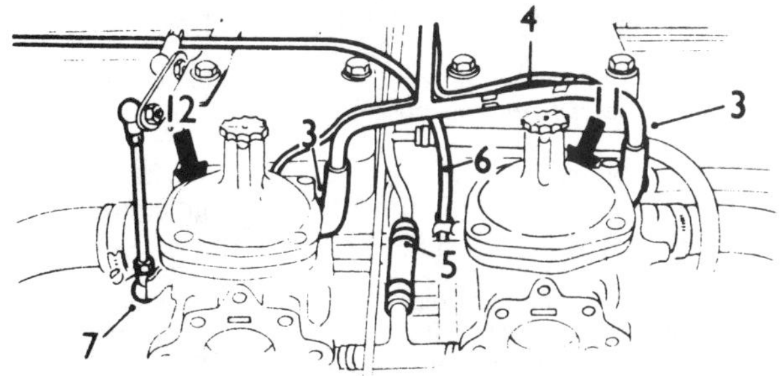

Fig. 3.20 Carburettor pipe connections (right-hand) on emission control cars (Sec 18)

3	*Balance pipe*	7	*Throttle linkage*
4	*Bypass valve inhibitor pipes*	12	*Carburettor mounting nuts*
5	*Fuel inlet pipe*		
6	*Choke cable (front carburettor)*		

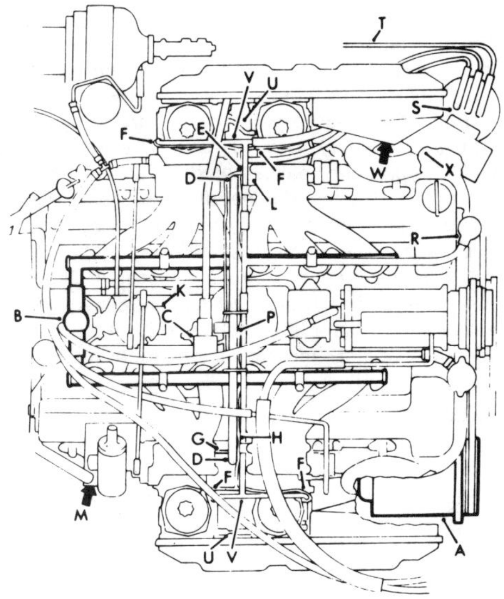

Fig. 3.21 Typical emission control arrangement (Sec 21)

A	*Air delivery pump*
B	*Non-return valve*
C	*Gulp valve*
D	*Cross-pipe*
E	*Rubber hose*
F	*Throttle bypass valve*
G	*Manifold pressure sensing point*
H	*Bypass valve actuating tube*
J	*Throttle edge tapping*
K	*Solenoid valve*
L	*Manifold pressure sensing point*
M	*Thermostatic vacuum switch*
P	*Bypass valve tube*
R	*Crankcase breather*
S	*Carbon canister*
T	*Fuel tank*
U	*Carburettor float chambers*
V	*Carburettor breather/balance system*
W	*Air pipe*
X	*Thermal override switch*

Fig. 3.22 Typical evaporative emission control arrangement within the engine compartment (Sec 21)

1	*Carburettors*	3	*Crankcase breather*
2	*Charcoal canister*	5	*Float chamber vents*

9 On cars with emission control, pull the bypass valve pipes from the carburettors and pull the vacuum pipes from the manifold stubs.
10 Release the manifold balance pipe.
11 Disconnect the choke cable and the throttle cross-rod from the bellcrank.
12 On right-hand drive cars, unbolt the throttle cable guide bracket.
13 Disconnect the radiator top hose and disconnect the induction housing bleed pipe.
14 Disconnect the engine cross-pipe from the thermostat housing.
15 Unbolt the thermostat housing and the engine lifting eye.
16 Unclip the induction housing bleed pipe.
17 On cars fitted with emission control, note the method of connection and then pull the vacuum pipes from the thermostatic vacuum switch. Unbolt the air rail clips from the induction manifold bosses. Unscrew the nut which holds the EGR pipe to the T-piece.
18 Unbolt the ballast resistor and ignition coil.
19 Unbolt the manifold/cylinder head branch pipe and engine lifting eye.
20 Unscrew the twelve nuts which hold the induction manifold to the cylinder head and withdraw the carburettor/manifold assembly.

Left-hand

21 Disconnect the left-hand fuel pipe from the valve and T-piece hoses. Plug the openings.
22 Pull off the carburettor balance branch pipe.
23 Detach the crankcase breather pipe from the cross-pipe and lay it across the engine.
24 Release the float chamber pipe from its clip.
25 On cars equipped with emission control systems, pull the bypass valve pipes from the carburettors. Unclip the throttle edge pipe and then pull the vacuum pipe from the rear end of the front induction manifold.
26 Disconnect the manifold balance pipe and the choke (cold start) cable.
27 Disconnect the throttle cross-rod from the bellcrank. On left-hand drive cars, unbolt the throttle cable guide bracket.
28 Disconnect the automatic transmission/heater system vacuum hose.
29 Pull the brake servo vacuum hose from the manifold and valve.
30 Disconnect the radiator top hose and the induction housing bleed pipe.
31 Disconnect the engine cross-pipe from the thermostat housing.
32 Unbolt the thermostat housing and engine lifting eye.
33 Unscrew the four bolts which secure the manifold/cylinder head branch pipe and engine lifting eye.
34 Disconnect the dipstick guide tube clip from the front carburettor.
35 On cars fitted with emission control, unbolt the air rail clips from the induction manifold bores, and release the nut which holds the EGR pipe to the T-piece.
36 Unscrew the twelve nuts which hold the induction manifold to the cylinder head and remove the carburettor/manifold assembly.

Both sides

37 Refitting of the right-hand and left-hand carburettor/manifold assemblies is a reversal of removal.

20 Carburettor – overhaul

1 Dismantle one unit at a time so that components will not become interchanged between the carburettors as many parts are individually matched during production.
2 With the carburettors removed from the engine as described previously, clean away all external dirt.
3 Prise out the soft plug from one of the cover screws.
4 Mark the relationship of the cover to the carburettor body, remove the four cover screws, lift off the cover and withdraw the spring.
5 Carefully withdraw the piston/diaphragm assembly. If the diaphragm is split or has hardened, remove the screws which secure the diaphragm retaining ring to the piston. Lift off the ring and discard the diaphragm.
6 *Do not remove the needle locking screw or needle unless essential.* If the needle must be renewed because it has become worn or distorted, then it can only be renewed with one of a similar type. The needle should appear biased to one side – this is correct.
7 Remove the float chamber screws and lift the float chamber from the carburettor body.
8 Do not remove the jet cover unless absolutely essential, in which case bend back the retaining lugs and withdraw the cover and O-ring. On reassembly, renew the jet cover, O-ring and float chamber gasket.
9 Disconnect the float pivot pin and detach the float.
10 Unscrew the fuel inlet needle valve.
11 Remove the nut, serrated and plain washers which secure the throttle lever to the throttle spindle. Withdraw the throttle lever, bush and actuating link.
12 Do not dismantle the throttle valve plate unless essential, in which case mark its relative position to the spindle, remove the securing screws and slide the plate from the slot in the spindle.
13 Withdraw the spindle, having noted the position of the spindle return spring.
14 Remove the screws and lockwashers which secure the bypass valve and cover to the carburettor body, discard the joint gasket. Do not separate the bypass valve cover from the body or its adjustment will be lost.
15 Prise the throttle spindle seals from the carburettor body and discard them.
16 Remove the screws which secure the temperature compensator to the carburettor body, withdraw the compensator and discard the seals.
17 Clean and examine all components, renewing any that are worn or damaged. Obtain a repair kit for each carburettor – part no 12883.
18 Reassembly is a reversal of dismantling, but observe the following points.
19 Check that the tapered plug is free to move in the temperature compensator housing. If it sticks, renew the assembly.
20 Fit all new seals and gaskets supplied in the kit.
21 Do not tighten the throttle valve plate screws until smooth and positive closure of the valve plate has been checked.
22 Once the float has been reassembled, invert the carburettor body so that the float arm closes the needle valve and then check the distance between the face of the carburettor body and the highest point on the visible surface of the float. This should be between 0.650 and 0.670 in (16.5 and 17.0 mm). Any adjustment should be carried out by bending the float arm. Make sure both floats are equal in height.
23 When reassembly is complete and the carburettors are installed to the engine, tune and adjust them, as described in Sections 15, 16 and 17.

21 Emission control system (carburettor engines) – description

1 One or more of the following systems may be encountered according to the vehicle operating territory.

Engine crankcase breather

2 This device causes blow-by and oil fumes to be drawn from the crankcase through the carburettor balance pipe when the engine is running. The gases are then burnt during the normal combustion cycle.

Evaporative emission control

3 This system stores fumes given off by fuel in the fuel tank and the carburettor float chambers and crankcase fumes while the engine is stationary.
4 The fumes are stored in a canister packed with activated carbon. Once the engine is running, the fumes are drawn from the canister and burnt during the normal engine combustion process.
5 The fuel tank venting system on USA Federal specification cars is modified to make sure that all vapour is vented through the control system even when the car is parked on a steeply inclined surface. A capacity limiting device built into the fuel tank ensures that the tank is never filled beyond a certain level in order to accommodate any increase in fuel level which would result from expansion of the fuel due to a rise in temperature.

Air intake temperature control

6 The carburettors operate most efficiently when the air intake temperature is 105°F (40°C). This temperature level is maintained by temperature sensor units on the air cleaner backplates and flap valves actuated by a vacuum motor controlled from the induction manifolds.
7 Cold and hot air (from around the exhaust manifolds) is mixed as necessary during normal running but under full throttle conditions, the flap valves admit only cold air. The air cleaners are operating correctly

Fig. 3.23 Typical evaporative emission control arrangement at rear fuel tanks (4) (Sec 21)

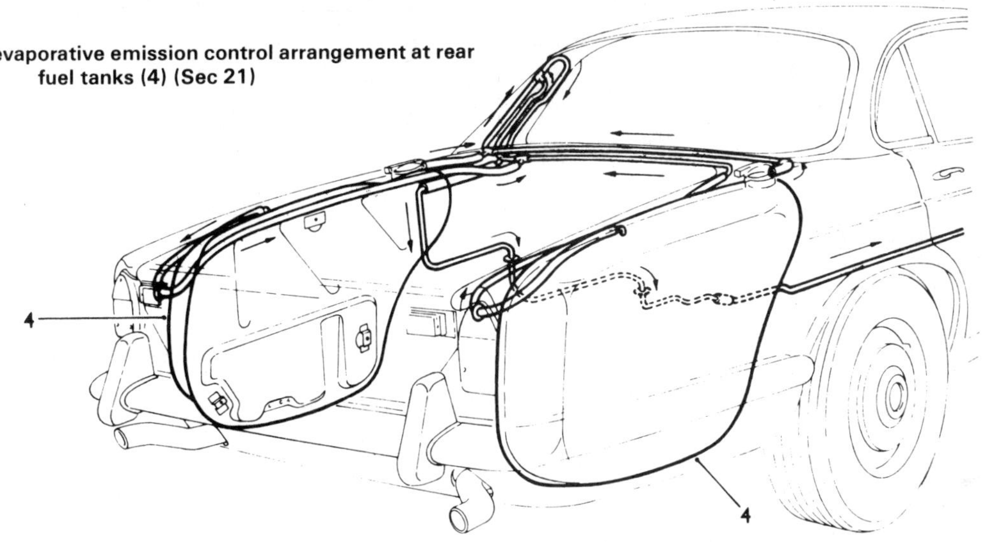

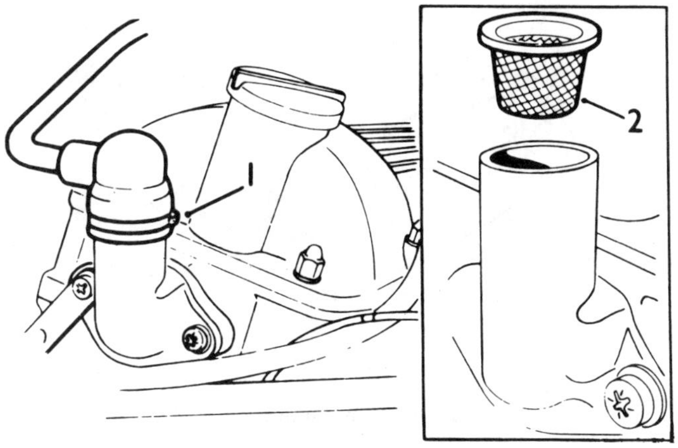

Fig. 3.24 Engine breather (Sec 22)

1 Rubber elbow *2 Filter*

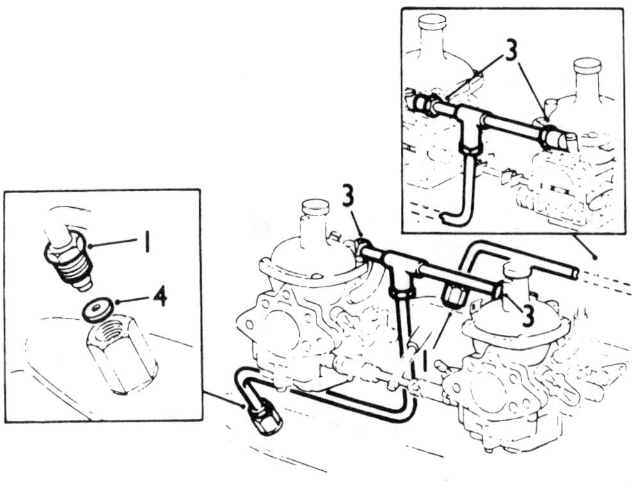

Fig. 3.25 EGR restrictor, T-piece and pipes (Sec 22)

1 Union nut *4 Restrictor*
3 Pipe assemblies and union nuts

if with the engine cold and off, the flap valve is parallel to the ram pipe. With the engine cold and running, the flap must be only open to hot air. With the engine hot and running, the flap must be only open to cold air.

Exhaust Gas Recirculation (EGR)

8 The system uses a proportion of the exhaust gas and injects it into the fuel/air mixture as a means of reducing the pollution level.

Air injection system

9 This system comprises a belt-driven air delivery pump, a non-return valve to prevent reverse flow in the air injection rail when exhaust gas pressure is high, and a gulp valve to admit extra air to the induction manifolds when closure of the throttle causes a sudden fall in manifold pressure. In addition, a throttle bypass valve is fitted to each carburettor, its purpose being to provide a completely combustible mixture during closed throttle, overrun conditions.

10 The air from the pump is injected into the exhaust ports just above the valve heads. This extra air combines with the exhaust gases to improve the oxidisation process and to provide lower emission levels of noxious gases.

Additional ignition retard

11 In addition to normal vacuum ignition advance control, an opposing vacuum retard mechanism is fitted. Vacuum is obtained from a tapping on the throttle edge of the left-hand rear carburettor on cars built to European specification. On cars produced for operation in North America, the vacuum sources are on the throttle edge of the left-hand rear carburettor and at the rear of the left-hand front manifold. A solenoid valve and pressure switch are incorporated to vary the vacuum source according to the increase in road speed which results in a rise in the automatic transmission governor pressure.

12 1974 cars are fitted with a thermal override switch which prevents the use of the throttle edge tapping at higher speeds until the engine has reached normal operating temperature.

13 A thermostatic vacuum switch protects the engine against overheating (caused by the additional vacuum retard) when the coolant temperature rises above a specified level. The switch also inhibits operation of the throttle bypass valves which would otherwise open as a result of the change in manifold pressure caused by the additional vacuum retard to the ignition.

22 Emission control system (carburettor engines) – maintenance

1 At regular intervals, check all hose, pipe and electrical connections for security. Any sudden increase in the CO content of the exhaust gas may be due to the failure of one individual emission control system or an individual component. Refer to Section 41 for fault diagnosis.

2 At the intervals specified in Routine Maintenance carry out the following operations.

Engine breather

3 Remove the clip which holds the rubber elbow to the filter housing. Withdraw the elbow and lift out the filter.
4 Clean the filter in fuel and let it dry before refitting it. Use a new clip to secure the elbow.

Carbon canister

5 Remove the left-hand front roadwheel.
6 Note the hose connections, marking them where necessary, and detach them from the canister studs.
7 Unclamp and remove the canister.
8 Fit a new canister and reconnect the hoses.

EGR restrictor, T-piece and pipes

9 Unscrew the union nut which secures the outlet pipe to the adaptor.
10 Remove both pairs of carburettors as described earlier in this Chapter.
11 Unscrew the union nuts and withdraw the pipe assembly. Extract the restrictor from the adaptor.
12 Using a wire brush, clean the pipes, the T-piece and the restrictor and blow them clean with air from a tyre pump.
13 Refit the components by reversing the removal operations. Never run the engine without the restrictor.

EGR inlet drilling

14 Remove the blanking screw from the top of the left-hand rear carburettor mounting flange.
15 Hold the throttle fully open and using a mild steel rod (8 in long x $\frac{1}{8}$ in diameter – 203 mm x 3.2 mm) carefully clear the carbon deposits from the inlet drilling.
16 Refit the blanking screw and then repeat the operations on the remaining carburettors.

23 Air injection system components – removal and refitting

Air pump

1 If a fault develops in the air pump then a factory reconditioned unit must be obtained as individual spare parts are not available.
2 Remove the right-hand air cleaner and the ram tube.
3 Slacken the air pump pulley bolts.
4 Remove the air silencer from the pump outlet elbow.
5 Release the mounting and adjuster screw locknuts, push the pump in towards the engine and slip off the drivebelt.
6 Remove the pulley bolts and withdraw the pulley using a suitable puller. Do not attempt to prise it off.
7 Unbolt and remove the elbow from the pump, then withdraw the pump mounting bolts and lift the pump from the engine.

Air rail (left-hand)

8 Remove the air cleaner.
9 Disconnect the throttle linkage at the throttle pedestal and swing it clear of the air rail.
10 Disconnect the accelerator and the kickdown switch from the pedestal and remove the switch (left-hand drive only).
11 Disconnect the hose from the inlet side of the gulp valve and lift out the delivery pipe.
12 Unbolt the gulp valve and disconnect the check valve outlet hose from it.
13 Unbolt the air rail from the inlet manifold.
14 Disconnect the carbon canister hoses (N America only) from the carburettor balance pipe and float chamber vent pipe.
15 Disconnect the bypass inhibitor pipes from the carburettors.
16 Remove the balance pipe after disconnecting it from the carburettors and breather pipe hose.
17 Disconnect the fuel return hose from the crossover pipe.
18 Disconnect the fuel inlet from the T-piece connector.
19 Disconnect the gulp valve delivery pipe from the inlet manifold.
20 Disconnect the engine breather pipe from the balance pipe hose.
21 Unbolt the feet of the air delivery pipe from the inlet manifolds. Lift the engine crossover pipes until the air delivery rail can be withdrawn together with feet, O-rings and washers.
22 Plug all pipe and manifold openings to prevent the entry of dirt.

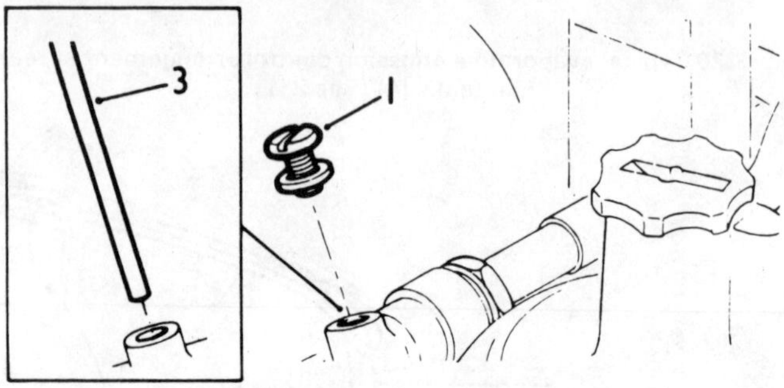

Fig. 3.26 EGR inlet drilling (Sec 22)

1 Blanking screw *3 Rod for decarbonising*

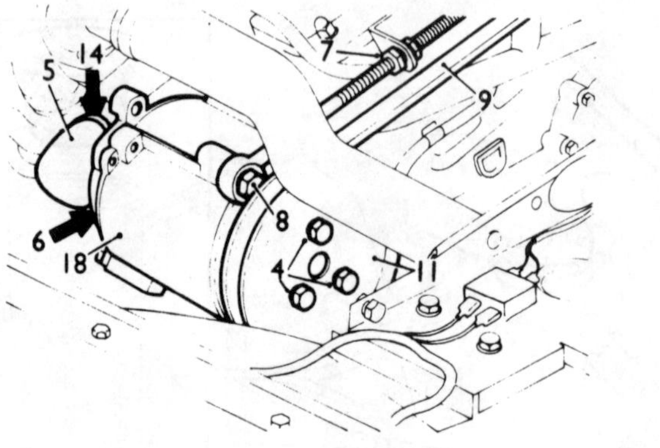

Fig. 3.27 Air pump removal (Sec 23)

4 Pulley bolts
5 Air silencer
6 Pump mounting nuts
7 Adjuster rod locknut
8 Adjuster rod trunnion bolt
9 Drivebelt
14 Outlet elbow
18 Air pump

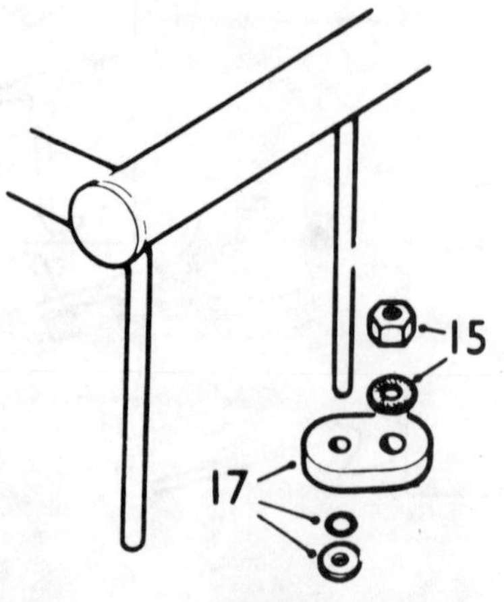

Fig. 3.28 Air rail delivery pipe connections to induction manifold (Sec 23)

15 Mounting nuts and washers *17 Foot, O-ring and washer*

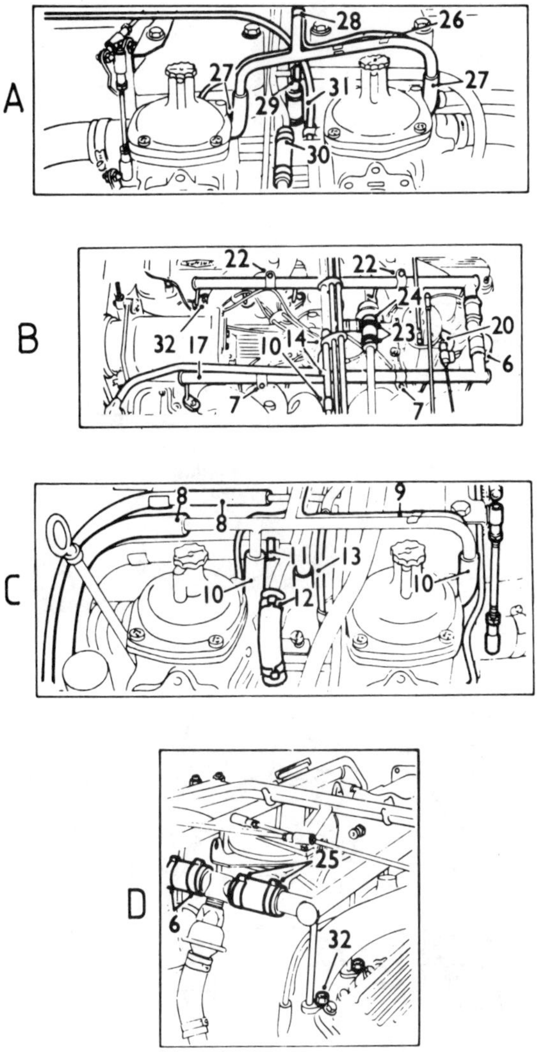

Fig. 3.29 Air rail disconnection (Sec 23)

A (right-hand rail):
- *26 Bypass inhibitor pipe*
- *27 Balance pipe hose*
- *28 Balance pipe retaining clip*
- *29 Fuel inlet hose*
- *30 Fuel crossover pipe*
- *31 Gulp valve delivery pipe*

B and D (Central components):
- *6 Non-return valve outlet hose*
- *7 Air rail fixing bolts*
- *10 Balance pipe*
- *14 Engine breather pipe*
- *17 Air rail*
- *20 Accelerator cable*
- *22 Air rail mounting feet*
- *25 Non-return valve outlet hose*
- *32 Delivery pipe feet*

C (left-hand rail):
- *8 Carbon canister hose*
- *9 Bypass inhibitor pipes*
- *10 Balance pipe*
- *11 Fuel return hose*
- *12 Fuel inlet hose*
- *13 Gulp valve delivery pipe*

Air rail (right-hand)

23 Repeat the operations given in paragraphs 8 and 9.
24 On right-hand drive cars, repeat paragraph 10.
25 Unbolt the brake servo vacuum pipe from the inlet manifold.
26 Repeat paragraphs 11, 12, 13 and 15.
27 Remove the balance pipe.
28 Disconnect the fuel inlet hose from the crossover pipe and the crossover pipe from the T-piece.
29 Repeat paragraphs 19, 21 and 22.

Non-return valve

30 Disconnect the air delivery rail hoses from the outlet stubs of the non-return valve, then disconnect the hose from the inlet stub of the valve.
31 Remove the valve.

Gulp valve

32 Disconnect the inlet hose from the gulp valve, also the outlet hose.
33 Detach the valve operating pipe.
34 Unbolt the valve from its mounting bracket, detach the valve and lift it away.

All components

35 Refitting of all components is a reversal of removal. Use new hose clips where necessary, fit new O-rings to the air rails and tension the air pump drivebelt (see Chapter 1).

24 Pressure switch (additional ignition vacuum retard) – testing, removal and refitting

1 Detach the green lead from the solenoid valve (Section 25).
2 Switch on the ignition and touch the lead onto the solenoid valve connector. The valve should be heard to operate.
3 Start the engine and run to normal operating temperature, reconnect the lead to the solenoid valve and switch off the ignition.
4 Connect a 12 volt test lamp with long leads, one lead to the exposed part of the solenoid valve connector and the other to a good earth on the engine. Position the lamp inside the car where it can be seen from the driving seat.
5 Switch on the ignition. The test lamp should not come on, but the solenoid should be heard to operate.
6 Run the car to a roadspeed of 40 mph (64 kph). The test lamp should come on between 35 and 40 mph (58 and 64 kph).
7 If the test lamp does not come on, the pressure switch or the thermal override switch is faulty. Eliminate the thermal override switch by testing it as described in Section 26.
8 If the pressure switch has been found to be faulty, disconnect the battery, disconnect the lead from the switch and unscrew it from the transmission casing.
9 When fitting the new switch, do not cross-thread or overtighten it.

25 Solenoid valve (additional ignition vacuum retard) – testing, removal and refitting

1 To test the operation of the switch, have the engine at normal operating temperature and drive the car along a level stretch of road with very light throttle application, accelerating gently until the transmission upshifts into top gear at about 28 mph (44 kph). Continue the gentle acceleration until the operation of the pressure switch and solenoid valve are felt to occur at between 30 and 40 mph (48 and 64 kph).
2 If this operation cannot be felt, it may be due to insensitivity on the part of the driver and the valve can be checked in the following way.
3 Pull the vacuum pipes from the solenoid valve.
4 Connect a length of tubing to the right-angled outlet stub on the valve body. Blow through the pipe: air should be ejected from the solenoid body.
5 Switch on the ignition and blow through the pipe once more. Air should be ejected from the pipe (5 in Fig. 3.32). If the tests are satisfactory, switch off the ignition and reconnect the vacuum hoses. If they are not, the valve is faulty and must be renewed.
6 To renew the valve, disconnect the battery, mark the leads and

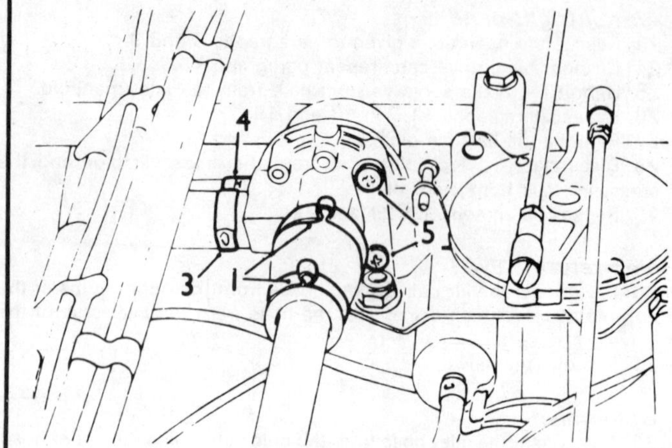

Fig. 3.30 Gulp valve (Sec 23)

1 *Inlet hose*
3 *Outlet hose*
4 *Operating pipe*
5 *Mounting screws*

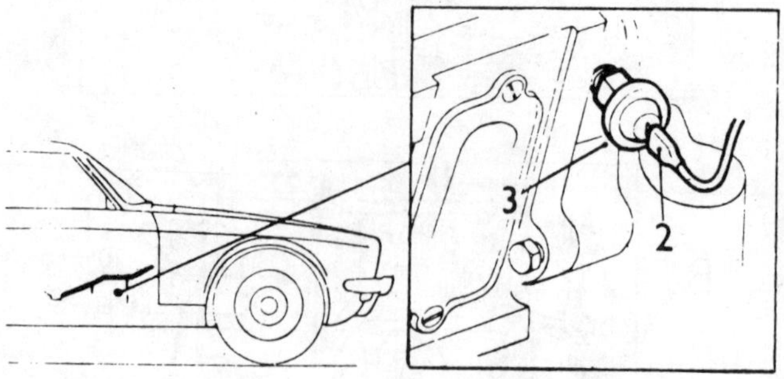

Fig. 3.31 Location of pressure switch (additional ignition vacuum retard) (Sec 24)

2 *Lead*
3 *Switch*

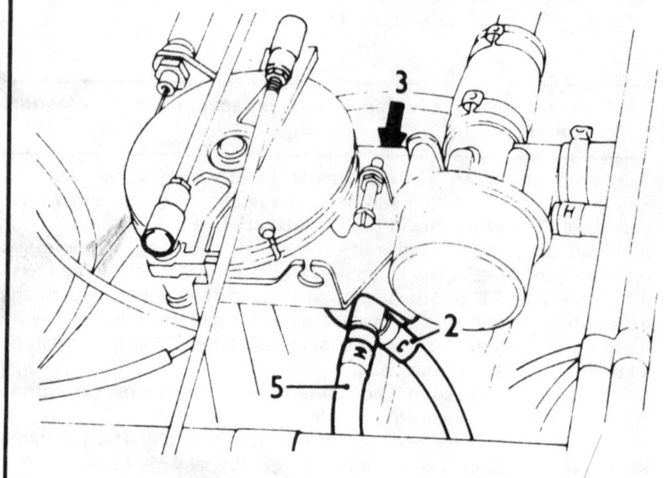

Fig. 3.32 Solenoid valve (Sec 25)

2 *Right-angled outlet*
3 *Test air ejection point*
5 *Air ejection pipe (test with ignition on)*

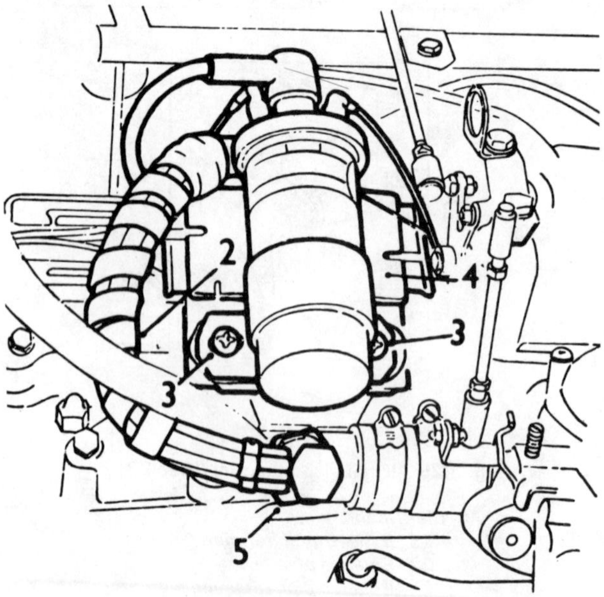

Fig. 3.33 Thermostatic vacuum switch (Sec 27)

2 *Vacuum pipes*
3 *Mounting screws*
4 *Ignition coil moved away from thermostatic switch*
5 *Switch and connecting union*

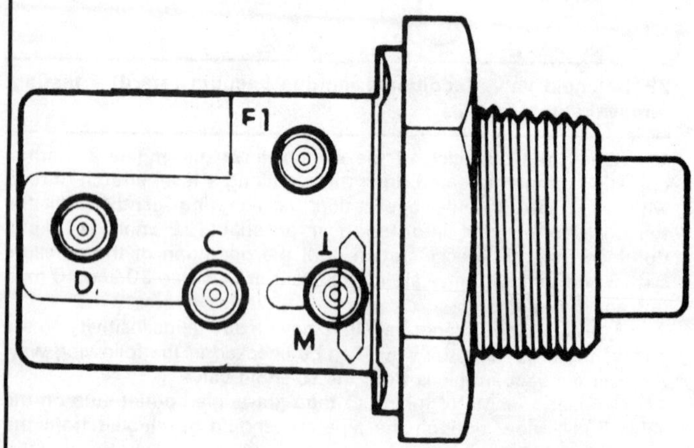

Fig. 3.34 Thermostatic vacuum switch toppings (Sec 27)

hose connections to the valve and then unbolt and remove it from the throttle pedestal top plate.
7 Refitting is a reversal of removal.

26 Thermal override switch (additional ignition vacuum retard) – testing, removal and refitting

1 Remove the left-hand air cleaner.
2 Disconnect the leads from the switch and with the engine cold, connect a continuity meter between the switch terminals. There should be a very low resistance.
3 Now run the engine to normal operating temperature, and repeat the meter test. A very high resistance should be registered.
4 If the readings are not as specified, the switch must be unscrewed and renewed. Apply sealing compound to the threads of the new switch.

27 Thermostatic vacuum switch (additional ignition vacuum retard) – removal, refitting and testing

1 Partially drain the cooling system.
2 Disconnect the vacuum hoses from the switch.
3 Unbolt the ignition coil and ballast resistor from their mounting bracket.
4 Unscrew the union nut and remove the switch from the manifold.
5 To test the switch connect lengths of tubing to the tappings C and D (Fig. 3.34). Blow into D, when air should be ejected from C. If air is not ejected, renew the switch. If air is ejected continue the test.
6 Place the switch bulb in a container of oil and raise the temperature to 220°F (104.4°C).
7 Blow into pipe D when air should be ejected from F1 and MT. If not, renew the switch.
8 If the original switch is being refitted, clean off all the test oil.
9 Smear the threads of the switch with jointing compound and fit it so that the pipe studs point horizontally to the rear of the car. Refill the cooling system.

28 Induction manifold (front) – removal and refitting

1 Disconnect the battery.
2 On emission control cars, unscrew the air rail setscrews.
3 Disconnect the hose from the right-hand brake servo non-return valve.
4 Unscrew and remove the four bolts which hold the induction manifold to the induction housing.
5 On emission control cars, remove the three nuts which hold the air rail feet to the rear manifold.
6 Remove the six nuts which hold the front manifold to the cylinder head.

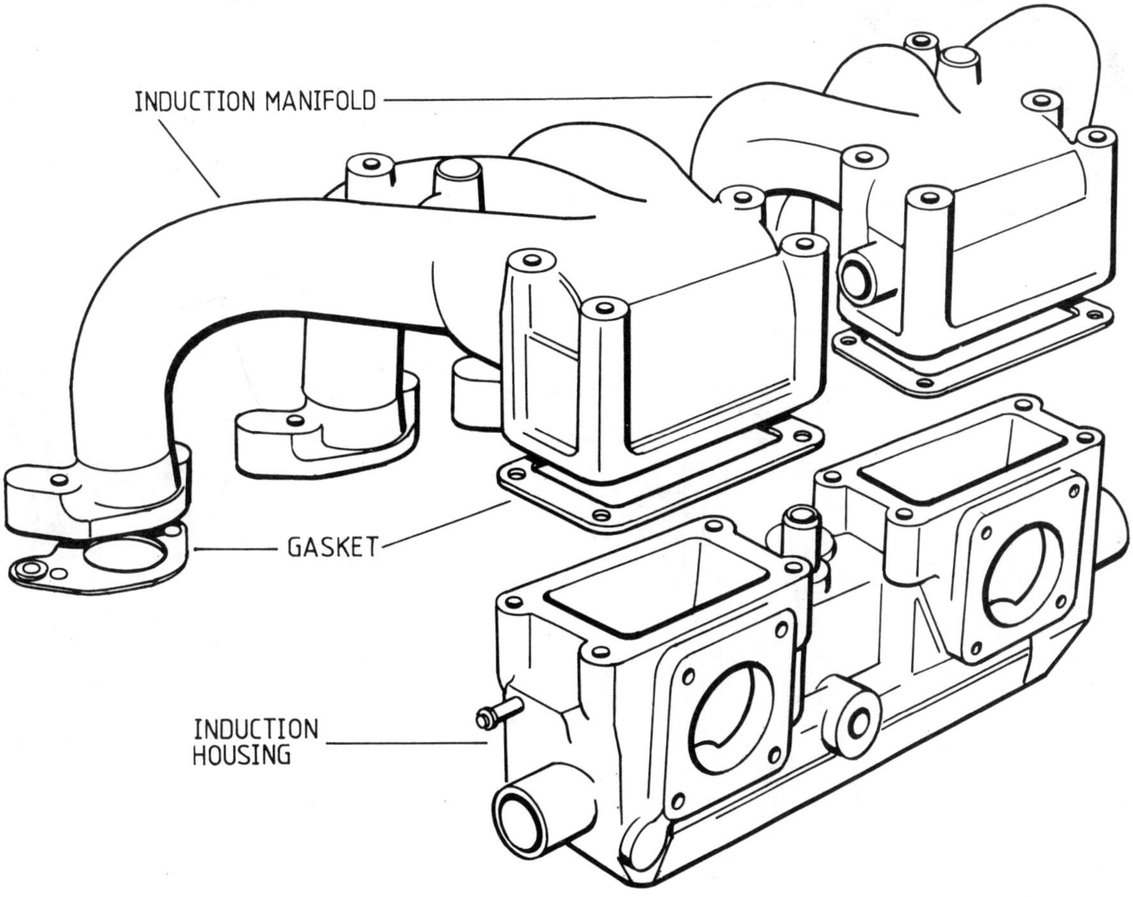

Fig. 3.35 Typical induction manifold and housing (Sec 28)

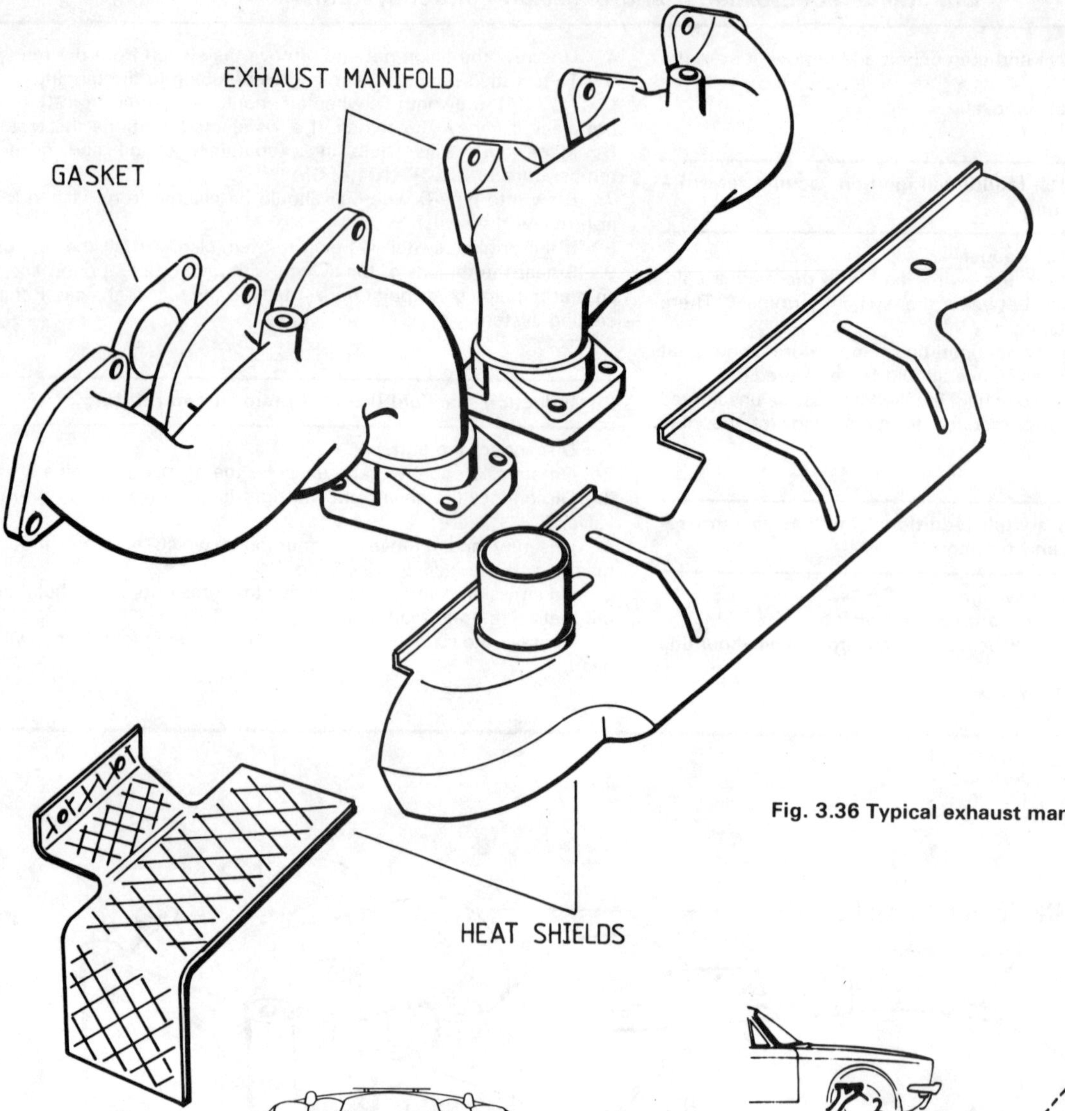

Fig. 3.36 Typical exhaust manifold (Sec 32)

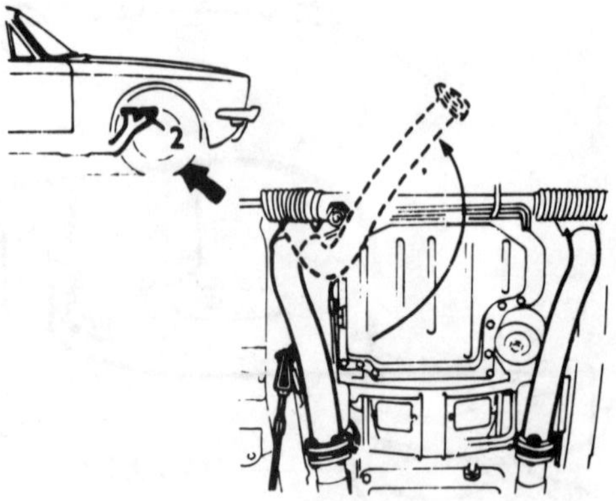

Fig. 3.38 Exhaust front downpipe removal (Sec 35)

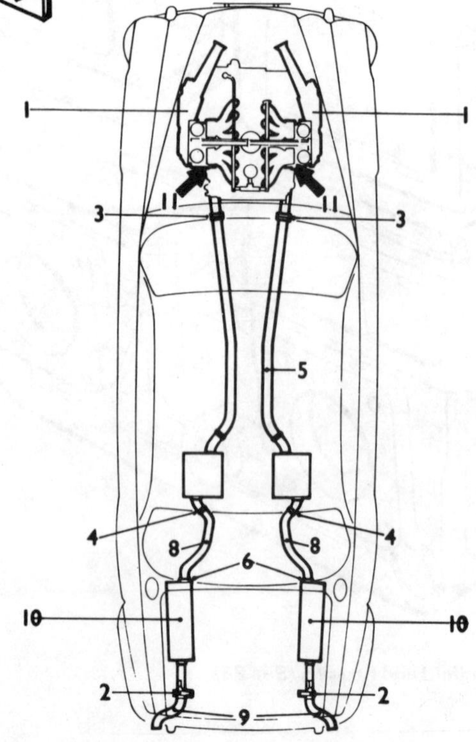

Fig. 3.37 Typical exhaust system (Sec 34)

1 Air cleaner
2 Rear silencer mounting nuts (in luggage boot)
3 Front to front intermediate pipe flange
4 Clamp
5 Front intermediate pipe
6 Clamp
8 Rear intermediate pipe
9 Tailpipe trim
10 Rear silencer
11 Manifold to downpipe flange

7 Pull the vacuum pipes from the manifold and then manoeuvre the manifold from the engine. Discard the gaskets and plug all openings to prevent the entry of dirt.
8 If a new manifold is being fitted, transfer the original brake servo vacuum non-return valve and stub pipe blanking caps.
9 Refitting is a reversal of removal; use new gaskets.

29 Induction manifold (rear) – removal and refitting

1 Disconnect the battery.
2 On emission control cars, unscrew the setscrews which hold the air rail.
3 Release the throttle pushrod from the bellcrank.
4 Disconnect the throttle cable. (On left-hand drive cars this is necessary only if the left-hand rear manifold is being removed, or on right-hand drive cars if the right-hand manifold is being removed).
5 If the left-hand manifold is being removed, pull the vacuum pipes from the manifold stubs.
6 On emission control cars, if the left-hand manifold is being removed, disconnect the tube from the throttle edge tapping.
7 Unscrew and remove the four bolts which hold the induction manifold to the induction housing.
8 On emission control cars, remove the three nuts which hold the air rail feet to the front manifold.
9 Unscrew and remove the six nuts which hold the manifold to the cylinder head.
10 On emission control cars, pull the vacuum pipes from the manifold.
11 Manoeuvre the manifold from the engine. Discard the gaskets and plug all openings to prevent the entry of dirt.
12 If a new manifold is being fitted, transfer the brake servo vacuum non-return valve from the original manifold, also the stub blanking caps.
13 Refitting is a reversal of removal; use new gaskets.

30 Induction housing (left-hand) – removal and refitting

1 Remove the carburettors as described in Section 18.
2 Drain the cooling system (Chapter 2).
3 Disconnect the manifold balance pipe.
4 Disconnect the top hose from the thermostat housing cover, then pull the hose from the engine cross-pipe clip. Also disconnect the hose on the front end of the induction housing.
5 Unbolt the thermostat housing and engine lifting eye from the cylinder head.
6 Disconnect the bleed pipe.
7 Pull the thermostat housing and hose from the induction housing.
8 Unscrew the setscrew which holds the transmission dipstick guide tube clip.
9 Release the hose from its clip at the rear end of the induction housing.
10 Unscrew and remove the eight bolts which hold the induction manifolds to the induction housing.
11 On USA emission control cars, release the union and swing the EGR pipe clear of the induction housing.
12 Draw the induction housing from the branch pipe.
13 Refitting is a reversal of removal; use new gaskets.

31 Induction housing (right-hand) – removal and refitting

1 Repeat the operations described in paragraphs 1 to 3 of Section 30.
2 Disconnect the top hose from the thermostat housing cover. Release the hose from the heater return pipe and the engine cross-pipe, also the clip on the front end of the induction housing.
3 Repeat the operations in paragraphs 5, 6 and 7 of Section 30, then follow with the remaining work detailed in paragraphs 9 to 13 of that Section.

32 Exhaust manifold (left-hand) – removal and refitting

1 Working under the car, remove the eight nuts and washers from the manifold/front downpipe studs.
2 Remove the three nuts and bolts which hold the front exhaust downpipe to the intermediate pipe.
3 Free the downpipe and let it rest on the suspension crossmember.
4 Disconnect the battery; remove it also if the exhaust manifold is being removed from the battery side.
5 Remove the complete carburettor/induction manifold/housing assembly (Section 19).
6 On USA emission control cars, slacken the EGR pipe union nut and remove the adaptor. Do not lose the restrictor.
7 Unbolt and remove the exhaust manifold heat shield.
8 Unbolt the front exhaust manifold from the cylinder head and lift the manifold from the engine compartment.
9 Remove the rear exhaust manifold in a similar way.
10 Refitting is the reverse of removal. Use new gaskets and fit the rear manifold first.

33 Exhaust manifold (right-hand) – removal and refitting

1 Carry out the operations described in Section 30, paragraphs 1 to 5.

34.10 Exhaust tailpipe trim screw (arrowed)

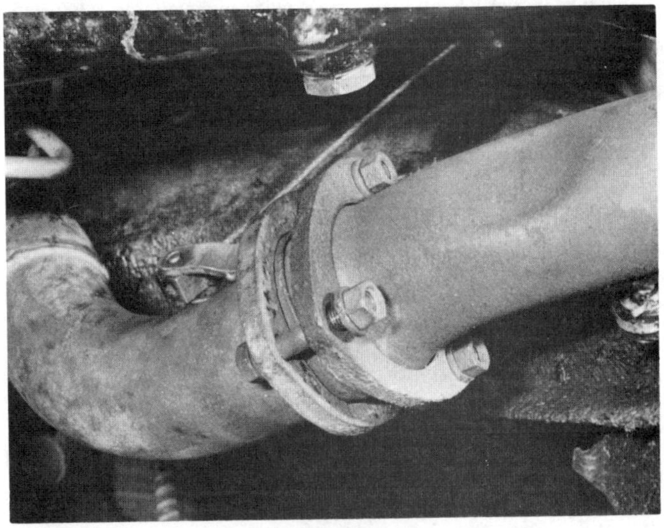

35.3 Exhaust joint (downpipe to front intermediate pipe)

2 Detach (two screws) the starter solenoid heat shield from the main heat shield.
3 Repeat the operations described in paragraphs 6 to 10 in Section 30.

34 Exhaust system (complete) – removal and refitting

1 If one or both of the dual exhaust systems is badly corroded, it is recommended that the complete system is withdrawn and a new system installed.
2 Where only one section of the system is in need of renewal then the section can be removed independently as described in Section 35.
3 Remove the air cleaner.
4 Working within the luggage boot, unscrew the two self-locking nuts which hold the rear silencer mounting.
5 Disconnect the front to front intermediate exhaust pipe flange.
6 Release the clamp at the front end of the silencer nearer the front of the car.
7 Separate the front intermediate pipe and front silencer from the rear intermediate pipe.
8 Release the rear silencer/tailpipe clamp and separate the rear silencer/tailpipe from the rear intermediate pipe.
9 Draw the rear intermediate pipe towards the rear of the car from its mounting rubber and suspension unit.
10 Use an Allen key to remove the tailpipe trim grub screw, pull off the trim and then withdraw the tailpipe/silencer forwards from the body (photo).
11 Unbolt the exhaust downpipe from the manifold and draw the pipe downward.
12 If the right-hand downpipe is being removed from a right-hand drive car, then apply full right steering lock. Conversely, if the left-hand pipe is being removed from a left-hand drive car, apply full left steering lock.
13 Do not damage the steering rack gaiter during removal.
14 Renew all clamps, mountings and other components as necessary.
15 Commence reassembly by offering the rear intermediate pipe into the rear suspension unit.
16 Attach the rear mounting bracket.
17 Fit the tailpipe and silencer into the mounting, apply exhaust jointing paste to the joint and clamp up.
18 The refitting operations for the remaining sections of the exhaust system are a reversal of removal.

35 Exhaust system – removal and refitting of individual sections

Front downpipe

1 Remove the air cleaner from the side concerned.
2 Unbolt the downpipe from the exhaust manifold.
3 Working under the car unbolt the front pipe from the front intermediate pipe (photo). On right-hand drive cars, if removing a right-hand pipe, apply full right steering lock before removal. Conversely, apply full left lock if a left-hand pipe is being removed from a left-hand drive car.

Intermediate pipe (front)

4 Unbolt the flange which connects with the front downpipe.
5 Release the clamp at the forward end of the front silencer.
6 Remove the intermediate pipe.

Front silencer

7 Remove the intermediate pipe as previously described.
8 Slacken the clamp and draw the silencer from the rear intermediate pipe.

Tailpipe and rear silencer

9 Extract the grub screw with an Allen key and pull off the trim from the tailpipe.
10 Release the clamp which holds the rear silencer to the rear intermediate pipe.
11 Draw the rear silencer and tailpipe towards the front of the car and downwards to clear the mounting rubber.

All sections

12 Refitting is a reversal of removal, but smear joints with exhaust

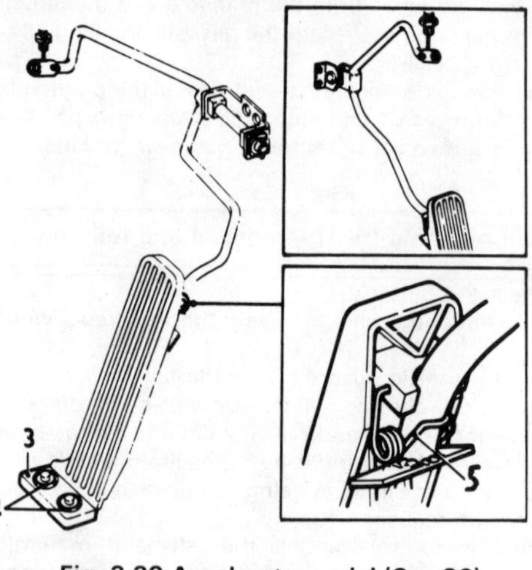

Fig. 3.39 Accelerator pedal (Sec 36)

2 Pedal mounting nuts
3 Pedal
5 Spring

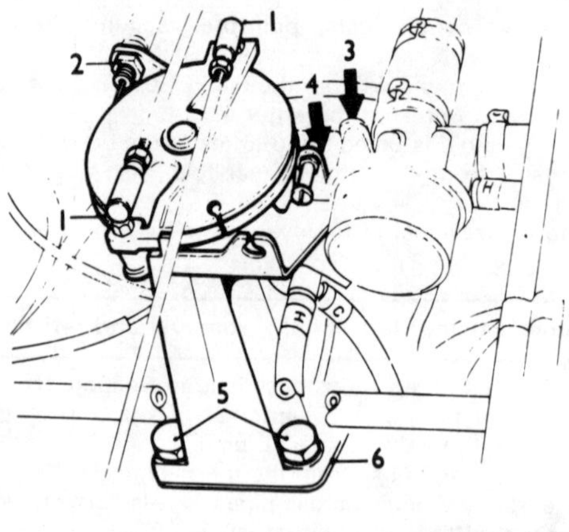

Fig. 3.40 Throttle pedestal (Sec 36)

1 Throttle pushrod
2 Cable locknut
3 Gulp valve (emission control cars only)
4 Solenoid valve (emission control cars only)
5 Mounting bolts
6 Jackshaft cover gasket

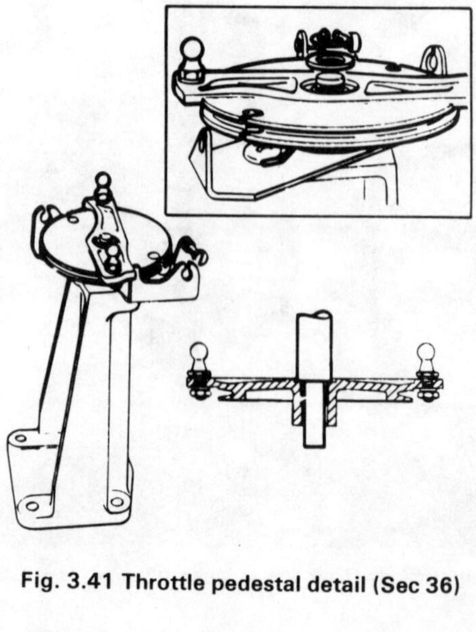

Fig. 3.41 Throttle pedestal detail (Sec 36)

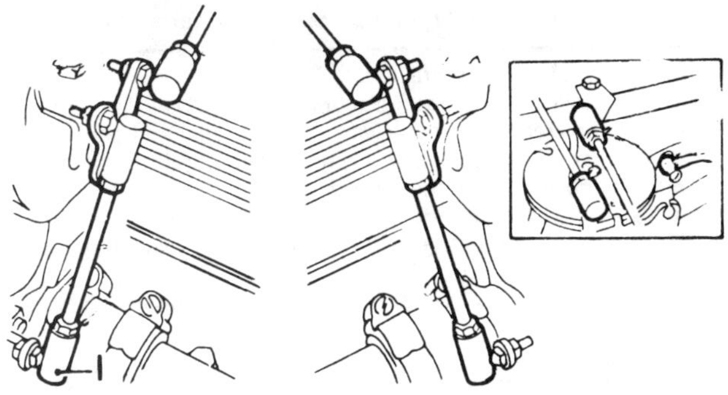

Fig. 3.42 Throttle linkage detail (Sec 37)

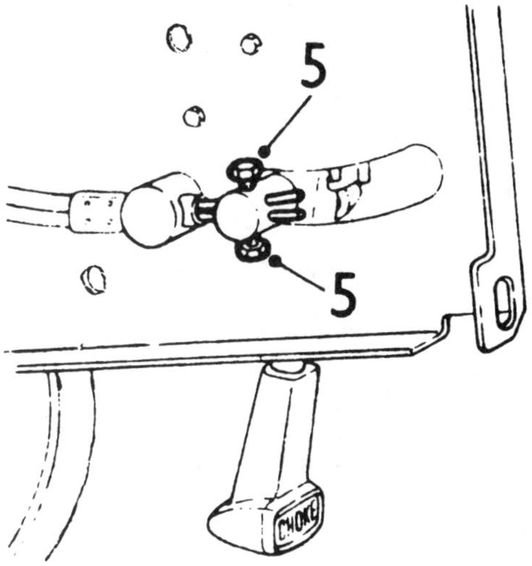

Fig. 3.43 Choke cable pinch-bolts (5) (Sec 38)

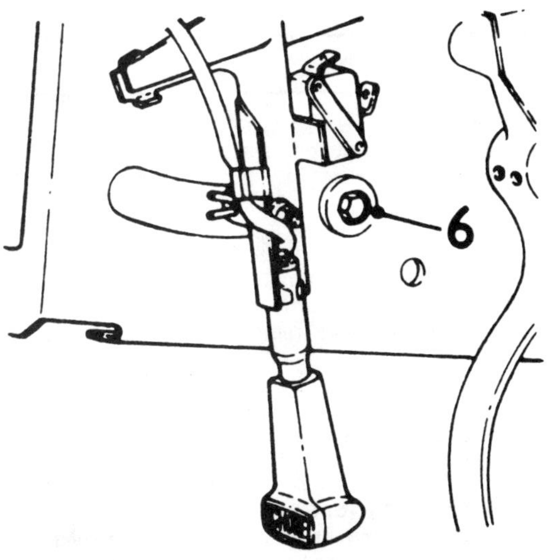

Fig. 3.44 Choke cable pivot block pinch-bolt (6) (Sec 39)

pipe jointing paste before connecting, renew seals, mountings and clamps as necessary.
13 On USA Federal Specification cars, there must be a clearance between the top surface of the exhaust trim and the lower surface of the energy absorbing beam of 1.5 in (38.0 mm).

36 Accelerator pedal and throttle linkage – removal and refitting

Accelerator pedal

1 Pull the carpet away from the base of the pedal and unscrew and remove the two securing nuts.
2 Withdraw the bottom of the pedal and disengage the spring and the rod from the pedal.

Throttle pedestal

3 Disengage the throttle pushrods from the platform on top of the pedestal.
4 Release the locknuts and disconnect the throttle cable.
5 On cars equipped with emission control, unscrew the three screws which secure the gulp valve and unbolt the solenoid valve from the pedestal top plate.
6 Remove the four setscrews which hold the oil pressure transducer mounting and the throttle pedestal. Lift the pedestal away.
7 Clean off the old gasket from the jackshaft cover.
8 The throttle pedestal can be overhauled once the circlip has been prised off.

Throttle cable

9 Disconnect the battery and pull the leads from the kickdown switch.
10 Release the locknuts and disconnect the throttle cable.
11 Working under the bonnet, slacken the locknut on the upper surface of the footwell.
12 Extract the split pin from the top end of the operating rod, then disengage the sleeve and nipple from the rod.
13 Remove the nut from the cable sheath and draw the throttle cable assembly into the engine compartment.

Throttle rod bushes

14 Remove the accelerator pedal as previously described.
15 Remove the under scuttle casing. On LHD cars, prise the spring clips from the cover on the steering column universal joint.
16 Extract the split pin from the top end of the operating rod, then disengage the sleeve and nipple from the rod.
17 Extract the split pin from the operating rod pivot, then pull the rod from the pivot and take off the washer.
18 Remove the bushes.

All components

19 Refitting of all components is a reversal of removal, but lubricate all pivots and bushes. Seal round the footwell locknut with suitable mastic.
20 On completion check the throttle linkage adjustment as described below, also the kickdown switch adjustment as described in Chapter 6.

37 Throttle linkage – adjustment

1 This work should be carried out after overhaul or the fitting of new components, or when wear has occurred.
2 Disconnect the throttle linkage from the throttle levers.
3 Check that the angle across the top of the left-hand bellcrank is exactly the same as that across the top of the right-hand one. If it is not, slacken the locknuts and while holding the platform in the 'throttle closed' position, turn the rod clockwise to increase the angle or anti-clockwise to decrease it.
4 When the correct angle has been obtained tighten the locknuts, making sure that the rod balljoints are at the centre of their areas of travel.
5 Now slacken the locknuts and adjust the lengths of the vertical links until they can be connected to the throttle levers without having to move the position of the levers. Tighten the locknuts, holding the balljoints in the centres of their areas of travel.
6 Release the throttle stop locknut. Open the throttle fully and screw

in the throttle stop until it just contacts the platform. Close the throttle and tighten the throttle stop locknut.

38 Choke operating inner cable – renewal

1 Remove the air cleaner from the appropriate side.
2 Working under the bonnet, disconnect the choke inner and outer cables from the carburettor.
3 If the crossover cable is being renewed, remove the outer cable from the nylon guides.
4 Remove the under scuttle casing.
5 Slacken the pinch-bolt on the choke cable and draw the cable from its sheath into the engine compartment.
6 Refitting is a reversal of removal, but enter the cable from the engine compartment. Check the fast idle setting (Section 17) on completion.

39 Choke cable assembly (complete) – removal and refitting

1 Remove both air cleaners.
2 Working under the bonnet, disconnect the choke inner and outer cables from the front right-hand and the rear left-hand carburettor.
3 Remove the crossover cable from the nylon guides.
4 Remove the under scuttle casing.
5 Slacken the two pinch-bolts on the choke lever.
6 Slacken the pinch-bolt on the cable pivot block abutment and press the cable from the block.
7 Withdraw the cable assembly rearwards through the bulkhead into the car.
8 Refitting is a reversal of removal. Use new grommets where necessary, and on completion check the fast idle setting as described in Section 17.

40 Fault diagnosis – carburettor fuel system

Symptom	Reason(s)
Excessive fuel consumption	Air filter choked Leakage from pump, carburettor or fuel lines or fuel tank Float chamber flooding Distributor weights or vacuum capsule faulty Mixture too rich Incorrect valve clearances Incorrect spark plug gaps Tyres under inflated Dragging brakes
Insufficient fuel delivery or weak mixture	Fuel tank air vent or pipe blocked or flattened Clogged fuel filter Float chamber needle valve clogged Faulty fuel pump valves Fuel pump faulty Fuel pipe unions loose Inlet manifold gasket or carburettor flange gasket leaking Incorrect adjustment of carburettor
Rough idling, hesitation or flat spot	Sticking piston Split diaphragm Faulty temperature compensator Perforated vacuum pipes Fuel level in float chamber too high Air filter choked Broken piston return spring

41 Fault diagnosis – carburettor emission control system

Symptom	Reason(s)
Fault in air injection system	Slack pump drivebelt Perforated or loose connecting hoses Choked air pump air filter
Fault in EGR system	Choked inlet drilling or restrictor
High CO content in exhaust gas	Faulty air temperature control in air cleaner Choked engine breather filter Faulty system switch or valve (refer to testing procedure in text)

PART B – FUEL INJECTION AND EMISSION CONTROL SYSTEMS

42 Description and operating principles

1 The electronic fuel injection system fitted to all models after 1975 is of the Bosch-Lucas D-Jetronic type.
2 The system can be divided into two parts both for ease of understanding and for maintenance and overhaul.

Fuel supply system (Sections 48 to 63)

3 This comprises rear mounted fuel tanks, and an electric fuel pump to keep a constant pressurised flow of fuel always available at the injectors.

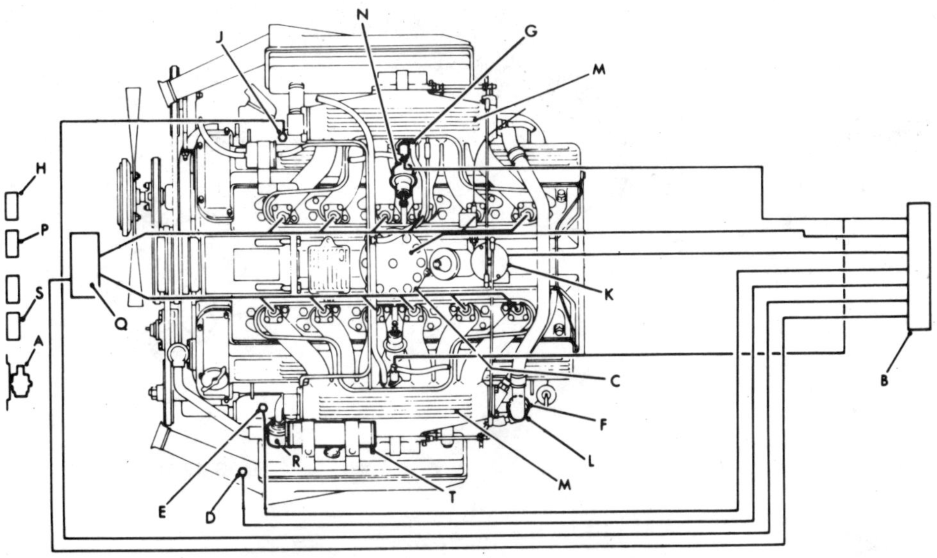

Fig. 3.45 Typical fuel injection system (Sec 42)

A Manifold pressure sensor
B Electronic control unit (ECU)
C Trigger unit
D Air temperature sensor
E Coolant temperature sensor
F Auxiliary air valve
G Cold start injector
H Cold start relay
J Thermotime switch
K Throttle switch
L Idle speed adjusting screw
M Induction manifolds
N Fuel pressure regulator
P Fuel pump relay
Q Power amplifier
R Overrun valve
S Main relay
T Fuel cooler

Sensing and control system (Sections 64 to 74)

4 This monitors the engine operating conditions of load, speed, temperature (coolant and intake air) and throttle movement, and by means of electrical pulses causes the injector solenoid valves to open for the exact time required to deliver the quantity of fuel which is required for any engine cycle.

5 The injectors are operated by an electrical control unit (ECU) in two groups of six, each group following the engine firing order.

6 The induction system is very similar to that used on an engine with carburettors.

7 The main components of the sensing and control part of the fuel injection system are explained below.

Pressure sensor

8 The position of the throttle pedal and the airflow into the engine determine the pressure within the plenum chamber. This pressure is converted by a pressure sensor into an electrical signal passed to the electronic control unit (ECU). The signal varies the duration of the injector operating pulse as necessary.

Trigger unit

9 This is fitted within the ignition distributor and utilises two switches 180° apart which close alternately at each revolution of the crankshaft. Each switch triggers the ECU to begin the timed pulse to a group of six fuel injectors.

10 The trigger pulse itself has no influence on the duration of the injection pulse, but the frequency of the trigger pulses modifies the duration of injection determined by the ECU.

Air temperature sensor

11 This is located in the air cleaner ram pipe and has a small effect to make sure that according to the temperature of the intake air (and in consequence its density), so the volume of fuel is varied to maintain the optimum fuel/air ratio.

Coolant temperature sensor

12 This operates in conjunction with the cold start system and the auxiliary air valve to form what is the equivalent of an automatic choke on a carburettor.

Cold start system (thermotime switch and cold start relay)

13 This is a system for injecting additional fuel into the induction manifolds. The cold start injectors are controlled by a cold start relay and thermotime switch. The thermotime switch senses coolant temperature and above a certain temperature level interrupts the relay earth connection. When the starter motor is operated, the cold start relay is energised through the thermotime switch. This switch also limits the duration of energising of the relay according to prevailing climatic conditions. The enrichment provided by this arrangement is in addition to that provided by the coolant temperature sensor. If the coolant temperature is above 95°F (35°C), the switch does not actuate as no additional enrichment will be required over and above the normal cranking enrichment (see next paragraph).

14 The ECU provides an increased pulse duration during engine cranking in addition to any enrichment resulting from the coolant temperature sensor or the cold start injectors.

Throttle switch

15 This is a rotary switch directly coupled to the throttle pulley. It signals the ECU as to the position and rate of movement of the throttle bufferfly valves.

Auxiliary air valve

16 This valve is controlled by coolant temperature and opens to allow air to bypass the throttles and so increase engine speed at cold start. This prevents stalling at cold start and cold idling. The valve incorporates an adjusting screw to regulate the air flow for idle speed adjustment. The valve is located on the left-hand cylinder bank rear coolant pipe.

43 Precautions and maintenance

1 Never allow the engine to run without the battery connected.

2 Do not use a high-speed battery charger as an aid to starting the car.

3 Always disconnect the battery before charging it from a mains charger.

4 A fuel flooding protection system is built in. If the ignition is switched on but the starter motor is not cranking the engine, then the fuel pump will run for a second or two to pressurise the fuel in the fuel rail. The pump is then automatically switched off by the ECU. Once the engine is turned by the starter motor the pump is switched on again. This arrangement prevents flooding with fuel should a fault develop in

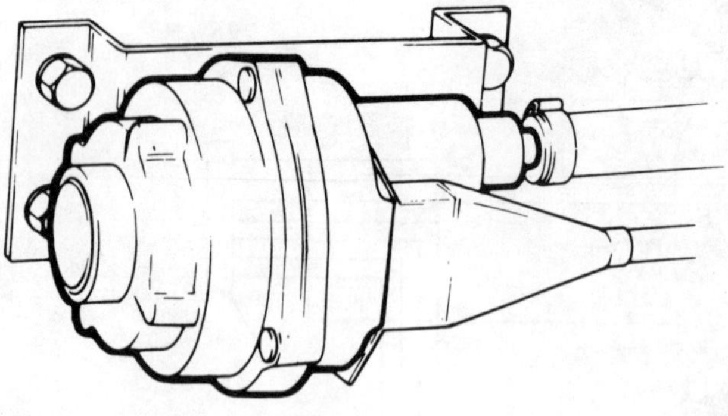

Fig. 3.46 Pressure sensor (Sec 42)

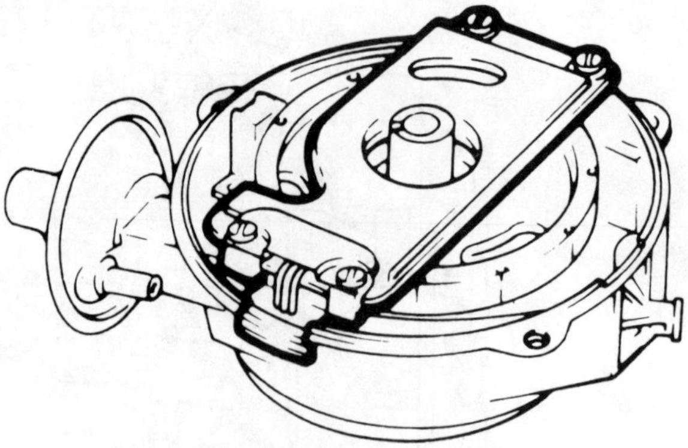

Fig. 3.47 Trigger unit (Sec 42)

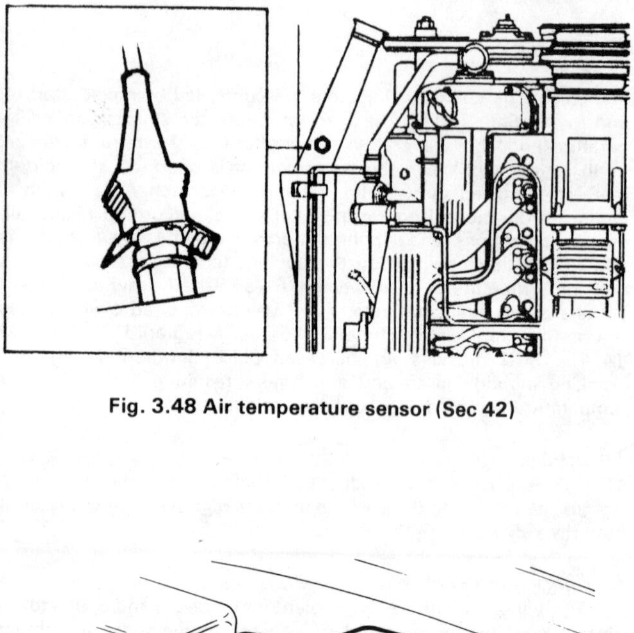

Fig. 3.48 Air temperature sensor (Sec 42)

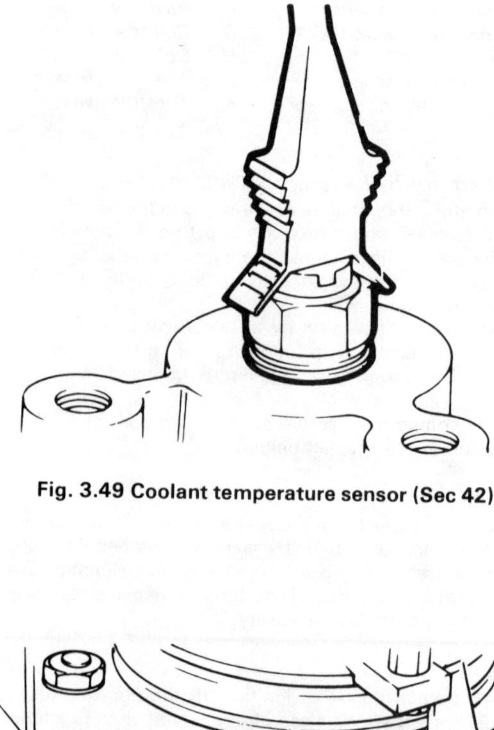

Fig. 3.49 Coolant temperature sensor (Sec 42)

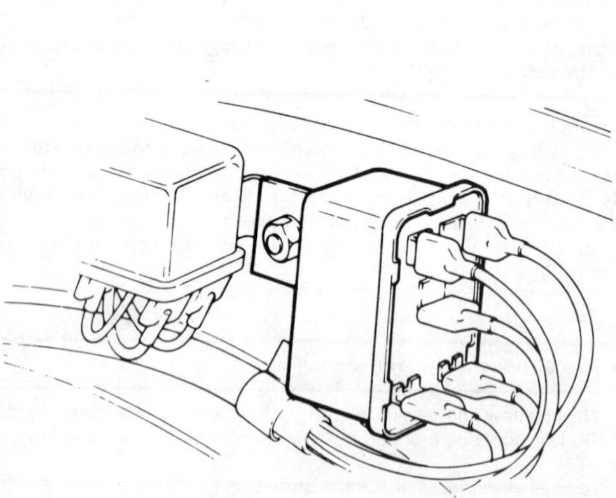

Fig. 3.50 Cold start relay (Sec 42)

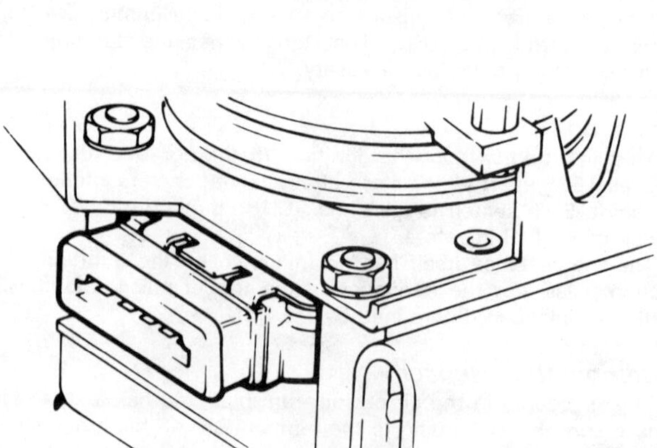

Fig. 3.51 Throttle switch (Sec 42)

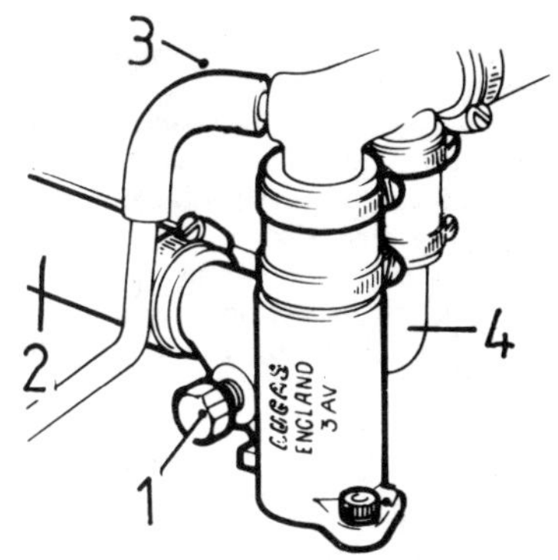

Fig. 3.52 Auxiliary air valve (Sec 42)

1 *Adjusting screw*
2 *Manifold bleed pipe*
3 *Air cleaner hose*
4 *Air balance pipe*

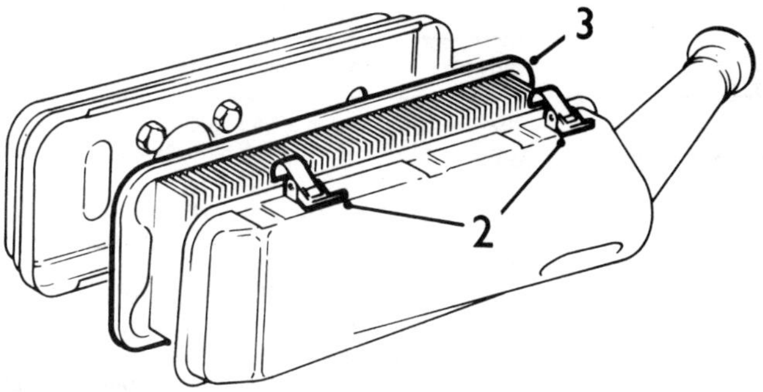

Fig. 3.53 Air cleaner (Sec 44)

2 *Toggle clips*
3 *Element*

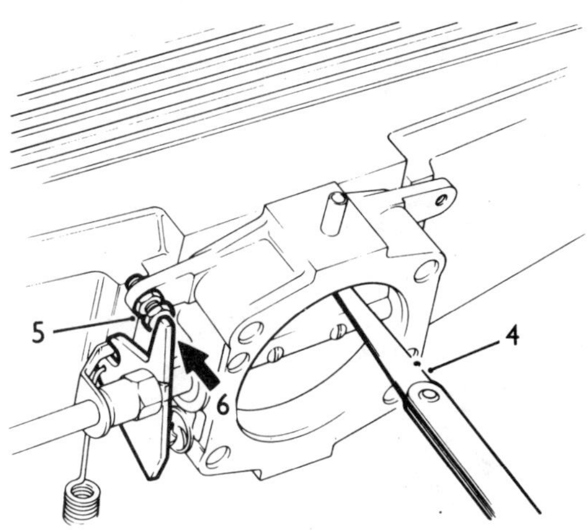

Fig. 3.54 Adjusting throttle butterfly valve (Sec 47)

4 *Feeler blade*
5 *Stop screw*
6 *Press arm against screw*

an injector whilst the ignition is on but the engine is not being cranked or running.

5 Maintenance consists of checking the security of all system hoses, pipes and electrical connections, and renewing the air and fuel filters at the specified service intervals.

44 Air cleaner – renewal of element

1 Disconnect the battery.
2 If the left-hand element is being renewed, disconnect the lead from the temperature sensor on the ram tube (photo).
3 Release the two toggle clips and remove the air cleaner cover.
4 Discard the filter element, wipe out the casing and check the condition of the seals.
5 Refit the new filter. Make sure that it is fitted the correct way round with the metal plate against the throttle housing (photo).
6 Refit the cover, reconnect the temperature sensor lead and the battery.

45 Air cleaner – removal and refitting

Left-hand

1 Disconnect the battery and the lead from the air temperature sensor on the ram tube.
2 Remove the air cleaner cover and filter element.
3 Disconnect the auxiliary air valve hose from the air cleaner backplate.
4 Disconnect the feed pipe hose from the positive crankcase ventilation (PCV) valve, also the engine breather hose.
5 Unbolt the air cleaner backplate from the throttle housing, pull it away and disconnect the overrun valve hose. Discard the flange gasket.
6 Refitting is a reversal of removal.

Right-hand

7 Repeat the operations described in paragraphs 2, 5 and 6 of this Section.

46 Idle speed – adjustment

1 Have the engine at normal operating temperature.
2 If the engine has been switched off after a run, re-start it and run it for two or three minutes.
3 Turn the idle speed screw (located on the auxiliary air valve) until the engine speed is 750 rpm.
4 If the idle speed fails to respond to turning the screw, check all manifold pipes and hoses for leakage, also the joint gaskets.
5 Check the security of the fuel injectors and cold start injectors.
6 Check the operation of the overrun valves (Section 62).
7 Check the auxiliary air valve (Section 61).
8 Check the adjustment of the throttle butterfly valves (Section 47).

47 Throttle butterfly valves – adjustment

1 Remove both air cleaners.
2 Slacken the locknut on the throttle butterfly stop screw and unscrew the screw.
3 Check that the throttle butterfly valve closes fully.
4 Insert a feeler blade (0.004 in (0.105 mm) for early models, 0.002 in (0.05 mm) for 1978 on) between the upper edge of the butterfly valve and the housing to hold the valve open.
5 Turn the stop screw until it just touches the stop arm, then tighten the locknut with the feeler in position. Pull out the feeler blade.
6 Press the stop arm against the stop screw and then carry out the foregoing operations on the opposite side of the engine.
7 Refit the air cleaners.
8 Check the throttle linkage adjustment (Section 37).
9 Check the operation of the throttle switch (Section 73).
10 Check the operation of the kickdown switch (Chapter 6).

48 Fuel system – depressurising

1 On XJS models remove the right-hand trim from within the luggage boot.
2 Pull the lead from terminal 85 of the fuel pump relay. Disconnect the ignition coil HT lead.
3 Switch on the ignition and operate the starter motor for a few seconds. The fuel system will now be depressurised.
4 After carrying out any work on the fuel system, reconnect the HT and relay leads.

49 Fuel tanks (XJ12 and Double Six) – removal and refitting

1 Refer to Section 14 after first depressurising the fuel system (Section 48).

50 Fuel tank (XJS) – removal and refitting

1 Remove the spare wheel and depressurise the fuel system (Section 48).
2 Disconnect and remove the battery.
3 Drain the fuel tank. To do this, remove the fuel pump cover from the battery tray and floor clips.
4 Clamp the fuel inlet hose at the pump to prevent loss of fuel and disconnect the hose from the pump.
5 Extract the grommet from the vent hole in the luggage boot floor. Connect a length of pipe to the inlet hose and pass the pipe through the hole in the floor.
6 Remove the fuel filler cap and after placing a container under the car, release the hose clamp and drain the tank.
7 Fold back the carpet from the fuel tank.
8 Clamp the fuel return hose to prevent loss of fuel and then disconnect the hose from the tank.
9 Disconnect the expansion tank supply hose from the rigid part of the pipeline and then disconnect the return pipe from the fuel tank.
10 Note the fuel tank vent pipe connections and disconnect them.
11 Disconnect the electrical leads from the fuel tank sender unit.
12 Disconnect the fuel filter assembly from the tank filler neck and then detach the assembly (three screws) from the body panel.
13 Release the fuel tank securing straps.
14 Remove the left and right-hand trim panels from inside the luggage compartment.
15 Remove the screws and lower the left-hand luggage compartment side panel from the body. Follow with the right-hand panel, but note the earth lead connections to the relay bracket and the pump relay.
16 Carefully remove the fuel tank.
17 The expansion tank supply pipe can now be detached, also the sender unit. To remove the sender unit, twist and unlock the locking ring with a suitable tool, turn the sender unit through 180° and withdraw it.
18 Never attempt to repair a fuel tank by soldering or welding. Always take it to a specialist repairer or renew the tank.
19 Refitting is a reversal of removal. Use new sealing rings and hoses where necessary. Do not fully tighten the tank securing straps until all connections have been made to it and it has been correctly located.

51 Fuel system filter – renewal

1 Depressurise the fuel system as described in Section 48.
2 Clamp the fuel inlet and outlet hoses either side of the filter to prevent loss of fuel.
3 Disconnect the hoses from the filter and then unbolt it from its bracket on the induction manifold (photo).
4 Remove the clamp from the filter and fit it to the new one. Discard the old filter.
5 Refitting is a reversal of removal.

52 Fuel pressure regulators – removal and refitting

1 Depressurise the fuel system as described in Section 48.
2 Disconnect the battery and then the lead from the cold start injector.
3 Unbolt the pressure regulator bracket, note which way round the regulator is fitted into the bracket and then lift the regulator upwards from the induction manifold.
4 Clamp the hoses which connect to the regulator in order to prevent loss of fuel and then detach them from it.
5 Unbolt the regulator from its bracket.
6 Refitting is a reversal of removal. If the original pressure regulator is being refitted, do not alter the setting of the adjuster screw and

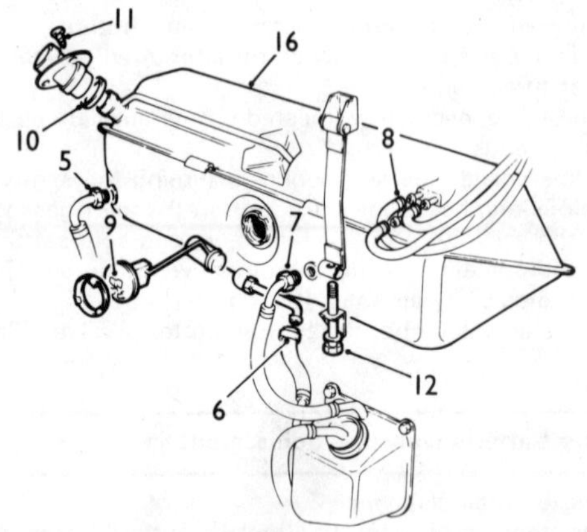

Fig. 3.55 Fuel tank (XJS) (Sec 50)

5 Fuel return
6 Expansion tank supply hose
7 Expansion tank return hose
8 Vent hoses
9 Tank sender unit
10 Filler hose
11 Filler neck screws
12 Mounting strap bolts
16 Fuel tank

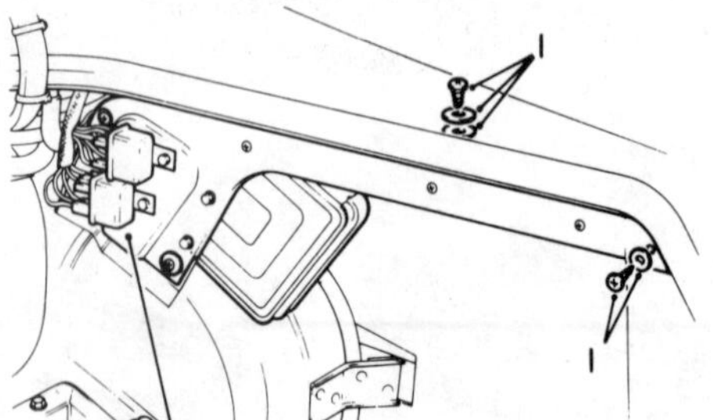

Fig. 3.56 Luggage compartment relay details (Sec 50)

1 Side panel screws
5 Pump relay plug
15 Earth to relay bracket

44.2 Left-hand air cleaner carries the temperature sensor

44.5 Air filter element

51.3 Fuel filter (1), fuel supply rail (2), right-hand (3) and left-hand (4) fuel rails

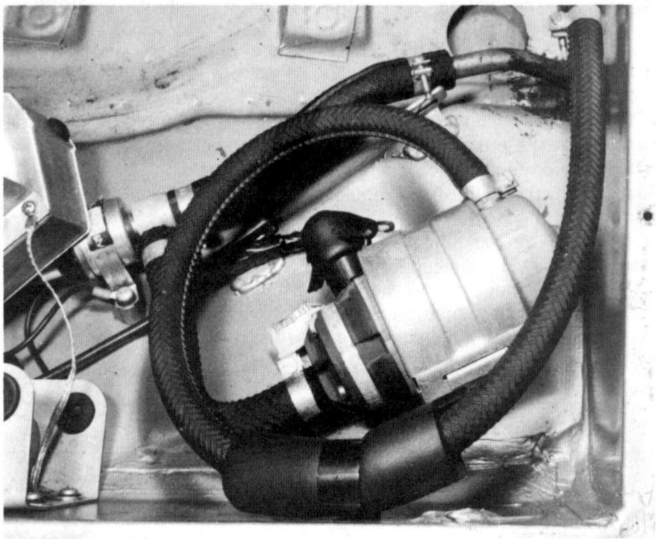

54.5 Fuel pump

58.1 Fuel cooler

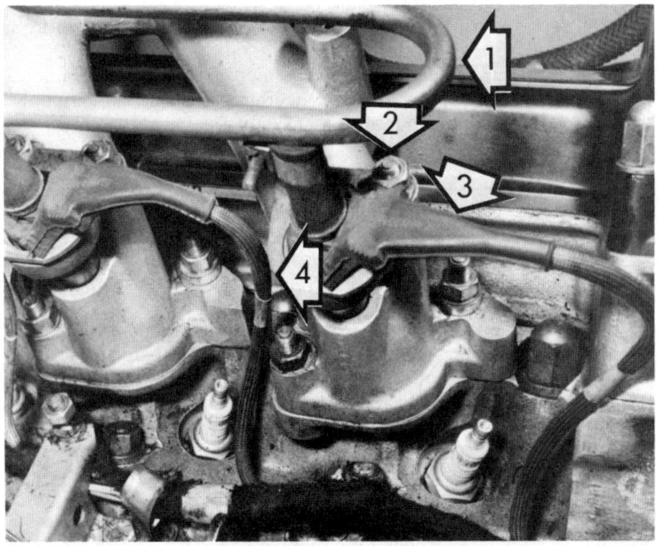

59.14 Fuel injector, showing fuel rail (1), injector clamp nut (2), electrical connector (3) and flexible fuel connecting hose (4)

locknut. If a new regulator is being fitted, it may require adjusting after checking as described in the next Section.

53 Fuel pressure regulators – checking and adjustment

1 Depressurise the fuel system as described in Section 48.
2 Disconnect the left-hand cold start injector supply pipe to the fuel rail and in its place connect a reliable pressure gauge.
3 Pull the negative LT lead from the ignition coil and switch the ignition on.
4 Earth terminal 85 of the fuel pump relay. The pressure gauge should indicate between 28.5 and 30.8 lbf/in^2 (2.0 and 2.2 kgf/cm^2).
5 The pressure indicated on the gauge may fall slowly, this is normal, but a rapid drop will indicate a fault in the system.
6 On the XJ12 and Double Six models only, operate the fuel changeover switch on the dash centre panel. Check the gauge pressure reading again as described in paragraph 4.
7 If the readings have proved satisfactory then both regulators are in good condition and the gauge can be removed and the original connections re-made.
8 Where one or both readings are outside the pressure specified then continue with the following adjustment procedure.
9 Unbolt both pressure regulators from the induction manifolds.
10 Clamp the fuel pipe between the left-hand pressure regulator inlet and the fuel rail.
11 Reconnect the negative LT lead to the ignition coil and start the engine.
12 Release the locknuts on both pressure regulators.
13 Turn the adjuster screw on the right-hand regulator until the reading on the pressure gauge is within the specified limits.
14 Release the clamp on the fuel pipe and transfer it to the right-hand fuel pipe. Turn the left-hand regulator adjuster screw until the pressure is within the specified limits.
15 Release the fuel pipe clamp and check that the pressure gauge still reads within the specified limits.
16 Without moving the adjuster screws, tighten the locknuts.
17 Switch off the ignition and again depressurise the fuel system so that the pressure gauge can be removed and the original connections re-made.

54 Fuel pump – removal and refitting

1 Depressurise the fuel system as described in Section 48.
2 Disconnect the battery.
3 Remove the spare wheel.
4 On XJS models, peel back the carpet and remove the fuel pump cover from within the luggage compartment.
5 Clamp the fuel inlet and outlet hoses at the pump and disconnect them (photo).
6 Disconnect the electrical plug.
7 Unbolt the pump mounting bracket, then release the pump from its clamping ring and remove it.
8 A faulty pump should not be overhauled but renewed complete.
9 Refit by reversing the removal operations. Make sure that the earth wire makes good metal-to-metal contact beneath one of the mounting screws.

55 Fuel pump relay – testing, removal and refitting

1 To test the relay, switch on the ignition. The pump should run for one or two seconds then stop. If the pump fails to operate or will not shut off, test by the following sequence.
2 Check that the inertia switch cut-out button is depressed (see Section 11) and that the connecting leads are secure. Check the switch for continuity when the button is depressed.
3 If the inertia switch is satisfactory, earth the pump relay terminal 85, switch on the ignition and check for battery voltage at terminal 86 of the main relay (see Section 56). If no reading is obtained, check the security of the electrical connections from the ignition switch through the inertia switch.
4 Now check for battery voltage at terminal 87 of the main relay. If no reading is obtained, check for battery voltage at the earth lead and connection from terminal 85 of the mains relay. If readings are obtained then the mains relay is faulty and should be renewed.
5 Check for battery voltage at terminal 86 of the fuel pump relay. If no reading is obtained, then an open circuit exists between terminal 87 of the main relay and 86 of the pump relay.
6 Check for battery voltage at terminal 87 of the pump relay. If no reading is obtained, check for battery voltage to earth and from terminal 85 of the pump relay. If these readings are satisfactory then the pump relay is faulty and must be renewed.
7 Finally, check all the supply and earth connections at the fuel pump.

Pump relay removal (XJ12 and Double Six)

8 Disconnect the battery and pull the leads from the pump relay, which is located second from the right on the radiator top rail.
9 Unscrew and remove the relay securing screw.

Pump relay removal (XJS)

10 Disconnect the battery and remove the right-hand trim panel from within the luggage compartment.
11 Identify the leads and disconnect the necessary ones from the main relay.
12 Extract the securing screw and remove the relay from the side panel of the luggage compartment.

Refitting

13 Refitting on all models is a reversal of removal.

56 Fuel system main relay – removal and refitting

1 The main relay on XJ12 and Double Six models is fitted at the extreme left-hand side of the radiator top rail.
2 On XJS models, the main relay is located adjacent to the fuel pump relay.
3 Removal is by means of extracting a single mounting screw. Mark the connecting leads before pulling them from the relay.
4 Refitting is the reverse of the removal procedure.

57 Fuel tank changeover valves (XJ12 and Double Six) – testing, removal and refitting

1 These valves are located adjacent to the fuel pump in the luggage compartment. The right-hand valve is the supply valve and is energised when the right-hand fuel tank is selected.
2 The left-hand valve is the return one and ensures that fuel in excess of the requirements of the engine is returned to the same tank. On later models, two solenoid operated return valves are fitted under the rear wheel arches.
3 To test a valve, disconnect the battery and remove the spare wheel.
4 Clamp the inlet and outlet hoses at the valve and then disconnect them.
5 Disconnect the electrical leads from the valve.
6 Push a length of rubber tubing onto the stub on the valve which is at right angles to its body. Blow through the tubing; air should be ejected from the outlet port at the larger diameter end of the valve body.
7 Energise the solenoid valve by applying a 12V current to the supply lead and earthing the remaining lead.
8 Blow through the rubber tubing again: air should be ejected from the outlet port at the smaller diameter end of the valve body.
9 Failure to operate as indicated will mean that the valve is faulty and must be renewed.
10 To remove the valve with the hoses disconnected, simply disconnect its securing clamp.
11 Refitting is a reversal of removal. Make sure that the earth is located beneath one of the clamp screws.

58 Fuel cooler – removal and refitting

1 This is fitted to cars which are equipped with an air conditioning system. It is essential to identify correctly the fuel lines before carrying out any dismantling operations (photo).
2 Depressurise the fuel system (Section 48).

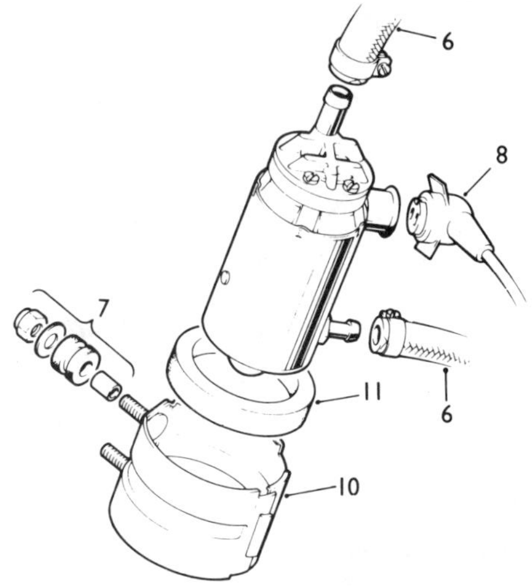

Fig. 3.57 Fuel pump (Sec 54)

6 *Fuel hoses*
7 *Mounting nuts and spacers*
8 *Electrical connector*
10 *Mounting clamp*
11 *Insulator*

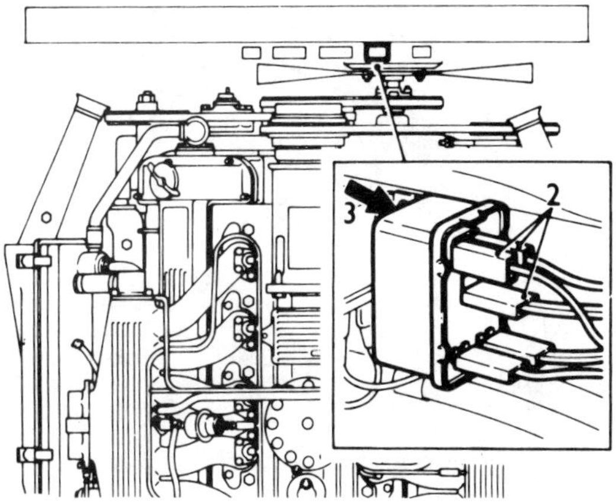

Fig. 3.58 Fuel pump relay (XJ12 and Double Six) (Sec 55)

2 *Lead connectors*
3 *Relay securing screw*

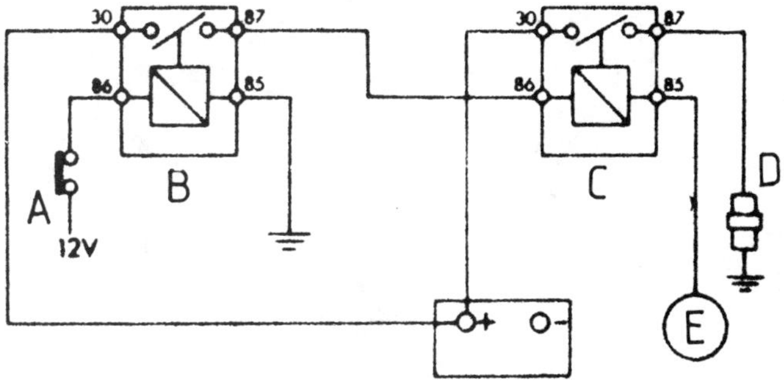

Fig. 3.59 Fuel system relay circuit diagram (Sec 55)

A *Inertia switch*
B *Main relay*
C *Pump relay*
D *Pump*
E *ECU*

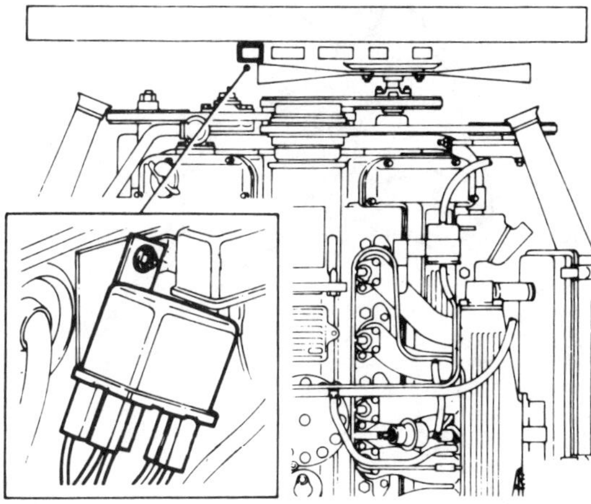

Fig. 3.60 Fuel system main relay (XJ12, Double Six) (Sec 56)

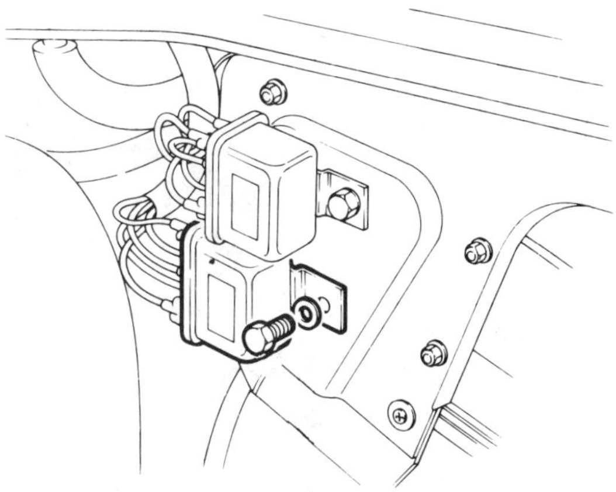

Fig. 3.61 Fuel system main relay (XJS) (Sec 56)

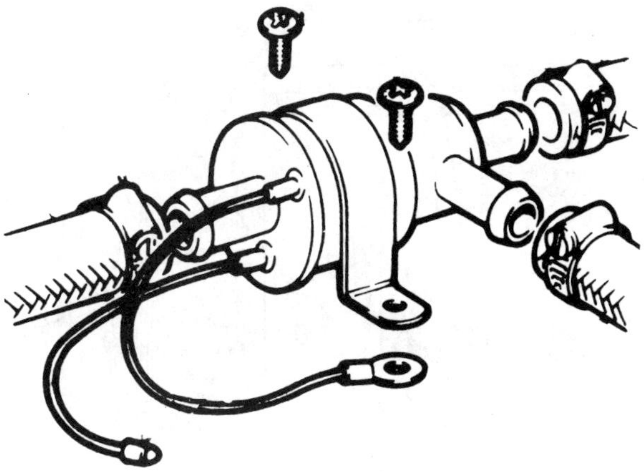

Fig. 3.62 Fuel tank changeover valve (XJ12, Double Six) (Sec 57)

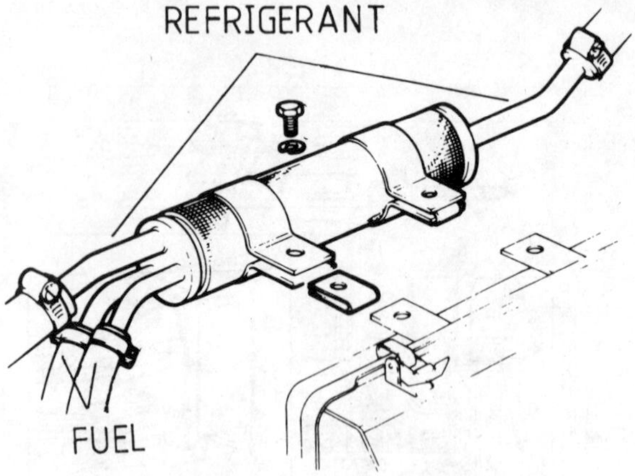

Fig. 3.63 Fuel cooler (Sec 58)

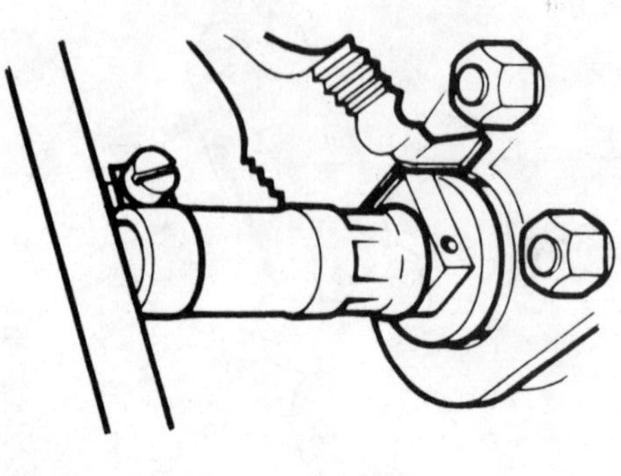

Fig. 3.64 Fuel injector attached to fuel rail (Sec 59)

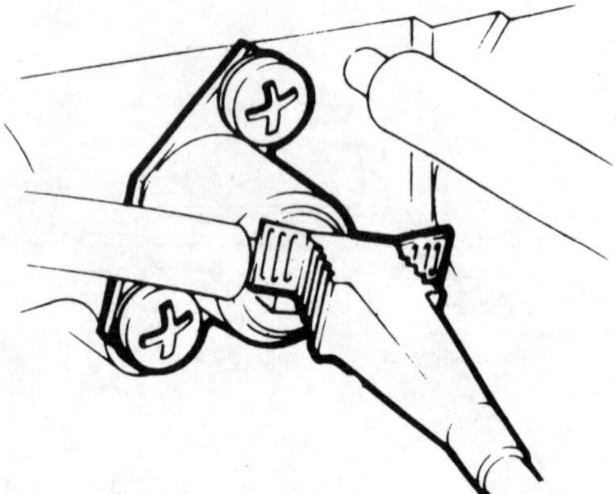

Fig. 3.65 Cold start injector (Sec 60)

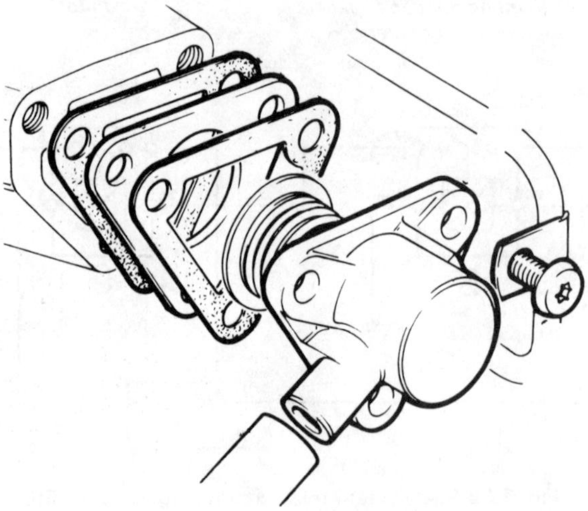

Fig. 3.66 Overrun valve (Sec 62)

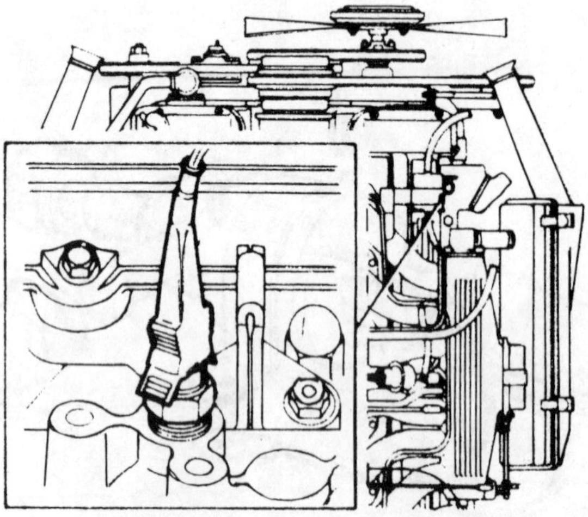

Fig. 3.67 Thermotime switch (Sec 65)

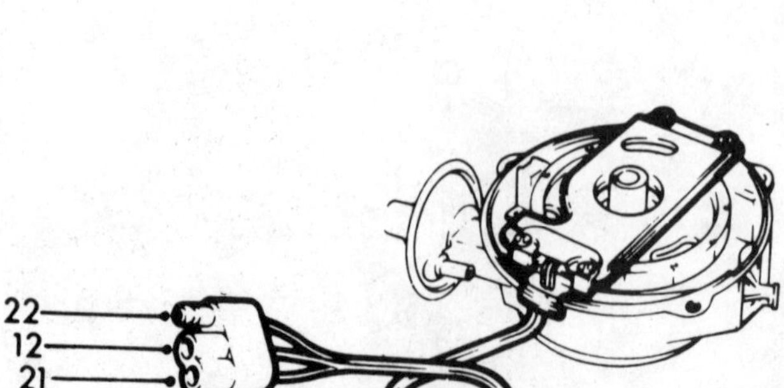

Fig. 3.68 Trigger unit plug terminals (Sec 67)

3 Clamp the fuel hoses on the end of the cooler to prevent loss of fuel and then disconnect them from the cooler.
4 If the refrigerant hoses must be disconnected then it is essential that the air conditioning system is discharged by your dealer beforehand. Refrigerant gas is very dangerous if allowed to escape into the atmosphere in an enclosed building.
5 The fuel cooler is attached to the air cleaner brackets by two setscrews.
6 Refitting is a reversal of removal. If the refrigerant was discharged by your dealer, have it recharged by him on completion of the work.

59 Fuel rail and injectors – removal and refitting

1 Depressurise the fuel system (Section 48) and then disconnect the battery.
2 Pull the manifold pressure pipe from the induction manifold.
3 Disconnect the throttle switch.
4 Disconnect the throttle cross-rods.
5 Clamp the fuel hose between the filter and the fuel supply rail.
6 Release the return fuel rail from the supply rail.
7 Extract the screws which hold the return fuel rail brackets to the induction manifolds. If the right-hand rail is being removed, note the longer space under the screw.
8 Release and pull the regulator to rail outlet hoses and the fuel return pipe from the fuel return rail.
9 Similarly release and pull the cold start injector and regulator inlet hoses from the fuel supply rail.
10 Release the clips that hold the fuel supply rail to the filter and to the main fuel rail.
11 Remove the supply and return fuel rails.
12 Release the wiring harness from the main fuel rail.
13 Pull the electrical connectors from the injectors, including the cold start injectors.
14 Unscrew and remove the twelve nuts which hold the injector clamps to the induction ram pipes. Lift the main fuel rail complete with injectors from the induction ram pipes. Mop up any spilled fuel with clean rag (photo).
15 Plug or tape over the injector holes to prevent dirt entering.
16 Release the clips which hold the injectors to the stubs on the main fuel rail. Pull the injectors from the rail and discard the O-ring seals.
17 Refitting is a reversal of removal. Make sure that the injectors are all fitted with new O-ring seals and their electrical connectors are fitted the correct way round (photo).

60 Cold start injector – removal and refitting

1 A cold start injector is mounted on each induction manifold.
2 Depressurise the fuel system (see Section 48).
3 Disconnect the battery.

59.17 Fuel injector O-ring seals (arrowed)

4 Clamp the fuel supply hose to the cold start injector which is to be removed. Detach the hose.
5 Pull the lead from the injector.
6 Unbolt the injector from the induction manifold. The securing screws may be setscrews, or socket screws requiring the use of an Allen key.
7 Refitting is a reversal of removal, but use a new gasket.

61 Auxiliary air valve – testing. removal and refitting

1 To test the valve, remove the filter element from the left-hand air cleaner.
2 Fully turn in the idle adjustment screw on the auxiliary air valve housing.
3 With the engine at normal running temperature, blocking the auxiliary air valve inlet should not affect the idling speed. If it does, continue the test in the following way after switching off the engine.
4 Carefully unscrew the expansion tank pressure cap, release any pressure and then refit the cap.
5 Disconnect the air balance pipe, the engine crankcase breather pipe and the manifold bleed pipe (XJS) from the valve.
6 Disconnect the air cleaner pipe from the auxiliary air valve.
7 Unbolt and remove the air valve from the coolant pipe and lift the valve clear.
8 Without damaging the seat, clean the old gasket from the coolant pipe.
9 Fully close the idle speed screw noting the number of turns needed to do so. Immerse the auxiliary air valve bulb in boiling water and watch the valve head through the side port. The valve should move smoothly to the closed position.
10 Take the valve from the water and quickly blow through the side port: no air should pass.
11 Let the valve cool and watch the valve head move smoothly back to open the main air passage.
12 If the movement of the valve is not satisfactory, renew the valve.
13 Refitting is a reversal of removal. Use a new gasket. Open the idle speed screw to approximately the same position as that originally set.
14 Check the coolant level in the expansion tank and top up if necessary.
15 Adjust the idle speed as described in Section 46.

62 Overrun valve – testing, removal and refitting

1 An overrun valve is fitted to each induction manifold. Each valve is designed to open and limit manifold depression under conditions of closed throttle overrun. This provides additional air to maintain a combustible fuel/air mixture under these conditions, so preventing an increase in exhaust emission levels.
2 To test the valve, remove the air cleaners, block the overrun valve pipes and start the engine.
3 If the idle speed is correct, stop the engine and unblock one valve inlet pipe only. Restart the engine. If the idle speed is correct, stop the engine again and unblock the second valve. Restart the engine. If the idle speed is now excessively fast, the last valve to be unblocked must be faulty and should be renewed.
4 To remove an overrun valve, extract the screws which hold it to the inlet manifold. Retrieve the spacer from the left-hand valve.
5 Disconnect the air cleaner hose and remove the valve complete with valve body.
6 Clean away all old pieces of gasket. Extract the valve from the valve body.
7 Refitting is a reversal of removal. Use a new gasket.

63 Fuel cut-off inertia switch

1 Refer to Section 11.

64 Coolant temperature sensor – testing, removal and refitting

1 Disconnect the battery.
2 Pull the lead from the coolant temperature sensor, which is located on the thermostat housing.

3 Connect an ohmmeter between the sensor terminals and note the resistance, which should correspond with those given in the following table according to the coolant temperature at the time of the test.

Coolant temperature	Resistance across terminals (kilohms)
14°F (-10°C)	*9.2*
32°F (0°C)	*5.9*
50°F (10°C)	*3.7*
68°F (20°C)	*2.5*
86°F (30°C)	*1.7*
104°F (40°C)	*1.18*
122°F (50°C)	*0.84*
140°F (60°C)	*0.60*
158°F (70°C)	*0.435*
176°F (80°C)	*0.323*
194°F (90°C)	*0.250*
212°F (100°C)	*0.190*

4 Disconnect the ohmmeter and then use it to check the resistance between each sensor terminal in turn and the sensor body. There should be a very high resistance shown on the ohmmeter. If not, renew the sensor as described in the following paragraphs.
5 Have the engine and coolant cold.
6 Disconnect the battery and pull the lead from the coolant temperature sensor.
7 Remove the expansion tank cap to release any residual pressure. Refit the cap.
8 Have the new sensor ready to hand with its threads smeared with jointing compound and a new sealing washer fitted.
9 Unscrew the original sensor and fit the new one as quickly as possible to avoid loss of coolant.
10 Reconnect the electrical leads and check and top up the coolant level.

65 Thermotime switch – testing, removal and refitting

1 Check the coolant temperature with a thermometer and record the reading. Note also the rating of the thermotime switch which is stamped on its body.
2 Disconnect the battery and the lead from the thermotime switch.
3 To test when the recorded coolant temperature is higher than that stamped on the switch, connect the ohmmeter between switch terminal W and earth. A very high resistance should be observed. If a low reading is observed, renew the switch.
4 To test when the recorded coolant temperature is lower than that stamped on the switch, connect the ohmmeter as previously described; a very low resistance should be observed.
5 If the switch is to be renewed, make sure that the engine is cold. Disconnect the battery and the lead from the switch. Have the new switch ready with a sealing washer fitted and its threads coated with jointing compound.
6 Remove the expansion tank cap and release any residual pressure. Unscrew and remove the switch from the thermostat housing. Quickly screw in the new switch.
7 Reconnect the electrical leads and top up the coolant level if necessary.

66 Air temperature sensor – testing, removal and refitting

1 This device is located in the left-hand air cleaner.
2 To test the sensor, disconnect the battery and pull the connector from the air temperature sensor.
3 Connect an ohmmeter between the sensor terminals and note the resistance, which should be very close to the readings in the following table according to the ambient air temperature at the time of the test.

Ambient air temperature	Resistance (ohms)
14°F (-10°C)	*960*
32°F (0°C)	*640*
50°F (10°C)	*435*
68°F (20°C)	*300*
86°F (30°C)	*210*
104°F (40°C)	*150*
122°F (50°C)	*108*
140°F (60°C)	*80*

4 Now check the resistance between each terminal and the body of the sensor. A very high resistance must be obtained, otherwise renew the sensor.
5 To renew the sensor, simply unscrew it from the air cleaner ram pipe.

67 Trigger unit – testing

1 An ohmmeter will be required for this work.
2 Disconnect the electrical lead from the fuel pump relay terminal 85.
3 Disconnect the negative LT lead from the ignition coil.
4 Separate the in-line connector which runs to the trigger unit.
5 Connect an ohmmeter between terminals 21 and 12 on the section of the in-line connector nearest the distributor.
6 Switch on the ignition and then operate the starter motor. The ohmmeter should indicate a regular even swing of its needle between low resistance and a very high resistance.
7 Reconnect the ohmmeter between terminals 22 and 12 and repeat the test. A similar reading must be obtained to the one previously described.
8 Any variation in the pattern of ohmmeter readings will mean that the trigger unit is faulty and must be renewed.

68 Trigger unit – removal and refitting

1 Disconnect the battery. Having identified the spark plug HT leads, disconnect them from all twelve spark plugs.
2 Disconnect the HT lead from the distributor.
3 On XJ12 and Double Six models, disconnect the manifold pressure sensor pipe at the T-piece and tie it away from the distributor cover.
4 Extract the three screws and lift the distributor cover away.
5 Remove the rotor arm.
6 Disconnect the trigger unit lead from the main wiring harness at the in-line connector.
7 Extract the four nylon screws and withdraw the trigger unit from the platform.
8 Remove the nylon clamp from the right-hand side of the unit. Release the trigger unit rubber seal and pull the unit from the distributor body.
9 Refitting is a reversal of removal.

69 Manifold pressure sensor – testing, removal and refitting

1 Disconnect the battery and pull the lead from the pressure sensor.
2 Connect an ohmmeter between the pressure sensor terminals and check that the indicated resistance is within the limits shown in the following table. If not, the sensor must be renewed.

Sensor terminals (see wiring diagrams)	Resistance (ohms)
7 and 15	*85.5 to 94.5*
8 and 10	*346.5 to 353.5*
7 or 15 and earth	*Open circuit ∞*
8 or 10 and earth	*Open circuit ∞*

3 To remove the pressure sensor, disconnect the electrical lead and hose and unbolt the sensor from its position, which is on the radiator top rail on XJ12 and Double Six models or on the wing valance on XJS models.
4 Refitting is a reversal of removal.

70 Cold start relay – removal and refitting

1 On XJ12 and Double Six models, the relay is mounted on the extreme right-hand side of the radiator top rail.
2 On XJS models, the relay is mounted on the front wing valance and the relay cover must first be removed.
3 Disconnect the battery, then identify the electrical leads and pull them from the cold start relay terminals.

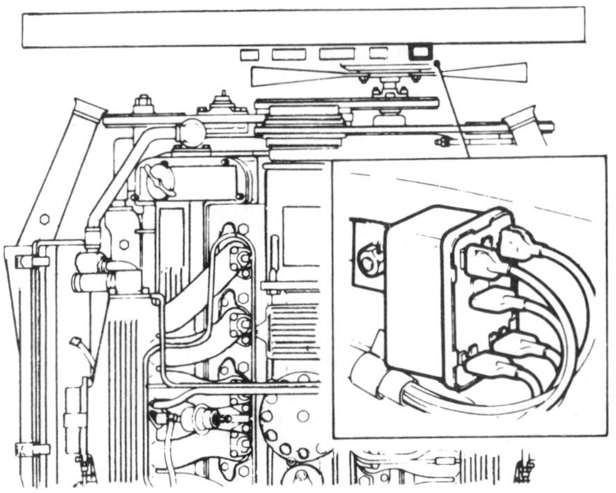

Fig. 3.69 Cold start relay (XJ12, Double Six) (Sec 70)

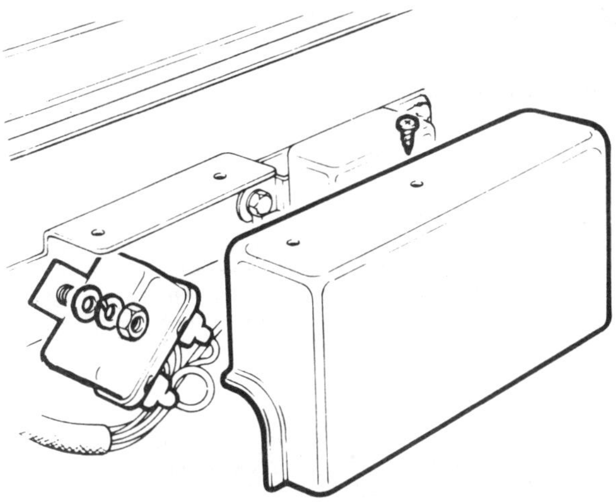

Fig. 3.70 Cold start relay (XJS) (Sec 70)

4 Unbolt and remove the relay. On right-hand drive XJS models, better access is obtained if the relay mounting bracket is unbolted and raised together with all the relays as one assembly.

71 Power amplifier – removal and refitting

1 The power amplifier is mounted on the radiator top rail (photo). Its purpose is to isolate the ECU from the large current draw which occurs when six fuel injectors are switched simultaneously.
2 Disconnect the battery and then separate the in-line connectors at the wiring harness.
3 Release the rubber grommet from the radiator top rail. Unbolt the amplifier and draw the wiring and plug through the hole in the rail.
4 Refitting is a reversal of the removal procedure.

72 Electronic control unit (ECU) – removal and refitting

1 The ECU is mounted within the luggage compartment and receives the input signals from the various fuel injection system sensors. The ECU then computes the period for which the injectors must open for each engine cycle.
2 Do not alter the setting of the idle fuelling potentiometer control knob on the amplifier unit or the idle CO level will be upset, see Section 82.
3 To remove the ECU, first disconnect the battery.
4 Remove the cover from the ECU which is located at the forward end of the luggage compartment (XJ12 and Double Six). On XJS models, remove the right-hand trim panel from the luggage compartment.
5 Release the clamp at the wiring harness entry, remove the clip and end cover and withdraw the harness plug.
6 Remove the ECU from its mounting bracket (photo).
7 Refitting is a reversal of removal. If a new unit has been fitted, check the CO level as described in Section 82.

73 Throttle switch – testing and adjusting

1 Check that the throttle linkage and throttle butterfly valve are correctly set (Sections 37 and 47).
2 Disconnect the battery and pull the electrical multi-connector from the throttle switch which is located underneath the throttle pulley.
3 Connect an ohmmeter between terminals 12/47 and 17 of the throttle switch. A very low resistance should be registered. If not, adjust in the following way.

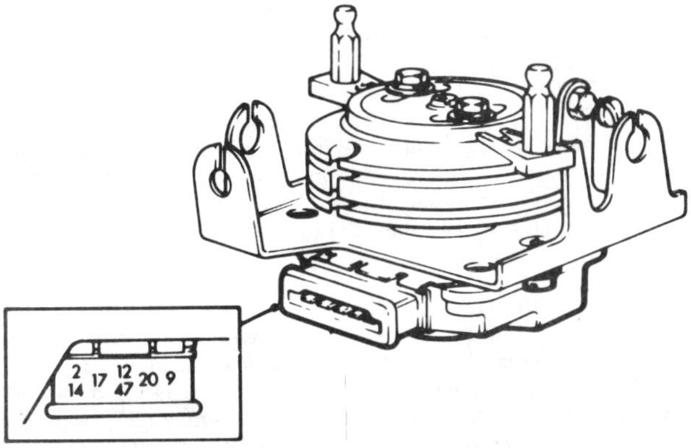

Fig. 3.71 Throttle switch terminal identification (Sec 73)

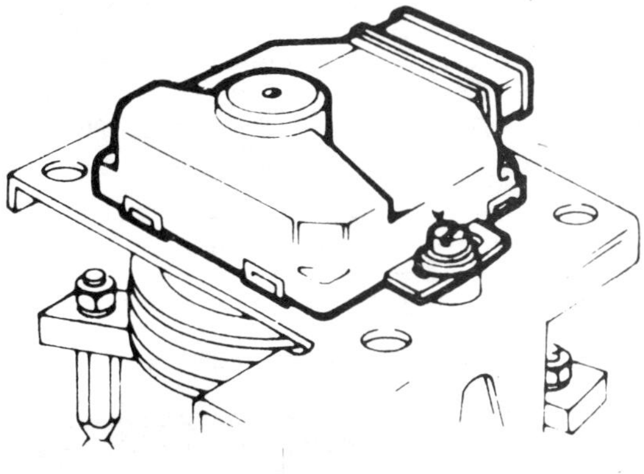

Fig. 3.72 Throttle switch correctly fitted (Sec 74)

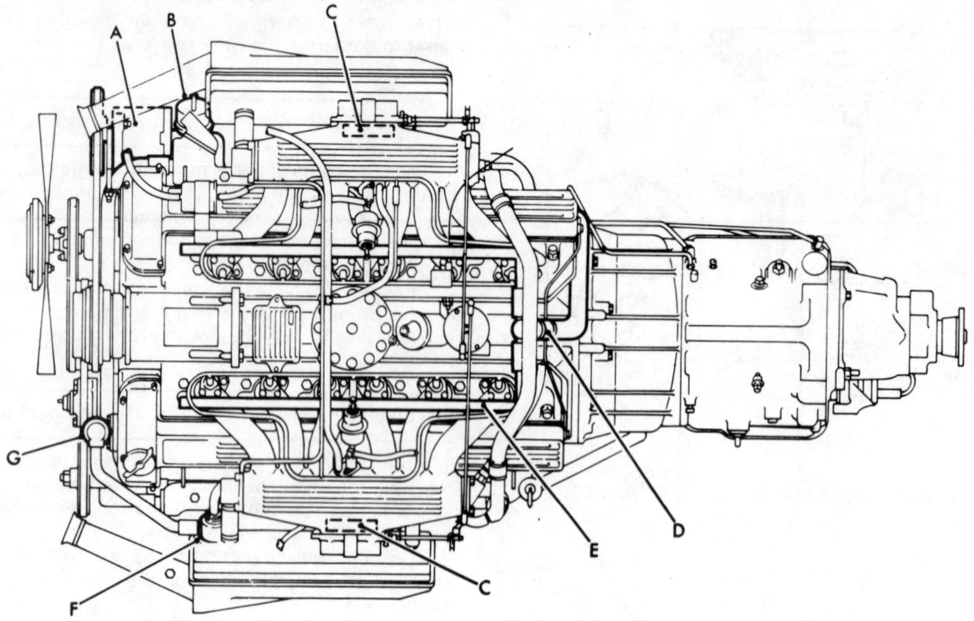

Fig. 3.73 Typical emission control system (Sec 75)

A Air pump
B Diverter valve
C EGR valves
D Non-return valve
E Air rail
F Positive crankcase ventilation valve
G Engine breather filter

4 Disconnect the pushrods from the throttle pulley (photo).
5 Unbolt and lift the throttle pulley from the pedestal. Disconnect the throttle switch plug.
6 Slacken the two throttle switch screws.
7 Insert a feeler blade (0.050 in (1.27 mm) thick for XJS or 0.030 in (0.76 mm) for XJ12 and Double Six) between the pulley and the closed throttle stop.
8 With the ohmmeter connected between terminals 12 and 17 of the throttle switch, turn the switch very slowly until the ohmmeter flicks to indicate a very low resistance. Tighten the two switch screws.
9 Remove the feeler blade and the ohmmeter should indicate a very high resistance when the pulley is closed against its stop. Remove the ohmmeter.
10 Reconnect the pushrods. If their balljoints will not connect to the bellcranks without displacing the latter, adjust the lengths of the rods. When tightening the rod locknuts, make sure that the balljoints are held at the centres of their arcs of travel.
11 With the throttle switch now correctly adjusted, continue the test in the following way.
12 Connect the ohmmeter between terminals 9 and 12/47 of the switch. Observe the ohmmeter and turn the throttle pulley by hand. The meter needle should swing regularly between very low and very high resistance ten times. If this does not happen, renew the switch.
13 If the test has been satisfactory, refit the multi-connector to the switch and reconnect the battery.

74 Throttle switch – removal and refitting

1 Carry out the operations described in paragraphs 2 and 4 of the preceding Section.
2 Slacken the nut which holds the throttle cable to the pedestal bracket.
3 Unbolt and lift the throttle platform from the pedestal.
4 Remove the two screws and lift the switch from its seat.
5 Refitting is a reversal of removal but make sure that the multi-connector socket faces towards the rear of the car (photo).

75 Emission control system (fuel injection engines) – description

1 Depending upon the operating territory, some or all of the following devices will be installed.

Air injection system

2 This comprises a belt-driven air delivery pump which supplies air through a diverter valve and non-return valve to the exhaust ports just above the exhaust valve heads.
3 This injected air mixes with the exhaust gases to continue the oxidisation process within the exhaust system.
4 The non-return valve prevents reverse flow in the injection rails when the exhaust gas pressure exceeds the air supply pressure.
5 The diverter valve operates when there is a sudden drop in manifold pressure, such as occurs when the throttle is closed quickly. Secondary air is diverted to atmosphere for between 2 and 3 seconds. This reduces the fuel/air ratio which would otherwise be too rich to burn and would cause a backfire in the exhaust system.

Thermostatic or part throttle vacuum ignition advance/retard systems

6 One of several different systems (depending upon operating territory) may be encountered. The purpose of the modified components as opposed to a conventional ignition distributor advance/retard mechanism is to vary the ignition timing according to coolant temperature and in conjunction with the throttle mode. On some versions, a signal is sent to the ECU to modify the fuel injection pulse at full throttle conditions.

Crankcase breather system

7 Blow-by gas from the crankcase is drawn into the engine while it is running by means of the induction manifold balance pipe.
8 A PCV (positive crankcase ventilation) valve is used to control part-throttle ventilation in the crankcase and to maintain a depression in the crankcase. On full throttle, a depression is maintained in the crankcase by the depression created on the clean side of the air cleaner.

Fuel evaporative control system

9 To prevent the emission of fuel vapour from the fuel tank to atmosphere, the vapour is stored in a carbon-filled canister when the engine is not running.

10 When the engine is running, the vapour in the canister is drawn into the induction manifold and burned during the normal combustion cycle.

11 The fuel tanks have an inbuilt expansion tank to accommodate the increase in fuel volume which occurs as the result of a rise in ambient temperature.

Exhaust Gas Recirculation (EGR)

12 In this system, exhaust gas is tapped from the exhaust downpipe and injected into the induction system. The system incorporates solenoid-operated valves which are controlled by an EGR controller to prevent valve operation under idle or full throttle conditions or during the warm-up period and at high roadspeeds.

Catalytic converters

13 These are fitted into the exhaust systems to further reduce CO or hydrocarbon emissions. Unleaded fuel only must be used on cars equipped with catalytic converters.

14 Under certain conditions, the temperature of the catalytic converter may be very high. To reduce the possibility of damage to the converter or the underside of the car generally, the following precautions should be observed.

(a) Do not continue to operate the car if the engine is misfiring or runs on after switching off
(b) Do not park in areas of long grass or other combustible materials
(c) Do not overload the car or pull excessively heavy trailer loads
(d) Do not operate the car downhill with the engine switched off
(e) Do not run the engine with a spark plug removed or HT lead disconnected
(f) Do not use a type of pump which can be screwed into a spark plug hole
(g) Do not push or tow start the car, use only battery jumper leads connected to the battery of another vehicle

76 Emission control systems – maintenance

1 Regularly inspect all hose and pipe connections. Check the air pump drivebelt tension as described in Chapter 1, Section 41.

2 At the intervals specified in Routine Maintenance, carry out the following operations.

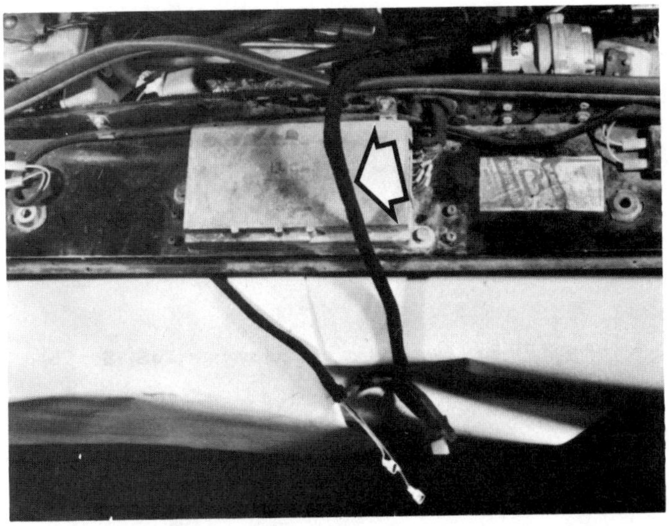

71.1 Power amplifier (arrowed)

72.6 Close-up of ECU and bracket

73.4 Throttle pulley and pushrods

74.5 Throttle pedestal and multi-connector sockets (induction manifolds removed)

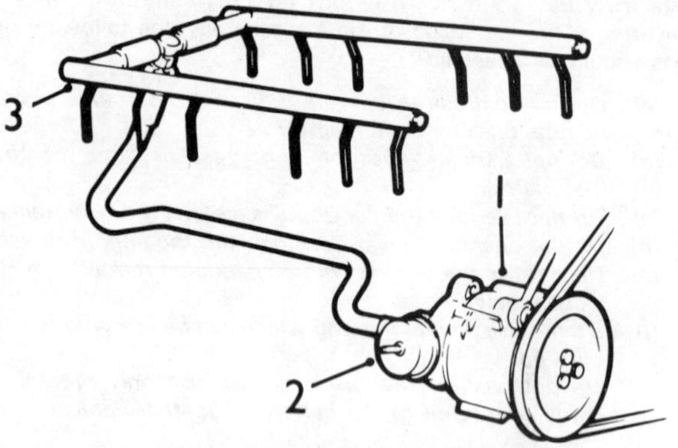

Fig. 3.74 Air injection system (diagrammatic) (Sec 75)

1 Air pump
2 Diverter valve
3 Non-return valve

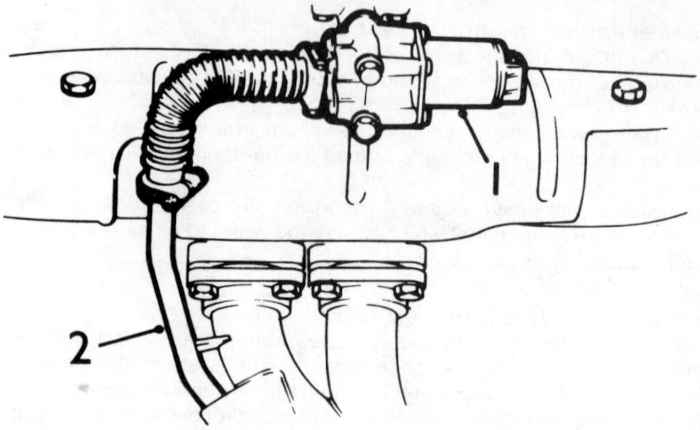

Fig. 3.75 EGR valve (Sec 75)

1 Valve assembly
2 Exhaust downpipe tapping

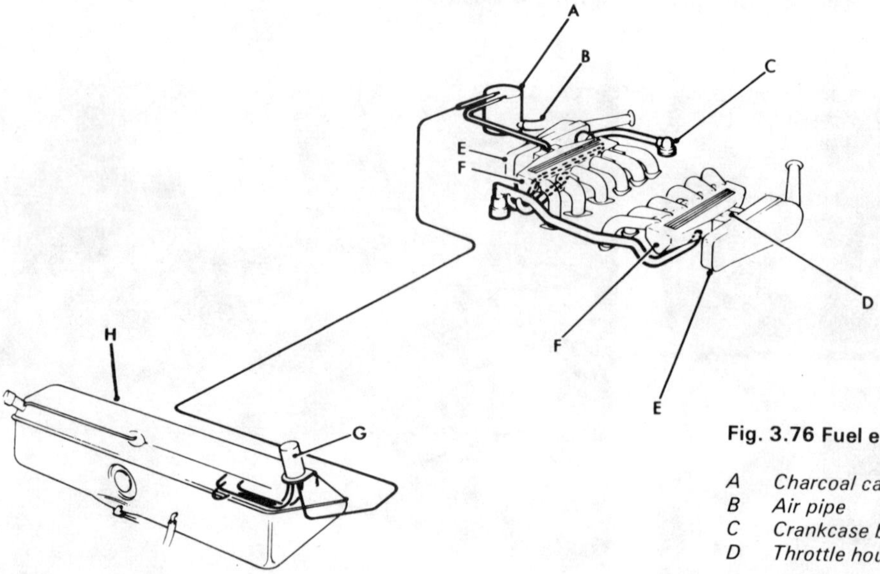

Fig. 3.76 Fuel evaporative control system (XJS) (Sec 75)

A Charcoal canister
B Air pipe
C Crankcase breather
D Throttle housings
E Air cleaners
F Induction manifolds
G Vapour separator
H Fuel tank

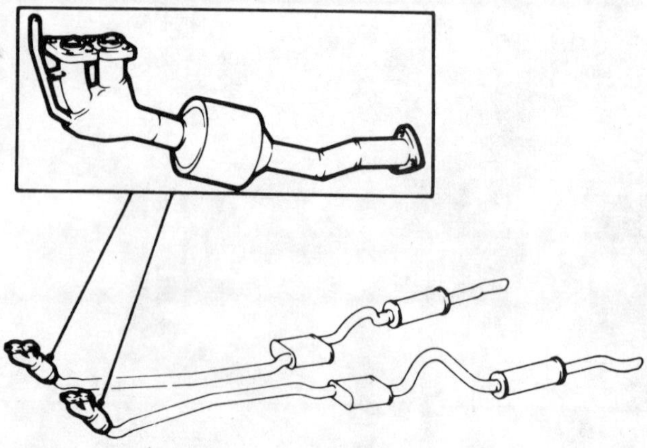

Fig. 3.77 Catalytic converter (Sec 75)

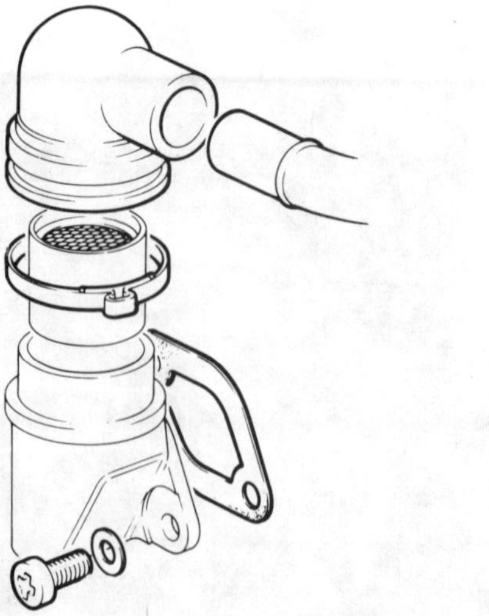

Fig. 3.78 Engine breather (Sec 75)

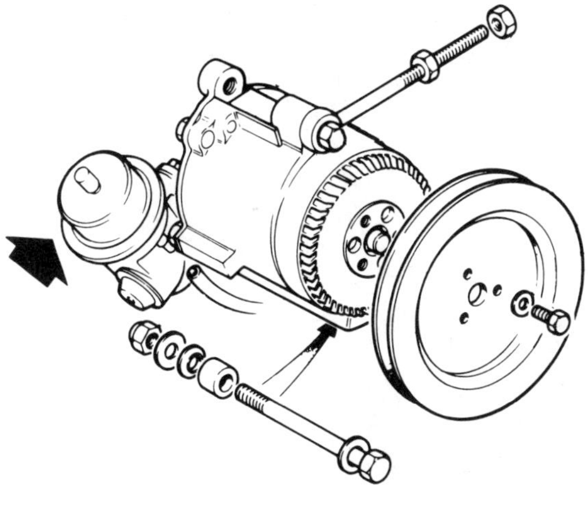

Fig. 3.79 Air pump and (arrowed) diverter valve (Sec 77)

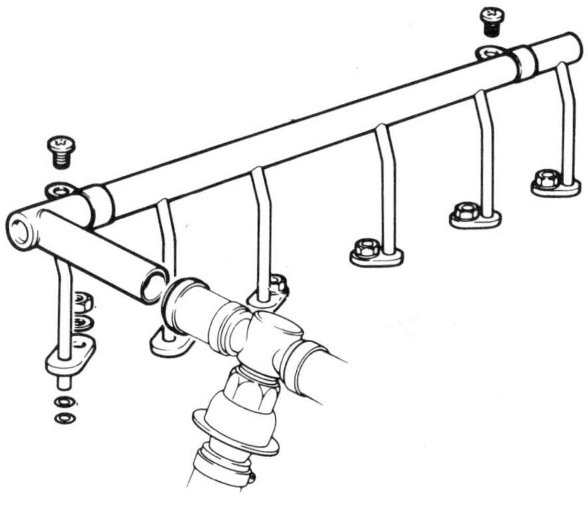

Fig. 3.80 Air rail (Sec 78)

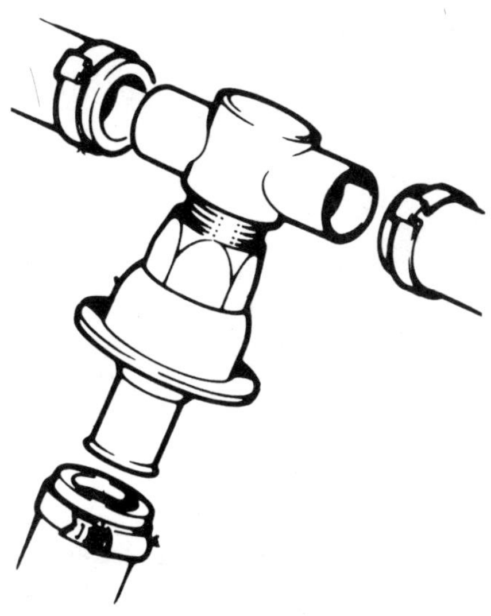

Fig. 3.81 Non-return valve (Sec 79)

Engine breather filter – cleaning

3 Release the clip and pull off the rubber cover from the breather housing.
4 Disconnect the pipe from the cover and clean away any sludge.
5 Lift out the filter, clean it in fuel, dry it and refit.
6 Reconnect the rubber cover.

Carbon canister – renewal

7 Raise the front of the car and remove the left-hand roadwheel.
8 On XJS models, unbolt and remove the access cover from the spoiler.
9 Identify the hoses and disconnect them from the canister.
10 Release the clamp and withdraw the canister.
11 Fit the new carbon canister by reversing the process just described.

Catalytic converter – renewal

12 On early models, the catalytic converter must be renewed at 25 000 mile (40 000 km) intervals. A service interval warning indicator is built into the centre switch panel and also indicates the service interval for the EGR system. A special key resets the indicator.
13 On later cars, a 50 000 mile (80 000 km) service interval is recommended and a reminder device is not installed.
14 To remove a catalytic converter, first withdraw the air cleaner element.
15 Release the EGR transfer pipe clamp at the take-off pipe and disconnect the transfer pipe.
16 Working under the car, remove the power steering rack bellows heatshield.
17 Support the front intermediate exhaust pipe and disconnect it from the downpipe.
18 Unbolt the downpipe and the heatshield from the exhaust manifold.
19 Remove the downpipe and catalytic converter. Removal will be made easier if the steering is turned as necessary.
20 Refitting is a reversal of removal, but use exhaust jointing compound at the joints and flanges.

EGR valve – cleaning and renewal

21 At 25 000 mile (40 000 km) intervals, the EGR valve, ports and transfer pipe should be removed as described later in this Chapter and all carbon deposits removed with a wire brush or scraper.
22 At 50 000 mile (80 000 km) intervals, the valve should be renewed.

77 Air pump and diverter valve (emission control) – removal and refitting

1 Remove the cover from the right-hand air cleaner.
2 Unbolt (three bolts) and remove the pulley from the pump. Do not prise the pulley off with a lever but pull it by hand only, otherwise the pump filter will be damaged.
3 Release the pump adjuster rod and swing the pump away from the engine.
4 Disconnect the vacuum pipe from the diverter valve, followed by the secondary air pipe. Discard the seal.
5 Unbolt the pump mountings and lift it from the engine.
6 Remove the elbow and diverter valve from the pump. Discard the gasket.
7 Refitting is a reversal of removal; use a new elbow gasket and secondary air pipe seal.
8 Tension the drivebelt as described in Chapter 1, Section 41.

78 Air rail (emission control) – removal and refitting

1 Depressurise the fuel system as described in Section 48.
2 Disconnect the battery.
3 Remove the fuel rail (Section 59).
4 Remove the fuel pressure regulators (Section 52).
5 Unbolt the air rail bracket from the induction manifold ram tubes.
6 If the right-hand air rail is being removed, disconnect the earth strap from the rear induction manifold ram tube.

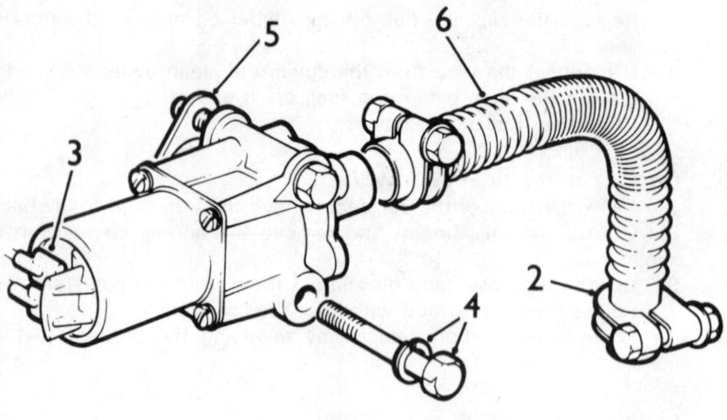

Fig. 3.82 EGR valve (Sec 80)

2 *Clamp*
3 *Electrical connectors*
4 *Mounting bolt and washer*
5 *Gasket*
6 *Transfer pipe*

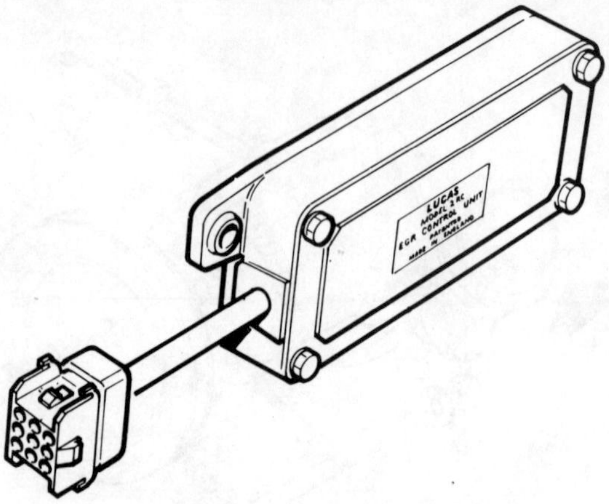

Fig. 3.83 EGR control unit (Sec 81)

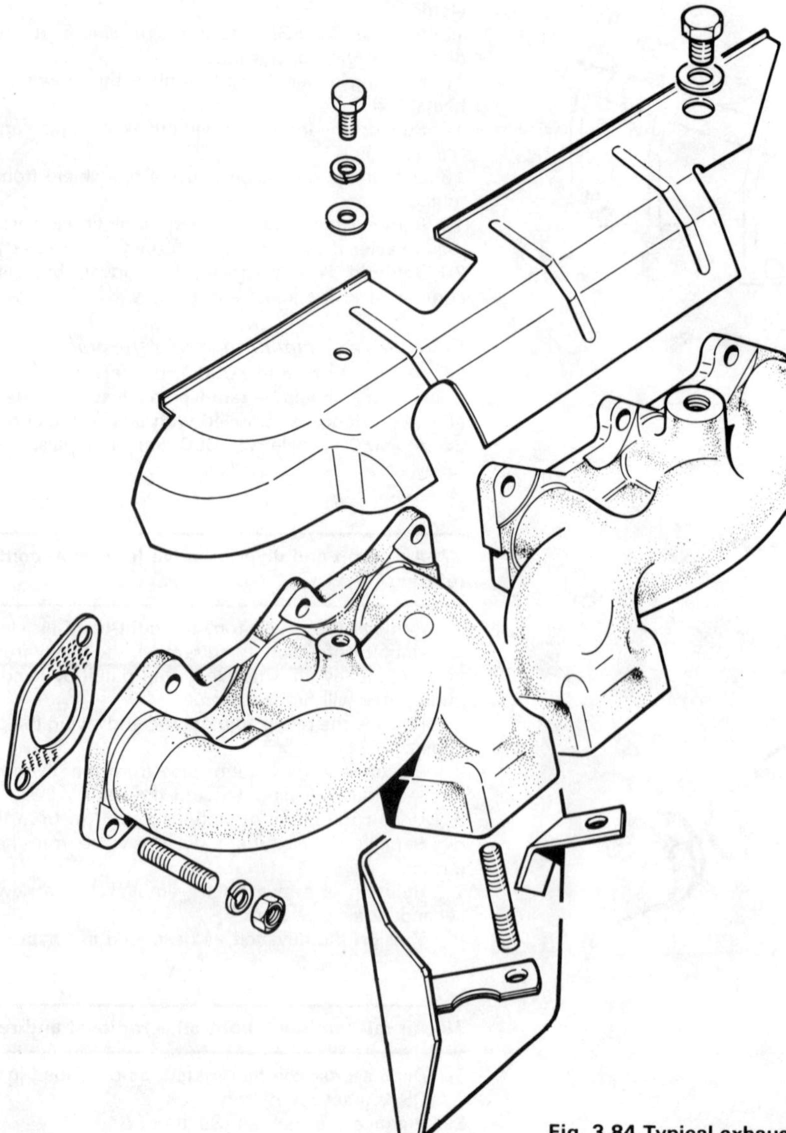

Fig. 3.84 Typical exhaust manifolds (Sec 85)

7 Unbolt the air rail and manifold stud spacers from the cylinder head.
8 Lift out the air rail and disconnect the non-return valve hose from it.
9 Refitting is a reversal of removal; use new rubber sealing rings.

79 Non-return valve (emission control) – removal and refitting

1 Note which way round the valve is fitted, release the hose clips and pull the hoses from the valve.
2 Refitting is a reversal of removal.

80 Exhaust gas recirculation (EGR) valve (emission control) – removal and refitting

1 Remove the cover from the air cleaner and disconnect the EGR valve transfer pipe.
2 Disconnect the electrical leads.
3 Unscrew and remove the valve mounting bolts.
4 Refitting is a reversal of removal, but use a new gasket.

81 Exhaust gas recirculation (EGR) control unit – removal and refitting

1 Disconnect the battery.
2 Remove the two nuts and washers which hold the rear right-hand lamp cluster. Disconnect the lamp earth lead and withdraw the cluster.
3 With the EGR control unit now accessible, pull off the multi-connector and remove the control unit.
4 Refitting is a reversal of removal.

82 CO level (mixture) – checking and adjusting

1 These operations will only be required if new components have been fitted to the fuel injection or emission control systems. It is essential to carry out this work immediately after renewal of the fuel injection electronic control unit (ECU).
2 Adjust the throttle butterfly valves (Section 47).
3 Adjust the idle speed (Section 46) with the engine at normal operating temperature.
4 Take off the cap from the air injection system diverter valve (Section 77) which will interrupt the air injection. Increase the engine speed to 2000 rpm for a period of 15 seconds, then allow it to return to idle speed.
5 Using an infra-red exhaust gas analyser, insert the probe into the sampling point at each end of the air injection rail. The CO reading should be within the specified limits. If necessary, adjust the idle potentiometer knob on the ECU until the correct reading is obtained.
6 Refit the diverter valve cap and reset the idle speed to the specified level.

83 Induction manifold (left-hand) – removal and refitting

1 Disconnect the battery and remove the air cleaner.
2 Depressurise the fuel system (Section 48).
3 Disconnect the fuel pipe from the overrun valves. Retrieve the spacer from the left-hand valve.
4 Disconnect the pressure regulator return hose from the fuel rail.
5 Disconnect the fuel crossover pipe from the fuel rail.
6 Disconnect the manifold pressure hose from the induction manifold.
7 Where fitted, disconnect the vacuum hose from the throttle housing.
8 On left-hand drive cars, disconnect the leads from the kickdown switch and the throttle cable from the throttle pedestal.
9 Disconnect the throttle pushrod from the bellcrank.
10 Unclip the wiring harness from the fuel rail.
11 Pull the electrical leads from the fuel and cold start injectors.
12 Disconnect the brake servo vacuum hose from the non-return valve.
13 Remove the throttle return spring.
14 Disconnect the manifold bleed pipe from the rubber elbow.
15 Unscrew and remove the twelve nuts which hold the induction manifold to the cylinder head. Under each outboard nut is fitted a spacer and washer, on inboard nuts, a washer only (photo).
16 Where fitted, detach the air rail clips from the manifold ram tubes, release the non-return valve hose, remove the air rail and discard the O-ring seals.
17 Where fitted, remove the EGR valve from the throttle housing.
18 Remove the six spacers from the manifold studs. Withdraw the manifold, at the same time easing aside the balance pipe and the fuel pipes.
19 Discard the manifold gaskets and obtain new ones. Note that the gaskets used originally are of composition type, while replacements are of sheet steal. These later type gaskets are handed left and right (photo). Plug the open ports to prevent the entry of dirt.
20 Refitting is a reversal of removal. Use new gaskets and injector sealing rings. Check the throttle linkage adjustment on completion (Section 37).

84 Intake manifold (right-hand) – removal and refitting

1 Disconnect the battery, remove the air cleaner and depressurise the fuel system (Section 48).
2 Disconnect the fuel filter and bracket from the manifold ram tube.
3 Repeat paragraph 3 of Section 83.
4 Disconnect the manifold pressure hose from the manifold and T-piece.
5 Repeat paragraph 5 of Section 83.
6 On RHD cars, disconnect the leads from the kickdown switch and the throttle cable from the throttle pedestal.
7 Release the throttle crossrod from the bellcrank and disconnect the vacuum hoses from the induction manifold (photo).
8 Disconnect the vacuum hoses from the throttle housing and the air balance pipe from the rubber elbow.
9 Unclip the wiring harness from the fuel rail and disconnect the electrical leads from the fuel and cold start injectors.
10 Release the earth strap from the manifold ram tube.
11 Disconnect the brake servo vacuum hose from the non-return valve.
12 Disconnect the heater vacuum hose from the manifold stub.
13 Where fitted, disconnect the diverter valve vacuum hose from its manifold stub.
14 Disconnect the automatic transmission vacuum hose from its rigid pipe section.
15 Repeat the operations described in paragraphs 13 and 15 to 20 of Section 83 (photo).

85 Exhaust manifold (left-hand) – removal and refitting

1 Disconnect the battery.
2 Remove the air cleaner.
3 Remove the exhaust front pipe by disconnecting it from the manifold and intermediate pipe flanges. The nuts are accessible from underneath the car using a socket and long extension.
4 Still working under the car, unbolt and remove the heatshields to give access to the manifold lower nuts. Unscrew and remove these nuts and their washers.
5 Working within the engine compartment, unbolt and remove the manifold heatshields.
6 Unscrew and remove the manifold upper securing nuts.
7 Withdraw the front section of the exhaust manifold first, followed by the rear section.
8 Discard the gaskets and clean the mating flanges.
9 Refitting is a reversal of removal, use new gaskets.

86 Exhaust manifold (right-hand) – removal and refitting

1 The operations are very similar to those described for the left-hand manifold in the preceding Section except that in addition, the starter motor heatshield must be removed before the rear manifold can be removed (photo).

83.15 Induction manifold washers (1) and spacers (2)

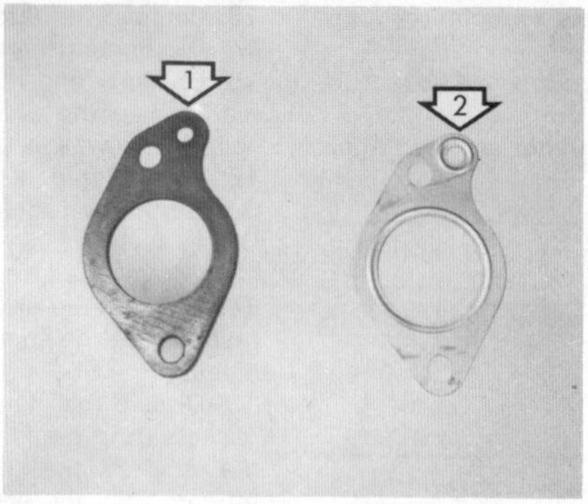

83.19 Induction manifold gaskets. 1 – Old type. 2 – New type

84.6 Vacuum hose connections to right-hand induction manifold

84.14 Tightening right-hand induction manifold nuts

86.1 Right-hand front exhaust manifold

87 Exhaust system – removal and refitting

1 Refer to Section 34 or 35.

88 Accelerator pedal and throttle linkage – removal and refitting accelerator pedal (XJS)

1 Extract the split pin and disconnect the cable from the pedal, after pulling off the sleeve.
2 Unbolt the pedal assembly from the bulkhead.
3 Remove the two circlips which secure the nylon bushes to the throttle pedal bracket. Turn the bushes through 45° and remove them. Remove the pedal from the bracket.

Throttle pedestal (all models)

4 Disconnect the throttle rods from the throttle pulley, then unscrew and remove the nut which holds the throttle cable to the pedestal bracket.
5 Rotate the pulley and release the throttle cable nipple.
6 Pull the multi-pin connector from the throttle switch.
7 Unscrew the nuts and lift the platform from the throttle pedestal.
8 Release the two screws and remove the switch operating rod from the throttle pulley.
9 Extract the circlip and remove the pulley from the platform.
10 Extract the bushes and remove and discard the return spring. Unscrew and remove the ballpins.

Throttle cable (XJS)

11 Release the cable from the accelerator pedal as previously described.
12 Unscrew the locknut and disconnect the cable from the pulley.
13 Disconnect the cable assembly from the bulkhead tube and then pull the cable through into the engine compartment. On RHD cars, the cable is secured to the bulkhead by a nut above the footwell on the driver's side.
14 Disconnect the leads from the kickdown switch.
15 Release the cable nipple from the pedestal and slacken the cable locknut at the pedestal bracket.
16 Remove the kickdown switch (two screws) from its mounting plate.

Accelerator pedal (XJ12 and Double Six)

17 Fold back the carpet and remove the pedal base nuts.
18 Withdraw the pedal and disconnect the retaining spring.

Throttle cable (XJ12 and Double Six)

19 Disconnect the battery and the kickdown switch plug.
20 Loosen the adjustment locknuts and the retaining locknut at the footwell, and detach the cable from the support bracket and pedestal.
21 Remove the operating rod split pin, disengage the sleeve and nipple, and withdraw the cable into the engine compartment after removing the nut from the sheath.

Refitting (all components)

22 Refitting of all components is a reversal of removal, but lubricate all pivots and bushes. Seal round the footwell locknut with mastic.
23 On completion, check the throttle linkage adjustment as described in Section 37.

89 Cruise control system – description

1 This device is optionally available on Series 3 models.
2 Its purpose is to maintain a set roadspeed with the foot released from the accelerator pedal. This is a most useful facility for long distance travel.
3 Immediate reversion to normal control is obtained once the brake

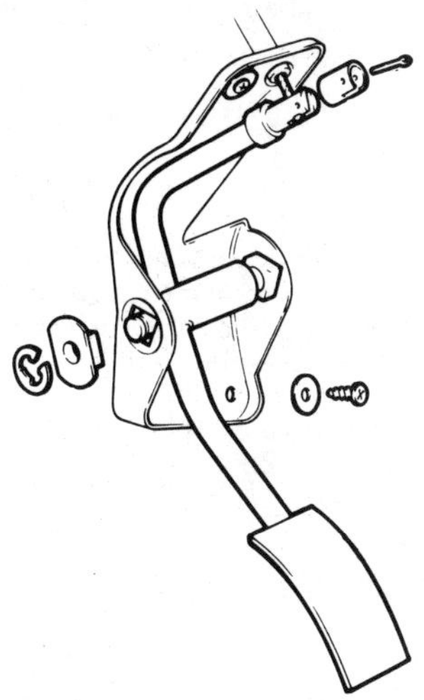

Fig. 3.85 Throttle pedal (LHD) (Sec 88)

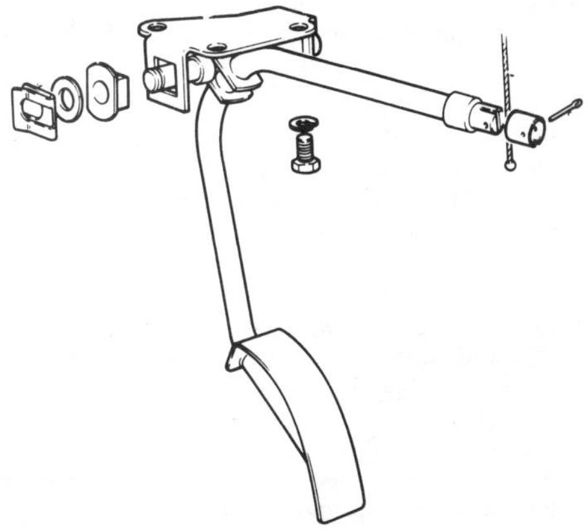

Fig. 3.86 Throttle pedal (RHD) (Sec 88)

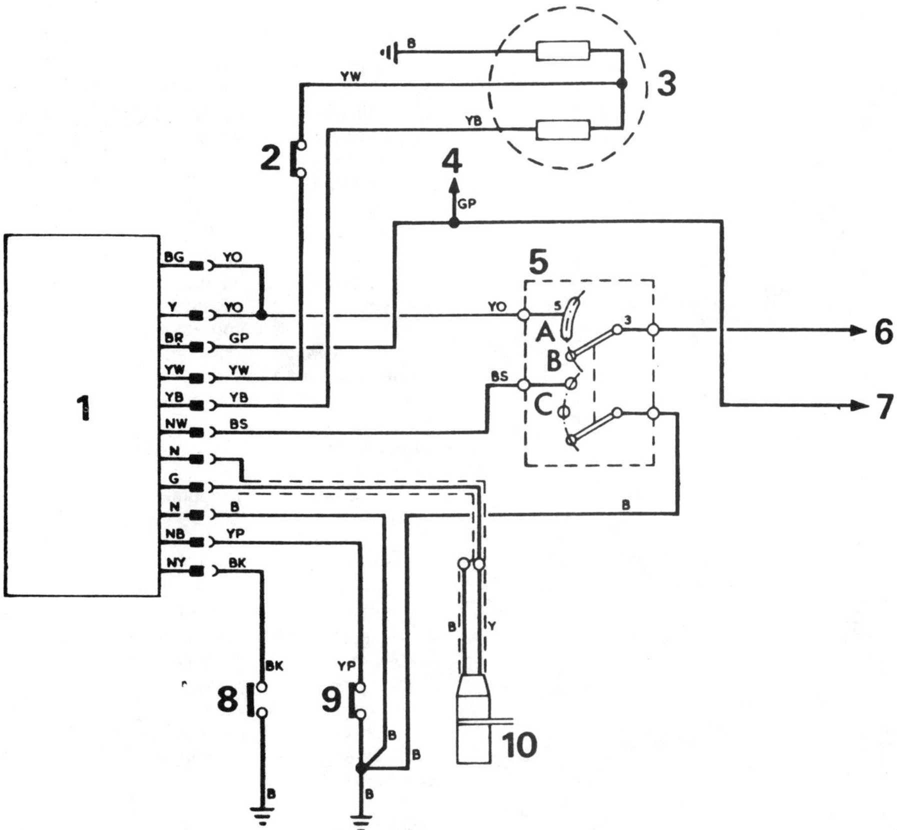

Fig. 3.87 Cruise control system wiring diagram (Sec 89)

1 Speed control switch
2 Brake operated switch
3 Actuator
4 Stoplamp bulb failure unit
5 Control switch:
A On
B Off
C Resume
6 Fuse No 12
7 Stoplamp switch
8 Set switch
9 Inhibit switch
10 Magnetic pick-up

pedal is operated and an inhibitor switch is incorporated to prevent the engine overrevving if the speed selector lever is moved to neutral while the cruise control system is operating.

4 The main components of the system include the following:

Control switch

5 This controls the system engagement and disengagement. Once actuated, the switch can be moved to the 'resume' position to actuate the ECU memory when the previously set roadspeed can be regained after an interruption due to braking or temporary change of speed.

Magnetic pick-up

6 This is located on the rear axle next to the propeller shaft flange. It consists of a magnetic signal unit which indicates to the ECU the roadspeed calculated from the rotational speed of the flange.

Set switch

7 This switch triggers the ECU to bring the cruise control system into operation.

Speed control unit

8 This is an electronic unit controlling the operation of the system. It operates solenoids which vary the vacuum used to open and close the throttle as necessary to maintain the preset roadspeed. 'Resume' and 'Off' modes are incorporated and the actuating vacuum is destroyed immediately the brake pedal is touched causing the throttle to close. The control unit also includes a circuit to prevent actuation of the system below 20 mph (32 kph).

90 Fault diagnosis – fuel injection system

Symptom	Reason(s)
Engine will not start when warm	Fuel tank(s) empty Clogged fuel filter Faulty fuel pump Faulty pressure regulator ECU connector loose Faulty auxiliary air valve Faulty cold start system Sticking throttle butterfly valves Faulty temperature sensor
Rough idle (cold engine)	Clogged fuel filter Faulty fuel filter Loose system electrical connections Sticking throttle butterfly valves Incorrect CO level (mixture) Blocked or leaking exhaust Unequal cylinder compressions Air leak at induction manifold Faulty auxiliary air valve Engine oil filler cap loose or poor seal Faulty ECU or throttle switch Choked carbon canister Faulty fuel injectors Faulty temperature sensors
Flat spot (hesitation)	Clogged fuel filter Faulty fuel pump Faulty pressure regulator Faulty throttle switch or ECU Loose system electrical connections Incorrectly adjusted throttle butterfly Sticking throttle butterfly Faulty auxiliary air valve Blocked or leaking exhaust system Air leak at induction manifold Blocked charcoal canister
Excessive fuel consumption	General leaks Faulty throttle switch or ECU Faulty cold start system Air leak at induction manifold Blocked exhaust system Engine oil filler cap loose or poor seal Charcoal canister blocked Faulty fuel injectors or pressure sensor Faulty temperature sensors
High idle speed and lack of engine braking	Air leak in induction manifold Sticking throttle butterfly Faulty auxiliary air valve Incorrect CO level (mixture) Leaks around throttle butterfly spindle Faulty overrun valve

Symptom	Reason(s)
Engine stalls at idling speed	Leaks in fuel system Clogged fuel filter Faulty pressure regulator Faulty fuel pump Loose electrical connections Faulty temperature sensors Faulty cold start system Clogged air cleaner element Sticking throttle butterfly Blocked or leaking exhaust Air leak in induction manifold Incorrect CO lever (mixture) Engine oil filler cap loose or poor seal Faulty ECU Charcoal canister blocked
Running on or pre-ignition (pinking)	Incorrect fuel grade Blocked hoses on crankcase or fuel vent systems Leaking cylinder head gasket Incorrect idle speed Engine overheating due to cooling system fault Over-advanced ignition
Backfire in exhaust	Fuel starvation due to faulty fuel pump, pressure regulator or blocked fuel filter Loose electrical connections Blocked air cleaner element Blocked or leaking exhaust Air leak in induction manifold Loose engine oil filler cap or poor seal Faulty diverter valve

91 Fault diagnosis – fuel injection emission control system

Symptom	Reason(s)
Fault in air injection system	Slack pump drivebelt Perforated or loose connecting hoses Choked air pump filter element
Fault in EGR system	Choked inlet drilling or restrictor
High CO content in exhaust gas	Faulty air temperatre control in air cleaner Choked engine breather filter Faulty system switch or valve (refer to testing procedure in text)

Chapter 4 Ignition system

Contents

Specifications

Ignition system type	Lucas OPUS contactless electronic

Distributor

Make and type	Lucas OPUS 36DE12
Rotor rotation (viewed from above)	Anti-clockwise
Pick-up module to timing rotor gap	0.020 to 0.022 in (0.50 to 0.55 mm)
Firing order	1A-6B-5A-2B-3A-4B-6A-1B-2A-5B-4A-3B

(A = right-hand bank, B = left-hand bank, No 1 cylinders at timing chain end)

Ignition timing

Australia and California (vacuum pipe connected, 1977/78)	4° ATDC @ 750 rpm
Sweden (vacuum pipe disconnected)	0° BTDC static or up to 750 rpm
All others (vacuum pipe disconnected)	10° BTDC static or up to 750 rpm
Centrifugal advance (vacuum pipe disconnected, crankshaft degrees and rpm)	No advance below 900rpm 22° to 26° @ 2000 rpm 29° to 33° @ 4000 rpm 34° to 38° @ 6200 rpm
Vacuum advance or retard (crankshaft degrees):	
UK models (typical)	Maximum 8° advance at 10 in (254 mm) Hg No advance below 6 in (152 mm) Hg
N American models (typical)	Maximum 18° retard with rising vacuum from 7 in to 10 in (178 mm to 254 mm) Hg. No retard below 1 in (25.4 mm) Hg

Ignition coil

Make and type	Lucas 13C12 or 22C12*
Primary resistance @ 20°C (68°F)	0.9 to 1.1 ohms
Ballast resistance	0.9 to 1.0 ohms

** From engine No 7P8169 special 'High Load' coil and amplifier fitted. 'High Load' coil must not be fitted with earlier amplifier*

Spark plugs

Type	Champion N10Y or equivalent
Electrode gap:	
All models up to 1977 (except N America)	0.025 in (0.64 mm)
N America (all models) and all models 1978 on	0.035 in (0.89 mm)

1 General description and maintenance

1 An electronic ignition system is fitted to all models. The main components include the distributor, an amplifer unit, ballast resistor and ignition coil.
2 The timing rotor and pick-up module, working in conjunction with the amplifier unit, are substitutes for the mechanical contact breaker on conventional distributors.
3 The timing rotor is a nylon disc with ferrite rods embedded in its outer edge corresponding with the number of cylinders.
4 The pick-up module is really a small transformer with input and output windings.
5 The timing rotor and pick-up coil generate a signal which is fed to the amplifier unit. The amplifier unit interprets the signal and feeds it to a power transistor in the printed circuit which functions as a switch in the ignition coil primary circuit.
6 A ballast resistor unit is wired in series with the ignition coil primary winding and is also associated with a function of one transistor in the amplifier unit.
7 When the engine is stationary, the timing rotor is in such a position that none of the ferrite rods are in alignment with the core of the pick-up module. Once the ignition is switched on, a transformer in the amplifier unit becomes conductive and the coil primary circuit is completed through electrodes of the power transistor. At the same time, a pulsating ac voltage is applied by the amplifier unit to the primary windings of the pick-up module. A small residual ac voltage is produced at the pick-up secondary windings, although at this time the pick-up is magnetically balanced. This voltage at the pick-up secondary terminals is applied to the amplifier unit, but is insufficient to affect the transistor circuits which control the switching off of the power transistor in the output stage of the amplifier unit.
8 Once the engine is cranked, one of the ferrite rods in the rotor which is in close proximity with the ferrite core of the pick-up module creates magnetic unbalance in the module core, so increasing the voltage at the module output terminals.
9 This voltage is then applied to the amplifier unit where it is rectified. The resulting direct current operates the transistor circuits which control the switching off of the power transistor in the output stage.
10 With the power transistor switched off, its electrodes no longer conduct and the ignition coil primary winding is disconnected. This causes a collapse of the primary winding magnetic field through the secondary windings of the ignition coil and as a result, high tension (HT) voltage is supplied at the HT terminal on the ignition coil.
11 On cars equipped with a fuel injection system, the distributor incorporates a trigger unit (refer to Chapter 3, Part B).
12 On cars equipped with a full emission control system, an additional ignition retard facility is built into the system (refer to Chapter 3, Section 21).
13 Routine maintenance has been virtually eliminated with this type of ignition system which does not have the conventional mechanical contact breaker. However, all connections should be checked, as should the ignition timing, at the intervals recommended in Routine Maintenance.

2 Distributor cap – removal and refitting

1 Check that the leads to the sparking plugs have a numbered sleeve on each of them. (A) denotes a lead running to the right-hand cylinder bank and (B) a lead to the left-hand cylinder bank (when viewed from the rear of the car).
2 Disconnect the leads from the spark plugs.
3 Disconnect the HT lead from the ignition coil.
4 Unscrew the three captive screws which hold the distributor cap and remove it.
5 With the cap removed, wipe the inside with a clean rag and check that the centre carbon brush is in good condition and moves freely on its spring.
6 Refit by reversing the removal operations.

3 Rotor arm and timing rotor – removal and refitting

1 Detach the distributor cap as described in the preceding Section and lay it to one side.
2 Pull off the rotor arm (photo).
3 On fuel injection models, withdraw the trigger unit (photo).
4 Extract the circlip and wave washer and withdraw the timing rotor (photo).
5 Refitting is a reversal of removal, but apply two or three drops of engine oil to the pad on top of the distributor shaft before pushing on the rotor arm. Make sure that the rotor arm is pressed fully home into its keyway.

4 Pick-up module – removal and refitting

1 Carry out the operations described in paragraphs 1 to 4 of the preceding Section.
2 Extract the two screws which hold the pick-up module to the pick-up arm.
3 Prise the cable grommet inwards out of its hole in the distributor body. Feed the cable through the hole and then remove the pick-up module.
4 To refit, pass the cable through the hole in the distributor body and fit the grommet.

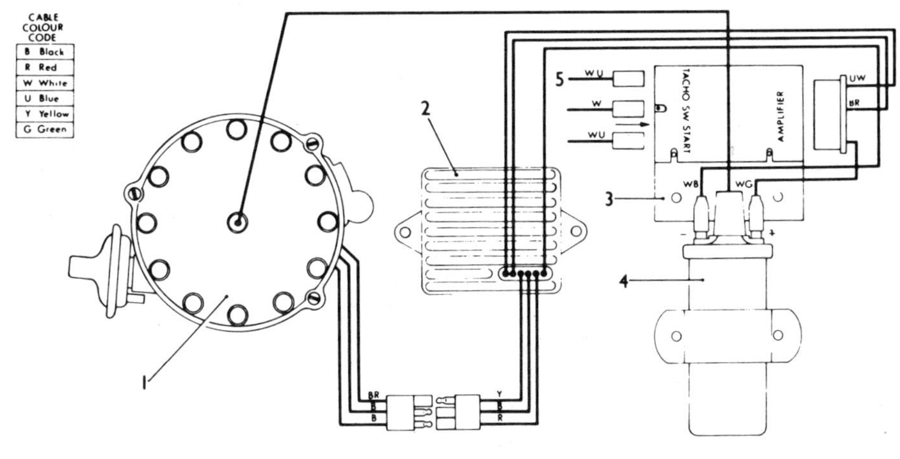

Fig. 4.1 Main components of the electronic ignition system (Sec 1)

1 Distributor
2 Amplifier unit
3 Ballast resistor
4 Ignition coil
5 Lead to tachometer

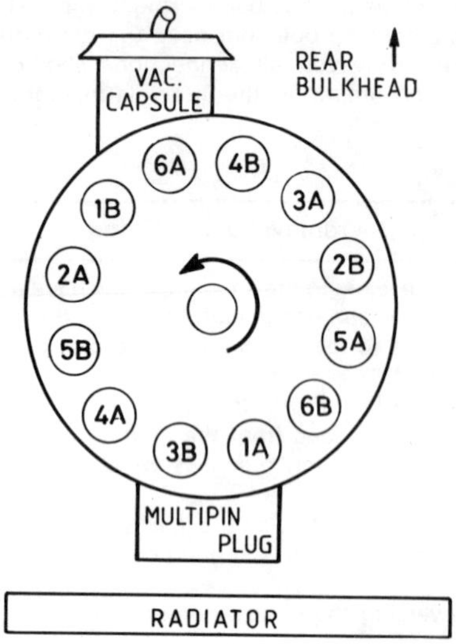

Fig. 4.2 Distributor cap spark plug HT lead connections (Sec 2)

A = right-hand cylinder bank
B = left-hand cylinder bank
Spark plugs numbered from front of engine

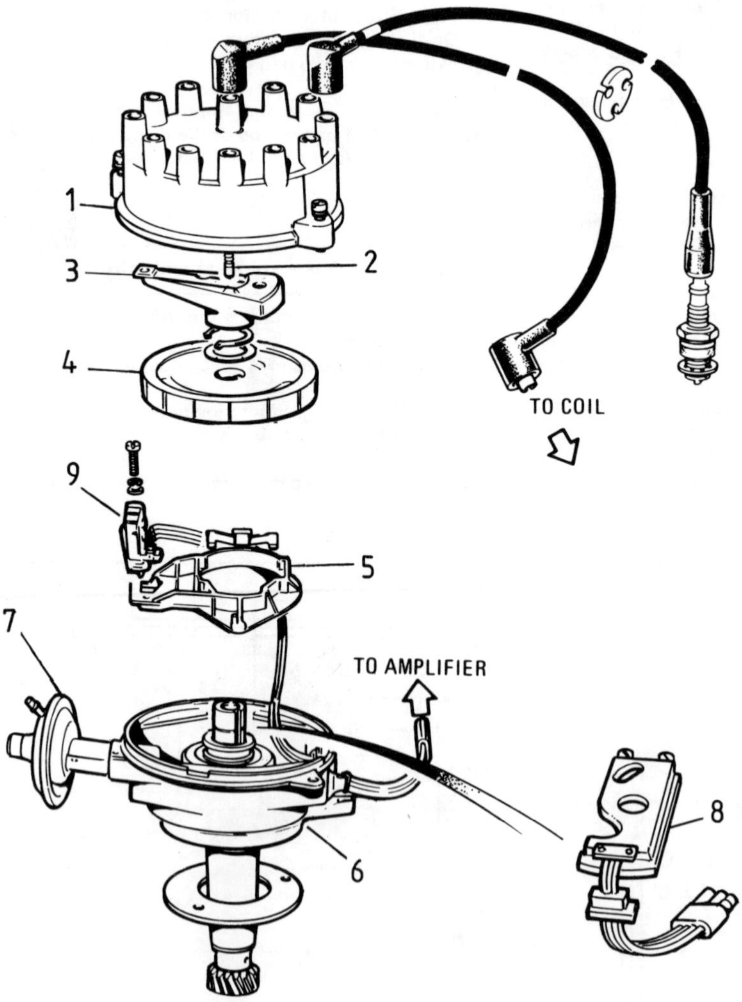

Fig. 4.3 Main components of the distributor (Sec 3)

1 Cap
2 Carbon brush
3 Rotor arm
4 Electronic timing rotor
5 Pick-up arm
6 Distributor body
7 Vacuum unit
8 Trigger unit
9 Pick-up module

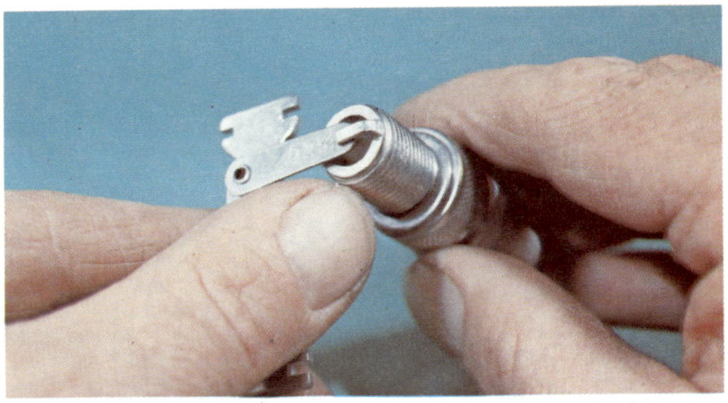

Measuring plug gap. A feeler gauge of the correct size (see ignition system specifications) should have a slight 'drag' when slid between the electrodes. Adjust gap if necessary

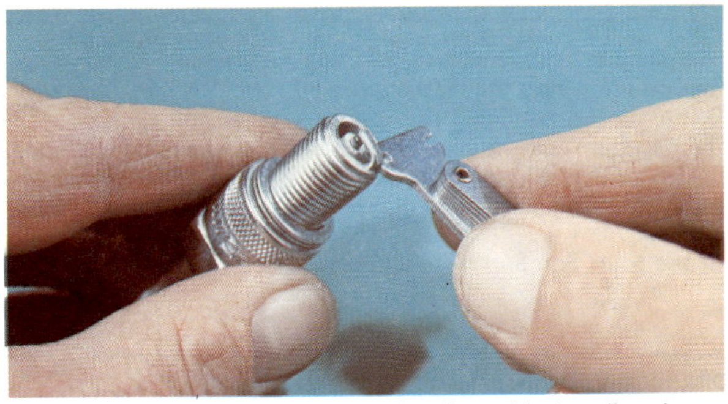

Adjusting plug gap. The plug gap is adjusted by bending the earth electrode inwards, or outwards, as necessary until the correct clearance is obtained. Note the use of the correct tool

Normal. Grey-brown deposits, lightly coated core nose. Gap increasing by around 0.001 in (0.025 mm) per 1000 miles (1600 km). Plugs ideally suited to engine, and engine in good condition

Carbon fouling. Dry, black, sooty deposits. Will cause weak spark and eventually misfire. Fault: over-rich fuel mixture. Check: carburettor mixture settings, float level and jet sizes; choke operation and cleanliness of air filter. Plugs can be re-used after cleaning

Oil fouling. Wet, oily deposits. Will cause weak spark and eventually misfire. Fault: worn bores/piston rings or valve guides; sometimes occurs (temporarily) during running-in period. Plugs can be re-used after thorough cleaning

Overheating. Electrodes have glazed appearance, core nose very white – few deposits. Fault: plug overheating. Check: plug value, ignition timing, fuel octane rating (too low) and fuel mixture (too weak). Discard plugs and cure fault immediately

Electrode damage. Electrodes burned away; core nose has burned, glazed appearance. Fault: pre-ignition. Check: as for 'Overheating' but may be more severe. Discard plugs and remedy fault before piston or valve damage occurs

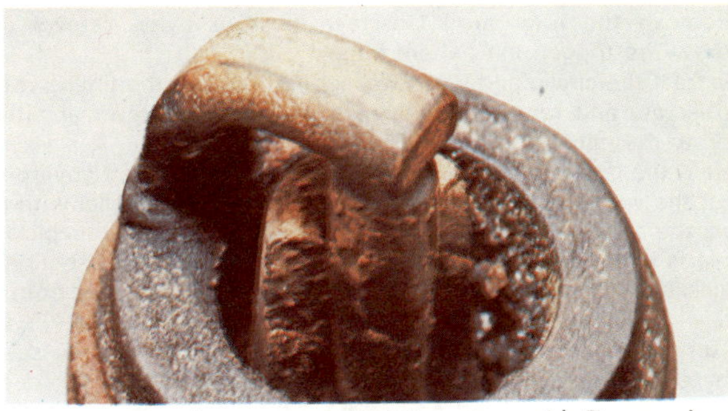

Split core nose (may appear initially as a crack). Damage is self-evident, but cracks will only show after cleaning. Fault: pre-ignition or wrong gap-setting technique. Check: ignition timing, cooling system, fuel octane rating (too low) and fuel mixture (too weak). Discard plugs, rectify fault immediately

5 The pick-up module should be fitted to the pick-up arm loosely with the core towards the distributor shaft.
6 Fit the electronic timing rotor, wave washer and circlip.
7 The gap between the pick-up module core faces and the edge of the electronic timing rotor must now be set. Use feeler blades to do this and when the gap is within the specified limits, tighten the module securing screws.
8 Fit the rotor arm and distributor cap.

5 Distributor – removal and refitting

1 Detach the distributor cover and lay it to one side.
2 Rotate the crankshaft until No 1 cylinder mark on the electronic timing rotor is in alignment with the mark on the pick-up module. The 'A' and 10° BTDC crankshaft timing marks should now be in alignment.
3 Disconnect the wiring to the distributor at the multi-pin plug.
4 Disconnect the vacuum pipe from the distributor.
5 Using an Allen key, insert it through the slots in the distributor electronic timing rotor and release the socket-headed screws. The distributor will have to be lifted at the same time as the screws are turned in order to fully release them (photo).
6 As soon as the screws are free, lift the distributor directly upward from the engine without restricting the rotation of the timing rotor with the fingers (photo).
7 Observe the timing mark on the periphery of the timing rotor and mark its position in relation to the distributor body. This work assumes that the timing rotor has not been moved from its 'withdrawn' setting.
8 Provided the position of the crankshaft has not been altered while the distributor has been out of the engine, then refitting can be carried out in the following way.
9 Hold the distributor over its hole in the jackshaft cover plate with the peripheral mark on the timing rotor in alignment with the distributor body mark made at removal. The distributor vacuum unit must be towards the rear of the engine and the timing mark on the pick-up module in alignment with the raised rib on the rear part of the jackshaft cover.
10 Without restricting the rotation of the timing rotor with the fingers, push the distributor directly downward, at the same time screwing in the three socket-headed screws evenly, so drawing the distributor gear into mesh with the one on the jackshaft. As the gears mesh, the timing rotor will turn (approximately 15°) and its peripheral mark will align with the one on the pick-up module.
11 If the crankshaft has been turned while the distributor has been out of the car, then re-position it by turning it until No 1 piston at the front end of the right-hand cylinder bank is rising on its compression stroke (verified by removing the spark plug and holding the finger over the hole), then continue to turn until the 'A' mark on the crankshaft damper is aligned with the 10° BTDC mark on the timing scale. Refit the distributor as previously described.
12 If a new distributor is being installed, or if the relative position of the mark on the timing rotor to the distributor body was not marked at time of removal, use the following method to fit the distributor. Set the crankshaft as previously described.
13 Remove the rotor arm. Unscrew the four nylon screws and withdraw the trigger unit (where fitted).
14 Extract the circlip and wave washer and remove the timing rotor.
15 Unscrew and remove the three spring-loaded screws and then withdraw the micro housing.
16 Hold the distributor body over its hole in the jackshaft coverplate so that the vernier adjuster projection on the body is parallel with the rib on the jackshaft cover on its forward section and the pick-up module is in alignment with the raised rib on the rearward section of the jackshaft cover plate. Temporarily push the timing rotor onto its shaft.
17 Turn the distributor timing rotor until the peripheral mark is 15° out of alignment with the mark on the pick-up module. Insert the distributor into its hole and as the gears mesh, the timing rotor will rotate to bring its mark into alignment with the one on the pick-up module. Insert and tighten the socket screws. Refit the micro housing but do not overtighten the spring-loaded screws (photos).
18 Refit the remaining components.
19 After installation of the distributor, always check the ignition timing as described in Section 7.

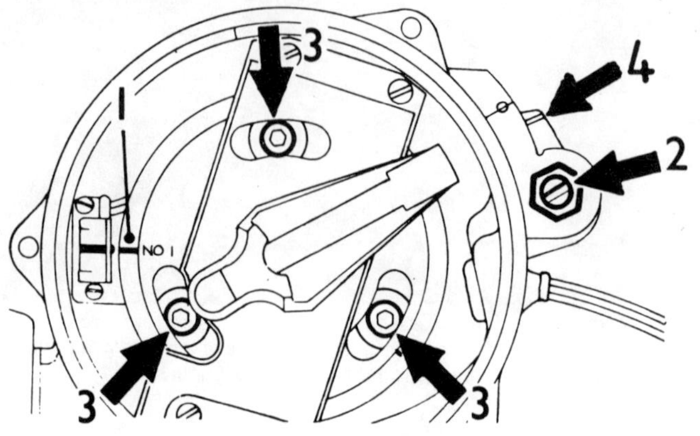

Fig. 4.4 Distributor securing screws (3) arrowed (Sec 5)

1 Pick-up to timing rotor alignment marks
2 Vernier adjuster
4 Vernier scale

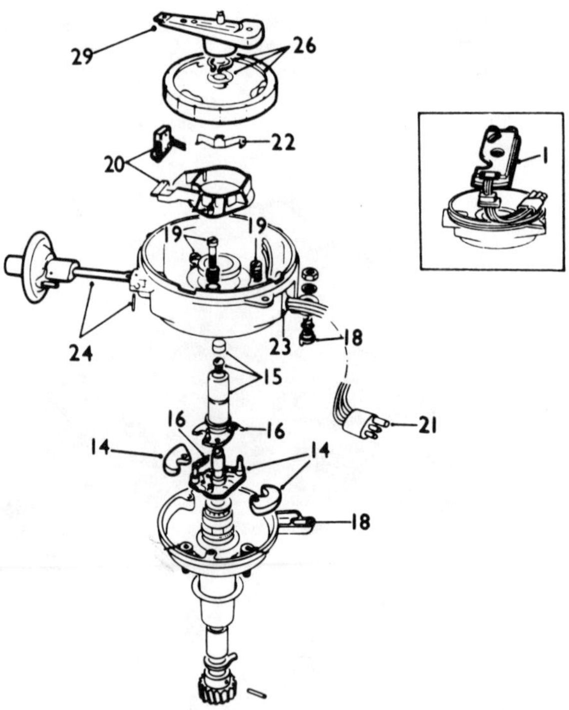

Fig. 4.5 Exploded view of distributor (Sec 6)

1 Trigger unit located above electronic timing rotor (fuel injection models)
14 Counterweight
15 Shaft, screw and felt lubrication pad
16 Counterweight retaining springs
18 Micro housing and eccentric peg
19 Securing screws
20 Pick-up module and arm
21 Harness multi-pin plug
22 Bearing spring
23 Cable grommet
24 Vacuum unit and roll pin
26 Electronic timing rotor, wave washer and circlip
29 Rotor arm

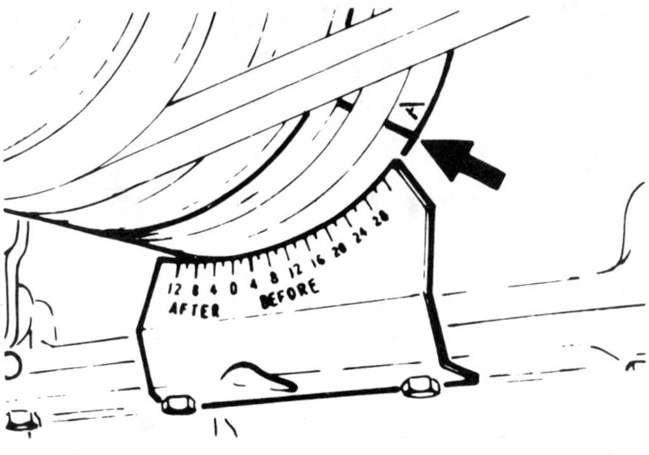

Fig. 4.6 Ignition timing scale and (arrowed) crankshaft timing mark (Sec 7)

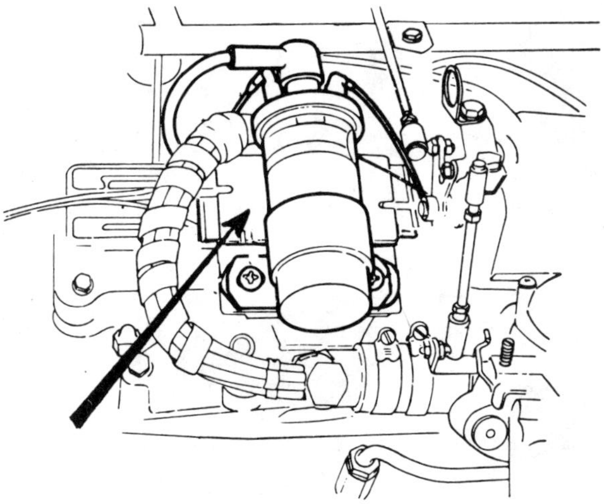

Fig. 4.7 Ignition coil mounting (carburettor engine) and ballast resistor (arrowed) (Sec 9)

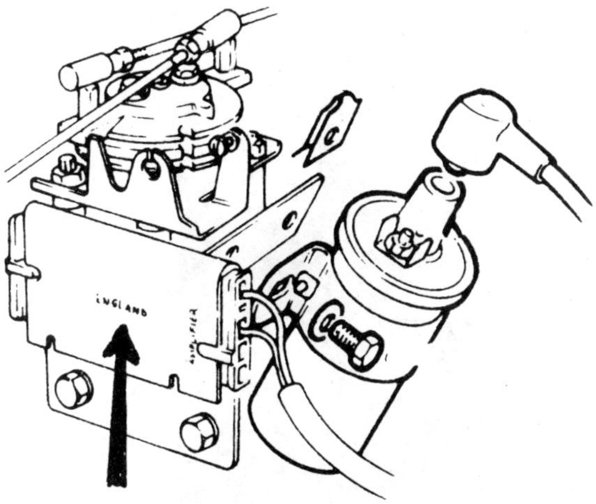

Fig. 4.8 Ignition coil mounting (fuel injection engine) and ballast resistor (arrowed) (Sec 10)

6 Distributor – overhaul

1 With the distributor removed from the car as previously described, clean away external dirt.
2 Remove the rotor arm.
3 On fuel injection models, remove the trigger unit.
4 Remove the electronic timing rotor.
5 Lift the vacuum operating rod from its peg on the pick-up arm (photo).
6 Prise the wiring grommet from the distributor body.
7 Remove the pick-up arm bearing spring, then slide the pick-up arm sideways to disengage it from its bearing. Lift the arm from the micro housing, drawing the wiring through the hole in the distributor body.
8 Detach the pick-up module.
9 Use a suitable punch to drive out the roll pin which secures the vacuum unit in the micro housing. Withdraw the vacuum unit.
10 Extract the three spring-loaded screws and lift the micro housing from the distributor body.
11 Prise the felt lubricating pad from the top of the distributor shaft and release the screw which is exposed.
12 Release the control springs from their fixing posts.
13 Lift the rotor carrier shaft from the distributor shaft and retrieve the centrifugal advance weights.
14 Inspect all components for wear. If the shaft or distributor body bushes are worn, a complete new distributor must be fitted.
15 Reassembly is a reversal of dismantling. Apply grease to the rotor carrier pivot posts before assembling the weights and smear the advance mechanism generally with grease.
16 When fitting the micro housing, make sure that the adjustment eccentric peg engages in its slot. Make sure also that the micro housing screws are really tight.
17 Adjust the pick-up module core gap as described in Section 4.

7 Ignition timing

1 Remove the distributor cap and rotor.
2 Rotate the crankshaft until the No 1 cylinder timing mark on the electronic timing rotor is about 0.25 in (6 mm) from the centre of the pick-up module housing (approaching in an anti-clockwise direction).
3 Slowly turn the crankshaft damper bolt until the timing mark on the damper is in alignment with the specified static mark on the timing scale (photo).
4 Release the adjuster screw locknut and turn the screw until the timing mark on the rotor is exactly opposite the centre of the pick-up module housing (photo). If there is insufficient adjustment the distributor must be repositioned after loosening the retaining screws as described in paragraph 7.
5 Tighten the vernier adjuster screw locknut and refit the distributor cap and rotor.
6 With the engine now started and brought to normal operating temperature, the ignition timing should be checked using a stroboscope connected in accordance with the maker's instructions.
7 Disconnect the vacuum pipe from the distributor vacuum unit if necessary – see Specifications and have the idling speed set to between 600 and 750 rpm on XJS models, 500 and 600 rpm on XJ12 and Double Six models. When the light is pointed at the specified timing scale/damper marks, they should appear stationary and in alignment. If they are not in alignment, then the distributor will have to be turned one way or the other to correct the timing by bringing them into alignment. This is achieved by using the vernier adjuster screw. If the timing is so badly out that the vernier does not provide sufficient adjustment, then the distributor cap will have to be removed and the socket-headed distributor screws released by pressing an Allen key through the slots in the timing rotor. Where this is necessary, make sure that with the ignition timing correctly set, the vernier adjuster is left in its central position. This will provide more scope for adjustment by means of the vernier on future occasions. Retighten the distributor securing screws.
8 Reconnect the distributor vacuum pipe if it was disconnected.
9 Readjust the idling speed where necessary (see Chapter 3).

8 Amplifier unit – removal and refitting

1 Disconnect the battery.

3.2 Distributor rotor arm (1), fuel injection trigger unit (2) and timing rotor (3)

3.3 Extracting a trigger unit securing screw

3.4 Timing rotor showing circlip

5.5 Releasing the distributor securing screws

5.6 Distributor removed, showing securing screws

5.17A Distributor body and securing screws

5.17B Micro housing spring loaded screws

6.5 Vacuum unit operating rod

7.3 Ignition timing marks set to 10° BTDC

7.4 Distributor vernier adjuster screw

10.2 Ignition coil is at the rear of the throttle pedestal. Ballast resistor is arrowed

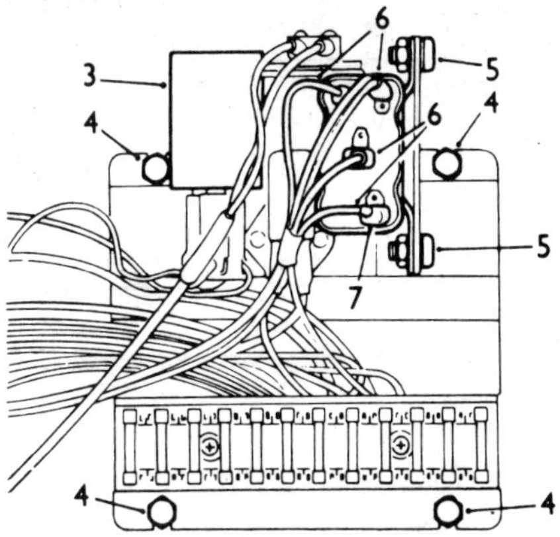

Fig. 4.9 Ignition protection relay (XJ12, Double Six) (Sec 11)

3 Flasher unit
4 Fuse block mounting screws
5 Relay mounting bolts to bracket
6 Connecting leads
7 Connecting leads

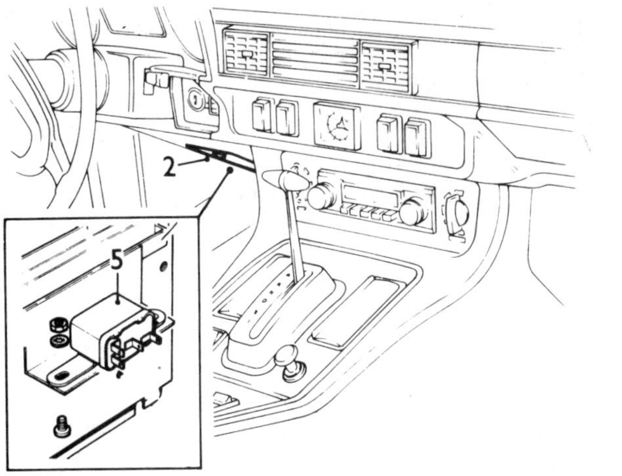

Fig. 4.10 Ignition/starter controlled relay (XJS) (Sec 12)

2 Cover to fuse block
5 Relay

2 Disconnect the wiring plug from the ballast resistor.
3 Disconnect the plug from the distributor/amplifier line.
4 Unscrew and remove the amplifier mounting screws and lift the unit from the top surface of the jackshaft cover plate on the engine.
5 It should be noted that commencing with engine number 7P8169, a revised type of coil and amplifier were fitted. If one component is being renewed, a late type amplifier is compatible with an early type coil, but if a new coil is being fitted then an old type amplifier will have to be renewed as well.
6 A fitting kit will be required for the later type amplifier which is mounted at 180° to the earlier type.
7 These later type components are identified by a label marked 'High Load'.

9 Ignition coil (carburettor engines) – removal and refitting

1 Disconnect the battery and the leads from the coil.
2 Unscrew and remove the two setscrews and lift the coil from its mounting bracket. Retrieve the ballast resistor distance pieces.
3 If a new coil is being fitted, refer to Section 8, paragraphs 5 to 7.
4 The ballast resistor can be removed from its location adjacent to the coil after extracting the mounting screws and disconnecting the wiring plugs.
5 Refitting is a reversal of removal.

10 Ignition coil (fuel injection engines) – removal and refitting

1 Disconnect the battery and the leads from the coil.
2 Unbolt the coil from the throttle pedestal (photo).
3 If the ballast resistor is to be removed from its location at the side of the coil, disconnect the electrical plugs from it, also the No 5 fuel injector lead for better access.
4 Disconnect the throttle rod at the bellcrank on the induction manifold and swing it to one side.
5 Extract the mounting screws and remove the resistor.
6 Refitting is a reversal of removal.

11 Ignition protection relay (XJ12, Double Six) – removal and refitting

1 Disconnect the battery and remove the under scuttle casing from the driver's side.
2 Remove the direction indicator/hazard warning flasher unit from the connector block.
3 Unscrew the four fuse box mounting nuts and ease the box down as far as it will go.
4 Unbolt the ignition protection relay from the mounting bracket, identify the cables and disconnect them.
5 Refitting is a reversal of removal.

12 Ignition/starter controlled relay (XJS) – removal and refitting

1 Disconnect the battery and remove the access cover from the fuse block on the driver's side under scuttle casing (see Chapter 12).
2 Remove the relay from its bracket above the fuse block, identify the leads and disconnect them.
3 Refitting is a reversal of removal.

13 Spark plugs and leads

1 The correct functioning of the spark plugs is vital for the correct running and efficiency of the engine. The plugs fitted as standard are listed on the Specifications page.
2 At intervals of 6000 miles (9600 km) the plugs should be removed, examined and cleaned. If worn excessively, renew the plugs at 12 000 miles (19 300 km). The condition of the spark plug will also tell much about the overall condition of the engine.
3 If the insulator nose of the spark plug is clean and white, with no deposits, this is indicative of a weak mixture, or too hot a plug. (A hot plug transfers heat away from the electrode slowly – a cold plug transfers it away quickly).
4 If the top and insulator nose is covered with hard black looking deposits, then this is indicative that the mixture is too rich. Should the plug be black and oily, then it is likely that the engine is fairly worn, as well as the mixture being too rich.
5 If the insulator nose is covered with light tan to greyish brown deposits, then the mixture is correct and it is likely that the engine is in good condition.
6 If there are any traces of long brown tapering stains on the outside of the white portion of the plug, then the plug will have to be renewed, as this shows that there is a faulty joint between the plug body and the insulator, and compression is being allowed to leak away.
7 Plugs should be cleaned by a sand blasting machine, which will free them from carbon more thoroughly than cleaning by hand. The machine will also test the condition of the plugs under compression. Any plug that fails to spark at the recommended pressure should be renewed.
8 The spark plug gap is of considerable importance, as, if it is too large or too small the size of the spark and its efficiency will be seriously impaired. The spark plug gap is given in the Specifications.
9 To set it, measure the gap with a feeler gauge, and then bend open, or close, the outer plug electrode until the correct gap is achieved. The centre electrode should never be bent as this may crack the insulation and cause plug failure, if nothing worse.

10 When refitting the plugs, remember to use new plug washers and refit the leads from the distributor in the correct firing order.

11 The plug leads require no attention other than being kept clean and wiped over regularly.

14 Ignition switch – removal and refitting

1 Refer to Chapter 11 where this is dealt with in conjunction with removal and refitting of the steering column lock.

15 Fault diagnosis – ignition system

Symptom	Reason(s)
Engine fails to start	Discharged battery Loose battery connections Disconnected leads Damp leads or distributor cap Cracked distributor cap
Engine misfires	Faulty spark plug Cracked distributor cap Cracked rotor Worn advance mechanism Incorrect spark plug gap Faulty coil Incorrect timing Poor earth connections Incorrect pick-up module core face to timing rotor gap
Engine overheats or lacks power	Seized centrifugal weights Leaking distributor vacuum pipe Incorrect ignition timing
Engine 'pinks'	Timing too far advanced Advance mechanism stuck in advance position Broken centrifugal weight spring Incorrect fuel octane rating

Chapter 5 Clutch

Contents

Specifications

Type ... Borg and Beck, single dry plate with diaphragm spring, hydraulically actuated

Driven plate diameter ... 10.5 in (266.7 mm)

Release bearing type ... Carbon thrust

Torque wrench settings

	lbf ft	Nm
Bellhousing bolts	44	60
Slave cylinder mounting bolts	25	34
Master cylinder to pedal box	12	16
Clutch cover bolts	25	34

1 General description

1 The clutch which is fitted in conjunction with the optional manual gearbox (XJS models only) is of single dry plate type and incorporates a diaphragm spring.
2 Actuation is hydraulic and the release bearing is of the carbon thrust type.

2 Clutch – adjustment

1 At the intervals specified in Routine Maintenance, check the clutch adjustment.
2 To do this, raise the car on ramps or place it over a pit and detach the return spring at the clutch slave cylinder.
3 Now check the total free movement of the slave cylinder pushrod by pushing the rod backwards and forwards. The correct free movement is 0.0625 in (15 mm).
4 If adjustment is required, fit an open-ended spanner to the flats on the pushrod and release the locknut.
5 Screw the push rod in or out as required and then retighten the locknut and reconnect the return spring.

3 Master cylinder – removal, overhaul and refitting

1 Remove the pedal box. To do this, first unbolt the wing stay from the engine compartment rear bulkhead on the pedal box side and swing it clear.
2 Disconnect the vacuum pipe from the brake servo unit.
3 Unbolt (but do not disconnect the fluid lines) the brake master cylinder from the servo unit.
4 On right-hand drive cars only, release the throttle cable from the throttle pedestal.
5 Unbolt the brake fluid reservoir from its mounting bracket and rest the reservoir on top of the engine.
6 Disconnect the hydraulic pipe from the clutch master cylinder. Plug the openings.
7 Release the nuts on the brake fluid reservoir bracket and swing it upwards from the pedal box.
8 Unscrew and remove the four nuts which hold the pedal box to the bulkhead.
9 Carefully ease the brake master cylinder from its mounting studs to clear the servo unit.
10 Withdraw the pedal box, complete with brake servo unit and clutch master cylinder, clear of the car.
11 Disconnect the return spring from the clutch pedal.
12 Extract the pushrod to pedal split pin, washer and clevis pin.
13 Unbolt the clutch master cylinder from the pedal box.
14 On right-hand drive cars, before the master cylinder can be completely withdrawn, the fluid reservoir bracket will have to be removed. When withdrawing the master cylinder, note the location of any mounting shims.
15 Drain the fluid from the fluid reservoir.
16 Clean away all external dirt and pull off the rubber dust-excluding boot.
17 Depress the pushrod sufficiently to be able to extract the circlip and then withdraw the piston/seal assembly with spring.
18 Note which way round the seal lips are fitted and then discard the seals.

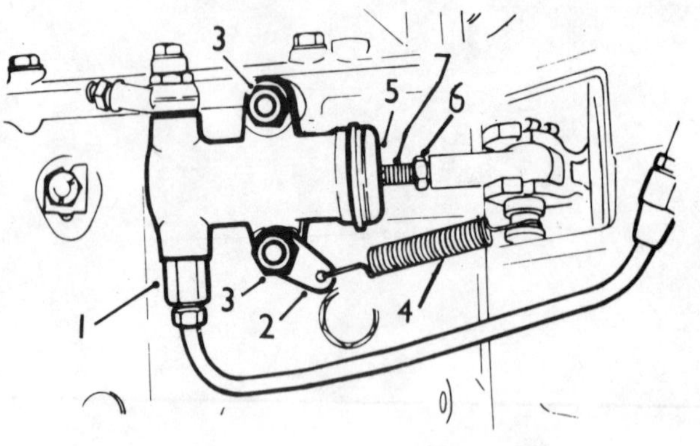

Fig. 5.1 Clutch slave cylinder (Sec 2 and 4)

1 *Fluid inlet union*
2 *Spring anchor plate*
3 *Cylinder mounting nut*
4 *Return spring*
5 *Rubber boot*
6 *Locknut*
7 *Pushrod*

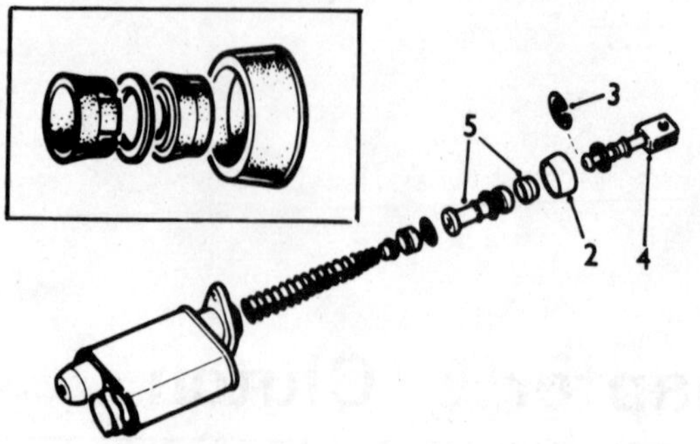

Fig. 5.2 Exploded view of the clutch master cylinder (Sec 3)

2 *Boot*
3 *Circlip*
4 *Pushrod and clevis fork*
5 *Secondary cup seal and piston*

Insert shows direction of seal fitting

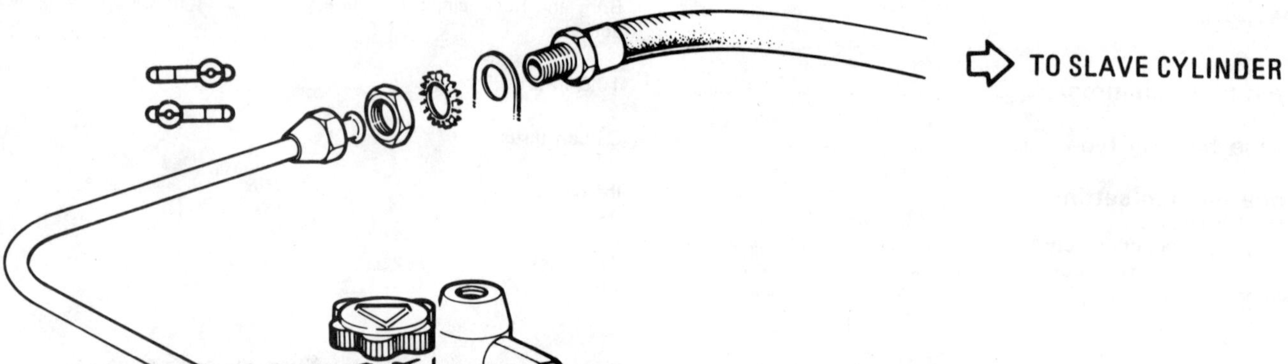

Fig. 5.3 Clutch master cylinder (Sec 3)

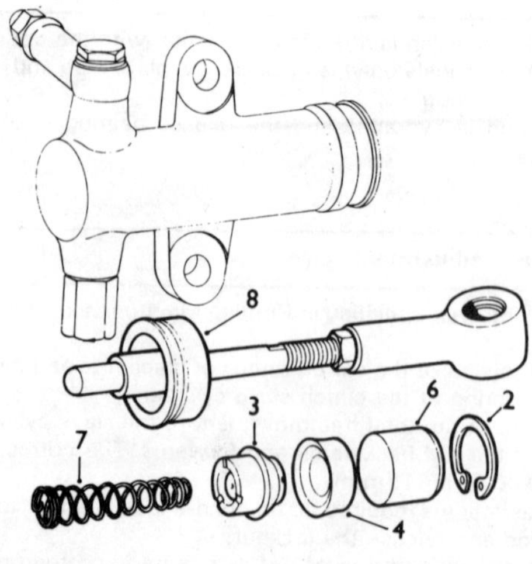

Fig. 5.4 Exploded view of clutch slave cylinder (Sec 4)

2 *Circlip*
3 *Cup filler*
4 *Cup seal*
6 *Piston*
7 *Spring*
8 *Dust-excluding boot*

19 Examine the cylinder bore for scoring or metal-to-metal rubbing. If this is evident, renew the complete master cylinder.
20 If the piston and cylinder are in good condition, clean the components in hydraulic fluid or methylated spirit (denatured alcohol) – nothing else.
21 Obtain a repair kit and fit the new seals, using the fingers only to manipulate them into position.
22 Reassemble, having first dipped the internal components in clean hydraulic fluid. Take care not to trap the lips of the seals as they enter the cylinder.
23 Refitting is a reversal of removal. Bleed the clutch hydraulic system on completion as described in Section 5.

4 Slave cylinder – removal, overhaul and refitting

1 Tape over the vent hole in the master cylinder fluid reservoir cap. This will reduce any loss of fluid when the hydraulic line is disconnected.
2 Disconnect the fluid pipe from the slave cylinder.
3 Note the position of the return spring anchor plate, unscrew the slave cylinder mounting nuts from the gearbox and then slide the spring anchor plate off its stud.
4 Pull the slave cylinder from its mounting studs and draw the cylinder off the pushrod.
5 Clean away external dirt, pull off the rubber dust-excluding cover and extract the circlip.
6 The internal components and piston assembly can now be ejected by tapping the end of the cylinder on a block of hardwood or by applying low air pressure from a tyre pump at the inlet port.
7 Wash all components in hydraulic fluid or methylated spirit (denatured alcohol) – nothing else.
8 Examine the piston and cylinder for scoring or metal-to-metal rubbing marks. If evident, renew the complete cylinder.
9 If the components are in good condition, discard the seal and obtain a repair kit.
10 Fit the new seal, making sure that the lips are the correct way round. Dip the internal components in clean hydraulic fluid before fitting them into the cylinder.
11 Reassembly and refitting are reversals of the preceding operations.
12 On completion of installation, bleed the hydraulic system as described in Section 5 and check and adjust the clutch free movement (Section 2).

5 Hydraulic system – bleeding

1 Remove the master cylinder fluid reservoir cap and top it up with specified hydraulic fluid.
2 Attach a bleed tube to the slave cylinder bleed nipple and immerse the other end of the tube in two or three inches of fluid poured into a glass jar.
3 Slacken the bleed nipple one half turn and have an assistant depress the clutch pedal fully and then release the pedal so that it returns unobstructed by the foot. Repeat this twice more and then top up the reservoir, using only clean fluid which has been stored in an airtight container and remained unshaken for 24 hours.
4 When air bubbles cease to be ejected from the open end of the bleed tube below the surface of the fluid, tighten the bleed screw while the pedal is on a downstroke or fully depressed.

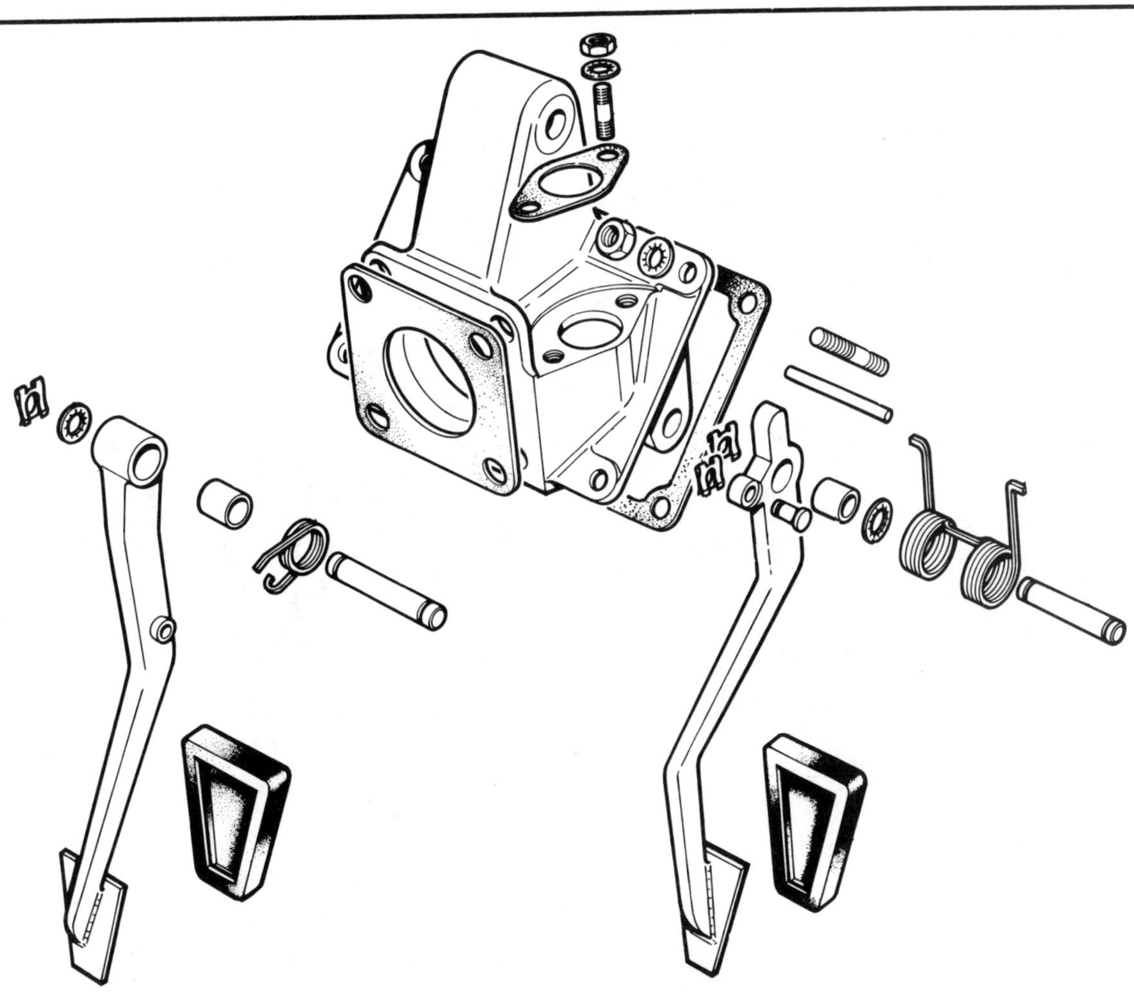

Fig. 5.5 The pedal box assembly (Sec 6)

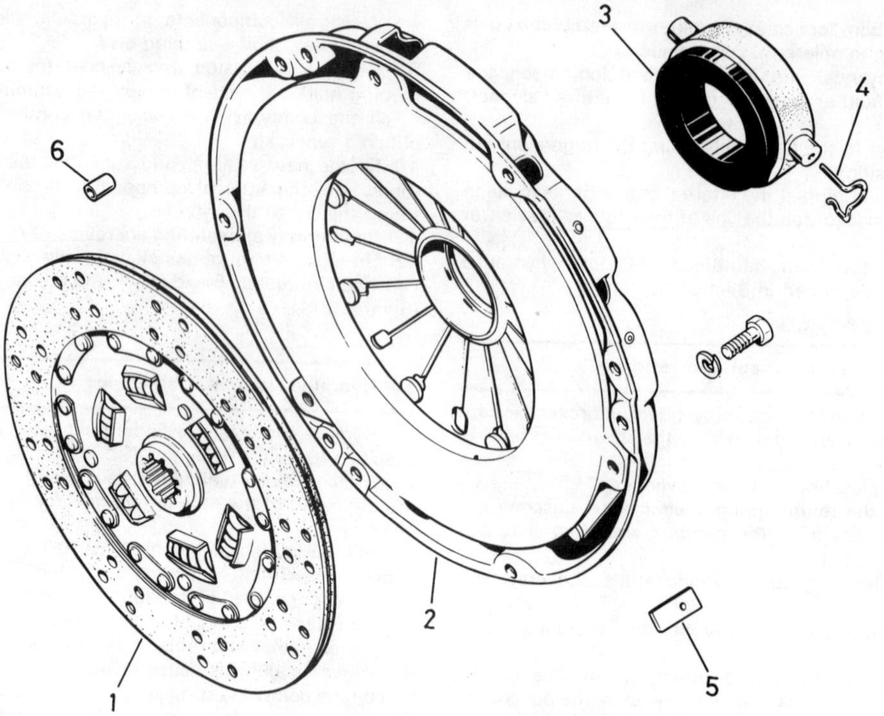

Fig. 5.6 The clutch components (Sec 8)

1 *Driven plate*
2 *Cover/pressure plate/diaphragm spring assembly*
3 *Carbon thrust bearing*
4 *Retaining spring*
5 *Balance weight*
6 *Crankshaft rear flange spigot bush*

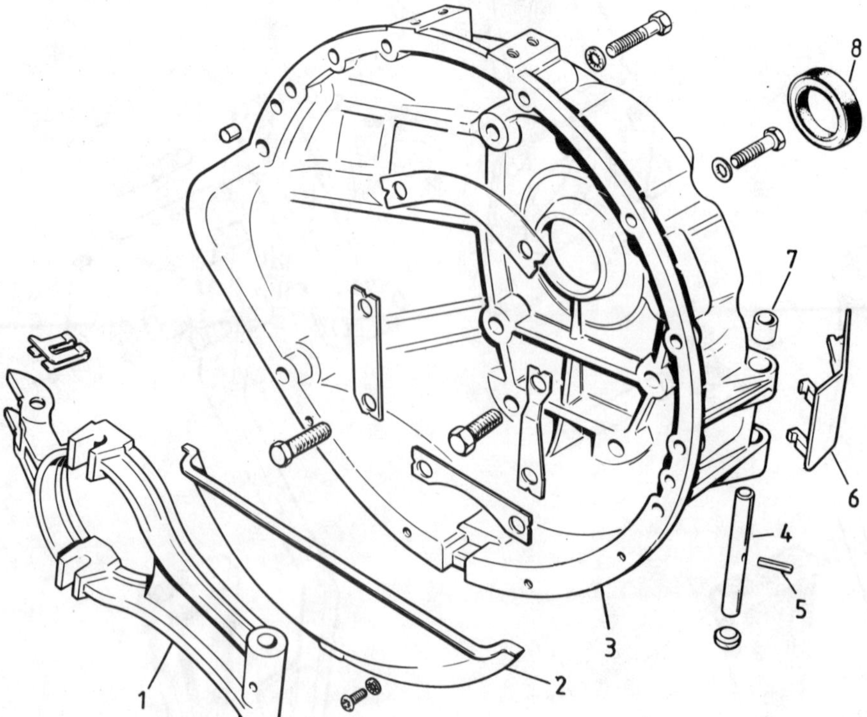

Fig. 5.7 Clutch release components (Sec 9)

1 *Withdrawal fork*
2 *Cover plate*
3 *Bellhousing*
4 *Pivot shaft*
5 *Roll pin*
6 *Blanking plug*
7 *Pivot shaft bush*
8 *Gearbox front oil seal*

5 Remove the bleed tube and jar and top up the reservoir and refit the cap. Do not re-use the fluid expelled from the system, but keep it only for covering the end of the bleed tube in the jar on a future occasion.

6 Clutch pedal – removal and refitting

1 Remove the pedal box as described in Section 3.
2 Using a large screwdriver, disengage the return spring from the pedal arm.
3 Disconnect the pedal arm from the master cylinder pushrod and then remove the locating pin.
4 Tap the clutch pedal cross-shaft out of the pedal box casting, retrieving the return spring and washers.
5 The shaft bearings can be renewed by pressing out the old ones and pressing in the new. As the new bushes have to be reamed to size, this is best left to your dealer.
6 Refitting is a reversal of removal, but apply grease to the cross-shaft and bushes before assembling.
7 Bleed the clutch hydraulic system once the pedal box has been refitted and the clutch master cylinder reconnected to the fluid lines.

7 Clutch – removal

1 Access to the clutch can only be obtained after removing the engine/transmission assembly as described in Chapter 1.
2 With the engine/transmission removed, unbolt the cover plate from the lower half of the front face of the clutch bellhousing.
3 Unbolt and remove the starter motor.
4 Unscrew and remove the bolts which hold the bellhousing to the engine cylinder block. Note the different lengths of these bolts.
5 Disconnect the gearbox breather pipe and then withdraw the gearbox from the engine, making sure that its weight does not hang upon the input shaft whilst the latter is still engaged in the splined hub of the clutch driven plate.
6 Mark the relative position of the clutch cover to the flywheel and then unscrew the securing bolts evenly, a few turns at a time, until the clutch diaphragm spring pressure has been relieved. Note the location of any balance weights. Remove the cover/pressure plate assembly and the driven plate.

8 Clutch – inspection and renovation

1 Due to the slow-wearing qualities of the clutch, it is not easy to decide when to renew it. The only positive indication something needs doing is when it starts to slip or when squealing noises on engagement indicate that the friction lining has worn down to the rivets. In such instances it can only be hoped that the friction surfaces on the flywheel and pressure plate have not been badly worn or scored.
2 A clutch will wear according to the way in which it is used. Much intentional slipping of the clutch while driving – rather than the correct selection of gears – will accelerate wear. It is best to assume, however, that the friction disc may need renewal after 50 000 miles (80 000 km), or earlier if it has been abused. The maintenance history of the car is obviously very useful in such cases.
3 Examine the surfaces of the pressure plate and flywheel for signs of scoring. If this is only light it may be left, but if very deep the pressure plate unit will have to be renewed. If the flywheel is deeply scored it should be taken off and advice sought from an engineering firm. Providing it may be machined completely across the face the overall balance of engine and flywheel should not be too severely upset. If renewal of the flywheel is necessary the new one will have to be balanced to match the original.
4 The friction plate lining surfaces should be at least $\frac{1}{32}$ in (0.8 mm) above the rivets, otherwise the disc is not worth putting back. If the lining material shows signs of breaking up or black areas where oil contamination has occurred it should also be renewed. If facilities are readily available for obtaining and fitting new friction pads to the existing disc this may be done but the saving is relatively small compared with obtaining a complete new disc assembly which ensures that the shock absorbing springs and the splined hub are renewed also. The same applies to the pressure plate assembly which cannot be readily dismantled and put back together without specialised riveting tools and balancing equipment. An allowance is usually given for exchange units.

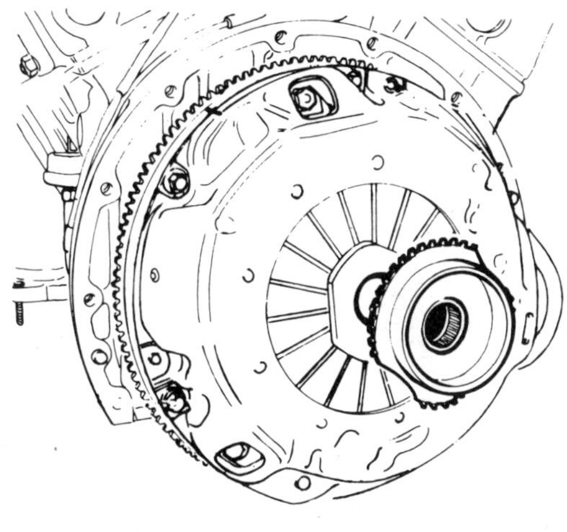

Fig. 5.8 Old input shaft being used to centralise driven plate (Sec 10)

9 Clutch release bearing and mechanism – overhaul

1 The clutch release bearing should always be renewed at the same time as the clutch to avoid dismantling again at a later date.
2 From inside the clutch bellhousing, release the spring clips which hold the release bearing to the withdrawal fork.
3 Remove the release bearing from the fork.
4 Further dismantling is only necessary if there is wear in the withdrawal fork pivot shaft or bushes. If there is, continue with the following operations.
5 Prise off the spring clip from the clutch pushrod clevis pin. Detach the return spring and withdraw the clevis pin.
6 Drive out the rollpin from the release fork pivot shaft.
7 Drill out the upper sealing plug from the pivot shaft so that the shaft can be tapped down and the withdrawal fork removed from the bellhousing.
8 If new bushes are fitted, they must be reamed after installation to accept the pivot shaft.
9 Refitting of all components is a reversal of removal. Use a new roll pin and sealing plugs on the withdrawal fork pivot shaft.

10 Clutch – refitting

1 Wipe the surfaces of the flywheel and pressure plate quite clean from oil or grease. Oil on these components will usually have come from a leaking oil seal at the front of the gearbox or from the crankshaft rear seal. Fit new seals before installing the new clutch assembly if oil seepage is evident.
2 Place the driven plate against the flywheel so that the greater projection which incorporates the torsion coil springs is away from the flywheel.
3 Place the clutch cover in position so that the marks made before removal are in alignment. Screw in the cover retaining bolts finger-tight.
4 The clutch driven plate must now be centralised. To do this, an old input shaft or alignment tool should be inserted through the hub in the driven plate and engaged in the spigot bush in the crankshaft rear flange. Move the tool as necessary to obtain a good sliding fit of the tool in the driven plate hub splines and then tighten the cover bolts to the specified torque in a diagonally opposite sequence.
5 Remove the alignment tool.
6 Refit the gearbox to the engine by reversing the removal operations given in Section 7 and then refit the engine/gearbox as described in Chapter 1.

11 Fault diagnosis – clutch

Symptom	Reason(s)
Judder when taking up drive	Loose engine or gearbox mounting Driven plate friction surfaces badly worn or oil-contaminated Worn splines on gearbox input shaft or driven plate hub Worn input shaft spigot bush in crankshaft rear flange
Clutch spin (failure to disengage) so that gears cannot be meshed	Incorrect clutch pushrod free movement Driven plate sticking on input shaft splines due to rust. May occur after car standing idle for long periods Damaged or misaligned pressure plate assembly
Clutch slip (increase in engine speed does not result in increase in car road speed)	Incorrect clutch pushrod free movement Friction surfaces worn out or contaminated with oil
Noise evident on depressing clutch pedal	Dry, worn or damaged release bearing Weak or broken pedal return spring Wear in driven plate hub or input shaft splines
Noise evident as clutch pedal released	Distorted driven plate Broken or weak driven plate cushion coil springs Weak or broken clutch pedal return spring Weak or broken pushrod return spring Distorted or worn input shaft Release bearing loose on its retainer hub

Chapter 6 Manual gearbox and automatic transmission

Contents

Specifications

Part A – Manual gearbox

Type ..... Four forward speeds, all with synchromesh, and reverse

Ratios

1st	3.238 : 1
2nd	1.905 : 1
3rd	1.389 : 1
4th	1.00 : 1
Reverse	3.428 : 1

Oil capacity ..... 3.0 Imp pints (3.6 US pints, 1.7 litres)

Part B – Automatic transmission (Borg Warner Type 12)

Type ..... Three element hydrokinetic torque converter with hydraulically operated planetary gear set to provide three forward gears and one reverse

Ratios

1st	2.40 : 1
2nd	1.46 : 1
3rd	1.00 : 1
Reverse	2.00 : 1

Gearchange speeds

3.07 : 1 axle ratio	**mph**	**kph**
Light throttle upshift:		
1 to 2	11 to 12	18 to 20
2 to 3	28 to 31	45 to 50

Kickdown		
1 to 2	55	89
2 to 3	97 to 100	157 to 161
3 to 2	82 to 90	132 to 145
3 to 1	23 to 30	37 to 48
Full throttle upshifts:		
1 to 2	21 to 27	34 to 43
2 to 3	62 to 70	100 to 113
Manually operated downshifts (throttle closed):		
2 to 1	18 to 23	29 to 37
3 to 1	21 to 32	35 to 53
Part throttle downshifts:		
3 to 2	19 to 23	31 to 37
3.31 : 1 axle ratio		
Light throttle upshift:		
1 to 2	5 to 13	8 to 20
2 to 3	25 to 29	40 to 46
Shut throttle downshifts:		
2 to 1	3 to 5	4 to 8
3 to 2	12 to 17	18 to 27
Full throttle upshifts:		
1 to 2	20 to 30	32 to 48
2 to 3	70 to 71	112 to 114
Manual shut throttle downshifts:		
2 to 1	20 to 21	32 to 34
3 to 1	26 to 33	41 to 53
Part throttle downshifts:		
2 to 1	16 to 20	25 to 32

Fluid capacity

From dry	16 Imp pints (19.2 US pints, 9.1 litres)
At service drain and refill	11 Imp pints (13.2 US pints, 6.3 litres)

Part C – Automatic transmission (GM400)

Type

Type	As Borg Warner

Ratios

1st	2.48 : 1
2nd	1.48 : 1
3rd	1.00 : 1
Reverse	2.07 : 1

Gearchange speeds

Up to and including transmission number 77ZA 4609 (UK)

	mph	kph
Light throttle upshift:		
1 to 2	10 to 15	16 to 24
2 to 3	17 to 18	27 to 29
Kickdown:		
1 to 2	57 to 60	92 to 97
2 to 3	87 to 93	140 to 150
3 to 2	77 to 86	124 to 138
3 to 1	31 to 32	50 to 51
Part throttle downshift:		
3 to 2	52	84
Closed throttle downshift (1 selected)	12	19
From transmission number 77ZA 4610 (UK)		
Light throttle upshifts:		
1 to 2	5 to 10	8 to 16
2 to 3	10 to 20	16 to 32
Full throttle upshifts:		
1 to 2	40 to 50	64 to 80
2 to 3	55 to 65	88 to 94
Full throttle kickdown:		
1 to 2	50 to 60	80 to 96
2 to 3	80 to 90	128 to 144
Kickdown:		
3 to 2	75 to 85	120 to 136
3 to 1	22 to 30	35 to 48
Manual downshift:		
2 to 1	13 to 18	21 to 29
Part throttle kickdown:		
3 to 2	8 to 12	13 to 19

Fluid capacity

From dry	$22\frac{1}{2}$ Imp pints (27 US pints, 12.75 litres)
At service drain and refill	16.5 Imp pints (19.8 US pints, 9.4 litres)

Torque wrench settings

	lbf ft	Nm
Manual gearbox		
Top cover bolts	14	19
Rear extension to gear casing	14	19
Clutch bellhousing to engine	44	60
Oil filler plug	25	34
Oil drain plug	25	34
Output flange nut	110	150
Reverse lever setscrew	25	34
Gear lever pivot nut	14	19
Mainshaft front and rear nuts	150	204
Input shaft nut	150	204
Automatic transmission (Borg Warner Type 12)		
Extension housing bolts	30	41
Oil pan bolts	13	18
Filler/guide tube union nut	25	34
Rear brake band screw locknut	44	60
Transmission casing to bellhousing bolts	60	82
Vacuum control unit	15	20
Driveplate to converter setscrews	30	41
Bellhousing to engine bolts	35	48
Output flange nut	50	68
Oil cooler pipe unions	21	29
Automatic transmission (GM400)		
Extension housing bolts	23	31
Oil pan bolts	12	16
Vacuum modulator retainer	18	25
Speedometer driveshaft nut	10	14
Torque converter housing to engine	35	48
Driveplate to torque converter setscrews	30	41
Output flange nut	50	68
Oil cooler pipe unions	21	29

PART A – MANUAL GEARBOX

1 General description

1 The manually-operated gearbox, which is fitted as an option to XJS models only, is of four-speed all synchromesh type with reverse gear.
2 The synchromesh units are of baulk ring type.
3 The gearshift control lever is of floor-mounted type.

2 Gearbox – removal and refitting

1 The gearbox can only be conveniently removed and refitted together with the engine as described in Chapter 1.
2 Once the engine/gearbox is out of the car, separate them as also described in Chapter 1.
3 If complete dismantling is to be carried out, the work should be done in the sequence of the following Sections, with the gearbox on the bench.

3 Gearbox rear extension – removal and dismantling

1 Insert two bolts into the holes in the output flange and then place a bar between them to restrain the flange from turning. Unscrew and remove the drive flange centre bolt and then tap off the flange.
2 Unscrew and remove the setscrew and withdraw the speedometer driven gear.
3 Unscrew and remove the seven setscrews which hold the rear extension to the main gearcase.
4 Draw the rear extension from the output shaft.
5 If the oil pump gear housing is to be removed, relieve the staking of the three countersunk head screws on the front face of the rear extension.
6 Insert two screws into the tapped holes provided and as they are tightened, the oil pump gear housing will be extracted.
7 Mark the gears on their visible faces with quick-drying paint to ensure correct refitting.
8 Retrieve the oil pump drive sleeve and distance tube.
9 Drive the rear oil seal from the rear extension housing.
10 Pull off the speedometer gear from the output shaft, followed by the ball bearing assembly.

4 Clutch bellhousing – removal

1 Remove the clutch release bearing and withdrawal fork as described in Chapter 5.
2 Inside the bellhousing, cut the locking wire from the setscrews, flatten the tabs of the lockplates and unscrew and remove the setscrews which hold the bellhousing to the gearcase.
3 Remove the bellhousing. Discard the gasket and the oil seal.

5 Gearbox top cover – removal and dismantling

1 Disconnect the breather pipe and set the gearshift lever in neutral.
2 Unscrew and remove the top cover bolts, noting the lengths and locations of the individual bolts and the wiring harness clips.
3 Lift the top cover from the gearcase. Do not try and tap it off sideways as it is located on hollow dowels.
4 Remove and discard the gasket.
5 Remove the gearshift lever. To do this, unscrew the self-locking nut and extract the coil spring, plain and fibre washers.
6 If worn, the bush can be pressed from the pivot jaw housing.
7 Cut the locking wire and extract the retaining screws from the selector forks and the retaining arm.
8 Withdraw the 3rd/4th selector rod and retrieve the fork, spacer tube and interlock ball.
9 Withdraw the 1st/2nd selector rod and retrieve the fork, spacer tube and the interlock pin.
10 Withdraw the reverse selector rod, the fork and the locating arm

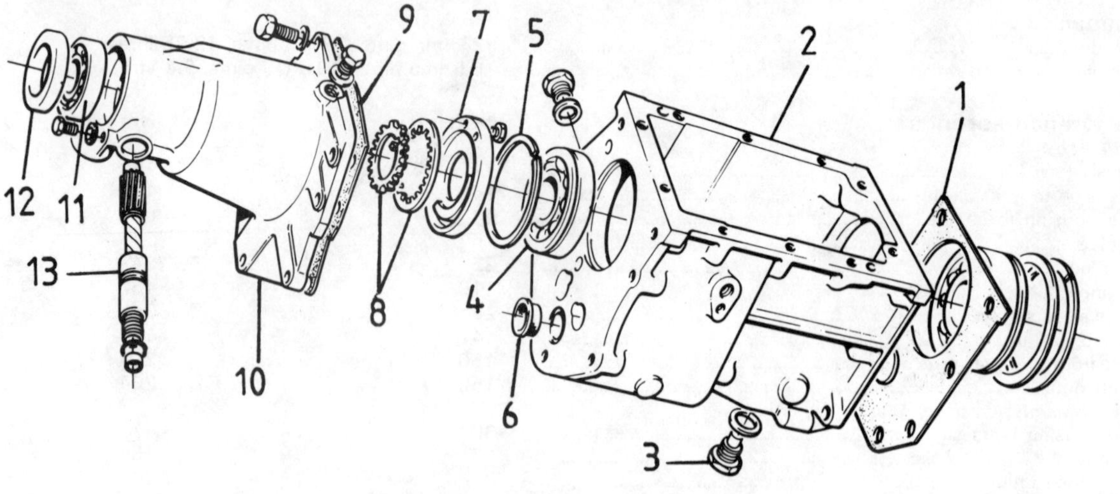

Fig. 6.1 Gearcase and rear extension housing (Sec 3)

1 Gasket
2 Gearcase
3 Drain plug
4 Mainshaft rear bearing
5 Bearing circlip
6 Filter
7 Oil pump housing
8 Oil pump gears
9 Gasket
10 Rear extension housing
11 Bearing
12 Oil seal
13 Speedometer driven gear

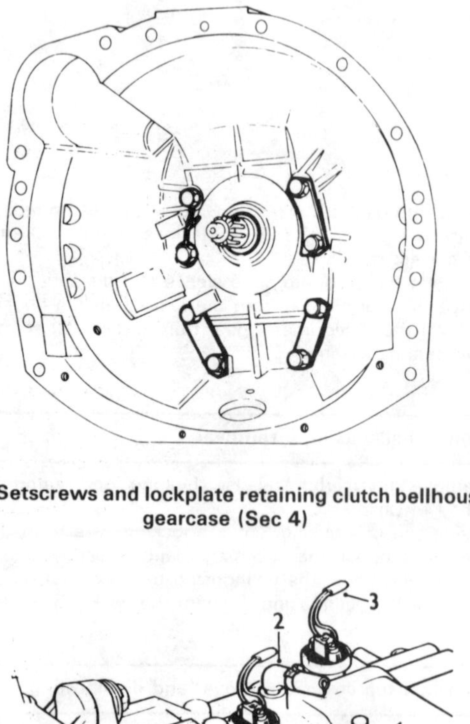

Fig. 6.2 Setscrews and lockplate retaining clutch bellhousing to gearcase (Sec 4)

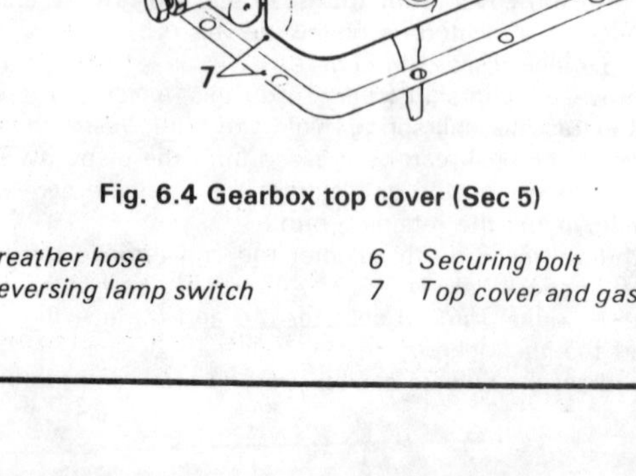

Fig. 6.4 Gearbox top cover (Sec 5)

2 Breather hose
3 Reversing lamp switch
6 Securing bolt
7 Top cover and gasket

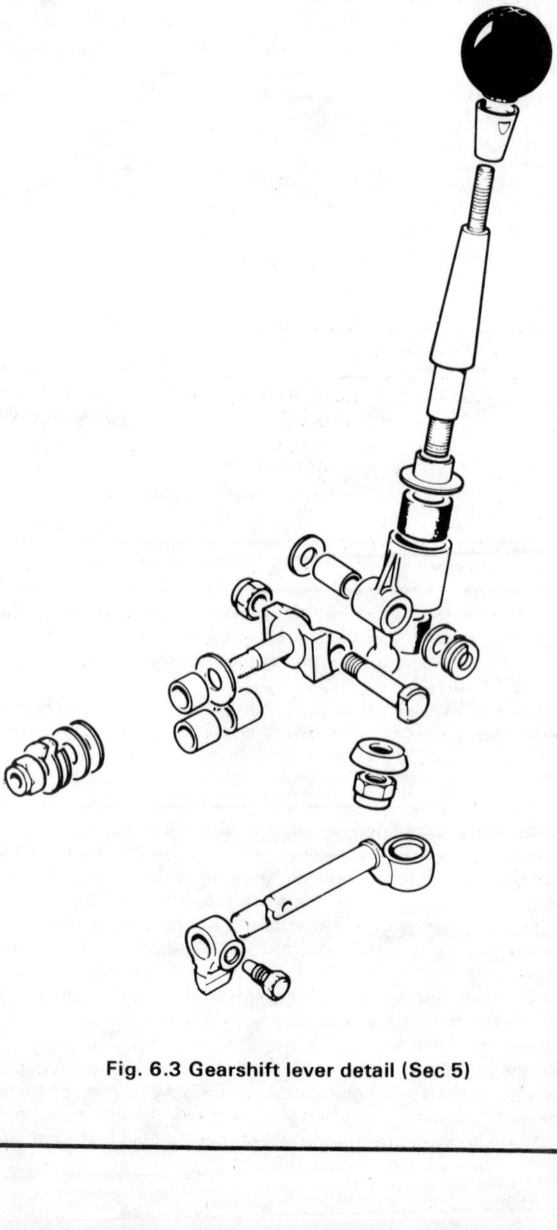

Fig. 6.3 Gearshift lever detail (Sec 5)

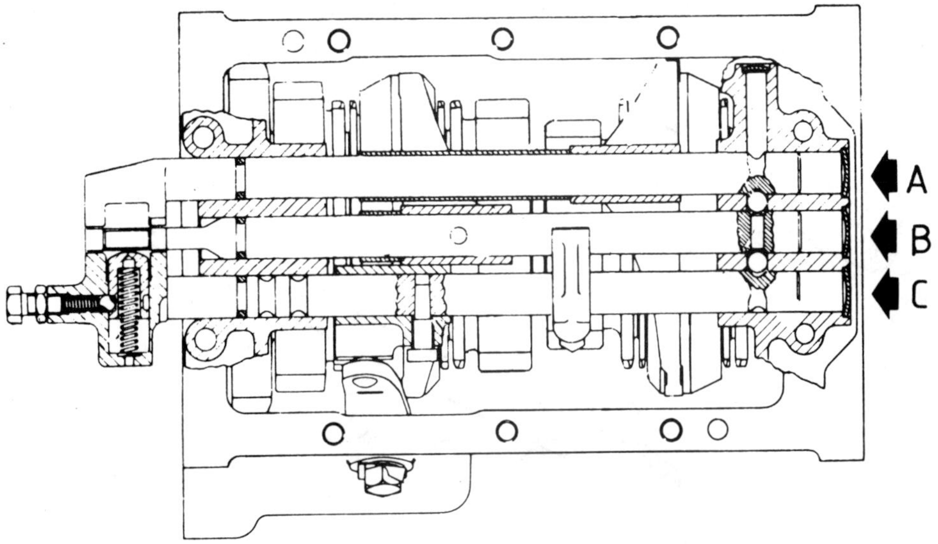

Fig. 6.5 Sectional view of selector mechanism (Sec 5)

A 3rd/4th selector rod
B 1st/2nd selector rod
C Reverse selector rod

and retrieve the detent plunger, ball and spring, also the interlock ball.
11 Release the locknut on the reverse selector and slacken the setscrew. Retrieve the detent plunger, stop spring, detent ball and the spring.

6 Geartrain – dismantling

1 Unscrew and remove the bolts which hold the adaptor plate. Remove the plate and discard the gasket.
2 Using a large screwdriver, move the synchro sleeves away from each other to lock up two gears at once.
3 Flatten the tab on the lockwasher and unscrew and remove the rear bearing nut.
4 Withdraw the countershaft and retrieve the Woodruff key. When pulling out the countershaft, make sure that the rear thrust washer which is pegged to the casing drops down in a clockwise direction (viewed from the rear of the gearbox), otherwise the washer may be trapped by reverse gear as the mainshaft is driven forward.
5 Prise out and discard the fibre plug from the front of the countershaft.
6 Rotate the input shaft unti' the cutaway parts of the gear are towards the top and bottom of the casing. Using two suitable levers, prise the input shaft and its bearing forward until the assembly can be withdrawn.
7 Retrieve the spacer ring and 4th gear synchro ring.
8 Extract the needle roller race from inside the input shaft.
9 If a new bearing is to be fitted to the input shaft, flatten the tab on the lockplate and remove the nut by gripping the shaft in a vice fitted with soft metal jaw protectors. Remove the oil thrower.
10 Tap the end of the input shaft sharply against a solid surface to dislodge the bearing.
11 Tap the reverse idler shaft so that it is ejected from the rear of the gearbox. Retrieve the Woodruff key.
12 Flatten the tab on the lockwasher and remove the bolt which holds reverse lever.
13 Turn the mainshaft until one of the large cutaway parts of the 3rd/4th synchro hub is in line with the countershaft gear and then tap the mainshaft forward through the rear bearing, making sure that reverse gear is kept pressed against 1st gear during the process.
14 Withdraw the rear bearing from the gearcase.
15 Fit a hose clip to the mainshaft to prevent reverse gear from sliding off as the mainshaft is withdrawn.
16 Lift out the mainshaft and the gears.
17 Lift out reverse idler gear.
18 Lift out the countergear assembly and retrieve the needle rollers, inner and outer thrust washers and the retaining rings.
19 Remove the temporary hose clip and withdraw reverse gear.
20 To dismantle the mainshaft, remove 1st speed gear and retrieve the needle rollers, spacer and sleeve.
21 Note the relative position of the 1st/2nd synchro unit to the baulk rings and then remove the synchro unit and the rings.
22 Withdraw 2nd speed gear together with the needle rollers and the spacer.
23 Flatten the tab on the lockwasher and unscrew and remove the nut which holds the 3rd/4th synchro. Note the relative position of the synchro unit to the baulk rings and remove the components including the thrust washer.
24 Withdraw 3rd speed gear, the needle rollers and the spacer.

7 Gearbox components – examination and renovation

1 With the gearbox completely stripped, clean the individual components and examine them for wear or damage.
2 Scoring of shafts or chipped gear teeth should be rectified by renewal of the components concerned.
3 If the countershaft rollers are worn, renew them as complete sets.
4 Check that the mainshaft oilways are clear.
5 Wear in the synchro assemblies will usually be determined before dismantling as a result of noisy gearshift or by the fact that the synchro is easily beaten during a fast gearshift.
6 It is recommended that a synchro assembly is renewed complete, but hubs and sleeves in good condition can be used again provided the springs, balls and plungers are renewed.
7 To dismantle a synchro unit, mark the relationship of hub to sleeve with quick-drying paint or a spirit marker. Cover the unit with a cloth to prevent the springs and balls flying out as the hub is pressed out of the sleeve.
8 To reassemble a synchro unit, locate the hub to the sleeve so that the longer projection on the hub is on the side opposite to the wider

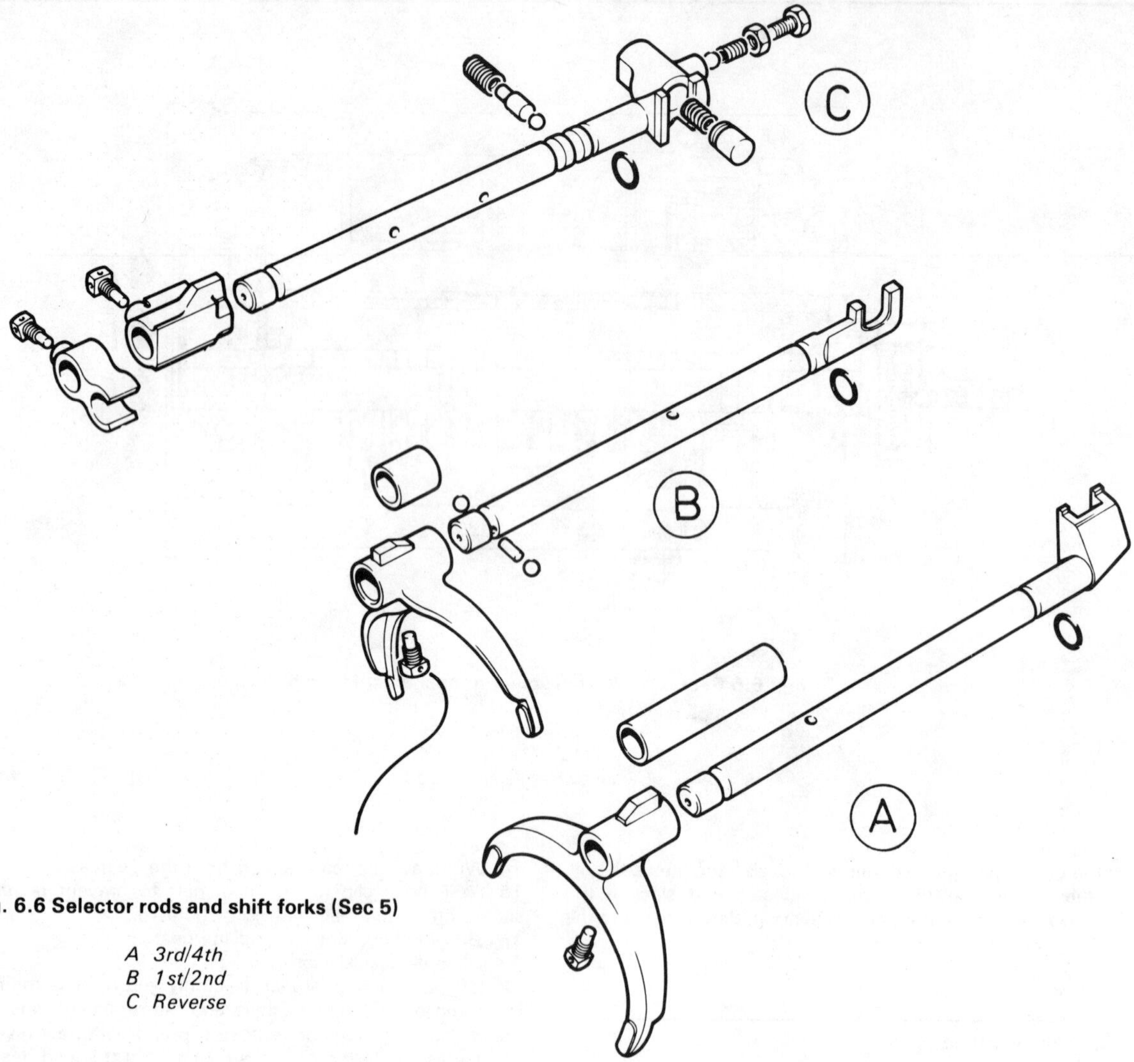

Fig. 6.6 Selector rods and shift forks (Sec 5)

A 3rd/4th
B 1st/2nd
C Reverse

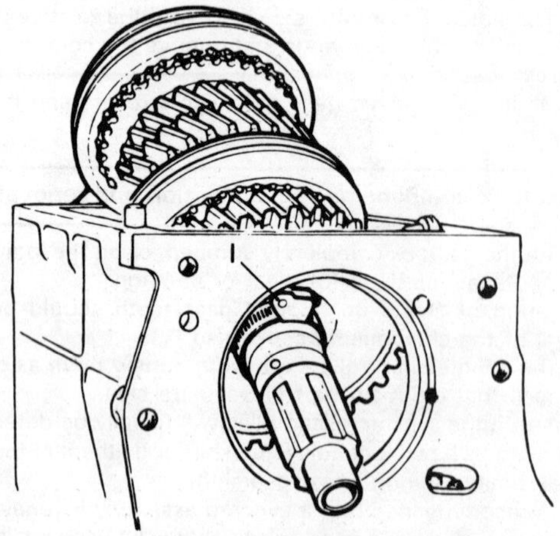

Fig. 6.7 Removing the mainshaft assembly (Sec 6)

1 *Temporary clip to retain reverse gear*

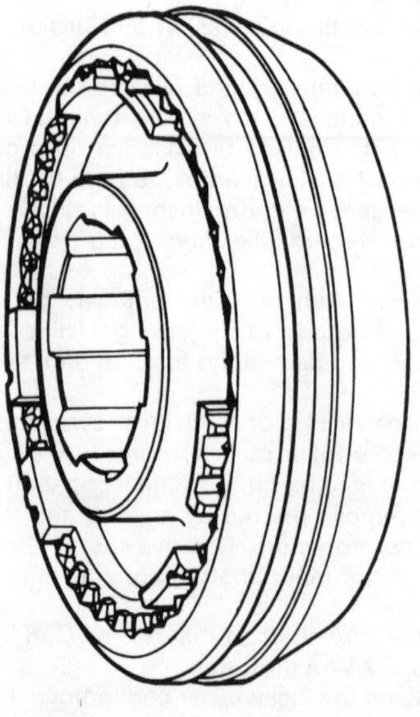

Fig. 6.8 Relationship of synchro sleeve to hub (Sec 6)

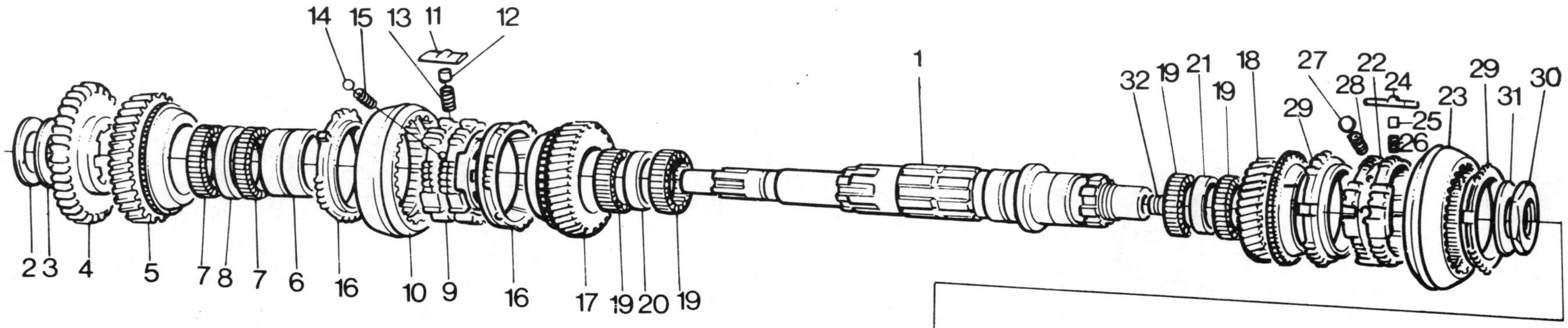

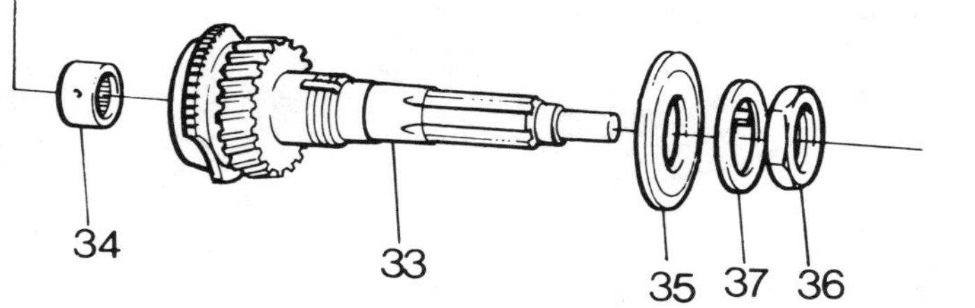

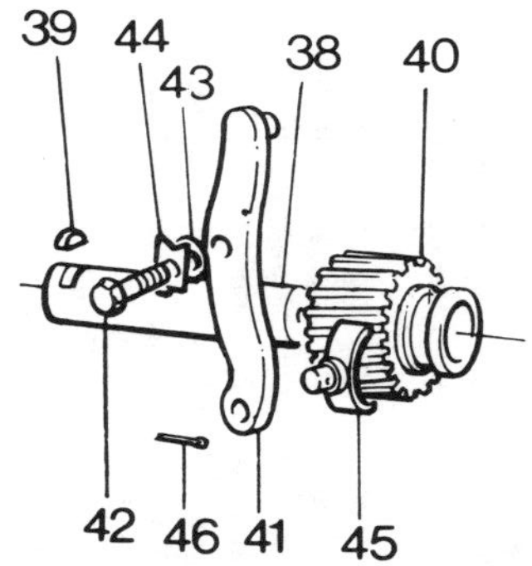

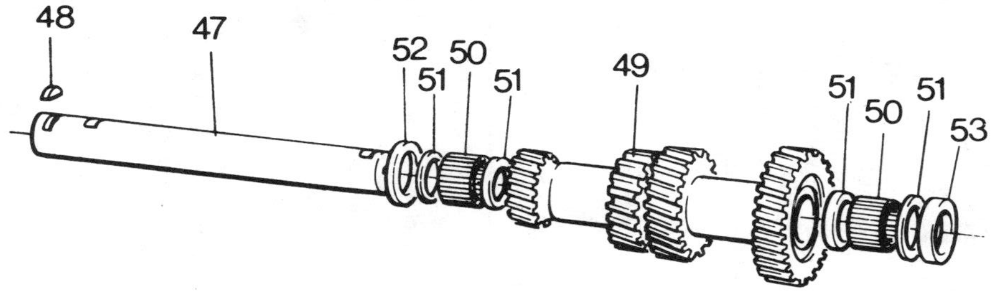

Fig. 6.9 Exploded view of the geartrain (Sec 6)

1	*Mainshaft*	28	*Spring*
2	*Nut*	29	*Synchro ring*
3	*Tab washer*	30	*Nut*
4	*Reverse gear*	31	*Tab washer*
5	*1st speed gear*	32	*Plug*
6	*Bearing sleeve*	33	*Input shaft*
7	*Needle rollers*	34	*Roller bearing*
8	*Spacer*	35	*Oil thrower*
9	*1st/2nd synchro hub*	36	*Nut*
10	*Synchro sleeve*	37	*Tab washer*
11	*Sliding key*	38	*Reverse idler shaft*
12	*Plunger*	39	*Key*
13	*Spring*	40	*Reverse idler gear*
14	*Detent ball*	41	*Lever assembly*
15	*Spring*	42	*Setscrew*
16	*Synchro ring*	43	*Fibre washer*
17	*2nd speed gear*	44	*Tab washer*
18	*3rd speed gear*	45	*Reverse slipper*
19	*Needle rollers*	46	*Split pin*
20	*Spacer*	47	*Countershaft*
21	*Spacer*	48	*Key*
22	*3rd/4th synchro hub*	49	*Countergear cluster*
23	*Synchro sleeve*	50	*Needle rollers*
24	*Sliding key*	51	*Retaining ring*
25	*Plunger*	52	*Thrust washer*
26	*Spring*	53	*Thrust washer*
27	*Detent ball*		

chamfer on the sleeve. Check that the hub slides smoothly in the sleeve.
9 With the unit on a bench, raise the hub in the sleeve until the holes in the hub are visible above the sleeve and insert the three springs, plungers and sliding keys into the holes. These particular springs are coloured red. Make sure that the ridge on each sliding key is visible when fitted to the hub.
10 Now fit the three springs which are not colour marked and the balls in alignment with the teeth on the synchro sleeve which have three detent grooves.
11 Compress and retain the springs in the hub using a hose clip or piston ring compressor.
12 With the hub resting on the sleeve, depress it slightly and push the sliding keys down until they engage in the neutral groove of the sleeve.
13 Using a plastic-faced mallet, tap the hub down squarely until the balls can be heard and felt to engage in the neutral groove (the second click).

8 Gearbox reassembly

1 Make sure that the gearcase is clean, with all traces of old gasket removed.
2 Using thick grease as an adhesive, stick one needle retaining ring into the hole in the larger gear of the countergear. Fit the needle rollers and the inner thrust washer. Make sure that the peg on the washer engages in the groove in the countergear.
3 Fit the similar needle roller assembly into the hole in the rear end of the countergear.
4 Using grease, stick a new (pegged) rear thrust washer into position on its boss. Stick the front thrust washer to the front of the countergear in a similar way.
5 Carefully lower the countergear into position in the gearcase with the larger gear towards the front of the casing. A dummy countershaft should now be inserted through the casing and countergear (without disturbing the needle bearings) to retain the countergear in position.
6 Using a feeler blade, check the clearance between the countershaft rear thrust washer and the face of the countergear. The endfloat must be between 0.004 and 0.006 in (0.10 and 0.15 mm). If the endfloat is not within the specified tolerance, the thrust washer will have to be changed for an oversize one.
7 A thin rod should now be substituted for the countershaft. Insert the rod by pressing out the countershaft, always keeping the rod in contact with the end of the shaft and at the same time supporting the weight of the countergear.
8 Fit the Woodruff key to the reverse idler shaft and then fit the reverse idler gear, the lever and the reverse idler shaft to the gearcase. Do not fit the retaining bolt at this stage.
9 Fit the needle roller race into the end of the input shaft.
10 Locate the oil thrower on the input shaft so that its raised centre part will be towards the bearing.
11 Fit the snap-ring into the groove in the input shaft bearing outer track.
12 Press the bearing squarely up to the shoulder on the input shaft.
13 Fit a new lockplate and tighten the input shaft nut to the specified torque.
14 Reassemble the mainshaft by fitting 3rd speed gear, the needle rollers and the wide spacer.
15 Fit 3rd/4th synchro, the baulk rings and the thrust washer. Fit a new lockplate and screw on and tighten the nut to the specified torque.
16 Fit 2nd speed gear, the needle rollers and the narrow spacer.
17 Fit 1st/2nd synchro and the baulk rings.
18 Fit 1st speed gear, the needle rollers, spacer and sleeve.
19 Refit reverse gear and temporarily fit a hose clip to retain it.
20 Lower the assembled mainshaft down through the top of the casing and then pass the rear end of the shaft through the bearing aperture. Take off the temporary hose clip.
21 Using thick grease, stick a new gasket to the front face of the gearcase.
22 Place the baulk ring on the front face of the 3rd/4th synchro hub.
23 Insert the input shaft through the front of the gearcase so that the cutaway parts of its gear are at the highest and lowest points.
24 Using a plastic-faced mallet, tap the input shaft into position making sure that the front end of the mainshaft enters the input shaft needle bearing squarely.

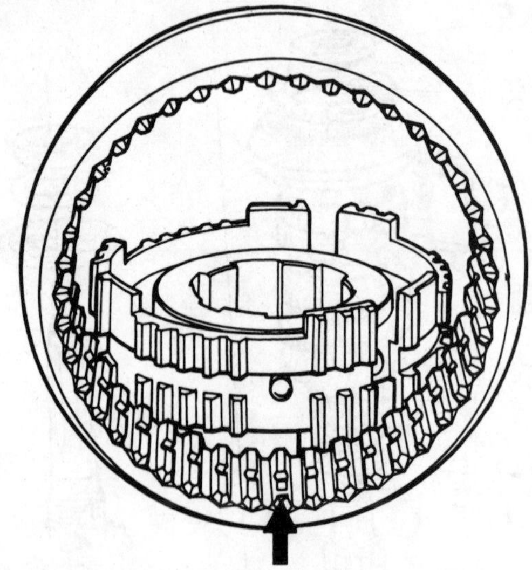

Fig. 6.10 Synchro sleeve tooth with three grooves (arrowed) (Sec 6)

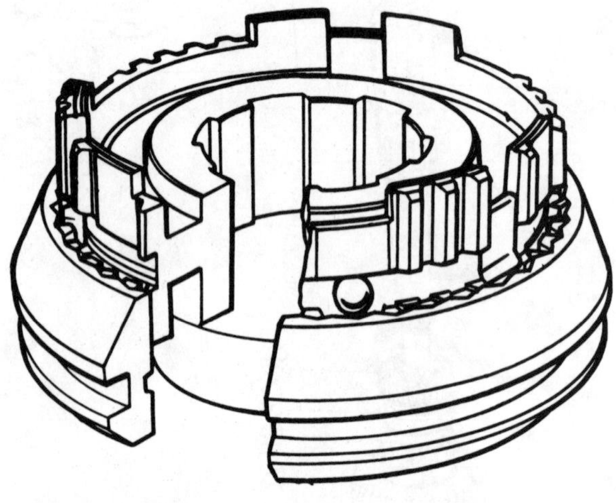

Fig. 6.11 Setting synchro hub on sleeve ready for insertion of balls and springs (Sec 6)

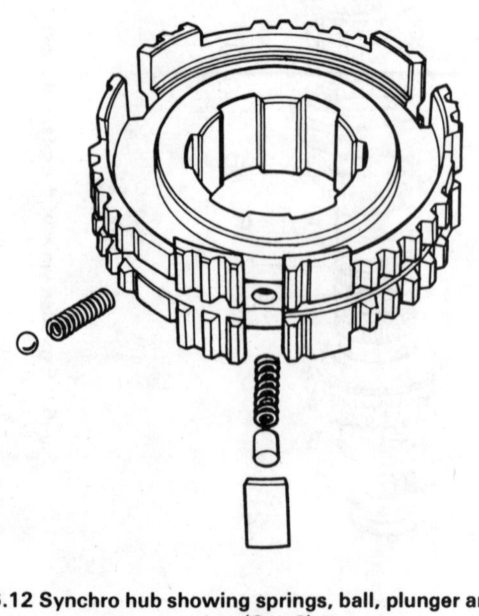

Fig. 6.12 Synchro hub showing springs, ball, plunger and sliding key (Sec 6)

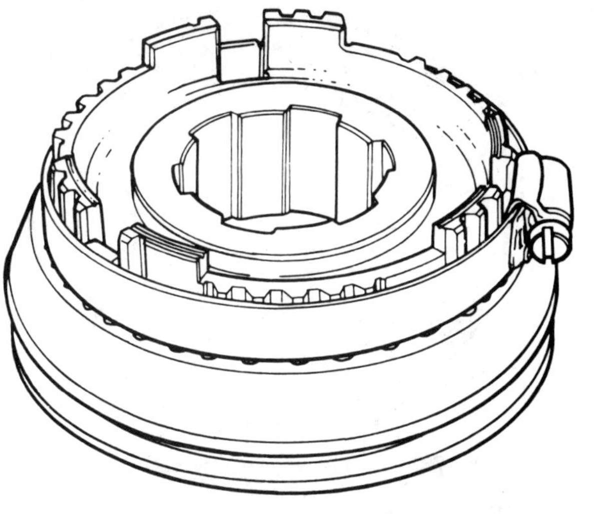

Fig. 6.13 Using a hose clip to compress the synchro coil springs (Sec 6)

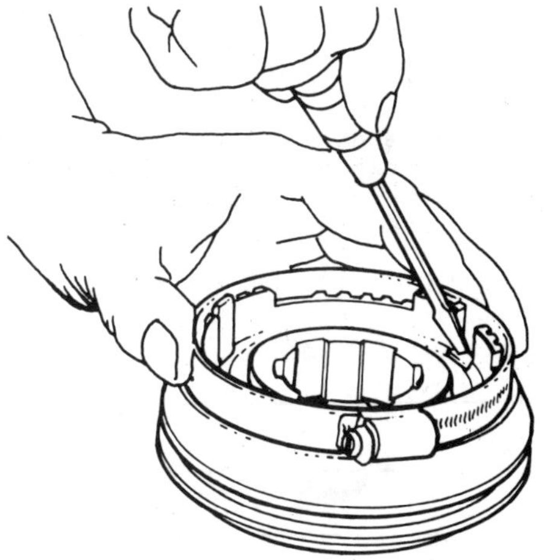

Fig. 6.14 Depressing the synchro sliding keys (Sec 6)

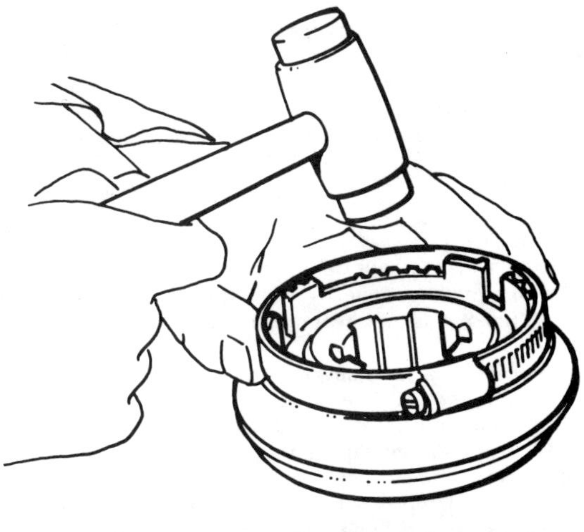

Fig. 6.15 Tapping the synchro hub fully into its sleeve (Sec 6)

25 Fit the snap-ring to the groove in the rear bearing.
26 Hold a block of hardwood against the front of the input shaft and carefully drive the mainshaft rear bearing forward onto the rear end of the mainshaft until it seats in the casing.
27 Insert the countershaft into the countergear, so displacing the thin rod. Keep the shaft and rod in end-to-end contact during this operation and slightly raise the countergear. Take care not to displace the needle roller assemblies.
28 Fit the Woodruff key to the countershaft and tap it fully home.
29 Fit a new fibre plug to the front of the countershaft.
30 Fit the reverse lever bolt, using a new lockplate.
31 Lock up two gears simultaneously by moving the synchro sleeves in opposite directions. Fit a new lockwasher and tighten the mainshaft rear bearing nut to the specified torque.
32 Refit the adaptor plate.
33 Complete the reassembly of the gearbox by refitting the top cover, the bellhousing and the rear extension as described in the following sections.

9 Gearbox top cover – reassembly and refitting

1 Fit the detent plunger and spring to the reverse selector rod.
2 Fit the detent ball, spring, setscrew and locknut.
3 Press the detent plunger fully home and tighten the setscrew to lock the plunger. Now slowly release the setscrew until the plunger is withdrawn far enough for the detent ball to engage in its groove. Tighten the locknut without allowing the setscrew to move.
4 Place the reverse selector rod detent spring, plunger and ball into their housing. Depress the plunger and fit the selector rod.
5 Fit the selector fork and locating arm to the reverse selector rod. Fit the retaining screws.
6 Fit the 1st/2nd selector rod into the top cover far enough to pick up the selector fork and spacer tube with the rod.
7 Position the top cover on its side, reverse selector rod at the bottom of the cover, and then push an interlock ball through the 1st/2nd selector rod hole at the front of the top cover. Manoeuvre the ball until it is against the groove in the reverse selector rod. Now push the 1st/2nd selector rod into its hole to retain the ball in its groove. Make sure that the ball is not displaced and is pushed ahead of the selector rod.
8 Fit the lockscrew to the 1st/2nd selector fork.
9 At this stage, check that if one selector rod is moved it will lock the other and that it is not possible to move the rods together at the same time.
10 Insert the interlock plunger through the 3rd/4th selector rod hole at the front of the top cover.
11 Gently manoeuvre the 1st/2nd selector rod until the plunger drops through.
12 Check that reverse and 1st/2nd selector rods are level and carefully push the 2nd interlock ball through the 3rd/4th hole to lie in the hole in the casting.
13 Pass the 3rd/4th selector rod through the hole in the top cover and fit the selector fork and spacer tube. Push the rod home to retain the ball in its groove. Fit the locking screw.
14 Check the interlock as described in paragraph 9.
15 Check the tightness of all the locking screws and fit a locking wire to them.
16 Fit a fibre washer to the gearshift lever pivot jaw pin. Locate the gearshift lever to the top cover.
17 Push the pivot pin through the bush in the top cover and then fit the second fibre washer, the plain washer, coil spring and self-locking nut.
18 Refit the top cover to the gear casing using a new gasket. Make sure that the synchro units are in the neutral mode and that the reverse idler gear is out of mesh. Check the latter by pushing the reverse lever towards the rear of the gearbox.

10 Clutch bellhousing – refitting

1 Refitting is a reversal of removal as described in Section 4, but observe the following points.
2 Make sure that the new oil seal is fitted with its lip towards the gearbox and then smear the lip with engine oil.
3 Tape over the input shaft splines to prevent them cutting into the

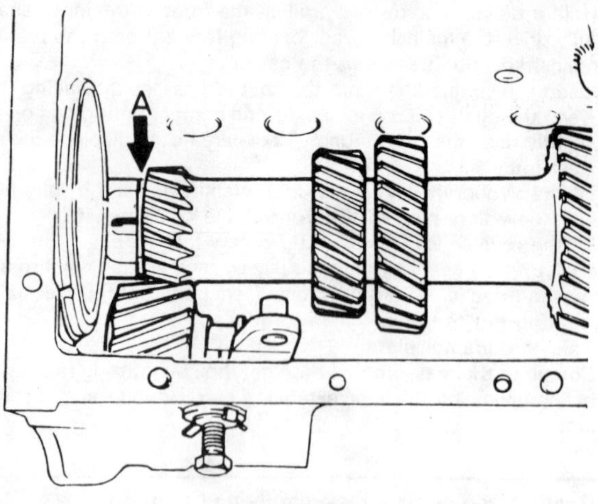

Fig. 6.16 Checking countergear endfloat (A) (Sec 8)

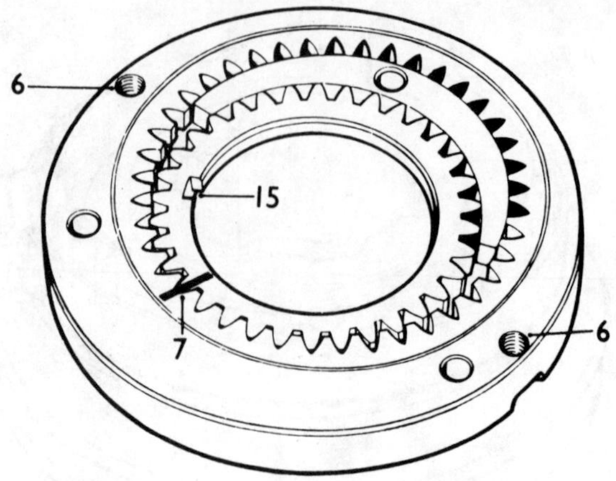

Fig. 6.17 Oil pump drivegear assembly (Sec 11)

6 Tappet holes for withdrawing gear housing
7 Alignment marks
15 Notch for oil pump drive sleeve pin

oil seal as the bellhousing is fitted.
4 Use new locking plates, tighten the setscrews to the specified torque and bend up the locktabs.

11 Gearbox rear extension - reassembly and refitting

1 Assemble the oil pump gears, making sure that the faces marked before dismantling are aligned.
2 Fit the oil pump housing to the gear casing using three counter-sunk-headed screws. Stake the screw heads.
3 Fit the oil pump drive sleeve to the oil pump gear so that the longer shoulder enters first.
4 Use a new paper gasket and fit the rear extension to the gear casing. During this operation, make sure that the oil pump drive sleeve pin engages with the gear.
5 Screw in and tighten the seven retaining setscrews.
6 Insert the spacer tube over the mainshaft through the rear end of the extension housing.
7 Tap the ball bearing race into the end of the rear extension housing.
8 Fit the speedometer drive gear to the end of the mainshaft.
9 Apply clean oil to the new oil seal and drive it squarely into the end of the extension housing.
10 Fit the speedometer driven gear assembly using the single setcrew.
11 Fit the output flange, tighten the nut to the specified torque and insert a new split pin.

12 Fault diagnosis – manual gearbox

Symptom	Reason(s)
Ineffective synchromesh	Worn baulk rings or synchro hubs
Jumps out of one or more gears (on drive or overrun)	Weak detent springs, worn selector forks, rods or gears
Noisy, rough operation, whining or vibration	Worn bearings or thrust washers
Noisy or difficult engagement of gears	Clutch fault

Note: It is sometimes difficult to decide whether it is worthwhile removing and dismantling the gearbox for a fault which may be nothing more than a minor irritant. Gearboxes which howl, or where the synchromesh can be 'beaten' by a quick gearchange, may continue to perform for a long time in this state. A worn gearbox usually needs a complete rebuild to eliminate noise because the various gears, if re-aligned on new bearings, will continue to howl when different wearing surfaces are presented to each other. The decision to overhaul therefore, must be considered with regard to time and money available, relative to the degree of noise or malfunction that the driver has to suffer.

PART B – AUTOMATIC TRANSMISSION (BORG WARNER TYPE 12)

13 General description

1 The automatic transmission which is fitted as standard equipment to all models up until 1978 is the Borg Warner Model 12.
2 All forward ratios are automatically engaged in accordance with accelerator position and car speed. Overriding control is still maintained by manual selection and a kick-down facility is provided for rapid change down.
3 Servicing and overhaul operations should be restricted to those described. Due to the complexity of the transmission unit and the need for special tools it is not recommended that major overhauls are undertaken.
4 In the event of a fault developing, always diagnose the problem **before** removing the unit from the car. This fault finding can be carried out either by referring to the Fault Diagnosis Sections in this Chapter or by consulting your Jaguar/Daimler dealer.
5 Factory reconditioned units are normally available through your dealer on an exchange basis, and in the case of a major fault developing in the original unit, this method of rectification can usually show an advantage compared with overhaul charges.

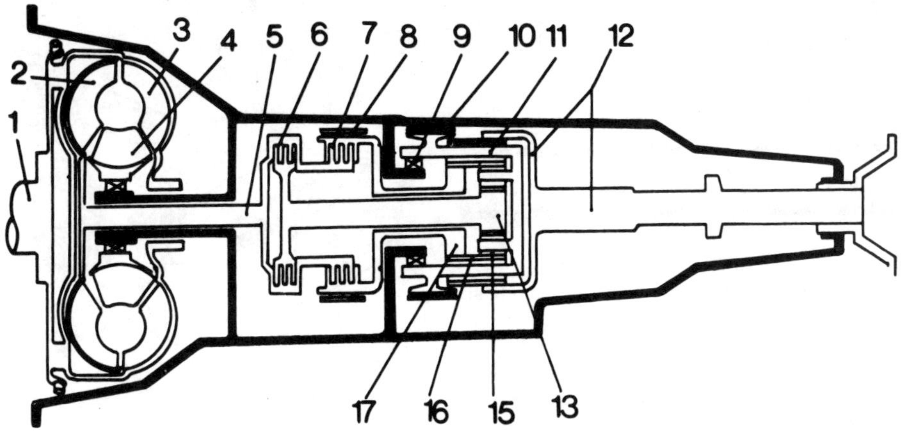

Fig. 6.18 Diagrammatic view of Borg Warner Type 12 transmission (Sec 13)

1 Engine crankshaft	*5 Input shaft*	*9 Uni-directional clutch*	*13 Sun gear and shaft*
2 Turbine	*6 Front clutch*	*10 Rear brake band*	*15 Planet pinion*
3 Impeller	*7 Rear clutch*	*11 Pinion carrier*	*16 Planet pinion*
4 Stator	*8 Front brake band*	*12 Ring gear and output shaft*	*17 Reverse sun gear*

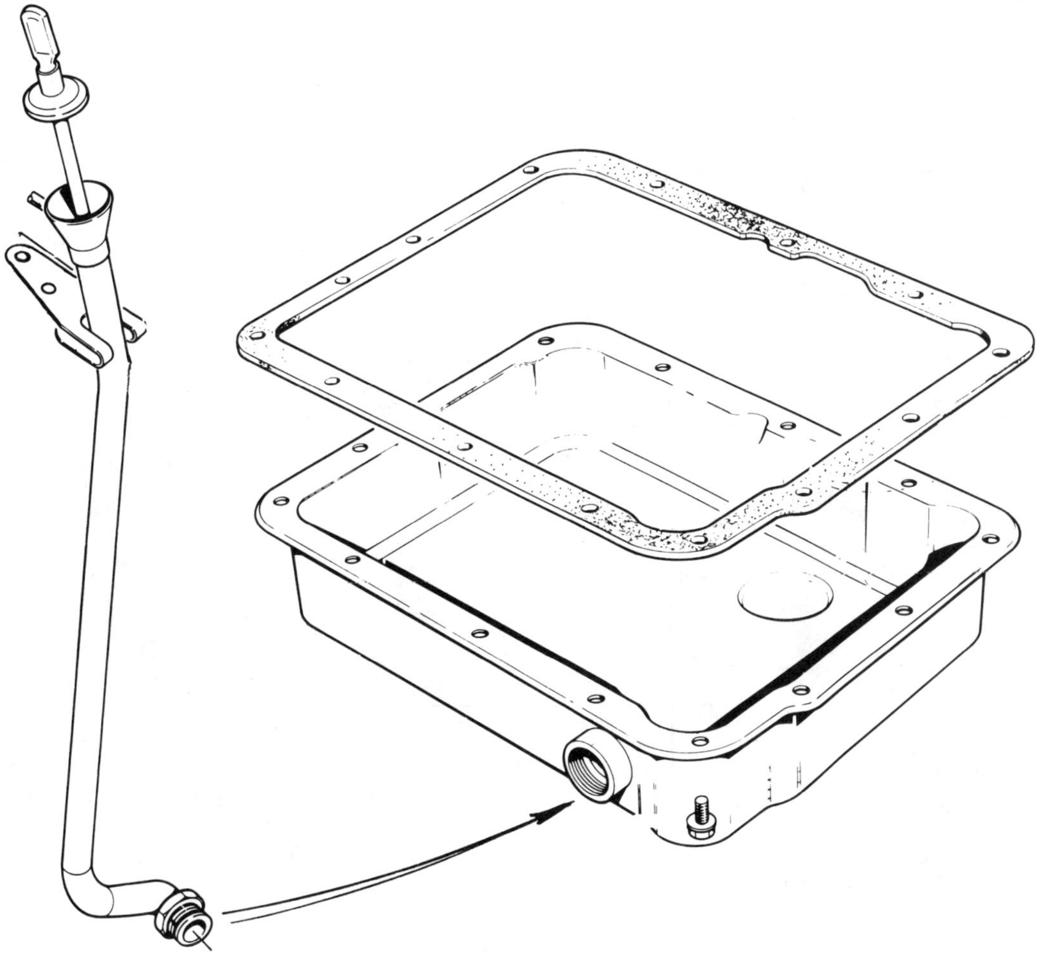

Fig. 6.19 Oil pan and dipstick guide/filler tube (Sec 15)

Fig. 6.20 Dipstick markings on Borg Warner transmission (Sec 14)

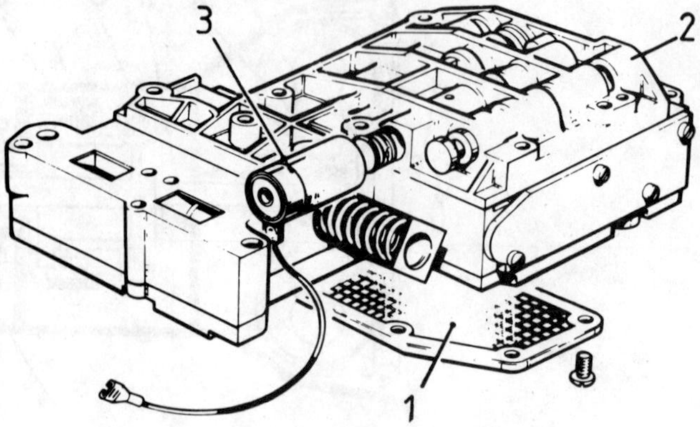

Fig. 6.21 Fluid strainer on valve block (Sec 15)

1 Strainer
2 Valve block
3 Kickdown solenoid

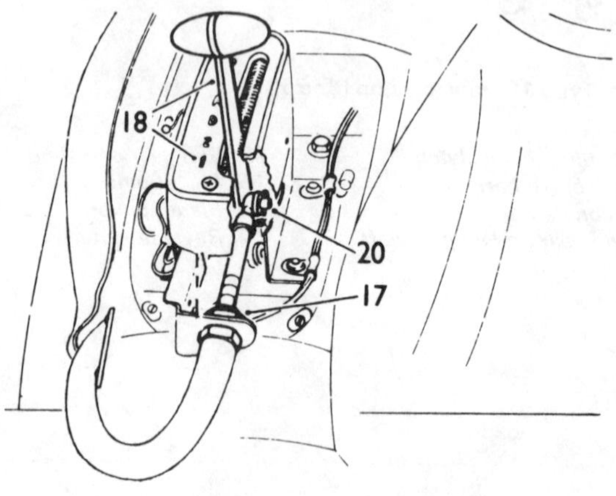

Fig. 6.22 Speed selector lever and cable (Sec 16)

17 Cable locknuts
18 Indicator plate
20 Cable attachment (split pin)

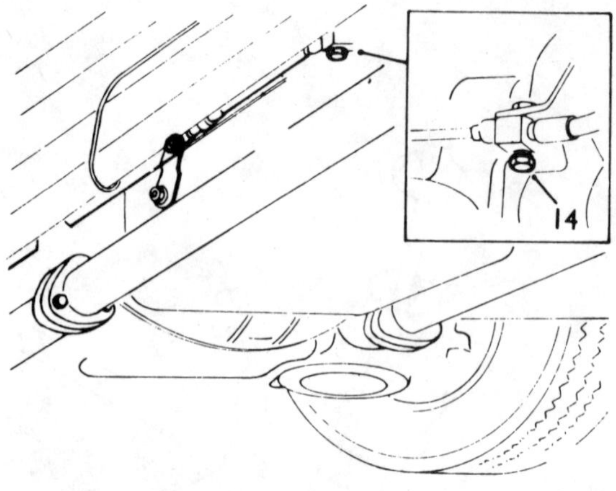

Fig. 6.23 Selector lever on transmission casing (Sec 16)

14 Cable trunnion bolt

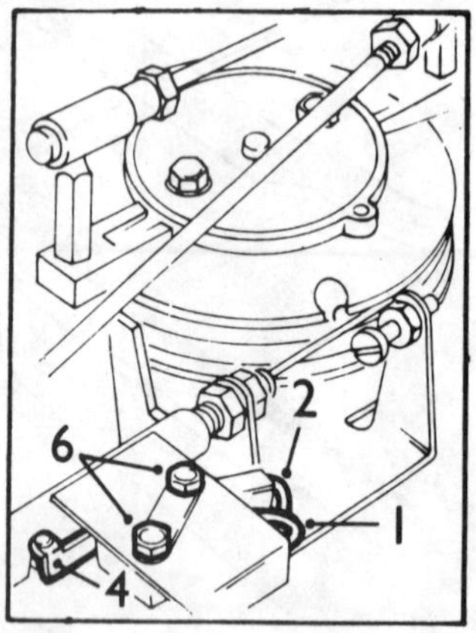

Fig. 6.24 Kickdown switch (Sec 18)

1 Switch terminal
2 Switch terminal
4 Switch arm
6 Switch securing bolts

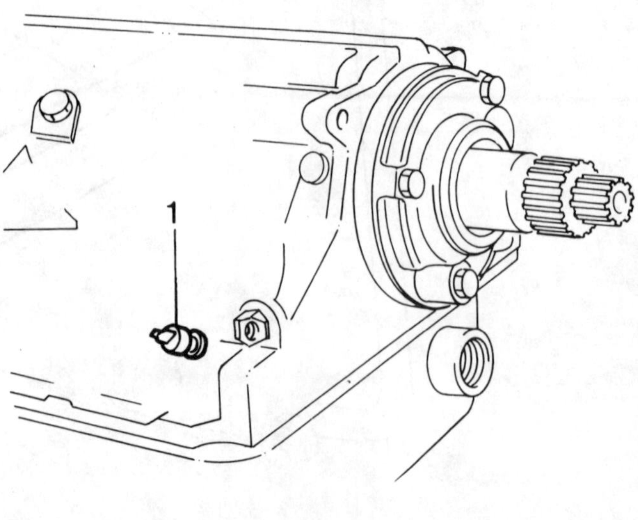

Fig. 6.25 Kickdown solenoid connector terminal (1) (Sec 19)

14 Maintenance and precautions

1 The most important maintenance task is the regular checking of the fluid level.
2 At the intervals specified in 'Routine Maintenance', operate the car on the road for at least 5 miles (8 km) and then place it on a level surface and with the engine still running, move the speed selector lever through all positions finally placing the lever in 'P'.
3 Withdraw the dipstick and wipe it clean on a piece of non-fluffy cloth. Re-insert it and then withdraw it for the second time and read off the fluid level.
4 If necessary, add specified fluid to the combined dipstick/oil filler tube to bring the level up to the 'FULL' mark. The difference between the 'LOW' and 'FULL' marks is equivalent to $1\frac{1}{2}$ Imp pints (1.8 US pints, 0.75 litres). Switch off the engine.
5 The only other maintenance items are to keep the exterior of the transmission casing clean to prevent the unit overheating and periodically to check the condition and security of the fluid flow and return pipes to the cooler located on the right-hand tank of the cooling system radiator.
6 If the car must be towed due to a fault in the engine, then an extra 3 Imp pts (3.6 US pints, 1.7 litres) of fluid must be added to the transmission, the speed selector lever must be placed in 'N' and the ignition key turned to the ACC position.
7 Restrict the towing speed to 30 mph (48 kph) and the distance towed to 30 miles (48 km).
8 If the car must be towed and there is a fault in the transmission then the rear wheels must be raised off the ground, or the propeller shaft must be disconnected from the final drive flange and the shaft tied securely to one side of the car underframe.

15 Transmission fluid – draining and refilling

1 Renewal of the automatic transmission fluid is not to be regarded as a routine service operation. It may be required however if the colour of the fluid on the dipstick is dark or if it smells burnt. This may be caused by overheating due to towing a trailer or overloading.
2 If the engine/transmission is being removed for overhaul then the fluid should be drained from the transmission unit before it is separated from the engine.

Draining

3 Place the car on ramps or over a pit.
4 Remove the left-hand intermediate exhaust pipe (XJ12 and Double Six).
5 As a drain plug is not fitted, unscrew the union nut which holds the combined filler/dipstick tube to the side of the oil pan. Fluid will now drain out and this should be collected in a large capacity container.
6 Unscrew and remove the nut which holds the collision plate to the engine rear mounting (XJS).
7 Unscrew and remove the nuts which secure the collision plate to its locating studs. Lower the plate, noting the location of the washers (XJS).
8 Extract the nuts and/or bolts which secure the oil pan to the transmission casing and lower the pan downward.
9 Remove and discard the gasket. Unbolt the strainer from the valve block and clean it. Refit the strainer.

Refilling

10 Refit the oil pan, using a new gasket.
11 Refit the fluid filler tube (and the collision plate on XJS models).
12 Due to the fact that the torque converter cannot be drained unless it is removed during overhaul, the quantity of fluid required to refill the transmission after draining is less than that required from dry. Refer to the Specifications where both quantities are given.
13 Apply the handbrake and select 'P'. Run the engine until normal operating temperature is reached and then check the fluid level as described in Section 14. Top up as necessary.

16 Speed selector cable – adjustment

1 Remove the centre console as described in Chapter 12.
2 Unscrew the two halves of the knob on the hand control lever (photo) and then set the lever to '1'.
3 Extract the screws and lift the speed selector indicator plate from the lever.
4 Extract the split pin which secures the cable to the base of the hand control lever and disconnect the cable.
5 Set the selector lever on the side of the transmission to '1'. The correct position of the lever can be established by pressing it as far as it will go towards the rear of the car.
6 Release the locknuts at the cable abutment and adjust their position until the selector cable can be connected to the hand control lever without having to disturb the previously set position of the hand control or transmission lever.
7 Tighten the locknuts and fit a new split pin.
8 Check for correct operation, particularly with regard to the operation of the reversing lamp and starter inhibitor switch. Refit the indicator plate, control lever knob, and the centre console.

17 Speed selector cable – removal and refitting

1 Remove the centre console as described in Chapter 12.
2 Refer to Chapter 1, Section 3, paragraph 34 and disconnect the cable trunnion block from the transmission casing.
3 The cable can now be disconnected from the lever on the side of the transmission casing and from the hand control lever.
4 Release the cable locknuts, unscrew and remove the one nearer the front of the car and draw the cable assembly through the mounting bracket at the hand control lever.
5 Refitting is a reversal of removal. On completion adjust the cable as described in the preceding Section.

18 Kickdown switch – checking and adjusting

1 Switch on the ignition and check that the input terminals on the switch are live. These terminals have the green coloured wires running to them.
2 Connect an earthed test lamp to the output terminal (green/white wire) and fully depress the throttle pedal. If the lamp does not light, release the pedal and gently depress the arm of the switch. If the lamp still does not light, renew the switch by unscrewing its mounting bolts.
3 If the lamp lights, loosen the retaining bolts and move the switch towards the cable so that the lamp lights by the switch action with the throttle pedal fully depressed.

19 Kickdown solenoid – testing, removal and refitting

1 The kickdown solenoid connector plug is screwed into the side of

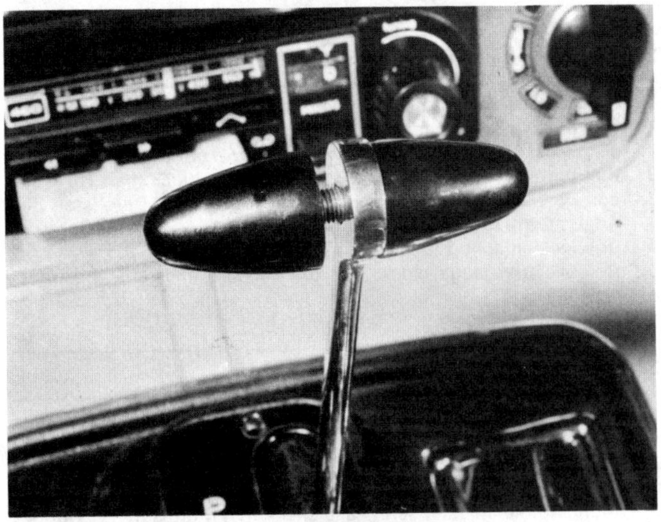

16.2 Automatic transmission speed select control lever

the transmission casing. Pull the wire from the connector terminal.
2 Using a jumper lead, momentarily connect the battery positive terminal to the terminal on the connector. If a click is heard, then the kickdown solenoid is operating correctly. If a click is not heard then the solenoid is faulty and must be renewed.
3 To renew the solenoid, remove the oil pan as described in Section 15, disconnect the lead from the connector terminal on the wall of the transmission casing, rotate the solenoid through 180° and remove it.
4 Refitting is a reversal of removal.

20 Vacuum control unit – testing, removal and refitting

1 A fault in the vacuum control unit will be indicated by one or more of the following symptoms:

(a) Smoky exhaust
(b) Low oil level in transmission requiring constant topping up
(c) Rough automatic gearshifts

2 To test the unit, first remove it from the transmission by disconnecting the hose, then unscrewing it and withdrawing the pushrod. A small panel is fitted to the left-hand side of the transmission tunnel for access.
3 If the unit is now connected to a vacuum source, the indicated vacuum should not fall below 18 in (46 cm) Hg, otherwise it will indicate a perforated diaphragm and a new unit will have to be fitted.
4 Once a new vacuum unit has been fitted, it must be adjusted immediately. To do this, connect a vacuum gauge and the original vacuum pipe to the unit using a 'T' piece.
5 Remove the small plug (0.125 in – 3.2 mm dia.) from the left-hand side of the transmission casing towards the front and connect a fluid pressure gauge (Part No CBW 1A-642 and STN 6752).
6 Have the engine/transmission at normal operating temperature, select 'D' and apply the hand and foot brakes.
7 Increase the engine speed until the vacuum gauge reads between 9 and 10 in (23 to 25 cm) Hg at 1200 rpm. Do not maintain this condition for longer than necessary – see paragraph 11.
8 The reading on the pressure gauge should now be between 70 and 95 lbf/in^2 (4.92 and 6.67 kgf/cm^2).
9 A pressure reading lower than that specified will cause clutch slip and transmission damage.
10 To adjust the vacuum control unit, remove the vacuum hose, insert a screwdriver into the pipe stub. Turn the adjusting screw clockwise to increase pressure or anti-clockwise to decrease it. Two complete turns of the screw will vary the pressure by 10 lbf/in^2 (0.7 kgf/cm^2). If when the adjustment is being checked, a rapid knocking noise is heard between 600 and 800 rpm, then the adjusting screw has been turned too far and has lost contact with the servo actuating rod.
11 When carrying out the foregoing adjustment, do not hold the engine speed for the pressure check (stall speed) for longer than 10 seconds at a time. The total stall period should not exceed one minute in every half hour.

21 Front brake band – adjustment

1 Remove the oil pan as described in Section 15.
2 Release the brake band adjusting screw until it no longer contacts the piston pin. *Note that the screw has a left-hand thread.*
3 Pull the front servo lever back until a gauge block (part No CBW 34) can be inserted between the adjusting screw and the piston pin.
4 Adjust the screw to a torque of 10 lbf in (0.12 kgf m), making sure that the locking spring is located in its retaining slot.
5 Remove the gauge block, refit the oil pass and refill the transmission.

22 Rear brake band – adjustment

1 This operation should be carried out when a new transmission has been installed and at 24 000 miles (38 600 km) intervals thereafter.
2 The adjuster screw is located on the right-hand side of the transmission casing. Release the locknut and unscrew it two turns.
3 Lubricate the adjuster screw and check that it turns freely. Tighten the screw to a torque of 10 lbf ft (1.4 kgf m) and then loosen it exactly 1¼ turns. Retighten the locknut to a torque of 44 lbf ft (6 kgf m).

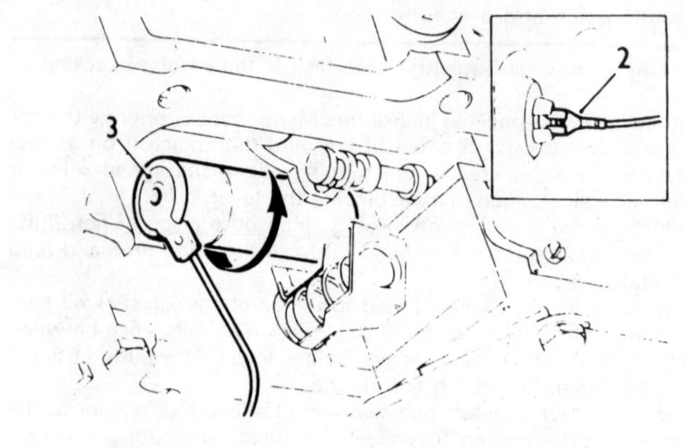

Fig. 6.26 Kickdown solenoid (3) and internal connection to connectors terminal (2) (Sec 19)

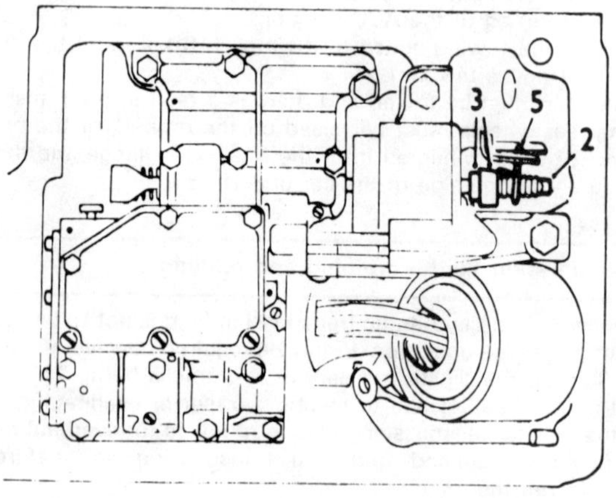

Fig. 6.27 Front brake band adjustment (Sec 21)

2 Adjusting screw
3 Gauge block (CBW 34)
5 Locking spring

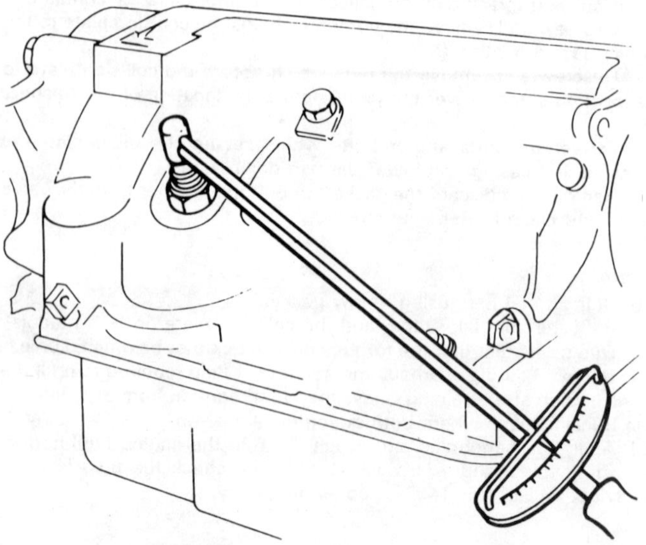

Fig. 6.28 Adjusting rear brake band (Sec 22)

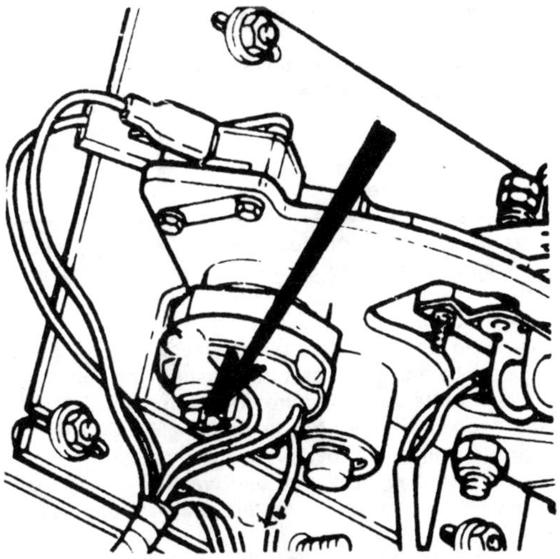

Fig. 6.29 Reversing lamp switch (arrowed) (Sec 23)

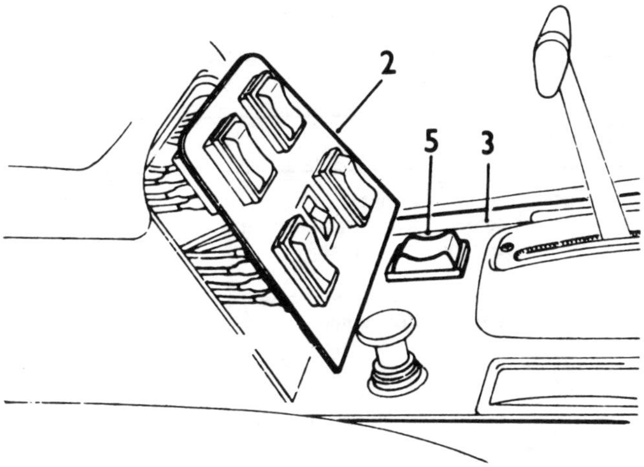

Fig. 6.30 Electric window switch panel (2), escutcheon (3) and door lock switch (5) (Sec 24)

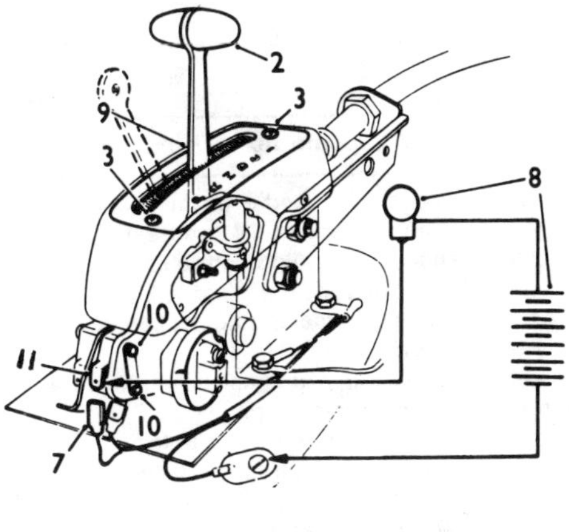

Fig. 6.31 Starter inhibitor switch test circuit (Sec 24)

2 Speed selector knob
3 Selector indicator screws
7 Switch leads
8 Test lamp circuit
9 Speed selector control lever
10 Switch securing nuts
11 Inhibitor switch

23 Reversing lamp switch – removal and refitting

1 Disconnect the battery.
2 Raise the lid on the centre console glove box and extract the console centre panel securing screw (XJS models only).
3 Remove the electric window lift control panel and the selector lever handgrip (XJ12 and Double Six models only).
4 Extract the centre panel screws and raise the panel until the leads to the various switches can be identified and disconnected. Remove the panel.
5 Unbolt and remove the selector indicator cover.
6 Identify the leads to the reverse switch terminals and disconnect them. Remove the switch, noting the washer and spacers.
7 Refitting is a reversal of removal.

24 Starter inhibitor switch – adjusting, removal and refitting

1 The starter motor should only operate if the ignition key is turned with the speed selector lever in 'N' or 'P'. If the starter operates with the selector lever in any other position, carry out the following adjustment.
2 Disconnect the battery.
3 Unscrew and remove the two halves of the selector control lever knob.
4 Extract the screws and draw the speed selector indicator off the hand control lever (XJS models only).
5 Prise the electric window switch panel away from the centre console without disconnecting the switches.
6 Extract the screws which hold the selector control escutcheon so that it can be slightly withdrawn to gain access to the cigar lighter and door lock switch terminals. Identify the wires and disconnect them. Remove the escutcheon.
7 Disconnect the supply cable from the starter inhibitor switch.
8 Connect a test lamp and battery in series with the switch and then move the selector lever to 'N'.
9 Slacken the switch locknuts and move the switch until the test lamp lights up. Tighten the locknuts.
10 Move the selector lever to 'P' and check that the test lamp is on but goes off when the lever is moved to any drive position.
11 Remove the battery and test lamp, re-make all the original connections and refit the components which were removed. Reconnect the battery.

25 Stall test

1 This test is only required if the performance of the transmission is suspect. The stall speed is the maximum engine rpm obtained whilst driving the impeller against the stationary turbine.
2 The engine must be in a correct state of tune and adjustment and the engine/transmission at normal operating temperature.
3 Fully apply the handbrake and the foot brake.
4 Start the engine, select 'D' and depress the accelerator pedal to the limit of its travel. Note the tachometer reading.
5 If the indicated rpm is under 1300 (XJS) or 1000 (XJ12 and Double Six) then the stator free wheel is slipping.
6 If the indicated rpm is between 1950 and 2050 (XJS) and 1600 and 1700 (XJ12 and Double Six) it can be assumed that the transmission is operating normally and is in good condition.
7 If the rpm is above 2400 (XJS) or 2100 (XJ12 and Double Six) then the transmission internal clutch is slipping.
8 To avoid overheating the transmission, *do not carry out the stall test for longer than ten seconds at a time.* The total stall period should not exceed one minute in every half hour.

26 Transmission unit – removal and refitting

1 The transmission is removed and refitted in conjunction with the engine as described in Chapter 1, Section 3, 4 or 5 as applicable.
2 The transmission should be separated from the engine as described in Section 6 of Chapter 1.

27 Torque converter housing and torque converter – removal and refitting

1 The operations described in this Section will normally only be required if a new or rebuilt transmission is to be installed. The original torque converter and converter housing can be fitted to the new transmission unit.
2 Remove the engine/transmission as described in Chapter 1.
3 Disconnect the oil cooler pipes.
4 Remove the breather pipe, dipstick and oil filler tube. Disconnect the pipe from the vacuum unit.
5 Drain the transmission fluid.
6 Unscrew and remove the four nuts which hold the transmission housing to the torque converter housing. Support the weight of the transmission and withdraw it.
7 Unbolt and remove the starter motor.
8 Unbolt and remove the cover plate from the lower half of the front of the torque converter housing.
9 Unbolt the converter housing from the engine cylinder block.
10 Remove the engine oil filter.
11 Extract the plug from the rear left-hand side of the crankcase to provide access to the driveplate-to-torque converter setscrews.
12 Turn the crankshaft until the first of the driveplate-to-torque converter setscrews comes into view.
13 Flatten the tabs on the lockplate and extract the setscrew. Continue to rotate the crankshaft until all the setscrews have been removed. Mark the driveplate-to-torque converter relationship and withdraw it.
14 Refitting is a reversal of removal, but make sure that the torque converter lugs engage with the cut-outs in the oil pump gear.

28 Rear oil seal – renewal

1 Leakage of fluid from the rear end of the transmission extension housing will almost certainly be from a worn output shaft oil seal.
2 Disconnect the front end of the propeller shaft (see Chapter 7) and place the shaft to one side.
3 Unscrew and remove the output shaft coupling flange nut. The nut may be secured by a split pin or a tab washer. The coupling flange will have to be held quite still while the nut is unscrewed. Make up a lever for this which can be bolted to the coupling flange using the original bolts which will still be in position in the flange.
4 Withdraw the coupling flange and washer.
5 Prise out the oil seal and then tap in a new one using a piece of tubing as a drift.
6 Apply grease to the coupling flange surfaces which will be in contact with the lips of the oil seal, install the coupling, tighten the nut to the specified torque and fit a new split pin or bend over the tab washer.
7 Reconnect the propeller shaft and then check and top up the fluid level in the automatic transmission unit.

29 Fault diagnosis – automatic transmission (BW type 12)

Symptom	Reason(s)
Engine will not start in 'N' or 'P'	Faulty starter or ignition circuit Incorrect speed selector linkage adjustment Incorrectly adjusted inhibitor switch
Engine starts in selector positions other than 'N' or 'P'	Incorrect speed selector linkage adjustment Incorrectly adjusted inhibitor switch
Severe bump when selecting 'D' or 'R' or excessive creep when handbrake released	Idling speed too high Vacuum circuit fault Solenoid fault
Poor acceleration and low maximum speed	Incorrect fluid level Incorrect linkage adjustment
No movement when 'R' selected	Incorrect rear band adjustment Low fluid level
Poor upshift quality	Front band requires adjustment
No movement in 'D'	Front brake band requires adjustment Fault in one-way clutch

PART C – AUTOMATIC TRANSMISSION (GM 400)

30 General description

1 This type of transmission is fitted as standard to XJ12 and Double Six models on Series 3 versions and to XJS models from 1979 cars onwards.
2 The transmission is fully automatic and incorporates a vacuum modulator and pressure regulator to monitor the position of the throttle so that the transmission is always engaged in the correct speed ratio.
3 The transmission can be distinguished from earlier Borg Warner units by the fact that the speed selector control lever has a longer travel between P and R, and that the torque converter bellhousing is cast in one piece with the transmission casing and cannot be detached from the casing.

31 Transmission fluid – topping up and renewal

1 The fluid level should be checked in a similar way to that described for the Borg Warner unit in Section 14 (photos).
2 Renewing the transmission fluid is not a routine service operation and should only be needed if the fluid on the dipstick appears discoloured or smells burnt. These conditions can be caused by towing a trailer or by overloading.
3 To drain the fluid, the oil pan must be removed as described in Section 35, there being no drain plug.
4 As the torque converter will not drain unless it is removed during overhaul, the quantity of fluid required to fill the transmission will be less than that required to fill from dry. Pour in the specified quantity of fluid and then check the fluid level as previously described. Top up as necessary but do not overfill.

32 Speed selector cable – adjustment

1 Remove the centre console as described in Chapter 12.

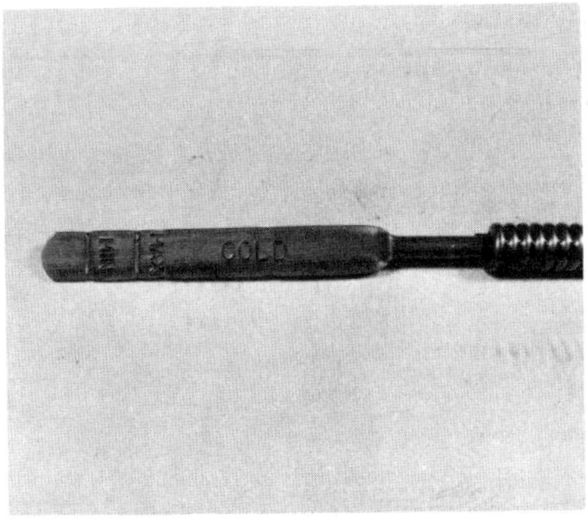

31.1A Dipstick marking (COLD side)

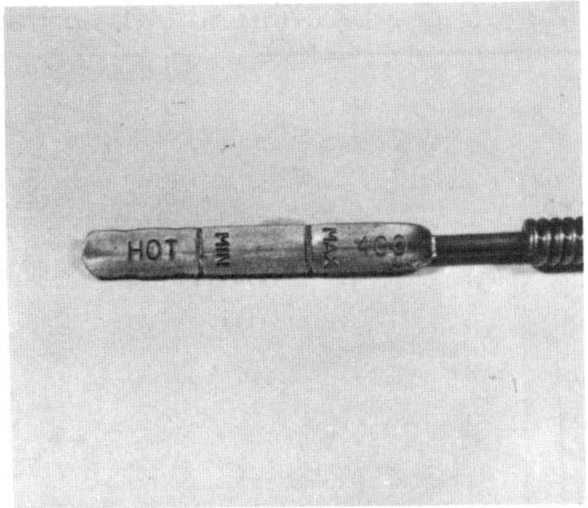

31.1B Dipstick marking (HOT side)

32.2 Selector quadrant details: 1 – Reversing lamp switch; 2 – Starter inhibitor switch; 3 – Index bulb; 4 – Operating cable locknuts

35.5 Removing the transmission oil pan – GM400 (transmission inverted on bench)

35.6A Unbolting the fluid filter – GM400 (transmission inverted on bench)

35.6B View of the GM 400 automatic transmission (filter removed)

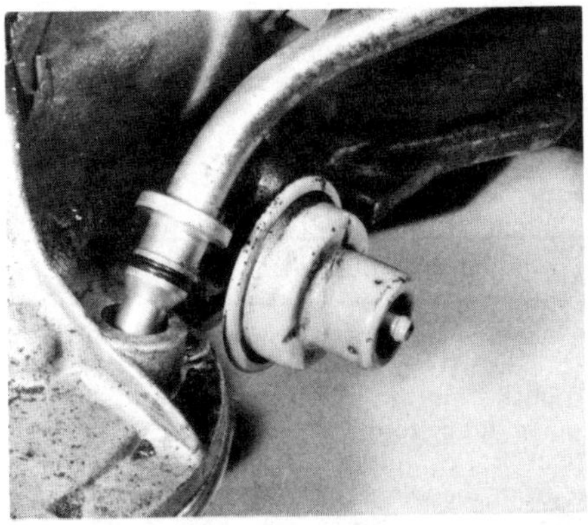

37.3 Removing the fluid dipstick guide tube

37.29 Rear mounting (GM 400 transmission)

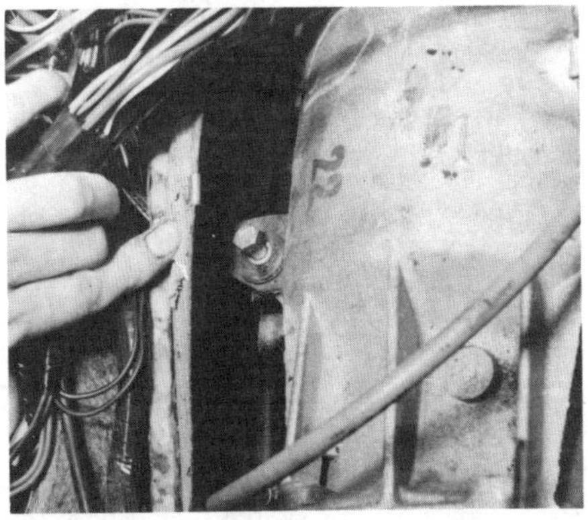

38.1 Speed selector cable trunnion bracket bolt

38.2A Trunnion bracket bolt removed (viewed from below)

38.2B Speed selector cable and trunnion bracket (transmission removed)

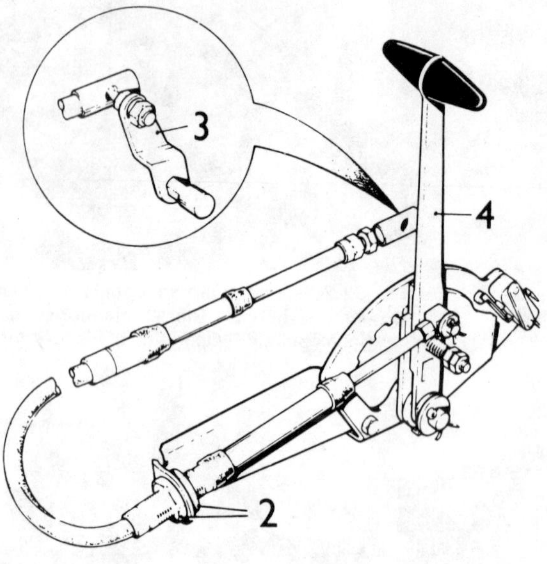

Fig. 6.32 Speed selector control cable (Sec 32)

2 Locknut
3 Transmission lever
4 Selector control lever

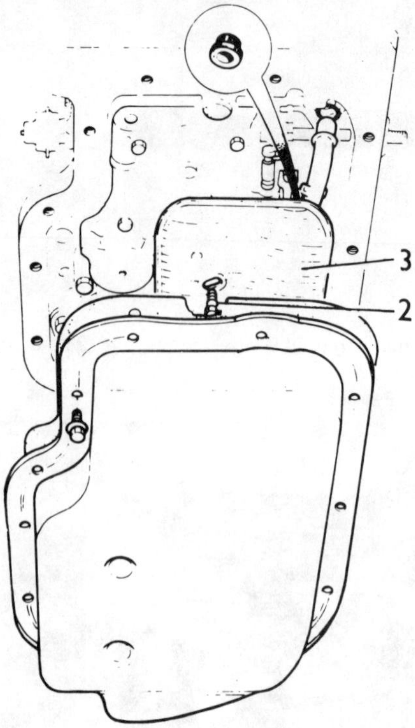

Fig. 6.33 Oil pan and filter (Sec 35)

2 Filter retaining screw
3 Filter

2 Slacken the locknuts at the cable abutment bracket just to the rear of the selector control lever (photo).
3 Set the control lever on the side of the transmission casing in the 'N' position. To do this, count the number of detents ('clicks') back from P or 1.
4 Now set the selector control lever in 'N'.
5 Without moving either lever from its centre of detent position, tighten the cable locknuts.
6 When correctly adjusted, a little free play should be evident at each selector position.

33 Kickdown switch – checking and adjusting

1 Refer to Section 18.

34 Starter inhibitor switch – adjusting, removal and refitting

1 Refer to Section 24.

35 Oil pan and filter – removal and refitting

1 Raise the car on ramps or place it over an inspection pit.
2 From the transmission casing unclamp the vacuum capsule, disconnect it and allow the fluid to drain into a container.
3 Reconnect and re-clamp the capsule.
4 Unscrew and remove all the oil pan bolts except for two at the front edge and one at the rear.
5 Place a container under the oil pan and press the oil pan upwards while the remaining bolts are removed and the oil pan tilted downward to allow the remaining fluid to drain. Discard the gasket (photo).
6 Unscrew and remove the oil filter securing bolt, remove the filter and discard it (photos).
7 Fit the new filter and tighten the securing screw.
8 Wipe out the oil pan with a non-fluffy rag, discard the old gasket and stick a new one to clean flanges using petroleum jelly as an adhesive.
9 Refit the oil pan and fill with fresh fluid as described in Section 31.

36 Stall test

1 Refer to Section 25. The information applies equally to the GM 400 transmission except that the stall speed for a transmission in good condition should be approximately 2400 rpm.

37 Transmission unit – removal and refitting

1 Place the car on ramps or over an inspection pit and disconnect the battery.
2 Withdraw the fluid dipstick from the transmission.
3 Unbolt the dipstick guide tube from the engine lifting eye and remove the upper tube (photo).
4 Unbolt the wing stays from the wings, release the pipe from one of the stays and then swing both stays away from the wings.
5 Using a suitable crossbeam (its ends located in the wing valance channels), and adjustable lifting hooks engaged in the rear lifting eyes, take the weight of the engine.
6 Disconnect the front exhaust pipes from the intermediate pipes by uncoupling the flanges.
7 Unbolt and remove the heat shields from the intermediate exhaust pipes. Remove the rear heat shield.
8 Pull the exhaust pipes outwards and tie them to the underframe.
9 Unbolt and remove the front heat shields.
10 Remove the centre nut from the transmission rear mounting. Remove the spacer.
11 Using a jack and a block of wood as an insulator, support the rear mounting plate of the transmission, then unscrew and remove the rear mounting bolts and spacers.
12 Lower the jack, remove the rear mounting and extract the crossmember bolts. Remove the crossmember.
13 Disconnect the front of the propeller shaft from the transmission output flange and tie the shaft to one side of the car.
14 Adjust the engine support hooks so that the engine is lowered by not more than one inch (25.4 mm).
15 Working under the car, disconnect the speedometer cable from the transmission.

16 Disconnect the speed selector cable from the lever on the side of the transmission and then release the cable trunnion pinch-bolt at the bracket on the transmission casing. Once the centre console is removed (Chapter 12), the speed selector cable can be drawn through the trunnion block and detached from the transmission if the cable loop to the rear of the selector lever is pulled rearward.
17 Disconnect the kickdown solenoid electrical lead and unclip the lead from the transmission.
18 Disconnect the vacuum pipe from the modulator capsule and then unclamp it. Allow the fluid which will run out to drain into a container.
19 Extract and discard the modulator O-ring.
20 Disconnect the transmission fluid cooler pipes from the transmission casing. Unclip them from the engine sump and move them carefully aside.
21 Unbolt and remove the cover plate from the front face of the torque converter bellhousing.
22 Extract the plug from the left-hand side of the front face of the converter bellhousing and insert a socket wrench to unscrew the setscrews which hold the torque converter to the driveplate. The crankshaft pulley nut will have to be turned to bring each setscrew into view in the plug hole.
23 On North American cars, unbolt and remove the right-hand heat shield from the steering rack gaiter.
24 If a catalytic converter is fitted, unbolt it from the right-hand manifold.
25 Unscrew and remove the bolts which hold the torque converter bellhousing to the engine, but leave the two lower left-hand ones and the lower starter motor bolt in position for the time being.
26 Remove the dipstick tube and slide the vacuum pipe bracket along the pipe.
27 The transmission is extremely heavy and the help of at least three assistants will be required to remove it. Take its weight, extract the remaining bolts and withdraw the transmission from the engine. As the unit is removed, take care to press the torque converter towards the rear of the transmission since if it disengages from the fluid pump, the oil seal may be damaged and loss of fluid can be expected.
28 If the original unit is being refitted, make up a clamp and bolt it to one of the bellhousing bolt holes to retain the torque converter rearwards.
29 If a new or rebuilt unit is being fitted, it will come complete with a new torque converter and retaining clamp. The latter must be removed just prior to installation of the transmission. Remove all blanking plugs from the new unit and take off any external components from the original unit which will be required for the new transmission. These will include the rear mounting (photo), the cooler pipe unions and the selector cable collar.
30 Refitting the transmission is a reversal of removal. Make sure that the torque converter is pushed fully rearward into engagement with the fluid pump drive keyways before coupling the transmission to the engine. It is imperative that just before the transmission is mated with the engine, the holes in the driveplate are aligned with the tapped holes in the torque converter. With the original torque converter, this is achieved by aligning the torque converter/driveplate paint spots. With a new torque converter, it is best to apply the paint spots in advance of reassembly. Failure to carry out this alignment before mating prevents insertion of the bolts as the rivet heads on the driveplate prevent rotation of the plate in relation to the torque converter once they are closely coupled.
31 Insert all the converter-to-driveplate bolts finger-tight before tightening them to the specified torque.
32 Jam the starter ring gear to prevent the torque converter turning while the bolts are fully tightened.
33 Fill the transmission with fresh fluid as described in Section 31, remembering that a larger quantity will be required if the transmission has been filled from dry using a new torque converter (see Specifications).

38 Speed selector cable trunnion bracket – removal and refitting

1 The speed selector cable trunnion bracket which is attached to the side of the transmission housing is bolted in position with a bolt entered from above (photo).
2 Although the cable can be withdrawn from the trunnion after disconnecting its front end and releasing the cable pinch-bolt, in the event of the trunnion bracket having to be removed due to fracture or breakage, then the centre console will have to be withdrawn as described in Chapter 12. If the main multi-pin plugs are now disconnected and some of the wiring harness clips released, it will be found that the screws which hold the transmission cover plate can be extracted and the plate complete with selector control can be lifted and removed rearwards from under the harness and other electrical leads. Once this is done the bolt which holds the selector cable trunnion to the gearcase can be unscrewed from above (photos).
3 If the foregoing operations have to be resorted to, make very sure that all wiring connections are clearly identified with masking tape onto which matching numbers or letters are written, or alternatively by noting their colour coding and switch terminal numbers before disconnecting them. There is such a profusion of wires under the centre console that it will be very time consuming to work out reconnections if the leads are pulled off in a haphazard fashion.
4 The transmission tunnel cover can be drilled with a hole large enough to accept a socket wrench and a rubber plug fitted to facilitate access to the selector cable trunnion block bolt on a future occasion.

39 Fault diagnosis – automatic transmission (GM400)

Symptom	Reason(s)
Delayed upshift or no upshift	Incorrect fluid level Faulty modulator Faulty detent solenoid Restricted exhaust system
No drive or slips in drive	Incorrect fluid level Incorrect selector cable adjustment
No reverse or slips in reverse	Incorrect fluid level Incorrect selector cable adjustment
No hold in 'P'	Incorrect selector cable adjustment
Drive in 'N'	Incorrect selector cable adjustment
Noisy operation	Incorrect fluid level Blocked filter Water in fluid (perforated cooler) Loose converter to driveplate bolts Cracked driveplate
Squeal during acceleration	Worn speedometer driven gear or O-ring seal

Chapter 7 Propeller shaft

Contents

Specifications

Type

XJ12 and Double Six	Two section, open, with universal joints and flexibly mounted centre bearing. Sliding joint on front section
XJS	Single section, open, with universal joints and sliding joint on front end

Torque wrench settings

	lbf ft	Nm
Propeller shaft flange nuts	34	46
Centre bearing baseplate bolts	18	25
Rear mounting spigot nut (XJS)	30	41

1 General description

1 The propeller shaft on XJ12 and Double Six models is of two section type with a centre bearing mounted to the bodyshell.
2 On XJS models, the propeller shaft is of one-piece construction. Some versions have a slightly larger diameter rubber damped shaft.
3 The universal joints are of conventional needle bearing type and are repairable.

2 Propeller shaft (XJ12 and Double Six) – removal and refitting

1 Place the car on ramps or over an inspection pit.
2 Disconnect the battery.
3 Support the weight of the engine, either on a jack with a wood block insulator under the sump, or with a crossbar and adjustable lifting hooks engaged in the engine rear lifting eyes as described in Chapter 1.
4 Remove the bolts securing the intermediate and rear heat shields.
5 Unbolt the exhaust intermediate pipe flanges and lower the exhaust pipes after removing the heat shields.
6 Jack up the rear mounting plate slightly and unscrew and remove the bolts which hold it to the bodyframe. Lower the jack and remove the strengthening bracket heat shields, the mounting plate, coil spring and washers. Refer to Chapter 1, Section 3, and remove the plate which covers the propeller shaft front flange.
7 Unbolt the propeller shaft front flange from the transmission output flange. Access to these flange nuts will be improved if the rear wheels are jacked up so that the propeller shaft can be turned (photo).
8 Unbolt the propeller shaft rear flange from the final drive companion flange (photo).
9 Unscrew and remove the propeller shaft centre bearing baseplate (photo), support and lower the complete propeller shaft and withdraw it from under the car.
10 Unbolt and remove the four self-locking nuts to release the heat shield from the centre bearing carrier.
11 Unscrew and remove the self-locking nut and the safety bolt from the centre bearing carrier.
12 Unscrew and remove the self-locking nuts which hold the centre bearing ring to the rubber mounting bracket. Retrieve the bump stop bracket and spacer studs complete.
13 Refitting is a reversal of removal, but check the bump stop setting and propeller shaft alignment as described in Sections 8 and 9.

3 Propeller shaft (XJS) – removal and refitting

1 The operations are very similar to those described in the preceding Section except that there is no centre bearing.
2 The gearbox rear mounting spigot should be removed to give better access to the propeller shaft front flange bolts.
3 Refitting is a reversal of removal, but tighten all bolts and nuts to the specified torque.

4 Propeller shaft front and rear sections (XJ12, Double Six) – removal and refitting

Front section

1 This can only be withdrawn from the rear of the propeller shaft after the complete assembly has been removed from the car.
2 Unscrew and remove the four nuts and bolts which hold the front and rear shaft flanges together and separate the sections.

Rear section

3 The rear section of the propeller shaft can be removed from the car without the need to disturb the rest of the propeller shaft assembly.
4 Unscrew and remove the four self-locking nuts which hold the

A Front section
B Rear section
1 Transmission
2 Shaft front flange
3 Universal joint
4 Sliding member
5 Rubber bellows
6 Splined section
7 Universal joint
8 Connecting flange to rear shaft section
9 Rear shaft front flange
10 Dust-excluder
11 Bearing ring (typical)
12 Centre bearing
13 Dust-excluder
14 Propeller shaft rear section
15 Universal joint
16 Shaft rear flange to final drive

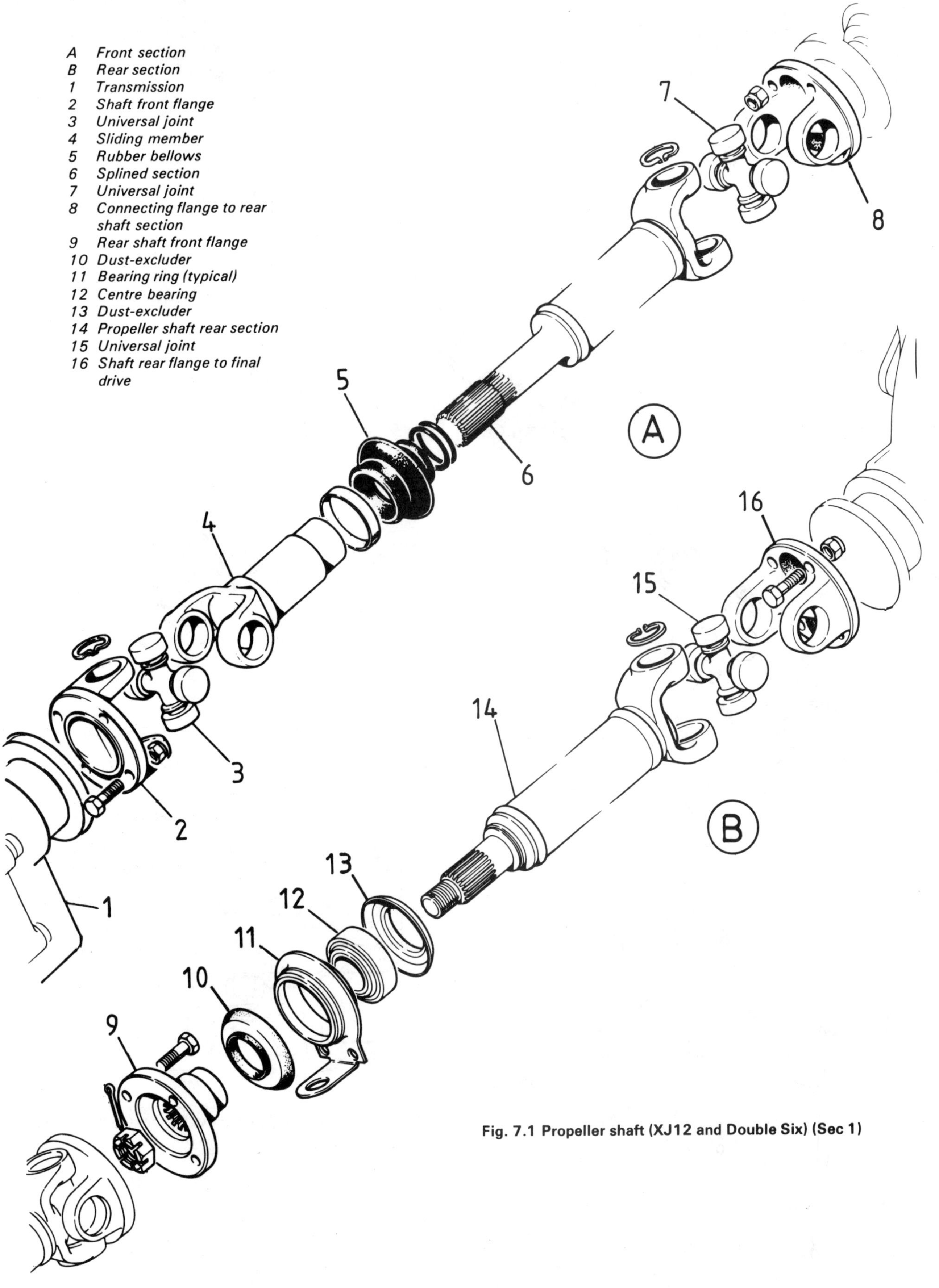

Fig. 7.1 Propeller shaft (XJ12 and Double Six) (Sec 1)

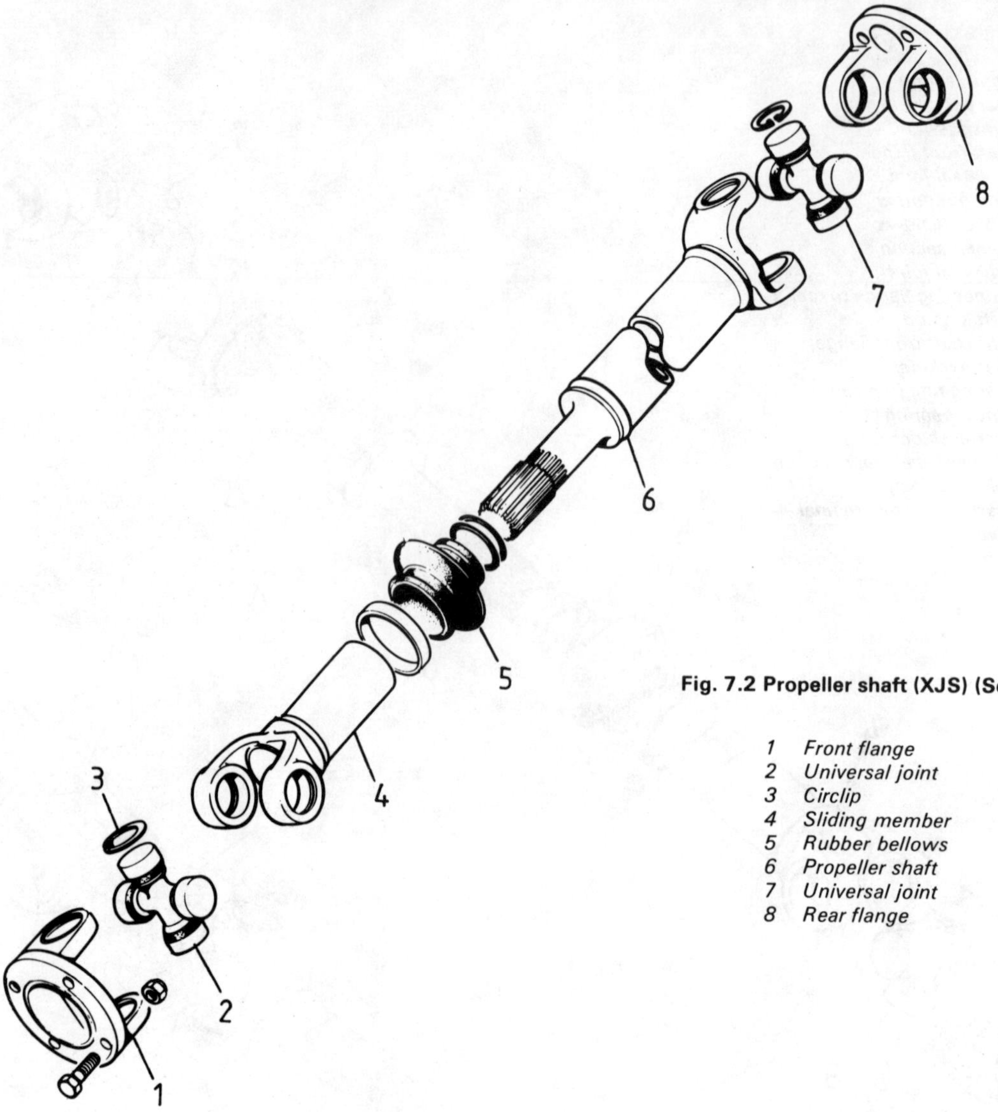

Fig. 7.2 Propeller shaft (XJS) (Sec 1)

1 *Front flange*
2 *Universal joint*
3 *Circlip*
4 *Sliding member*
5 *Rubber bellows*
6 *Propeller shaft*
7 *Universal joint*
8 *Rear flange*

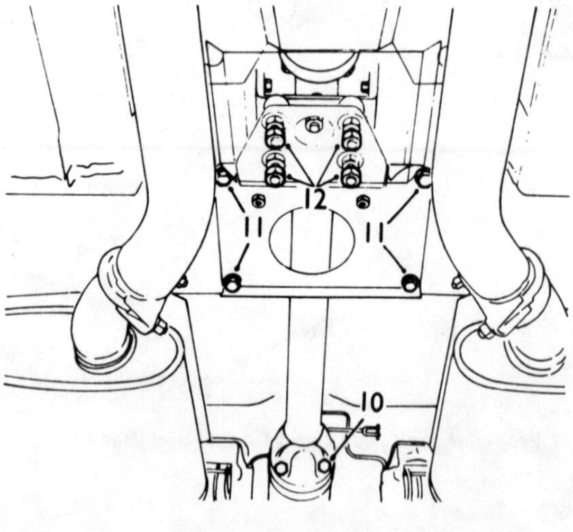

Fig. 7.3 Centre bearing mounting (XJ12, Double Six) (Sec 2)

10 *Rear flange bolts*
11 *Baseplate screws*
12 *Heat shield self-locking nuts*

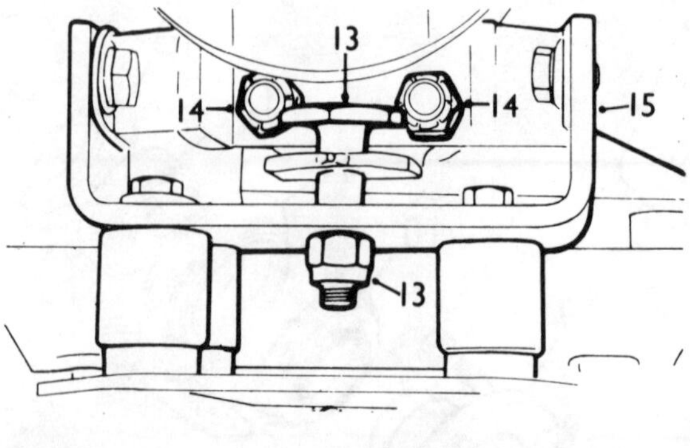

Fig. 7.4 Centre bearing carrier (XJ12, Double Six) (Sec 2)

13 *Safety bolt and self-locking nut*
14 *Self-locking nuts (centre bearing ring to rubber mounting bracket)*
15 *Bump stop bracket*

heat shield to the centre bearing carrier.

5 Unbolt the rear shaft flange from the front shaft flange.

6 Unbolt the rear end of the propeller shaft from the final drive pinion flange.

7 Support the rear shaft section and unbolt the centre bearing baseplate.

8 Repeat the operations described in paragraphs 11 and 12 of Section 2.

9 Refitting is a reversal of removal, but check the bump stop setting and propeller shaft alignment as described in Sections 8 and 9.

5 Universal joints – overhaul

1 Wear in the needle roller bearings is characterised by judder and vibration in the transmission on over-run, 'clonks' on taking up the drive, and in extreme cases of lack of lubrication, metallic squeaking and ultimately grating and shrieking sounds as the bearings break up.

2 It is easy to check if the needle roller bearings are worn; with the propeller shaft in position, try to turn the shaft with one hand and with the other hand the rear axle flange and repeat this procedure for the other joints. Any movement between the shaft and the front, centre or rear couplings is indicative of bearing failure and/or wear in the spider. The old bearings will have to be discarded and replaced by a new universal joint assembly.

3 Remove the propeller shaft, in the manner described in Sections 2 or 3.

4 Thoroughly clean all dirt from the snap rings and the top of the bearing surfaces.

5 Remove all the circlips by pinching with a pair of pliers and at the same time prising out with a screwdriver. If a ring proves difficult to remove it may be because it is jammed by the end of the bearing race, so slightly tap the end of the race to relieve the pressure.

6 Hold the joint in the hand and with a hide-faced or other type of

2.7 Propeller shaft front joint

2.8 Propeller shaft rear joint

2.9 Propeller shaft centre bearing mounting (typical)

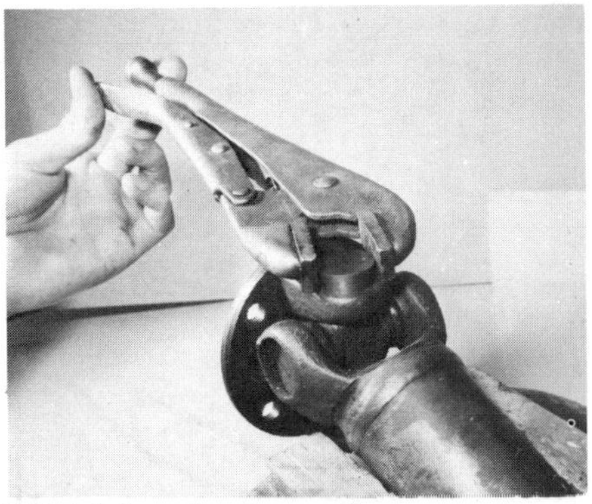

5.6 Twisting a bearing cup from a yoke

5.10 Typical universal joint repair kit

5.13 Alternative method of fitting a bearing cup using a socket and vice

5.15 Fitting a bearing cup clip

5.16 Propeller shaft sliding joint

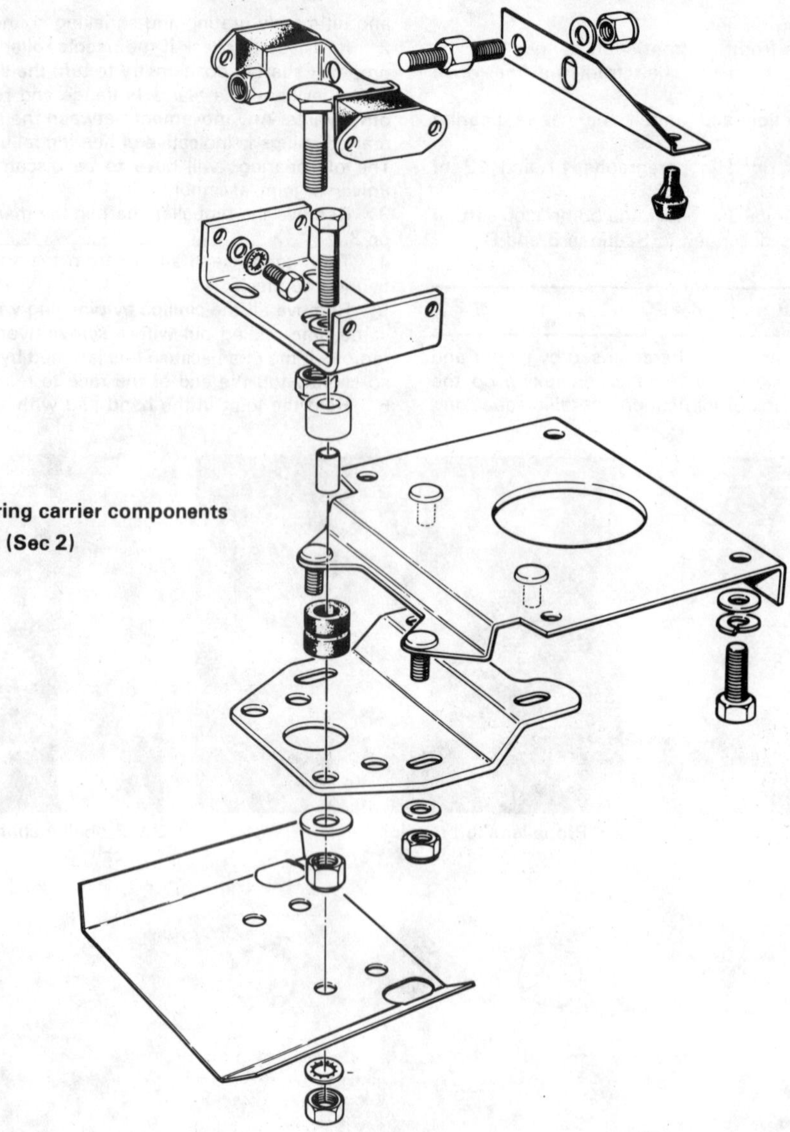

Fig. 7.5 Centre bearing carrier components (typical) (Sec 2)

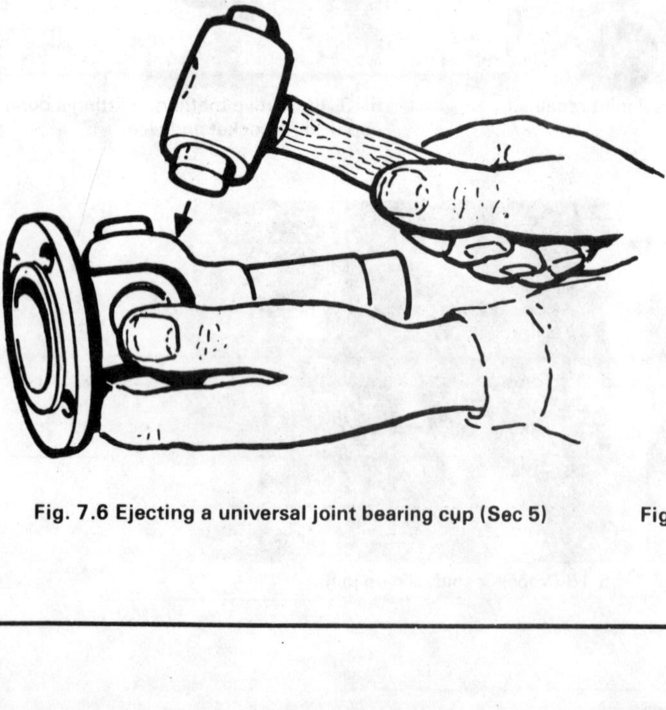

Fig. 7.6 Ejecting a universal joint bearing cup (Sec 5)

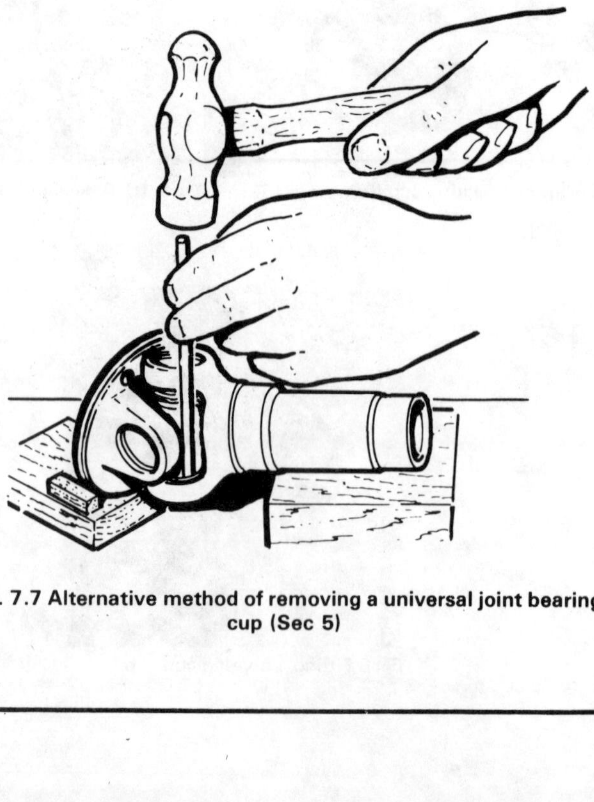

Fig. 7.7 Alternative method of removing a universal joint bearing cup (Sec 5)

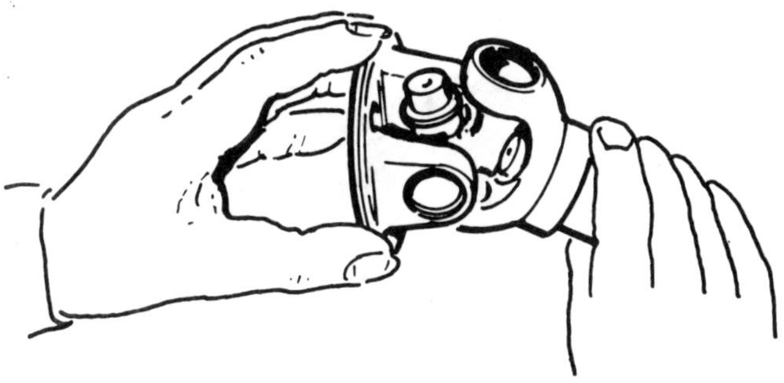

Fig. 7.8 Separating a universal joint yoke from spider (Sec 5)

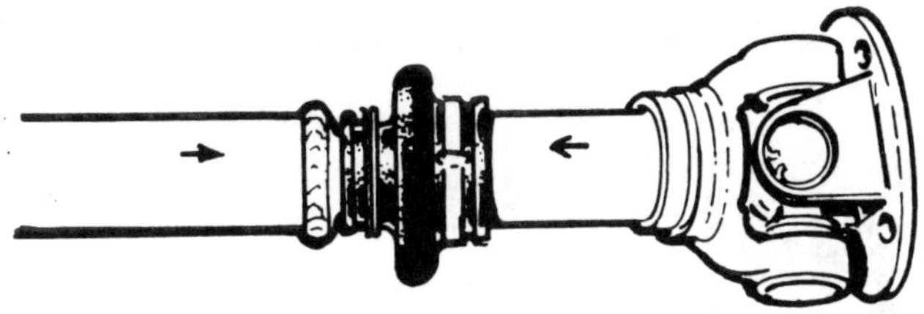

Fig. 7.9 Propeller shaft sliding joint alignment marks (Sec 5)

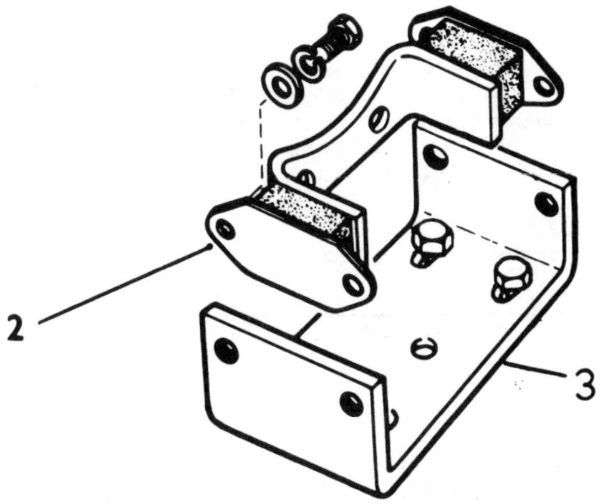

Fig. 7.10 Centre bearing mounting (XJ12, Double Six) (Sec 7)

2 Mounting
3 Carrier

soft hammer, tap the yoke lug as shown in Fig. 7.6. This will cause the top bearing to work outwards until it can finally be removed with the fingers. If the top bearing proves obstinate it can be tapped out from inside with a small diameter punch (photo) (Fig. 7.7).
7 Repeat the above procedure for the opposite bearing.
8 The splined sleeve yoke to flange can now be separated from the shaft yoke.
9 Rest the two trunnions which are now exposed on wood blocks, and tap the yoke with a soft-nosed hammer to remove the two remaining races.
10 It is now advisable to look carefully at the yoke cross holes. It is a very rare event but these holes have been known to wear to a certain degree of ovality. If this has occurred the defective item will have to be renewed. Otherwise, obtain a universal joint repair kit (photo).
11 Renew the cork gaskets and retainers.
12 Smear the wall of the race with grease to keep the rollers in position in the housing for assembly.
13 Insert the spider in the yoke holes, place the bearings in position and then lightly tap it home using a soft flat-faced drift slightly smaller than the yoke in diameter. Alternatively, press the bearings in using a vice (photo).
14 Repeat the above for the opposite bearing in the yoke.
15 Fit new circlips to the bearings and ensure they are correctly located in the grooves (photo).
16 Now place the mating yoke in position on the spider and fit the bearings and circlips in the same manner as described above. It is essential that the sliding joint is refitted with its fixed yoke in line with the fixed yoke at the end of the propeller shaft; arrows are stamped on the two items to facilitate alignment. Apply grease to the mating surfaces of the sliding section of the shaft. Fit a new gaiter and clips (photo).
17 Make sure that the joint moves freely in all direction, if it appears to bind tap lightly with a wooden mallet to relieve any pressure of the bearings on the end of the spider.

6 Centre bearing (XJ12 and Double Six) – removal and refitting

1 Remove the rear section of the propeller shaft as described in Section 4.
2 Extract the split pin and unscrew and remove the castellated nut.
3 Draw the drive flange off the propeller shaft.
4 Support the bearing ring on the open jaws of a vice and using a plastic-faced hammer, drive the shaft downwards out of the ring.
5 Raise the dust-excluding ring from the bearing using a sharp cold chisel and hammer.
6 Drive the bearing off the shoulder of the propeller shaft.
7 Fit the new bearing using a piece of tubing applied to the centre track of the bearing.
8 Tap the bearing ring onto the bearing outer race until the shoulder on the ring seats on the bearing.
9 Clean the shaft splines thoroughly and coat sparingly with thread locking compound.
10 Fit the dust-excluder to the drive flange and then tap the flange onto the shaft splines. Make sure that the closer and wider spaced flange holes are in the same relative alignment as the holes in the flange at the other end of the propeller shaft.
11 Tighten the castellated nut and fit a new split pin, then reform the dust excluder with a suitable hammer.

7 Centre bearing mounting (XJ12 and Double Six) – removal and refitting

1 Remove the rear section of the propeller shaft as described in Section 4.
2 Unscrew and remove the four setscrews which hold the centre bearing mounting to the centre bearing carrier.

8 Bump stop (XJ12 and Double Six) – checking and adjusting

1 Unscrew and remove the four self-locking nuts which hold the centre bearing carrier heat shield.
2 Check the clearance betwen the bump stop rubber and the

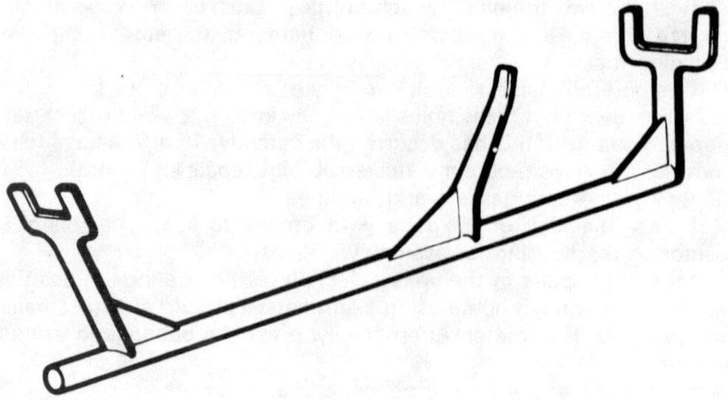

Fig. 7.11 Alignment gauge JD46 (Sec 9)

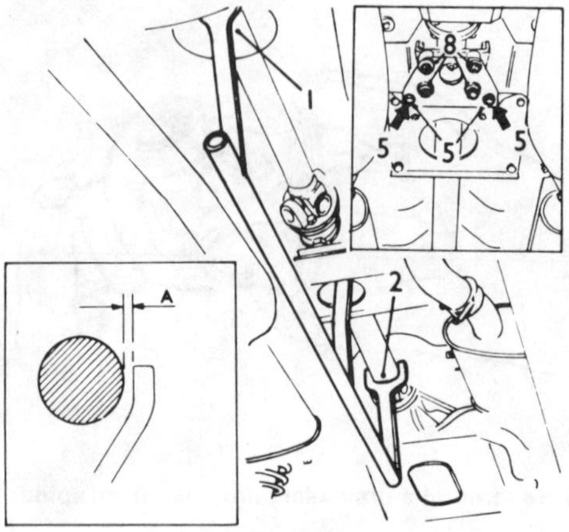

Fig. 7.12 Checking propeller shaft alignment (Sec 9)

1 Small yoke of gauge
2 Large yoke of gauge
5 Carrier-to-baseplate bolts
8 Carrier plate plain nuts
A Clearance of alignment gauge to propeller shaft

baseplate. This should be 0.125 in (3.18 mm).

3 If the clearance is incorrect, working from under the rear of the car, reach over the top of the centre bearing baseplate and release the bump stop bracket self-locking nuts.

4 Place a piece of flat metal sheet or bar (0.125 in (3.18 mm) thick) between the baseplate and the bump stop rubber. Now tighten the self-locking nuts on the securing bracket until the temporary gauge can just be withdrawn.

5 Refit the heat shield, making sure that it is fitted to extend under the coupling flange.

9 Propeller flange (XJ12 and Double Six) – alignment

1 Whenever the propeller shaft or its rear section is removed and refitted, the shaft alignment should be checked.

2 A special gauge (JD46) will be required for this. If one cannot be borrowed then your dealer will have to do the job as quickly as is convenient after the shaft has been fitted to the car, otherwise vibration during running may occur.

3 First check and adjust the bump stop setting as described in the preceding Section.

4 Place the small yoke of the alignment gauge against the front section of the propeller shaft just forward of its shoulder.

5 Place the larger yoke against the rear section of the propeller shaft.

6 The clearance between the centre arm of the gauge and the side of the propeller shaft (A in Fig. 7.12) should be 0.09 in (2.38 mm).

7 If adjustment is needed, unbolt the heat shield from the centre bearing carrier.

8 Slacken the four self-locking nuts which hold the centre bearing carrier to the baseplate.

9 Grip the propeller shaft and move it vigorously in all directions. Make sure that the centre bearing rubber mounting is not under any fore and aft pre-load.

10 Tighten the four self-locking nuts.

11 Grip the bolt heads and release the four nuts at the carrier plate. Now adjust the position of the centre bearing until the alignment is as specified. Tighten the carrier plate nuts.

12 Refit the heat shield to the centre bearing carrier.

10 Fault diagnosis – propeller shaft

Symptom	Reason(s)
Judder on take-off	Shaft out of alignment
Vibration when vehicle running on road	Out of balance or distorted propeller shaft Backlash in splined shaft Loose flange securing bolts Worn universal joint bearings Worn centre bearing

Chapter 8 Driveshafts and final drive

Contents

Specifications

Final drive type

Salisbury 4HU incorporating 'Powr Lok' differential. Independently mounted with open universally jointed driveshafts

Final drive ratio

N America	3.31 : 1
All other models	3.07 : 1

Oil capacity

2¾ Imp pints (3.3 US pints, 1.6 litres)

Torque wrench settings

	lbf ft	Nm
Caliper mounting bracket bolts	75	102
Bottom tie plate bolts	18	25
Caliper mounting bolts	50	68
Crossmember to final drive bolts	70	95
Wishbone bracket setscrews	62	84
Driveshaft inboard flange nuts	52	71
Wishbone pivot shaft nut	50	68
Shock absorber mounting nuts	35	48
Final drive rear cover bolts	20	27
Differential bearing cap bolts	65	88
Crownwheel bolts	85	115

1 General description

1 The final drive unit incorporates a limited-slip differential and is mounted on a crossmember which in turn is flexibly mounted to the bodyframe.

2 Power is transmitted to the roadwheels through universally jointed open driveshafts.

3 In view of the special tools and gauges required for any overhaul of the final drive unit, any work should be limited to the operations described in this Chapter. Otherwise, take the unit to your dealer or obtain a new or rebuilt assembly.

2 Rear hub – removal, overhaul and refitting

1 Jack up the rear end of the car and support it securely under the bodyframe on axle stands. Remove the roadwheel.

2 Remove the suspension outer pivot grease nipple, withdraw the split pin and unscrew and remove the castellated nut and washer from the end of the axle driveshaft.

3 Using a suitable extractor withdraw the hub and hub carrier assembly from the splined end of the driveshaft. Note the location of the inner oil seal track and the endfloat spacer.

4 Unscrew and remove one nut from the end of the lower wishbone outer pivot shaft (arrowed Fig. 8.3) and drive out the pivot shaft. Remove the hub and hub carrier.

5 Turn the hub carrier upside-down so that the hub inner bearing is at the top and then press out the hub. Discard the outer oil seal.

6 Remove the three setscrews and withdraw the water deflector. Prise out the inner oil seal and remove the inner track from the inner bearing.

7 Drive out the inner and outer bearings if these are to be renewed. Use a suitable extractor to withdraw the inner track of the outer bearing.

8 If new hub bearings are being fitted, press the new outer tracks of the inner and outer bearings into the hub carrier. Apply wheel bearing grease to the bearing components.

9 Hold the hub carrier so that the outside bearing is at the top. Locate the inner race of the outer bearing and then press a new outer oil seal into its recess.

10 Fit the water deflector and press the hub complete with outer seal

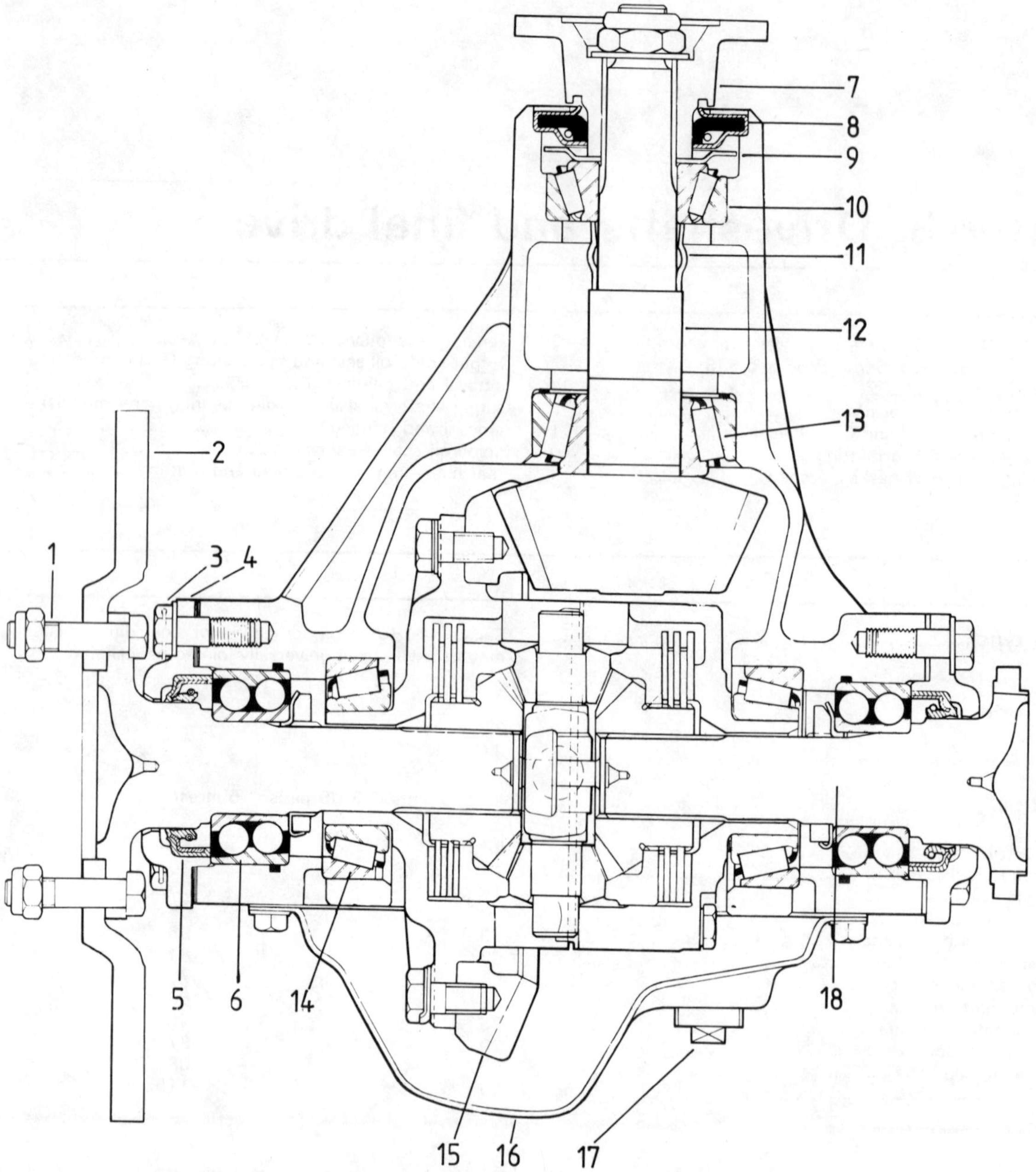

Fig. 8.1 Sectional view of final drive unit with ball type output shaft bearings (Series 1) (Sec 1)

1 Driveshaft connecting bolts
2 Brake disc
3 Caliper mounting bracket bolt
4 Caliper mounting bracket
5 Oil seal
6 Ball bearing
7 Pinion drive flange
8 Oil seal
9 Oil thrower
10 Tapered roller bearing (outer)
11 Collapsible spacer
12 Pinion shaft
13 Tapered roller bearing (inner)
14 Differential side bearing
15 Crownwheel
16 Rear cover plate
17 Filler/level plug
18 Output shaft

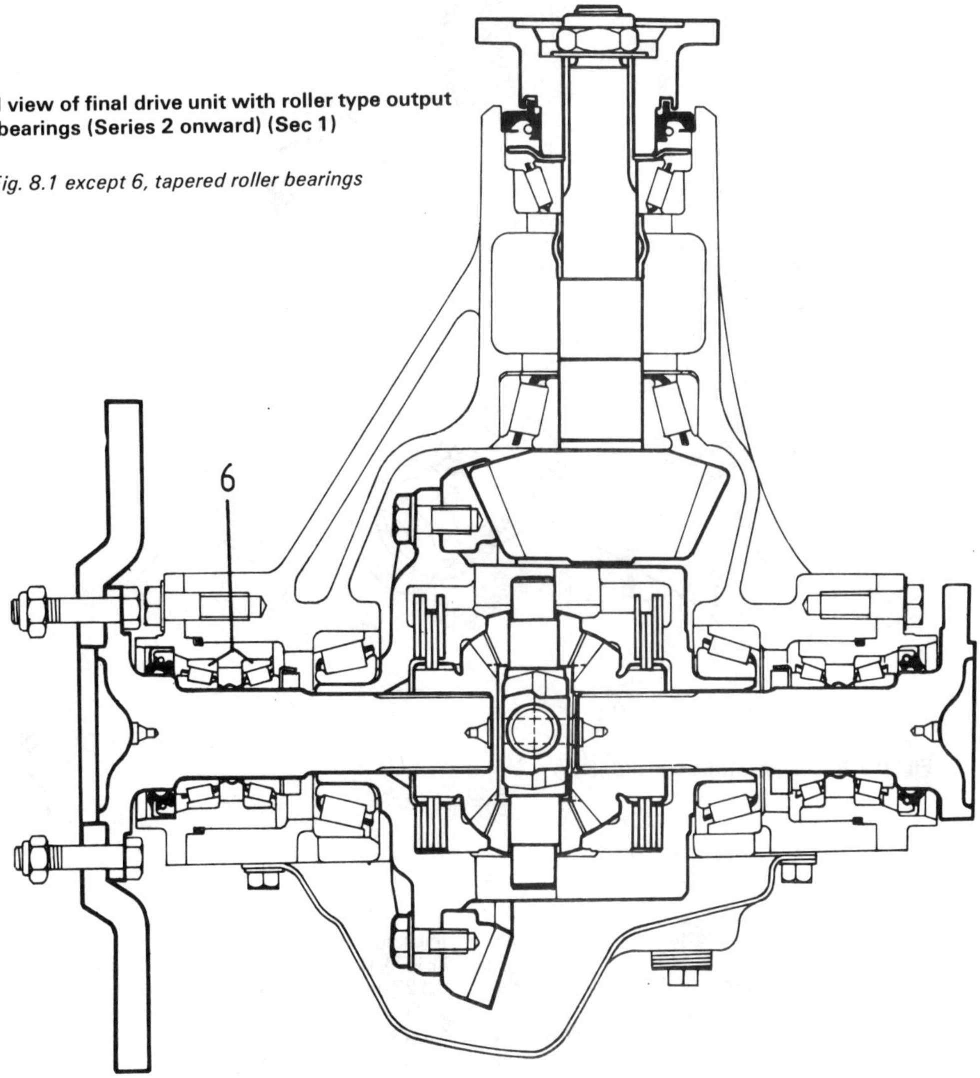

Fig. 8.2 Sectional view of final drive unit with roller type output shaft bearings (Series 2 onward) (Sec 1)

Key as for Fig. 8.1 except 6, tapered roller bearings

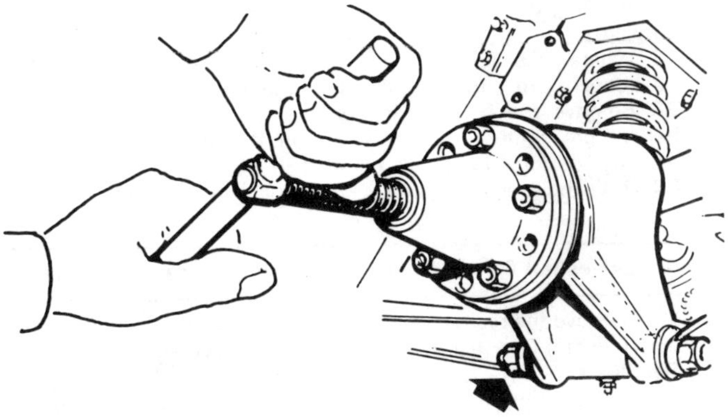

Fig. 8.3 Rear hub showing hub extractor and (arrowed) wishbone outboard pivot shaft (Sec 2)

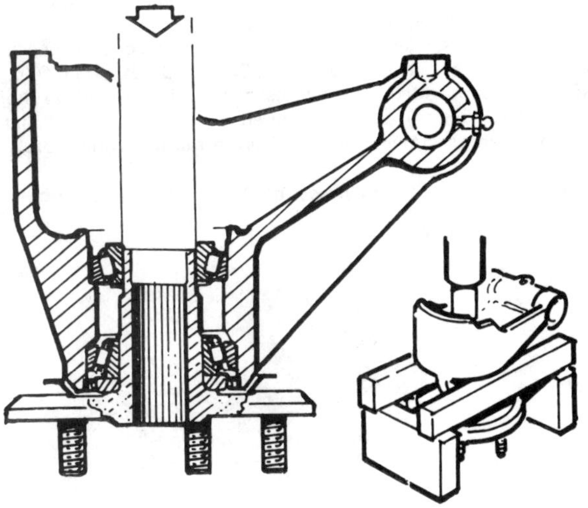

Fig. 8.4 Pressing the rear hub from the carrier (Sec 2)

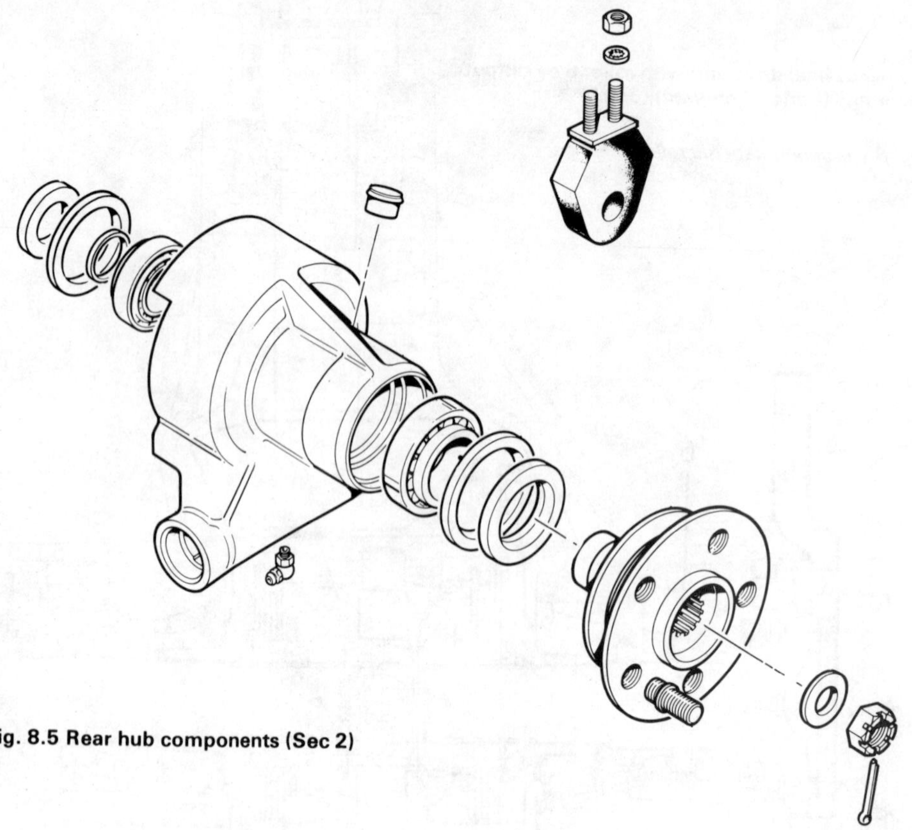

Fig. 8.5 Rear hub components (Sec 2)

track into the inner track of the outer bearing until the hub is fully home.

11 Hold the hub and hub carrier vertically so that the inner end of the hub is uppermost.

12 Locate the inner track of the inner bearing on the hub followed by the special collar of the official tool no. JD15. Press the track onto the hub until its inner face is flush with the special collar.

13 Mount a dial gauge as shown in Fig. 8.7. Tap the hub carrier downwards, zero the dial gauge and then use two levers inserted between the hub and hub carrier to move the carrier upwards. Record the maximum reading on the dial gauge.

14 Remove the special collar and then fit a spacer (if necessary) to give endfloat of between 0.001 and 0.003 in (0.025 and 0.076 mm). Spacers are supplied in thicknesses of 0.109 to 0.151 in steps of 0.003 in (0.076 mm) and are lettered 'A' (smallest) to 'R' (largest) omitting letters 'I', 'O' and 'N', as given in the following table:

Letter	Thickness in	Thickness mm
A	*0.109*	*2.77*
B	*0.112*	*2.85*
C	*0.115*	*2.92*
D	*0.118*	*3.00*
E	*0.121*	*3.07*
F	*0.124*	*3.15*
G	*0.127*	*3.23*
H	*0.130*	*3.30*
J	*0.133*	*3.38*
K	*0.136*	*3.45*
L	*0.139*	*3.53*
M	*0.142*	*3.61*
P	*0.145*	*3.68*
Q	*0.148*	*3.75*
R	*0.151*	*3.84*

15 For example, assume that the endfloat measured with the collar in position is 0.25 in (0.64 mm). Take the mean permissible endfloat as 0.002 in (0.05 mm) and subtract this from the measured endfloat, giving 0.023 in (0.59 mm). The special collar is 0.150 in (3.81 mm) thick so the thickness of the spacer to be fitted will be 0.150 - 0.023 in ie 0.126 in (3.22 mm). The nearest spacer in thickness to this is 0.127 in (3.23 mm) so fit a letter 'G' spacer in place of the special collar.

16 Fit the inner oil seal and its seating ring.

17 Locate the hub assembly between the jaws of the suspension wishbone, install the pivot shaft and nuts.

18 Clean the splines of the hub and shaft with a suitable solvent and then apply a thin coating of thread locking compound to the splines.

19 Engage the hub with the shaft splines, fit the washer and castellated nut and tighten to the specified torque.

20 Fit a new split pin to the castellated nut and refit the outer pivot grease nipple.

21 It is worth rechecking the hub bearing endfloat again at this stage by attaching the dial gauge as shown in Fig. 8.8 and levering the hub outwards.

22 Where possible, do not drive the car for a period of between 4 and 12 hours in order to allow the thread locking compound to harden.

23 Remove the hub bearing grease cap (photo) and inject wheel bearing grease until no more will go in. Do not pressurise the grease, or it will be forced past the oil seals. Refit the cap.

24 Refit the roadwheel and lower the car to the ground.

3 Driveshaft (XJ12, Double Six, Series 1) – removal and refitting

1 Remove the rear suspension assembly, as described in Chapter 11 and then remove the hub assembly as described in the preceding Section.

2 Remove the rear shock absorber which is nearest the front of the car. To do this, remove the upper and lower mounting pivot nuts and drive out the pivot pin until the shock absorber mounting is released.

3 Unscrew and remove the four self-locking nuts which secure the driveshaft inner universal joint to the output flange of the final drive unit and brake disc.

4 Withdraw the driveshaft. Extract and note the exact location of any shims which are used for camber purposes and are fitted between the shaft flange and the brake disc.

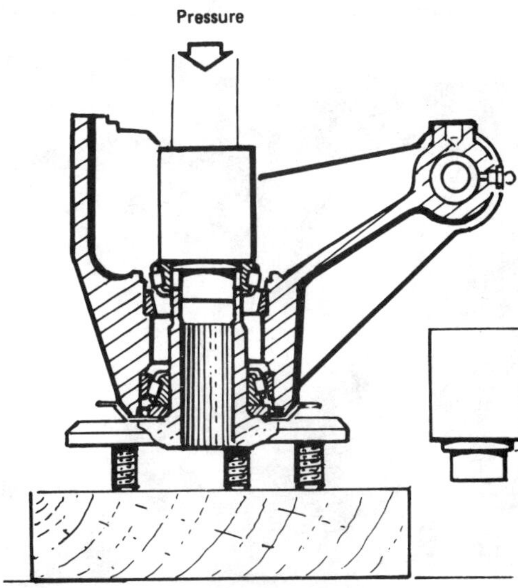

Fig. 8.6 Pressing inner track of rear hub inner bearing using collar of special tool (Sec 2)

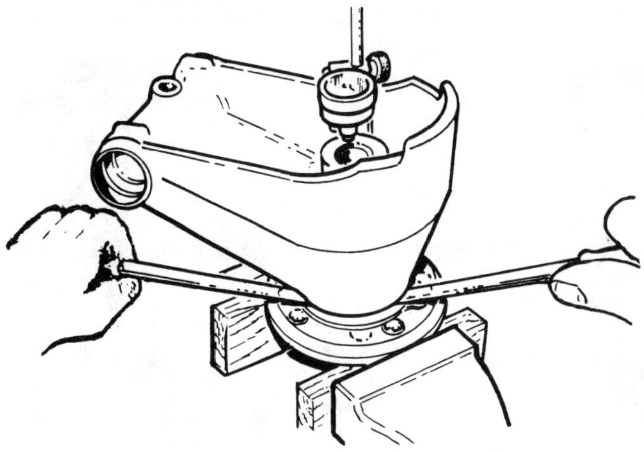

Fig. 8.7 Checking the rear hub bearing endfloat on the bench (Sec 2)

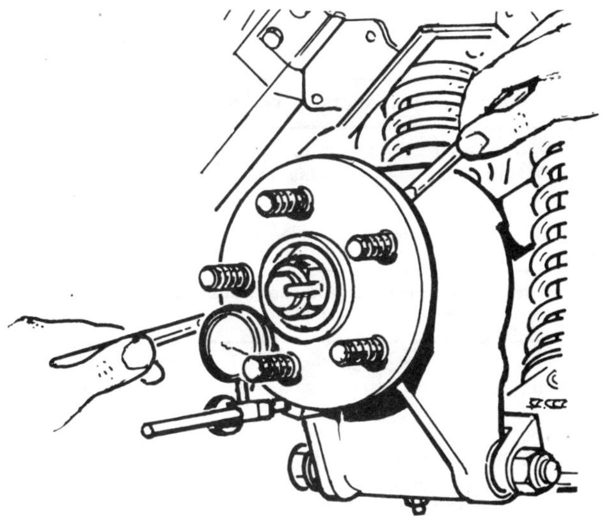

Fig. 8.8 Checking the rear hub bearing endfloat with hub installed on car (Sec 2)

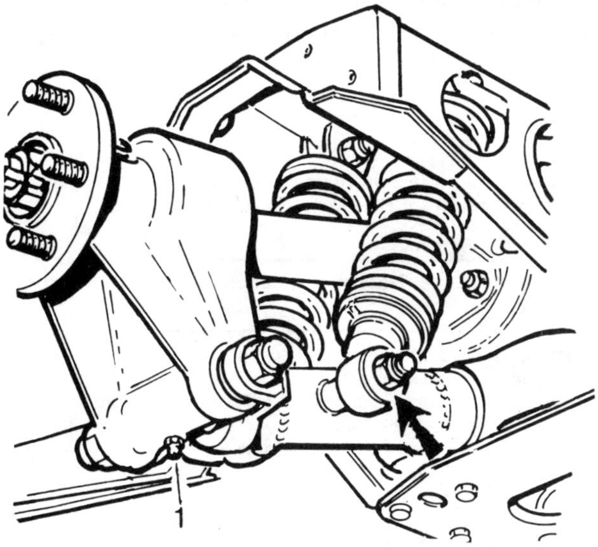

Fig. 8.9 Shock absorber lower mounting (arrowed) and pivot shaft grease nipple (1) (Sec 3)

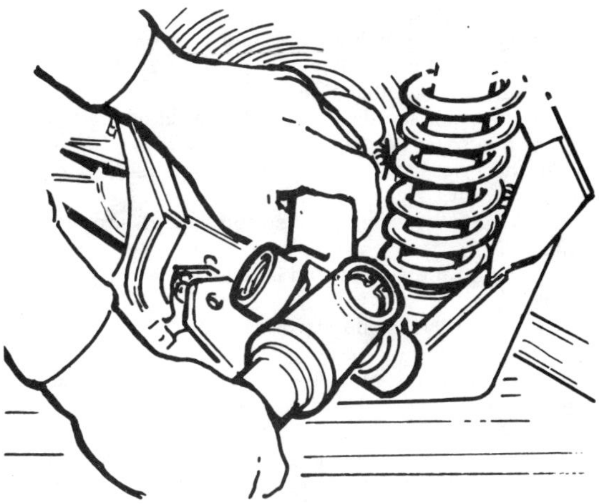

Fig. 8.10 Withdrawing a driveshaft (Sec 3)

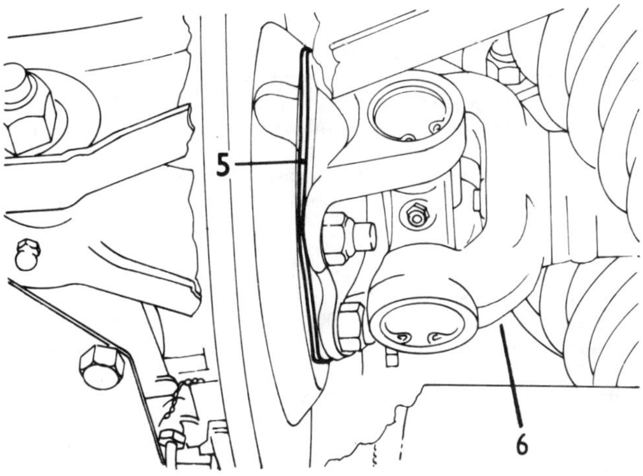

Fig. 8.11 Location of rear wheel camber shims (5) (Sec 3)

6 Driveshaft

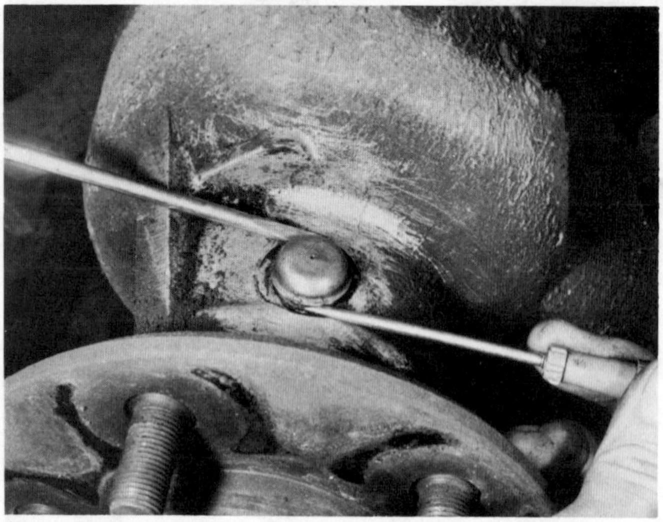

2.23 Removing a rear hub grease cap

4.3 Driveshaft inboard shroud and clip

5 Refitting is a reversal of removal, but make sure that the camber shims are returned to their original locations.

4 Driveshaft (XJ12, Double Six, Series 2 on and XJS) – removal and refitting

1 Jack up the rear of the car and support it securely on axle stands.
2 Remove the roadwheel.
3 Slacken the clip on the driveshaft inboard shroud (photo) and slide the shroud away from the flange.
4 Unscrew and remove the flange nuts.
5 Extract the split pin and unscrew and remove the castellated nut and washer from the end of the driveshaft at the hub.
6 Unscrew and remove the grease nipple from the hub carrier.
7 Fit a suitable extractor to the hub and draw the hub from the splined end of the driveshaft.
8 Pivot the hub assembly on its shaft.
9 Remove the nut from the shock absorber mounting. Detach the lash-down bracket, then drive the pin forward and release the lower end of the damper.
10 Withdraw the driveshaft, noting carefully the camber control shims which are located between the driveshaft inner flange and the brake disc.
11 If a new driveshaft is being fitted, then the original shrouds, oil seal track and spacer should be removed and fitted on the new shaft. The shrouds are secured with pop rivets and when fitted should have their seams sealed with suitable mastic. Make sure that the inner oil seal track chamfer clears the round edge on the driveshaft.
12 Refit the inboard end of the driveshaft, replacing the original camber shims onto clean surfaces. Do not fully tighten the nuts at this stage.
13 Reconnect the shock absorber and the lash-down bracket.
14 Apply thread locking compound to the splines of the driveshaft, raise the hub carrier and insert the end of the driveshaft into it.
15 Use a piece of tubing to drive the hub fully onto the shaft, fit the washer and tighten the castellated nut to the specified torque. Insert a new split pin.
16 Check the hub bearing endfloat as described in Section 2.
17 Screw in the hub carrier grease nipple.
18 Tighten the driveshaft nuts at the inboard flange to the specified torque.
19 Slide the inboard driveshaft shroud into position and tighten the clip.
20 Refit the roadwheel and lower the car to the ground.
21 Check the rear wheel camber at the earliest opportunity (see Chapter 11).

5 Driveshaft universal joints – overhaul

1 The procedure is very similar to that described in Chapter 7 for the overhaul of propeller shaft universal joints, to which reference should be made.

6 Output shaft, oil seal and ball bearing (earlier models) – removal and refitting

1 Remove the driveshaft as described in Section 3.
2 Cut the locking wire and unbolt the brake caliper from the final drive unit.
3 Remove the brake disc.
4 Cut the locking wire and unbolt the caliper mounting bracket.
5 Withdraw the output shaft together with the caliper mounting bracket shims, the bearing assembly and the square section oil seal from the final drive casing.
6 Flatten the tab of the lockwasher and unscrew and remove the nut from the output shaft.
7 Draw the ball bearing assembly and the caliper mounting bracket from the output shaft.
8 Commence reassembly by pressing a new square section oil seal into the groove in the final drive casing. Do not attempt to cut off the projecting part of the oil seal (Fig. 8.13).
9 Apply oil to the seal lips, the four special flange bolts and locate the caliper mounting bracket and the oil seal over the driveshaft.
10 Slide the ball bearing onto the output shaft, then fit a new lockplate and nut.
11 Tighten the nut to the specified torque and turn up the tab of the lockplate.
12 Smear oil on the splines and insert the output shaft into the final drive casing.
13 Screw in the five mounting bracket bolts finger-tight only at this stage.
14 Using feeler blades, measure between the inner face of the caliper mounting bracket and the differential housing. When finally assembled, there must be a compression (nip) of 0.003 in (0.076 mm) on the oil seal and ball bearing, so deduct this from the measured dimension and then select shims to suit from the following thicknesses available:

0.003 in (0.076 mm)
0.005 in (0.127 mm)
0.010 in (0.254 mm)
0.030 in (0.762 mm)

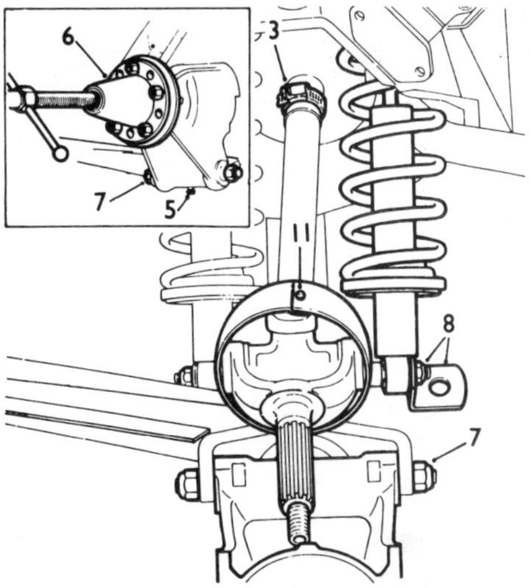

Fig. 8.12 Driveshaft removal (Sec 4)

3 Shroud clip
5 Grease nipple
6 Hub puller
7 Pivot shaft
8 Shock absorber lower mounting and lash-down bracket
11 Shroud pop rivet

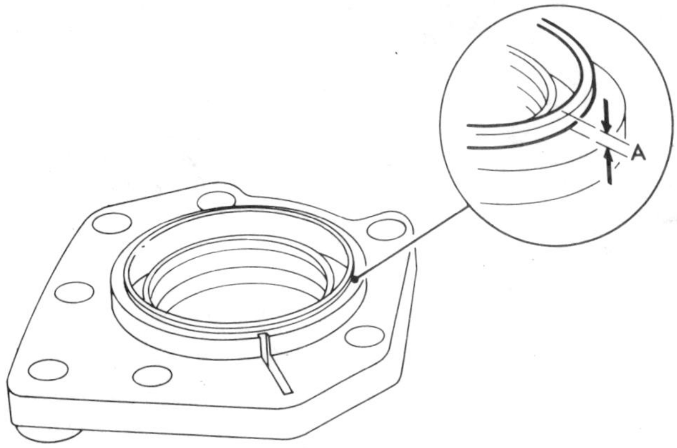

Fig. 8.13 Output shaft oil seal (early type) (Sec 6)

A Projection of seal above casing

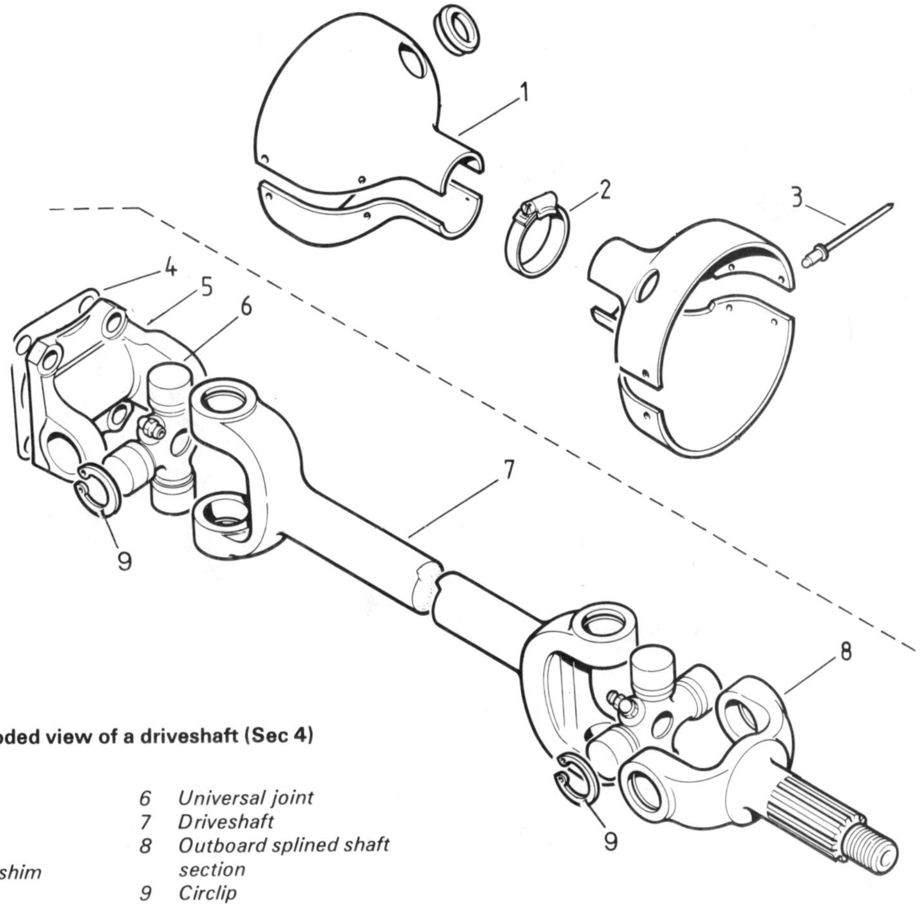

Fig. 8.14 Exploded view of a driveshaft (Sec 4)

1 Shroud
2 Shroud clip
3 Pop rivet
4 Camber control shim
5 Inboard flange
6 Universal joint
7 Driveshaft
8 Outboard splined shaft section
9 Circlip

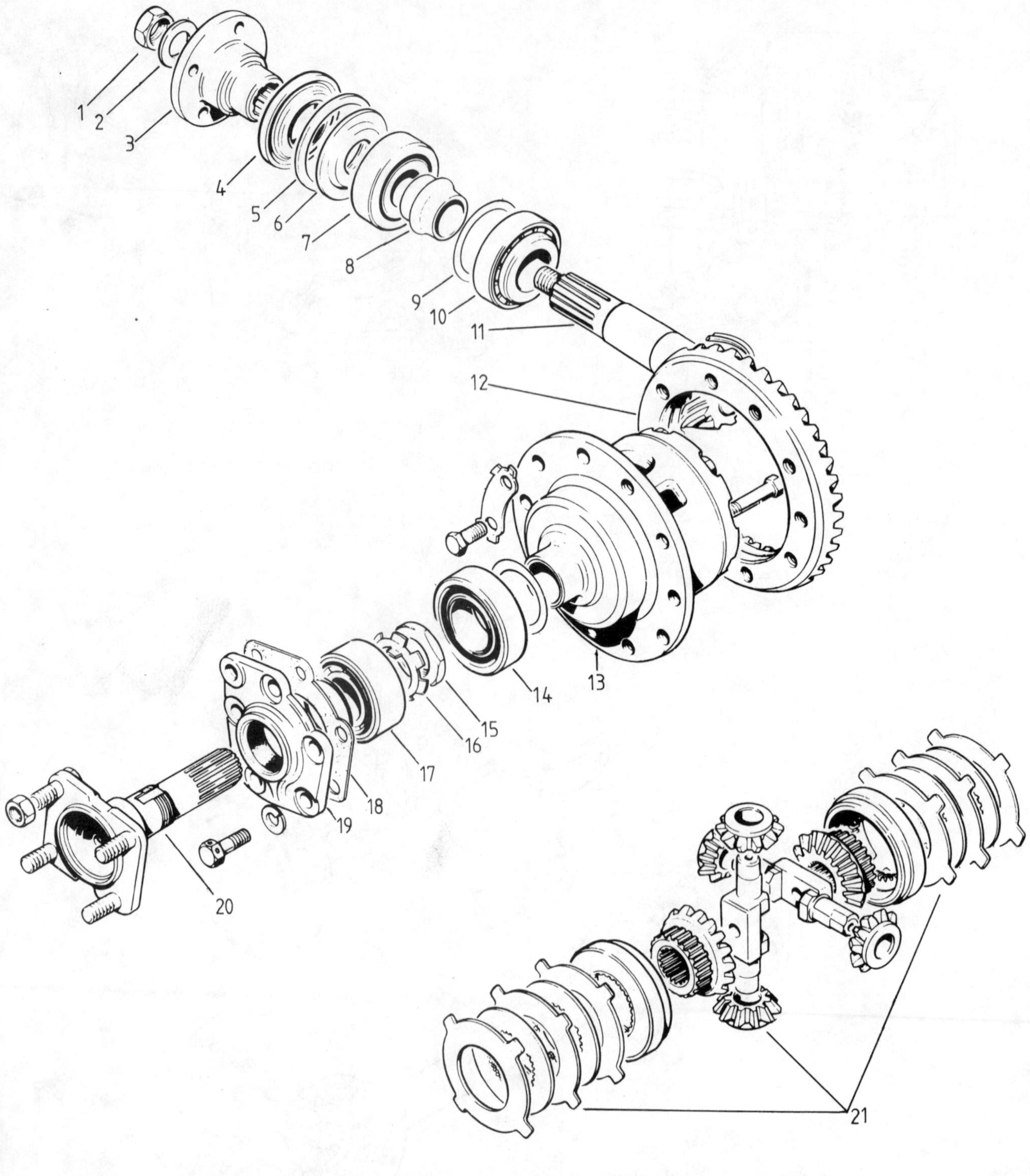

Fig. 8.15 Exploded view of the final drive unit (Sec 7)

1 Pinion nut
2 Washer
3 Pinion drive flange
4 Oil seal
5 Spacer
6 Oil thrower
7 Outer pinion bearing
8 Collapsible spacer
9 Shim
10 Pinion inner bearing
11 Pinion shaft
12 Crownwheel
13 Differential case
14 Ouput shaft inner bearing
15 Output shaft nut
16 Nut lockplate
17 Output shaft outer bearing
18 Caliper centralising shim
19 Caliper mounting bracket
20 Output shaft
21 Differential assembly

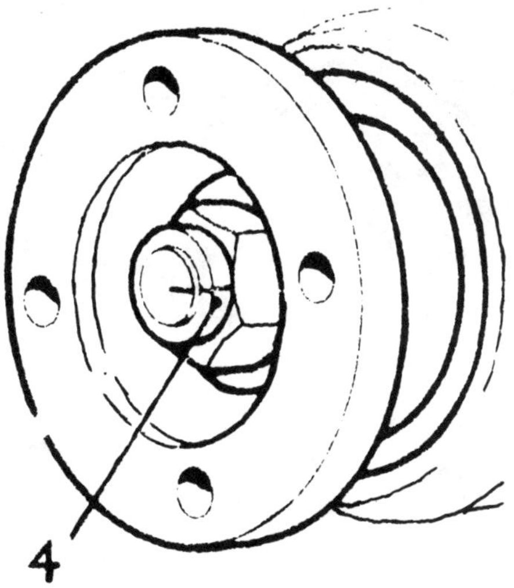

Fig. 8.16 Pinion nut markings (4) (Sec 8)

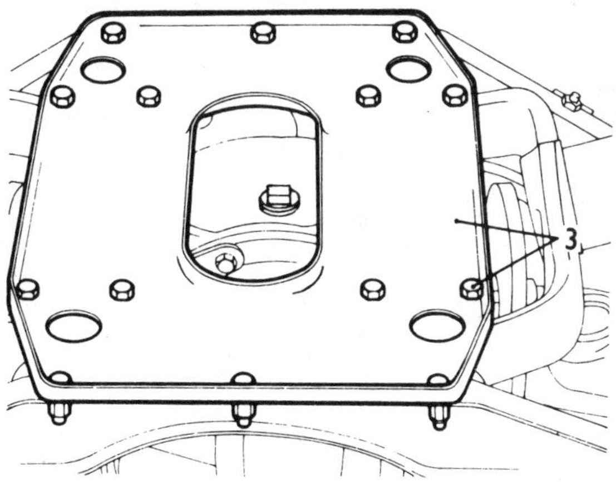

Fig. 8.17 Tie plate and securing bolts (3) (Sec 10)

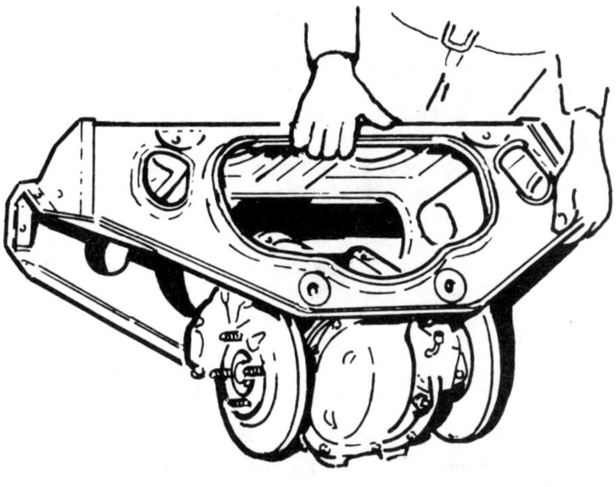

Fig. 8.18 Separating the crossmember from the final drive unit (Sec 10)

15 Withdraw the output shaft and fit the shims, having first applied jointing compound to the shim and flange mating faces. Refit the output shaft and tighten the five securing bolts to the specified torque in diagonal sequence. Fit a new locking wire to the bolt heads.
16 Fit the brake disc with the original camber shims.
17 Fit the caliper to the mounting bracket using two bolts and lockwashers.
18 Check that the brake disc is central in the jaws of the caliper. This can be done using feeler blades. Any adjustment which may be required should be done by altering the thickness of the shim pack which is located between the output shaft flange and the brake disc. If this shim pack is altered, then the camber shims will have to be varied in order to compensate (refer to Chapter 11).
19 Wire the caliper bolts and refit the driveshaft.

7 Output shaft, oil seal and roller bearing (later models) – removal and refitting

1 Remove the driveshaft as described in Section 4.
2 Remove the brake disc and the shims which may be fitted to either side of it.
3 Cut the lockwire and unscrew and remove the five bolts which hold the caliper mounting bracket to the final drive casing.
4 Withdraw the output shaft and discard the O-ring seal.
5 Provided the shaft nut is not disturbed, the assembly can be refitted using a new O-ring.
6 If new bearings or an oil seal are to be fitted, then proceed in the following way.
7 Clamp the caliper mounting bracket in the jaws of a vice, flatten the tab of the lockplate and unscrew and remove the shaft nut.
8 Withdraw the output shaft from the caliper mounting bracket and catch the inner bearing and track. Remove and discard the collapsible spacer.
9 Prise the oil seal from the caliper mounting bracket, discard the seal and retrieve the outer bearing and track.
10 Using a brass drift, drive the bearing outer tracks from the housing.
11 Remove the caliper mounting bracket from the vice.
12 Clean all components and press all new bearing outer tracks into position.
13 Press grease into the outer bearing and fit it with its inner track into position.
14 Press a new oil seal into position (lips to bearing) and fill the oil seal lip groove with grease.
15 Clamp the caliper mounting bracket in the jaws of the vice and make sure that the brake disc bolts are in position in the output shaft flange. Pass the shaft through the oil seal and the outer bearing.
16 To the shaft fit a new collapsible spacer, inner bearing assembly and new lockplate.
17 Screw on the shaft nut, finger tight only.
18 Using a torque wrench or spring balance, check and record the torque required to start the output shaft turning in the oil seal/mounting bracket.
19 Tighten the shaft nut very carefully to the point where bearing endplay is just eliminated. Recheck the turning torque, which should not have changed. If necessary, alter the position of the nut slightly until the turning torque is as originally checked.
20 Tighten the nut by not more than $\frac{3}{16}$ in (5.0 mm) measured at the perimeter of the nut. Check the turning torque which should have increased by between $4\frac{1}{2}$ and $5\frac{1}{2}$ lbf in (0.052 and 0.063 kgf m). If this is the case then the correct bearing preload has been achieved. If not, turn the nut fractionally more and re-check the turning torque. If the turning torque exceeds 6 lbf in (0.07 kgf m) then the nut has been overtightened and the assembly must be dismantled, a new collapsible spacer fitted and the setting operations started again. The collapsible spacer will not regain its original length if the shaft nut is backed off and when overcompressed, must be discarded and a new one fitted.
21 Once the correct preload has been set, bend down two tabs on the lockplate to lock the shaft nut
22 Refit the output shaft assembly as described in the following paragraphs.
23 Fit a new O-ring seal into the bearing housing groove.
24 Oil the shaft splines and insert the assembly into the final drive housing.
25 Using the five bolts, secure the caliper mounting bracket to the

final drive unit, tightening the bolts to the specified torque. Lock the bolt heads with wire.
26 Refit the brake disc and shims. Check the rear wheel camber angle (Chapter 11).

8 Pinion oil seal – renewal

1 A leaking oil seal can be renewed without the need to remove the final drive unit from the car.
2 Raise the rear of the car and disconnect the driveshaft inboard flanges from the final drive unit, noting the number and the location of any camber control shims.
3 Disconnect the rear end of the propeller shaft from the final drive pinion compression flange.
4 Use a suitable torque wrench (lbf in) or wind a cord round the companion flange of the pinion and attach it to a spring balance. Check and record the force required to start the flange moving. Take the average of several recordings.
5 Mark the relative position of the pinion nut to the end of the pinion shaft (Fig. 8.16).
6 Make up a suitable lever, 3 to 4 ft (0.9 to 1.2 m) in length and drilled so that by bolting it to the companion flange, the flange can be held still while the flange is unscrewed.
7 Unscrew and remove the pinion nut and washer and withdraw the companion flange. Use an extractor if necessary.
8 Prise out the faulty oil seal and install the new one.
9 Refit the companion flange (complete with propeller shaft flange bolts) and the washer and screw on the pinion nut. The pinion threads should be clean with thread locking compound applied to them.
10 Tighten the pinion nut very carefully until it takes up its previously marked position. Hold the flange still with the long restraining lever.
11 Check the rotating force required to turn the flange using the cord and spring balance. Tighten the pinion nut, *only a fraction of a turn at a time,* until the force recorded on the spring balance exceeds that recorded before dismantling by between 5 and 10 lbf in (0.06 and 0.12 kgf m).
12 The correct turning torque of the pinion flange should be between 25 and 30 lbf in (0.29 and 0.35 kgf m). If the required torque is lower than specified, tighten the nut slightly. If it is higher (above 45 lbf in, 0.52 kgf m maximum) then the collapsible spacer which is located between the pinion bearings will be overcompressed and a new spacer will have to be fitted. It is no good attempting to reduce the preload by backing off the nut. A new spacer can only be fitted after almost complete dismantling of the final drive unit.
13 Reconnect the propeller shaft and the driveshafts and lower the car. Check and top up the oil in the final drive.

9 Final drive casing rear cover gasket – renewal

1 A leaking rear cover gasket can be renewed in the following way.
2 Raise the rear of the car and support it on axle stands.
3 Unbolt the bottom tie plate from the crossmember and inner fulcrum brackets.
4 Drain the oil from the final drive unit.
5 Unscrew and remove the ten setscrews and detach the rear cover and gasket.
6 Refitting is a reversal of removal, but clean the mating flanges and smear the new gasket with grease.
7 Apply thread locking compound to the cover setscrews.
8 Fit the drain plug and fill the final drive unit with specified oil to the level of the filler plug hole. Recheck the level when the car has been lowered to the ground.

10 Final drive unit – removal and refitting

1 Remove the rear suspension as described in Chapter 11. Drain the oil from the final drive unit.
2 Invert the suspension assembly on the bench and remove the 14 bolts which secure the tie plate.
3 Disconnect the four shock absorber/roadspring assemblies but do not dismantle them.
4 Remove the four self-locking nuts which secure the driveshaft

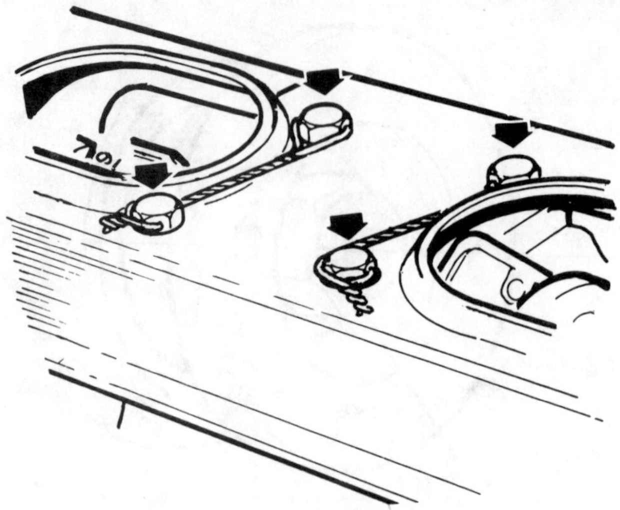

Fig. 8.19 Final drive to crossmember bolts (arrowed) and locking wire (Sec 10)

inner universal joint flange to the brake disc and final drive output flanges (remove the shrouds first on later models).
5 Pull the driveshafts aside, noting the number and location of the camber shims.
6 Remove a nut from one end of the suspension inner wishbone pivot shafts and drive out the shafts.
7 Withdraw the hubs, driveshafts and radius arm assemblies.
8 Disconnect the handbrake levers from the compensator.
9 Disconnect the brake lines from the caliper units.
10 Turn the final drive assembly over and cut the locking wire from the differential carrier bolts. Unscrew the bolts and remove the crossmember from the carrier by tilting the crossmember forward over the nose of the pinion.
11 Cut the lockwires and unbolt the wishbone pivot brackets from the final drive unit. Note the location and number of any shims.
12 Cut the caliper locking wire and unbolt and remove the calipers.
13 Remove the brake discs, noting the location and number of shims.
14 Commence refitting by placing the caliper centralising shims onto the face of the output flange of the final drive unit, followed by a brake disc. Secure with two nuts.
15 Fit a caliper, tighten the mounting bolts and check that the disc runs centrally in the caliper jaws. If it does not, transfer a shim from one side of the disc to the other.
16 Tighten the caliper bolts and lock them with wire.
17 Refit the opposite brake disc and caliper in a similar way.
18 Remove the nuts from both discs.
19 Place the crossmember over the final drive unit, refit the bolts and tighten to the specified torque. Lock the bolt heads with wire.
20 Refit the handbrake lever return springs.
21 Invert the complete assembly on the bench and offer the wishbone pivot brackets to the final drive unit. Secure each loosely with two setscrews.
22 Insert the shims removed at dismantling between the wishbone pivot brackets and the final drive unit.
23 Tighten the bracket setscrews to the specified torque and lock them with wire.
24 Refit the camber shims to one side onto the brake disc studs. Refit the driveshaft and tighten the nuts to the specified torque.
25 Fit the spacer tube between the lugs of the wishbone pivot bracket on one side of the final drive unit.
26 Lubricate the wishbone bearings. Offer up the wishbone to the pivot bracket and insert a dummy shaft to retain the bearing components.
27 Now drive the pivot shaft into position, keeping its end in close contact with the dummy shaft as the latter is displaced.
28 Tighten the pivot shaft nut to the specified torque.
29 Re-locate and fix the driveshaft shroud.
30 Refit the shock absorber with spacer and lash-down bracket.

Tighten the nuts to the specified torque.
31 Repeat the operations described in paragraphs 20 to 30 on the opposite side of the final drive unit.
32 Refit the bottom tie plate and tighten the bolts to specified torque.
33 Refit the rear suspension unit as described in Chapter 11.
34 On completion of installation, bleed the brakes (Chapter 9), check the rear wheel camber (Chapter 11) and check and top up the oil in the final drive unit.

11 Fault diagnosis – final drive and driveshafts

Symptom	Reason(s)
Noise on drive or overrun	Low oil level Loose crownwheel bolts Loose bearing cap bolts General wear in bearings or gear teeth
Noise on turn	Seized broken or damaged pinion or side gear or thrust washers
Knock during gearshift or when taking up drive	Excessive crownwheel to pinion backlash Worn gears Worn driveshaft splines Drive pinion nut loose Loose crownwheel bolts or bearing cap bolts Worn side gear splines Wear in driveshaft universal joints

Chapter 9 Braking system

Contents

Specifications

Front brakes

Type	Girling ventilated disc, bridge type calipers
Disc diameter	11.18 in (284.0 mm)
Disc thickness	0.95 in (24.13 mm)

Rear brakes

Type	Girling inboard damped disc, bridge type calipers incorporating mechanically operated handbrake caliper
Disc diameter	10.375 in (263.5 mm)
Disc thickness	0.50 in (12.7 mm)

Hydraulic system

Master cylinder bore diameter:	
XJS	0.938 in (23.83 mm)
XJ12 and Double Six	0.875 in (22.23 mm)
Fluid type	Universal to exceed SAE 1703D
Servo unit	Girling Supervac 100

Torque wrench settings

	lbf ft	Nm
Brake pedal box to body	13	18
Master cylinder mounting nuts	20	27
Servo unit to pedal box	10	14
Rear flexible hose bracket to crossmember	18	25
Vacuum reserve tank to body nuts	18	25
Front disc to hub bolts	35	48
Front caliper mounting bolts	20	27
Tie plate bolts and nut	18	25
Rear caliper mounting bolts	55	75
Master cylinder banjo bolts	23	31
Master cylinder tipping valve nut (early models)	40	54
Handbrake mounting bolts:		
XJS	18	25
XJ12 and Double Six	7	10

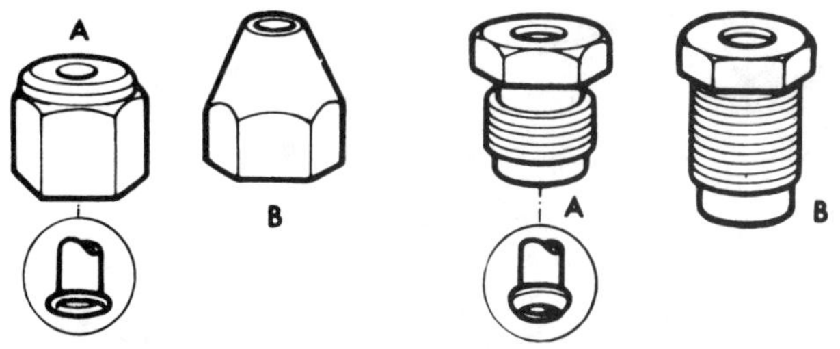

Fig. 9.1 Brake pipe union nuts identification (Sec 2)

A Metric
B UNF

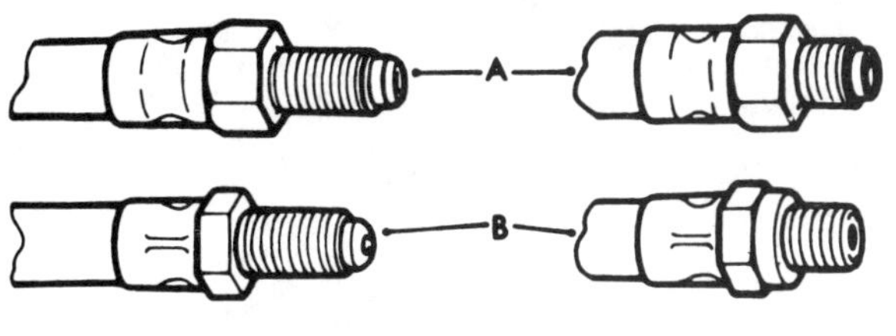

Fig. 9.2 Flexible brake hose end fittings – identification (Sec 2)

A Metric
B UNF

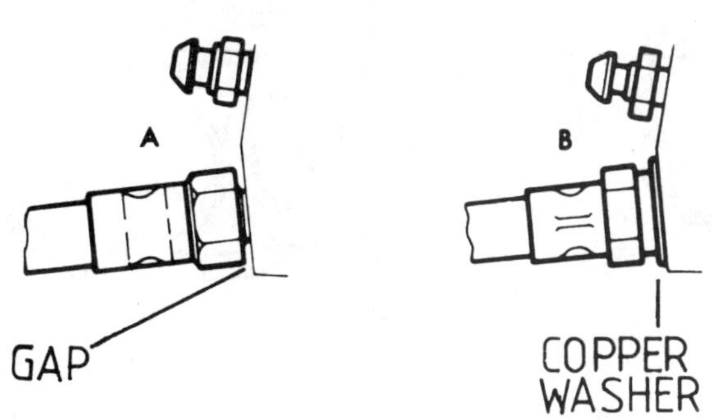

Fig. 9.3 Flexible hoses installed – identification (Sec 2)

A Metric
B UNF

1 General description

1 The braking system is of four-wheel disc type. The hydraulic system is of dual type with a tandem master cylinder. Servo assistance is provided.
2 The rear calipers and discs are mounted inboard on the differential housing and output flanges.
3 The handbrake operates through mechanical linkage to the rear calipers which incorporate automatically adjustable handbrake mechanism.
4 Later models differ from earlier cars in respect of the following:

(a) Redesigned master cylinder
(b) Redesigned pressure differential warning actuator
(c) Four piston type front calipers
(d) Partial metrication of the system (see Section 2)

5 Cars incorporating the new components can be identified by the plastic adaptors which connect the reservoir fluid lines to the master cylinder, or on very late versions by the reservoir being mounted directly on the master cylinder (photo).

2 Precautions

1 When topping up or bleeding the system, always use hydraulic fluid which meets SAE J1703/D specification.
2 When dismantling and cleaning internal components of the system, use only hydraulic fluid or brake cleaning fluid – nothing else, otherwise the seals will be ruined.
3 On later cars with partial metrication of the brake hydraulic system, the following components do not yet have metric threads or connections, but retain UNF threads:

(a) Rear calipers
(b) Handbrake calipers
(c) Hydraulic pipes from the rear three-way connector to rear calipers and the rear three-way connector itself

4 For safety reasons, always screw any component of the hydraulic system into position using the fingers only initially to test that the threads are compatible.
5 Identification of UNF and metric components can be made after reference to the accompanying illustrations.
6 Always discard fluid which has been bled from the system and top up the system with fluid which has been stored in an airtight container and has remained unshaken for the preceding 24 hours.

3 Disc pads – inspection and renewal

1 At the intervals specified in Routine Maintenance, examine the thickness of the friction material on the disc pads.
2 In the case of the front brakes, remove the roadwheels.
3 The pads are clearly visible through the aperture in the caliper units and if the friction material has worn down to $\frac{1}{8}$ in (3.2 mm) or less then they must be renewed.
4 Always renew the pads in axle sets.
5 Withdraw the spring clips and pull out the pad retaining pins (photo). Extract the anti-chatter springs (front pads).
6 Withdraw the pads from the caliper, gripping their edges with a pair of pliers if they are hard to remove (photo). Do not depress the brake pedal while the pads are out of the caliper or the pistons will be ejected.
7 Brush out any dust from the interior of the caliper and then depress the caliper pistons squarely into their bores in order to accommodate the new, thicker pads (photo). Depressing the pistons will cause the fluid level to rise in the master cylinder reservoir and eventually overflow, so it is advisable to draw off some of the hydraulic fluid from the reservoir before commencing operations. A poultry baster or an old hydrometer is useful for drawing off some fluid. Do not spill any hydraulic fluid on the paintwork as it acts as a paint stripper!
8 Install the new pads making sure that the friction lining is against the disc. Insert the retaining pins, the spring clips and the anti-chatter springs (front pads).
9 Apply the footbrake several times to bring the pads into contact with the discs and then top up the fluid reservoir to the indicated level.
10 For renewal of handbrake friction pads, see Section 18.

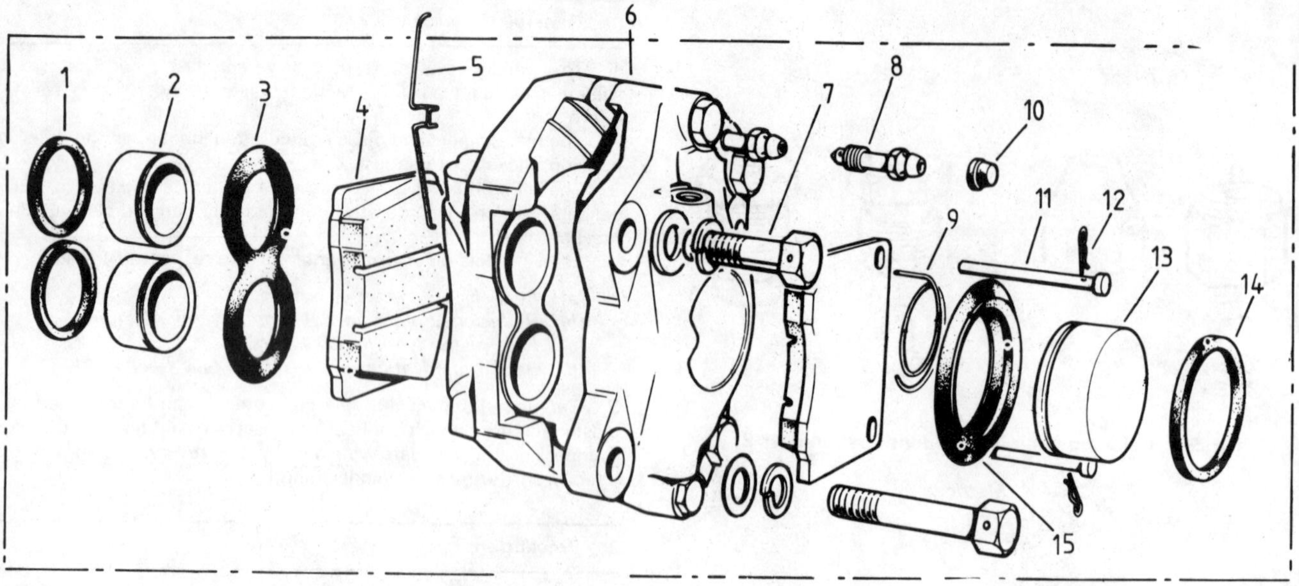

Fig. 9.4 Three-piston type front caliper (Sec 4)

1 *Piston seal*
2 *Piston*
3 *Dust-excluding boot*
4 *Disc pad*
5 *Anti-chatter spring*
6 *Caliper*
7 *Caliper mounting bolt*
8 *Bleed nipple*
9 *Dust-excluding boot clip*
10 *Bleed nipple cap*
11 *Pad retaining pin*
12 *Pin clip*
13 *Piston*
14 *Piston seal*
15 *Dust-excluding boot*

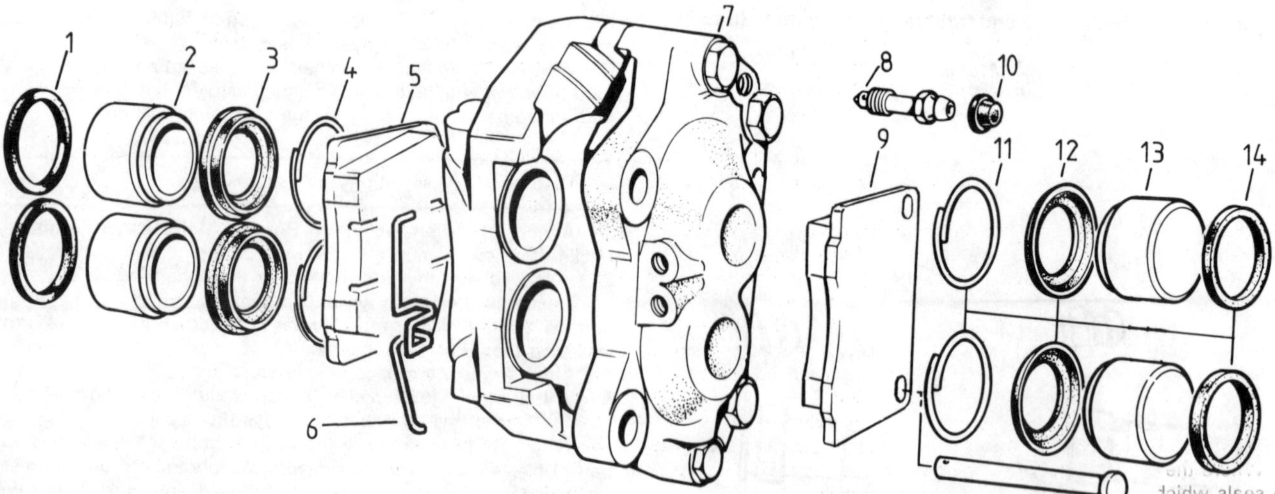

Fig. 9.5 Four-piston type front caliper (Sec 4)

1 *Piston seal*
2 *Piston*
3 *Dust-excluding boot*
4 *Dust-excluding boot clip*
5 *Disc pad*
6 *Anti-chatter spring*
7 *Caliper*
8 *Bleed nipple*
9 *Disc pad*
10 *Bleed nipple cap*
11 *Dust-excluding boot clip*
12 *Dust-excluding boot*
13 *Piston*
14 *Piston seal*
15 *Pad retaining pin*
16 *Pin clip*

1.5 Reservoir mounted directly onto master cylinder

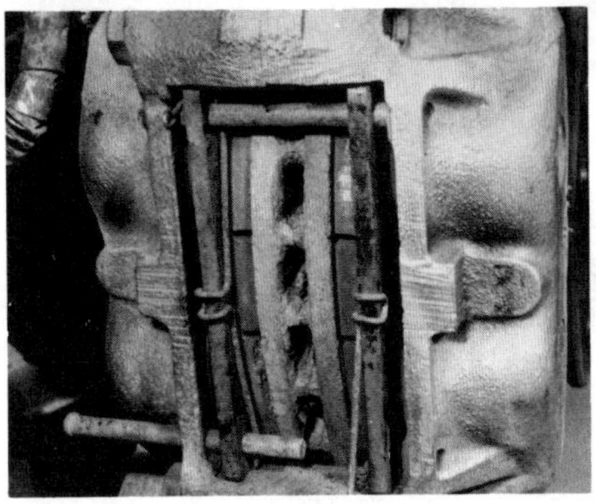
3.5 Front disc pads

3.6 Pads being withdrawn

3.7 Pads removed

5.4A Rear disc caliper

5.4B Withdrawing rear disc pads

4 Front caliper – removal, overhaul and refitting

1 Jack-up the front of the car and remove the roadwheel.
2 Disconnect the hydraulic hose at the junction with the rigid brake pipe (see Section 8). Plug the pipes.
3 Cut the locking wire, remove the caliper mounting bolts and after noting the location of any shims, withdraw the caliper. Withdraw the disc pads.
4 Clean away all external dirt. **On no account unscrew the bolts which secure the two halves of the caliper body together.**
5 Detach the rubber dust excluders from the locating grooves.
6 Place a pad of rag between the piston end faces and apply air from a tyre pump to the fluid union on the caliper body. This will eject the pistons far enough so that they can be extracted with the fingers. There are two outer pistons and one inner, on calipers fitted to early cars; later cars are fitted with four-piston calipers.
7 Examine the surfaces of the pistons and the cylinders for scoring or bright wear areas. If these are evident, renew the caliper complete.
8 Where the components are in good condition, extract and discard the seals which are located in the cylinder grooves.
9 Obtain a repair kit which will contain the new seals and other renewable items. Manipulate the new seals into their cylinder grooves using the fingers only.
10 Dip each piston in clean hydraulic fluid and enter it squarely into its cylinder.
11 Refit the dust excluders and engage their lips in the cylinder grooves. Depress the pistons fully into their cylinders.
12 Refit the caliper to the stub axle carrier and refit the shims. Add or remove shims if necessary to centralise the caliper jaws on the disc. Tighten the bolts to the specified torque wrench setting. Lock the bolts with new wire.
13 Refit the disc pads.
14 Reconnect the hydraulic hose and bleed the front circuit, as described in Section 16.
15 Refit the roadwheel and lower the car to the ground.

5 Rear caliper – removal, overhaul and refitting

1 Jack up the rear of the car, or place it over an inspection pit or on ramps.
2 Remove the handbrake caliper as described in Section 18.
3 Disconnect the hydraulic line from the caliper and plug the open ends to prevent loss of fluid and entry of dirt.
4 Withdraw the disc pads from the caliper and then cut the locking wire from the caliper mounting bolts and unscrew and remove the bolts (photos).
5 Slide the caliper around the brake disc and withdraw it through the gap exposed by removal of the tie plate.
6 Overhaul of the caliper is similar to that described for the front caliper except that only two pistons are employed in the rear unit.
7 To refit the caliper, locate it in position and secure it with two mounting bolts. Lock the bolts with new wire. Check that the brake disc is central within the caliper opening. If necessary, adjustment can be carried out by adding or removing brake disc shims. To do this, the caliper and disc will have to be removed and a shim added or removed from the pack located between the brake disc and the final drive output shaft flange.
8 Once the caliper has been centralised on the disc, the camber control shims must be adjusted. These are located between the brake disc and the driveshaft flange. If a caliper shim was removed then an equivalent camber shim must be added. If a caliper shim was added then a camber shim of equivalent thickness must be removed.
9 Reverse the rest of the removal operations and when refitting is complete, bleed the rear brake circuit as described in Section 16.

6 Master cylinder (early type) – removal, overhaul and refitting

1 Remove the cap from the master cylinder reservoir and draw off as much fluid as possible by syphoning or using a poultry baster or old hydrometer.

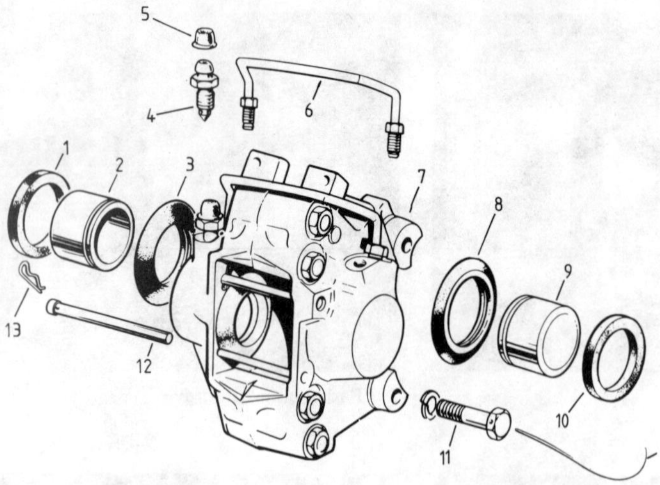

Fig. 9.6 Rear caliper (typical) (Sec 5)

1 Piston seal
2 Piston
3 Dust-excluding boot
4 Bleed nipple
5 Bleed nipple cap
6 Bridge pipe
7 Caliper
8 Dust-excluding boot
9 Piston
10 Piston seal
11 Caliper mounting bolt
12 Pad retaining pin
13 Pin clip

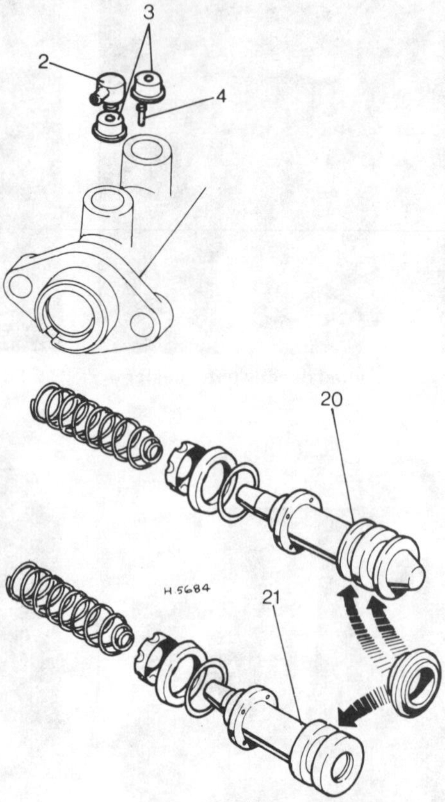

Fig. 9.7 Exploded view of later type master cylinder (Sec 7)

2 Fluid pipe adaptor
3 Grommets
4 Lock pin
20 Secondary piston
21 Primary piston

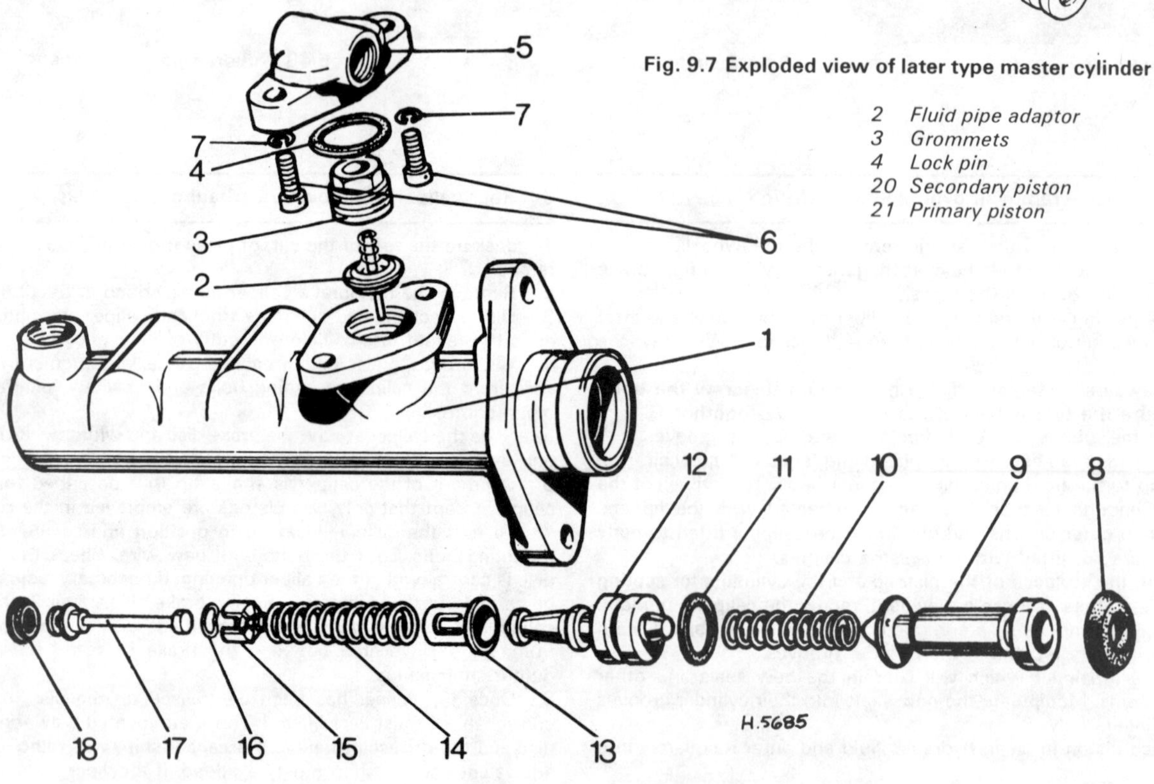

Fig. 9.8 Exploded view of early type master cylinder (Sec 6)

1 Body
2 Tipping valve
3 Tipping valve securing nut
4 Tipping valve cover seal
5 Cover
6 Screws
7 Spring washers
8 Gland seal
9 Primary plunger
10 Intermediate spring
11 Ring seal
12 Secondary plunger
13 Thimble
14 Spring
15 Valve spacer
16 Spring washer
17 Valve stem
18 Valve seal

2 Disconnect the brake lines from the master cylinder body.
3 Unscrew and remove the two flange nuts and withdraw the master cylinder from the front face of the vacuum servo unit.
4 Clean away all external dirt.
5 Extract the two screws and their washers and withdraw the tipping valve cover and seal.
6 Remove the tipping valve securing nut, depress the primary plunger and withdraw the tipping valve.
7 Eject the remainder of the internal components, either by carefully shaking them out or by applying air pressure from a tyre pump at one fluid inlet union while holding a finger over the second inlet.
8 Examine the surfaces of the plungers and the cylinder bore for scoring or bright wear areas. If these are evident, renew the master cylinder complete.
9 If these components are in good condition then separate the plungers and intermediate spring. Lift the leaf of the spring retainer and withdraw the spring and valve sub-assembly from the secondary plunger.
10 Extract the spring, valve spacer and spring washer from the valve stem, also the seal from the valve head.
11 Discard all rubber seals and obtain a repair kit which will contain all the renewable items.
12 Install the new seals, using the fingers only to manipulate them into position on the primary and secondary plungers.
13 Fit the valve seal (smallest diameter first) onto the valve head. Position the spring washer on the valve stem so that it faces away from the valve stem shoulder.
14 Fit the valve spacer, legs first, then attach the spring retainer to the valve stem so that the key hole end is first.
15 Slide the secondary spring over the retainer and then position the sub-assembly on the secondary plunger. The spring must be compressed whilst the leaf of the retainer is depressed behind the head of the plunger. This operation will be made easier if the sub-assembly is carefully secured in a vice and the vice jaws closed to compress the spring until it is nearly coil bound. Use a small screwdriver to press the spring retainer back against the secondary plunger. Depress the leaf of the retainer behind the head of the plunger.
16 Fit the intermediate spring between the primary and secondary plungers. Dip the plungers in clean hydraulic fluid and insert them into the cylinder bore (valve end leading).
17 Depress the primary plunger from the bore and install the tipping valve assembly. Fit the seal and screw in the tipping valve securing nut to the specified torque. Install the tipping valve cover and a new seal.
18 Fit the master cylinder to the vacuum servo unit.
19 Reconnect the brake lines and bleed the complete hydraulic system (both circuits), as described in Section 16.

7 Master cylinder (later type) – removal, overhaul and refitting

Note: *Destroy the vacuum in the brake servo unit by depressing the foot pedal ten times before commencing the operations below.*
1 Slacken the clips which secure the reservoir hoses to the master cylinder adaptors, disconnect the hoses and plug them.
2 Disconnect the rigid brake lines from the master cylinder body and plug the lines.
3 Unbolt the master cylinder from the servo unit.
4 Clean away all external dirt.
5 Prise the reservoir hose adaptors from their sealing grommets on the master cylinder body. Prise out the grommets.
6 Depress the primary piston into the bore of the master cylinder and extract the secondary piston stop pin from the grommet housing nearest the front of the master cylinder.
7 Extract the circlip from the end of the master cylinder and tap the flange end on a block of wood to eject the primary piston and spring and the secondary piston and spring. If these components are difficult to remove, apply air from a tyre pump at the fluid outlet port.
8 Keep the piston assemblies separate, noting that the secondary piston spring is thicker and longer than the primary spring.
9 Examine the surfaces of the pistons and cylinder bore for scoring or bright wear areas. If these are evident, renew the master cylinder complete.
10 If these components are in good condition, remove the spring, spring seat, recuperating seal and washer from the secondary piston. Also prise the seals from the rear of the secondary piston.
11 Dismantle the primary piston in a similar way.
12 Discard all the seals and obtain a repair kit.
13 Use only the fingers to manipulate the seals into position and commence reassembly by fitting the secondary piston inner seal into its groove so that its lip faces the front of the master cylinder.
14 Install the second seal to the secondary piston with its lip in the reverse direction to the first one fitted.
15 Fit the washer, recuperating seal, spring seat and the spring over the front end of the secondary piston.
16 Install the primary piston rear seal (lip away from circlip) and then fit the washer, recuperating seal, spring seat and spring over the front end of the piston.
17 Apply hydraulic fluid to the piston assemblies and insert the secondary piston and spring into the master cylinder followed by the primary piston. Depress the piston and fit the circlip.
18 Depress the primary piston and fit the secondary piston stop pin.
19 Refit the grommet and adaptors and refit the master cylinder to the servo by reversing the removal operations. Bleed the system (Section 16).

8 Flexible hydraulic hoses – inspection, removal and refitting

1 Periodically, inspect the condition of the flexible brake hoses. If they appear swollen or chafed, or if when bent double with the fingers tiny cracks are visible, then they must be renewed.
2 Make sure that a replacement hose has the same type of thread (metric or UNF) as the old one. Refer to Section 2 for details.
3 Always uncouple the rigid pipe from the flexible hose first, then release the end of the flexible hose from the support bracket. Now unscrew the flexible hose from the caliper or connector. If this method is followed, no kinking of the hoses will occur.
4 When refitting the hose, always use a new copper sealing washer if one was originally fitted.
5 When installation is complete, check that the flexible hose does not rub against the tyre or other adjacent components. Its attitude may be altered to overcome this by releasing its bracket support locknut and twisting the hose in the required direction by not more than one quarter turn.
6 Bleed the hydraulic system (Section 6).

9 Rigid brake lines – inspection, removal and refitting

1 At regular intervals wipe the steel brake pipes clean and examine them for signs of rust or denting caused by flying stones.
2 Examine the fit of the pipes in their insulated securing clips and bend the tongues of the clips if necessary to ensure a positive fit.
3 Check that the pipes are not touching any adjacent components or rubbing against any part of the vehicle. Where this is observed, bend the pipe gently away to clear.
4 Any section of pipe which is rusty or chafed should be renewed. Brake pipes are available to the correct length and fitted with end unions from most Jaguar/Daimler dealers and can be made to pattern by many accessory suppliers. When installing the new pipes use the old pipes as a guide to bending and do not make any bends sharper than is necessary.
5 Make sure that the unions on the new pipes are of the same type (metric or UNF) as on those removed. Refer to Section 2 if in doubt.
6 Bleed the hydraulic system on completion (Section 16).

10 Front brake disc – inspection, removal and refitting

1 Jack up the front of the car and remove the roadwheels.
2 Withdraw the disc pads.
3 Examine the discs for deep grooves or scoring or cracks. If these are evident, renew the disc. Light scoring is normal.
4 Check the disc for run-out. A dial guage should be used for this although feeler blades placed between the face of the disc and a fixed point are a satisfactory substitute.
5 Turn the disc and check that the run-out or out-of-true does not exceed 0.004 in (0.10 mm). If it does the disc must be renewed.
6 It is most important that for optimum brake efficiency the hub endfloat is as specified in Chapter 11.

Removal – XJ12 and Double Six models

7 Unbolt the hub from the disc. the bolts can be reached using a socket inserted through the aperture in the disc shield.

8 Tap off the hub grease cap, extract the split pin, remove the nut and the thrust washer and withdraw the hub with the hand. On models fitted with the four-piston type caliper, remove the water deflector as described in Section 11.

9 The brake disc can now be slid out of the caliper jaws, over the end of the stub axle and removed. There is no need to remove the caliper or to disconnect the hydraulic brake hose for this operation.

Removal – XJS models

10 Remove the disc pads as described in Section 3.

11 Remove the hub as described in paragraphs 7 and 8 and tap off the water deflector. This can be done by passing a drift through the hole in the disc shield.

12 Cut the locking wire and unbolt the caliper, noting the location of any shims fitted between the steering arm and the caliper.

13 Slacken the bolt which holds the steering arm to the hub carrier.

14 Ease the caliper to one side without disconnecting the hydraulic brake hose and withdraw the disc.

Refitting – all models

15 Refitting is a reversal of removal, but if the disc is not central in the jaws of the caliper, adjust the number of shims which are located between the caliper and the steering arm. Always add or remove the same number of shims at each mounting bolt. Adjust the hub endfloat as described in Chapter 11, Section 5.

11 Front disc shield – removal and refitting

1 Jack up the car and remove the roadwheel.

2 Slacken the upper bolt which holds the steering arm to the stub axle carrier.

3 Cut the lockwire from the caliper mounting bolts and remove the upper mounting bolt.

4 Remove the disc shield clips or nuts and bolts, and withdraw the shields.

5 Remove the hydraulic feed pipe that runs between the flexible pipe and the caliper. Plug the openings.

6 Remove the locknut which holds the hydraulic hose union to the shield. Remove the hose from the bracket.

7 Withdraw the disc shield.

8 Refitting is a reversal of removal, but use new self-locking nuts on the shield lower studs and on completion bleed the hydraulic circuit.

12 Rear brake disc – inspection, removal and refitting

1 Refer to paragraphs 3, 4 and 5 of Section 10. If the brake disc must be renewed, jack up the car and remove the roadwheel from the side of the car concerned.

2 Support the bodyframe securely on stands.

3 Remove the brake caliper, as previously described.

4 Drive out the shock absorber lower mounting pin and then cut the locking wire from the radius arm locking bolt and remove the bolt.

5 Unscrew and remove the grease nipple from the hub pivot shaft and then support the hub on wooden blocks.

6 Lever the radius arm from the spigot anchor point.

7 Release the clip which secures the driveshaft inner universal joint shroud and slide it clear of the joint.

8 Disconnect the inner universal joint from the brake disc, by unscrewing the securing nuts, tapping the bolts towards the final drive unit and carefully retaining the camber shims.

9 Lift out the brake disc. It may be necessary to jack up the car a little higher to facilitate removal of the disc.

10 Refitting is a reversal of removal, but the disc must run central in the caliper aperture. If this is not the case, add or remove shims located between the aisc and the final drive output flange. Compensate for this by adding or subtracting a shim of similar thickness from the camber angle shim pack. (Refer to Section 5, paragraph 8).

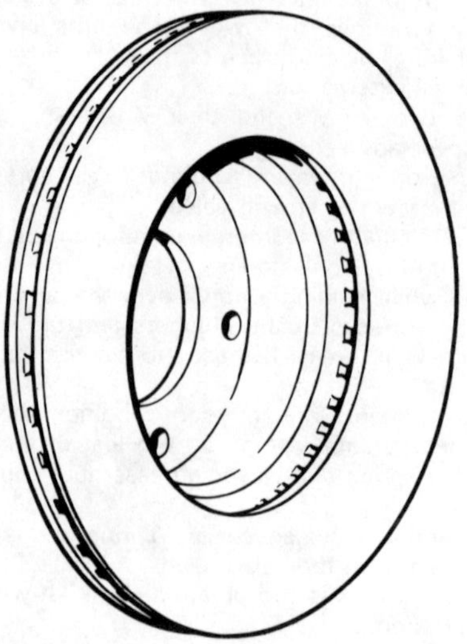

Fig. 9.9 Typical ventilated type front disc (Sec 10)

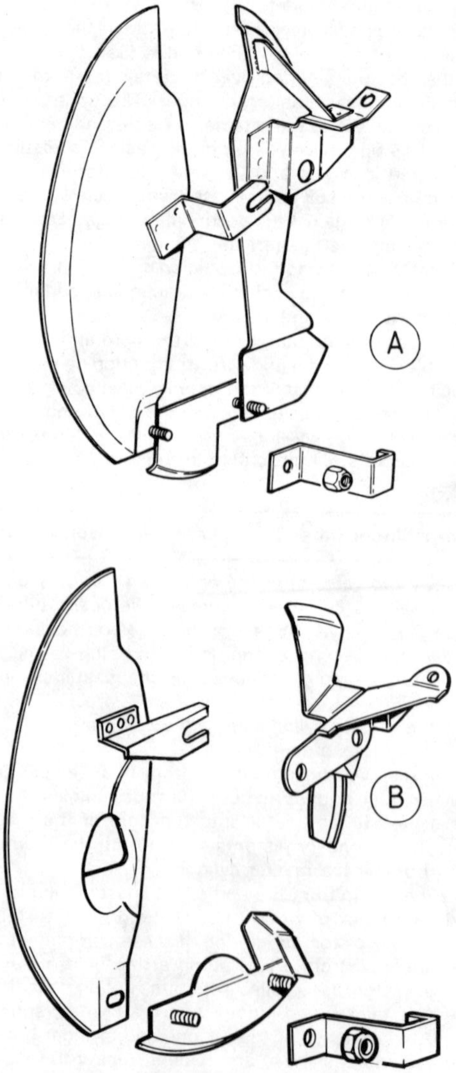

Fig. 9.10 Front disc shields (Sec 11)

A Three-piston caliper type
B Four-piston caliper type

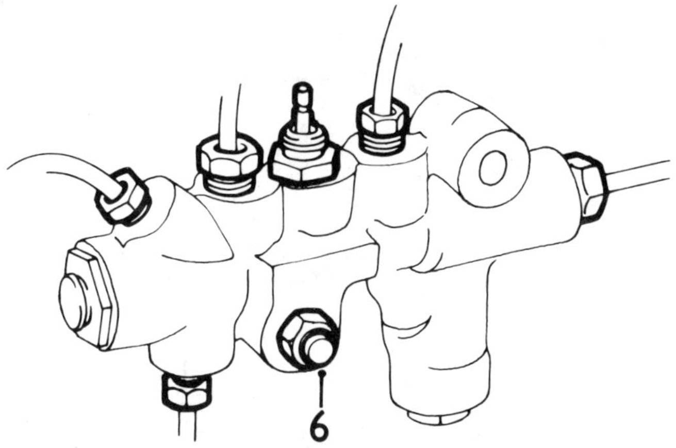

Fig. 9.11 Combination valve (Sec 13)

6 *Mounting stud*

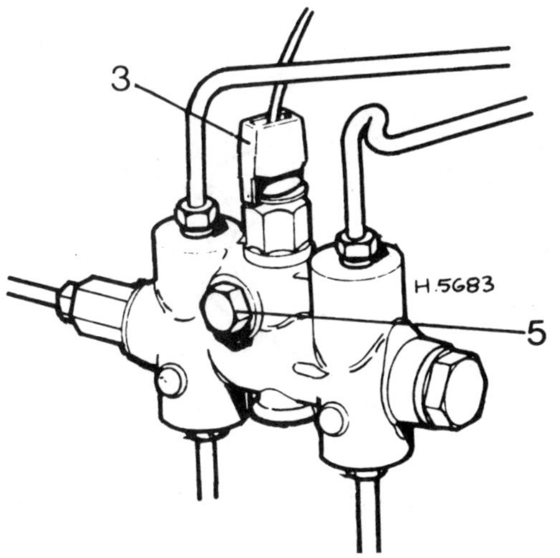

Fig. 9.12 Pressure differential warning actuator (PDWA) (Sec 14)

3 *Switch*
5 *Mounting bolt*

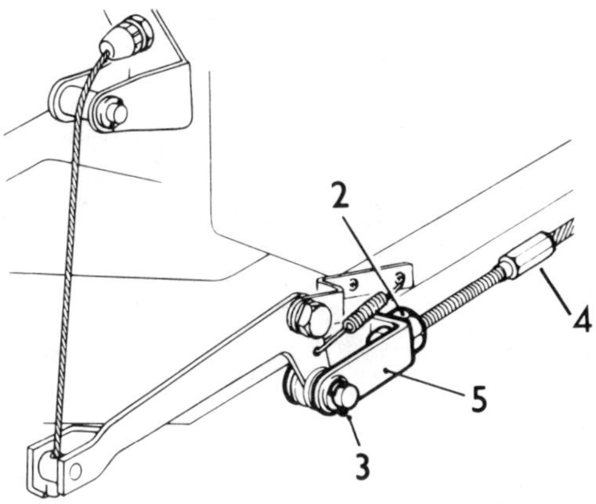

Fig. 9.13 Handbrake cable adjustment (early XJ12, Double Six) (Sec 17)

2 *Locknut*
3 *Split pin and clevis pin*
4 *Adjuster*
5 *Yoke*

13 Combination valve (incorporating pressure differential warning actuator – description

1 This device, fitted to earlier models, incorporates two valves: the pressure differential warning actuator (PDWA) and the pressure conscious reducing valve (PCRV). The PDWA monitors front and rear brake circuit pressures and gives a visual warning to the driver if there is a fall in either pressure. The PCRV reduces the pressure in the rear brake circuit progressively during application of the brakes to prevent the rear roadwheels locking.
2 The PDWA valve is essentially a piston which is kept in balance by the equal pressures of the two circuits of the hydraulic system. When one pressure falls, the piston is displaced and completes an electrical circuit to illuminate a warning lamp.
3 The PDWA valve is automatically reset during bleeding operations.
4 A faulty combination valve must be renewed complete, it cannot be repaired or overhauled.

14 Pressure differential warning actuator (PDWA) – description

1 On later models, this device is fitted as an independent unit and in conjunction with a pressure reducing valve as on earlier cars (photo).
2 Its purpose and operation are as described in the preceding Section.

15 Combination valve and PDWA – testing, removal and refitting

1 Check and top up the brake reservoir fluid.
2 Switch on the ignition and fully apply the handbrake. The brake warning lamp should come on.
3 Start the engine and let it idle. Release the handbrake, apply the footbrake fully and keep it depressed. Select 'P' on automatic transmission models.
4 Have an assistant release any one of the brake bleed nipples and catch the ejected fluid in a jar. The brake warning lamp should immediately illuminate. Close the bleed nipple.
5 Release the footbrake and then depress it again, when the warning lamp should go out.
6 Switch off the engine, apply the handbrake and top up the fluid reservoir.
7 Failure of the switch to operate can only be rectified by renewing the combination valve (early cars) or actuator (later cars) in the following way.
8 Disconnect the battery and remove the air cleaner cover and filter element.
9 Disconnect the electrical leads and all the hydraulic pipes from the unit. Cap or plug the pipes to prevent loss of fluid.
10 Unscrew and remove the single securing bolt and remove the valve or actuator.
11 Refitting is a reversal of removal. Bleed the hydraulic system on completion.

16 Hydraulic system – bleeding

1 If any of the hydraulic components in the braking system have been removed or disconnected, or if the fluid level in the master cylinder has been allowed to fall appreciably, it is inevitable that air will have been introduced into the system. The removal of all this air from the hydraulic system is essential if the brakes are to function correctly, and the process of removing it is known as bleeding.
2 There are a number of one-man, do-it-yourself, brake bleeding kits currently available from motor accessory shops. It is recommended that one of these kits should be used wherever possible as they greatly simplify the bleeding operation and also reduce the risk of expelled air and fluid being drawn back into the system.
3 If one of these kits is not available then it will be necessary to gather together a clean jar and a suitable length of clear plastic tubing which is a tight fit over the bleed screw, and also to engage the help of an assistant.
4 Before commencing the bleeding operation, check that all rigid pipes and flexible hoses are in good condition and that all hydraulic unions are tight. Take great care not to allow hydraulic fluid to come

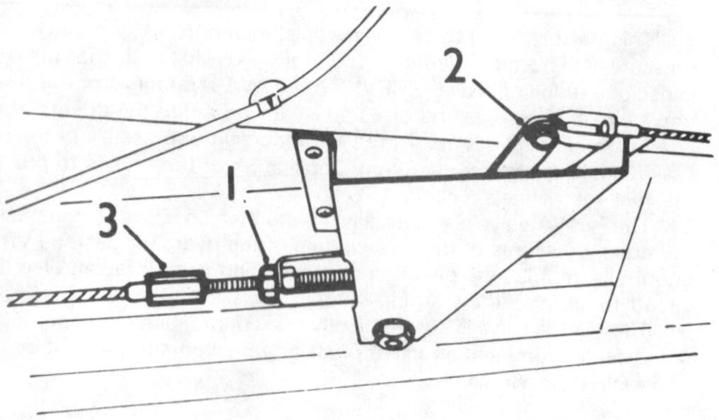

Fig. 9.14 Handbrake cable adjustment (later XJ12, Double Six) (Sec 17)

1 *Locknut*
2 *Clevis pin*
3 *Adjuster*

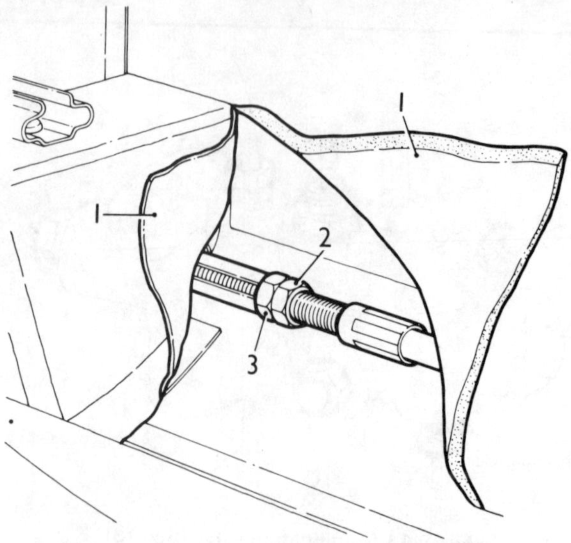

Fig. 9.15 Handbrake cable adjustment (XJS) (Sec 17)

1 *Carpet at sill*
2 *Locknut*
3 *Adjusting nut*

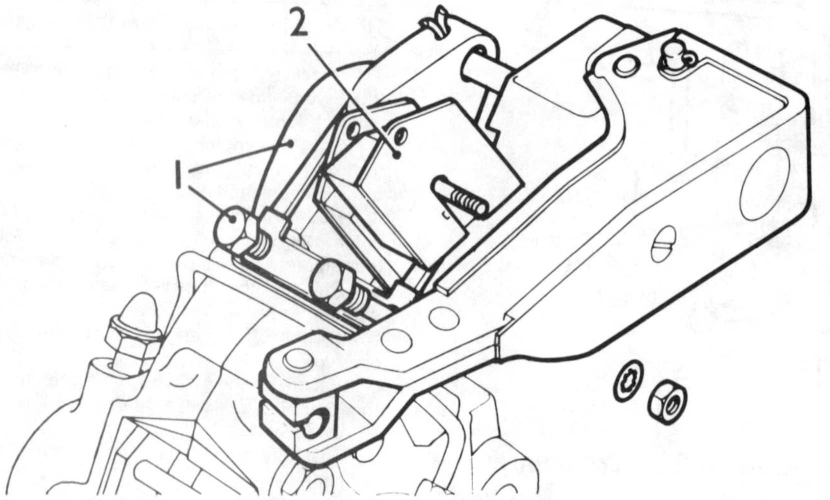

Fig. 9.16 Handbrake caliper (Sec 18)

1 *Mounting bolts*
2 *Brake pad*

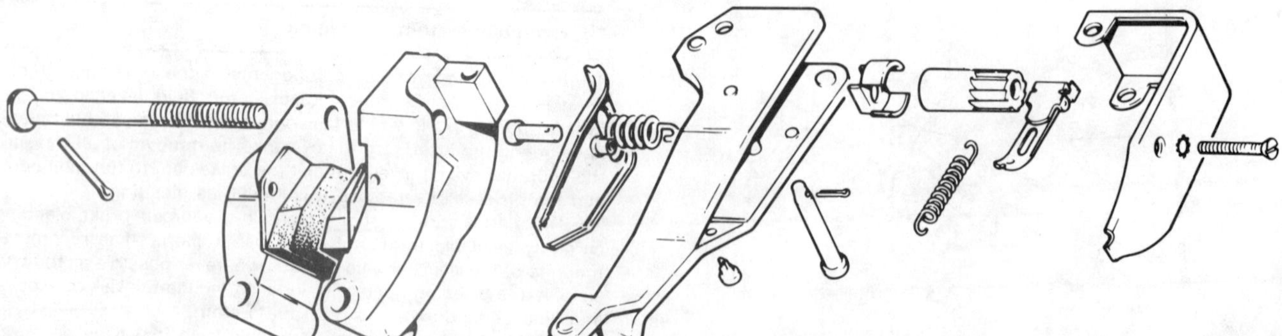

Fig. 9.17 Exploded view of a handbrake caliper (Sec 18)

into contact with the vehicle paintwork, otherwise the finish will be seriously damaged. Wash off any spilled fluid immediately with cold water.
5 If hydraulic fluid has been lost from the master cylinder, due to a leak in the system, ensure that the cause is traced and rectified before proceeding further or a serious malfunction of the braking system may occur.
6 To bleed the system, clean the area around the bleed screw at the caliper(s) to be bled. If the hydraulic system has only been partially disconnected and suitable precautions were taken to prevent further loss of fluid, it should only be necessary to bleed that part of the system. However, if the entire system is to be bled, start at the caliper furthest away from the master cylinder.
7 Remove the fluid reservoir filler cap and top up the reservoir. Periodically check the fluid level during the bleeding operation and top up as necessary. If the level of fluid is allowed to fall to the point where air is drawn into the system, it will be necessary to recommence the bleeding procedure.
8 It is advantageous to have the engine idling during bleeding so that servo assistance is available to give a good flow of fluid. Take precautions against the build-up of exhaust fumes and remember that the exhaust system may be hot.
9 If a one-man braking bleeding kit is being used, connect the outlet tube to the bleed screw and then open the screw half a turn. If possible position the unit so that it can be viewed from the car, then depress the brake pedal to the floor and slowly release it. The one-way valve in the kit will prevent expelled air from returning to the system at the end of each stroke. Repeat this operation until clean hydraulic fluid, free from air bubbles, can be seen coming through the tube. Now tighten the bleed screw and remove the outlet tube.
10 If a one-man brake bleeding kit is not available, connect one end of the plastic tubing to the bleed screw and immerse the other end in the jam jar containing sufficient clean hydraulic fluid to keep the end of the tube submerged. Open the bleed screw half a turn and have your assistant depress the brake pedal to the floor and then slowly release it. Tighten the bleed screw at the end of each downstroke to prevent expelled air and fluid from being drawn back into the system. Repeat this operation until clean hydraulic fluid, free from air bubbles, can be seen coming through the tube. Tighten the bleed screw at the end of a downstroke and remove the tube.
11 If the entire system is being bled the procedures described above should now be repeated at each wheel, finishing at the wheel nearest to the master cylinder. Do not forget to recheck the fluid level in the master cylinder at regular intervals and top up as necessary.
12 When completed, recheck the fluid level in the master cylinder, top up if necessary and refit the cap. Check the 'feel' of the brake pedal which should be firm and free from any 'sponginess' which would indicate air still present in the system.
13 Discard any expelled hydraulic fluid as it is likely to be contaminated with moisture, air and dirt which makes it unsuitable for further use.
14 With the ignition on and the handbrake released, check that the brake pressure drop warning light is extinguished. If it fails to go out after firm pressure has been applied to the brake pedal, either further bleeding is required or the PDWA switch is defective.

17 Handbrake cable – adjustment

1 Under normal circumstances, the handbrake is self-adjusting through the integral automatic adjuster of the handbrake caliper. No further adjustment is required. However, due to cable stretch, some supplementary adjustment may be needed after high mileages when the handbrake control has excessive travel when applying the brake fully.

Early cars (XJ12 and Double Six)

2 Release the handbrake control lever fully.
3 Working under the car, slacken the locknut on the front yoke (photo).
4 Extract the split pits, the washer and the clevis pin which holds the yoke to the bellcrank lever.
5 Check that the levers on the handbrake calipers are fully released.
6 Adjust the position of the yoke on the threaded rod until it can be connected to the bellcrank lever, using the clevis pin, with a very slight amount of slackness evident in the cable. Do not remove all the slackness so that the cable is taut when connected.
7 Refit the clevis and new split pins and tighten the yoke locknut.

Later cars (XJ12 and Double Six)

8 Working under the car, slacken the locknut at the forked end of the cable threaded adjuster.
9 Extract the split pin, clevis pin and washer and disconnect the fork from the handbrake lever.
10 Check that the handbrake actuating arms at the rear calipers are fully released by pressing them in towards the calipers.
11 Unscrew the clevis fork on the end of the handbrake cable until it can be reconnected to the handbrake lever and the clevis pin inserted without any tendency for the cable to pull on the caliper actuating levers.
12 Refit the washer and a new split pin to the clevis pin.

XJS models

13 A floor-mounted handbrake lever is fitted at the side of the front seat on these models. Access to the cable adjuster is obtained by peeling back the sill carpet just to the rear of the driver's seat.
14 Release the handbrake control lever fully and release the cable adjuster locknut.
15 Tighten the adjusting nut so that all slackness is just removed from

14.1 Pressure differential warning actuator on later models

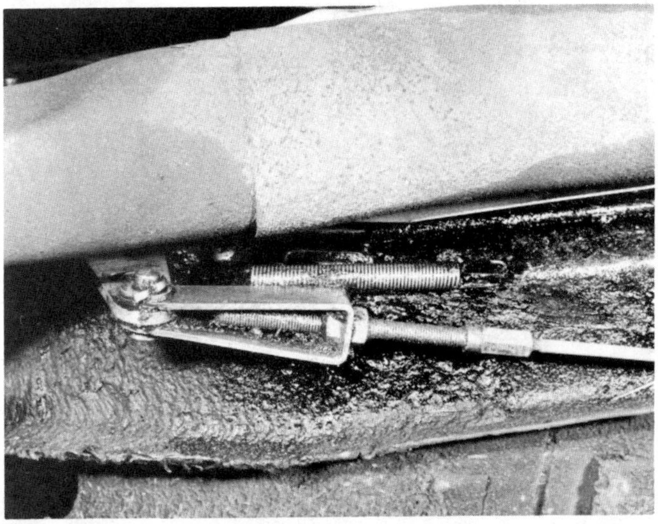

17.3 Handbrake cable adjuster

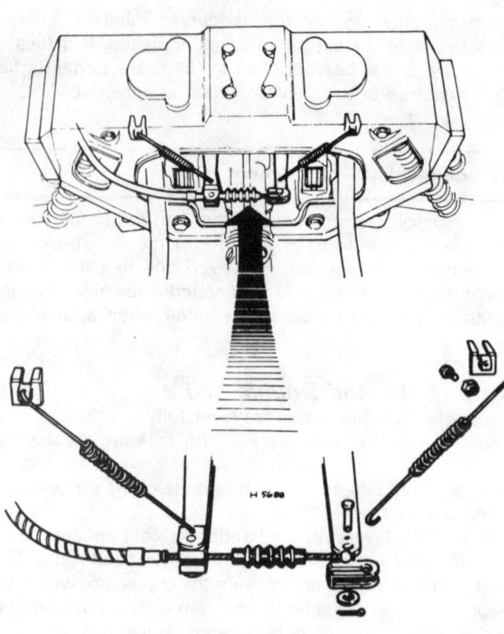

Fig. 9.18 Handbrake cable connections to caliper levers (Sec 18)

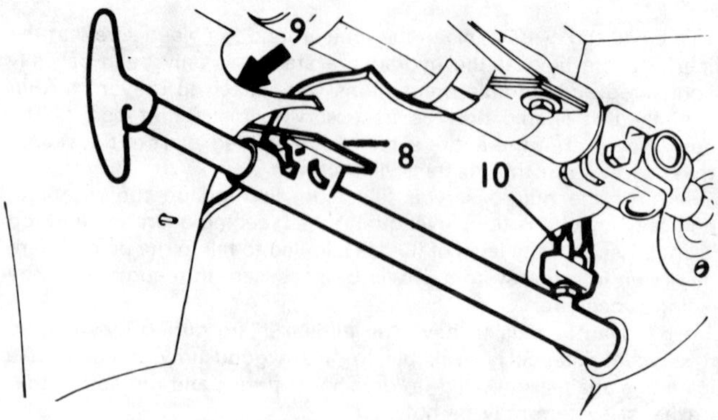

Fig. 9.19 Pull out type handbrake control lever mounting (Sec 19)

8 Mounting bracket
9 Trim
10 Warning switch

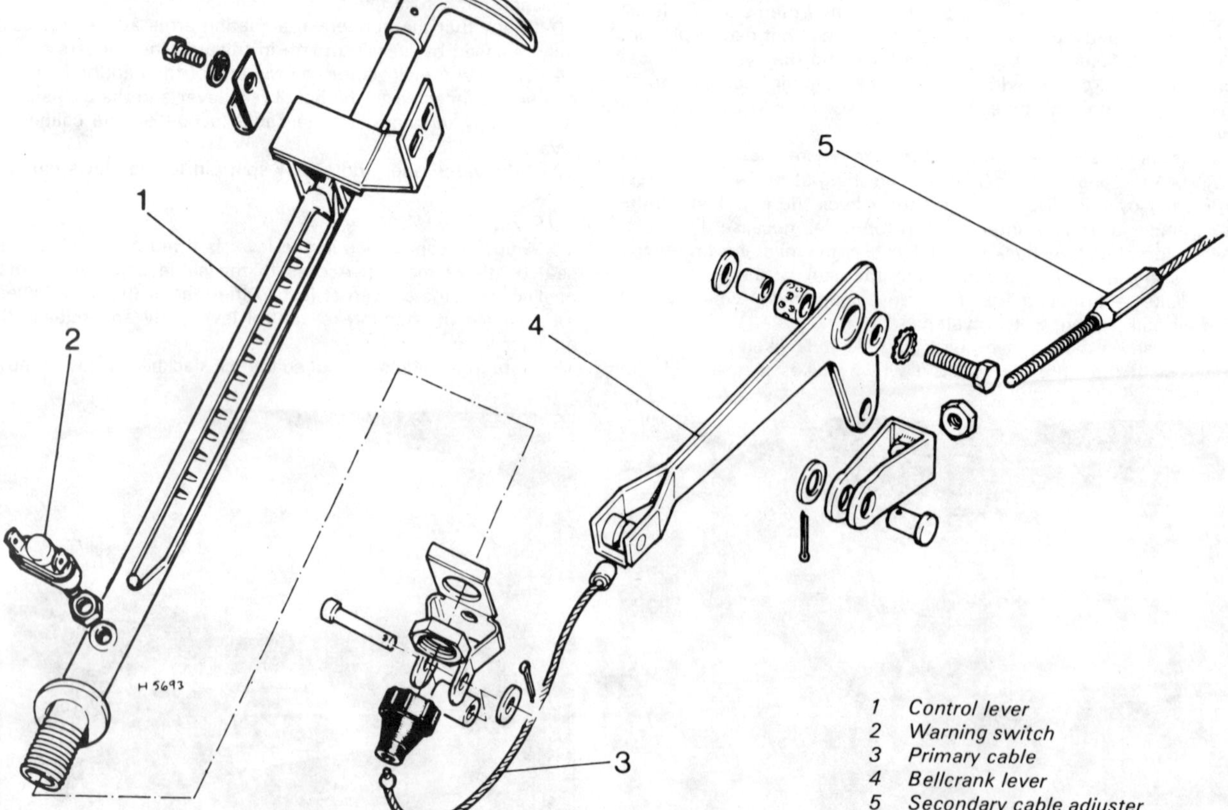

1 Control lever
2 Warning switch
3 Primary cable
4 Bellcrank lever
5 Secondary cable adjuster

Fig. 9.20 Handbrake control lever (XJ12, Double Six) (Sec 19)

18.3 Rear supsension tie plate

18.6 Handbrake caliper lever and cable

18.8 Handbrake caliper mounting bolts, lock-plate and retraction lever

18.9A Withdrawing the handbrake caliper

18.9B Cover plates within the luggage boot

18.10 Handbrake caliper

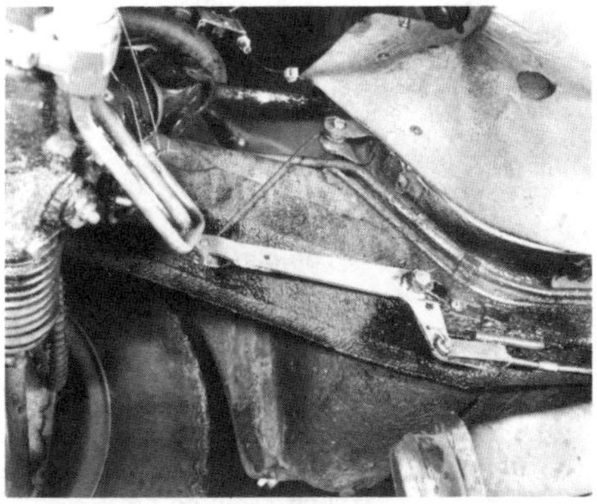

19.2 Handbrake primary cable, pulley and lever

19.5 Handbrake control lever

the cable, then turn the nut back just enough to introduce the smallest amount of slackness into the cable.

16 Tighten the locknut and replace the carpet.

18 Handbrake friction pads and caliper – removal and refitting

1 The friction pads for the handbrake are quite separate from the disc pads which are actuated by the hydraulic system. Under normal conditions, the handbrake pads will last indefinitely. Where they are in need of renewal then the handbrake caliper must first be removed as described below.

2 Raise the rear of the car on ramps or place it over an inspection pit.

3 Unbolt and remove the tie plate from the suspension unit (photo).

4 Release the handbrake control lever fully.

5 Extract the split pin and clevis pin which hold the handbrake cable to one caliper operating lever.

6 Detach the cable from the other operating lever (photo).

7 Unclip the return spring from the operating lever.

8 Bend the tabs down on the caliper mounting bolt lockplate and unscrew and remove the bolts, the lockwasher and the retraction lever which has a forked end (photo).

9 Slide the caliper around the brake disc and withdraw it through the aperture exposed by the removal of the tie plate. This aperture is at the rear of the car. Any surface rust on the brake discs will make the job of sliding the calipers more difficult. As an aid to manoeuvring the handbrake calipers, the small cover plates can be removed from the spare wheel recess in the luggage boot and the hands inserted (photos).

10 To renew the pads, remove the nuts and the spring washers which hold the pads to the carriers. Withdraw the pads (photo).

11 Hold one of the pad carriers and wind the remaining one out two or three turns. Insert the new pads using a new nut and spring washer.

12 If new pads have been fitted, then adjust the caliper by holding one pad carrier while rotating the other one to give a gap between the surfaces of the pads of 0.75 in (19.05 mm).
13 Refit the caliper by passing it through the aperture left by the removal of the tie plate.
14 Fit the retraction lever (engaging the fork in the holes), then fit new lockplates and the caliper mounting bolts.
15 Operate the actuating lever on the caliper until the ratchet ceases to click. The pads are then correctly set.
16 Refit the return spring to the handbrake operating lever.
17 Reconnect the handbrake cable to both levers.
18 Refit the tie plate to the suspension.

19 Handbrake control lever and cables (XJ12, Double Six) – removal and refitting

Control lever

1 Disconnect the battery.
2 Disconnect the handbrake primary cable from the bellcrank lever (photo).
3 Remove the nylon roller, over which the primary cable runs, from its support bracket.
4 Remove the driver's side dash liner (see Chapter 12).
5 Release the trim cover from the steering column and peel back the cover to expose the handbrake control lever bracket bolts (photo).
6 Unscrew the bolts which hold the handbrake assembly to the footwell side panel.
7 Identify the leads at the handbrake warning switch and disconnect them. Remove the handbrake control lever far enough to be able to slip the cable nipple from the sliding member.

Cables

8 The primary cable is removed in conjunction with the handbrake control lever as described above.
9 To remove the main (secondary) cable, release the control lever fully and disconnect the front end of the cable from the bellcrank lever.
10 Remove the inner and outer cable guides from under the car, also the guide spring.
11 Extract the split pin and the clevis pin and disconnect the rear end of the cable from the caliper lever. Slip the cable out of the opposite caliper lever and remove the cable.

Refitting

12 Refitting the control lever and the primary and secondary cables is a reversal of removal but observe the following points:

(a) Adjust the handbrake warning switch (see Section 21)
(b) Use new split pins in the clevis pins
(c) Adjust the cable as described in Section 17

20 Handbrake control lever and cable (XJS) – removal and refitting

Control lever

1 Disconnect the battery.
2 Remove the driver's seat.
3 Extract the bolt which holds the handbrake control lever pivot cover.
4 Slide the cover up and off the lever.
5 Identify the leads and disconnect them from the handbrake warning switch.
6 Peel back the carpet at the sill and slacken the nuts on the handbrake cable.
7 Detach the nipple from the cable.
8 Unbolt and remove the control lever assembly, noting the location of the earth lead and the tubular spacers on the mounting bolts.
9 Detach the cable from the control lever and lift the lever from the car.

Cable

10 Carry out the operations described in paragraphs 2 to 7.
11 Detach the cable from the handbrake control lever.
12 Disconnect the rear end of the cable from the levers on the handbrake calipers.
13 Cut the clips which secure the protective sleeve to the outer cable and slide the sleeve from the cable.
14 Remove the protective cover from the outer cable.
15 Withdraw the cable into the car from the control lever end, extracting it from its body guide tube.

Refitting

16 Refitting of the control lever and the cable is a reversal of removal, but adjust the cable as described in Section 17.

21 Handbrake switch – adjustment

Pull-out type control lever (XJ12, Double Six)

1 Pull the footwell side casing carpet to one side clear of the handbrake control lever.
2 Slacken the switch locknut, mark and detach the leads.
3 With the control lever fully off, screw in the switch until the warning lamp just goes out (ignition switched on).
4 Make sure that the longer dimension of the switch is parallel with the control lever and tighten the locknut.
5 Check the adjustment by operating the hand control lever.

Floor-mounted type control lever (XJS)

6 Slide the handbrake control lever cover from the base of the lever as described in Section 20.
7 Slacken the switch setscrews and with the ignition on, move the switch (with the control lever fully off) until the warning lamp just goes out.
8 Tighten the switch screws, check the operation of the switch and refit the cover.

22 Brake fluid level warning switch – removal and refitting

1 All types of master cylinder fluid reservoirs have a low level warning switch built into the filler cap.
2 Any malfunction in the switch (assuming the fluid level is correct and the warning lamp bulb is not blown) can only be rectified by renewal.
3 Disconnect the battery.
4 Peel back the black rubber cover from the reservoir cap, disconnect the cables and unscrew the lid.
5 Renew the lid complete, reconnect the leads and fit the rubber cover.

23 Brake stoplamp switch – adjustment

1 The switch is located at the brake pedal arm.
2 Slacken the switch securing bolt.
3 Switch on the ignition and move the switch until, when the brake foot pedal is just depressed, the stoplamps come on, and when the pedal is released, the lamps are out.
4 Tighten the switch bolt and turn off the ignition.

24 Brake pedal box (XJ12, Double Six) – removal and refitting

1 Disconnect the battery and remove the air cleaner.
2 Disconnect the hydraulic pipes from the master cylinder and cap the pipes to prevent loss of fluid.
3 On RHD cars, disconnect the vacuum hoses from the servo elbow pipe.
4 On LHD cars, disconnect the vacuum hose from the servo adaptor.
5 Disconnect the leads from the switch in the fluid reservoir cap.
6 Unbolt or disconnect (dependent upon type) the fluid reservoir and remove it. Take care not to drip fluid on the paintwork.
7 On LHD cars, continue from paragraph 11. On RHD cars, unbolt the throttle cable guide bracket from the right-hand rear intake manifold.

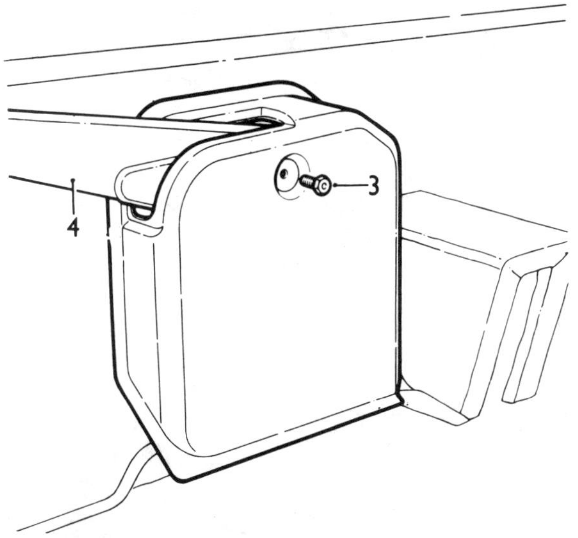

Fig. 9.21 Handbrake control lever pivot cover (XJS) (Sec 20)

3 Securing screw
4 Control lever

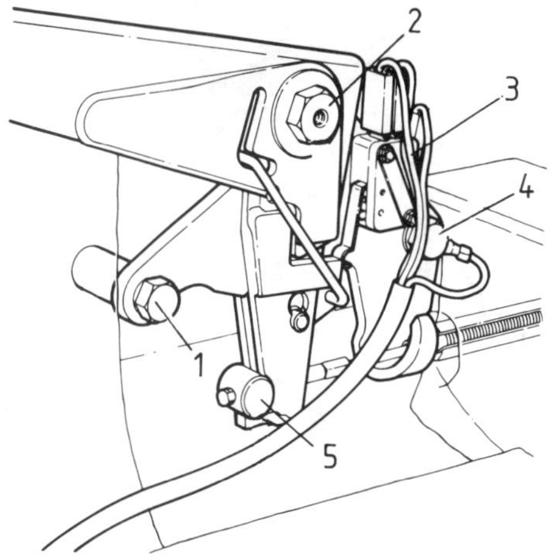

Fig. 9.22 Handbrake control lever attachments (XJS) (Sec 20)

1 Mounting bolt
2 Pivot bolt
3 Warning switch
4 Earth connection
5 Handbrake cable end nipple

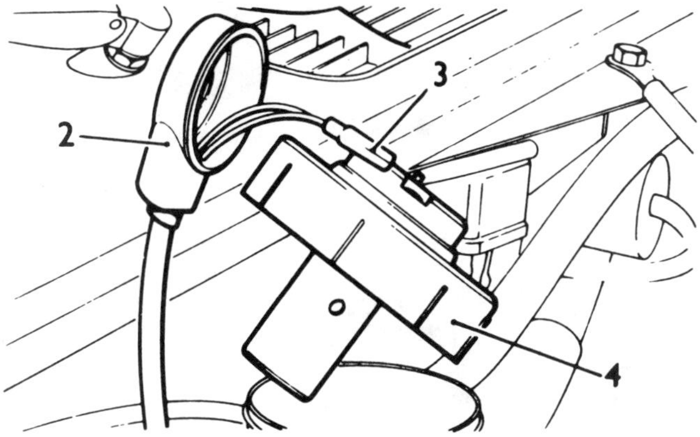

Fig. 9.23 Fluid reservoir cap removed (Sec 22)

2 Rubber cover
3 Electrical connector
4 Cap

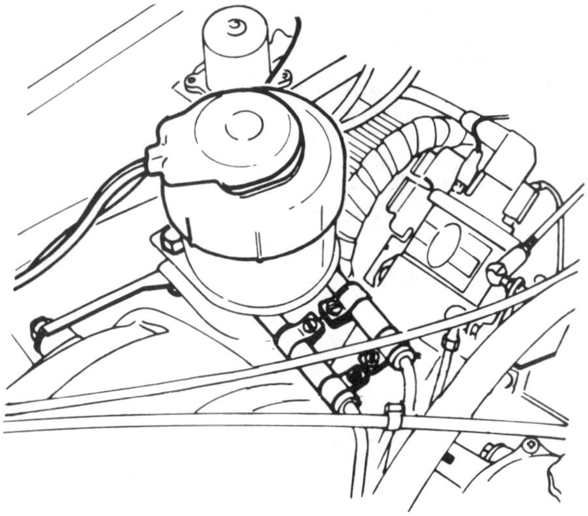

Fig. 9.24 Remotely mounted brake fluid reservoir (Sec 22)

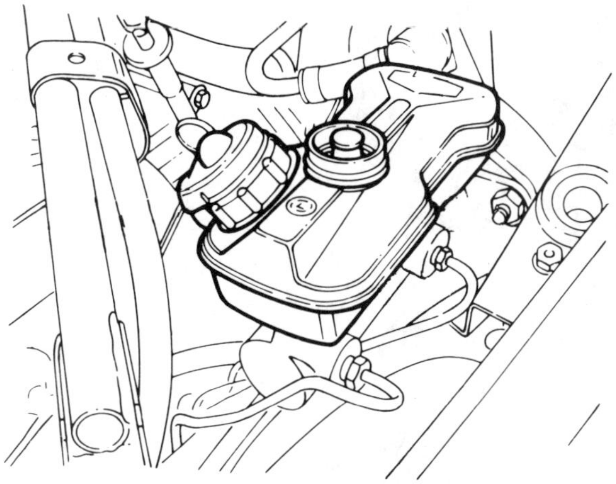

Fig. 9.25 Directly mounted brake fluid reservoir (Sec 22)

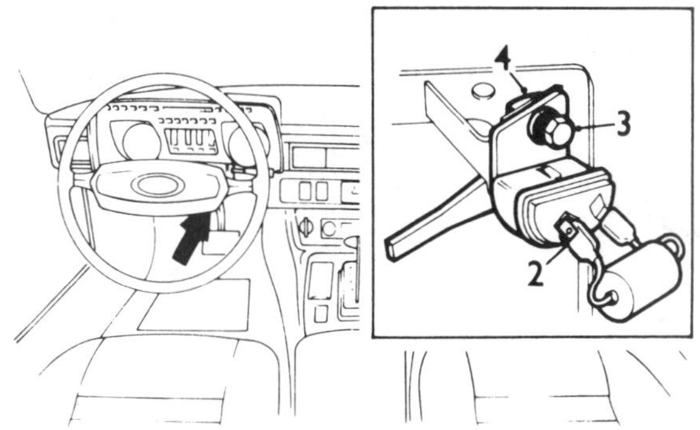

Fig. 9.26 Typical brake stoplamp switch (LHD shown, RHD similar) (Sec 23)

2 Electrical connector
3 Mounting bolt
4 Keep plate

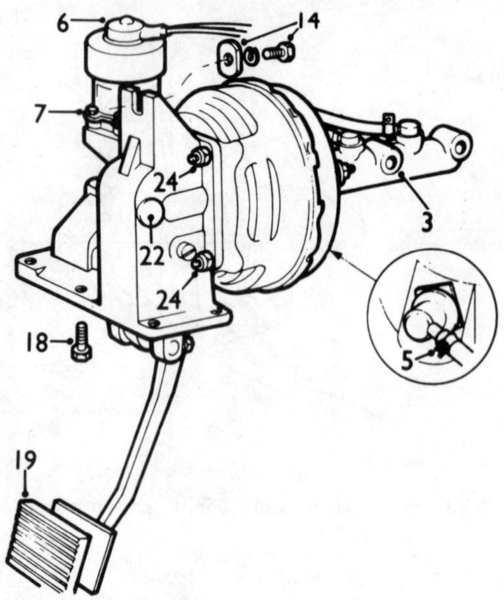

Fig. 9.27 Brake pedal box assembly (XJ12, Double Six) (Sec 24)

3 *Master cylinder*
5 *Vacuum hose to servo unit*
6 *Fluid reservoir cap*
7 *Reservoir mounting bolts*
14 *Pedal box upper mounting bolt*
18 *Pedal box base bolts*
19 *Brake pedal pad*
22 *Rubber sealing plug*
24 *Servo mounting nuts*

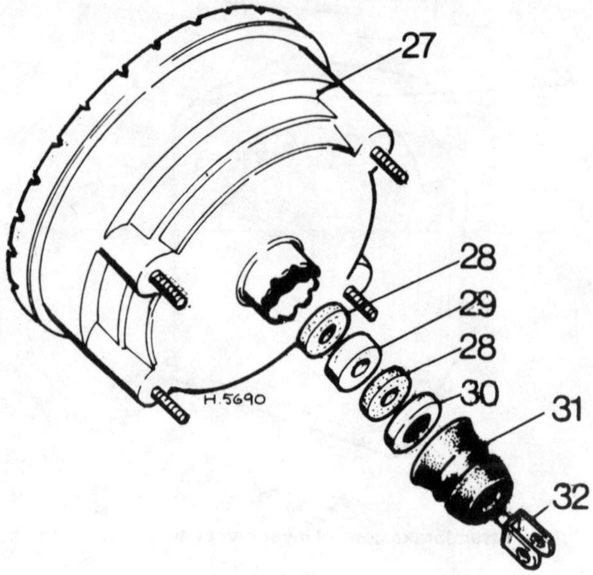

Fig. 9.28 Typical brake servo air filter components (Sec 27)

27 *Rear shell*
28 *Filter felts*
29 *Air filter*
30 *Filter retainer*
31 *Dust cover*
32 *Clevis fork*

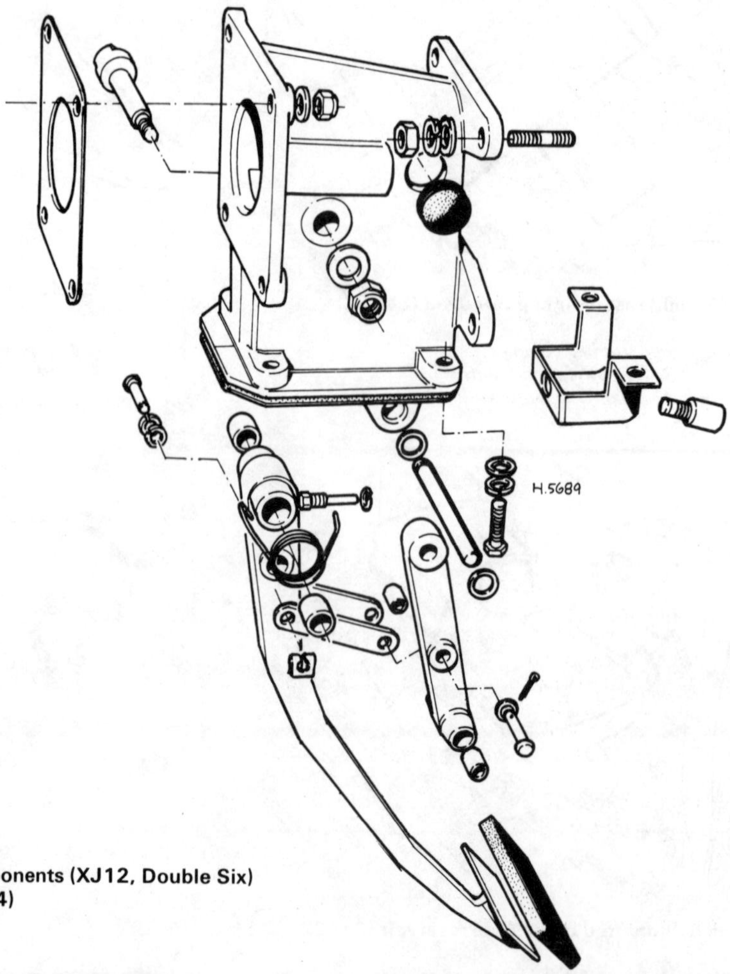

Fig. 9.29 Brake pedal box components (XJ12, Double Six) (Sec 24)

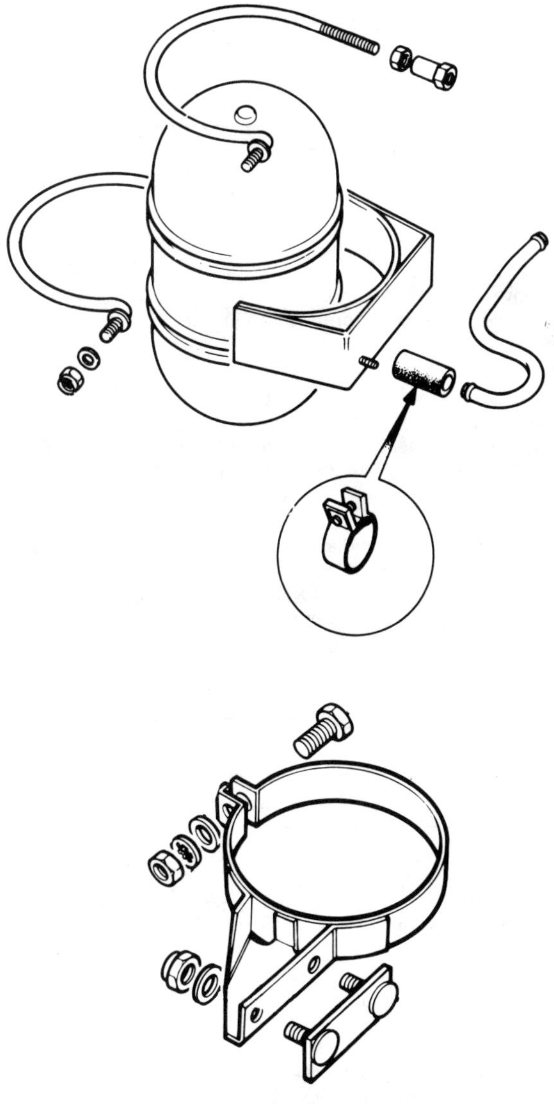

Fig. 9.30 Vacuum reservoir tank with alternative mountings (Sec 30)

8 Disconnect the leads from the kickdown switch.
9 Slacken the locknut that holds the kickdown switch and the throttle cable to the pedestal. Disengage the cable from the pulley and move it away from the servo unit.
10 Remove the self-locking nut which holds the steering column lower mounting bracket to the pedal box.
11 Unbolt the upper section of the pedal box from the bulkhead.
12 Unbolt the fluid reservoir mounting bracket from the servo unit.
13 Move the driver's seat as far as possible to the rear. Extract the single screw from the front of the seat cushion and lift out the cushion.
14 Remove the carpets from the footwell.
15 Remove the brake stoplamp switch.
16 Unbolt the lower section of the pedal box from the bulkhead.
17 On cars with carburettors, move the choke cables clear of the servo unit.
18 Lift the combined servo unit, pedal box and master cylinder upwards and remove it forwards from the car.
19 Extract the two rubber plugs from the sides of the pedal box.
20 Disconnect the servo operating rod from the brake pedal arm.
21 Unbolt the pedal box from the servo unit.
22 The pedal box can be dismantled for renewal of bushes and thrust washers. Apply grease to shafts, bushes and washers on reassembly.
23 Refitting is a reversal of removal. Bleed the hydraulic system on completion (see Section 16).

25 Brake pedal box (XJS) – removal and refitting

1 Removal of the pedal box from cars fitted with manual transmission is covered in Chapter 5, Section 3, paragraphs 1 to 14, in conjunction with the clutch pedal.
2 On cars equipped with automatic transmission, the operations are identical except that any reference to clutch actuating components should be ignored.
3 Refitting is a reversal of removal. On manual transmission cars, bleed the clutch hydraulic system on completion.

26 Vacuum servo unit – description and testing

1 A vacuum servo is fitted into the brake hydraulic circuit in series with the master cylinder, to provide assistance to the driver when the brake pedal is depressed. This reduces the effort required by the driver to operate the brakes under all braking conditions.
2 The unit operates by vacuum obtained from the induction manifold and comprises basically a booster diaphragm and non-return valve. The servo unit and hydraulic master cylinder are connected together so that the servo unit piston rod acts as the master cylinder pushrod. The driver's braking effort is transmitted through another pushrod to the servo unit piston and its built in control system. The servo unit piston does not fit tightly into the cylinder, but has a strong diaphragm to keep its edges in constant contact with the cylinder wall, so assuring an air tight seal between the two parts. The forward chamber is held under vacuum conditions created in the inlet manifold of the engine and, during periods when the brake pedal is not in use, the controls open a passage to the rear chamber so placing it under vacuum conditions as well. When the brake pedal is depressed, the vacuum passage to the rear chamber is cut off and the chamber opened to atmospheric pressure. The consequent rush of air pushes the servo piston forward in the vacuum chamber and operates the main pushrod to the master cylinder.
3 The controls are designed so that assistance is given under all conditions and, when the brakes are not required, vacuum in the rear chamber is established when the brake pedal is released. All air from the atmosphere entering the rear chamber is passed through a small air filter.
4 Under normal operation conditions the vacuum servo unit is very reliable, but should a fault develop then the complete assembly must be renewed as repair kits or internal components are no longer supplied. Operations must therefore be restricted to the maintenance tasks described in the next Section.
5 It must be emphasised that failure of a servo unit will not affect the safety of the braking system, merely cause higher pedal pressures than those normally required.
6 A vacuum reserve tank is fitted to all models.
7 To test the efficiency of the servo system, jack up a front roadwheel and check that it turns without binding.
8 Start the engine, allow time for vacuum to build up and apply the brake pedal several times. Have an assistant turn the roadwheel immediately the brake pedal is released. If the brake binds then an internal fault in the servo is indicated.
9 With the engine running, apply the brake pedal several times. If the pedal is slow to return, check for damaged hoses or a clogged servo air filter, see next Section.
10 Allow the engine to idle for a few minutes to build up vacuum. Switch off the engine and apply the brake pedal two or three times. The vacuum 'hiss' should be heard on each application. If not, a faulty non-return valve or a leak in the system is indicated.
11 With the engine switched off, apply the footbrake pedal several times to destroy the vacuum in the system. Apply light foot pressure to the brake pedal and start the engine. If the servo is operating correctly, the foot pedal will move nearer the floor. If it does not move then the system is leaking.

27 Vacuum servo unit – maintenance

1 Occasionally check the security and condition of the vacuum hose to the inlet manifold.
2 At specified intervals (see Routine Maintenance) or when the foot brake pedal seems to be sluggish in operation, renew the air filter in the following way.
3 Remove the brake vacuum servo unit, as described in Section 24 or 25.
4 Remove the dust cover, detach the end cap and withdraw the filter and filter felt rings. Cut the filter rings to permit them to pass over the clevis fork.
5 Fit the new filter felts by cutting them cleanly so that they will pass over the clevis fork. Ensure that the cuts in the various filter rings are not in line, but stagger their position.
6 Refit the end cap and dust cover.
7 Refit the brake vacuum servo unit.

28 Vacuum servo unit – removal and refitting

1 The vacuum servo unit is removed and refitted in conjunction with the pedal box as described in Section 24 or 25.

29 Vacuum servo non-return valve – removal and refitting

1 Disconnect the vacuum flexible hose from the non-return valve on the intake manifold.
2 Unscrew and remove the non-return valve and its copper washer.
3 The valve can be tested by blowing through it, first in one direction and then in the other. Air should only pass one way.
4 Refit by reversing the removal operations, but use a new copper washer.

30 Vacuum reserve tank – removal and refitting

1 Jack up the front of the car and remove the right-hand front roadwheel.

XJ12 and Double Six

2 Remove the horn relay.
3 Disconnect the hose from the vacuum tank.

XJS

4 Extract the screws which hold the lower edge of the diaphragm panel to the front skirt panel.
5 Prise out the plastic studs which hold the top of the diaphragm panel to the inner wing. Remove the diaphragm panel.

All models

6 Disconnect the tank mounting clamp or straps and withdraw the tank from the car. On XJS models the vacuum pipe must be disconnected from the tank before it can be completely withdrawn.
7 Refitting is a reversal of removal.

31 Fault diagnosis – braking system

Symptom	Reason(s)
Pedal travels almost to floor before brakes operate	Brake fluid level too low Caliper leaking Master cylinder leaking (bubbles in master cylinder fluid) Brake flexible hose leaking Brake line fractured Brake system unions loose Pad linings over 75% worn
Brake pedal feels springy	New pads not yet bedded-in Brake discs badly worn or cracked Master cylinder securing nuts loose
Brake pedal feels spongy and soggy	Caliper leaking Master cylinder leaking (bubbles in master cylinder reservoir) Brake pipe line or flexible hose leaking Unions in brake system loose
Excessive effort required to brake car	Pad linings badly worn New pads recently fitted – not yet bedded-in Harder pads fitted than standard causing increase in pedal pressure Pads or discs contaminated with oil, grease or hydraulic fluid Servo unit inoperative or faulty
Brakes uneven and pulling to one side	Pads or discs contaminated with oil, grease or hydraulic fluid Tyre pressures unequal Brake caliper loose Brake pads fitted incorrectly Different type of pads fitted at each wheel Anchorages for front suspension or rear suspension loose Brake discs badly worn, cracked or distorted
Brakes tend to bind, drag or lock-on	Air in hydraulic system Caliper pistons seized Handbrake cables too tight Fault in servo unit

Chapter 10 Electrical system

Contents

Specifications

System type	12 volt, negative earth
Battery capacity	
XJ12 and Double Six	70 Ah at 20-hour rate
XJS	68 Ah at 20-hour rate
Alternator	
Make and type	Lucas 20 ACR or 25 ACR, or Motorola 9AR 2512P
Cut-in voltage	13.5V
Cut-in speed	950 to 1500 (alternator) rpm
Maximum output	66A
Maximum operating speed	15 000 (alternator) rpm
Starter motor	
Make and type	Lucas M45G pre-engaged
Windscreen wiper motor	
Make and type	Lucas 16W, two-speed

Lamp bulbs

The bulbs listed below are typical, but precise details may vary according to model year and operating territory. For exact specification consult the operator's handbook supplied with the vehicle.

	Bulb No	Wattage
Headlamp:		
Main and dip	411	60/45
Main beam only	411	50
Halogen	H1	55
N America	15602	37.5/50
Front flasher and parking (N. America)	GLB 380	21/6
Front flasher	GLB 382	21
Front parking	GLB 207	5
	or GLB 989	6
Reversing lamp	GLB 273	21
Rear number plate	GLB 989	6
	or GLB 254	
Rear flasher	GLB 382	21
Tail	GLB 207	5
Stop/tail	GLB 380	21/6
Map reading	GLB 254	6
Interior and pillar	GLB 272	10
Luggage boot	GLB 989	6
Clock	GLB 987	2.2
Warning lamps	Capless	1.2
Opticell	GLB 989	6
Speedometer	GLB 981	2.2
Tachometer	GLB 987	2.2
Choke warning	GLB 987	2.2
Choke handle	GLB 281	2
Main beam warning	GLB 987	2.2
Safety belt warning	GLB 987	2.2
Heater control panel	GLB 280	1.5
Automatic transmission indicator	GLB 281	2
Foglamp or spotlamp (Cibie)	H2	55
Cigar lighter	G70112	2.2
Warning lamp (catalytic converter)	GLB 281	2

1 General description

1 All models have a 12 volt negative earth system.
2 The major components of the system comprise a battery, a belt-driven alternator and a pre-engaged type starter motor.
3 On cars equipped with an air-conditioning system, a heavy duty alternator is fitted.
4 The battery supplies a steady current for the ignition, lighting and other electrical circuits and provides a reserve of electricity when the current consumed by the electrical equipment exceeds that being produced by the charging system.
5 Although full instructions for the periodic overhaul and minor servicing of the various electrical components are given in this Chapter it must be appreciated that rectification of major faults will require specialised knowledge and equipment and therefore, where such faults arise, the defective item should be removed and replaced with a serviceable item which can usually be obtained on an exchange basis.
6 Wiring diagrams covering the various models will be found at the end of the Chapter.

2 Battery – maintenance and inspection

1 On XJ12 and Double Six models, the battery is located within the engine compartment against the rear bulkhead (photo).
2 On XJS models, the battery is located in the luggage compartment

under a cover held in place by two screws.
3 Keep the top of the battery clean by wiping away dirt and moisture.
4 Remove the plugs or lid from the cells and check that the electrolyte level is just above the separator plates. If the level has fallen, add only distilled water until the electrolyte level is just above the separator plates. Where a Lucas Pacemaker battery is fitted, lift the vent cover and check that electrolyte is visible in all the filling tubes. If it is, do not add any more. If any tube is empty, add distilled water into the filler trough to the indicated level, then refit the vent cover.
5 As well as keeping the terminals clean and covered with petroleum jelly, the top of the battery, and especially the top of the cells, should be kept clean and dry. This helps prevent corrosion and ensures that the battery does not become partially discharged by leakage through dampness and dirt.
6 If topping up the battery becomes excessive and the case has been inspected for cracks that could cause leakage, but none are found, the battery is being over-charged and the voltage regulator within the alternator will have to be checked.
7 At three-monthly intervals, measure the electrolyte specific gravity with a hydrometer to determine the state of charge and condition of the battery. There should be very little variation between the different cells and if a variation in excess of 0.25 is present it will be due to either:

(a) *Loss of electrolyte from the battery at some time caused by spillage or a leak, resulting in a drop in the specific gravity of electrolyte when the deficiency was replaced with distilled water instead of fresh electrolyte*
(b) *An internal short circuit caused by buckling of the plates or a similar malady pointing to the likelihood of total battery failure in the near future*

8 The specific gravity of the electrolyte for fully charged conditions at the electrolyte temperature indicated, is listed in Table A. The specific gravity of a fully discharged battery at different temperatures of the electrolyte is given in Table B.

Table A

Specific Gravity – Battery Fully Charged

1.268 at	*100°F or 38°C electrolyte temperature*
1.272 at	*90°F or 32°C electrolyte temperature*
1.276 at	*80°F or 27°C electrolyte temperature*
1.280 at	*70°F or 21°C electrolyte temperature*
1.284 at	*60°F or 16°C electrolyte temperature*
1.288 at	*50°F or 10°C electrolyte temperature*
1.292 at	*40°F or 4°C electrolyte temperature*
1.296 at	*30°F or-1.5°C electrolyte temperature*

Table B

Specific Gravity – Battery Fully Discharged

1.098 at	*100°F or 38°C electrolyte temperature*
1.102 at	*90°F or 32°C electrolyte temperature*
1.106 at	*80°F or 27°C electrolyte temperature*
1.110 at	*70°F or 21°C electrolyte temperature*
1.114 at	*60°F or 16°C electrolyte temperature*
1.118 at	*50°F or 10°C electrolyte temperature*
1.122 at	*40°F or 4°C electrolyte temperature*
1.126 at	*30°F or-1.5°C electrolyte temperature*

3 Battery – removal and refitting

XJ12 and Double Six

1 The battery incorporates a cooling fan. Remove the battery in the following way.
2 Peel back the flexible covers from the battery terminals, release the pinch-bolts and disconnect the leads from the battery terminals.
3 Disconnect the leads to the battery cooling fan by detaching them at the snap connectors.
4 Slacken the battery holding down bolts.
5 Prise the flexible outlet pipe from the cooling jacket grommet.
6 Detach the battery positive lead from the clip on the cooling jacket.
7 Ease the battery and its cooling jacket forward until the jacket can be withdrawn from the battery (photo).
8 Lift the battery from the car.
9 The cooling fan can be removed from the cooling jacket after withdrawing the seven securing screws. The nylon impeller can be levered from the motor shaft (photo).
10 Reassembly and refitting are reversals of removal and dismantling.

XJS

11 Release the two screws and lift the cover from the battery.
12 Peel back the battery terminal covers, release the clamp bolts and disconnect the leads.
13 Release the battery filler cover securing strap and remove the filler cover.
14 Unscrew the battery clamp nuts and remove the clamp.
15 Keeping the battery level, lift it from the luggage compartment.

4 Electrolyte replenishment (battery)

1 If the battery is in a fully charged state and one of the cells maintains a specific gravity reading which is 0.25 or more lower than the others, then it is likely that electrolyte has been lost from the cell with the low reading at some time.
2 Top up the cell with a solution of 1 part sulphuric acid to 2.5 parts of water. If the cell is already fully topped up draw some electrolyte out of it with a hydrometer. Do not mix the electrolyte yourself, but obtain it from your dealer or service station ready mixed. Recharge the battery and check the hydrometer readings.
3 If the specific gravity reading is still not satisfactory a new battery will have to be obtained, as the design of the intercell connectors prevents any further tests with, for example, a high rate discharge meter.

2.1 Battery (XJ12, Double Six) in cooling jacket

3.7 Battery with cooling jacket removed

3.9 Interior of battery cooling jacket

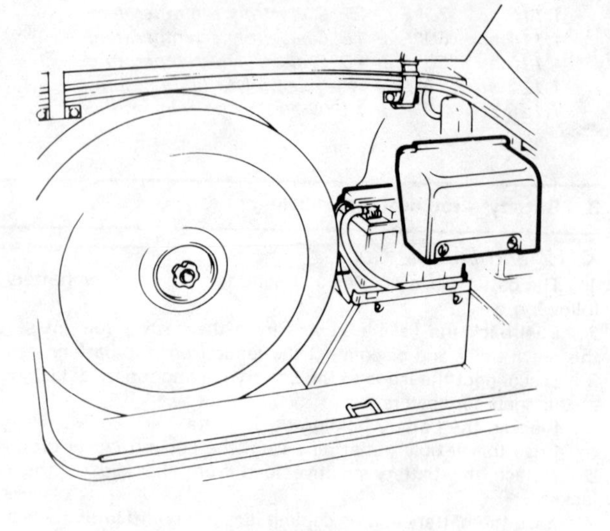

Fig. 10.1 Battery and cover in the luggage compartment (XJS) (Sec 2)

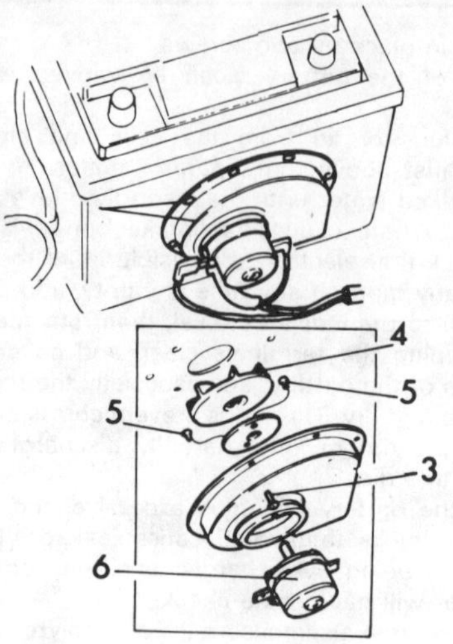

Fig. 10.2 Battery and cooling fan (XJ12, Double Six) (Sec 3)

3 *Fan securing screw*
4 *Fan*
5 *Keeper plate screws*
6 *Fan motor*

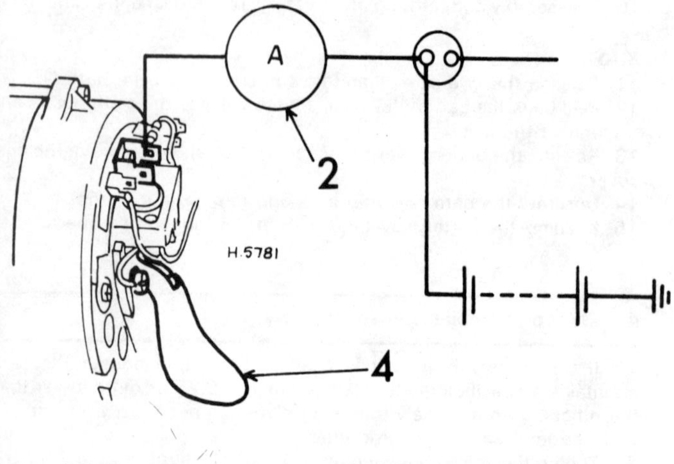

Fig. 10.3 Alternator output test (Lucas type) (Sec 8)

2 *Ammeter*
4 *Jump lead*

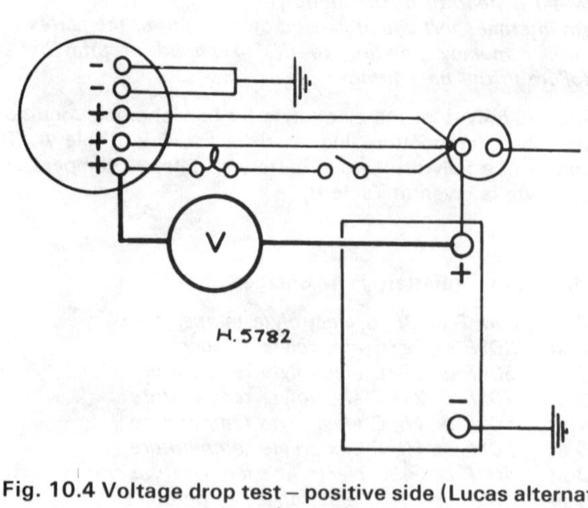

Fig. 10.4 Voltage drop test – positive side (Lucas alternator) (Sec 8)

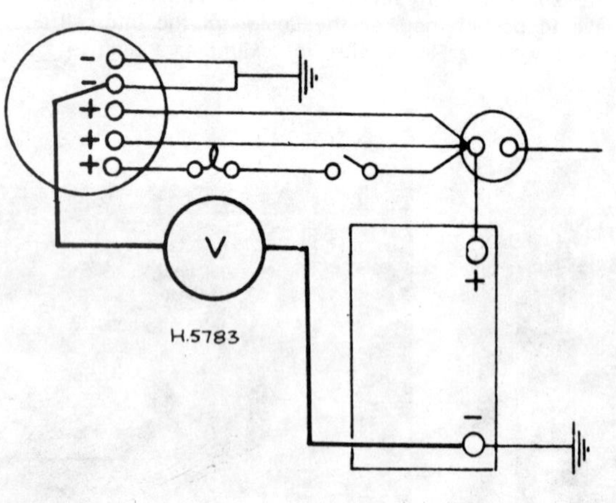

Fig. 10.5 Voltage drop test – negative side (Lucas alternator) (Sec 8)

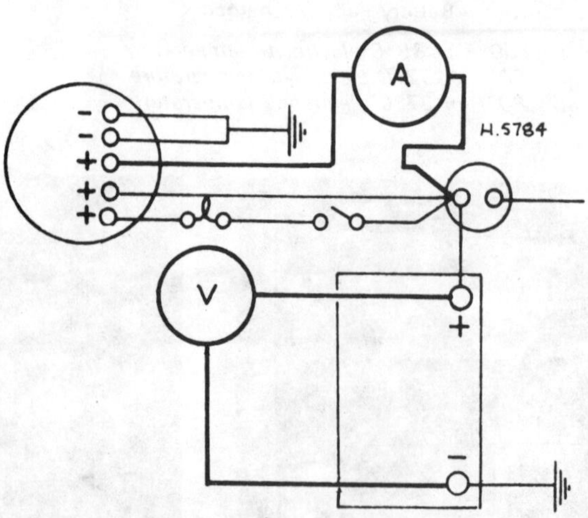

Fig. 10.6 Control unit test (Lucas alternator) (Sec 8)

5 Battery – charging

1 In winter time when heavy demand is placed upon the battery, such as when starting from cold, and much electrical equipment is continually in use, it is a good idea to have occasionally the battery fully charged from an external source at the rate of 3.5 or 4 amps (see Section 7).
2 Continue to charge the battery at this rate until no further rise in specific gravity is noted over a four hour period.
3 Alternatively, a trickle charger at the rate of 1.5 amps can be safely used overnight.
4 Specially rapid 'boost' charges which are claimed to restore the power of the battery in 1 to 2 hours are most dangerous as they can cause serious damage to the battery plates.

6 Alternator – general description and maintenance

1 Briefly the alternator comprises a rotor and stator. Current is generated in the coils of the stator as soon as the rotor revolves. This current is three-phase alternating which is then rectified by positive and negative silicon diodes and the level of voltage required to maintain the battery charge is controlled by a regulator within the alternator.
2 Maintenance consists of occasionally wiping away any oil or dirt which may have accumulated on the outside of the unit.
3 No lubrication is required as the bearings are grease sealed for life.
4 Check the drivebelt tension periodically to ensure that its specified deflection is correctly maintained. The correct tension of the belt is indicated when the midpoint of the top run of the belt can be depressed $\frac{1}{2}$ in (12.7 mm). Adjustment is carried out by releasing the alternator pivot mounting bolts and the adjustment link bolts and moving the alternator away from or towards the engine. Retighten the bolts on completion.
5 On cars which are equipped with power steering and air-conditioning the drivebelt arrangement is complex and although all the belts should be tensioned as just described, renewal of an inner belt will necessitate removal of the outer belts first; refer to Chapter 1, Section 51.

7 Alternator – special precautions

Take extreme care when making circuit connections to a vehicle fitted with an alternator and observe the following. When making connections to the alternator from a battery always match correct polarity. Before using electric-arc welding equipment to repair any part of the vehicle, disconnect the connector from the alternator and disconnect the negative battery terminal. Never start the car with a battery charger connected. Always disconnect both battery leads before using a mains charger. If boosting from another battery, always connect in parallel using heavy cable.

8 Alternator (Lucas) – testing in the car

1 The Lucas 20 or 25 ACR alternator, is fitted, dependant upon the equipment (air-conditioner etc) specified for the particular model.
2 A moving coil ammeter and a moving coil voltmeter will be required to carry out these tests.
3 If the engine is cold, run it at 3000 rpm for 3 or 4 minutes, then stop the engine.
4 Disconnect the lead from the battery negative terminal.
5 Connect the ammeter in series with the alternator main outut cable and starter solenoid.
6 Remove connectors from the alternator, detach the moulded end cover and then re-make the connections.
7 Connect a jump lead to short out the 'F' and '–' terminals of the control unit.
8 Reconnect the lead to the battery negative terminal.
9 Switch on all the car lights with the headlamps on main beam. Switch on the ignition and check that the warning lamp is on.
10 Start the engine, slowly increase its speed to 3000 rpm. The reading on the ammeter should be equivalent to the alternator maximum rated output which is 66 amps. If it is not, the alternator requires overhaul and reconditioning.
11 Having completed the output test, remake the original connections and check for voltage drop.
12 Connect a voltmeter between the battery positive terminal and the alternator main output terminal.
13 Switch on all the car lights including the headlamps on main beam. Start the engine and run at 3000 rpm. Record the voltmeter reading and then switch off the engine.
14 Transfer the voltmeter connections to the battery negative terminal and the alternator negative terminal.
15 Repeat the operations described in paragraph 13, and again note the reading on the voltmeter. The readings recorded should not exceed 0.5 volts. Higher readings indicate high resistance in the circuit.
16 To test the control unit, first make sure that all connections are clean and secure and that the battery is in a fully charged condition (charge from an outside source if necessary).
17 Connect an ammeter in series with the starter solenoid and the alternator main output cable.
18 Connect the voltmeter between the battery terminals.
19 Start the engine and run it at 3000 rpm until the ammeter reads less than 10 amps. The voltmeter reading should be between 13.6 and 14.4 volts. If the reading fluctuates or is outside the range specified then the control unit is faulty.

9 Alternator (Motorola) – testing in the car

1 Before carrying out the tests, make sure that the battery is fully charged. An accurate voltmeter and ammeter will be required.
2 Switch off the ignition. Check the voltage on one of the three phases of the stator windings by passing a probe of the voltmeter through the ventilation hole as shown.
3 Connect the voltmeter between a phase and earth, then between a phase and the positive terminal. Observe the correct polarity. If the reading is anything but zero on the voltmeter then there is a defective positive rectifier diode. Renew the diode bridges.
4 Switch on the ignition but do not start the engine. Carry out a check of the field circuit. Do this by extracting the regulator securing screws and touching the voltmeter probe on the field terminal EX. If the voltmeter reading exceeds 2 volts then the field circuit is defective. First check the movement of the brushes in their holders and examine them for wear. Check that the brush leads are not frayed and that the slip rings are clean. If the voltmeter reads zero, check the security of connections to the regulator, the ignition switch and the ignition indicator lamp.
5 Now check the regulator circuit by detaching its green wire from the field EX terminal and measuring the voltage across the field windings. This should not exceed 2 volts. If it is between 8 and 12 volts then the alternator is faulty. If the voltage is correct, switch on the ignition and start the engine. Have the engine speed faster than the normal idle. Check the output voltage at the alternator B+ terminal and then at the battery positive terminal. The correct reading at both checking points should be 14.2V ± 0.5V at an ambient temperature of 77°F (25°C). If the difference between the two readings is more than 0.3V, check all wiring connections for security and absence of corrosion.
6 With the field lead disconnected, the regulator disconnected and the output terminal shorted to the field terminal, run the engine at fast idle and check the regulator and diodes.
7 Check the voltage between the output terminal B+ and earth. If the voltage rises to between 14 and 16V but did not attain 14V in the second test described in paragraph 5 then the regulator is defective and should be renewed.
8 If the voltage does not rise but the field circuit has been tested and found to be satisfactory (paragraph 4) then either the alternator stator or the rectifier diodes are defective.
9 The removal of any defective components from the alternator is described in Section 13.

10 Alternator (XJ12, Double Six) – removal and refitting

1 Disconnect the battery.
2 Remove the right-hand air cleaner (Chapter 3).
3 Where fitted, remove the air pump (Chapter 3).
4 Release the alternator mounting bolt and the adjuster link nut.
5 Slacken the adjuster trunnion block to bracket bolt.

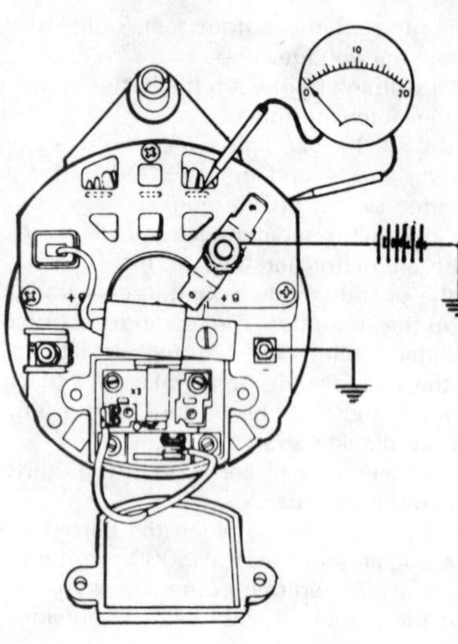

Fig. 10.7 Test circuit (phase to earth) – Motorola alternator (Sec 9)

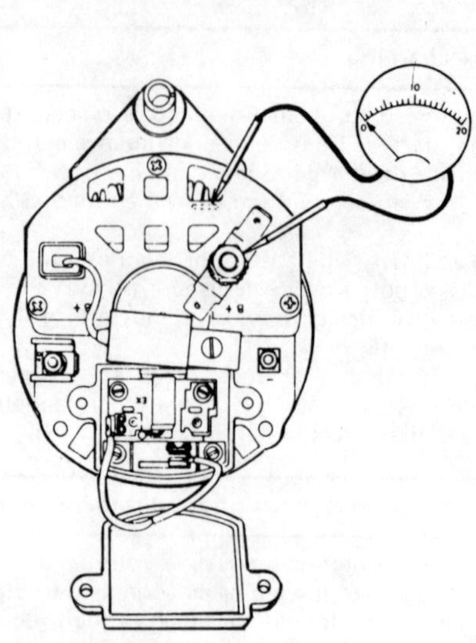

Fig. 10.8 Test circuit (winding to positive terminal) – Motorola alternator (Sec 9)

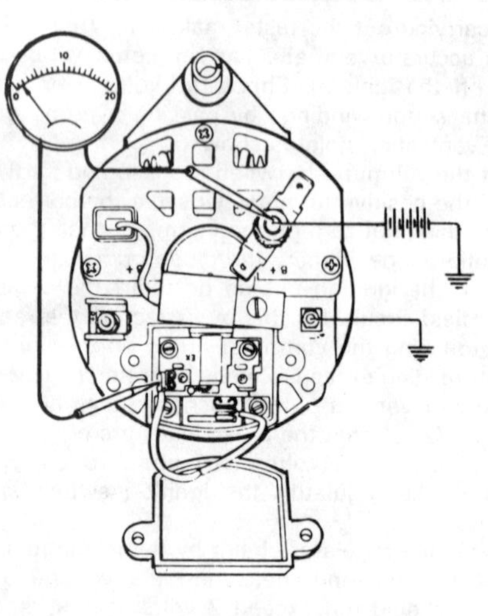

Fig.10.9 Test circuit (field winding check) – Motorola alternator (Sec 9)

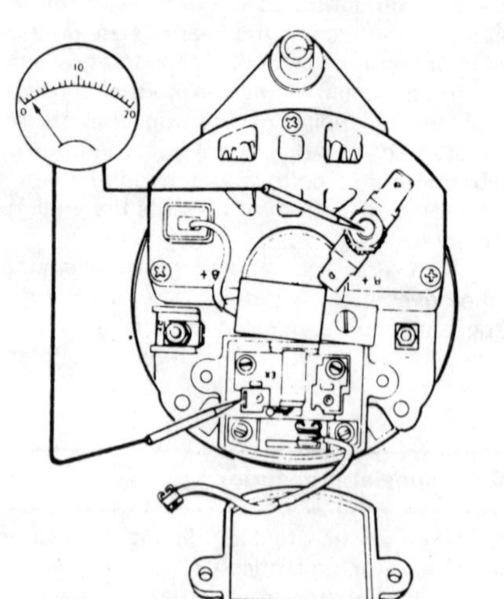

Fig. 10.10 Test circuit (regulator) – Motorola alternator (Sec 9)

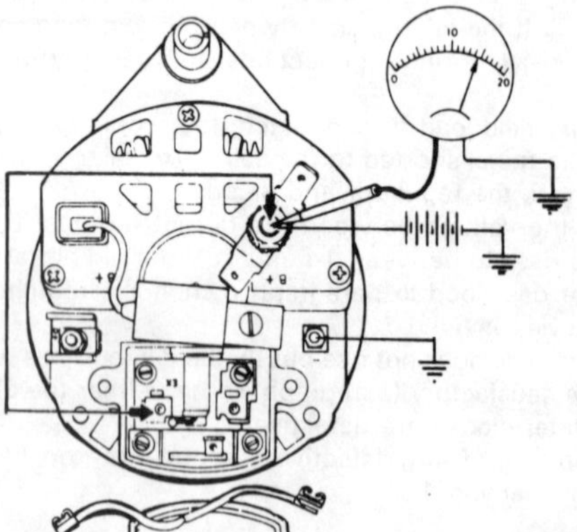

Fig. 10.11 Test circuit (diode) – Motorola alternator (Sec 9)

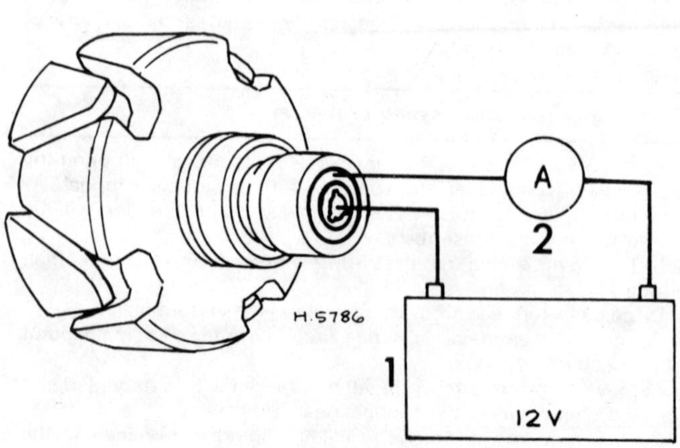

Fig. 10.12 Checking slip ring resistance (Lucas alternator) (Sec 12)

1 Battery
2 Ammeter

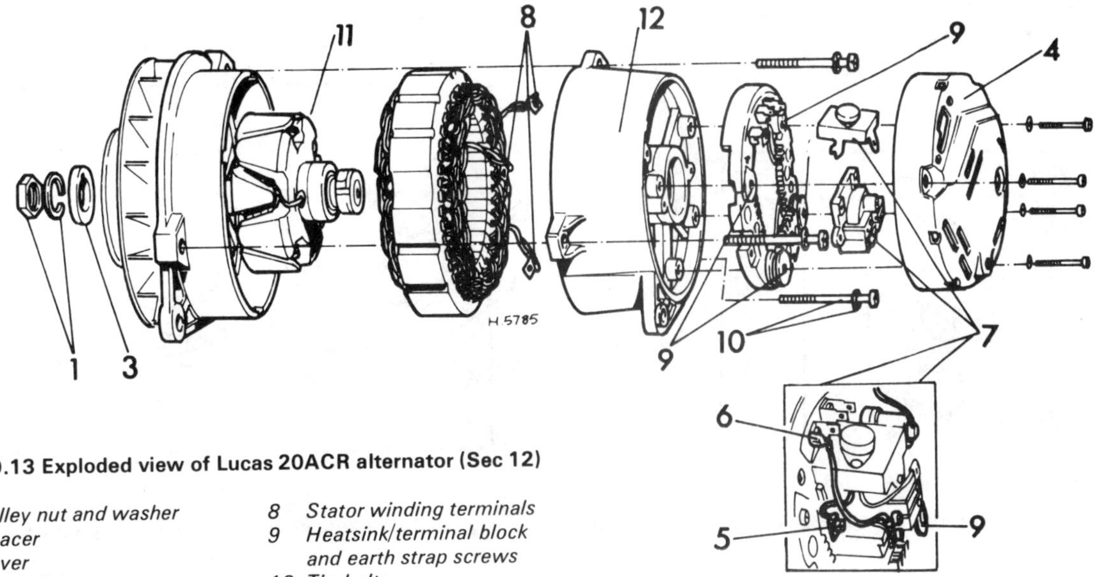

Fig. 10.13 Exploded view of Lucas 20ACR alternator (Sec 12)

1 *Pulley nut and washer*
3 *Spacer*
4 *Cover*
5 *Brush fixing screw*
6 *Leads to 'Ind' and '+' terminals*
7 *Brush moulding and control box*
8 *Stator winding terminals*
9 *Heatsink/terminal block and earth strap screws*
10 *Tie-bolts*
11 *Rotor/drive end bracket*
12 *Slip ring end bracket*

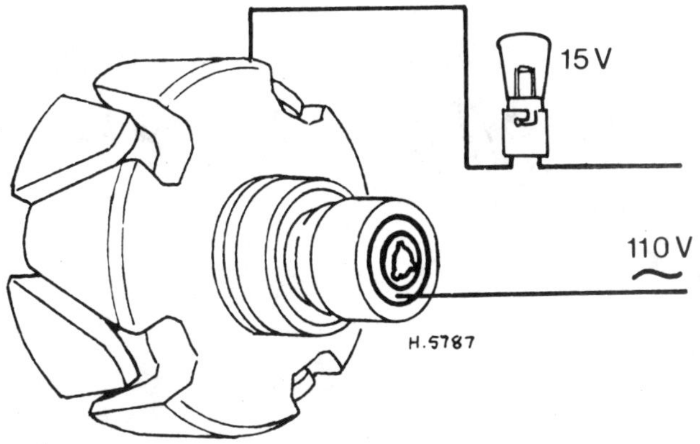

Fig. 10.14 Checking slip ring and rotor insulation (Lucas alternator) (Sec 12)

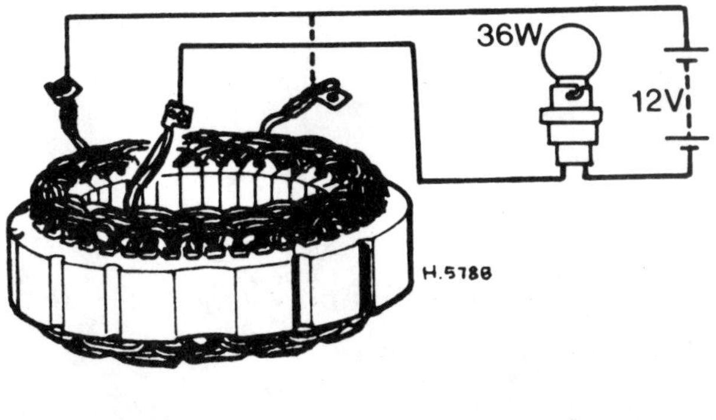

Fig. 10.15 Checking stator continuity (Lucas alternator) (Sec 12)

6 Pull out the electrical connector plug from the back of the alternator.
7 Release the adjuster link locknuts and move the alternator in towards the engine until the drivebelt can be slipped off the pulley.
8 Unscrew and remove the alternator front and rear mounting pivot bolts and lift the alternator from the engine compartment.
9 If the alternator drivebelt must be renewed, then the old belt can only be removed if the fanbelt is removed first by releasing the jockey pulley (see Chapter 1, Section 51) on models without air conditioning, or the fanbelt and the compressor belt on models with air conditioning.
10 Refitting is a reversal of removal. Tension the drivebelts as described in Chapter 1, Section 51.

11 Alternator (XJS) – removal and refitting

1 The operations are very similar to those described in the preceding Section, except that only the air cleaner cover and filter element should be removed to gain access to the alternator.

12 Alternator (Lucas) – overhaul

1 There are detail differences between the 20 and 25 ACR alternators but this overhaul procedure applies equally to both types.
2 With the alternator removed from the car, remove the pulley retaining nut and washer and draw off the pulley. Remove the fan, spacer and Woodruff key.
3 Remove the moulded cover plate.
4 Unscrew the brush holder screws, noting that they also secure the radio interference suppression capacitor and black earth cable.
5 Disconnect the red leads from the 'IND' and '+' terminals of the alternator.
6 Withdraw the brush moulding complete with control box.
7 Disconnect the three stator windings from their respective heatsinks.
8 Remove the four screws which secure the heatsink/terminal block assembly and the small screw which connects the earth strap to the alternator frame.
9 Unscrew and remove the three tie bolts from the alternator frame.
10 Separate the slip ring end bracket and stator from the rotor and drive end bracket. To do this, insert a lever and prise them apart.
11 With the alternator dismantled, check the brushes for wear. The brushes must protrude beyond the holder by at least 0.32 in (8 mm), otherwise renew them, noting the location of the leaf spring at the side of the inner brush.
12 The slip rings should normally only require cleaning with a fuel soaked cloth but if essential, they can be burnished with finest grade glasspaper (not emery).

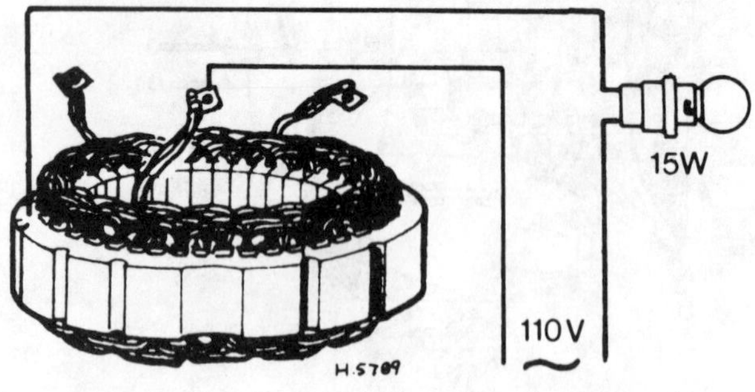

Fig. 10.16 Checking stator insulation (Lucas alternator) (Sec 12)

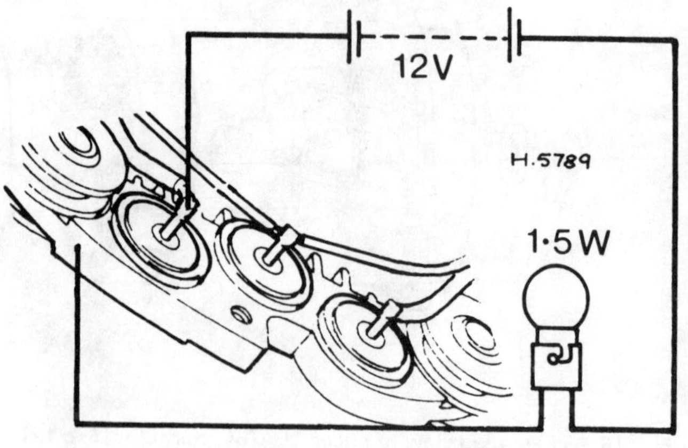

Fig. 10.17 Testing diodes (Lucas alternator) (Sec 12)

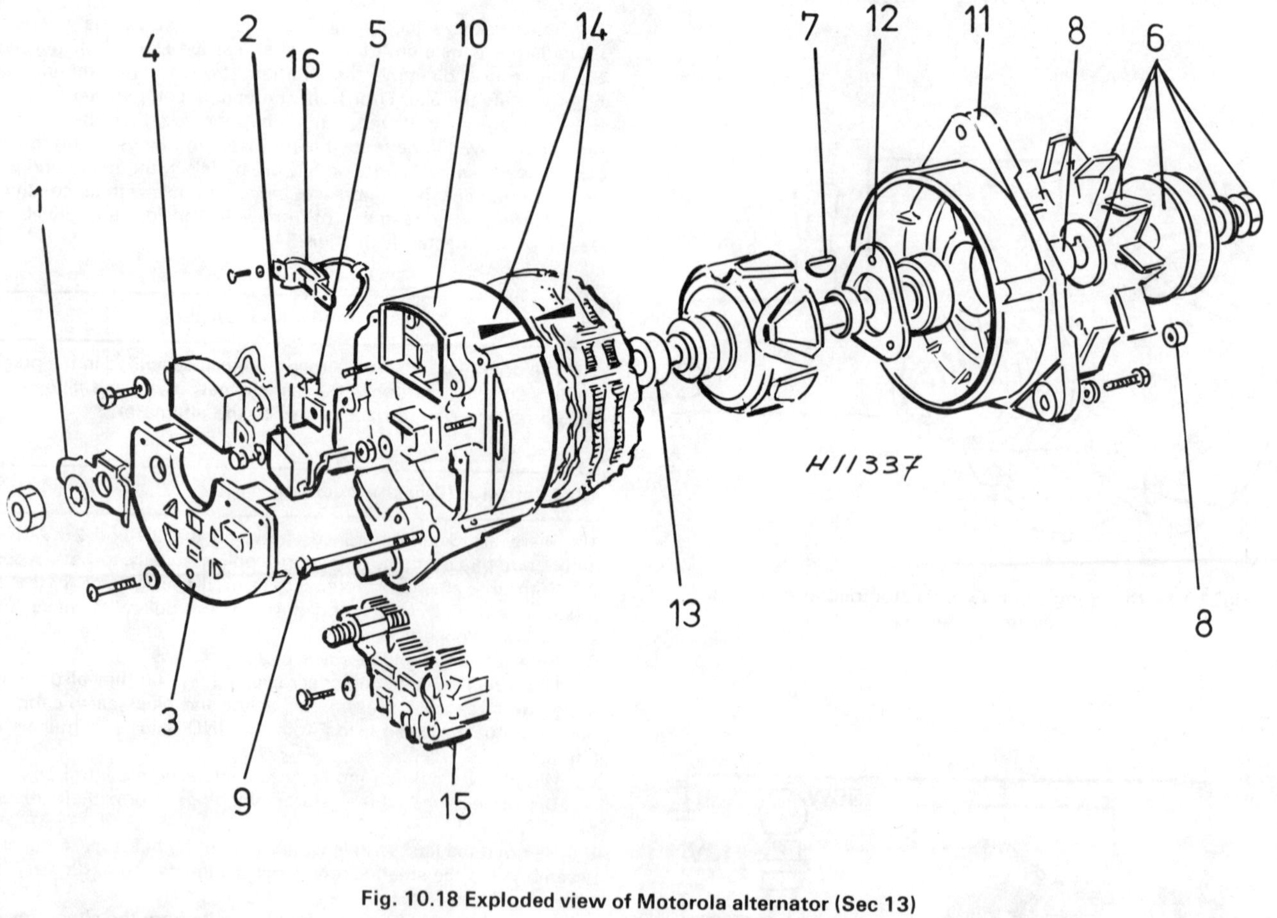

Fig. 10.18 Exploded view of Motorola alternator (Sec 13)

1 B+ terminal
2 Capacitor
3 Moulded rear cover
4 Regulator
5 Brush holder
6 Pulley/fan components
7 Woodruff key
8 Spacer
9 Tie-bolt
10 Rear housing
11 Front housing
12 Front bearing retainer
13 Rear bearing
14 Stator and alignment marks
15 Diode bridge
16 D+ lead assembly

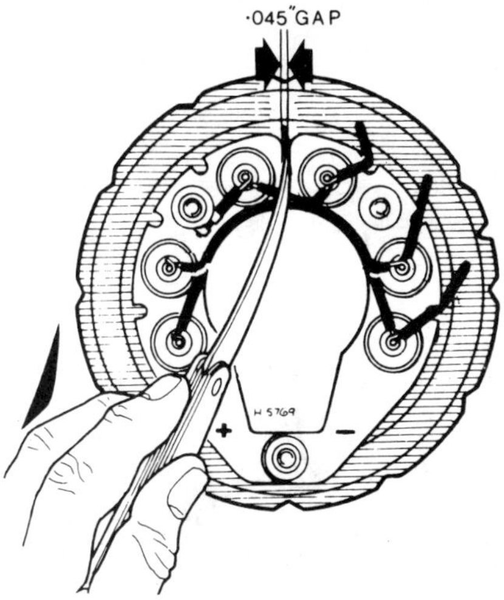

Fig. 10.19 Slip ring end cover (typical) on Lucas alternator (Sec 12)

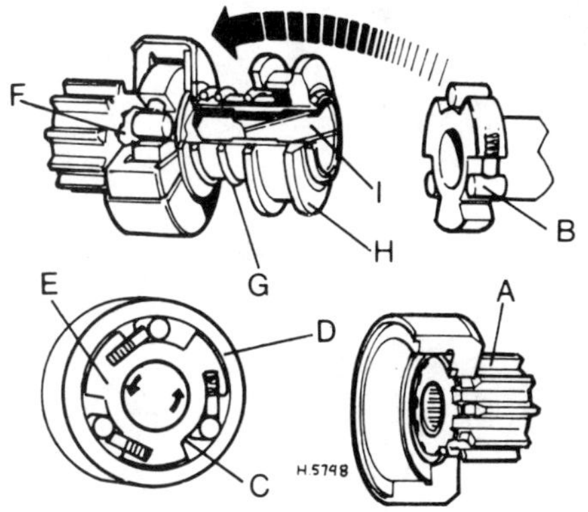

Fig. 10.20 Starter motor drive/clutch components (Sec 19)

A *Alternative construction (pinion pressed and snap-ringed into driven member)*
B *Spring-loaded rollers*
C *Cam tracks*
D *Driven member (with pinion)*
E *Driving member*
F *Bush*
G *Engagement spring*
H *Operating bush*
I *Driving sleeve*

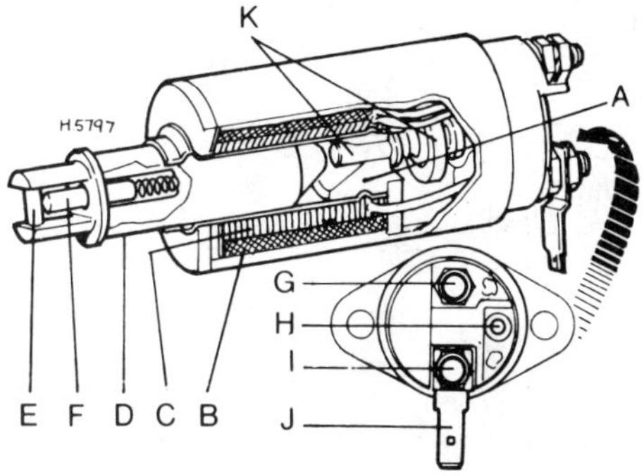

Fig. 10.21 View of typical starter motor solenoid (Sec 19)

A *Core*
B *Shunt winding*
C *Series winding*
D *Plunger*
E *Clevis pin*
F *'Lost motion' device*
G *Starter terminal*
H *Solenoid terminal*
I *Battery terminal*
J *Accessories terminal*
K *Spindle and moving contact assembly*

13 To test the servicability of the rotor, connect an ohmmeter between the slip rings. Resistance should be 3.6 ohms at 20° C (68°F). Alternatively, where an ohmmeter is not available, connect an ammeter and 12 volt supply between the slip rings; the ammeter should indicate about 3 amps.

14 To test for defective insulation between the slip rings and the rotor a 110 volt supply will be needed and without a suitable transformer this part of the test will have to be left to your dealer or automotive electrician. Where a suitable voltage supply is available, connect it with a 15W test lamp between the slip rings and rotor poles in turn. If the lamp lights then the coil is earthed to the rotor core. In this event a new rotor/slip ring assembly will be required.

15 The stator can be tested for continuity by connecting any two of the three stator cables in series with a 12 volt battery supply and a 36 watt test lamp. The lamp should light up.

16 Repeat the test by moving the test lamp circuit to the third stator cable. Failure of the lamp to light on either of these tests indicates an open circuit and the stator must be renewed.

17 The insulation of the stator can be checked with a 110 volt test lamp rig. Connect the leads to the laminated yoke and to any one of the three stator cables. If the lamp lights up, the stator coils are earthed and the stator must be renewed.

18 To test the diodes, connect one battery terminal to the heatsink under test. Connect the other battery terminal in series with the test lamp (1.5W) and each diode pin in turn. Reverse the connections between the heatsinks and the diode pins in turn. The lamp should light in one direction only. If the lamp lights in both directions or does not light light up at all, a new rectifier/heatsink assembly is needed.

19 When soldering the diode assemblies, use 'M' grade 45/55 tin/lead solder. Be careful not to overheat the diodes or bend their pins. It is advisable to lightly grip the diode pins with a pair of long nosed pliers when soldering so that the pliers will absorb excess heat. After soldering, the connections must be neatly arranged around the heatsinks and tacked down with 'MMM' EC 1022 adhesive where shown in the figure in order to ensure adequate clearance for the rotor.

20 Reassembly is a reversal of dismantling but the following points must be observed.

21 If the rotor and drive end bracket have been separated, support the inner track of the drive end bearing using the distance collar. Do not use the drive end bracket as a support while fitting the rotor to it or it may crack.

22 Tighten the tie-bolts evenly and make sure that the brushes are correctly located before refitting the brush moulding.

23 It is very important that the aluminium casing of the control unit does not touch the alternator body when it is installed in its final position. This would cause the field circuit to be fully switched on and the alternator would then supply maximum output irrespective of battery charge conditions.

13 Alternator (Motorola) – overhaul

1 With the alternator removed from the car, remove the B+ terminal from the end cover.

2 Detach the capacitor from the alternator casing.

3 Remove the rear cover (three screws).

4 Detach the regulator (two screws).

5 Lift out the brush holder (two setscrews).

6 Unscrew the pulley nut and draw off the pulley. An old drivebelt engaged in the pulley groove and gripped in the jaws of a vice close to the pulley will stop the pulley turning as the pulley nut is unscrewed. Remove the Woodruff key and spacer.

7 Remove the four tie-bolts and retain the captive nuts.

8 Pull off the rear housing complete with the stator and diode bridge. The rear bearing will remain on the rotor spindle.

9 Draw off the front housing and take off the short spacer next to the rotor.

10 If essential, the front bearing can be removed if the retaining plate (3 screws) is removed and the bearing pressed out.

11 The rear bearing can be withdrawn from the rotor spindle using a suitable puller.

12 Mark the relationship of the stator ring to the rear housing to make sure that it is refitted during reassembly in its original position.

13 Unsolder the leads of the three phase windings and the D+ lead from the diode bridge. Use a pair of long-nosed pliers as a heatsink when unsoldering the leads, otherwise the heat may be transmitted to

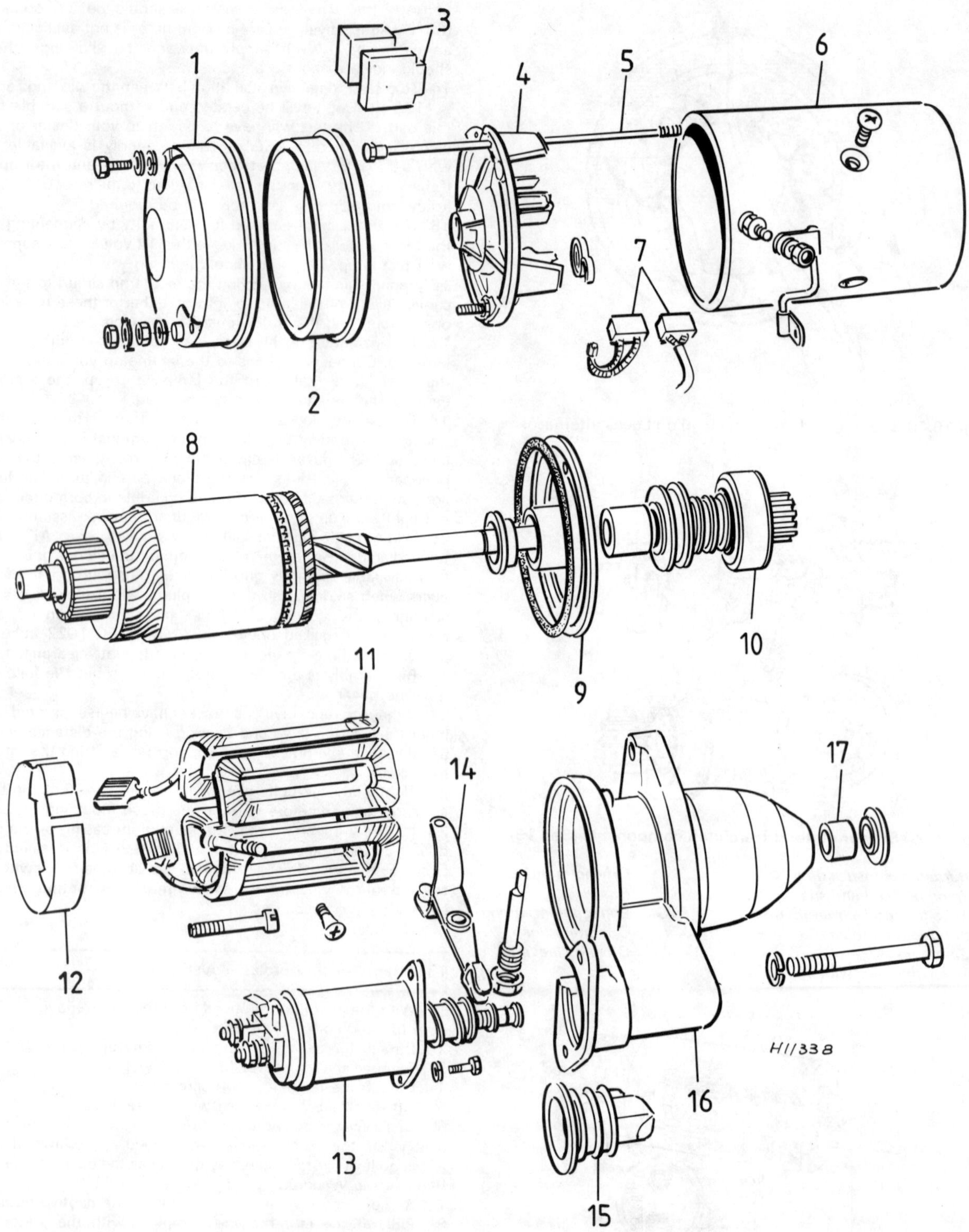

Fig. 10.22 Exploded view of the starter motor (Sec 19)

1 Cover	*6 Yoke*	*10 Clutch/drive assembly*	*14 Engagement lever*
2 Seal	*7 Brushes*	*11 Field coils*	*15 Dust-excluding boot*
3 Plugs	*8 Armature*	*12 Spacer ring*	*16 Drive end housing*
4 Commutator end bracket	*9 Front end bracket*	*13 Solenoid*	*17 Bush*
5 Tie-bolt			

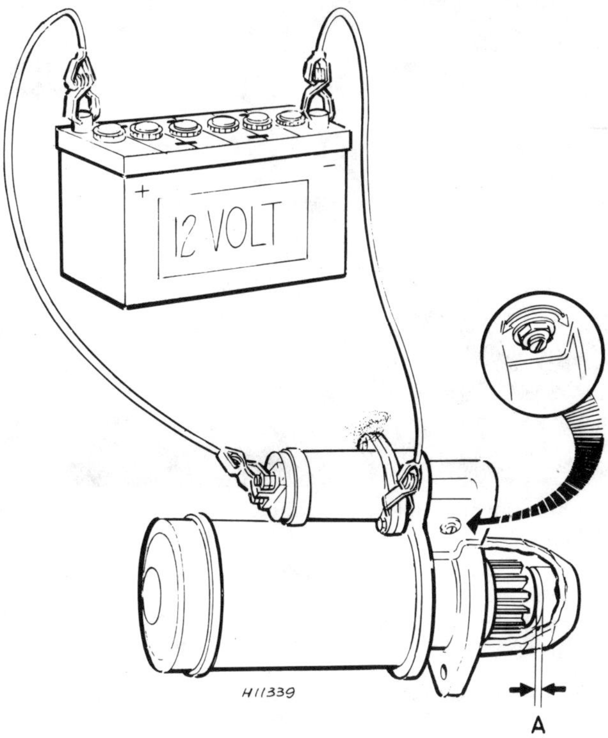

Fig. 10.23 Setting the starter motor drive pinion (Sec 19)

A See text

the diodes and damage them.
14 Lift out the diode bridge (two setscrews).
15 Withdraw the alternator housing from the stator, detach the two terminals and remove the D+ lead complete.
16 Extract the O-ring from the bearing housing.
17 Commence reassembly by fitting a new O-ring into the recess in the rear bearing housing.
18 Fit the D+ red lead assembly into the rear housing. Bolt it into position and pass the loose end of the lead through the hole below the D+ terminal.
19 Align the stator with the housing in the previously marked position so that the three leads pass through the housing. Place the stator with the housing resting on top of it on a clean surface.
20 Lower the diode bridge with the terminals and the capacitor fitted into position in the housing so that the three leads pass through the gaps between the fins. Secure with the two setscrews, trapping the capacitor connector under the right-hand one.
21 Solder the three phase winding leads and the D+ lead to the diode bridge, again using pliers to grip each terminal in turn to act as a heatsink.
22 If the rear bearing was removed, press a new one onto the rotor spindle and then press the spindle/bearing into the rear housing.
23 Place the short spacer over the front end of the spindle making sure that the larger inside diameter is next to the rotor.
24 If the front bearing was removed, press a new one into the front housing and secure with a retaining plate. The retaining plate screws should have their threads smeared with thread locking compound.
25 Fit the alternator front housing. Apply thread locking compound to the tie bolt threads and tighten them to secure the assembly, but do not overtighten.
26 Fit the plain washer to the rotor spindle, and insert the Woodruff key. Fit the large washer, the fan, the pulley, the small washer and the nut in that order. Tighten the pulley nut to 29 lbf ft (39 Nm).
27 Refit the brush holder, the regulator, the rear cover, the capacitor and the B+ terminal components.

14 Starter motor – description

1 The pre-engaged type of starter motor incorporates a solenoid mounted on top of the starter motor body. When the ignition switch is operated, the solenoid moves the starter drive pinion, through the medium of the shift lever, into engagement with the flywheel or driveplate starter ring gear. As the solenoid reaches the end of its stroke and with the pinion by now fully engaged with the starter ring gear, the main fixed and moving contacts close and engage the starter motor to rotate the engine. This fractional pre-engagement of the starter drive does much to reduce the wear on the starter ring gear.
2 In order to prevent damage to the starter pinion teeth or flywheel ring gear, once the key has been turned to 'START' and the starter motor is rotating, it is not possible to move the key again to 'START' unless the key is first returned to the 'ACC' position. This facility allows the starter motor to come to rest between consecutive circuit completions.

15 Starter motor – testing in position in the car

1 Switch on the lights and the ignition. Ensure that the selector lever of automatic models is in the 'P' or 'N' position.
2 Operate the starter control. If the lights go dim but the motor is not heard to operate, it shows that current is flowing through the motor windings but that, for some reason, the armature is not rotating.
3 If, when the starter is operated, the lamps retain their full brilliance and the motor does not operate, check the circuit for continuity starting with the battery connections (especially the earth connection), then look carefully at the engine earth connection followed by the connections to the motor and the starter switch. If it is established that voltage is getting to the motor when the switch is operated, an internal fault in the motor is indicated.
4 Sluggish or a slow action of the motor is usually caused by a loose connection resulting in high resistance in the circuit, check as described in paragraph 3.
5 If the motor is heard to operate but it does not turn the engine, a fault in the drive is indicated which will involve removal of the motor for rectification.

16 Starter motor (XJ12 and Double Six, RHD) – removal and refitting

1 Disconnect the battery, set the front roadwheels and the steering wheel in the straight-ahead position.
2 Slacken two bolts from the steering column upper universal joints.
3 Disconnect the fluid pipes from the power steering pump at the pinion housing and then unclip the pipes from the steering rack. Plug the openings.
4 Remove the steering column lower universal joint pinch-bolt.
5 Push the steering lower column upwards from the pinion housing.
6 Using a suitable balljoint separator, disconnect the steering tie-rods.
7 Slacken the steering rack housing lower mounting bolts and unscrew and remove the upper mounting bolt.
8 Remove the exhaust front downpipe.
9 Move the steering rack downwards as far as it will go.
10 Disconnect the starter cables from the terminal post and the starter solenoid relay (photo). Tie the cables to the top of the engine.
11 Unscrew and remove the starter motor mounting bolts (photo), pull the starter motor forward, rotate it until the solenoid is underneath and then lift the starter motor from the engine compartment.
12 Refitting is a reversal of removal. With the front roadwheels at the steering wheel in the straight-ahead position, the universal joints should be connected to the column and shaft so that the pinch-bolts pass smoothly through the groove in the splined sections.
13 Fill and bleed the power steering system on completion as described in Chapter 11.

17 Starter motor (XJ12 and Double Six, LHD) – removal and refitting

1 Disconnect the battery.

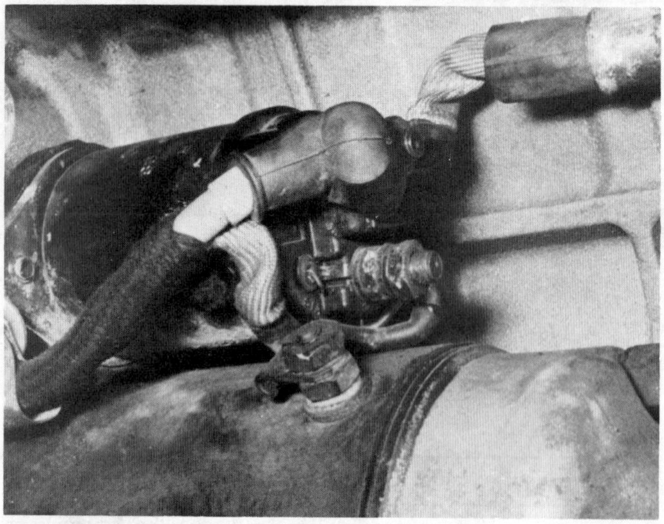

16.10 Starter solenoid connections

2 Remove the right-hand front exhaust downpipe.
3 Disconnect the starter cables from the right-hand terminal post and the solenoid relay.
4 Tie the cables to the top of the engine.
5 Unscrew and remove the starter motor mounting bolts and lift the motor from the engine compartment.
6 Refitting is a reversal of removal.

18 Starter motor (XJS) – removal and refitting

1 Disconnect the battery and set the front roadwheels and steering wheel in the straight-ahead position.
2 Unscrew and remove the steering column universal joint pinch-bolts.
3 Unbolt and remove the heat shield from the steering gaiter.
4 Unscrew and remove the pinch-bolt which connects the universal joint to the pinion shaft of the steering unit.
5 Working inside the car, release the clip from the steering column draught-excluding collar. Disengage the universal joints and ease the steering shaft/joint assembly through the engine compartment rear bulkhead into the car.
6 Disconnect the power steering fluid pipes from the steering housing and drain into a suitable container, then plug the openings.
7 Disconnect the exhaust downpipe from the intermediate pipe on the steering pinion shaft side of the engine.
8 Remove the front exhaust underfloor heat shield.
9 Slacken the lower bolts which hold the steering rack housing to the front suspension assembly.
10 Unbolt the rack heat shield mounting bracket from the suspension.
11 Lower the steering rack carefully, easing it past the sump. Retrieve the packing washers from under the steering rack top mounting joint.
12 Unbolt and remove the exhaust downpipe from the manifold.
13 Remove the starter motor heat shield and cable clip.
14 Disconnect the feed cable from the alternator at the starter motor.
15 Disconnect the starter motor solenoid connector from the terminal post and tie it to the wing stay. Disconnect the cable from the spade terminal on the bulkhead.
16 Unscrew and remove the starter motor mounting bolts.
17 Before lifting the starter motor out of the engine compartment, tie a long piece of string to the end of the cable which is temporarily attached to the wing stay. Detach the cable from the wing stay and remove the starter motor: the string will be drawn through the cable conduit to facilitate refitting.
18 Refitting is a reversal of removal. With the front roadwheels and the steering wheel in the straight-ahead position, the universal joints should be connected to the column and shaft so that the pinch-bolts pass smoothly through the grooves in the splined sections.
19 Fill and bleed the power steering system as described in Chapter 11.

16.11 Starter motor with top and bottom mounting bolts partly withdrawn

19 Starter motor – overhaul

1 With the starter motor removed from the car, clean away external dirt.
2 Remove the link connecting the solenoid to the yoke terminal.
3 Release the solenoid from its mounting bracket and retrieve the gasket.
4 Disconnect the solenoid plunger from the top of the drive engagement lever.
5 Remove the end cover.
6 Unscrew and remove the two through bolts.
7 Lift the brushes from their boxes and detach the commutator end bracket from the yoke.
8 Withdraw the yoke and field coil assembly from the armature and intermediate bracket. Retrieve the sealing ring.
9 Slacken the locknut and remove the drive engagement pivot pin from the fixing bracket.
10 Remove the drive end bracket and then the engagement lever.
11 Using a piece of tubing, drive the thrust collar up the armature shaft to expose the jump ring.
12 Prise out the jump ring.
13 Remove the roller clutch drive assembly.
14 Remove the intermediate bracket.
15 Clean and examine all components.
16 The commutator should appear in a burnished condition, free from pitting or burning. It may be cleaned with a fuel soaked cloth or polished with fine glass paper if absolutely necessary. Do not undercut the insulators between the segments.
17 The porous bronze bearings in the commutator and drive end brackets should be renewed if they are worn. They are best removed by tapping a thread into them and then screwing in a bolt to extract them.
18 Soak the new bearings in clean engine oil for 24 hours before installing them; no reaming is required.
19 Check the length of the brushes: if they have worn down to 0.313 in (8.0 mm) or less, renew them. To do this, cut off the worn brush connectors about 0.125 in (3.0 mm) from the original connecting joints to the field coils.
20 Open and tin the loop of the new brush, place it over the stub of the connector, pinch together and solder. Work quickly, using pliers as a heat sink to prevent too much heat travelling up the field coil wires.
21 Examine the roller clutch drive assembly. If it is in good condition it should take up the drive instantaneously in one direction and should rotate easily and smoothly in the other. There should be no roughness or tendency to bind in movement around or along the shaft splines. Similarly, the operating bush must be free to slide smoothly along the driving sleeve when the engagement spring is compressed. Make sure that the trunnion blocks pivot freely on the pegs of the engaging lever.
22 Reassembly is a reversal of dismantling, but on completion, check the pinion movement in the following way and adjust if necessary.

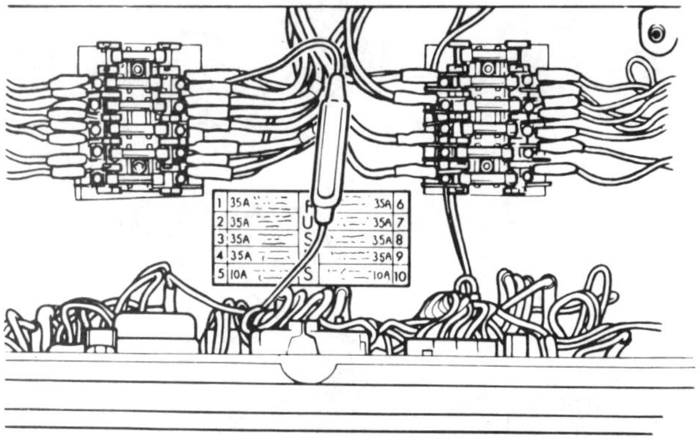

Fig. 10.24 Fuse arrangement (XJ12, Double Six – Series 1) (Sec 20)

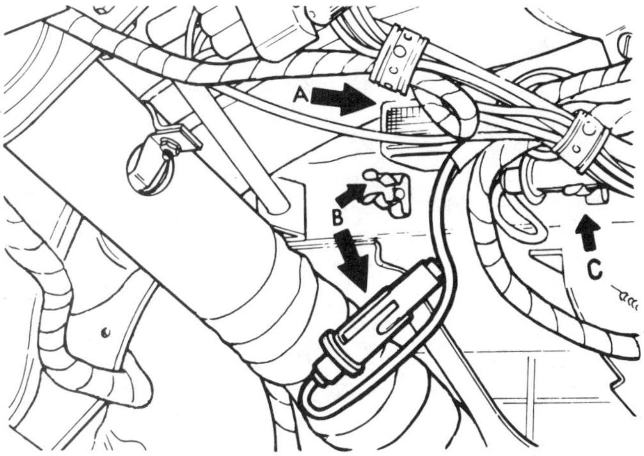

Fig. 10.25 Hazard warning flasher (A), flasher fuse (B) and reversing lamp fuse (C) on XJ12, Double Six Series 1 (Sec 20)

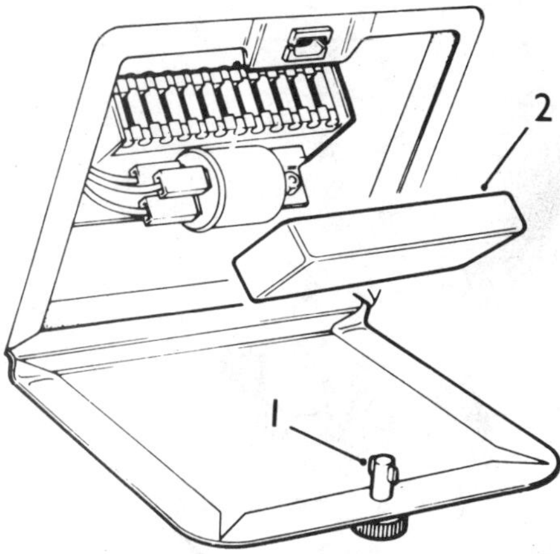

Fig. 10.26 Fuse box (XJ12 and Double Six, Series 2 on, and XJS) (Sec 21)

1 *Quick release screw*
2 *Cover*

23 To check pinion movement, refer to Fig. 10.23 and connect a 10 volt supply between the starter motor body and the Lucar connector on the solenoid (10 volts is specified because it is the approximate level to which the car battery voltage falls during normal starter operation. If a 12 volt battery with external cell connectors is available, it is a simple enough matter to attach jump leads across 5 of the 6 cells and so obtain 10 volts. If not, the error arising from using a 6 or a 12 volt supply may be acceptable).
24 Measure the distance between the pinion and the thrust washer on the extension of the armature shaft when the pinion is lightly pressed towards the armature. This dimension (A in Fig. 10.23) should be 0.005 in to 0.015 in (0.13 to 0.38 mm).
25 If the setting is outside those limits, disconnect the battery.
26 Now adjust the setting by first slackening the nut on the eccentric pivot pin (inset at Fig. 10.23) and then turn the pin clockwise to decrease and anticlockwise to increase the gap. The head of the arrow stamped on the end of the pin should be set only between the limits of the arrows cast in the drive end bracket.
27 Tighten the pin securing nut and then reconnect the battery and recheck the setting.

20 Fuses (XJ12 and Double Six, Series 1)

1 The main fuses are located behind the instrument panel and access to them is gained by extracting the two instrument panel retaining screws from the top corners of the panel and then hinging the panel down to expose the fuses and 'circuits protected' information. Circuits protected and fuse ratings are as follows:

Fuse No	Circuits protected	Amps
1	*Screen washer, instruments, horn relay, tachometer*	*35*
2	*Map reading, interior lamps, cigar lighter, air conditioner relay*	*35*
3	*Windscreen wiper, direction indicators, heater motor, stoplamps*	*35*
4	*Horns*	*35*
5	*Side/tail lamps (LH)*	*10*
6	*Main (outer) headlamps*	*35*
7	*Inner headlamp*	*35*
8	*Outer (dipped) headlamp (LH)*	*35*
9	*Outer (dipped) headlamp (RH)*	*35*
10	*Side/tail lamps (RH)*	*10*

2 In-line fuses are used to protect certain other circuits and their location and ratings are given below.
3 *Hazard warning.* 35 Amp, in plastic fuse holder behind side facia panel on the drivers' side.
4 *Reversing lamp.* 8 Amp, in plastic fuse holder adjacent to hazard warning fuse holder.
5 *Heated rear window.* 25 Amp, in plastic fuse holder exposed when facia centre panel is lowered.
6 *Seat belt warning system.* 5 Amp, located behind centre panel.
7 *Key warning system.* 8 Amp, located in clip behind facia below the windscreen pillar.
8 Refer to paragraphs 7 and 8 of Section 21.

21 Fuses (XJ12 and Double Six, Series 2 on and XJS)

1 The main fuse block is located below the instrument panel on the driver's side.
2 Turn the quick-release pin knob through a quarter of a turn and lower the access panel until its lower edge can be detached (photo).
3 Remove the fuse block cover. A list of fuse ratings and circuits protected will be found within the cover, but will generally conform to the following:

Fuse No	Circuits protected	Amps XJ12	Amps XJS
1	*Fog lamps*	*20*	*25*
2	*Hazard warning lamps*	*15*	*15*
3	*Map, interior and seat belt lamps, clock, cigar lighter, electric aerial*	*35*	*35*
4	*Panel lights*	*15*	*10*
5	*Direction indicators*	*15*	*15*

6	*Reversing lamps*	*35*	*10*
7	*Panel switches, cigar lighter lamp, rear number plate lamp, luggage boot lamp, fibre optic unit, gear selector indicator lamp*	*15*	*10*
8	*Side/tail lamps (LH)*	*15*	*10*
9	*Side/tail lamps (RH)*	*15*	*10*
10	*Air conditioner motor*	*50*	*50*
11	*Windscreen wipers, air conditioner relay and clutch, windscreen washer, horn relay, cooling fan relay*	*50*	*35*
12	*Heated rear window*	*35*	*35*

4 Headlamp fuses (main beam 25A, low beam 10A) are mounted separately from the main fuses.
5 On XJ12 and Double Six models, the headlamp fuses are located at each end of the radiator top rail. Lift the lid to expose the fuse cartridges.
6 On XJS models, the headlamp fuses are located on the left-hand front wing valance, just forward of the cooling system expansion tank.
7 A separate in-line fuse is normally used for radio and cassette players.
8 Always renew a fuse with one of similar rating. If it blows again immediately, trace and rectify the fault before using another one. Never be tempted to fit a fuse of greater rating in an effort to overcome the problem, or bypass a fuse with metal foil or wire.

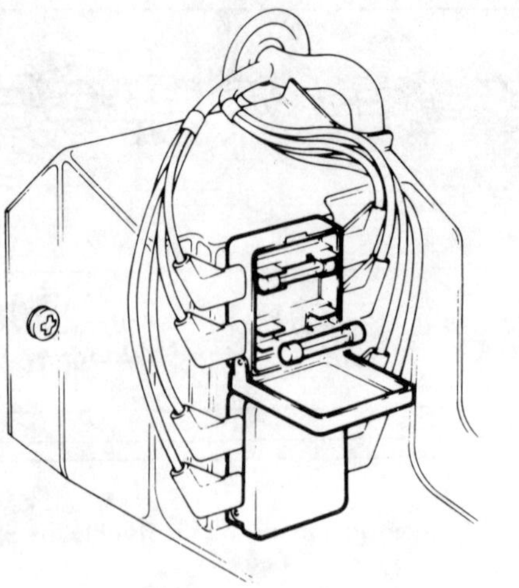

Fig. 10.27 Headlamp fuses (XJS) (Sec 21)

22 Relays (XJ12 and Double Six, Series 1)

1 The purpose of this Section is to identify the location of the various relays. Testing can only be carried out by the substitution of new units. Refer also to Chapter 2 for details of the cooling fan relay.
2 Disconnect the battery before removing or refitting a relay. Always identify cables before disconnecting them from their relay terminals.

Air conditioner blower motor power relay

3 The relay is located on the engine compartment rear bulkhead.

Main air conditioner relay

4 The relay is located on the rear face of the radiator top rail.

Air conditioner blower motor override relay

5 The relay is inside the car, under the facia crash roll.
6 To obtain access to the relay, disconnect the battery, remove the facia crash roll and lower the centre instrument panel.

Electrically-operated window relay control box

7 This is located within the car, behind the left-hand kick panel forward of the front seat.

Horn relay

8 This is located on the right-hand wing valance within the engine compartment.

Ballast resistor starter relay

9 This is located adjacent to the air conditioner blower motor relay on the engine compartment rear bulkhead.

Aerial relay

10 This is fitted in conjunction with a power operated radio aerial. The relay is accessible if the luggage boot floor is removed, then the spare wheel and the fuel pump cover.

Fig. 10.28 Air conditioner blower motor power relay (XJ12 and Double Six, Series 1) (Sec 22)

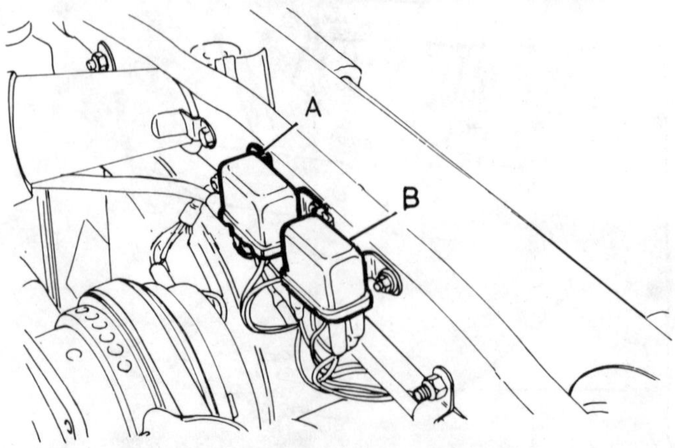

Fig. 10.29 Main air conditioner relay (XJ12 and Double Six, Series 1) (Sec 22)

A Air conditioner relay
B Headlamp relay

23 Relays (XJ12 and Double Six, Series 2 on)

1 The purpose of this Section is to identify the location of the various relays (photo). Testing can only be satisfactorily carried out by substitution of a new unit.
2 Always identify cables before detaching them from their relay terminals and disconnect the battery.
3 Refer also to the following Chapters:

Chapter 2 – Radiator electric fan motor relay
Chapter 3 – Cold start relay, fuel pump relay and fuel system main relay

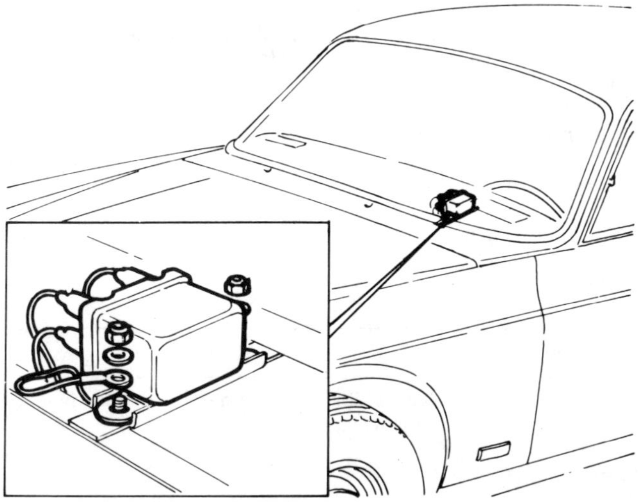

Fig. 10.30 Air conditioner blower motor override relay (XJ12 and Double Six, Series 1) (Sec 22)

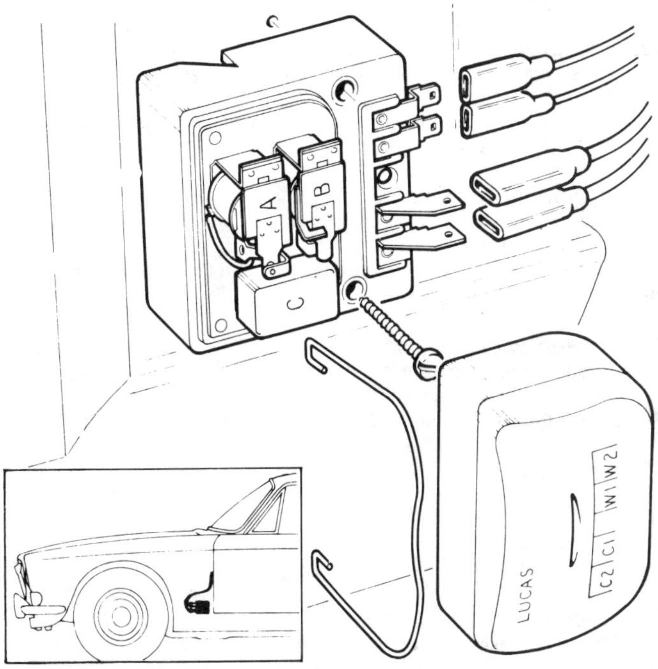

Fig. 10.31 Electric window relay control box (Sec 22)

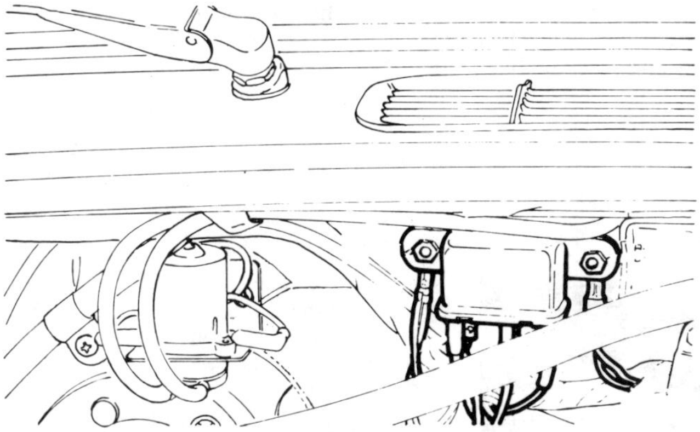

Fig. 10.32 Ballast resistor starter relay (XJ12 and Double Six, Series 1) (Sec 22)

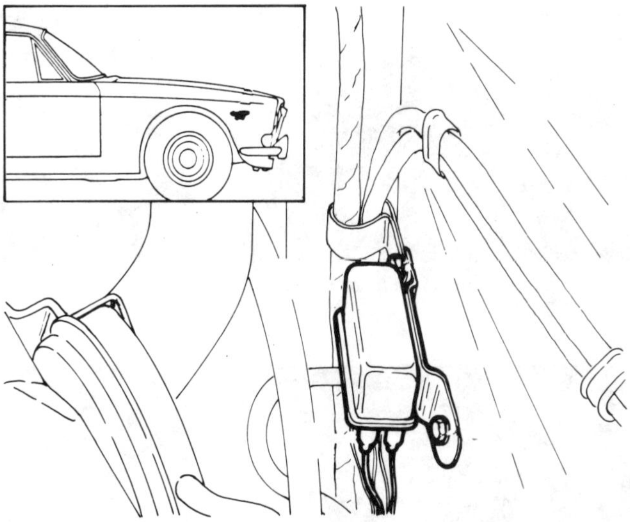

Fig. 10.34 Horn relay (XJ12 and Double Six, Series 1) (Sec 22)

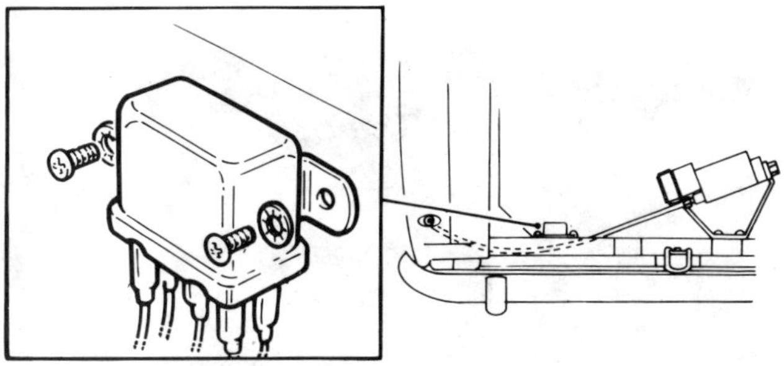

Fig. 10.33 Aerial relay (XJ12 and Double Six, Series 1) (Sec 22)

Chapter 4 – Ignition protection relay and starter solenoid/ballast coil relay
Chapter 12 – Air conditioning system

4 The power aerial relay is located within the luggage boot, near the spare wheel and adjacent to the aerial motor.

Heater motor relay

5 This is located within the car just forward of the centre console (photo).
6 Access to the relay is obtained by removing the left-hand side casing from the centre console and then detaching the air outlet duct.

Air conditioner blower motor relay

7 To obtain access to the relay, remove the left-hand panel and air vent from the centre console.
8 Pull the relay directly downward to disconnect it from its mounting block.

Windscreen wiper motor relay

9 To reach the relay, first remove the dash casing from the passenger side (see Chapter 12)
10 Release the relay securing clip and pull it from its connector block.

Window lift relay

11 This is located underneath the centre console, which will have to be removed to reach it.
12 The relay is attached, by means of a bracket, to the automatic transmission selector quadrant (photo).

Door lock solenoid relays

13 To remove these relays, push the left-hand front seat fully forward.
14 Remove the cushion from the rear seat.
15 Pull the carpet and sound deadening felt away from the transmission tunnel and the box section which supports the rear seat cushion.
16 The relays will have to be supported through the hole in the crossmember while their mounting screws are extracted. Withdraw the complete relay assembly through the hole in the crossmember, disconnect the leads and release the relays from the mounting bracket (photo).

Horn relay

17 Located on the right-hand wing valance, the relay on earlier models was rectangular but on later versions it is cylindrical.

Headlamp relay

18 This is located adjacent to the headlamp fuse box within the engine compartment.

24 Relays (XJS)

1 The location of relays is similar to that described in the preceding Section except for the following.

Window lift relay

2 To obtain access to the relay, remove the under scuttle casing (Chapter 12) from the passenger side.
3 Unbolt the relay mounting plate from the fan motor unit.
4 The relay is mounted back-to-back with the low coolant control unit, except on North American versions when it is located on the rear of the mounting plate.

Door lock solenoid relay

5 Remove the dash liner from the passenger side and the screws from the footwell side casing.
6 Detach the relay mounting bracket from the body side panel.

21.2 Fuse panel. Note spare fuses in cover

23.1 Relays on the radiator top rail:

1 *Headlamp relay*
2 *Manifold pressure sensor*
3 *Fuel system main relay*
4 *Air conditioner relay*
5 *Radiator fan relay*
6 *Fuel pump relay*
7 *Cold start relay*

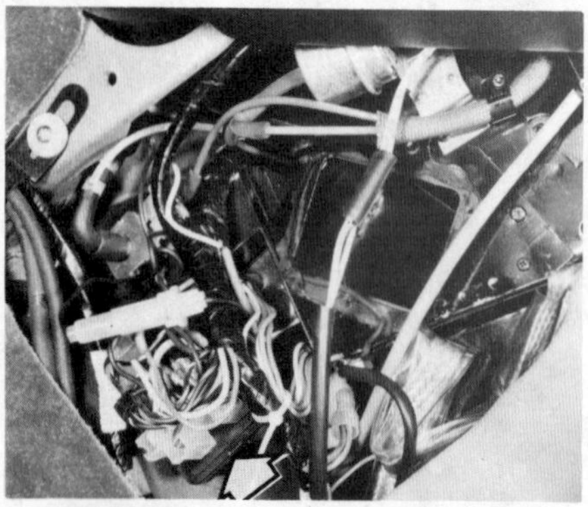

23.5 Heater motor and air conditioner blower motor relay (arrowed)

23.12 Window lift relay (arrowed)

23.16 Door lock solenoid relays

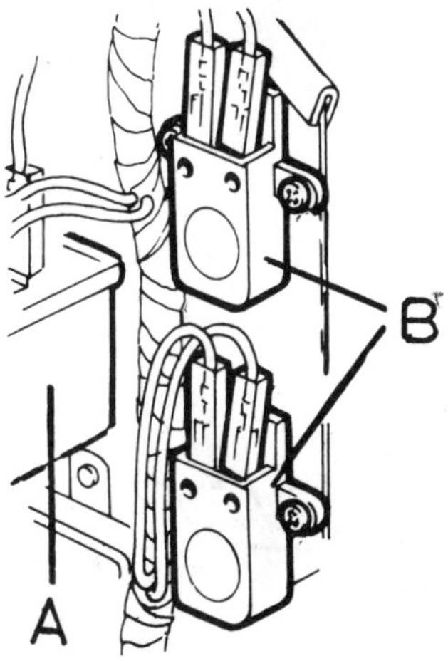

Fig. 10.35 Window lift relay (A) and door lock circuit breakers (B) on XJS models (Sec 24)

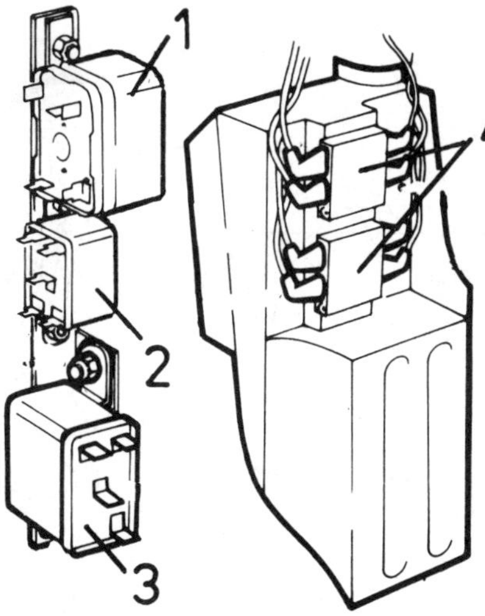

Fig. 10.36 Horn, fan and headlamp relays (XJS) (Sec 24)

1 *Headlamp dip*
2 *Radiator fan*
3 *Horn*
4 *Headlamp fuses*

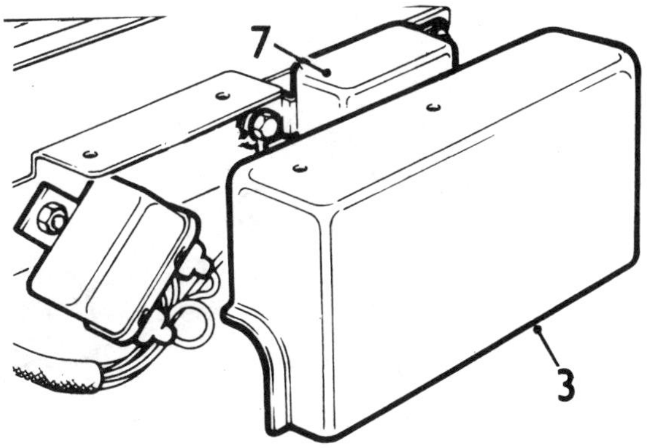

Fig. 10.37 Starter relay (7) and cover (3) on XJS (Sec 24)

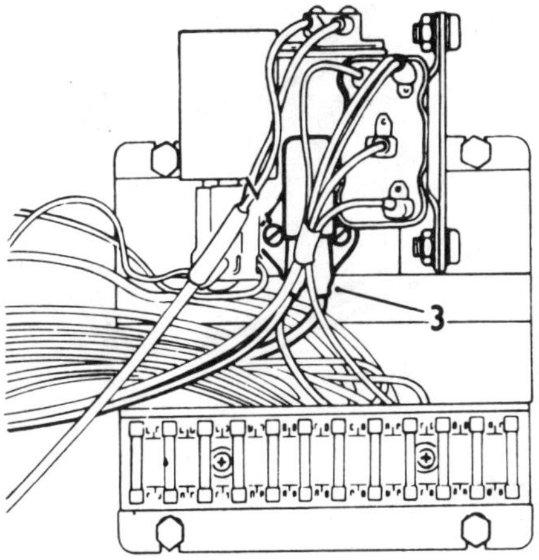

Fig. 10.38 Door lock circuit breakers (3) on fuse block (XJ12, Double Six) (Sec 25)

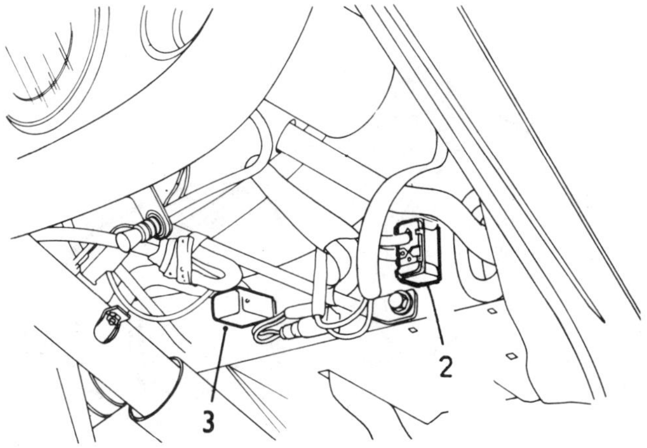

Fig. 10.39 Direction indicator flasher unit (2) and hazard warning flasher unit (3) and XJ12 and Double Six, Series 1 (Sec 27)

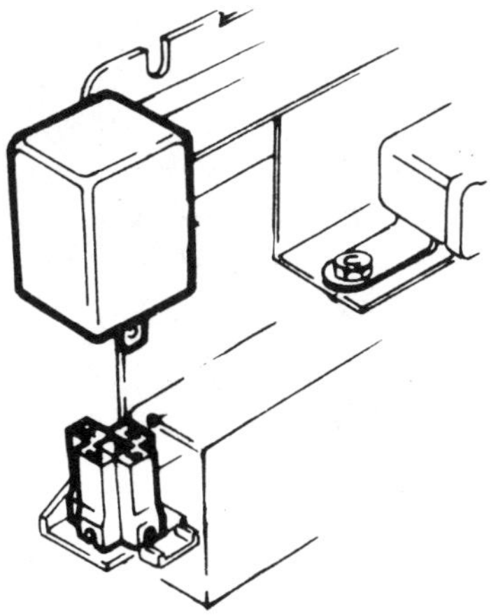

Fig. 10.40 Direction indicator/hazard warning flasher unit (XJS) (Sec 28)

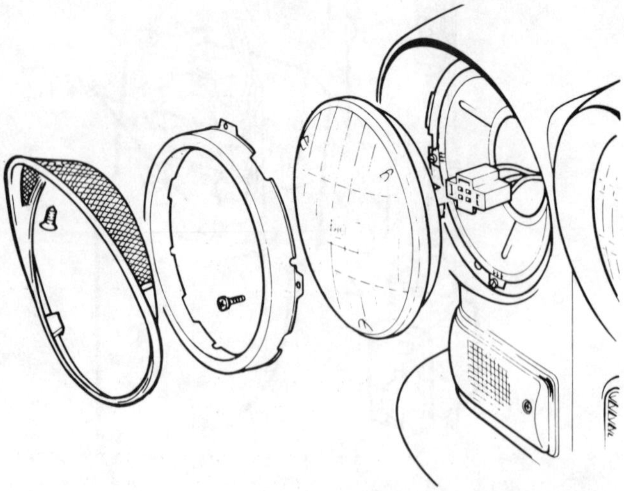

Fig. 10.41 Outer sealed beam headlamp (XJ12, Double Six) (Sec 29)

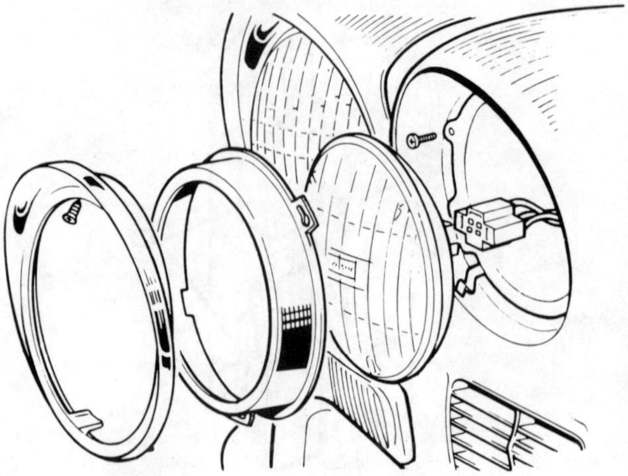

Fig. 10.42 Inner sealed beam headlamp (XJ12, Double Six) (Sec 29)

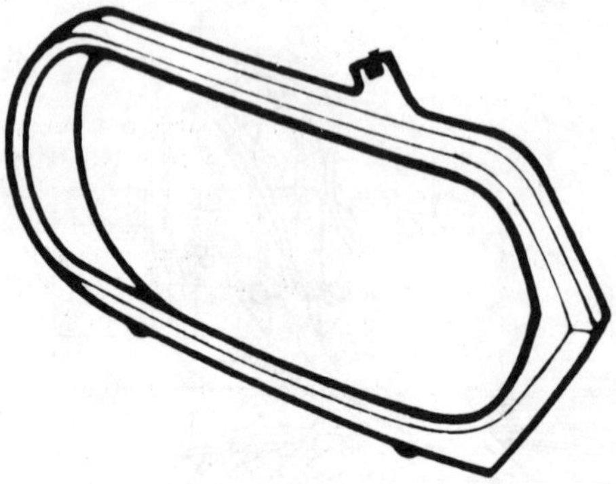

Fig. 10.43 Headlamp rim finisher (XJS except N America) (Sec 31)

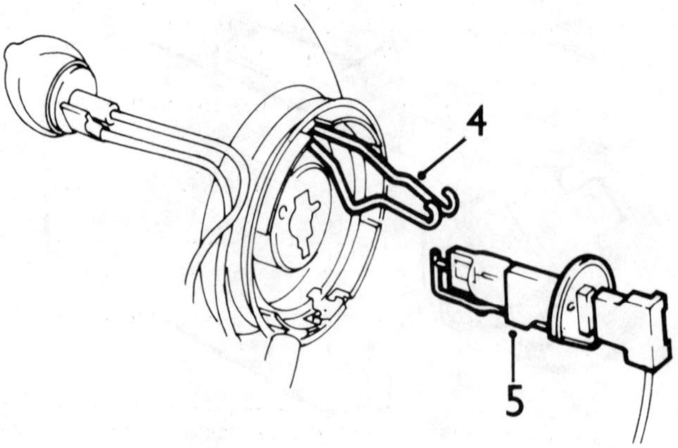

Fig. 10.44 Headlamp bulb (Halogen) on XJS models (Sec 31)

4 Bulb securing clip
5 Bulb

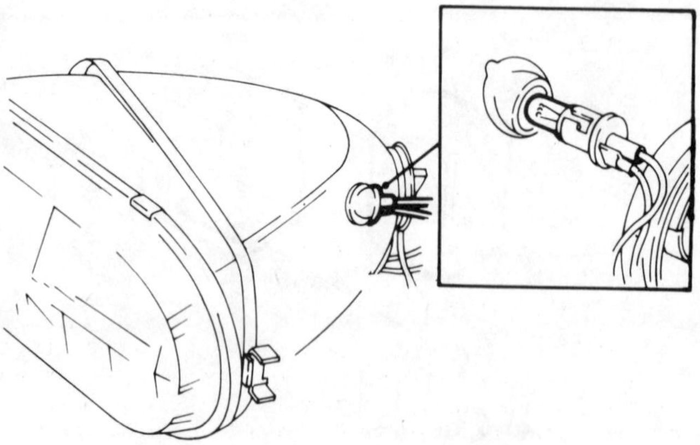

Fig. 10.45 Front parking lamp bulb (XJS, except N America) (Sec 31)

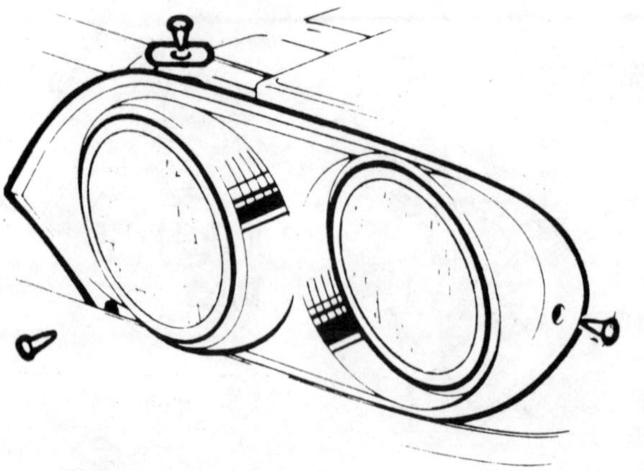

Fig. 10.46 Headlamp rim finisher (XJS, N America) (Sec 32)

7 Identify the leads and disconnect them from the relay. Unbolt the relay from its bracket.

Horn relay and headlamp relays

8 Identify the leads to the headlamp fuse box and disconnect them from the fuse box terminals at the left-hand wing valance.
9 Extract the two retaining screws and lift off the relay cover.
10 The lower (horn) relay can now be unbolted and removed. The upper relays are the headlamp relays.

Starter relay

11 The starter relay is located at the rear end of the right-hand wing valance, within the engine compartment.
12 To remove the relay, disconnect the battery, then extract the securing screw and lift the cover from the relay.
13 Extract the screw which holds the relay and its mounting plate to the wing valance.
14 Unscrew and remove the nut and lockwasher which hold the earth terminal and the relay to the mounting plate.
15 Identify the electrical leads and then disconnect them from the terminals on the base of the relay.

25 Circuit breakers (XJ12, Double Six)

1 Circuit breakers are fitted in conjunction with the electrically operated door locks. Rapid, repeated operation of the door locks will cause the thermal cut-out type circuit breaker to operate. After a few moments, the circuit breaker will reset automatically and the door lock system will again become operative.
2 The circuit breakers are mounted on the fuse block and can be reached after removing the driver's side under scuttle casing.

26 Circuit breakers (XJS)

1 The purpose of the circuit breakers is as described in the preceding Section.
2 The circuit breakers are mounted adjacent to the window lift relays (see Section 24).

27 Hazard warning and direction indicator flasher units (XJ12 and Double Six, Series 1)

1 These are fitted as separate units under the dash panel. They are reached by removing the lower dash casing (two screws).
2 Grip the flasher unit firmly and pull it from its connector block.
3 Before renewing a flasher unit always check for a blown fuse, faulty bulb or loose wiring connections.

28 Hazard warning and direction indicator flasher unit (XJ12 and Double Six, Series 2 on, and XJS)

1 A single unit is used on these models to control both functions. Access to it is obtained by removing the under scuttle casing from the driver's side.
2 Grip the flasher unit firmly and pull it from its socket which is adjacent to the fuse block.
3 Before renewing a flasher unit, always check for a blown fuse, faulty bulb or loose wiring connections.

29 Headlamp sealed beam unit (XJ12, Double Six) – renewal

Outer unit

1 Extract the single retaining screw and remove the headlamp hood.
2 Remove the three screws and withdraw the rim which retains the headlamp sealed beam unit (photo).
3 Pull the unit forward until the connecting plug at its rear can be pulled off.
4 Refitting is a reversal of removal, but make sure that the new unit is of exactly similar type to the original. Provided the headlamp beam setting screws have not been altered, then no adjustment should be required on the new unit.

Inner unit

5 The operations are basically similar to those just described for the outer unit, except that the rim retaining screws should only be slackened and not removed. The rim can then be removed if it is turned in an anti-clockwise direction so that the larger diameter of the keyhole clears the head of the screw (photo).

30 Headlamp bulb (XJ12, Double Six) – renewal

1 Some models are equipped with bulb type headlamps (photo).
2 Access to the bulb holder is obtained in a similar way to that described in the preceding Section. Parking lamp bulbs are incorporated in the outer headlamps on later models (photo).
3 To release the bulb holder, prise out the spring retaining clips (photo).
4 When fitting the new bulb, make sure that the notch in the bulb collar plate engages with the projection on the bulb holder.

31 Headlamp bulb (XJS) – renewal

1 Bulb type headlamp units are fitted to all models except those having North American specification.
2 Raise the bonnet and extract the screw which holds the finisher to the top of the headlamp housing.
3 Pull the top of the finisher forward then upwards to disengage the bottom locating spigots.
4 Depress the nylon tabs which retain the lamp unit, pull the unit forward until the connecting plug can be detached.
5 Release the clips securing the bulb and withdraw it. Do not touch the bulb with the fingers if it is to be used again. Similarly, do not touch a new bulb with the fingers when fitting it as the natural grease in the skin will reduce the life of the bulb. If the bulb is touched inadvertently, clean it with a rag dipped in methylated spirit (denatured alcohol).
6 The front parking lamp bulb may be removed from the reflector of the headlamp simply by pulling it from its rubber grommet.
7 Refitting is a reversal of removal.

32 Headlamp sealed beam unit (XJS) – renewal

1 Cars built to North American specification are equipped with sealed beam headlamp units.
2 Raise the bonnet and remove the three screws which secure the headlamp finisher.
3 Slacken, but do not remove, the three screws which hold the lamp unit bezel. Turn the bezel anti-clockwise and remove it.
4 Pull the lamp unit forward until the connector plug can be detached from its rear.
5 Renew the unit with one of similar type. Provided that the adjusting screws have not been disturbed, the beam alignment of the new unit will be the same as the original.

33 Headlamp beam setting

1 It is recommended that this work is left to your dealer, as accurate setting requires the correct optical equipment.
2 However, in an emergency, the following operations will produce an acceptable result.
3 Place the car on a level surface with its front end 25 ft (7.6 m) from, and square to, a wall or screen. The conditions should be as dark as possible so that the light patterns can be clearly seen.
4 Switch the headlamps to full (main) beam. The centres of all four oval light patterns should be at the same height from the ground as the centres of the lamp units on the car, and at the same distance apart.
5 If adjustment is required, remove the finishers from the headlamp units as described in earlier Sections and turn the adjustment screws. On XJ12 and Double Six models, the screws are located at the lamp unit retaining ring. On XJS models, the adjustment screws are integral with the nylon retainer clip blocks.

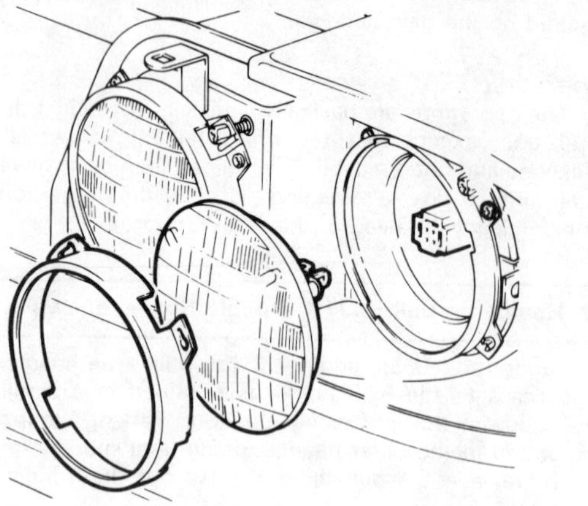

Fig. 10.47 Headlamp sealed beam unit (XJS, N America) (Sec 32)

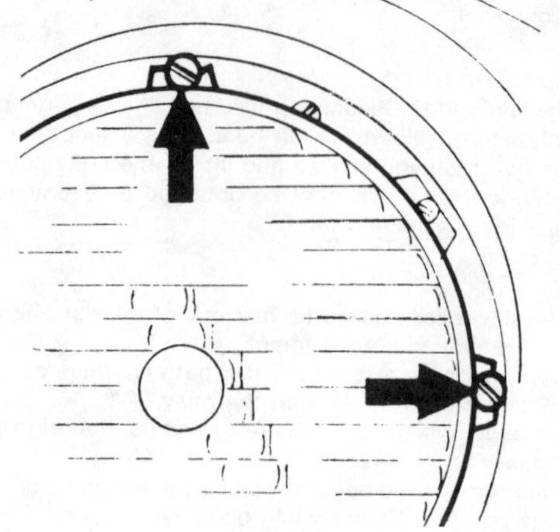

Fig. 10.48 Typical outer headlamp adjusting screws (Sec 33)

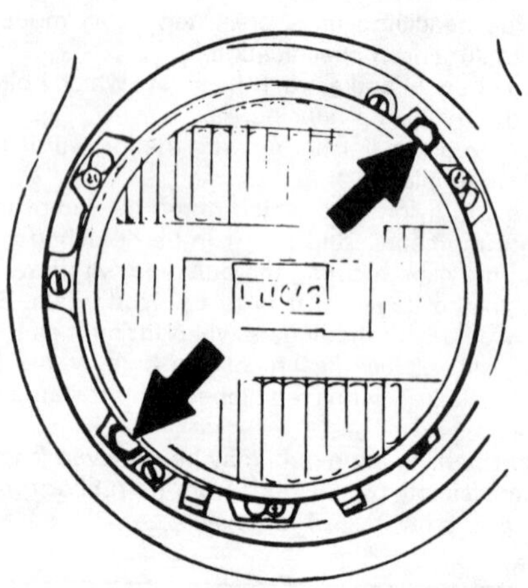

Fig. 10.49 Typical inner headlamp adjusting screws (Sec 33)

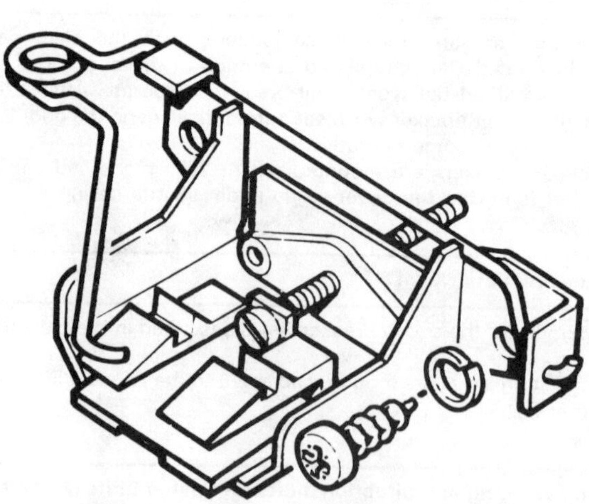

Fig. 10.50 Lamp retaining blocks with integral adjustment screws (XJS) (Sec 33)

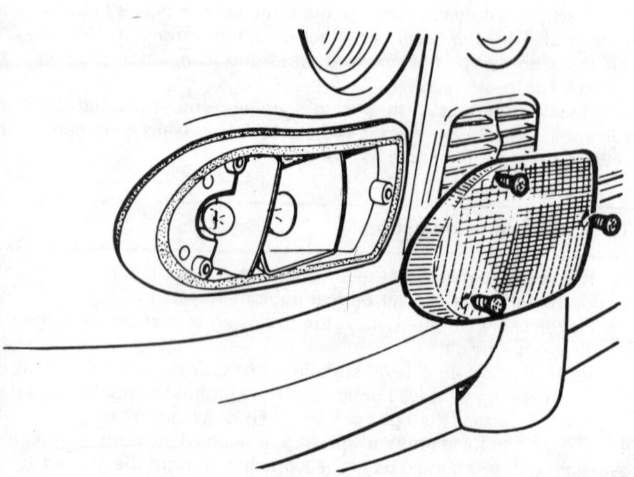

Fig. 10.51 Front parking/direction indicator lamp (XJ12 and Double Six, Series 1) (Sec 34)

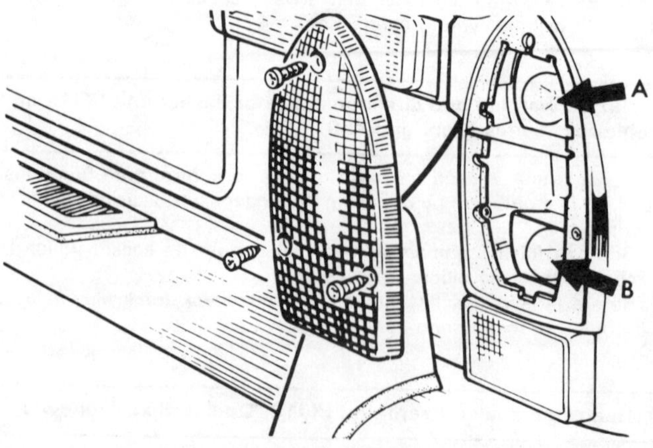

Fig. 10.52 Rear lamp cluster (XJ12 and Double Six, Series 1) (Sec 34)

A Direction indicator bulb
B Stop/tail bulb

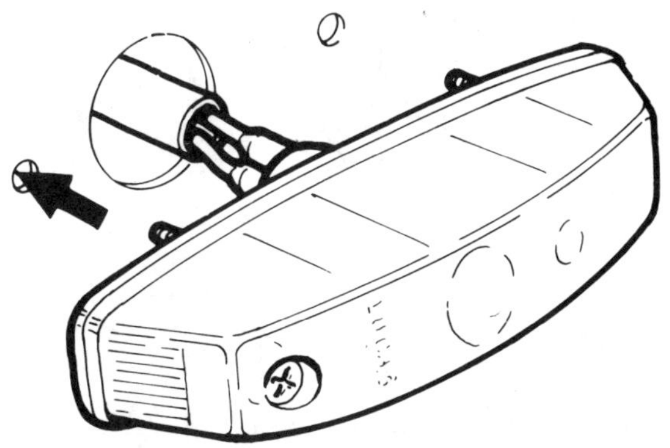

Fig. 10.53 Front direction indicator repeater (XJ12 and Double Six, Series 1) (Sec 34)

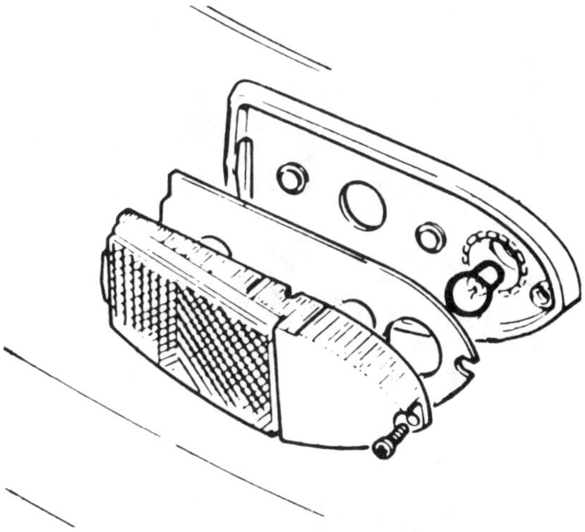

Fig. 10.54 Side marker lamp (XJ12 and Double Six, Series 1) (Sec 34)

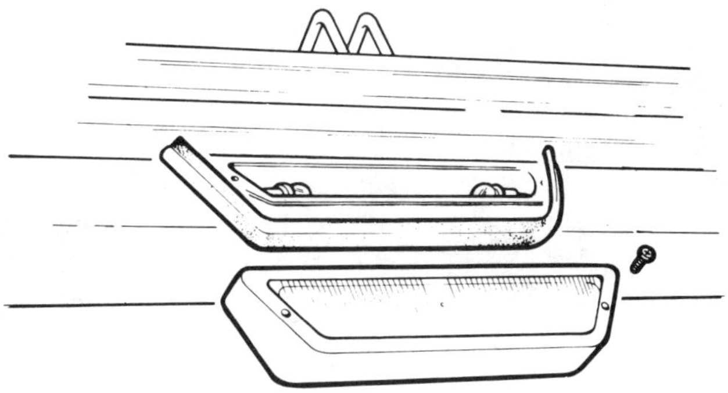

Fig. 10.55 Rear number plate lamp (XJ12 and Double Six, Series 1) (Sec 34)

34 Bulbs (XJ12 and Double Six, Series 1) – renewal

Front parking/direction indicator

1 Remove the three lens retaining screws and the lens itself.
2 Release the bulbs, which are of bayonet fitting type.

Rear lamp cluster

3 Remove the three lens securing screws and the lens itself.
4 The tail/stop and direction indicator bulbs are now exposed. Depress, twist and remove the bayonet fitting bulbs.
5 When fitting a stop/tail lamp bulb, note that it can only be fitted one way as its pins are offset.

Front direction indicator repeater lamp

6 The bulb is accessible after extracting the two lens retaining screws and the lens.

Side marker lamp

7 A single screw retains the lens, the opposite end of the lens is held by a tab moulded onto it.
8 Remove the lens for access to the bayonet fitting bulb.

Rear number plate lamp

9 Extract the two screws from the lamp embellisher.
10 Remove the lens which has now been freed and remove one or both bulbs from their holders.

Reversing lamp

11 Remove the lens (two screws) and carefully pull the festoon type bulb from its spring contacts.

Interior pillar lamp

12 Pull off the snap-on type lens/cover.
13 Pull the festoon type bulb from its spring contacts.

Map reading lamp

14 Press the bulb holder side clips inwards and withdraw the holder downwards.
15 Pull the festoon type bulb from the holder.

Luggage boot lamp

16 The bulb is immediately accessible within the small aperture in the underside of the luggage boot lid.

Speed selector indicator lamp

17 Unscrew the two halves of the control lever knob.
18 Remove the escutcheon panel for the window lift switches and then remove the console escutcheon.
19 Unbolt and slide the selector cover up the control lever.
20 Remove the bulb shroud and withdraw the bulb from its holder.

Instrument panel lamps

21 Unscrew and remove the two knurled retaining screws from the centre instrument panel. Lower the panel.
22 Turn the bulb holder in an anti-clockwise direction to release it, then extract the bulb.

Individual instrument lamps and main beam warning lamp

23 Access to these is described, together with removal of the instrument concerned, in Sections 62, 64 or 65 of this Chapter.

Cigar lighter bulb

24 Disconnect the battery.
25 Lever off the electric window switch panel escutcheon plate.
26 Remove the console escutcheon (four screws).
27 Lift the console escutcheon, together with the window lift switch panel, away from the centre console.
28 Press the sides of the cigar lighter bulb holder together and withdraw the complete cigar lighter assembly.
29 Remove the bulb from its holder.

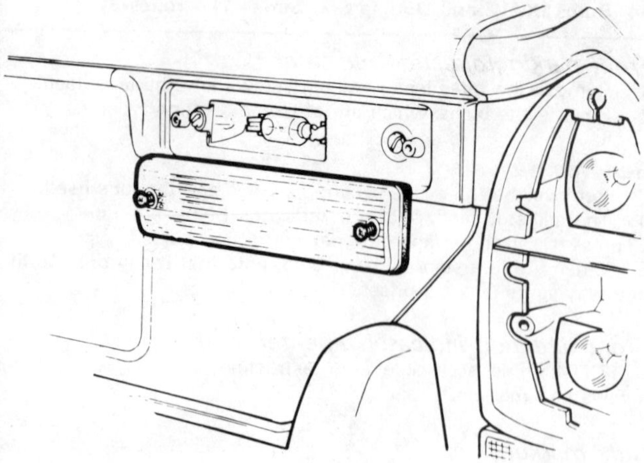

Fig. 10.56 Reversing lamp (XJ12 and Double Six, Series 1) (Sec 34)

Fig. 10.57 Interior pillar lamp (XJ12 and Double Six, Series 1) (Sec 34)

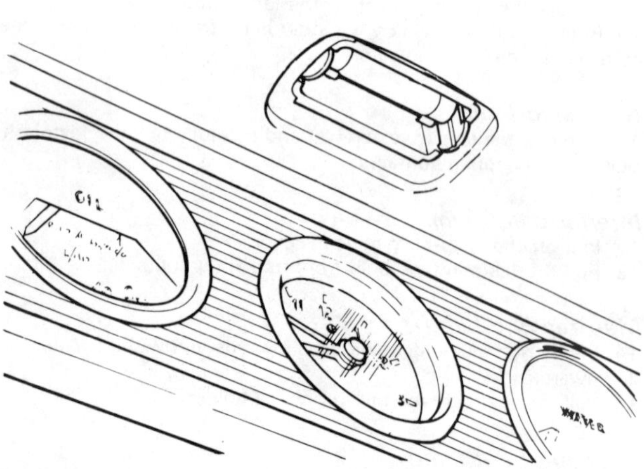

Fig. 10.58 Map reading lamp (XJ12 and Double Six, Series 1) (Sec 34)

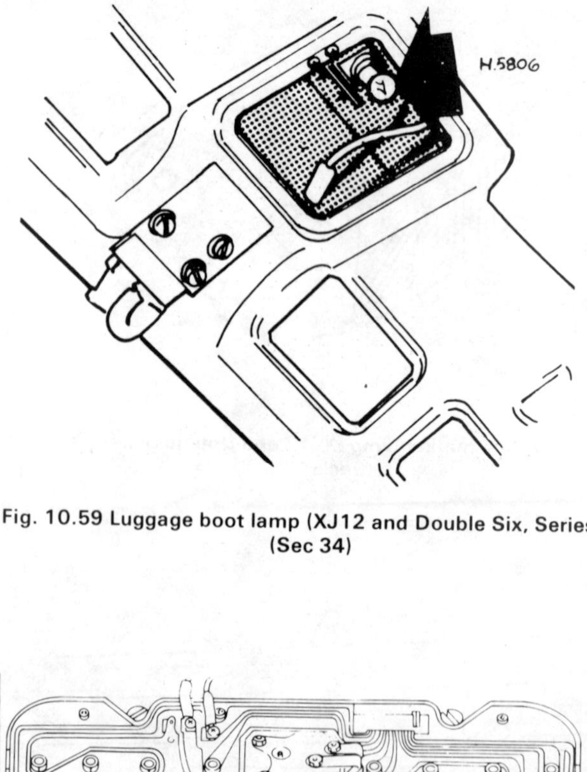

Fig. 10.59 Luggage boot lamp (XJ12 and Double Six, Series 1) (Sec 34)

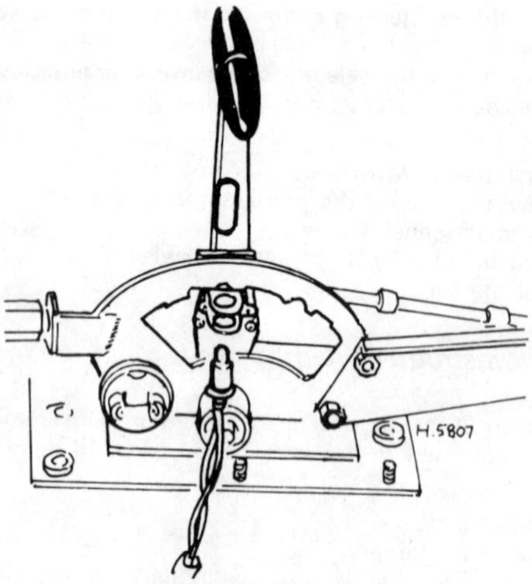

Fig. 10.60 Speed selector indicator lamp bulb (XJ12 and Double Six, Series 1)

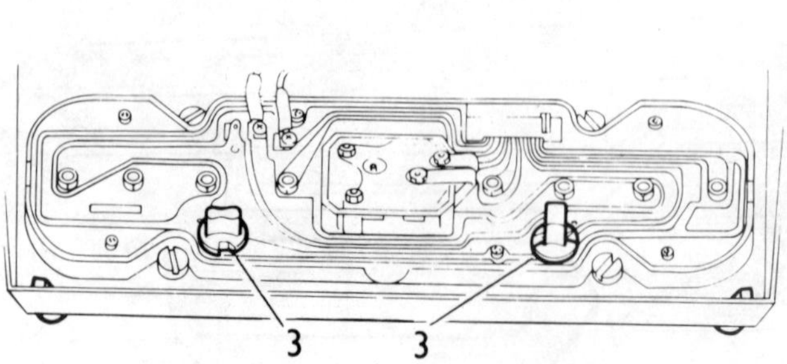

Fig. 10.61 Instrument panel lamp holders (3) (XJ12 and Double Six, Series 1) (Sec 34)

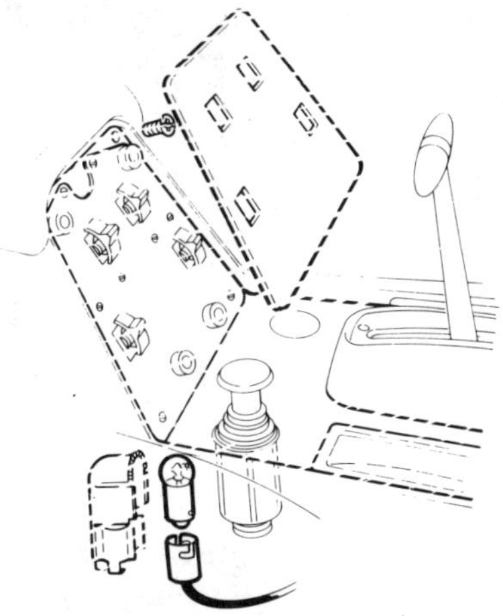

Fig. 10.62 Cigar lighter bulb renewal (XJ12 and Double Six, Series 1) (Sec 34)

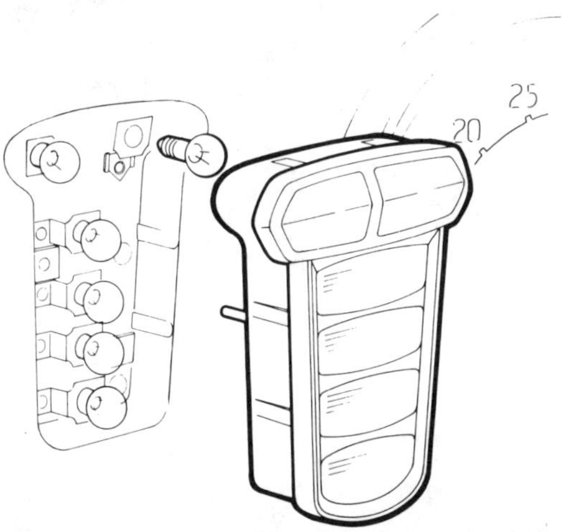

Fig. 10.63 Instrument panel warning lamp cluster (XJ12 and Double Six, Series 1) (Sec 34)

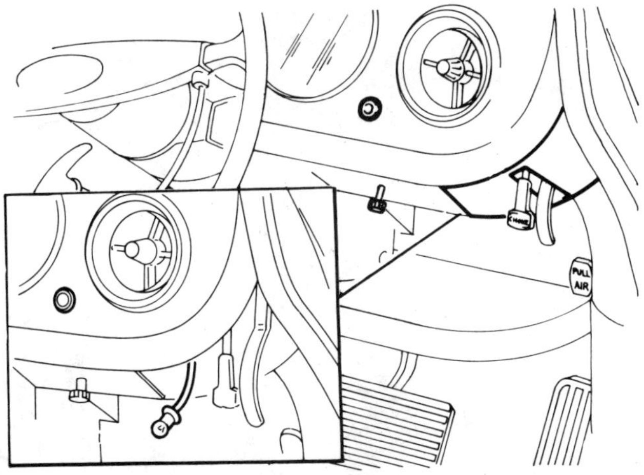

Fig. 10.64 Choke warning lamp (XJ12 and Double Six, Series 1) (Sec 34)

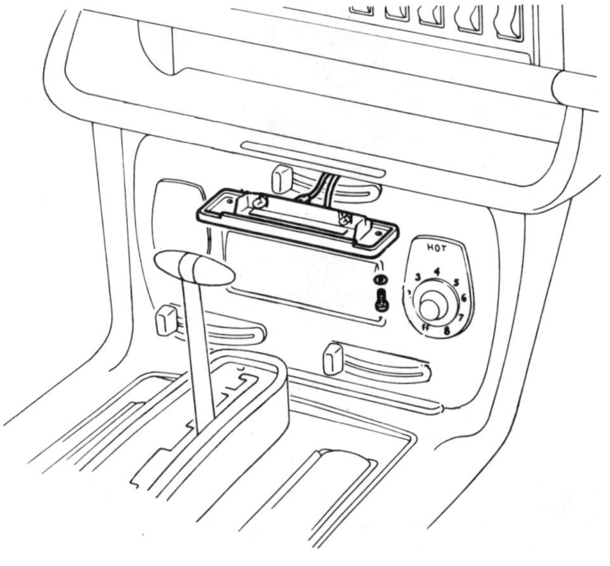

Fig. 10.65 Heater panel lamp (XJ12 and Double Six, Series 1) (Sec 34)

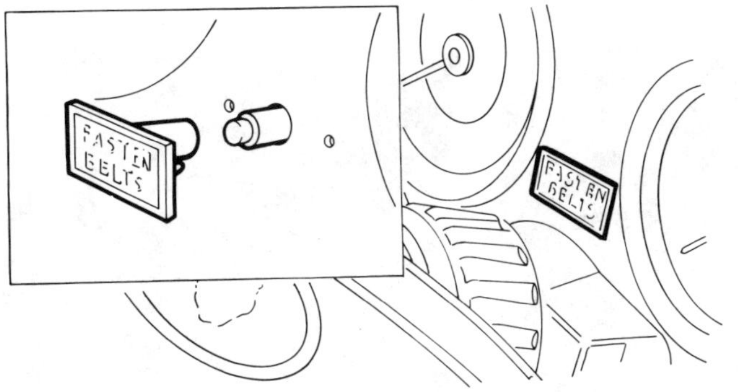

Fig. 10.66 Seat belt warning lamp (XJ12 and Double Six, Series 1) (Sec 34)

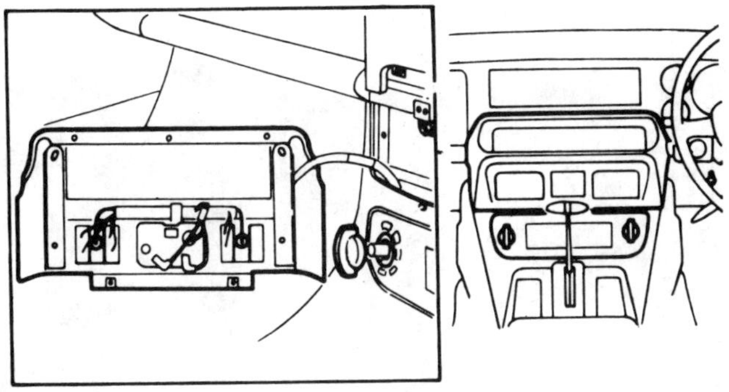

Fig. 10.67 Switch panel lamp (XJ12, Double Six – Series 2 on) (Sec 35)

29.2 Removing headlamp (outer)

29.5 Inner headlamp rim retaining screw (arrowed)

30.1 Bulb type headlamp unit

30.2 Outer headlamp unit showing parking lamp bulb

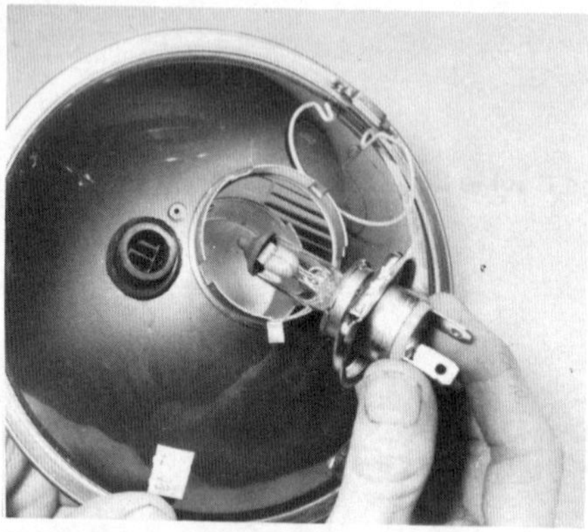
30.3 Headlamp bulb holder and retaining clip

35.1A Front parking/flasher lamp

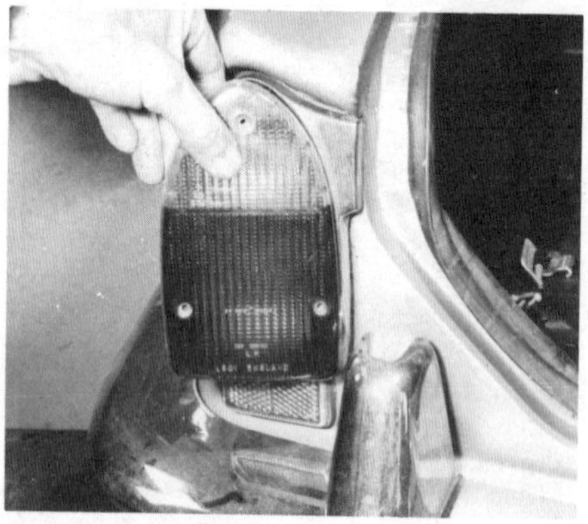
35.1B Rear lamp cluster

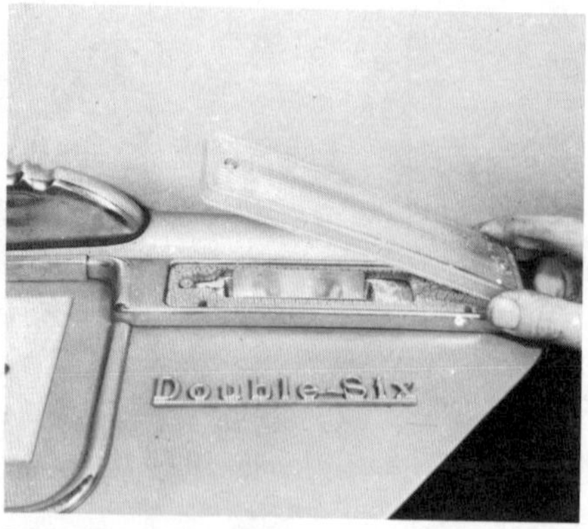

35.1C Reversing lamp

35.1D Rear number plate lamp

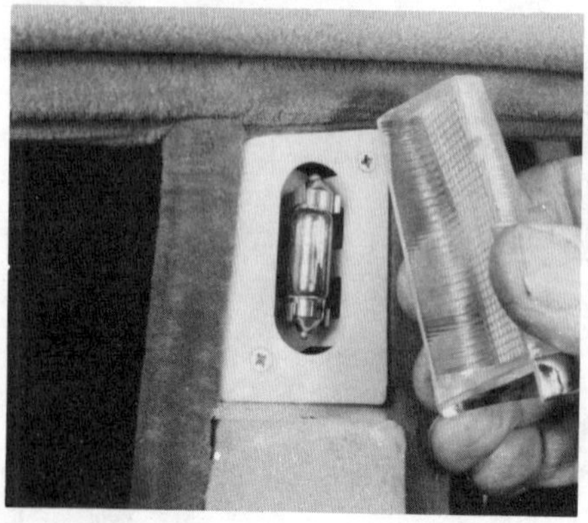
35.5 Interior pillar lamp

35.13 Clock bulb holder

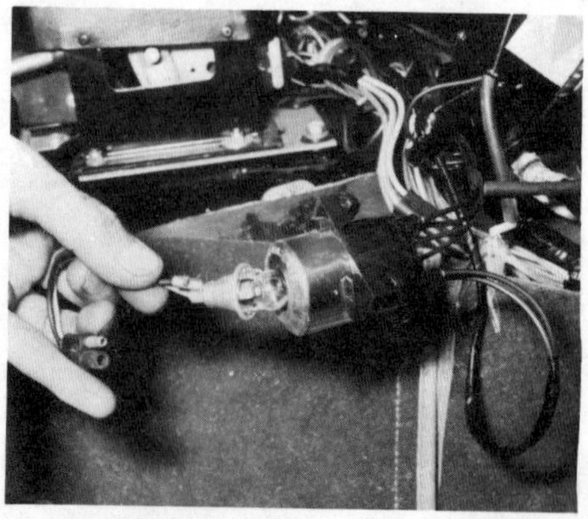
38.6 Opticell unit

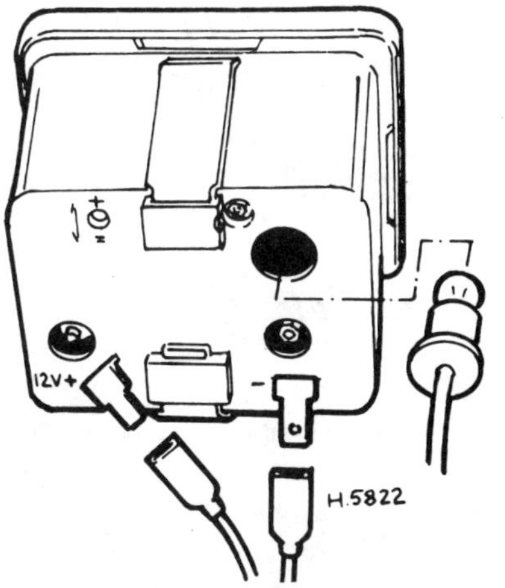

Fig. 10.68 Clock bulb (XJ12, Double Six – Series 2 on) (Sec 35)

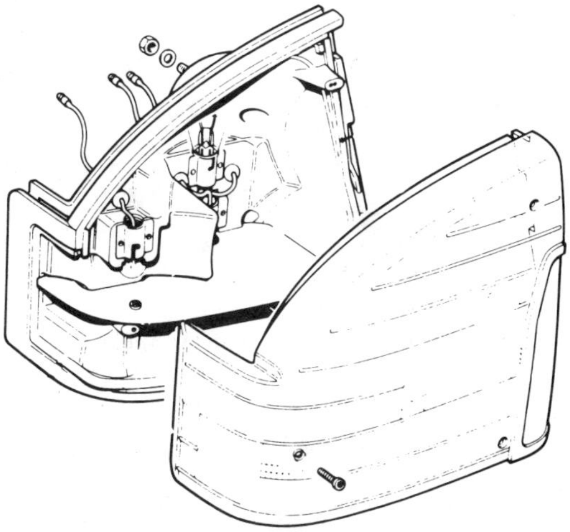

Fig. 10.69 Tail lamp lens and bulbs (XJS) (Sec 36)

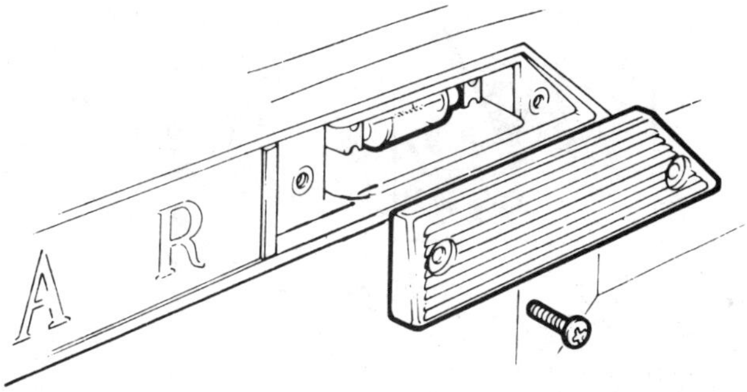

Fig. 10.70 Reversing lamp lens and bulb (XJS) (Sec 36)

Warning lamp cluster

30 Using two thin screwdriver blades, carefully lever the cover from the bulb holder casing.

31 Individual screw-in type bulbs can be renewed as necessary.

Choke warning lamp

32 Disconnect the battery and remove the under scuttle casing (two screws) as described in Chapter 12.

33 Pull the bulb holder from the lens carrier.

Heater panel bulb

34 Unscrew the two screws and withdraw the escutcheon.

35 Remove the two screws inside the escutcheon to expose the bulb.

Seat belt warning lamp

36 Prise the indicator plate from the facia. The plate is held in position by two friction nylon bushes.

37 Pull the bulb holder from the lamp unit and remove the bulb.

35 Bulbs (XJ12 and Double Six, Series 2 on) – renewal

1 Access to the bulbs in all the following lamps is obtained by extracting the lens securing screws and removing the lens (photos):

Front flasher/parking lamp
Front flasher repeater lamp
Side marker lamp
Rear lamp cluster
Reversing lamps
Rear number plate lamp
Foglamp (bulbs not to be handled with the fingers).

2 The bulbs may be of conventional bayonet fitting, capless or of festoon type. This can be determined by inspection or by reference to the Specifications at the beginning of this Chapter.

Interior lamps (2-door models)

3 One of these lamps is fitted above each door.

4 Access to the festoon type bulb is obtained by carefully levering the lamp assembly from its recess.

Interior lamp (4-door models)

5 Refer to Section 34 (photo).

Map reading lamp

6 Refer to Section 34.

Luggage boot lamp

7 Refer to Section 34.

Speed selector indicator lamp

8 Refer to Section 34.

Switch panel lamp

9 Pull off the control knobs from the heater/air conditioner. Remove the radio aperture escutcheon.

10 Extract the four screws which hold the centre oddments tray and lift the tray forward.

11 Pull the bulb holder from the diffuser assembly.

12 A miniature bayonet fitting type bulb is used at this position.

Clock bulb

13 Pull the centre oddments tray forward as described in paragraphs 9 and 10 (photo).

14 The bulb holder can now be pulled directly from the rear of the clock case.

Warning lamp cluster

15 Carefully lever off the cover plate.

16 The individual capless type bulbs can be removed by giving them a straight pull, do not twist.

Direction indicator warning lamp

17 The lamps are incorporated in the speedometer and tachometer.

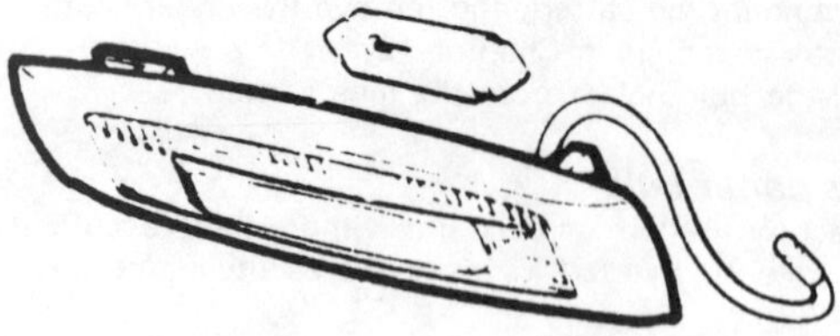

Fig. 10.71 Roof interior lamp (XJS) (Sec 36)

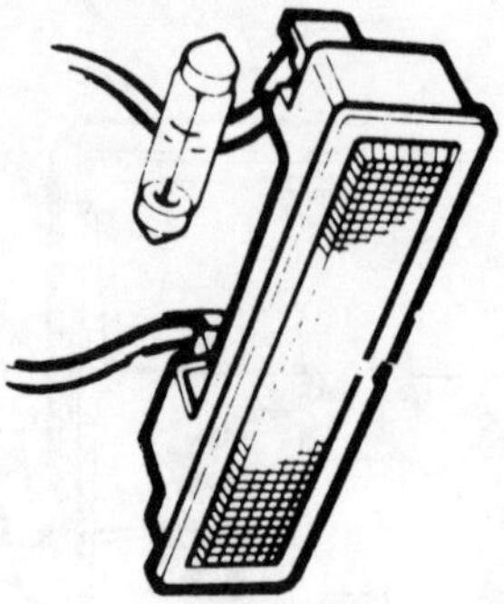

Fig. 10.72 Map reading lamp (XJS) (Sec 36)

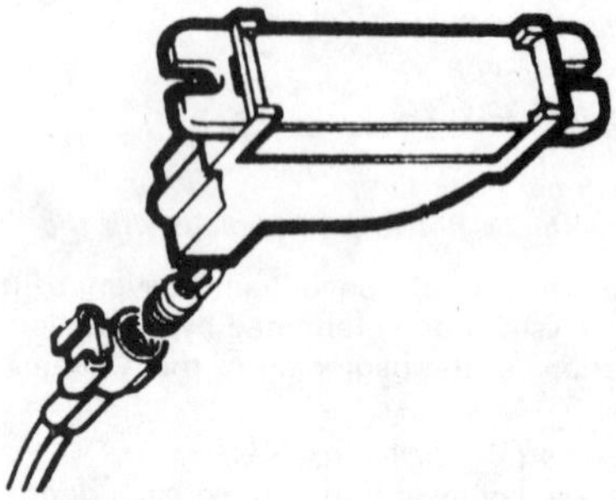

Fig. 10.73 Switch panel bulb (XJS) (Sec 36)

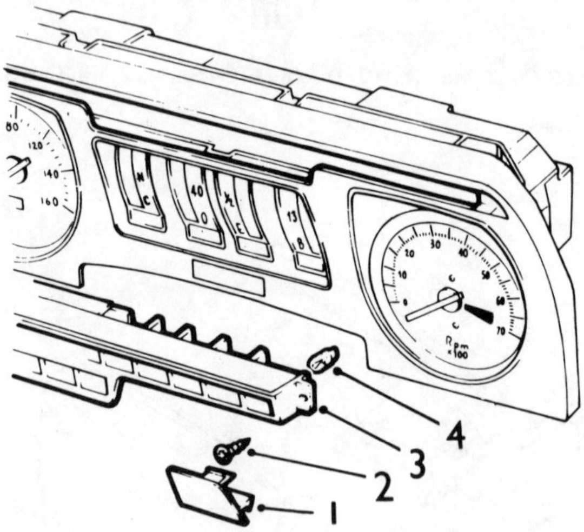

Fig. 10.74 Warning lamp bulb (XJS) (Sec 36)

1 End cover
2 Screw
3 Warning lamp strip
4 Bulb

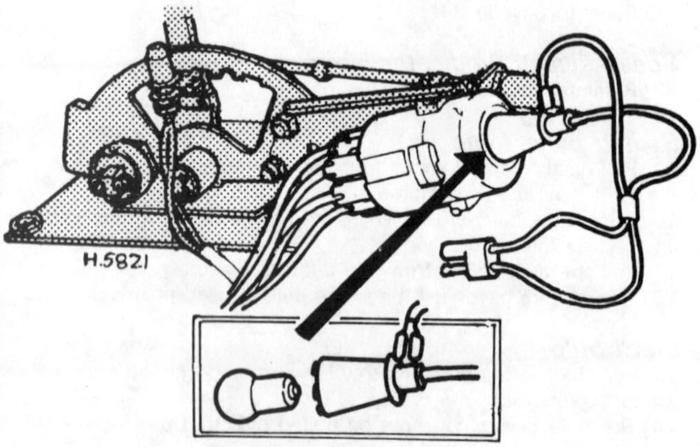

Fig. 10.75 Opticell unit (XJ12, Double Six) (Sec 38)

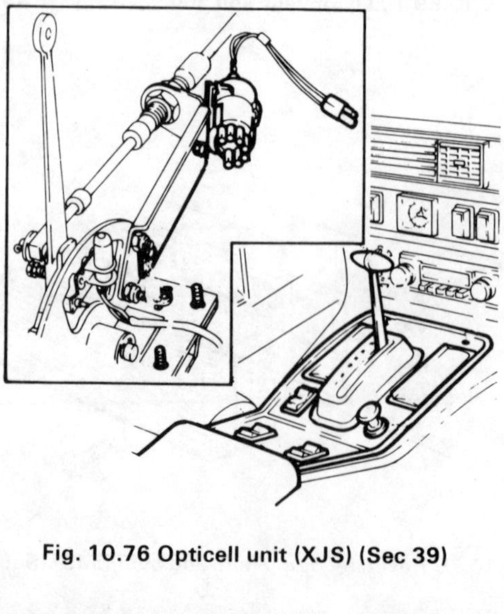

Fig. 10.76 Opticell unit (XJS) (Sec 39)

18 The particular instrument must be removed as described in Section 66 before a bulb can be renewed.

Speedometer and tachometer illumination

19 The individual instrument must be removed (see Section 66) before the bulb can be renewed.

36 Bulbs (XJS) – renewal

1 Access to the bulbs in all the following lamps is obtained by extracting the lens securing screws and removing the lens:

Front flasher lamp
Side flasher repeater lamp
Side marker lamp
Rear lamp cluster
Rear number plate lamp
Reversing lamps

2 The bulbs may be of conventional bayonet fitting, capless or of festoon type. This can be determined by inspection or by reference to the Specifications at the beginning of this Chapter.
3 Models having bulb type headlamps incorporate the parking lamp bulb in the headlamp reflector (refer to Section 31).

Interior roof lamp

4 Prise the lamp assembly from its recess in the headlining.
5 Remove the shroud from the back of the lamp and pull the festoon type bulb from its contacts.

Map reading lamp

6 Located on the passenger side in the facia side casing, the lamp acts also as an interior lamp.
7 It can be prised from its recess to renew the festoon type bulb.

Luggage boot lamp

8 The bulb is immediately accessible in the underside of the luggage boot lid.

Switch panel bulb

9 Prise the switch panel from the facia.
10 Pull the bulb holder from the diffuser assembly.
11 Remove the bulb from the holder.

Speed selector indicator lamp

12 Raise the lid of the centre console glovebox lid.
13 Unscrew and remove the three screws which hold the centre panel tothe console.
14 Raise the centre panel until the electrical leads can be identified and disconnected from the door lock switch and the cigar lighter.
15 Pull the centre panel up the selector lever. If necessary, unscrew the two halves of the lever knob and draw the panel off the lever to enable the nuts of the selector quadrant cover to be unscrewed.
16 Raise the cover, remove the hood from the lamp and withdraw the bulb.

Instrument illumination

17 These bulbs are accessible after removal of the instrument panel as described in Section 69.

Clock bulb

18 Prise the clock mounting panel from the facia.
19 Pull the bulb holder from the back of the clock and withdraw the bulb from the holder.

Warning lamps

20 Slacken the adjustment ring on the steering wheel and pull the wheel upwards as far as possible
21 Prise out the cover from both ends of the warning lamp strip.
22 Unscrew the lens cover from the instrument panel, remove the cover and the bulb.

37 Opticell unit – description

1 This device is fitted to all later models and comprises a centralised light source to illuminate certain areas by means of fibre elements and diffuser lenses.
2 The components illuminated in this way include the ignition switch, the lighting switch and the heater/air conditioner control switches.

38 Opticell unit (XJ12, Double Six) – removal and refitting

1 Disconnect the battery.
2 Remove the screws from the centre console top finisher panel. Withdraw the window lift switch panel and the finisher panel far enough to be able to reach the opticell unit.
3 Extract the two screws which hold the opticell unit to the speed selector lever quadrant.
4 Disconnect the fibre elements by pulling them from the opticell lens hood.

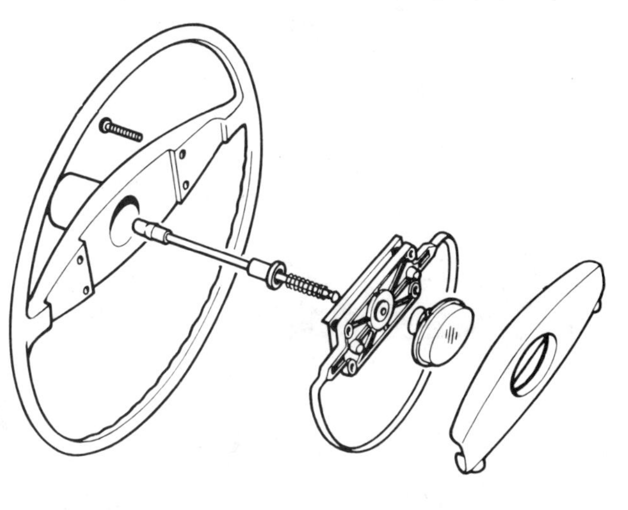

Fig. 10.77 Horn switch arrangement (XJ12 and Double Six, Series 1) (Sec 40)

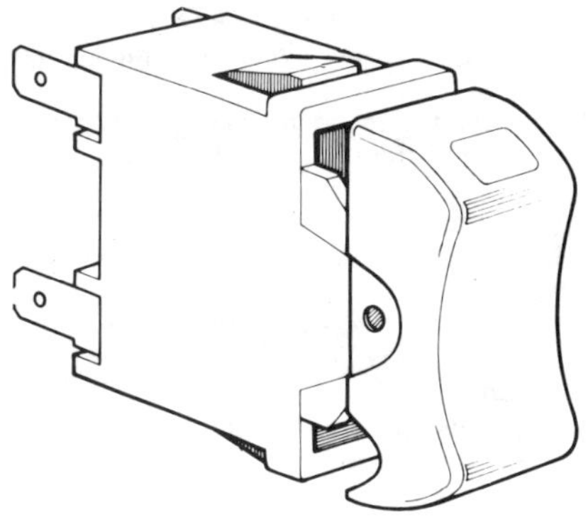

Fig. 10.78 Panel switch (XJ12 and Double Six, Series 1) (Sec 40)

5 Disconnect the electrical leads from the unit.
6 The opticell bulb is of miniature bayonet fitting type and is retained in the unit by a holder which is a push fit (photo).
7 Refitting is a reversal of removal.

39 Opticell unit (XJS) – removal and refitting

1 Disconnect the battery and then raise the lid of the centre glovebox.
2 Extract the three screws which hold the console centre panel.
3 Remove the speed selector lever knob by unscrewing its two halves (automatic) or by unscrewing the knob from the gearshift lever (manual).
4 Lift the centre panel from the console.
5 Identify and disconnect the electrical leads from the door lock selector switch, also the cigar lighter cable at its snap connector.
6 On automatic transmission models, remove the four nuts and lift the cover from the speed selector quadrant.
7 Unbolt the opticell unit. Pull the fibre elements and the bulb holder from it and disconnect the electrical leads.
8 Refitting is a reversal of removal.

40 Switches (XJ12 and Double Six, Series 1) – removal and refitting

1 Reference should also be made to earlier Chapters of this manual for details of special switches:

Oil pressure	*Chapter 1*
Coolant temperature	*Chapter 2*
Reversing lamp	*Chapter 6*
Fuel cut-off	*Chapter 3*
Brake system switches	*Chapter 9*

2 Before attempting to remove any of the switches, disconnect the battery.

Horn switch
3 Prise off the horn push cover from the centre of the steering wheel.
4 Extract the four screws from the rear face of the steering wheel spokes and remove the horn ring/switch assembly.

Panel switches
5 Release the two knurled screws and lower the instrument panel.
6 Disconnect the leads from the switch that is to be removed, depress the switch locking tabs and withdraw it.
7 It should be noted that if the parking lamp switch is to be removed then the headlamp switch will have to be withdrawn first.

Instrument panel rheostat
8 Remove the under scuttle casing screws.
9 Using a thin rod, depress the spring-loaded plunger and pull off the rheostat knob.
10 Unscrew the rheostat bezel, identify and disconnect the leads and remove the rheostat from the under scuttle casing.

Headlamp dipswitch
11 The switch is mounted on the floor to the left of the brake pedal.
12 Peel back the carpet and unscrew the two switch setscrews.
13 Identify and disconnect the leads from the switch.

Door pillar switch
14 This switch controls the interior lamps and is actuated by the opening and closure of the door.
15 It can be levered from its locating hole using a screwdriver.
16 Tape the connecting lead to the pillar before disconnecting it to prevent the lead slipping back into the interior of the pillar.
17 In order to reduce corrosion on the switch, smear the plunger with petroleum jelly before refitting.

Luggage boot lamp switch
18 The switch is part of the lamp assembly and is accessible as described in Section 34.

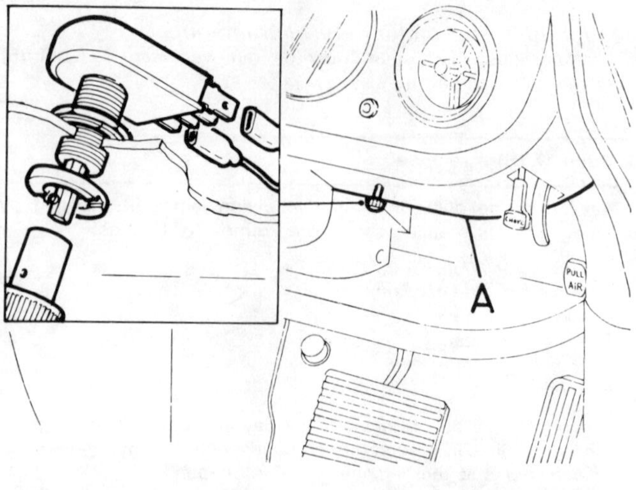

Fig. 10.79 Instrument panel rheostat (XJ12 and Double Six, Series 1) (Sec 40)

A Underscuttle casing

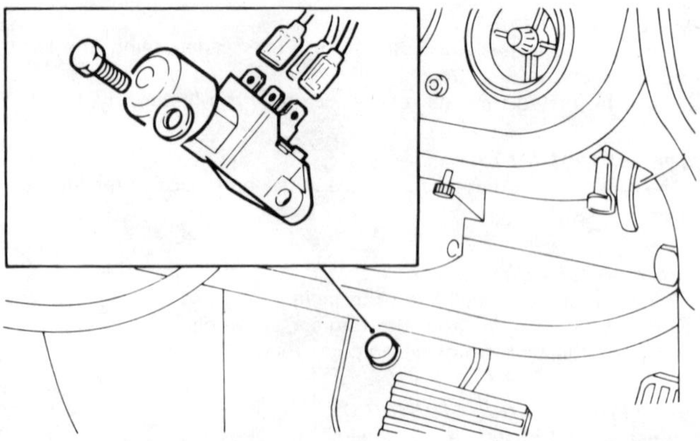

Fig. 10.80 Headlamp dipswitch (XJ12 and Double Six, Series 1) (Sec 40)

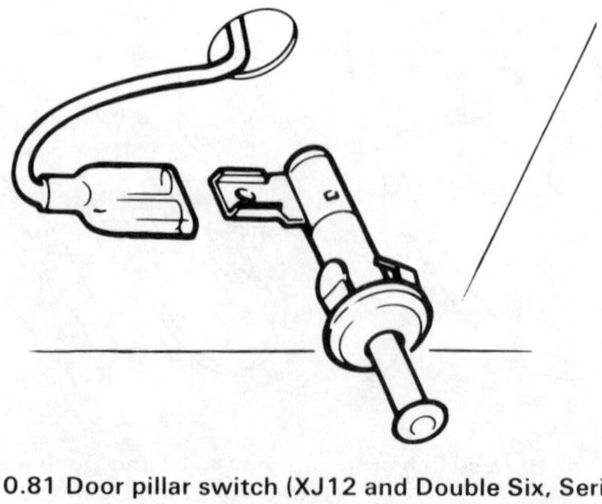

Fig. 10.81 Door pillar switch (XJ12 and Double Six, Series 1) (Sec 40)

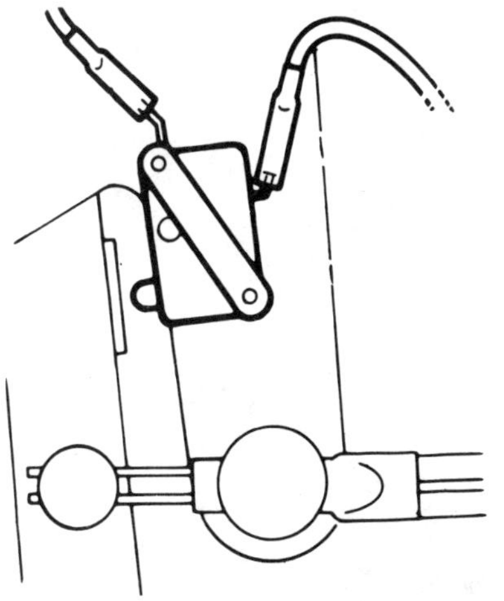

Fig. 10.82 Choke warning switch (XJ12 and Double Six, Series 1) (Sec 40)

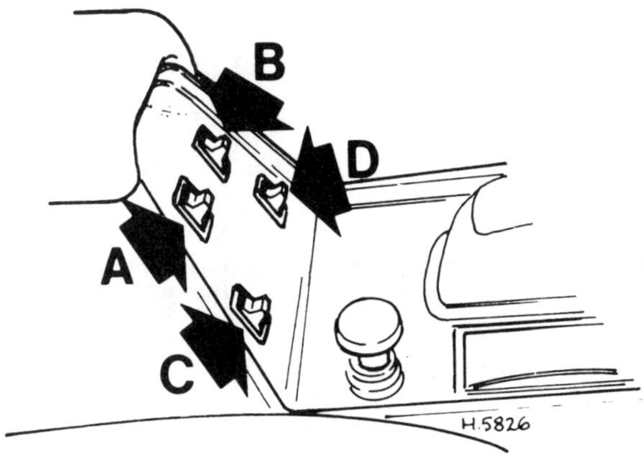

Fig. 10.83 Window lift switches (XJ12 and Double Six, Series 1) (Sec 40)

A/B Rear windows
C/D Front windows

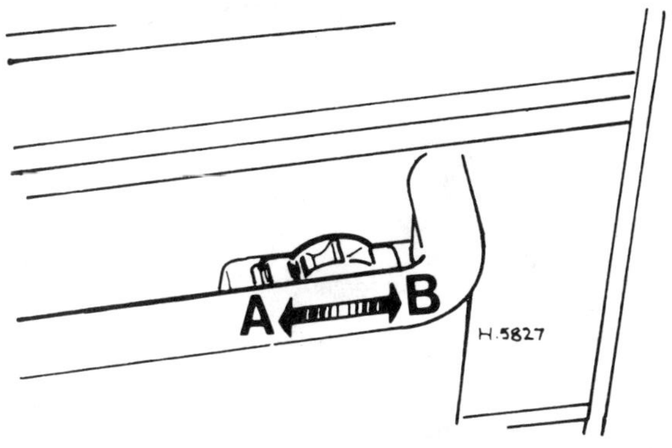

Fig. 10.84 Rear passenger window control switches (XJ12 and Double Six, Series 1) (Sec 40)

A Lower
B Raise

Key alarm switch

19 This switch is mounted in the centre pillar and is retained by a single screw.

Seat belt warning system switches

20 Refer to Section 46.

Choke warning switch

21 This switch is accessible after removal of the under scuttle casing.
22 The switch can be adjusted so that the warning lamp comes on when the choke control knob is pulled out.

Window lift switches – front

23 The switches can be removed if the panel escutcheon is prised out from its nylon retaining bushes.
24 Now slacken the upper centre retaining screw on the centre console top escutcheon.
25 Extract the two screws forward of the console ashtrays, lift the console escutcheon and push it forward to gain access to the switch carrier panel.
26 Unscrew and remove the four screws which hold the switch panel.
27 Identify the connecting leads before disconnecting them from the switch terminals. Note which way up the switches are installed to the panel.

Window lift switches – rear

28 Remove the screws from the lower edge of the armrest on the rear door. Raise the armrest to release it from its keyhole type fixings.
29 Identify the leads and disconnect them from the switch terminals. Remove the switch escutcheon plate and withdraw the switch.

Refitting (all switches)

30 Refitting of all switches is a reversal of removal. Reconnect the battery and check for correct operation on completion.

41 Switches (XJ12 and Double Six, Series 2 on) – removal and refitting

1 Refer to paragraphs 1 and 2 of Section 40.

Front window lift switches

2 Lever the switch mounting panel from the centre console.
3 Identify the cables and the way round that the switch is fitted into the panel. Disconnect the cables.
4 Depress the switch retaining tags and remove it.

Rear window lift switches

5 The operations are very similar to those described for the front switch panel.

Door lock selector switch

6 Lever the switch panel from the centre console.
7 Unscrew and lift the centre console escutcheon far enough to be able to disconnect the switch cables.
8 Depress the switch retaining tags and remove the switch.

Horn switch

9 Extract the two screws from the rear face of the steering wheel spokes and lift the horn push from the steering wheel.
10 Unscrew and remove the four screws now exposed on the horn push backplate.
11 The horn push contact assembly can be removed after peeling the trim pad away.

Master lighting switch

12 Remove the under scuttle casing from the driver's side.
13 Slacken the two screws which hold the master switch legend plate.
14 Remove the switch control knob by depressing the retaining plunger.
15 Remove the switch shroud and push the switch through the mounting plate.
16 Disconnect the multi-pin plug and socket.

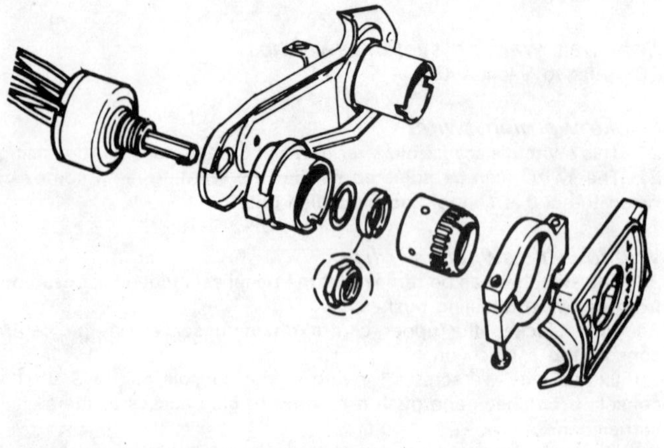

Fig. 10.85 Master lighting switch (XJ12 and Double Six, Series 2 on) (Sec 41)

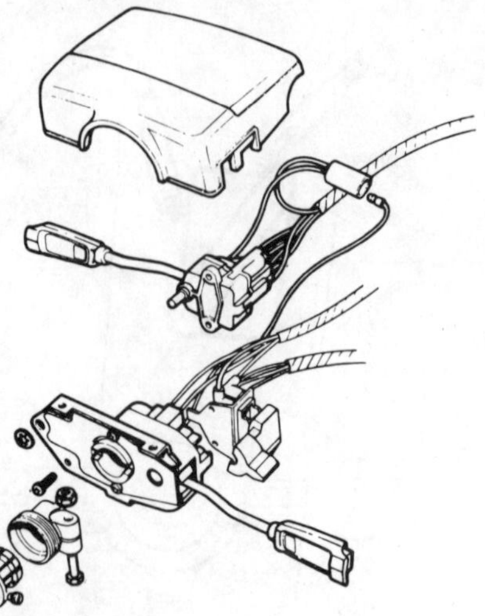

Fig. 10.86 Windscreen washer/wiper switch (XJ12 and Double Six, Series 2 on) (Sec 44)

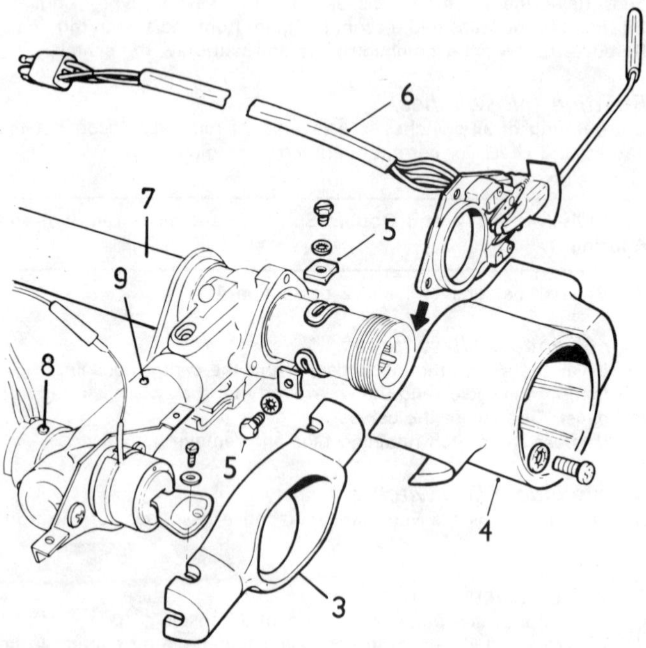

Fig. 10.87 Direction indicator/headlamp flasher switch (XJ12 and Double Six, Series 1) (Sec 43)

3 *Lock shroud*
4 *Column shroud*
5 *Switch cancelling bar studs*
6 *Wiring harness*
7 *Steering upper column*
8 *Ignition switch retaining screw*
9 *Lock retaining shear bolt*

Panel switches

17 On early models, remove the heater/air conditioner control knobs. Pull the radio escutcheon forward.
18 Remove the four screws from the centre oddments tray and pull the tray forward.
19 Identify the leads and disconnect them from the related pair of switches.
20 Withdraw the pair of switches together with the oddments tray.
21 Depress the switch spring retaining clips and push the switch through the mounting panel.
22 On later cars, the switch mounting panel can be removed simply by levering it from its surround or the switches themselves withdrawn after depressing the retaining clips (photo).

Instrument panel rheostat

23 Refer to Section 40, paragraphs 8 to 10.

Door pillar switch

24 Refer to Section 40, paragraphs 14 to 17.

Key alarm switch

25 Refer to Section 40, paragraph 19.

Seat belt warning system switches

26 Refer to Section 47.

Choke warning switch

27 This is fitted to models which have a carburettor fuel system.
28 Remove the under scuttle casing from the driver's side.
29 Release the nut which holds the choke cable conduit to the facia bracket.
30 Pull the choke handle holder from the handle.
31 Disconnect the choke cable from the handle.

32 Extract the two screws which hold the micro switch and retrieve the keep plate.
33 Disconnect the leads at the snap connectors and remove the switch.

Refitting (all switches)

34 Refitting of all switches is a reversal of removal. Reconnect the battery and check for correct operation on completion.

41.22 Switch removed from mounting panel (later type)

42 Switches (XJS) – removal and refitting

1 Removal and refitting of all switches is as described for XJ12 and Double Six models in the preceding Section, but the following points should be noted.
2 When removing the master lighting switch, the switch shroud will have to be detached from the facia instrument module and lower mounting bracket to give access to the switch knob retaining plunger.
3 A grommet is provided in the under scuttle casing for access to the panel light rheostat knob retaining plunger.
4 The door pillar switches are retained by a small screw.

43 Steering column switches (XJ12 and Double Six, Series 1) – removal and refitting

Direction indicator/headlamp flasher switch

1 Disconnect the battery.
2 Remove the steering wheel as described in Chapter 11.
3 Extract the three screws which secure the column shroud and remove the shroud.
4 Remove the indicator cancelling bar studs.
5 Disconnect the wiring harness multi-pin connector.
6 Withdraw the switch assembly.

Ignition switch/steering lock

7 Disconnect the battery.
8 Remove the steering wheel (Chapter 11).
9 Remove the shroud from around the ignition lock.
10 Remove the shroud from around the steering column.
11 Remove the under scuttle casing from the driver's side.
12 Disconnect the wiring harness multi-pin plug and socket. Remove the upper steering column (see Chapter 11).
13 Extract the screws and pull out the ignition switch component from the switch housing.
14 To remove the steering lock assembly, the fixing bolts will have to be drilled and a screw extractor used.

Refitting (all switches)

15 Refitting of all switches is a reversal of removal. When fitting the steering column lock, use new shear head bolts and tighten them until their heads break off.

44 Steering column switches (XJ12 and Double Six, Series 2 on) – removal and refitting

Windscreen washer/wiper switch

1 Disconnect the battery.
2 Remove the steering column lower shroud.
3 Remove the steering wheel (Chapter 11).
4 Remove the under scuttle casing from the driver's side (Chapter 12).
5 Disconnect the steering column switch wiring harness at the plugs.
6 Slacken the clamp bolt and pull the complete switch assembly from the steering column, together with the steering column upper shroud.
7 The washer/wiper switch can be detached by removing two screws and a spire washer.

Hazard warning switch

8 Carry out the operations described in paragraphs 1 to 6.
9 The hazard warning switch can be pushed out of its mounting plate once the retaining tags have been depressed.

Direction indicator/headlamp flasher switch

10 Repeat the operations described in paragraphs 1 to 6 and then separate the hazard warning and washer/wiper switches as described earlier.
11 Do not try to separate the direction indicator/headlamp flasher switch from the mounting plate. A new switch is supplied as a complete assembly including the plate.
12 Refitting is a reversal of removal.

Ignition switch/steering column lock

13 Remove the under scuttle casing from the driver's side.
14 Pull off the ring which retains the ignition switch component to the steering lock housing.
15 Pull the wiring harness plug from the socket and withdraw the harness and ignition switch.
16 To remove the steering column lock, the upper column must be withdrawn as described in Chapter 11.
17 Drill some indentations round the periphery of the retaining bolt and unscrew it by tapping it with a drift and hammer.
18 Refitting is a reversal of removal. Tighten a new lock securing bolt until its head breaks off.

45 Steering column switches (XJS) – removal and refitting

Windscreen wiper/washer switch

1 Disconnect the battery.
2 Slacken the steering wheel adjustment ring and pull the wheel upwards to the limit of its travel.
3 Extract the screws and remove the steering column lower shroud.
4 Remove the steering wheel (Chapter 11).
5 Extract the screw which holds the upper shroud to the bracket on the steering column.
6 Release the clamp screw from the switch assembly.
7 Pull the switch and upper shroud from the steering column, detach the shroud and disconnect the wiring harness at the block connector.
8 Release the switch from the mounting plate and disconnect the earth cable at the snap connector.

Direction indicator/headlamp flasher switch

9 Carry out the operations described in paragraphs 1 to 7.
10 Do not try to separate the switch from the mounting plate. A new switch is supplied complete with mounting plate.

Ignition switch/steering column lock

11 Disconnect the battery.

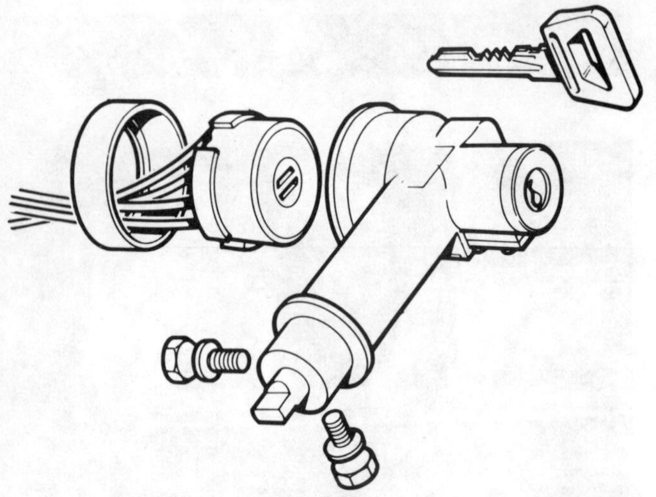

Fig. 10.88 Steering column lock/ignition switch (typical) (Sec 44)

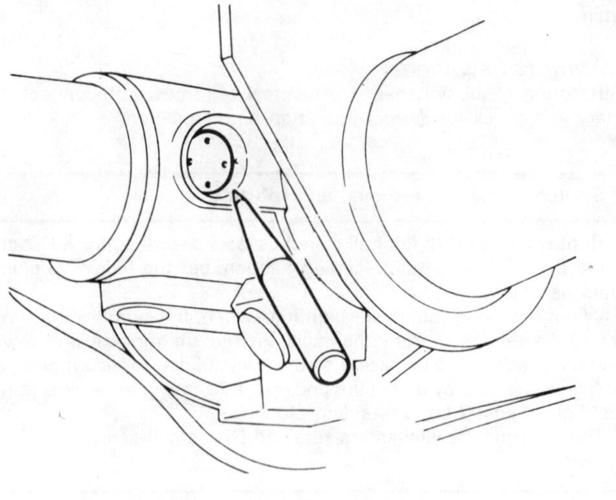

Fig. 10.89 Removing a shear head steering column lockbolt (Sec 44)

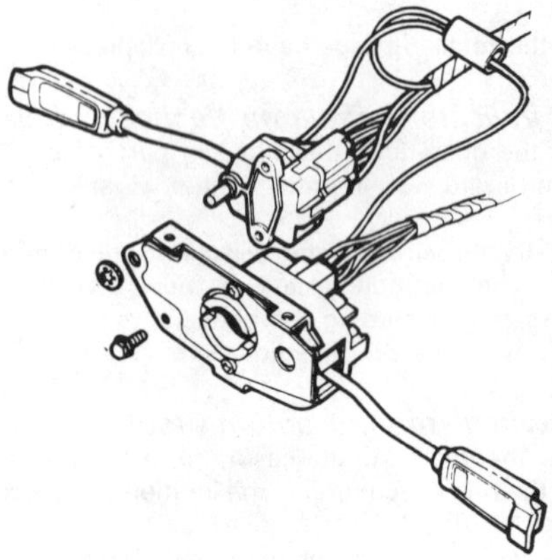

Fig. 10.90 Windscreen wiper/washer switch and headlamp dipswitch (XJS) (Sec 45)

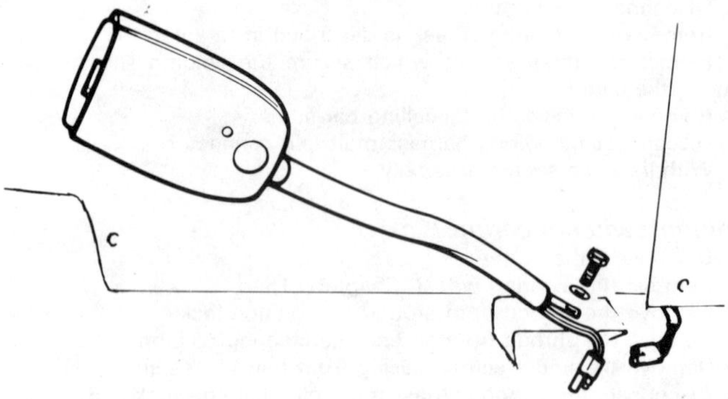

Fig. 10.91 Safety belt anchorage switch (XJ12 and Double Six, Series 1) (Sec 46)

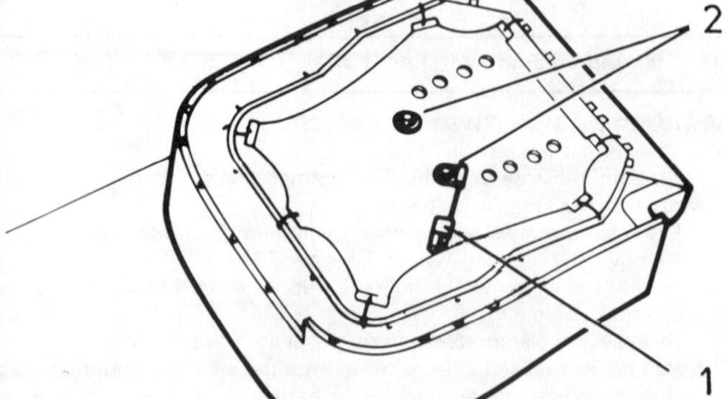

Fig. 10.92 Seat weight-sensitive switch (XJ12 and Double Six, Series 1) (Sec 46)

1 Connector
2 Switch retaining screws

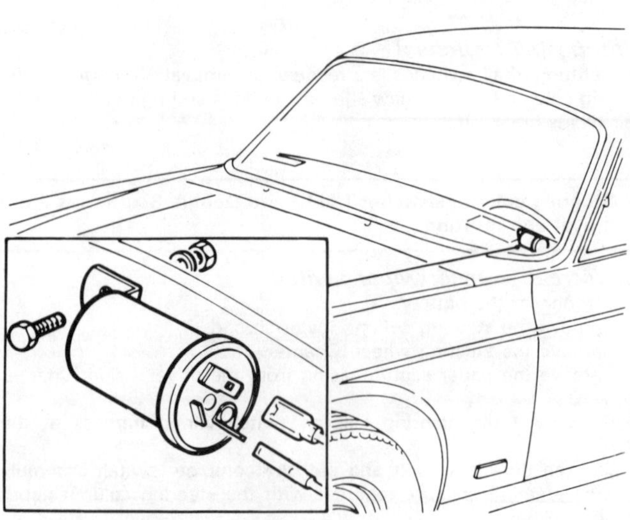

Fig. 10.93 Safety belt warning buzzer (XJ12 and Double Six, Series 1) (Sec 46)

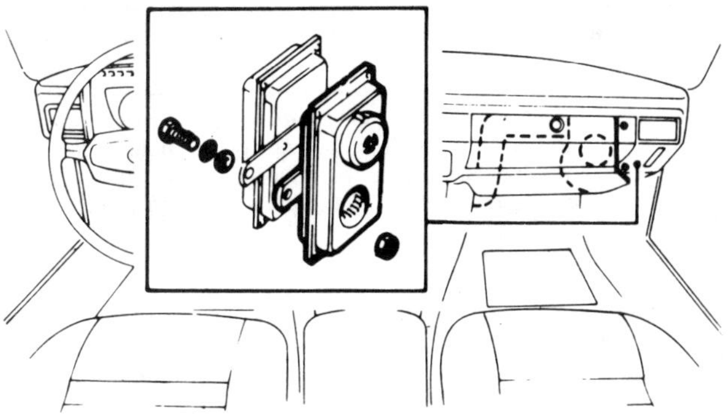

Fig. 10.94 Safety belt warning buzzer control unit (XJS) (Sec 48)

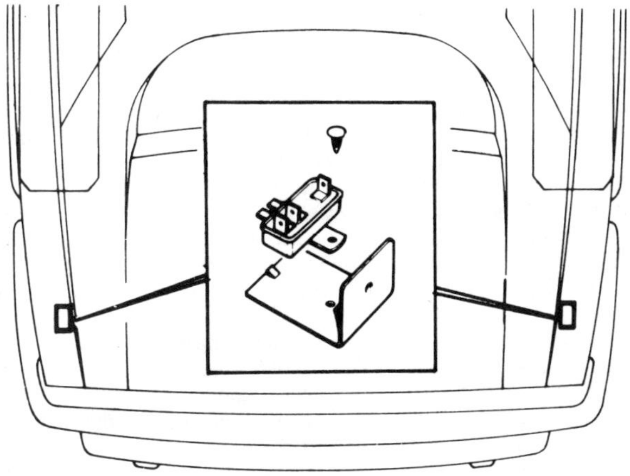

Fig. 10.95 Parking lamp failure sensor (XJS) (Sec 50)

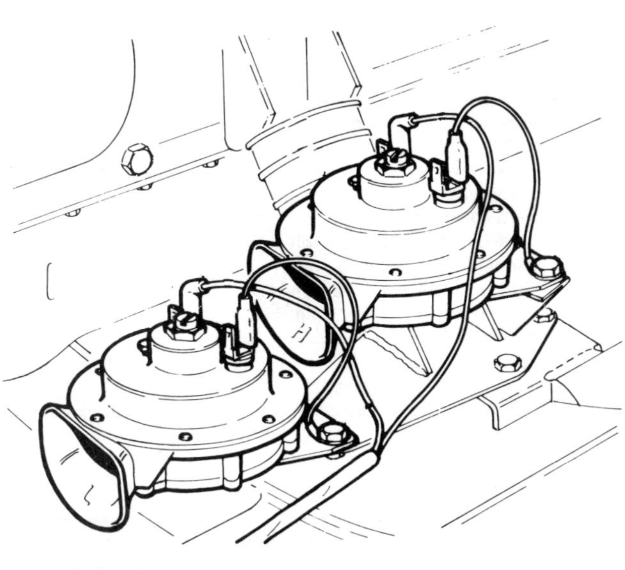

Fig. 10.96 Dual horn arrangement (XJ12, Double Six) (Sec 52)

12 Remove the under scuttle casing from the driver's side (Chapter 12).
13 Disconnect the steering column shroud from the facia, the instrument module at the mounting bracket by extracting the fixing screws.
14 Ease the shroud away until the grub screw which holds the ignition switch to the steering lock housing can be removed.
15 Disconnect the wiring harness connectors and remove the switch.
16 Removal of the steering column lock is as described in Section 44.

Refitting (all switches)

17 Refitting is a reversal of the removal procedure. Reconnect the battery and check for correct operation on completion.

46 Safety belt system (XJ12 and Double Six, Series 1)

1 Inertia reel safety belts are fitted as standard for the driver and the front passenger.
2 A warning is given both by an indicator lamp and by a buzzer if either of the front belts is left unfastened when, with the engine running, the speed selector lever is moved to a 'Drive' position and the seats are occupied.
3 The main components of the system are a belt (anchorage) switch, a seat cushion weight-sensitive switch and a buzzer mounted at the facia top rail crash roll.

47 Safety belt system (XJ12 and Double Six, Series 2 on)

1 The system used on these models is of the sequential start interlock type. The engine will not start unless the correct starting procedure is first carried out. This is:

(a) Sit in car and apply handbrake fully
(b) Set the selector lever to N or P
(c) Fasten the seat belts

2 Failure to comply with the starting sequence will not only prevent the car starting but will also start a warning buzzer and illuminate a warning lamp.
3 If a passenger leaves the car temporarily while the engine is running, the lamp and buzzer will operate for a seven second period and again when the passenger resumes his seat and a 'Drive' position is selected.
4 To start the engine for tuning or maintenance purposes, reach in through the window. By this means, the seat (weight-sensitive) switches will not be actuated to operate the warning system.
5 The system includes belt anchorage switches, seat cushion (weight-sensitive) switches, and an inhibitor switch at the speed selector lever. The latter is fitted adjacent to the starter inhibitor switch and reference should also be made to Chapter 6. The seat belt inhibitor switch should be so adjusted that the warning lamp and buzzer will operate if the lever is moved to a 'Drive' position, either forward or reverse.

48 Safety belt system (XJS)

1 The inertia reel belts incorporate belt anchorage switches and a buzzer control unit which is mounted behind the under scuttle casing on the passenger side.
2 Failure to have connected either of the front seat belts when the ignition is switched on and the seats are occupied, will actuate a warning lamp and a buzzer for a period of ten seconds.

49 Anti-theft (ignition key warning) system

1 A warning buzzer sounds if the driver's door is opened without having first removed the ignition key from the steering column lock.
2 The buzzer is the same unit used for the safety belt warning system and is actuated by the switch in the body door pillar.

50 Sensors (XJS)

Low coolant control unit

1 In the event of a low coolant level occurring due to a leak, a warning lamp will illuminate and a buzzer will sound. The buzzer control unit is located back-to-back with the unit for the seat belt/anti-theft systems, refer to Section 48.

Stoplamp failure sensor

2 This is located under the console centre panel.
3 To reach it, first disconnect the battery and then raise the console glove box lid for access to the centre panel rear securing screw.
4 Extract the centre panel screws, lift the panel and identify and disconnect the leads from the door lock switch.
5 Remove the speed selector or gearshift lever knob and withdraw the panel over the lever.
6 Identify and disconnect the leads from the sensor and unbolt it from its mounting bracket.

Front and rear parking lamp failure sensor

7 The sensor units are mounted either behind the under scuttle casing (see Chapter 12) on the passenger side or on the body side panel just forward of the rear lamp assemblies. The rear mounted sensors are secured by a plastic spigot to a mounting bracket.
8 The parking lamp arrangement which the sensor controls depends upon the vehicle specification for different operating territories.

51 Cigar lighter – removal and refitting

1 Access to the cigar lighter is described in the bulb renewal operations of Section 34.

52 Horns (XJ12, Double Six) – removal, refitting and adjustment

1 Disconnect the battery and remove the left-hand air cleaner.
2 Disconnect the leads from the horn terminals and unbolt the horns from their mounting brackets.
3 Refitting is a reversal of removal, but note the earth lead under the mounting bolts.
4 The horn adjustment screw is normally sealed. The purpose of the screw is to take up wear, not to vary the pitch of the horn note.
5 To adjust the horn, clean out the head of the adjustment screw and disconnect the feed cable from the horn.
6 Connect a 0 to 25 amp ammeter and a switch in series with the horn and the feed cable.
7 Depress the horn button and turn the adjustment screw until the horn just becomes inaudible. Now turn the screw clockwise until the horn draws a current of between 6.5 and 7.0 amps.

53 Horns (XJS) – removal, refitting and adjustment

1 The horns are mounted below the front bumper apron.
2 Disconnect the battery, disconnect the leads from the horns and unbolt and remove them.
3 Refitting is a reversal of removal. Adjust for a satisfactory note and performance by means of the diaphragm tension screw on the top of each horn.

54 Windscreen wiper blades and arms (XJ12, Double Six) – removal and refitting

1 To remove a wiper blade, release the small tag which secures it to the wiper arm and pull the blade from the arm (photo).
2 The wiper arms can be removed from the splined driving spindles after first pulling the arms away from the windscreen until they lock (photo).
3 When refitting the wiper arms, make sure that the wiper motor is in the parked position, having been switched off by the wiper control switch (not the ignition key) and set the arms complete with blades, parallel with the lower edge of the windscreen before pressing the arm fully onto its spindle.

55 Windscreen wiper blades and arms (XJS) – removal and refitting

1 Pull the wiper arm from the windscreen, depress the blade retaining clip and slide the blade spigot out of the hole in the arm.
2 To remove a wiper arm, note its angle in relation to the bottom edge of the windscreen and then lift the plastic cover from the driving spindle nut.
3 Unscrew and remove the spindle nut and pull the arm from the spindle splines.
4 Refitting is a reversal of removal but make sure that the wiper motor is in the parked position, having been switched off by the wiper control switch not the ignition key. Set the arms complete with blades parallel with the bottom edge of the screen.

56 Windscreen wiper motor and linkage (XJ12, Double Six) – removal and refitting

1 Remove the wiper arms from their driving spindles.
2 Disconnect and remove the battery, unbolt and remove the cover panel from the left rear corner of the engine compartment (photo).
3 Unscrew the large nut which connects the driving cable conduit to the wiper motor.
4 Withdraw the electrical plug connector from the socket in the motor.
5 Remove the two setscrews, washers and clamp strap and then withdraw the motor and driving cable by drawing the cable through its conduit.
6 If the driving spindle assemblies are worn they can only be removed after first withdrawing the screen rail facia. To do this, insert a thin blade under the edge of the loudspeaker grille and lever up the facia. The grille is retained by plastic pegs. Remove the two screws now exposed, also the two other screws from the underside of the screen facia roll (just above the fresh air outlets).
7 Unscrew and remove the two nuts which secure the wheelbox backplate and withdraw the cable drive conduit.
8 Unscrew the nuts which secure the wheelbox to the scuttle and withdraw the wheelbox, spacer and seals.
9 Refitting the wheelboxes is a reversal of removal, except that the flared ends of the conduit tube must register with the narrow slots in the cover plate.
10 After refitting the wiper motor, the wiper arms must be installed in the following way.
11 Switch on the ignition and then switch on the wiper switch to slow speed. Switch off the wiper switch so that the driving spindles will stop in the 'Parked' position. Install the wiper arms so that they lie parallel with the lower edge of the windscreen.

57 Windscreen wiper motor and linkage (XJS) – removal and refitting

1 Remove the wiper arms and blades as previously described.
2 Disconnect the battery.
3 Unscrew and remove the air inlet grille securing nuts. Raise the grille and wiper assembly until the washer jet tube and the wiring harness multi-plug connector can be disconnected.
4 Unbolt the motor from the grille, invert the grille and remove the wheelbox driving spindle nuts.
5 Unbolt and remove the rack cover plate and withdraw the rack assembly.
6 Remove the motor shroud and disconnect the wiring harness at the connector on the wiper motor gearbox.
7 Refitting is a reversal of removal.

58 Windscreen wiper motor – overhaul

The following operations must be regarded as typical as it is becoming increasingly difficult to obtain individual spare parts and the wiper motor assemblies also differ in detail according to model of car

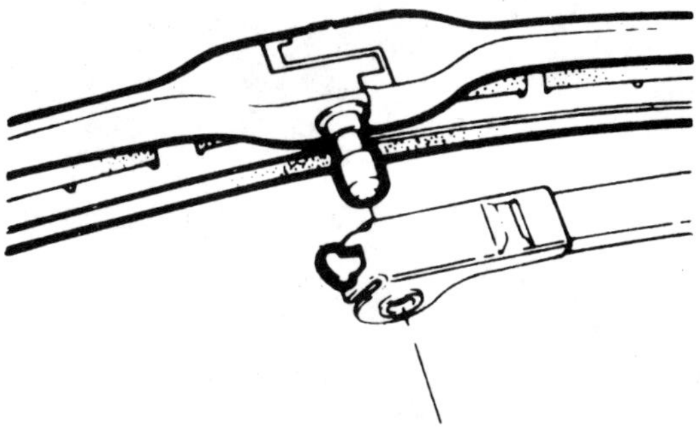

Fig. 10.97 Wiper blade attachment to arm (XJS) (Sec 55)

Fig. 10.98 Wiper arm attachment (XJS) (Sec 55)

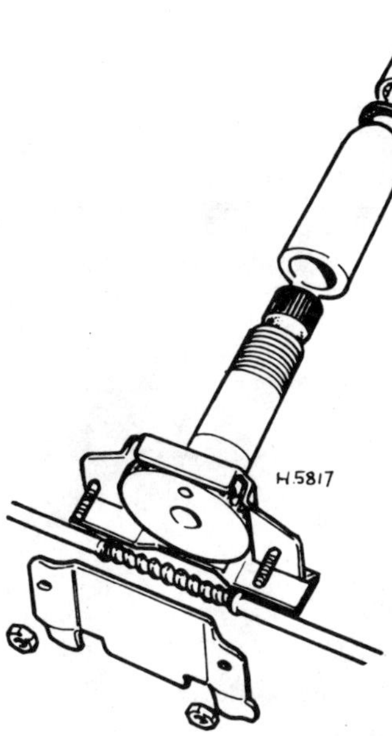

Fig. 10.99 Windscreen wiper wheel box (XJ12, Double Six) (Sec 56)

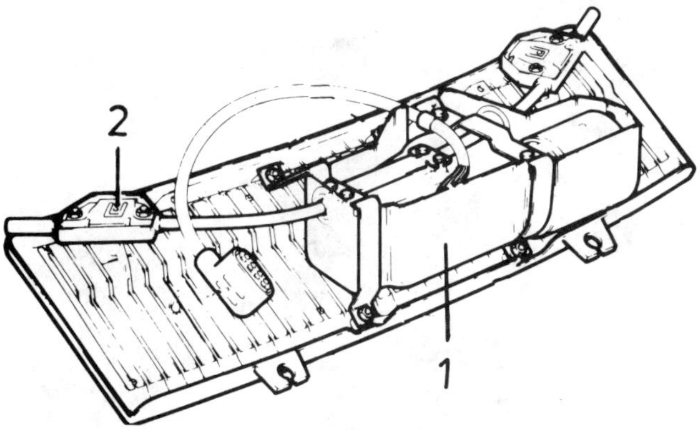

Fig. 10.100 Windscreen wiper motor and linkage (XJS) (Sec 57)

1 Motor and shroud
2 Rack assembly

and production date. In view of the normally long life of a wiper motor it is recommended that a new unit is obtained rather than to attempt to repair an old assembly which has become faulty or worn.

1 With the motor removed from the car as described earlier, withdraw the gearbox cover screws and remove the cover.

2 Prise the circlip from the groove in the gearwheel crankpin and extract the flat washer, conical spring, friction plate, connecting rod assembly and its flat washer.

3 Remove the circlip and washer which secure the shaft to the gearbox.

4 Draw the gear from the shaft, collecting the dished washer from the underside of the gearwheel.

5 Note the gearbox to yoke alignment marks and then withdraw the two fixing bolts and detach the yoke assembly and the armature from the gearbox. Take care that once removed, the yoke does not come near any swarf or iron filings which might be attracted to its pole pieces.

6 Mark the location of the moulded slider block in relation to the terminal assembly as this controls the wiper parking position.

7 Remove the screws which secure the brushgear and the terminal and limit switch assembly and withdraw the assemblies.

8 Inspect the brushes for wear. The main (diametrically opposite) brushes should be renewed if they are worn to $\frac{3}{16}$ in (4.8 mm) or less. If the narrow section of the third brush is worn to the full width of the brush, it must be renewed. Check that the brushes move freely in their holders.

9 Clean the commutator of the armature with a fuel soaked rag or polish it with very fine glasspaper.

10 Renew any gearbox components which are worn.

11 Reassembly is a reversal of dismantling but check the following points.

12 Before refitting the armature to the yoke, check that the thrust disc and felt lubricating disc are in position in the yoke bearing. The thrust disc should be located flat against the endface of the bearing, followed by the felt washer which has a hole in its centre to allow the ball in the end of the armature shaft to contact the thrust disc. Prior to fitting the components, apply oil to the felt washer.

13 Apply grease liberally to all gearbox components.

14 If new parts have been fitted, check the armature endfloat which must be between 0.002 and 0.008 in (0.05 and 0.2 mm). With the wiper motor completely assembled and the thrust screw released and in the uppermost position, tighten the screw until it just makes contact

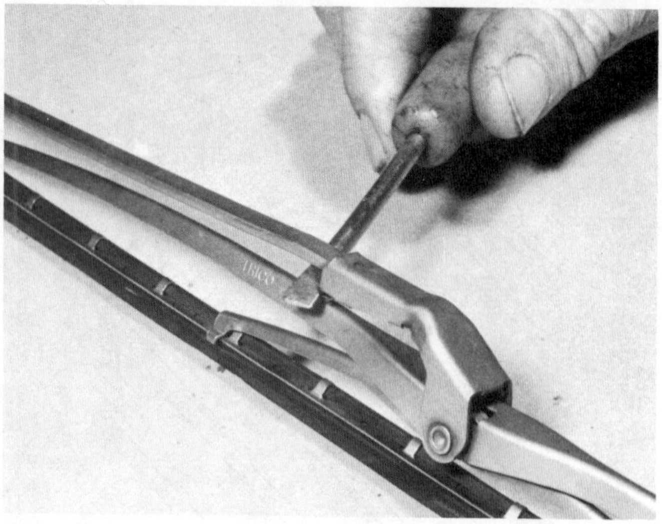

54.1 Depressing a wiper blade securing tag

56.2 Windscreen wiper motor is located next to the battery

and then unscrew it one quarter of a turn and tighten the locknut.

59 Windscreen washer (XJ12, Double Six) – description and jet adjustment

1 The windscreen washer reservoir is located towards the front of the engine compartment on the left-hand valance.
2 Use washer fluid additive, particularly in cold weather, which will prevent the fluid freezing. Never add engine anti-freeze to the reservoir, but in an emergency or in severe weather, methylated spirit (denatured alcohol) may be added to the fluid.
3 The washer pump is located on the engine compartment rear bulkhead (Series 1) or on the bumper support strut on later models (photo).
4 The washer jets are located on the air intake grille at the base of the windscreen. They can be cleaned with thin wire, removed by unscrewing them with a screwdriver or adjusted to provide the best wash pattern by moving them with a screwdriver blade inserted into their slots.

60 Windscreen washer (XJS) – description and jet adjustment

1 On this model, the washer reservoir is located at the left rear

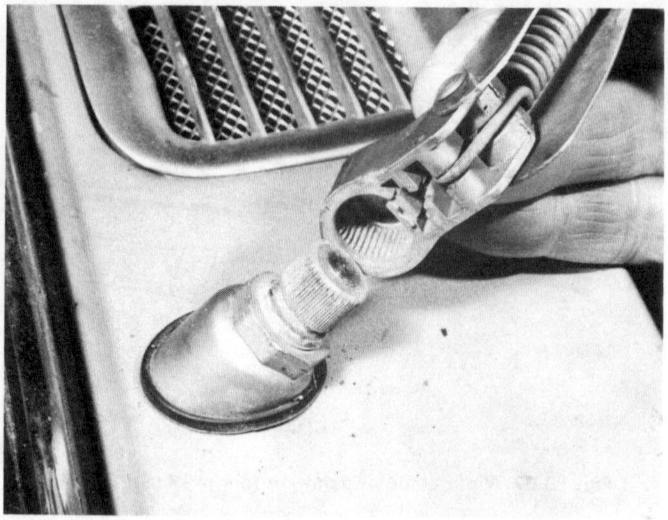

54.2 Wiper arm removed from its spindle

59.3 Windscreen washer pump

corner of the engine compartment.
2 The electric washer pump is attached to the reservoir mounting clamp band.
3 The jets are located in the air intake grille and can be removed after detaching the grille and raising it slightly. Jet adjustment is similar to that described in the preceding Section.

61 Headlamp wash/wipe mechanism

1 This equipment, fitted to later models (optional extra on some), comprises the following main assemblies:

Washer reservoir and pump

2 This is located under the front left-hand wheel arch and supplies both the windscreen and headlamp washer systems.
3 To remove the reservoir, jack up the front of the car and take off the left hand roadwheel.
4 The washer pump is mounted close to the reservoir on the bumper support strut.

Washer jets and supply tubes

5 The headlamp washer jets and supply tubes can be removed in the

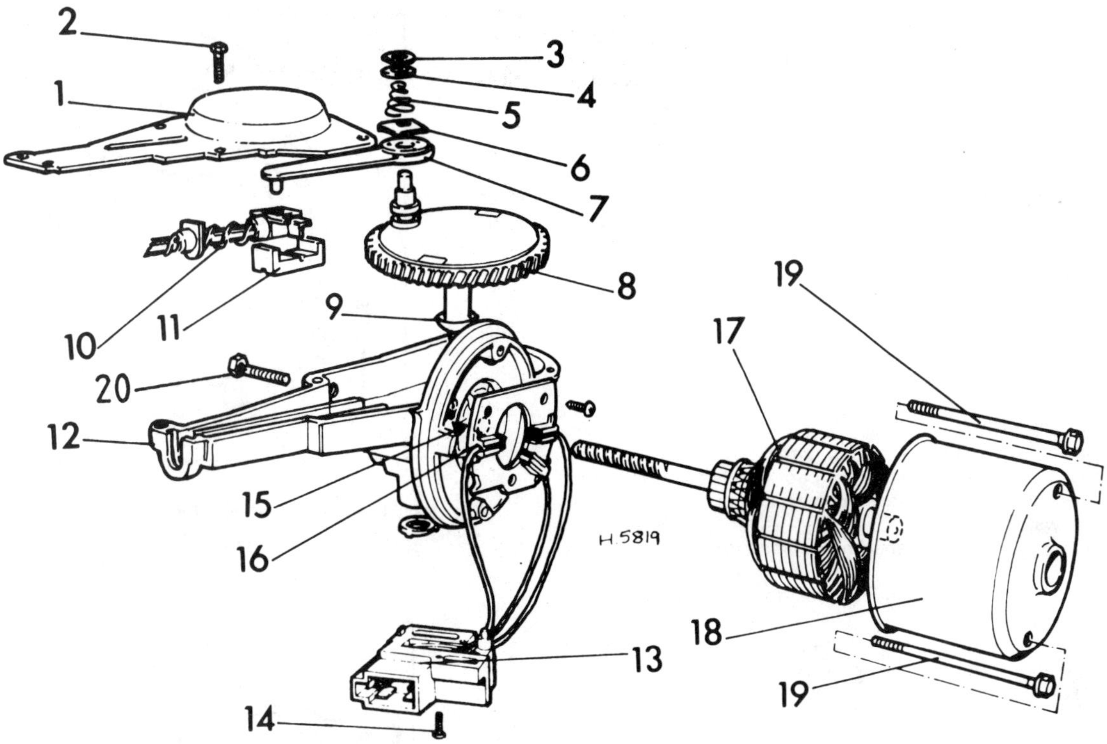

Fig. 10.101 Exploded view of typical windscreen wiper motor (Sec 58)

1 Gearbox cover
2 Screw
3 Circlip
4 Washer
5 Spring
6 Friction plate
7 Crankarm
8 Gear
9 Dished washer
10 Cable rack
11 Slider block
12 Gearbox
13 Limit switch
14 Screws
15 Bush
16 Brush gear
17 Armature
18 Yoke
19 Tie-bolts
20 Armature endfloat adjuster screw and locknut

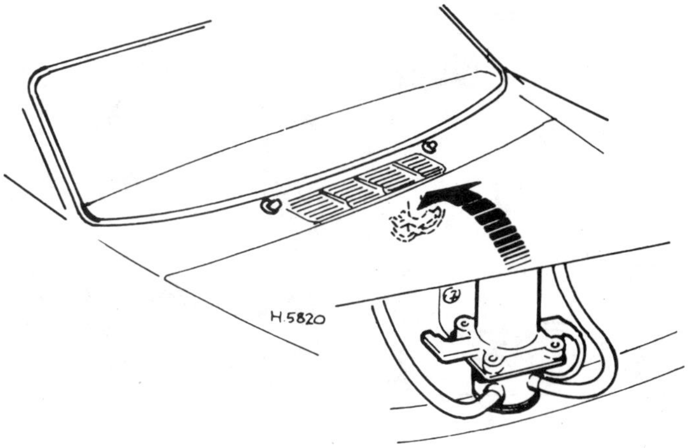

Fig. 10.102 Windscreen washer pump location (XJ12 and Double Six, Series) (Sec 59)

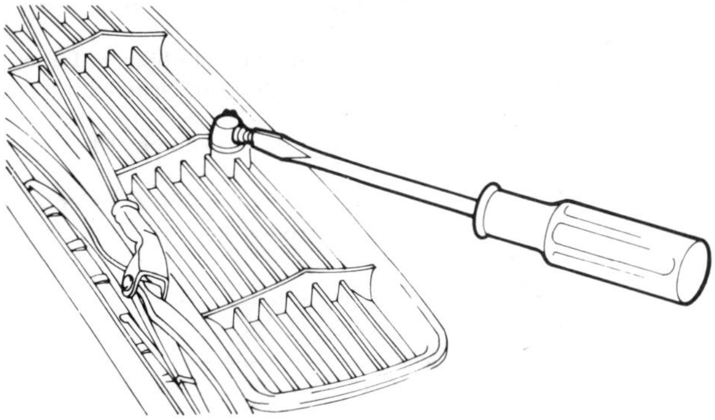

Fig. 10.103 Adjusting a washer jet (Sec 59)

following way.
6 Lift the bonnet and carefully pull the supply tubes from the jets. Hold the jets outside the car with the hand and unscrew the nuts which secure the jet assemblies to the headlamp panel.
7 The fluid supply tubes are secured in spring clips to the flange below the lower grille.

Wiper arm

8 The headlamp wiper arm is removable after unscrewing the pivot screw. Press the wiper arm towards the headlamp glass and remove it together with the spacer cup.

Washer/wiper switch

9 The headlamp washer/wiper switch is mounted in the centre console top panel. The panel can be removed for access to the switch after extracting the screws.

Wiper motor and rack

10 The headlamp wiper motor is located within the engine compartment. To remove the motor, first disconnect the battery and then remove the cover plate from the rack drive section of the motor (four self-tapping screws).
11 Remove the nylon channel and lift the rack drive peg from its recess.
12 Unbolt the motor from its mounting plate, disconnect the electrical leads and withdraw the motor.
13 The motor gear can be withdrawn if the two screws are removed from the cover plate on the gear housing. Detach the circlip from the spindle, remove the gear and plain and conical washers.
14 The rack drive cables are simply removed by withdrawing them from their conduits.
15 The wiper wheel boxes and rack tubes can be removed if the headlamp outer rim finisher is first withdrawn. Extract the three screws which hold the headlamp rim and rack tube. Ease the rim and tube forward and slacken the collet nut. Draw the rim away and let the wiper blade rotate as the rack is withdrawn.
16 Refitting of all the headlamp wash/wipe components is a reversal of removal, but when fitting the wiper arm, turn the blade to the parked position (in alignment with the drive tube) and hold it from moving with the hand while tightening the pivot screw.

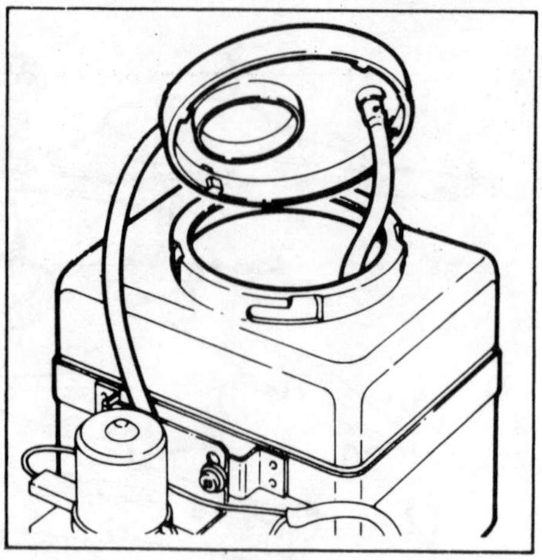

Fig. 10.104 Windscreen washer reservoir and pump (XJS) (Sec 60)

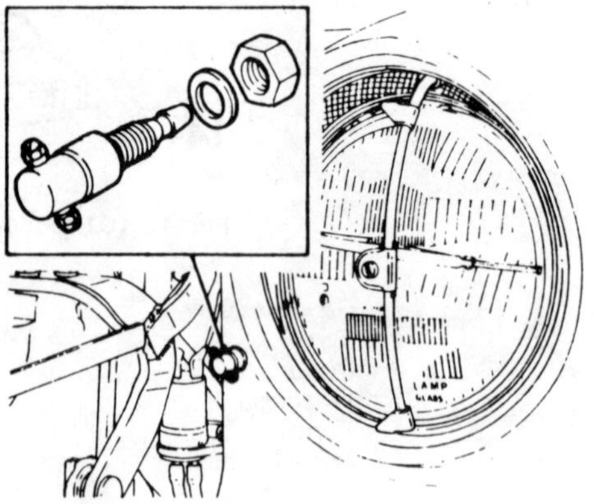

Fig. 10.105 Headlamp wash/wipe arrangement (typical) (Sec 61)

62 Speedometer (XJ12 and Double Six, Series 1) – removal and refitting

1 Disconnect the battery.
2 Remove the under scuttle casing (two screws).
3 Reach up behind the speedometer and disconnect the drive cable by unscrewing the knurled retaining ring.
4 Disconnect the trip reset cable by unscrewing the knurled ring.
5 Apply hand pressure to the speedometer bezel and turn the instrument in an anti-clockwise direction until it is felt to release from its bayonet fixing.
6 From the speedometer casing, pull out the bulb holders for the illumination of the instrument and the warning lamp(headlamp main beam).
7 Disconnect the earth lead and remove the speedometer from the instrument panel.
8 Wear in the right-angled gearbox at the rear of the speedometer can only be rectified by fitting a new unit. The unit can be detached by unscrewing its knurled retaining ring.
9 Refitting is a reversal of removal.

63 Speedometer inner cable (XJ12 and Double Six, Series 1) – renewal

1 Remove the speedometer as described in the preceding Section.
2 It is now possible to grip the end of the inner cable with a pair of pliers and pull it from the cable conduit.
3 If the cable has broken, then the assembly will have to be disconnected at the transmission end to extract the lower section.
4 Lubricate the lower two thirds of the cable with thin grease, sparingly, before inserting it from the speedometer end of the conduit.

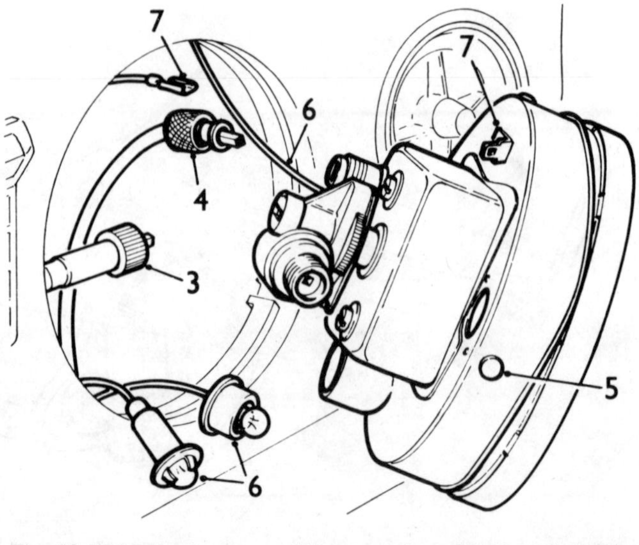

Fig. 10.106 Speedometer cable connections (XJ12 and Double Six, Series 1) (Sec 62)

3 Drive cable
4 Trip reset cable
5 Bayonet fitting pin
6 Warning lamp leads and bulb holders
7 Earth lead and terminal

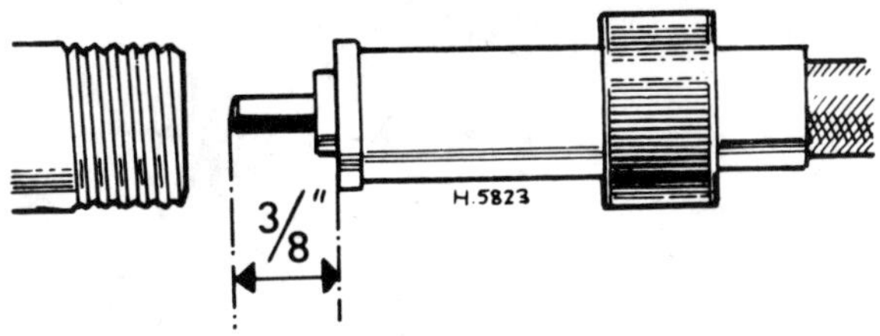

Fig. 10.107 Correct speedometer inner cable projection (Sec 63)

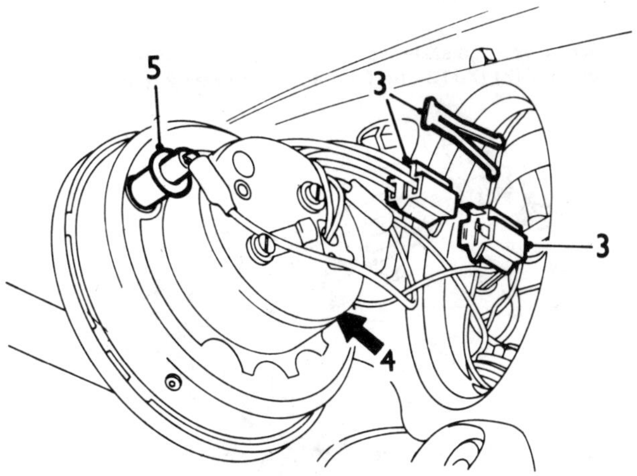

Fig. 10.108 Tachometer removal (XJ12 and Double Six, Series 1) (Sec 64)

3 *Plug and socket*
4 *Earth connection*
5 *Tachometer illumination bulb*

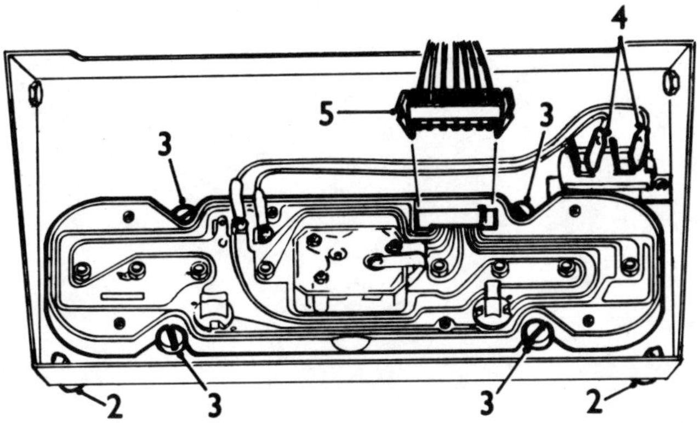

Fig. 10.109 Rear view of instrument panel (XJ12 and Double Six, Series 1) (Sec 64)

2 *Knurled retaining screws*
3 *Cheese-headed screws*
4 *Voltage stabiliser*
5 *Multi-pin harness connector*

The upper end of the inner cable should project by $\frac{3}{8}$ in (9.52 mm) to ensure correct engagement.

64 Tachometer (XJ12 and Double Six, Series 1) – removal and refitting

1 Disconnect the battery.
2 Apply hand pressure to the front of the instrument and turn it anti-clockwise until its bayonet fixing is released.
3 Withdraw the tachometer until the bulb holder for instrument illumination can be pulled from the casing. Disconnect the multi-pin plug and socket and the earth lead.
4 Refitting is the reverse of removal.

65 Supplementary instruments (XJ12 and Double Six, Series 1) – removal and refitting

1 The following instruments can be removed as a complete sub panel:

Battery condition indicator
Clock
Oil gauge
Coolant temperature gauge

2 Disconnect the battery.
3 Remove the two knurled retaining screws and lower the instrument panel.
4 Pull the leads from the instrument voltage stabiliser and withdraw the wiring harness connector plug from its socket.
5 Unscrew and remove the four setscrews and lift the sub panel away.
6 Extract the six screws which hold the back panel to the sub panel. Disconnect the clock leads and withdraw the back panel complete with instruments.
7 The individual instruments can be removed from the back panel if the two securing nuts are unscrewed.
8 The printed circuit board is removable once the instruments have been withdrawn.
9 A faulty instrument voltage stabiliser can give rise to incorrect readings on the instruments, and should be suspected if the fuel contents and coolant temperature gauges malfunction at the same time.
10 Refitting is a reversal of removal. Take care not to damage the gauge needles as the gauges are pushed into the housing, and do not scratch the printed circuit.
11 Do not reverse the leads to the electric clock. The clock must be re-started as soon as the battery is re-connected otherwise it may be damaged. To start the clock and reset the time, pull out the knob on the front of the clock, turn to the correct time and release it. Fast or slow correction is made by turning the small slotted screw on the back of the clock.

66 Speedometer, inner cable and tachometer (XJ12 and Double Six, Series 2 on) – removal and refitting

1 The operations are as described for earlier models in Sections 62, 63 and 64.

67 Supplementary instruments (XJ12 and Double Six, Series 2 on) – removal and refitting

1 The following instruments can all be removed individually from the facia panel using the same method:

Battery condition indicator
Oil pressure gauge
Coolant temperature gauge
Fuel gauge

2 Disconnect the battery.
3 Remove the speedometer or tachometer as necessary to gain access to the instrument holding strap and knurled nut. Remove the nut and strap.

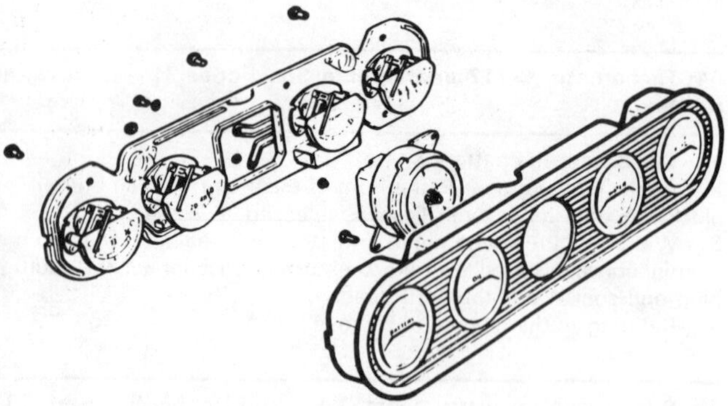

Fig. 10.110 Instrument housing (XJ12 and Double Six, Series 1) (Sec 65)

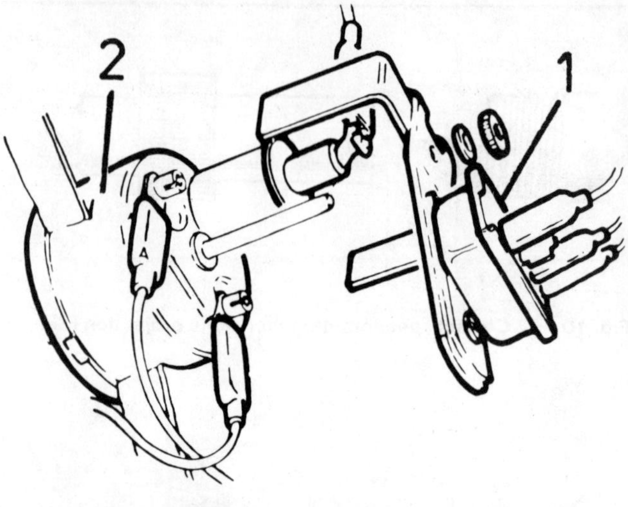

Fig. 10.111 Voltage stabiliser (1) attached to battery condition indicator (2) (XJ12 and Double Six, Series 2) (Sec 67)

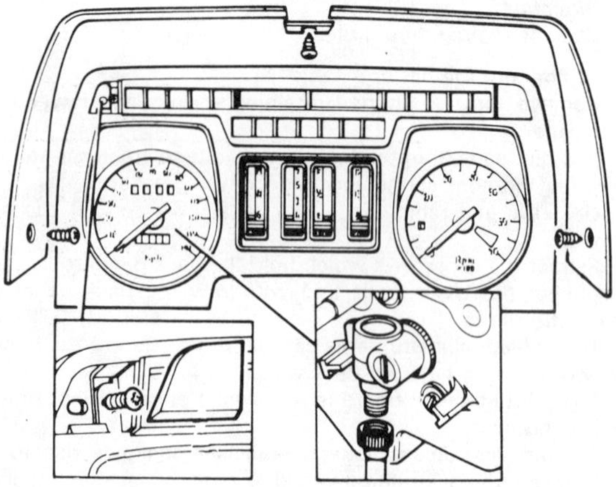

Fig. 10.112 Instrument panel and gauges (XJS) (Sec 69)

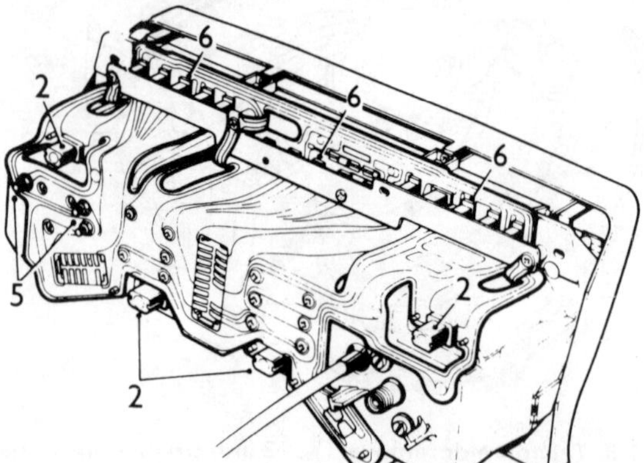

Fig. 10.113 Rear view of instrument panel (XJS) (Sec 69)

2 *Illumination bulb holders*
5 *Printed circuit-to-tachometer fixing nuts*
6 *Warning lamp bulb holders*

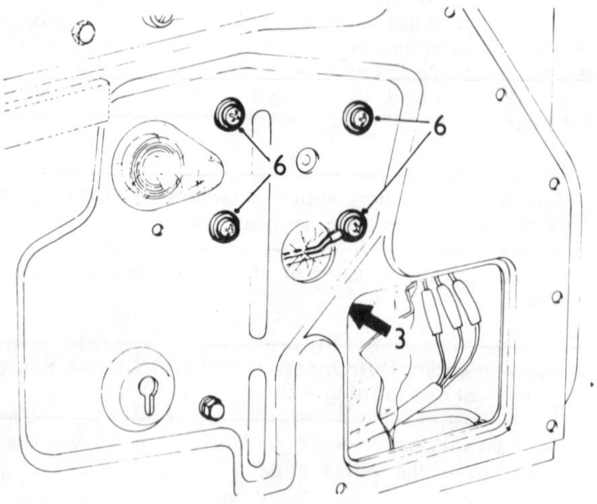

Fig. 10.114 Front window lift motors (XJ12 and Double Six, 4-door) (Sec 72)

3 *Harness plug and socket*
6 *Regulator mounting screws*

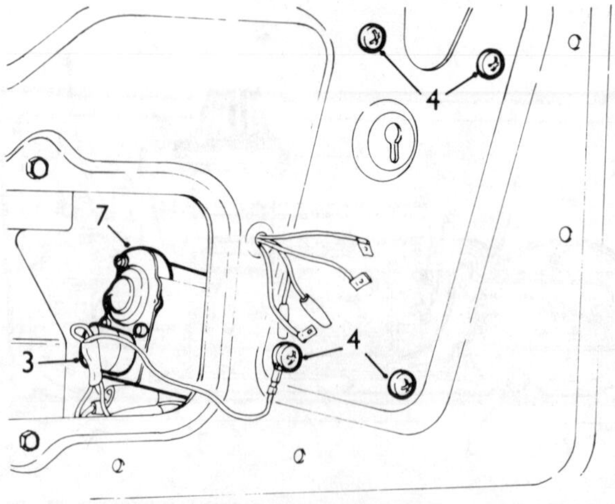

Fig. 10.115 Rear window lift motors (XJ12 and Double Six, 4-door) (Sec 72)

3 *Harness plug*
4 *Regulator mounting screws*
7 *Motor*

4 Withdraw the instrument from the facia panel until the electrical leads and illumination bulb holder can be detached from it.
5 The instrument voltage stabiliser is attached to the mounting strap of the battery condition indicator. Refer to Section 65, paragraph 9.
6 The clock can be removed simply by levering it from the facia panel. Note the position of the leads before disconnectimg them.
7 Refitting is a reversal of removal, but refer to Section 65, paragraph 11 in respect of the electric clock.

68 Speedometer inner cable (XJS) – renewal

1 Remove the under scuttle casing from the passenger side (see Chapter 12).
2 Reach up behind the instrument panel and disconnect the cable from the speedometer by unscrewing the knurled nut which holds the cable to the right-angled drive unit.
3 Grip the end of the inner cable and withdraw it from its conduit. If the inner cable has broken, the transmission end of the conduit will have to be disconnected to retrieve the lower section of the inner cable.
4 Insert the new cable from the speedometer end, having applied thin grease sparingly to the lower two thirds of its length.

69 Instrument panel and gauges (XJS) – removal and refitting

1 Disconnect the battery.
2 Remove the under scuttle casing from the driver's side.
3 Extract the screws and the surround from around the instrument panel.
4 Prise off the covers from the screw heads at each end of the warning lamp strip. Unscrew and remove the screws which will release the instrument panel from the facia.
5 Pull the panel forward until the speedometer cable can be disconnected from the rear of the speedometer and the wiring harness disconnected.
6 Slacken the adjustment ring on the steering wheel and pull it upwards as far as possible to provide clearance for the complete removal of the instrument panel.
7 Extract the seven screws and remove the lens from the panel.
8 The individual instruments (excluding the speedometer) can be removed if the screws or nuts holding the printed circuit to the instrument are first withdrawn and then the mounting screws or spire nuts extracted. Take care not to scratch or damage the printed circuit board.
9 The speedometer can be removed from the panel if the right-angled drivegear assembly is first detached by unscrewing the knurled ring.
10 Refitting is a reversal of removal.

70 Clock (XJS) – removal and refitting

1 Disconnect the battery and prise the clock out of the switch panel.
2 Pull the bulb holder from the rear of the clock casing and disconnect the electrical leads.
3 The hands of the clock are set by depressing the reset knob at the right-hand lower corner of the face. Adjustment for fast or slow correction is by means of the small screw on the back of the casing.

71 Heated rear window

1 The heating element on all cars is applied to the inside surface of the glass. Great care must be taken not to damage the element with sharp objects or, when cleaning the glass, with rings on the fingers.
2 Use only water to clean the glass and never stick labels onto the inside of the rear window if they are likely to cover any of the fine wires of the element.

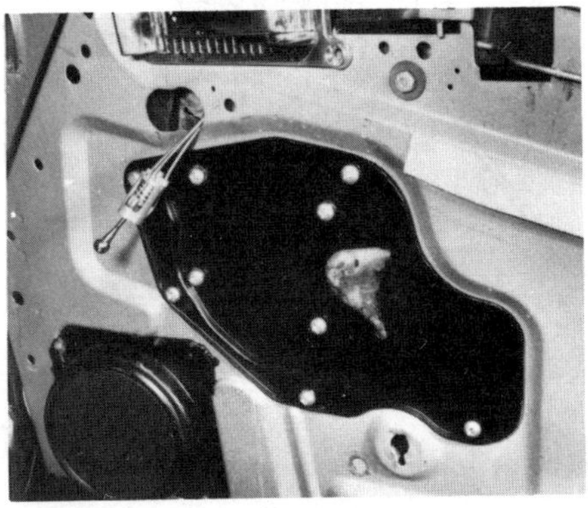

72.5A Front door window lift motor mounting plate

72.5B Front door window lift motor and regulator

72.7 Window lift motor/regulator removed

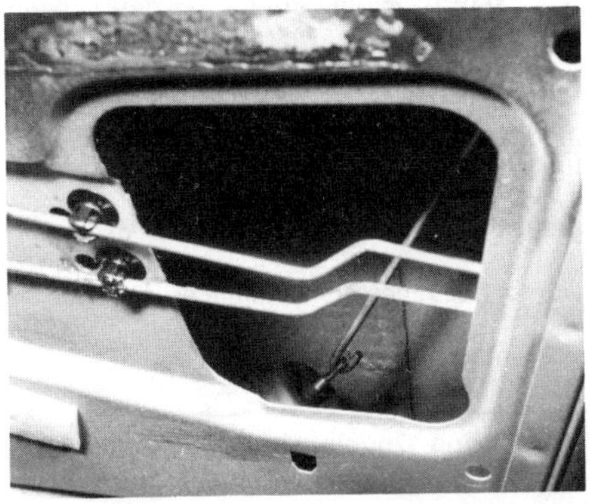

75.3A Door lock solenoid attached to pushrod

75.3B Removing door lock solenoid from a front door

78.2 Power operated aerial motor and relay within luggage boot (XJ12, Double Six – Series 3)

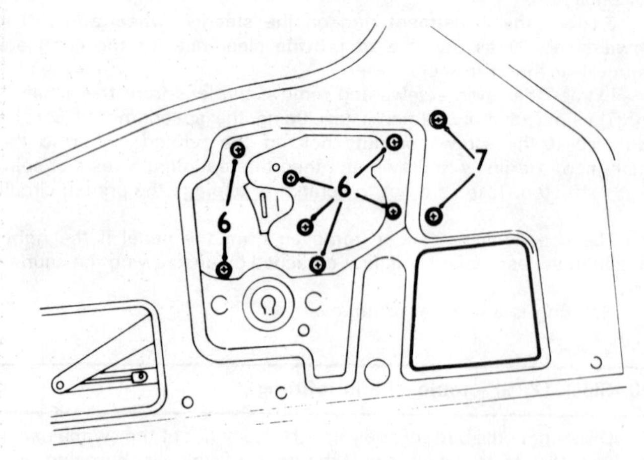

Fig. 10.116 Window lift motors (XJ12 and Double Six, 2-door) (Sec 73)

6 *Regulator mounting plate screws*
7 *Motor mounting bracket*

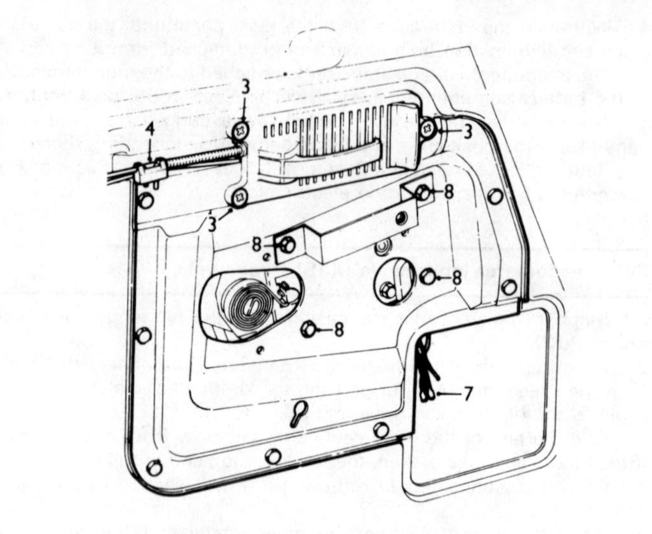

Fig. 10.117 Window lift motor (XJS) (Sec 74)

3 *Door inner handle screws*
4 *Control lever to handle connection*
7 *Motor electrical harness*
8 *Motor mounting screws*

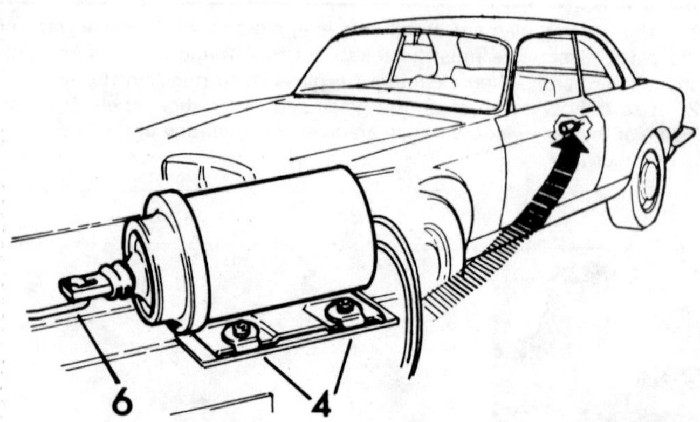

Fig. 10.118 Typical door lock solenoid (Sec 75)

4 *Mounting screws*
6 *Piston/rod connection*

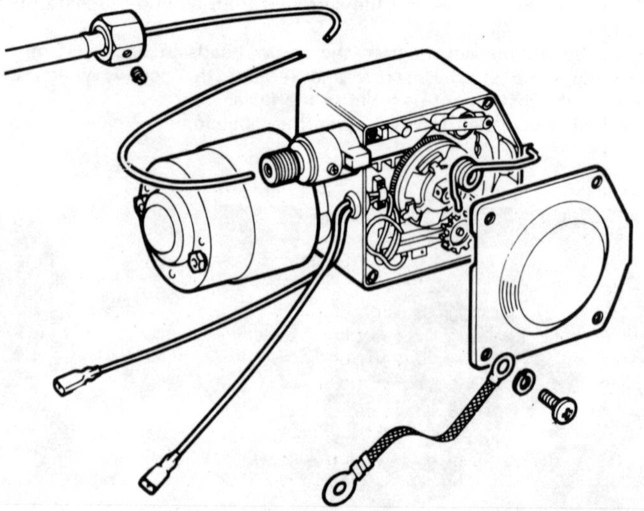

Fig. 10.119 Typical power-operated radio aerial (Sec 78)

72 Window lift motors (XJ12 and Double Six, 4-door models) – removal and refitting

Front

1 Disconnect the battery.
2 Remove the door interior trim panel and armrest as described in Chapter 12.
3 Disconnect the motor wiring harness by separating the multi-pin plug from the socket.
4 Remove the upper bolt which holds the glass channel to the door inner panel.
5 Extract the outer ring of pan-headed screws to release the window regulator mounting panel from the door panel (photos).
6 Slide the regulator towards the hinge side of the door until the arm roller clears its channel.
7 Raise the regulator arm so that it passes over the outer side of the glass channel and then remove the regulator through the aperture in the door inner panel (photo).
8 The electric motor can now be separated from the regulator mechanism after withdrawing the three setscrews.

Rear

9 Disconnect the battery.
10 Remove the door interior trim panel and armrest as described in Chapter 12.
11 Remove the four pan-headed setscrews and detach the regulator/motor from the door inner panel. Move the assembly until the regulator arm can be slipped out of its channel.
12 Withdraw the assembly through the aperture in the door inner panel, raising the glass if necessary to enable it to pass.
13 Separate the motor from the regulator mechanism by extracting the three setscrews.
14 If the motor is faulty, it must be renewed complete as it is a sealed unit.
15 Refitting is a reversal of removal.

73 Window lift motor (XJ12 and Double Six, 2-door models) – removal and refitting

Front

1 Remove the door interior trim panel and armrest as described in

Chapter 12.
2 Lower the window to 1 in (25 mm) above the door and then disconnect the battery.
3 Remove the two nuts which hold the window lift arm bobbin channel. Slide the channel from the bobbin.
4 Unscrew and remove the seven setscrews and one drive screw from the regulator mounting plate.
5 Remove the two setscrews from the motor mounting bracket, disconnect the electrical leads and withdraw the motor/regulator through the aperture in the door panel.
6 If the regulator is to be separated from the motor, clamp the regulator lifting arm and quadrant firmly together in the jaws of a vice to prevent the spring disengaging suddenly, which could cause personal injury.

Rear

7 Remove the side trim from the rear compartment and lower the window until it is horizontal.
8 Disconnect the battery.
9 Support the window with a block of wood and remove the four motor retaining screws.
10 Disconnect the wiring, detach the motor from the window channel, and withdraw the assembly through the aperture.
11 Observe the warning given in paragraph 6.

74 Window lift motor (XJS) – removal and refitting

1 Lower the window glass to its lowest position and disconnect the battery and remove the door interior trim pad as described in Chapter 12.
2 Remove the door inner handle screws and disengage the remote control levers from the handle.
3 Pull the waterproof sheet away from the motor connections and then disconnect the leads.
4 Unscrew and remove the motor mounting bolts and move the regulator assembly towards the rear edge of the door, at the same time disengaging the regulator from its channel.
5 Raise the glass and either wedge it or have an assistant retain it.
6 Extract the seven screws and remove the mounting plate.
7 Withdraw the motor/regulator assembly through the aperture in the door panel.
8 If the motor is to be separated from the regulator, clamp the regulator arm and quadrant firmly together in the jaws of a vice to prevent the spring disengaging suddenly, which could cause injury.
9 Refitting is a reversal of removal.

75 Door lock solenoid – removal and refitting

1 Raise the window to its fully closed position and then disconnect the battery.
2 Remove the door interior trim panel and armrest as described in Chapter 12.
3 Unscrew and remove the two setscrews that hold the solenoid to the door stretcher, unhook the solenoid piston from the door lock pushrod and withdraw it until the electrical leads can be disconnected. Remove the solenoid completely (photos).
4 Refit by reversing the removal operations.

76 Radio – removal and refitting

1 The following operations must be regarded as typical only. Unless the radio or cassette player has been installed as standard or factory-fitted option, the type of equipment fitted and its location may vary according to the individual manufacturer's recommendations.
2 Disconnect the battery and then remove the knobs from the radio, heater and air conditioner control levers. These usually simply pull off.
3 Remove the radio control spindle nuts and the escutcheon, then extract the screws from the front face of the radio which hold it to its mounting bracket.
4 Withdraw the radio until the aerial, power and earth leads can be disconnected from it, then lift it away.
5 Refitting is a reversal of removal.

77 Speaker – removal and refitting

1 Disconnect the battery.
2 Remove the door interior trim panel, armrest and casing.
3 Disconnect the leads from the speaker and unbolt the speaker flange from the door panel and remove the speaker.
4 The speaker grille can be levered from the trim panel, but take care not to damage the trim.
5 Refitting is a reversal of removal.

78 Power-operated aerial – removal and refitting

1 Fully extend the aerial and then disconnect the battery.
2 Remove the luggage compartment floor, the spare wheel and the cover from the fuel pump (photo).
3 Release the aerial motor mounting clip and disconnect the electrical leads.
4 Remove the cover plate from the motor gearbox, detach the earth strap and then carefully release the pressure roller spring.
5 Release the grub screw and nut which secure the flexible drive and then pull the nylon drive from the motor gearbox.
6 Retract the aerial by hand and unscrew the aerial retaining nut. Remove the curved adaptor plate and the weather seal.
7 The rear lamp cluster may have to be removed before the aerial can be withdrawn from inside the rear wing.
8 Refitting is a reversal of removal.

79 Fault diagnosis – electrical system

Symptom	Reason(s)
Starter fails to turn engine	Battery discharged Battery defective internally Battery terminal leads loose or earth lead not securely attached to body Loose or broken connections in starter motor circuit Starter motor switch or solenoid faulty Starter brushes badly worn, sticking, or brush wires loose Commutator dirty, worn or burnt Starter motor armature faulty Field coils earthed
Starter turns engine very slowly	Battery in discharged condition Starter brushes badly worn, sticking or brush wires loose Loose wires in starter motor circuit
Starter spins but does not turn engine	Pinion or flywheel gear teeth broken or worn Battery discharged

Symptom	Reason/s
Starter motor noisy or excessively rough engagement	Pinion or flywheel gear teeth broken or worn Starter motor retaining bolts loose
Battery will not hold charge for more than a few days	Battery defective internally Electrolyte level too low or electrolyte too weak due to leakage Plate separators no longer fully effective Battery plates severely sulphated Alternator drivebelt slipping Battery terminal connections loose or corroded Alternator not charging Short in lighting circuit causing continual battery drain Alternator internal regulator unit not working correctly
Ignition light fails to go out, battery runs flat in a few days	Alternator drivebelt loose and slipping or broken Alternator brushes worn, sticking, broken or dirty Alternator brush springs weak or broken Internal fault in alternator

Failure of individual electrical equipment to function correctly is dealt with alphabetically, item by item, under the headings listed below

Electrically-operated windows

Complete system failure	Faulty control box Blown fuse Overloaded circuit breaker
Driver's window normal, remainder inoperative	Sticking switch Circuit earthed
Failure of one window only	Faulty switch Poor electrical connection Stiff mechanism or sticking window

Horn

Horn emits intermittent or unsatisfactory noise	Cable connections loose Horn incorrectly adjusted
Horn fails to operate	Blown fuse Cable or cable connection loose, broken or disconnected Horn has an internal fault
Horn operates all the time	Horn push either earthed or stuck down Horn cable to horn push earthed

Lights

Lights come on but fade out	If engine not running battery discharged Wire connections loose, disconnected or broken Light switch shorting, disconnected or broken Light switch shorting or otherwise faulty
Lights do not come on	If engine not running, battery discharged Wire connections loose, disconnected or broken Light switch shorting or otherwise faulty
Lights give very poor illumination	Lamp glasses dirty Lamps badly out of adjustment
Lights work erratically – flashing on and off, especially over bumps	Battery terminals or earth connection loose Lights not earthing properly Contacts in light switch faulty

Wipers

Wiper motor fails to work	Blown fuse Wire connections loose, disconnected or broken Brushes badly worn Armature worn or faulty Field coils faulty
Wiper motor works but wiper blades remain static	Wiper motor gearbox parts badly worn Stripped splines on wheelbox spindles

Symptom	Reason/s
Wiper motor works slowly and takes little current	Brushes badly worn Commutator dirty, greasy or burnt Armature badly worn or faulty
Wiper motor works very slowly and takes excessive current	Commutator dirty, greasy or burnt Armature bearings dirty or unaligned Armature badly worn or faulty

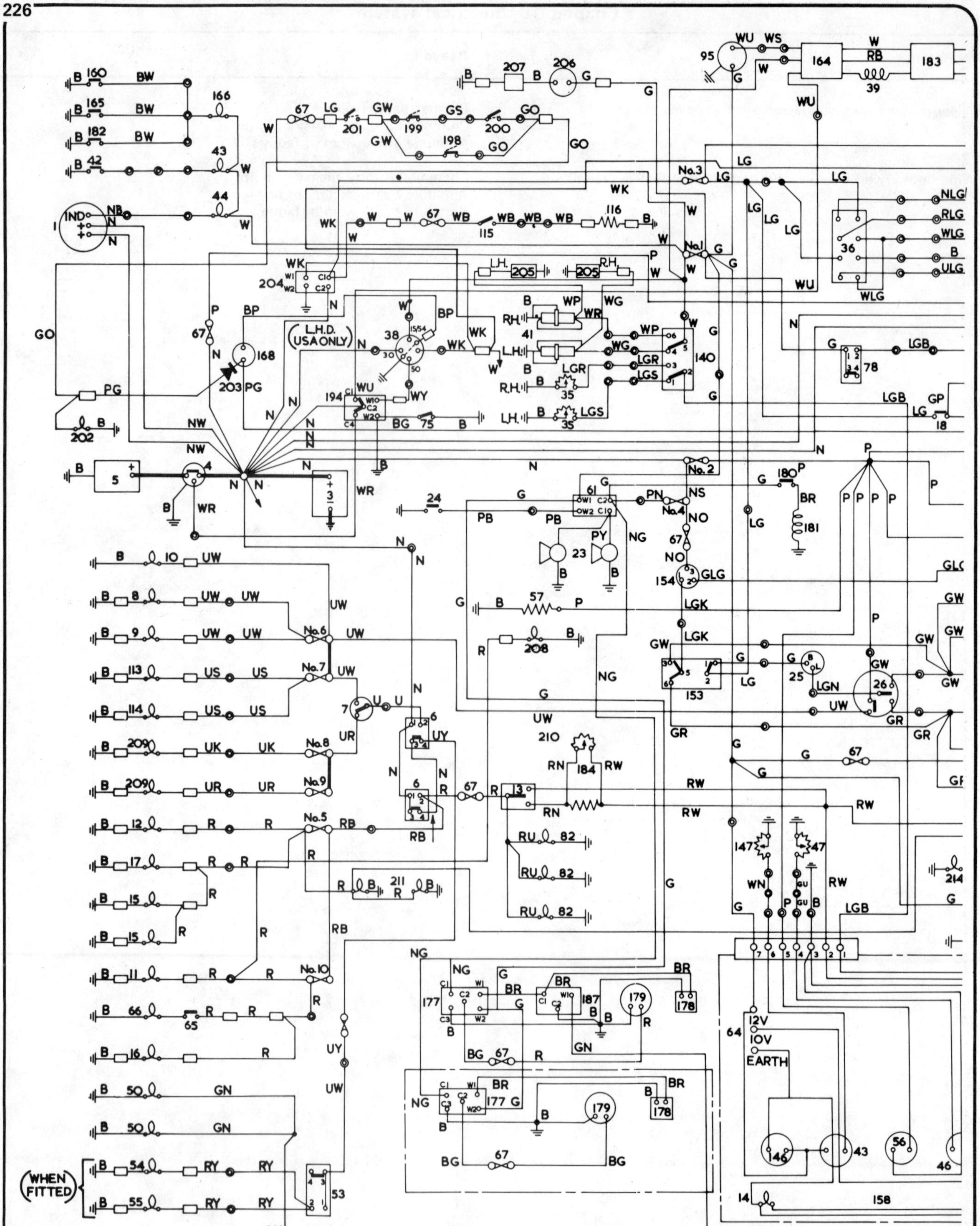

Fig. 10.120 Wiring diagram for XJ12 and Double Six, Series 1

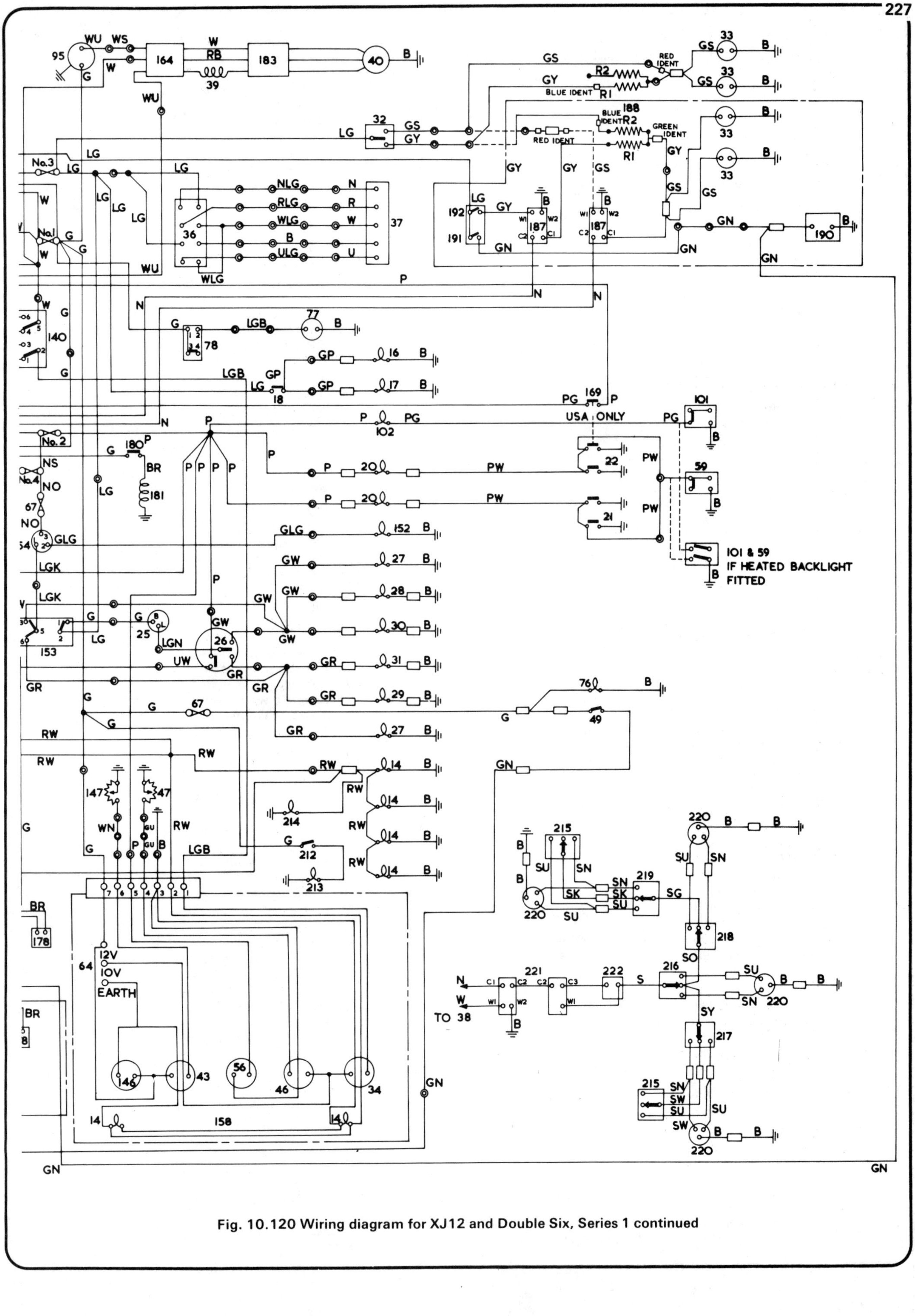

Fig. 10.120 Wiring diagram for XJ12 and Double Six, Series 1 continued

Fig. 10.120 Wiring diagram for XJ12 and Double Six, Series 1

1 Alternator
3 Battery (12V)
4 Starter solenoid
5 Starter motor
6 Lighting switch
7 Headlamp dipswitch
8 RH headlamp
9 LH headlamp
10 Main beam warning lamp
11 RH sidelamp
12 LH sidelamp
13 Panel lamps switch
14 Panel lamps
15 Number plate illumination lamps
16 RH stop & tail lamp
17 LH stop & tail lamp
18 Stop lamp switch
20 Interior lights
21 RH door switch
22 LH door switch
23 Horns
24 Horn push
25 Flasher unit
26 Direction indicator switch
27 Direction indicator warning lamp
28 RH front flasher lamp
29 LH front flasher lamp
30 RH rear flasher lamp
31 LH rear flasher lamp
32 Heater or fresh air motor switch
33 Heater or fresh air motors
34 Fuel gauge
35 Fuel gauge tank unit
36 Windscreen wiper switch
37 Windscreen wiper motor
38 Ignition switch
39 Ignition coil
40 Distributor
41 Fuel pumps
42 Oil pressure switch
43 Oil pressure warning lamp or gauge
44 Ignition or no charge warning lamp
46 Water temperature gauge
47 Water temperature transmitter
49 Reversing lamp switch
50 Reversing lamps
53 Fog lamp switch
54 RH fog lamp
55 LH fog lamp
56 Clock
57 Cigar lighter
59 Interior light switch
61 Horn relay
64 Bi-metal instrument voltage stabiliser
65 Boot light switch
66 Boot light
67 Line fuse
75 Automatic gearbox safety switch
76 Automatic gearbox selector indicator lamp
77 Electric windscreen washer
78 Electric windscreen washer switch
82 Switch illumination lamps
95 Tachometer
101 Map light switch
102 Map light
113 RH headlamp inner (4 headlamps)
114 LH headlamp inner (4 headlamps)
115 Rear window demist switch
116 Rear window demist unit
140 Fuel tank changeover switch
146 Battery condition indicator
147 Oil pressure transmitter
152 Hazard warning lamp
153 Hazard warning switch
154 Hazard warning flasher unit
158 Printed circuit instrument panel
160 Split brake differential switch
164 Ballast resistor
165 Handbrake switch
166 Handbrake warning lamp
168 Ignition key warning buzzer
169 Buzzer door switch
177 Radiator cooling fan relay
178 Radiator cooling fan thermostat
179 Radiator cooling fan motor
180 Auto transmission kickdown switch
181 Auto transmission kickdown solenoid
182 Brake fluid level switch
183 Opus ignition amplifier
184 Panel light resistor
187 Air conditioning relay
188 Air conditioning resistor
190 Air conditioning compressor
191 Air conditioning thermostat switch
192 Air conditioning control switch
194 Starter solenoid/ballast coil relay
198 Driver's seat belt switch
199 Passenger's seat belt switch
200 Passenger's seat switch
201 Seat belt warning gearbox switch
202 Seat belt warning lamp
203 Blocking diode-seat belt warning
204 Ignition protection relay
205 Fuel solenoid valves
206 Battery cooling fan motor
207 Battery cooling thermostat
208 Cigar lighter illumination
209 Left-right hand dipped beam
210 Panel light rheostat
211 Heater panel illumination
212 Choke warning light switch
213 Choke warning light
214 Choke control illumination
215 Window lift master switch
216 Window lift switch (front) RH
217 Window lift switch (rear) RH
218 Window lift switch (front) LH
219 Window lift switch (rear) LH
220 Window lift motor
221 Window lift safety relay
222 Window lift circuit breaker

Colour code for wiring diagrams

N	Brown	B	Black
U	Blue	O	Orange
R	Red	P	Purple
K	Pink	G	Green
W	White	L	Light
Y	Yellow	S	Slate

When a cable has two colour code letters, the first denotes the main colour and the second the tracer colour

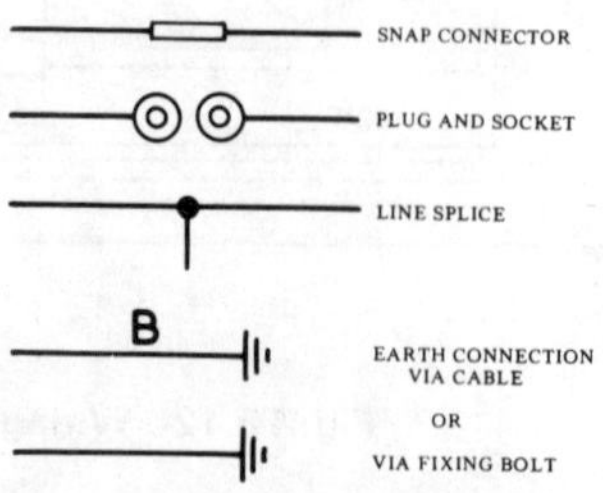

Fig. 10.121 Wiring diagram for XJ12 and Double Six, Series 2

Component	Grid Ref	No	Component	Grid Ref	No
Alternator	*DE2*	*1*	*Ignition coil*	*N1*	*39*
Aerial Motor	*K7*	*185*	*Ignition protection relay*	*G7*	*204*
Aerial motor relay	*J7*	*186*	*Ignition switch*	*H2*	*38*
Air conditioning/Heater Circuit (to)	*J7*	*139*	*Ignition warning lamp*	*B2*	*44*
Air conditioning relay	*K12*	*187*	*Inertia switch*	*N3*	*250*
Automatic gearbox kickdown solenoid	*J12*	*181*	*Interior lights*	*Q10*	*20*
Automatic gearbox kickdown switch	*J12*	*180*	*Interior light switch*	*T10*	*59*
Automatic gearbox safety switch	*J1*	*75*	*Left & Right hand dipped beam lamps*	*B3*	*209*
Ballast resistor	*MN1*	*164*	*Lighting switch*	*E5*	*6*
Battery	*E1*	*3*	*Line fuse*	*G3*	*67*
Battery condition indicator	*MN2*	*146*	*Main beam warning lamp*	*B5*	*10*
Battery cooling fan motor	*E12*	*206*	*Main relay*	*Y7*	*304*
Battery cooling fan thermostat	*E12*	*207*	*Map light*	*Q9*	*102*
Bi-metal instrument voltage stabiliser	*L2*	*64*	*Map light switch*	*R9*	*101*
Blocking diode – Brake warning	*B2*	*256*	*Number plate lamps*	*B7*	*15*
Blocking diodes – direction indicators	*C10*	*289*	*Oil pressure switch*	*A2*	*42*
Boot light	*B8*	*66*	*Oil pressure transmitter*	*P1*	*147*
Boot light – switch	*C8*	*65*	*Oil pressure warning lamp or gauge*	*M1*	*43*
Brake fluid level switch	*A1*	*182*	*Output unit*	*U3*	*292*
Cigar lighter	*M10*	*57*	*Overdrive control switch*	*S2*	*72*
Cigar lighter illumination	*E7*	*208*	*Overdrive gearbox switch*	*S2*	*73*
Clock	*P11*	*56*	*Overdrive solenoid*	*S3*	*71*
Cold start relay	*U7*	*299*	*Panel lamps*	*Q8*	*14*
Cold start valve i	*U8*	*300*	*Panel lamps rheostat*	*N7*	*210*
Cold start valve ii	*U8*	*301*	*Pressure sensor*	*V8*	*302*
Control unit	*U3*	*292*	*Pump relay*	*Y7*	*305*
Direction indicator switch	*D10*	*26*	*Radiator cooling fan motor*	*M11*	*179*
Direction indicator warning lamps	*B10*	*27*	*Radiator cooling fan thermostat*	*K11*	*178*
Distributor	*Q1*	*40*	*Radiator fan motor relay*	*K11*	*177*
Door lock solenoid	*Q6*	*257*	*Radio*	*H6*	*60*
Door lock solenoid relay	*N6*	*258*	*Rear fog guard lamp*	*A8, B8*	*288*
Door lock switch	*M6*	*260*	*Rear fog guard switch*	*B8*	*286*
Door switch LH	*R10*	*22*	*Rear fog guard warning lamp*	*C9*	*287*
Door switch RH	*R10*	*21*	*Rear window demist switch*	*F8*	*115*
EGR Control box	*U1*	*291*	*Rear window demist unit*	*F10*	*116*
EGR Valves	*U2*	*294*	*Rear window demist warning light*	*B12*	*150*
EGR Warning diode	*B1*	*284*	*Reversing lamps*	*T2*	*50*
EGR Warning lamp	*C1*	*278*	*Reversing lamp switch*	*S1*	*49*
EGR Warning switch	*A1*	*277*	*Revolution counter*	*K1*	*95*
Electric windscreen washer	*F12*	*77*	*Seat belt switch – driver*	*L4*	*198*
Electric windscreen washer switch	*D12*	*78*	*Seat belt warning lamp*	*K5*	*202*
Emission control valve solenoid	*J12*	*252*	*Seat belt warning control unit*	*REV*	*290*
Emission control valve switch	*J12*	*253*	*Side lamp LH*	*B6*	*12*
Fibre optics illumination lamp	*P8*	*255*	*Side lamp RH*	*B7*	*11*
Flasher unit	*E9*	*25*	*Split brake differential switch*	*A1*	*160*
Flasher lamp, Front, LH	*B10*	*29*	*Split brake test switch & warning lamp*	*B1*	*159*
Flasher lamp, Front RH	*B9*	*28*	*Starter Motor*	*D1*	*5*
Flasher lamp, Rear, LH	*B11*	*31*	*Starter solenoid*	*F1*	*4*
Flasher lamp, Rear, RH	*B9*	*30*	*Starter solenoid/Ballast coil relay*	*H1*	*194*
Fog lamp, LH	*B5*	*55*	*Stop and tail lamp LH*	*B11*	*17*
Fog lamp, RH	*B5*	*54*	*Stop and tail lamp RH*	*B11*	*16*
Fuel gauge	*M2*	*34*	*Stoplamp switch*	*D11*	*18*
Fuel gauge tank unit	*R2,3*	*35*	*Temperature sensor, air*	*T8*	*297*
Fuel injectors	*U4*	*296*	*Temperature sensor, coolant*	*Y8*	*307*
Fuel pump	*R3*	*41*	*Thermal circuit breaker*	*L6*	*259*
Fuel pump solenoid	*S3*	*205*	*Thermal override switch*	*H12*	*285*
Fuel tank changeover switch	*Q3*	*140*	*Thermo switch EGR*	*U2*	*295*
Handbrake switch	*A2*	*165*	*Thermo time switch*	*U8*	*298*
Handbrake warning lamp	*B2*	*166*	*Throttle switch*	*W8*	*303*
Handbrake warning flasher unit	*E9*	*154*	*Trigger unit*	*X8*	*306*
Hazard warning lamp	*B9*	*152*	*Water temperature gauge*	*N2*	*46*
Hazard warning switch	*D9*	*153*	*Water temperature transmitter*	*Q2*	*47*
Headlamp dip switch	*E3*	*7*	*Window lift master switch*	*N4*	*215*
Headlamp, Inner, LH	*B4*	*114*	*Window lift motor*	*PQRT4*	*220*
Headlamp, Inner, RH	*B4*	*113*	*Window lift safety relay*	*M5*	*221*
Headlamp, Outer, LH	*B4*	*9*	*Window lift switch, Front, LH*	*Q5*	*218*
Headlamp, Outer, RH	*B4*	*8*	*Window lift switch, Front RH*	*P5*	*216*
Headlamp relay	*D4*	*231*	*Window lift switch, Rear, LH*	*R5*	*219*
Horns	*H12*	*23*	*Window lift switch, Rear, RH*	*R5*	*217*
Horn push	*G12*	*24*	*Windscreen wiper motor*	*M9*	*37*
Horn relay	*G11*	*61*	*Windscreen wiper relay*	*K8*	*251*
Ignition amplifier – OPUS	*P1*	*183*	*Windscreen wiper switch*	*K9*	*36*

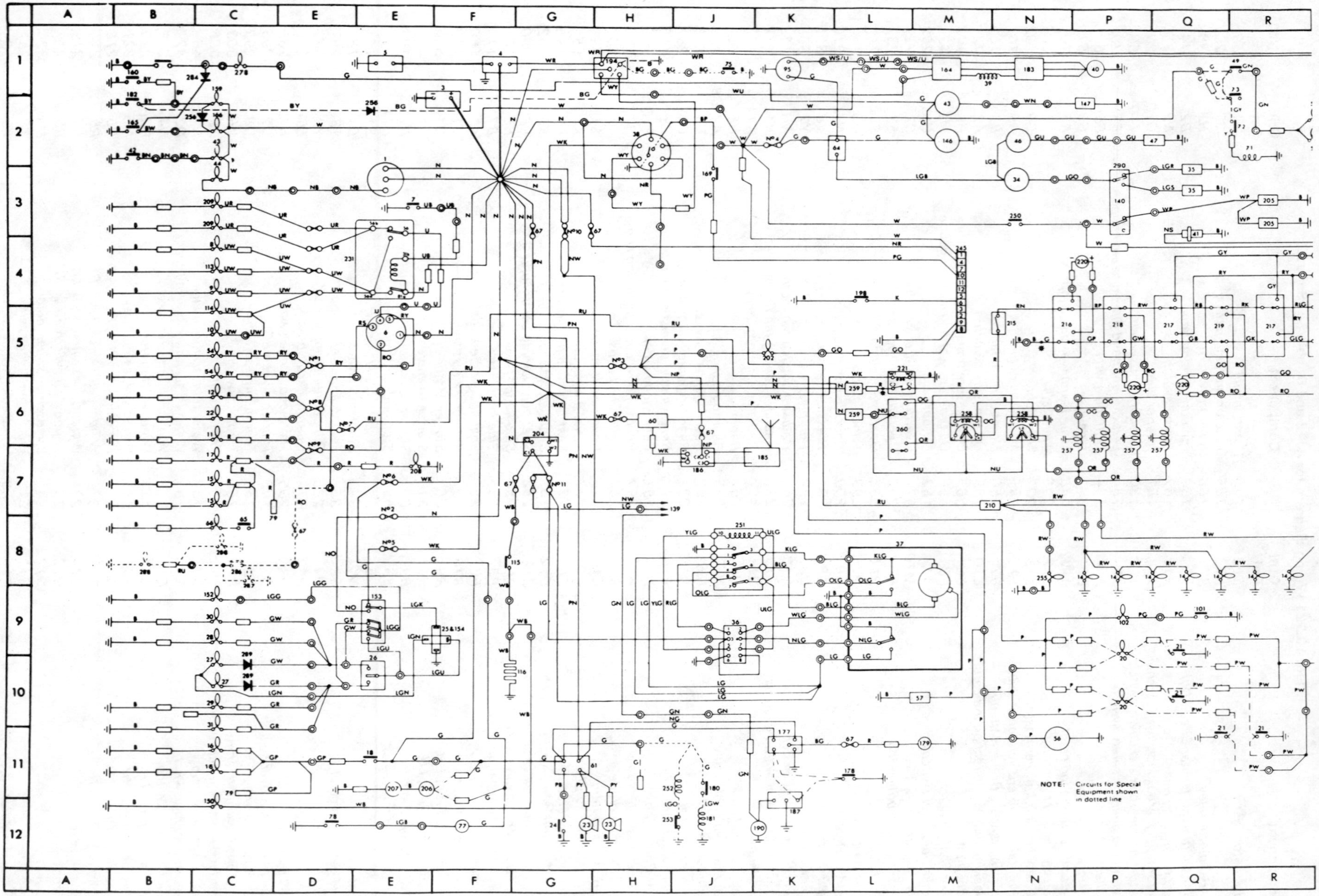

Fig. 10.121 Wiring diagram for XJ12 and Double Six, Series 2

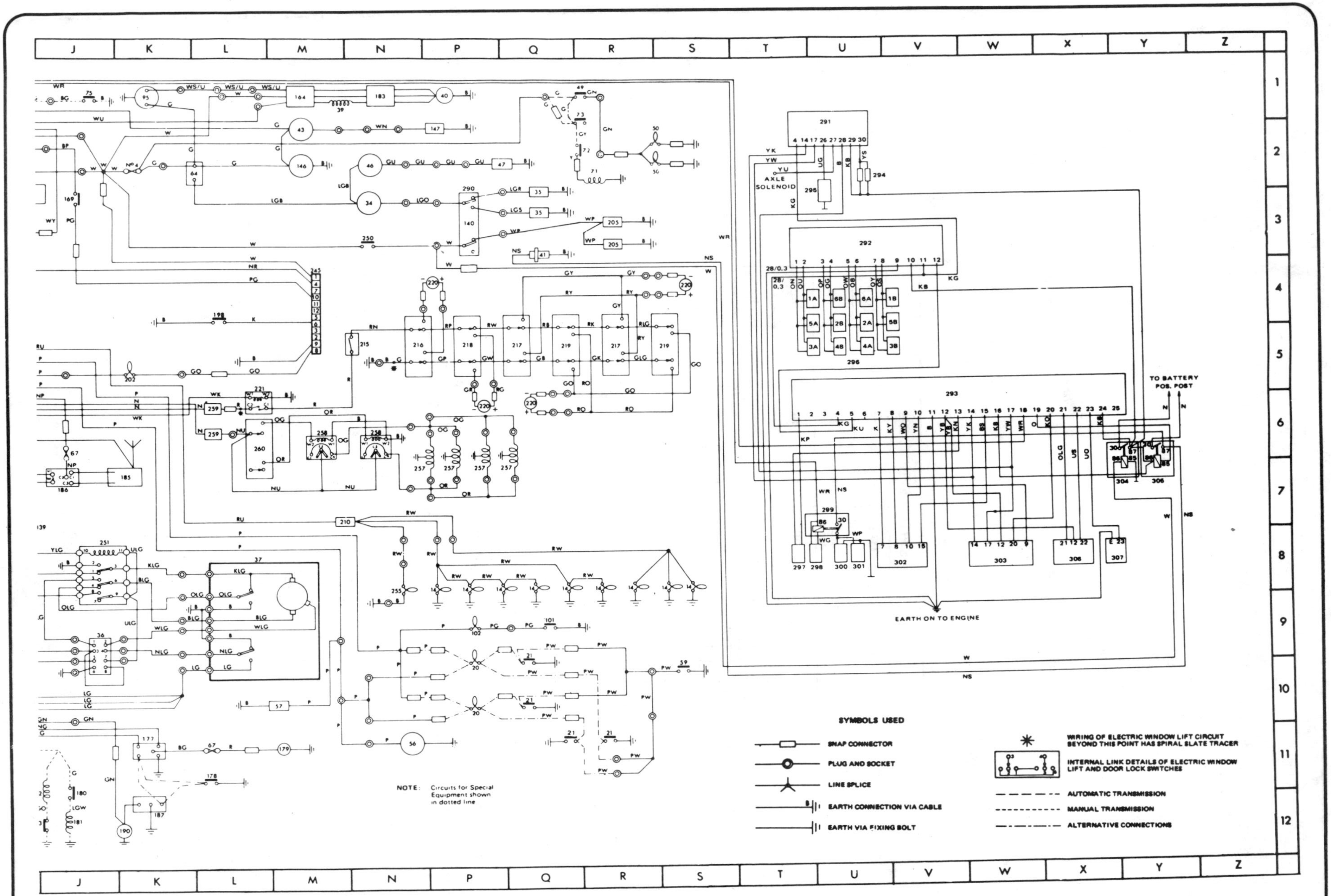

Fig. 10. 121 Wiring diagram for XJ12 and Double Six, Series 2 (continued)

Fig. 10.122 Wiring diagram air conditioning system, Series 2 cars

33 Blower motors
47 Water temperature transmitter
187 Air conditioning relays
188 Air conditioning resistors
190 Air conditioning compressor
191 Air conditioning thermostat
192 Air conditioning control switches
261 Air conditioning amplifier unit
262 Air conditioning servo control unit
263 Vacuum solenoid valve
264 In car temperature sensor
265 Ambient temperature sensor

SWITCH FUNCTIONS						
MICRO SWITCH		OFF	LO	AUTO	HI	DEF
A	DEFROST	nc	nc	nc	nc	no
B	HIGH SPEED	no	nc	no	nc	nc
C	ON/OFF	no	nc	nc	nc	nc
D	LOW SPEED	no	no	nc	nc	nc

nc - NORMALLY CLOSED
no - NORMALLY OPEN

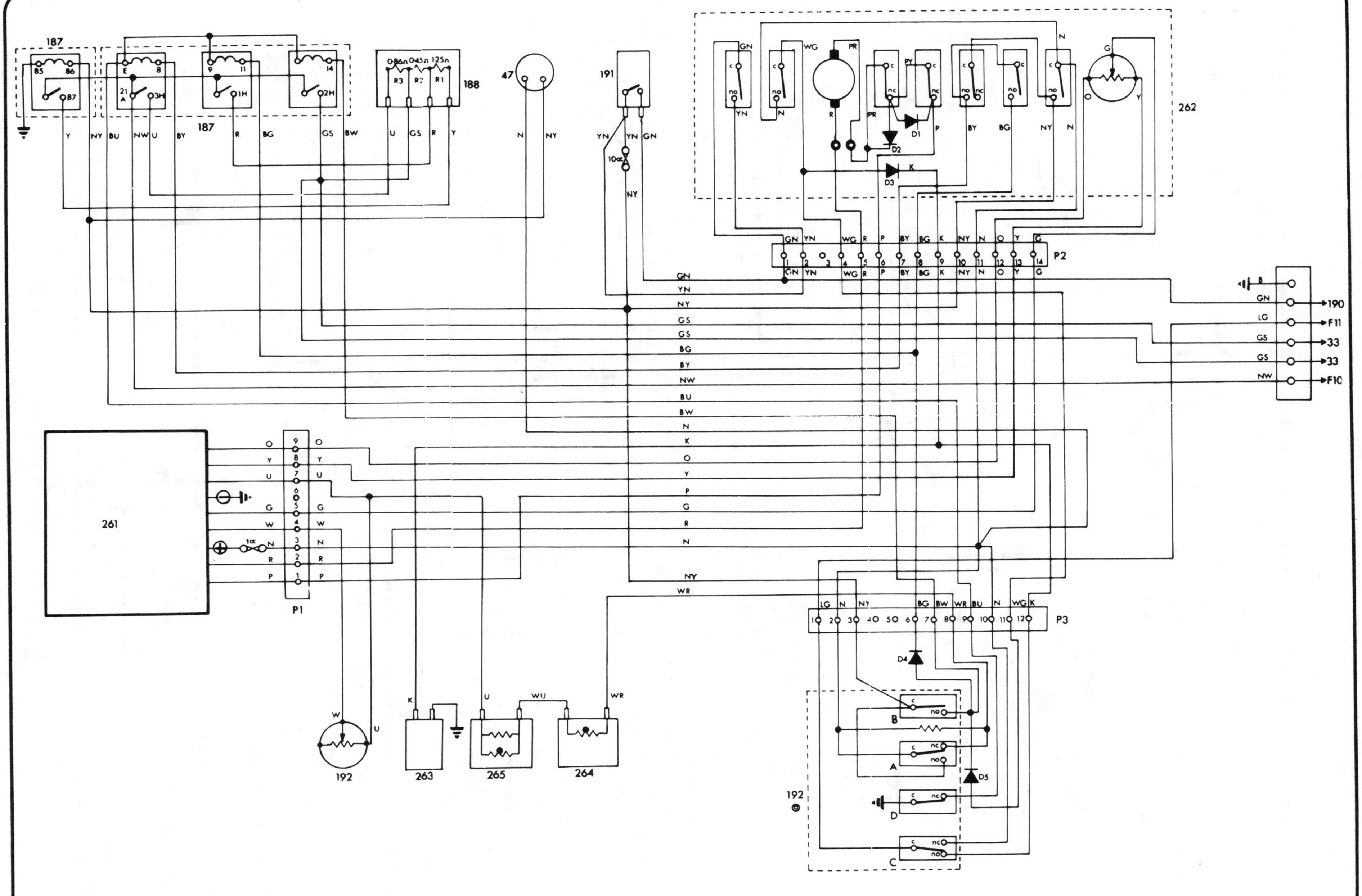

Fig. 10.122 Wiring diagram air conditioning system, Series 2 cars

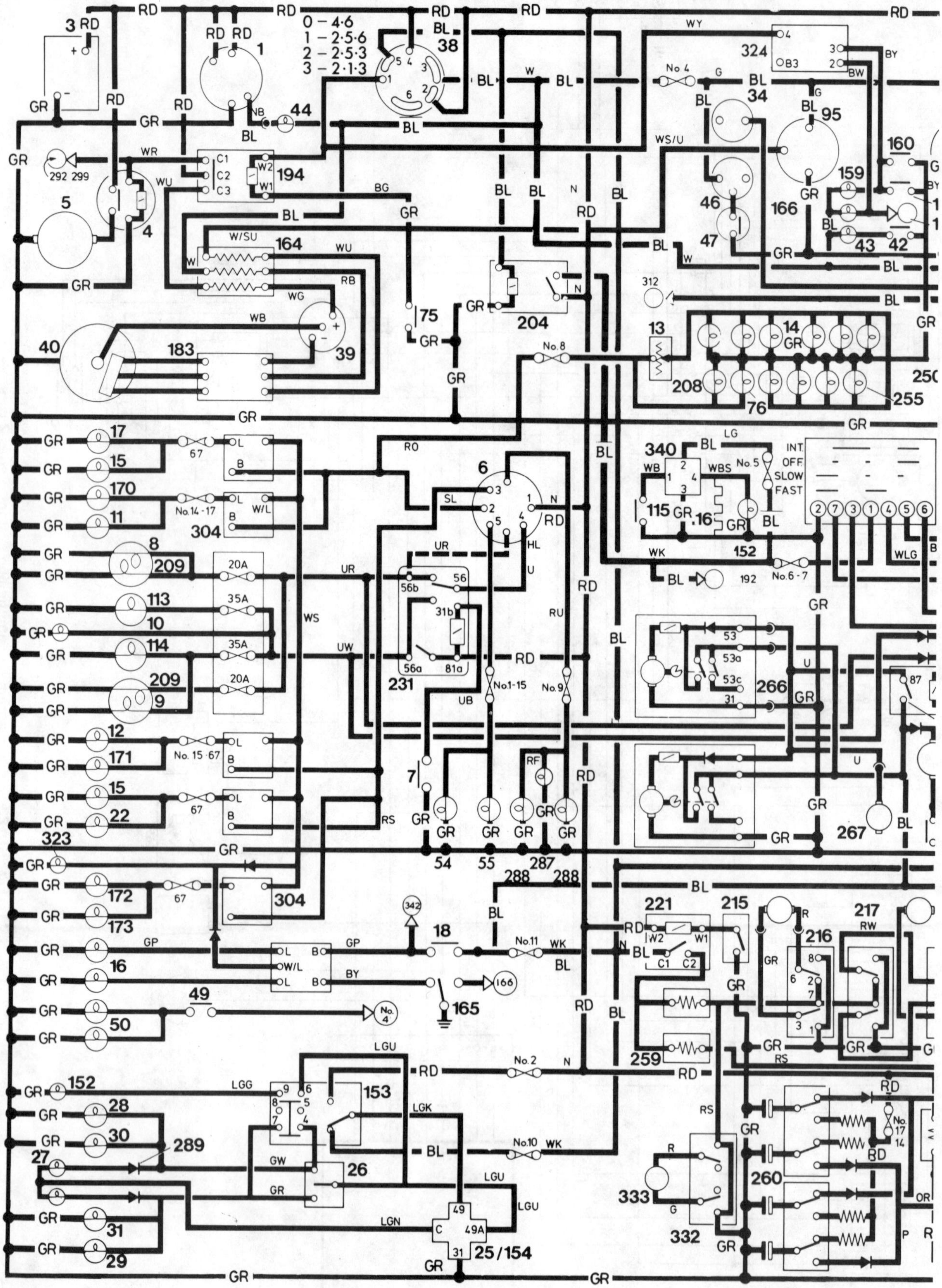

Fig. 10.123 Wiring diagram for XJ12 and Double Six, Series 3

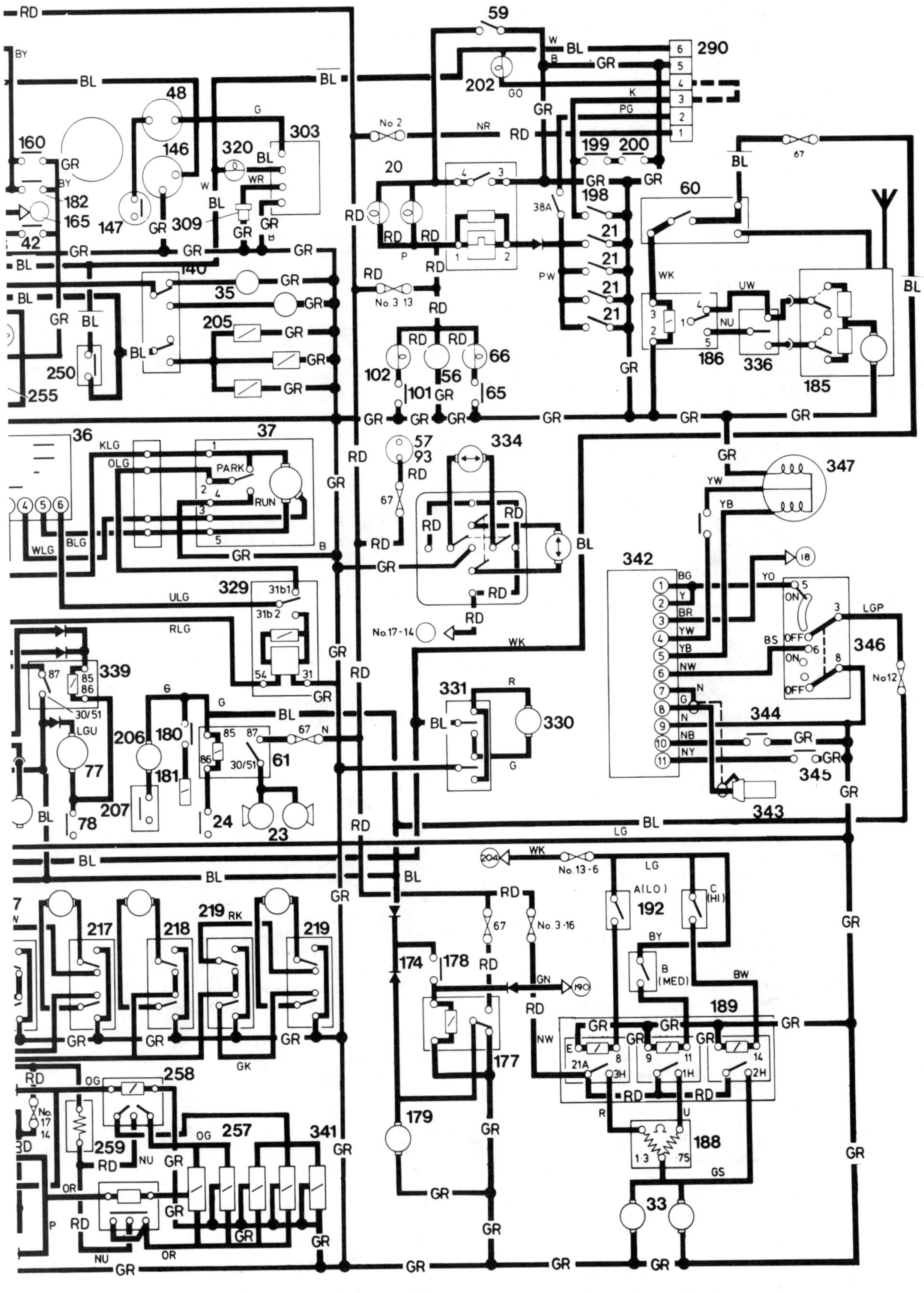

Fig. 10.123 Wiring diagram for XJ12 and Double Six, Series 3 - continued

Fig. 10.123 Wiring diagram for XJ12 and Double Six, Series 3

1 Alternator
3 Battery
4 Starter solenoid
5 Starter motor
6 Master lighting switch
7 Headlamp flash switch
8 Headlamp beam RH
9 Headlamp beam LH
10 Main beam warning light
11 RH Sidelamp
12 LH Sidelamp
13 Panel lamp rheostat
14 Panel lamps
15 Number plate illumination lamp(s)
16 Stop lamp(s)
17 Tail lamp RH
18 Stoplamp switch
19 Fuse box(es)
20 Interior light(s)
21 Door switch
22 Tail lamp LH
23 Horn(s)
24 Horn push
25 Flasher unit (part of 154)
26 Direction indicator switch
27 Direction indicator warning lights
28 RH front flasher
29 LH front flasher
30 RH rear flasher
31 LH rear flasher
34 Fuel gauge
35 Fuel gauge tank unit
36 Windscreen wiper switch
37 Windscreen wiper motor
38 Ignition/starter switch
38A Key switch (part of 38)
39 Ignition coil
40 Distributor
42 Oil pressure switch
43 Oil pressure warning light
44 Ignition warning light
46 Coolant temperature gauge
47 Water temperature transmitter
48 Oil pressure gauge
49 Reversing lamp switch
50 Reversing lamp(s)
54 Fog lamp RH
55 Fog lamp LH
56 Clock
57 Cigar lighter socket
59 Interior light switch
60 Radio
61 Horn relay
65 Boot light switch
66 Boot light
67 Line fuse
75 Automatic transmission safety switch
76 Automatic transmission selector lamp
77 Windscreen washer pump
78 Windscreen washer switch
93 Charging and inspection lamp socket
95 Tachometer
101 Map light switch
102 Map light
113 Headlamp inner RH
114 Headlamp inner LH
115 Rear window demist switch
116 Rear window demist unit
140 Fuel changeover switch
146 Battery condition indicator
147 Oil pressure transmitter
150 Rear window demister warning light
152 Hazard warning light
153 Hazard warning switch
154 Hazard warning flasher unit
159 Brake fluid level warning light
160 Brake differential pressure switch
164 Ballast resistor
165 Handbrake switch
166 Handbrake warning light
170 Side markers RH front
171 Side markers LH front
172 Side markers RH rear
173 Side markers LH rear
174 Radiator cooling fan diode(s)
177 Radiator cooling fan relay
178 Radiator cooling fan thermostat (in pump)
179 Radiator cooling fan motor
180 Kickdown switch
181 Kickdown solenoid
182 Brake fluid level switch
183 Ignition amplifier (OPUS)
185 Aerial motor
186 Aerial motor relay
194 Starter solenoid ballast coil relay
198 Seat belt switch – driver
199 Seat belt switch – passenger) Non
200 Seat switch – passenger) Federal
202 Seat belt warning light
204 Ignition protection relay
205 Fuel solenoid valves
206 Battery cooling fan
207 Battery cooling fan thermostat
208 Cigar lighter illumination
209 Headlamp dip beam RH & LH
215 Window lift master switch
216 Window lift switch RH front
217 Window lift switch LH front
218 Window lift switch RH rear
219 Window lift switch LH rear
220 Window lift motor(s)
221 Window lift relay
231 Headlamp relay
250 Inertia switch
255 Fibre optics illumination bulb
257 Door lock solenoid
258 Door lock solenoid relay
259 Thermal circuit breaker
260 Door lock switch
266 Headlamp wiper motor
267 Headlamp wash motor
287 Fog guard warning light
288 Fog guard lamp
289 Direction indicator blocking diode
290 Seat belt logic unit (Federal)
301 Stoplamp failure sensor
303 Low coolant control unit
304 Park lamp failure sensor
309 Low coolant sensor
320 Low coolant warning light
323 Lamp failure warning light
324 Invertor
329 Timer Relay-wipers
330 Seat adjuster motor
331 Seat adjuster switch
332 Sliding roof switch
333 Sliding roof motor
334 Electric door mirror
335 Interior lamp delay
336 Aerial adjusting switch
339 Headlamp wiper relay
340 Heated back-light delay
341 Boot lock solenoid
342 Speed control unit
343 Magnet pick-up
345 Set switch
346 Switch control unit
347 Actuator

Fig. 10.124 Wiring diagram for fuel injection – Series 3 cars

41 *Fuel pump*
291 *EGR control unit*
292 *Fuel injection amplifier*
293 *Fuel injection control unit (ECU)*
296 *Fuel injectors*
297 *Air temperature sensor*
298 *Thermotime switch*
299 *Cold start relay*
300 *Cold start injector*
305 *Coolant temperature sensor*
306 *Trigger unit*
307 *EGR valve*
308 *EGR thermo switch*
310 *Throttle switch*
312 *Main relay*
314 *Fuel pump relay*
315 *Blocking diode – inhibit incorrect polarity (part of 312)*
318 *Manifold pressure sensor*

Fig. 10.125 Wiring diagram for air conditioning – Series 3 cars

33 *Blower motors*
47 *Coolant temperature sensor*
188 *Resistor*
189 *Blower speed relay*
190 *Compressor clutch*
191 *Thermostat*
192 *Control switch*
261 *Amplifier*
262 *Servo*
263 *Vacuum valve*
264 *In car sensor*
265 *Ambient sensor*
327 *Temperature selector*
350 *Overtemperature switch*
351 *Thermal fuse*

Fig. 10.126 XJS wiring diagram – power supply, ignition, instruments and fuel supply

1 *Alternator*
3 *Battery*
4 *Starter solenoid*
5 *Starter motor*
6 *Master lighting switch*
19 *Fuse box(es)*
21 *Door switch*
34 *Fuel gauge*
38 *Ignition/Starter switch*
39 *Ignition coil*
40 *Distributor (OPUS)*
41 *Fuel pump*
42 *Oil pressure switch*
43 *Oil pressure gauge*
46 *Coolant temperature gauge*
47 *Water temperature transmitter*
67 *Line fuse*
75 *Automatic gearbox safety switch*
79 *Trailer socket*
95 *Tachometer*
146 *Battery condition indicator*
147 *Oil pressure transmitter*
159 *Brake level warning light*
160 *Split brake differential switch*
164 *Ballast resistor*
165 *Handbrake switch*
166 *Handbrake warning light*
180 *Kickdown switch*
182 *Brake fluid level switch*
183 *Ignition amplifier (OPUS)*
190 *Air conditioning compressor*
194 *Starter solenoid ballast coil relay*
202 *Seat belt warning light*
204 *Ignition protection relay*
250 *Inertia switch*
256 *Brake warning diode*
259 *Thermal circuit breaker*
302 *Over voltage control unit*
303 *Low coolant control unit*
309 *Low coolant sensor*
310 *Fuel injection power amplifier*
311 *Fuel injection control unit*
312 *Main relay, fuel injection*
314 *Fuel pump relay*
319 *Fuel level warning light*
320 *Low coolant warning light*
321 *Over voltage warning light*

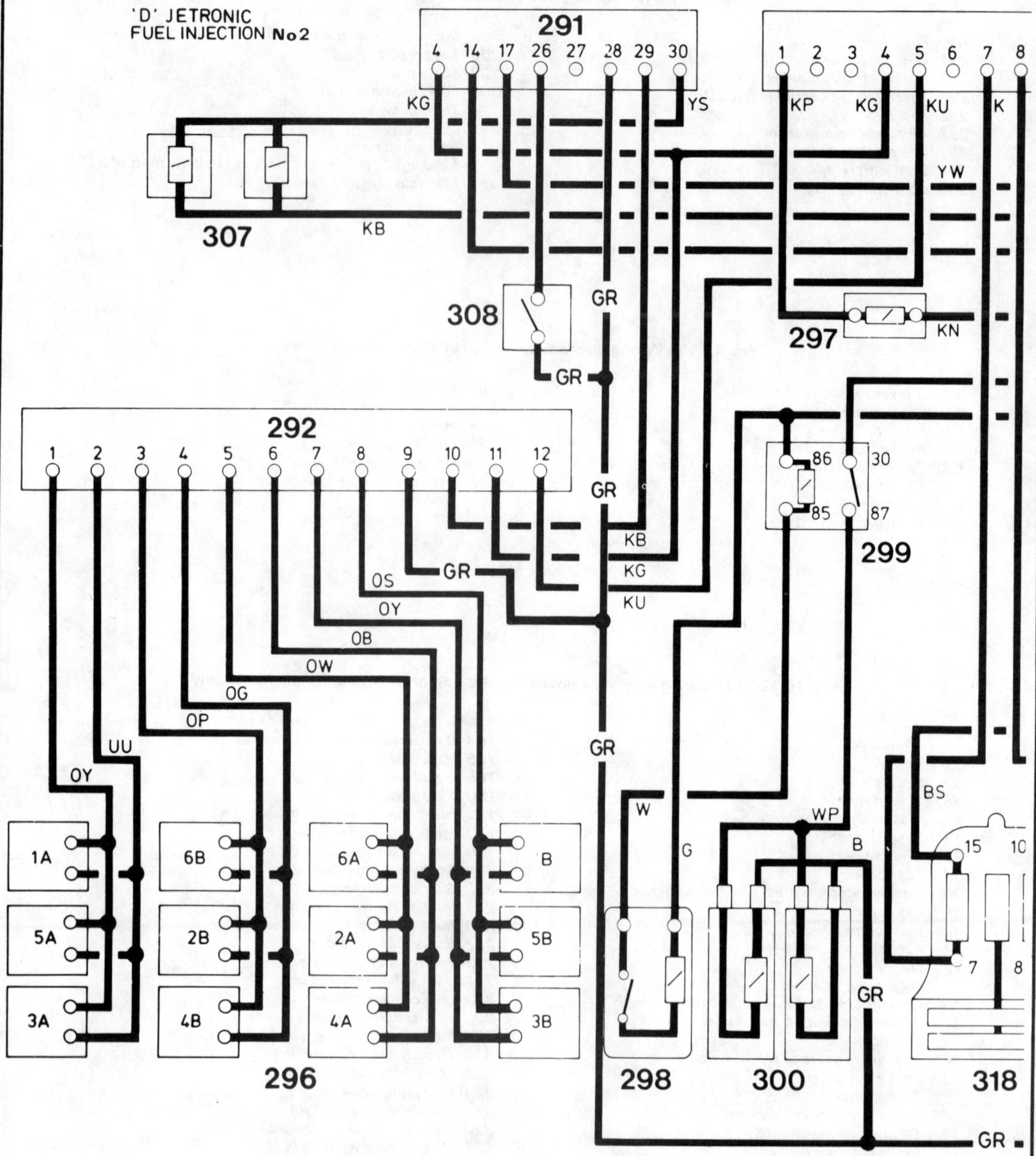

Fig. 10.124 Wiring diagram for fuel injection – Series 3 cars

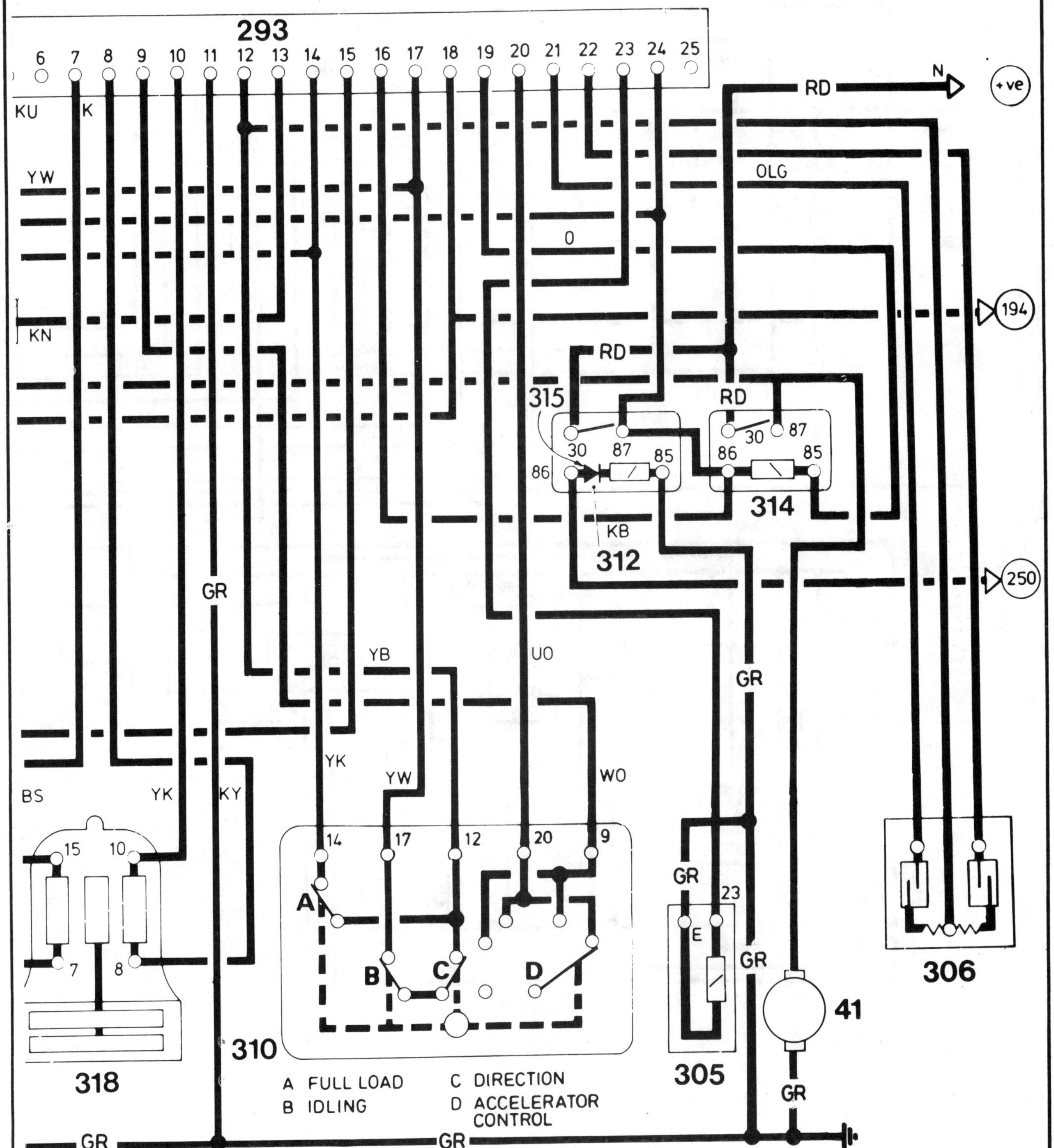

Fig. 10.124 Wiring diagram for fuel injection – Series 3 cars – continued

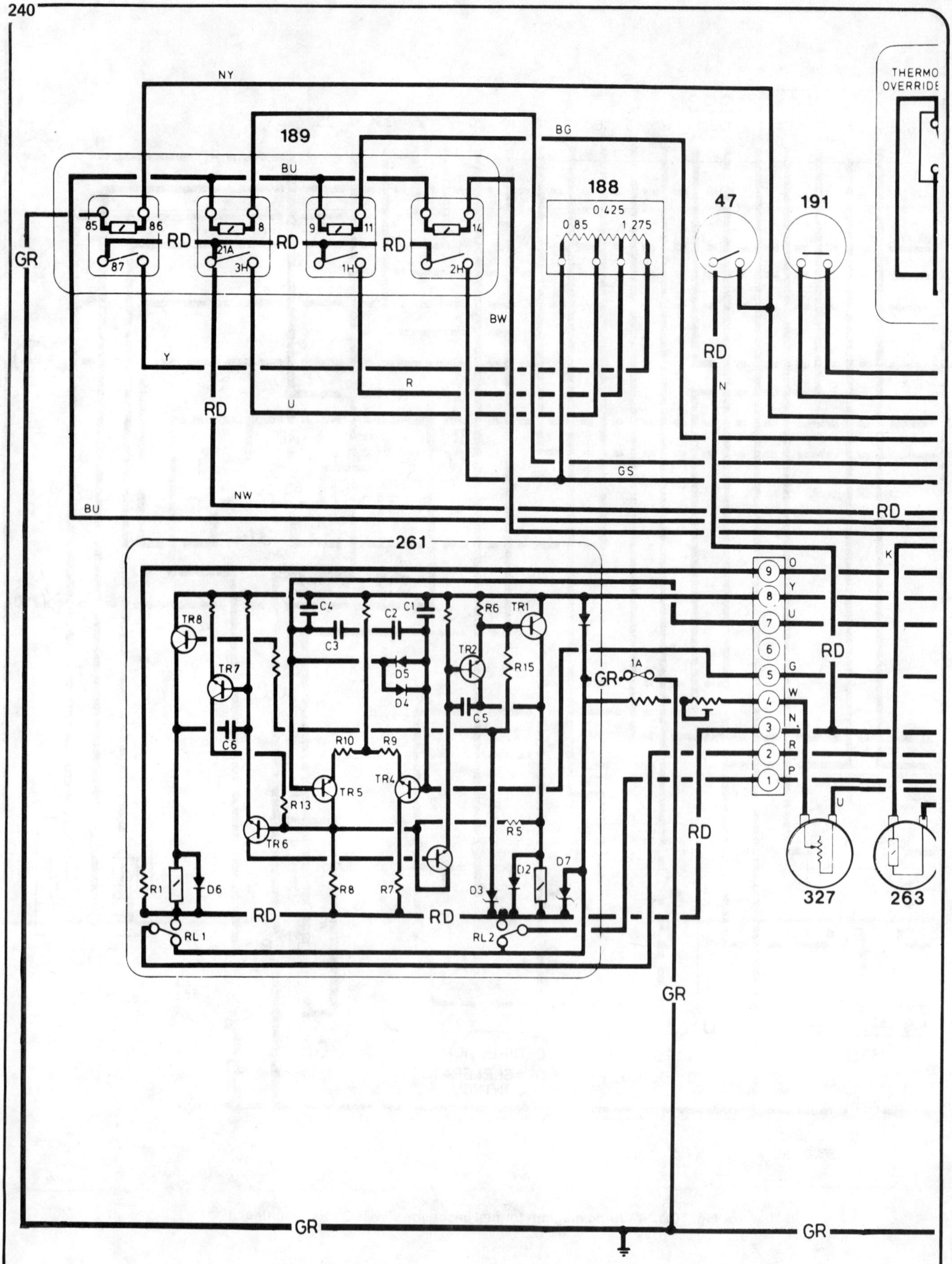

Fig. 10.125 Wiring diagram for air conditioning – Series 3 cars

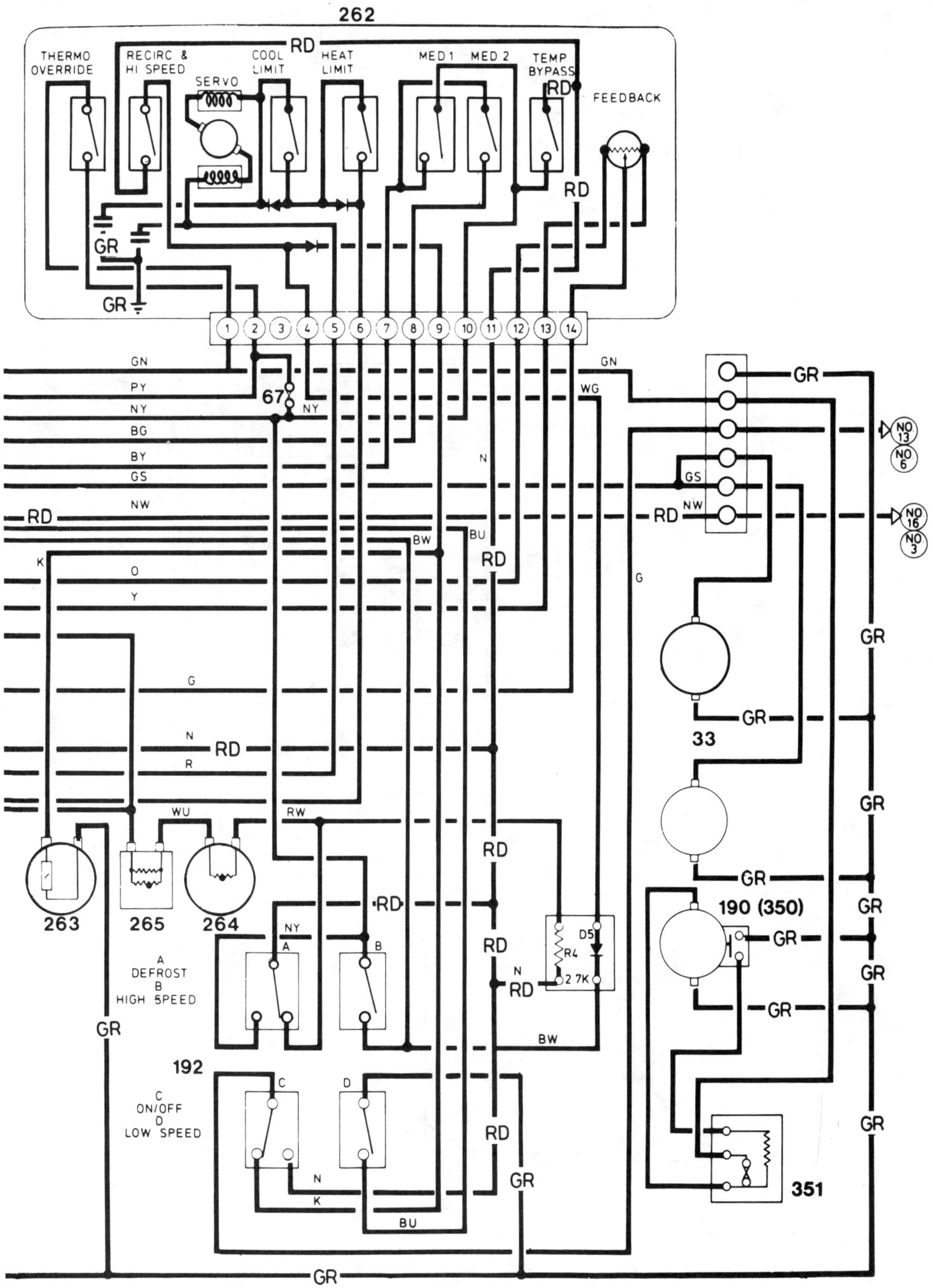

Fig. 10.125 Wiring diagram for air conditioning – Series 3 cars – continued

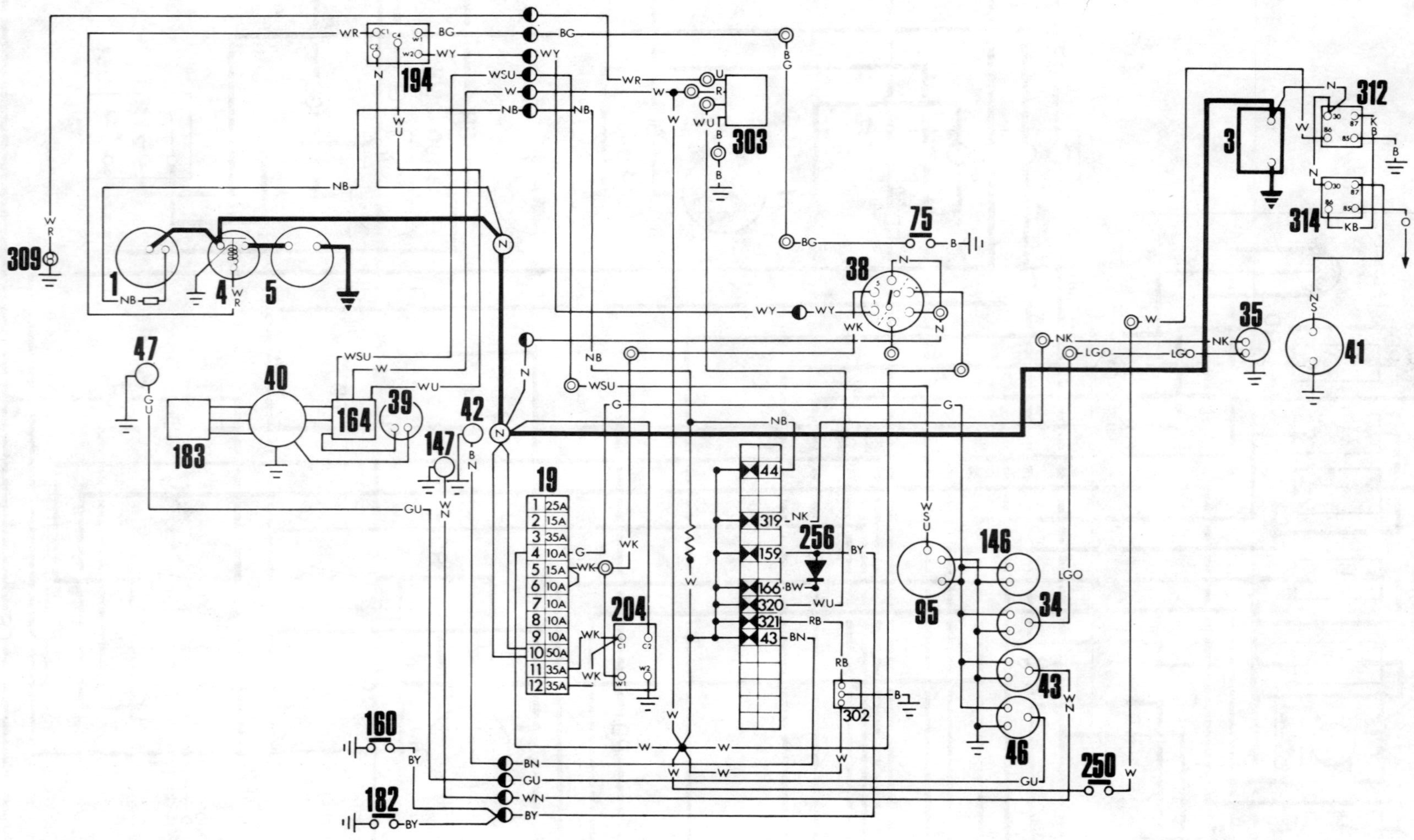

Fig. 10.126 Wiring diagram – power supply, ignition, instruments and fuel supply – XJS

Fig. 10.127 XJS wiring diagram – external lighting. Insets show alternative connections

3 Battery
6 Master lighting switch
7 Combined headlamp/dip/flash and direction indicator switch
8 Headlamp dip beam
9 Headlamp main beam
11 RH Side lamp
12 LH Side lamp
15 Number plate illumination lamp(s)
16 Stop lamp(s)
17 Tail lamp RH
18 Stop lamp switch
19 Fuse box(es)
22 Tail lamp LH
25 Flasher unit
26 Direction indictor switch (see No 7)
27 Direction indicator warning lights
28 RH Front flasher
29 LH Front flasher
30 RH Rear flasher
31 LH Rear flasher
38 Ignition/Starter switch
45 Headlamp flasher switch (see No 7)
49 Reverse lamp switch
50 Reverse lamp(s)
54 Fog lamps
65 Boot light switch
66 Boot light
67 Line fuse
79 Trailer socket
153 Hazard warning switch
154 Hazard warning flasher unit
159 Brake level warning light
160 Split brake differential switch
165 Handbrake switch
166 Handbrake warning light
170 Side markers
182 Brake fluid level switch
231 Headlamp relay
256 Brake warning diode
286 Rear fog guard switch
288 Rear fog guard lamp
289 Direction indicator diode
291 Brake warning relay
293 Fog lamp warning light
304 Park lamp failure sensor(s)

Fig. 10.128 XJS wiring diagram – interior lighting and auxiliary equipment. Insets show alternative connections

3 Battery
6 Master lighting switch
13 Panel lamp rheostat
14 Panel lamps
20 Interior light(s)
21 Door switch
23 Horn(s)
24 Horn push
37 Windscreen wiper motor
56 Clock
57 Cigar lighter
59 Interior light switch
60 Radio
61 Horn relay
67 Line fuse
76 Automatic gearbox selector lamp
77 Windscreen washer motor
79 Trailer socket
101 Map light switch
102 Map light
105 Rear interior lights
115 Rear window demist switch
116 Rear window demist unit
118 Combined windscreen wiper/washer switch
139 To air conditioning circuit
150 Rear window demist warning light
177 Radiator cooling fan relay
178 Radiator cooling fan thermostat
179 Radiator cooling fan motor
185 Aerial motor
186 Aerial motor relay
190 Air conditioning compressor
198 Seat belt switch, driver
202 Seat belt warning light
208 Cigar lighter illumination
216 Window lift switch, RH
218 Window lift switch, LH
220 Window lift motor(s)
221 Window lift relay
222 Window lift circuit breaker
245 Seat belt logic unit
255 Fibre optics illumination bulb
256 Brake warning diode
257 Door lock solenoid
258 Door lock solenoid relay
259 Thermal circuit breaker
260 Door lock switch
278 Service interval warning light

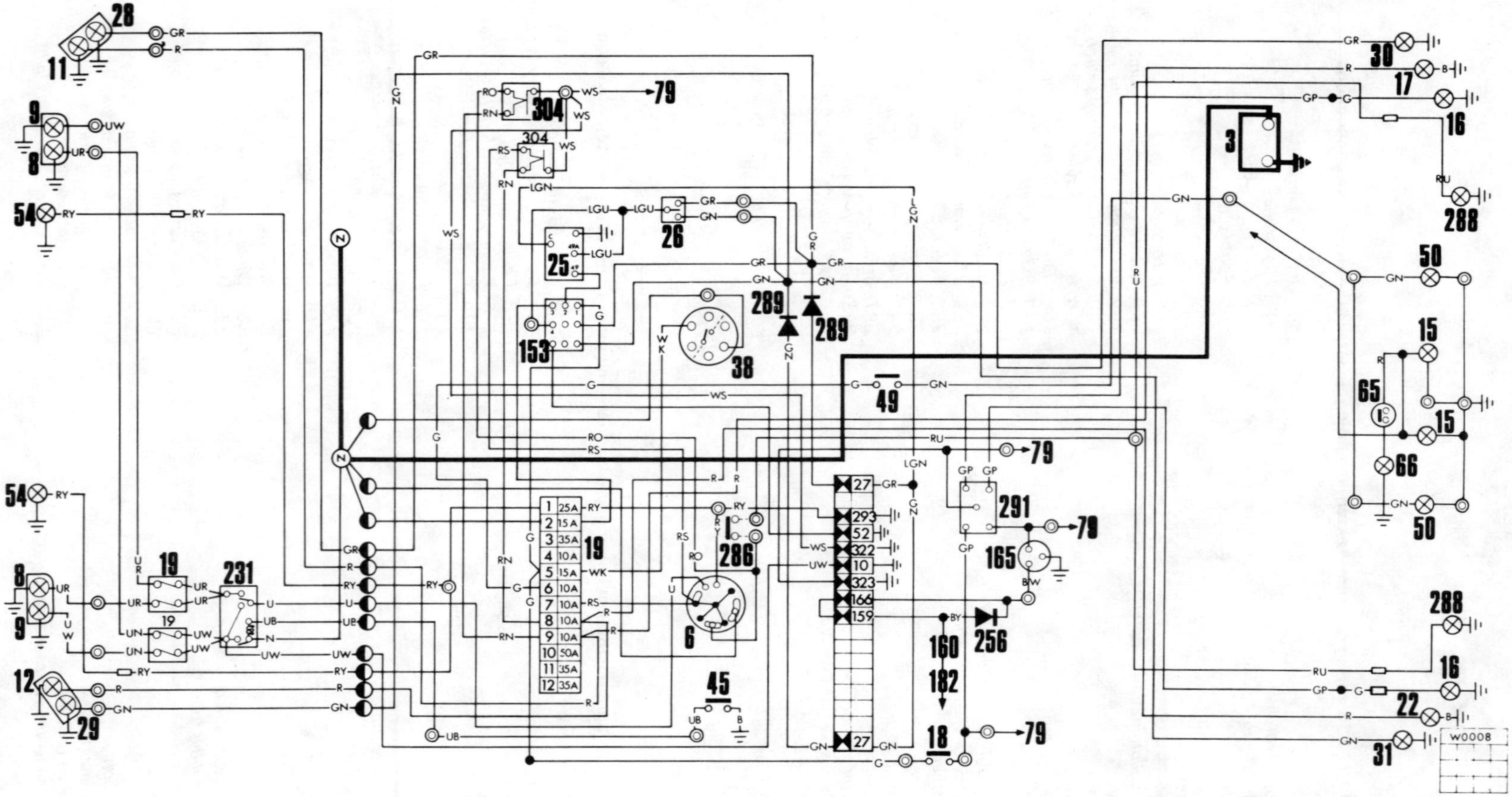

Fig. 10.127 Wiring diagram – external lighting. Insets show alternative connections – XJS

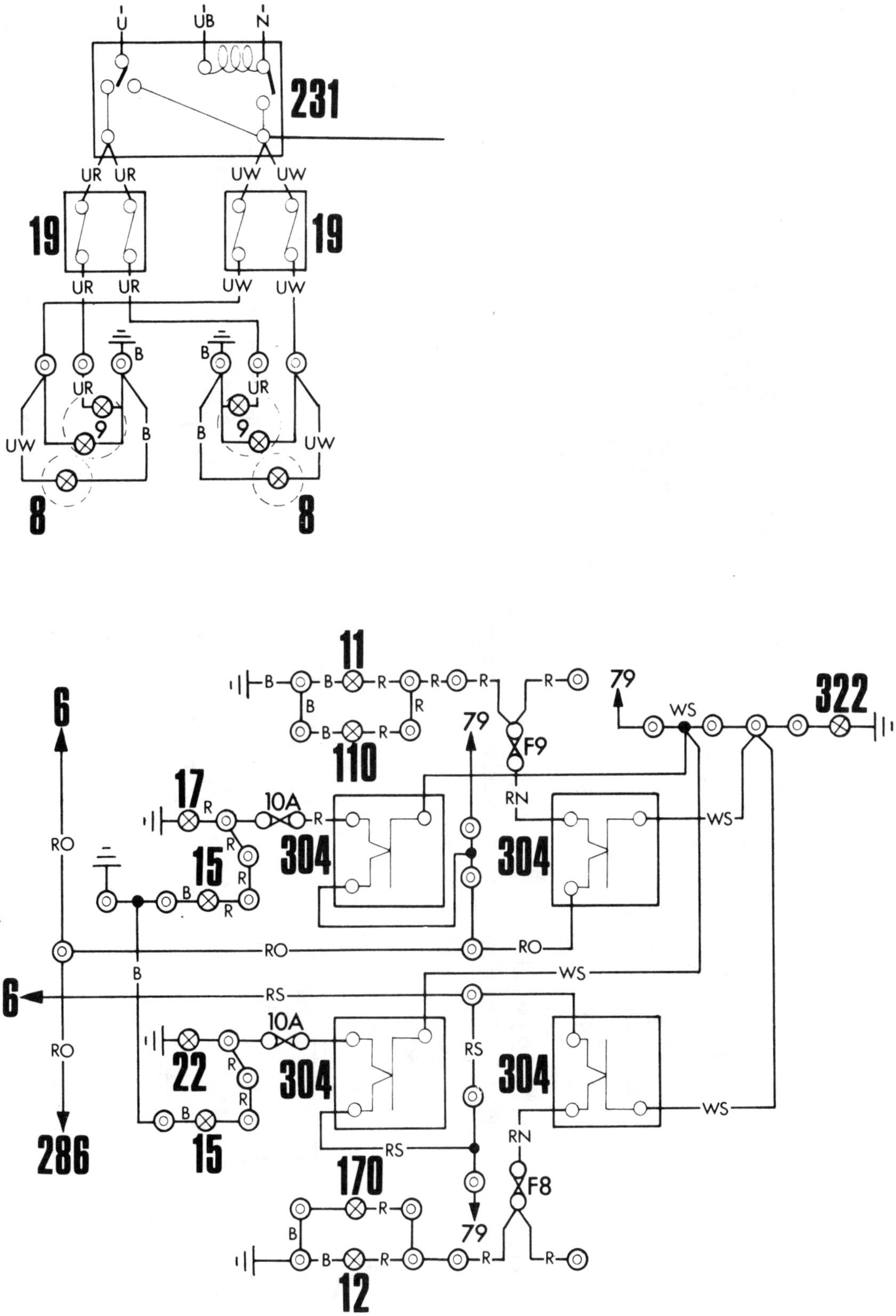

Fig. 10.127 Wiring diagram – external lighting. Insets show alternative connections – XJS continued

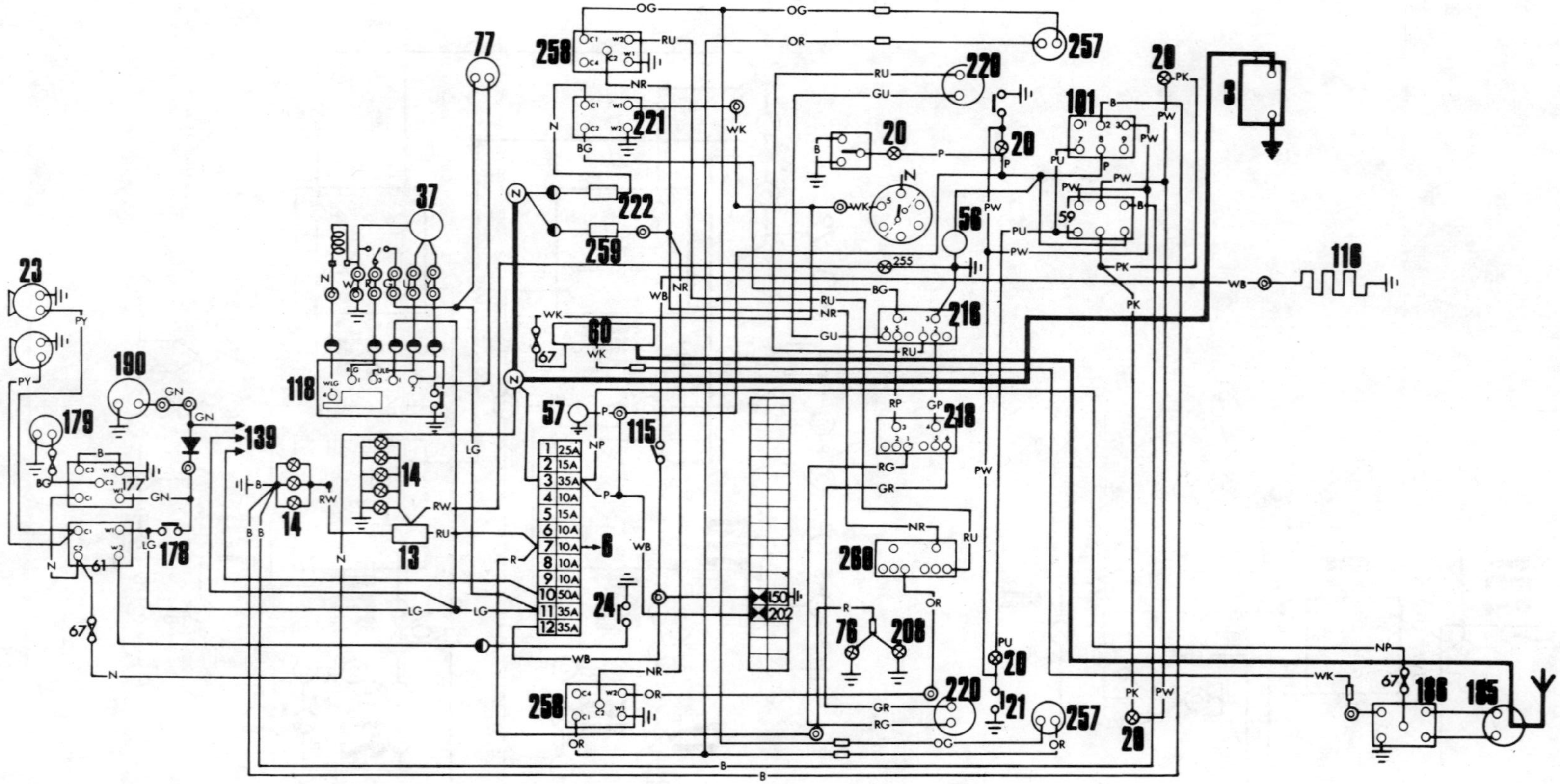

Fig. 10.128 Wiring diagram – interior lighting and auxiliary equipment. Insets show alternative connections – XJS

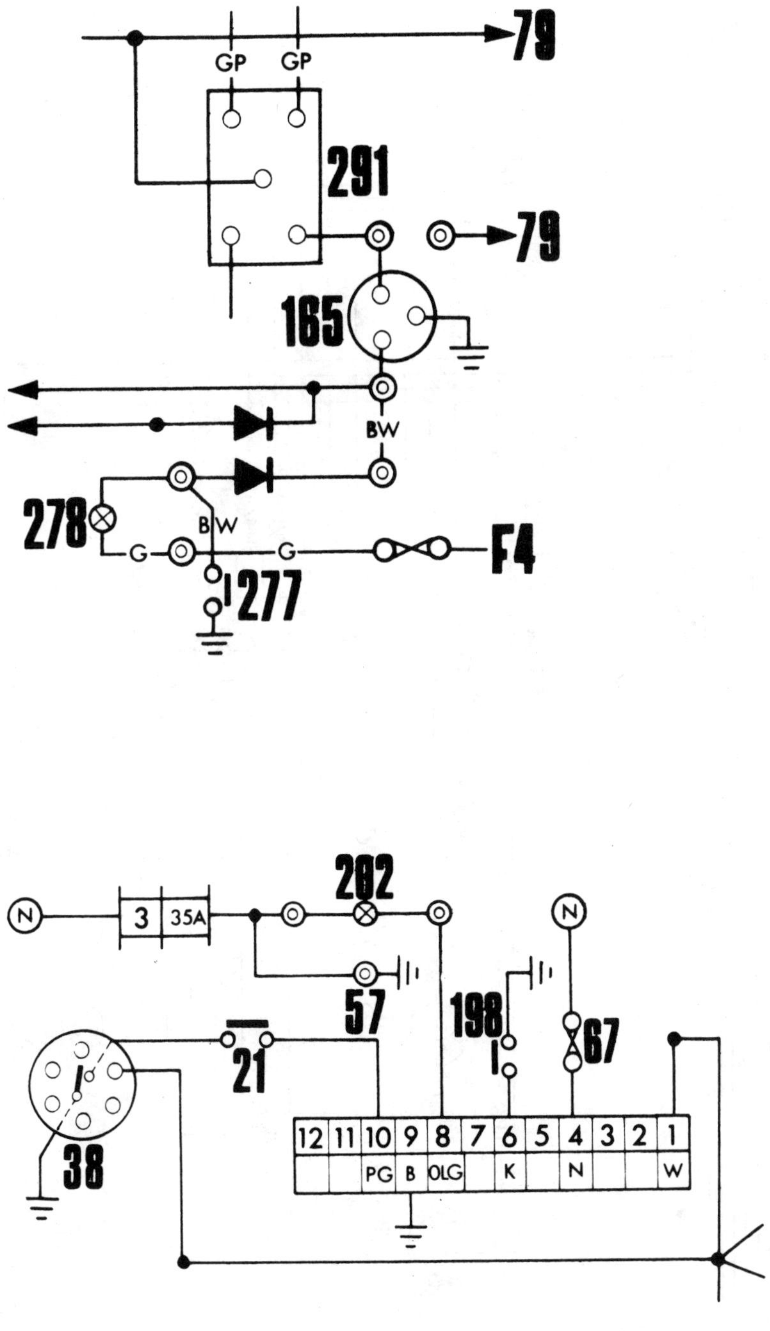

Fig. 10.128 Wiring diagram – internal lighting and auxiliary equipment. Insets show alternative connections – XJS – continued

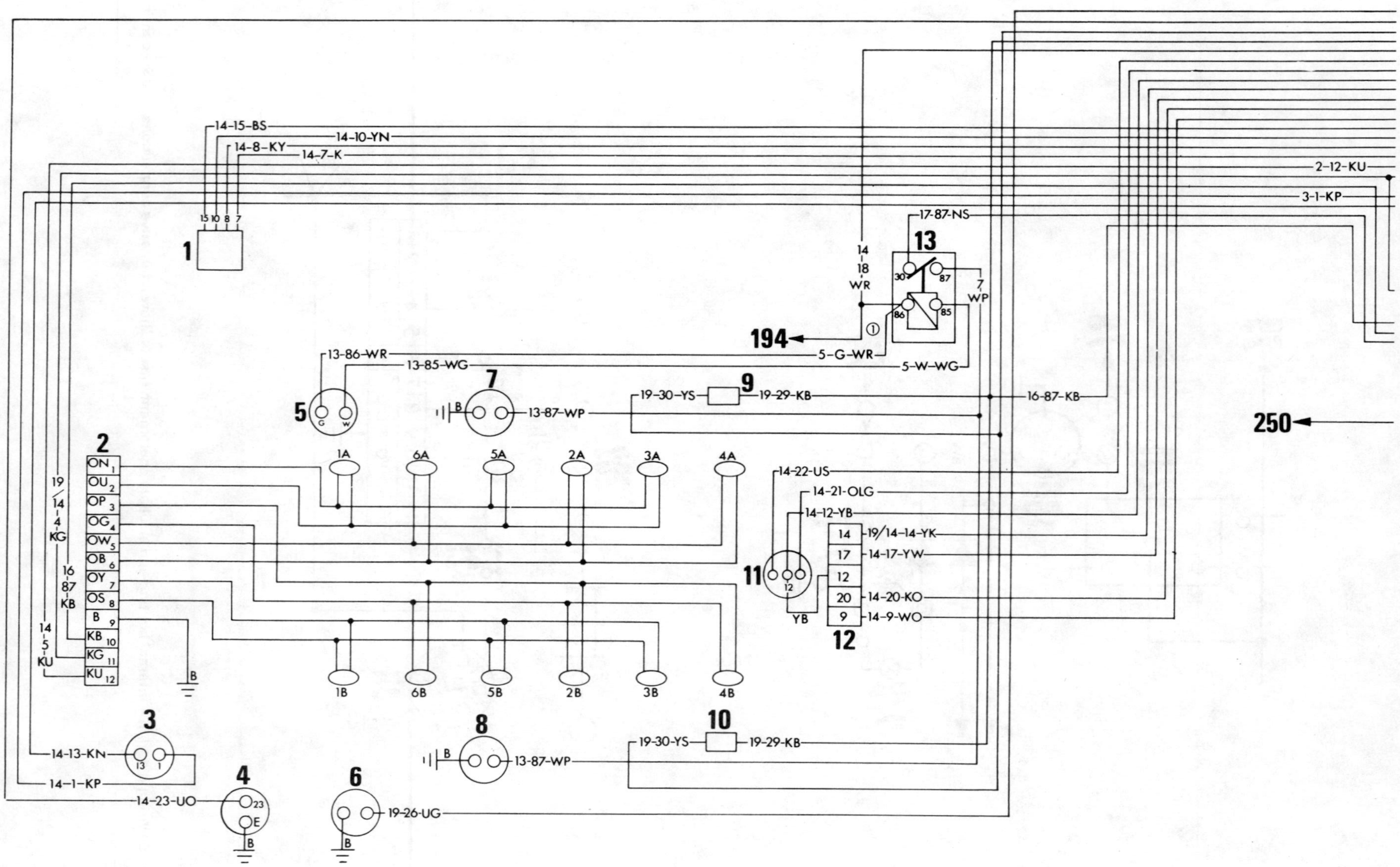

Fig. 10.129 Wiring diagram – fuel injection XJS

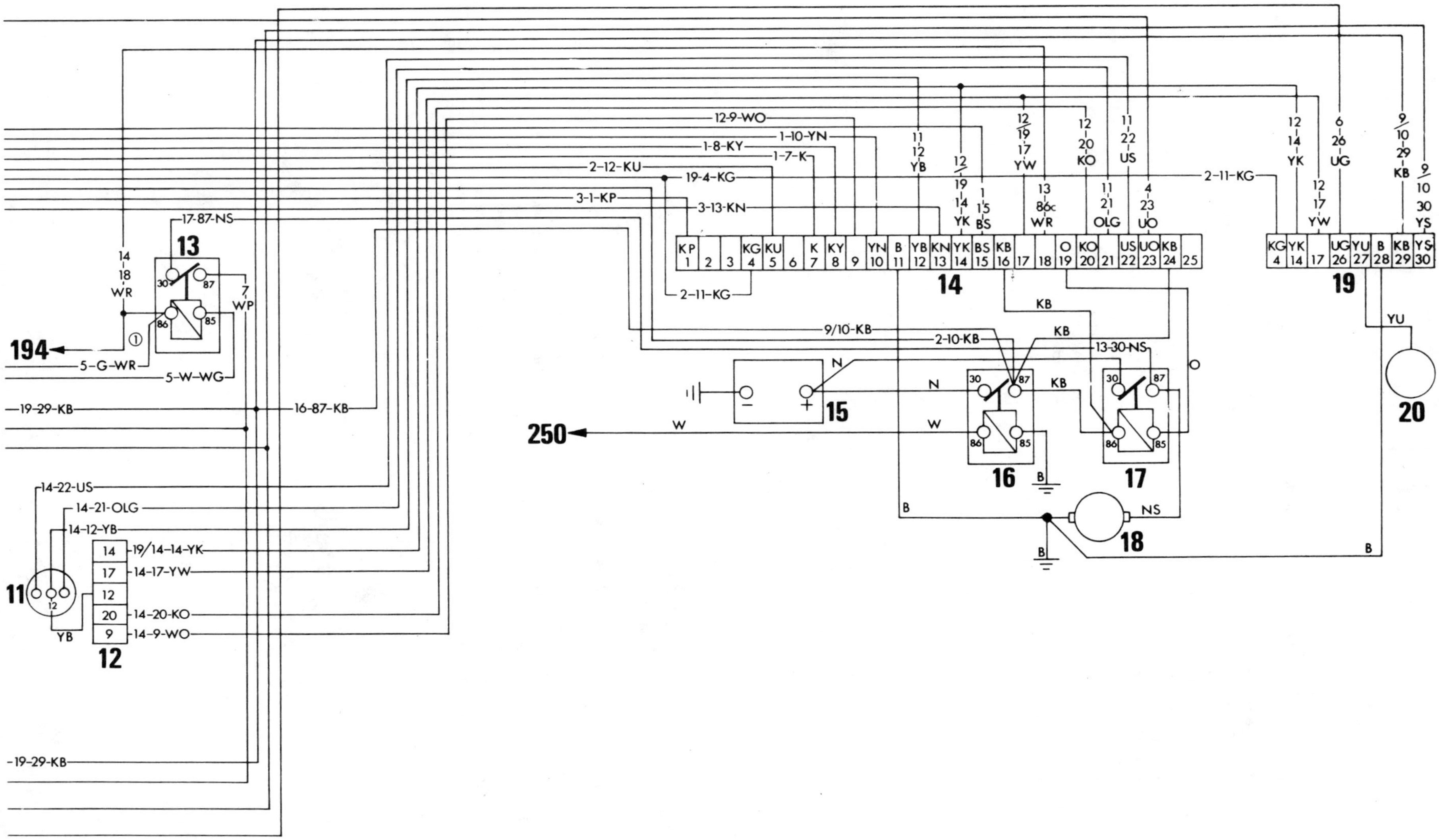

Fig. 10.129 Wiring diagram – fuel injection XJS – continued

Fig. 10.129 XJS wiring diagram – fuel injection

1 Pressure sensor
2 Power amplifier
3 Air temperature sensor
4 Coolant temperature sensor
5 Thermotime switch
6 EGR thermo switch (if fitted)
7 Cold start valve
8 Cold start valve
9 EGR valve
10 EGR valve
11 Trigger unit
12 Throttle switch
13 Cold start relay
14 Electronic control unit
15 Battery
16 Main relay
17 Pump relay
18 Fuel pump
19 EGR control unit
20 Axle solenoid
194 Starter solenoid ballast resistor relay
250 Fuel cut-off inertia switch
1A to 6B Fuel injectors

Fig. 10.130 XJS wiring diagram – air conditioning

33 Blower motors
47 Water temperature transmitter
187 Air conditioning relays
188 Air conditioning resistors
190 Air conditioning compressor
191 Air conditioning thermostat
192 Air conditioning control switches
261 Air conditioning amplifier unit
262 Air conditioning servo control unit
263 Vacuum solenoid valve
264 In car temperature sensor
265 Ambient temperature sensor

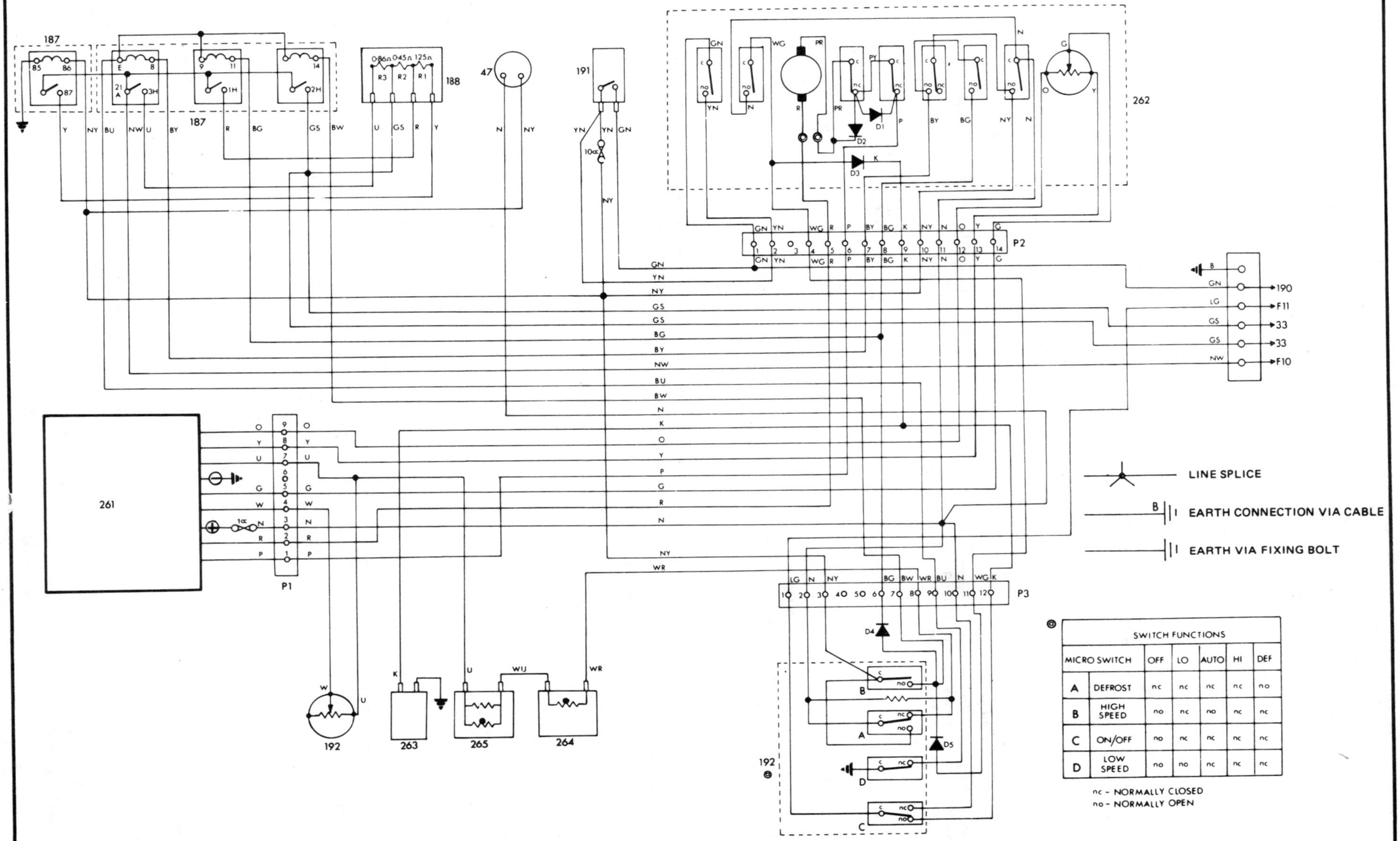

SWITCH FUNCTIONS

MICRO SWITCH		OFF	LO	AUTO	HI	DEF
A	DEFROST	nc	nc	nc	nc	no
B	HIGH SPEED	no	nc	no	nc	nc
C	ON/OFF	no	nc	nc	nc	nc
D	LOW SPEED	no	no	nc	nc	nc

nc – NORMALLY CLOSED
no – NORMALLY OPEN

Fig. 10.130 Wiring diagram – air conditioning XJS

Chapter 11 Suspension and steering

Contents

Specifications

Front suspension

Type ... Independent with wishbones, coil springs, telescopic shock absorbers and anti-roll bar

Steering angles

Castor:
- XJ12 and Double Six, Series 1 ... 2° to $2\frac{1}{2}$° positive
- All other models ... $3\frac{1}{4}$° to $3\frac{3}{4}$° positive

Camber (all models) ... $\frac{1}{4}$° to $\frac{3}{4}$° positive

Front wheel alignment (toe):
- XJ12 and Double Six, Series 1 and Series 2 with carburettors, and XJS ... $\frac{1}{16}$ to $\frac{1}{8}$ in (1.6 to 3.2 mm) toe-in
- XJ12 and Double Six with fuel injection ... 0 to $\frac{1}{16}$ in (0 to 1.6 mm) toe-out

Steering system

Type ... Rack-and-pinion, power-assisted with safety column

Number of turns lock to lock:
- XJ12 and Double Six ... 3.15
- XJS ... 2.9

Turning circle:	
XJ12 and Double Six, Series 1	39 ft (11.9 m)
XJ12 and Double Six, Series 2 on:	
Standard wheelbase	38 ft 8 in (11.79 m)
Long wheelbase	40 ft (12.2 m)
XJS	36 ft 3 in (11.05 m)

Rear suspension

Type	Independent, with coil springs and telescopic shock absorbers. Anti-roll bar on XJS models
Camber (all models)	$\frac{1}{2}$° to 1° negative
Roadwheel alignment (all models)	$\frac{1}{32}$ in (0.8 mm) toe-in to $\frac{1}{32}$ in (0.8 mm) toe-out

Roadwheels

Type and size	Pressed steel, 6JK15, or alloy die cast

Tyres

Size (all models)	205/70VR15	
Pressures in lbf/in^2 (kgf/cm^2)*:	**Normal conditions**	**High speed/full load**
XJ 12 and Double Six:		
Series 1, front and rear	26 (1.83)	34 (2.4)
Series 2 on, front	28 (1.97)	36 (2.5)
Series 2 on, rear	26 (1.83)	36 (2.5)
XJS:		
Front	26 (1.83)	32 (2.2)
Rear	24 (1.69)	30 (2.1)

**Refer also to individual vehicle tyre pressure label*

Torque wrench settings

	lbf ft	Nm
Front suspension		
Stub axle to stub axle carrier	85	115
Steering arm to stub axle carrier	50	68
Disc to hub	35	48
Caliper to stub axle carrier	55	75
Upper swivel balljoint to stub axle carrier	50	68
Lower swivel balljoint to lower wishbone	50	68
Upper wishbone pivot shaft nuts	50	68
Lower wishbone pivot shaft nuts	45	61
Upper swivel balljoint to wishbone	30	41
Upper pivot shaft to crossmember	50	68
Spring pan bolts	30	41
Shock absorber mounting bracket	30	41
Shock absorber upper mounting	30	41
Shock absorber lower mounting	34	46
Buffers to spring pan	10	14
Upper wishbone rebound rubbers	10	14
Anti-roll bar bracket to body	30	41
Anti-roll bar to link and link to wishbone	18	25
Suspension crossmember clamp bolt	30	41
Suspension crossmember front mounting bolt	100	136
Vee mounting to body	25	34
Vee mounting to crossmember	25	34
Rear suspension		
Tie-plate to crossmember	18	25
Inner pivot bracket to final drive unit	60	82
Final drive to crossmember	75	102
Caliper mounting bolts	50	68
Wishbone inner pivot shaft nuts	50	68
Wishbone outer pivot shaft nuts	100	136
Driveshaft inner flange bolts	50	68
Driveshaft to hub carrier	100	136
Radius rods to wishbone	65	88
Radius rods to body	40	54
Radius rod safety strap bolts	40	54
Radius rod safety strap to floor panel	30	41
Shock absorber upper mounting	35	48
Shock absorber lower mounting	35	48
Vee mounting to body	30	41
Vee mounting to crossmember	18	25
Bump stop rubber to body	18	25
Anti-roll bar bracket to body (XJS only)	18	25
Steering		
Pinion housing cover plate	18	25
Rack balljoints	50	68

	lbf ft	Nm
Tie-rod end locknuts	140	190
Tie-rod end balljoint to steering arm	45	61
Steering gear mounting bolts	18	25
Universal joint pinch-bolts	18	25
Steering wheel to shaft	28	38
Steering column to lower bracket	18	25
Lower column to body	18	25
Column to upper bracket	18	25
Fluid pipe adaptor on rack housing	50	68
Wheels		
Roadwheel nuts	45	61

1 General description

The front suspension assembly comprises a pressed steel crossmember to which is attached the steering mechanism and the upper and lower suspension wishbones.

The front suspension incorporates coil springs, hydraulic telescopic (gas-pressurised) shock absorbers (photo) and an anti-roll bar fitted between the two lower wishbones.

The rear suspension assembly also comprises a pressed steel crossmember, rubber mounted to the body and located by radius arms. The open driveshafts are located in the transverse plane by two links. The suspension incorporates four coil springs which enclose hydraulic telescopic shock absorbers, which are gas pressurised.

On XJS models, an anti-roll bar is fitted at the rear as well as to the front of the car.

The steering gear is of rack and pinion type with power assistance on all models. The steering column is of collapsible type incorporating shear plugs and two universal joints.

There are differences in detail between many of the components used on XJ12, Double Six and XJS models.

2 Maintenance and inspection

1 At the intervals specified in Routine Maintenance, apply grease to the four top and bottom swivel balljoints of the front suspension.
2 Remove the hub caps from the front roadwheels and apply the grease gun to the exposed nipple. A bleed hole is provided to indicate when sufficient grease has been injected.
3 Check and adjust the front hub bearings (Section 5) and the front wheel alignment (Section 49).
4 Grease the inner and outer pivot bearings of the rear suspension. Remove the rear hub grease plug and fill (but do not pressurise) with grease.
5 Check the reservoir oil level in the steering pump and lubricate sparingly the rack and pinion assembly using the nipple provided.
6 Give four or five strokes of the grease gun to the track rod end grease nipples. A bleed hole is provided, covered with a nylon disc which will lift when sufficient grease has been injected.
7 Check the security of all suspension and steering nuts and bolts, examine rubber dust excluders and gaiters for splits or cuts and renew as necessary. Check steering linkage and balljoints for wear and adjust or renew as described in this Chapter.

3 Front shock absorbers – removal, testing and refitting

1 The shock absorbers should be removed and tested whenever the cornering or roadholding characteristics of the car appear to have deteriorated, if there is evidence of oil on the shock absorber casing, or at 30 000 mile (48 000 km) intervals.
2 To remove a shock absorber, disconnect the upper mounting nuts and cushions which are accessible within the engine compartment. Jack up the front of the car and remove the roadwheel.
3 Unscrew and remove the self-locking nut from the lower mounting and withdraw the bolt.
4 Compress the shock absorber and remove it from the car.
5 Grip the shock absorber lower mounting in the jaws of a vice so that the shock absorber is held vertically. Now fully extend and contract the unit ten or twelve times. If there is any lack of resistance in either direction or seizure, then the unit (which is sealed) must be renewed. Never attempt to dismantle a shock absorber, particularly the gas-pressurised type.
6 Refitting the shock absorber is a reversal of removal but if the original unit is being refitted, check the rubber bushes and cushions for deterioration and renew, if necessary.

4 Front anti-roll bar – removal and refitting

XJ12, Double Six

1 Place the car over a pit or raise and support it securely on stands placed under its front end. Remove both front roadwheels.
2 Remove the two self-locking nuts which secure the anti-roll bar link to the bracket on the front suspension lower wishbone.
3 Remove the four setscrews which secure the keeper plates to the front crossmember. Lift the anti-roll bar away.
4 The link arm bush can be renewed by pressing it out of the link arm eye. The rubber support bushes are split to enable them to be removed easily. Their splits should face the rear of the car.
5 Refitting is a reversal of removal, but do not fully tighten the nuts and setscrews until the weight of the car has been lowered onto the roadwheels.

XJS

6 Jack up the front of the car and support the side members on stands. Remove both front roadwheels and place a jack under the centre of the front crossmember.
7 Prise out the plastic fasteners which secure the stoneguards under the wheel arches.
8 Remove the two screws and thirteen plastic fasteners which hold the spoiler undertray to the body and the spoiler proper.
9 Using a balljoint separator, disconnect the left-hand tie-rod from the steering arm.
10 Remove the self-locking nuts and disconnect the links from the anti-roll bar on both sides of the car.
11 Unscrew and remove the mounting bolts from the front suspension assembly. Lower the jack until the spacers, bushes and sleeves can be removed.
12 Unbolt the anti-roll bar clamp plates from the bodyframe and detach the rubber insulators.
13 Withdraw the anti-roll bar past the left-hand front hub.
14 Refitting is a reversal of removal, but observe the following points.
15 Locate the rubber insulators so that their splits are towards the rear of the car.
16 Do not fully tighten connecting nuts and bolts until the weight of the car has been lowered onto its roadwheels.
17 When refitting the spoiler undertray and the stoneguards, use new plastic fasteners.
18 Tighten all bolts and nuts to the specified torque.
19 The anti-roll bar mounting clamp rubber insulators and link cushions can be renewed without having to withdraw the anti-roll bar from the car if the securing nuts are released and the bar prised away. Use rubber lubricant or soapy water to ease refitting.

5 Front hub – overhaul and adjustment

1 Apply the handbrake fully, jack up the front of the car and remove

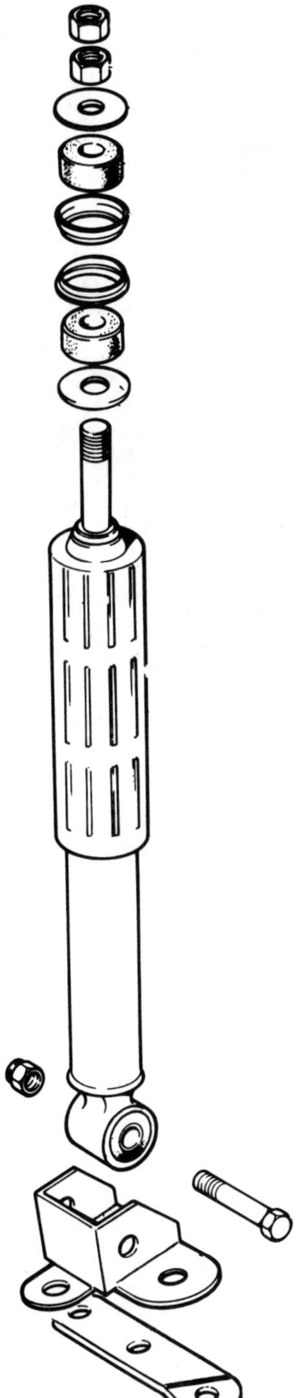

Fig. 11.1 Typical front shock absorber (Sec 3)

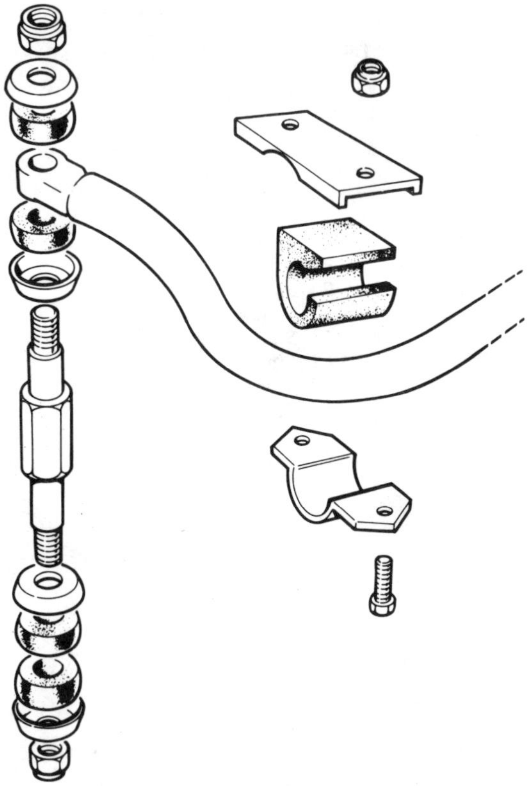

Fig. 11.2 Front anti-roll bar end link and clamp (Sec 4)

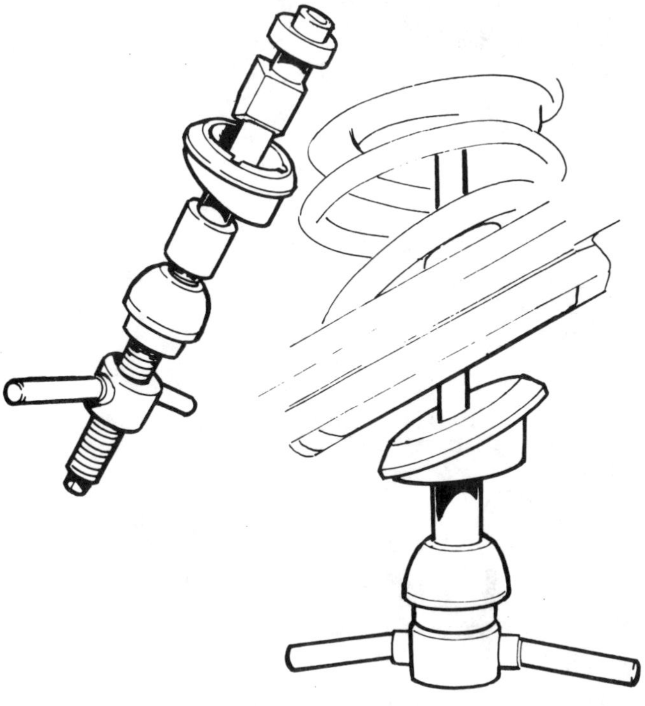

Fig. 11.3 Typical coil spring, compressor (Sec 6)

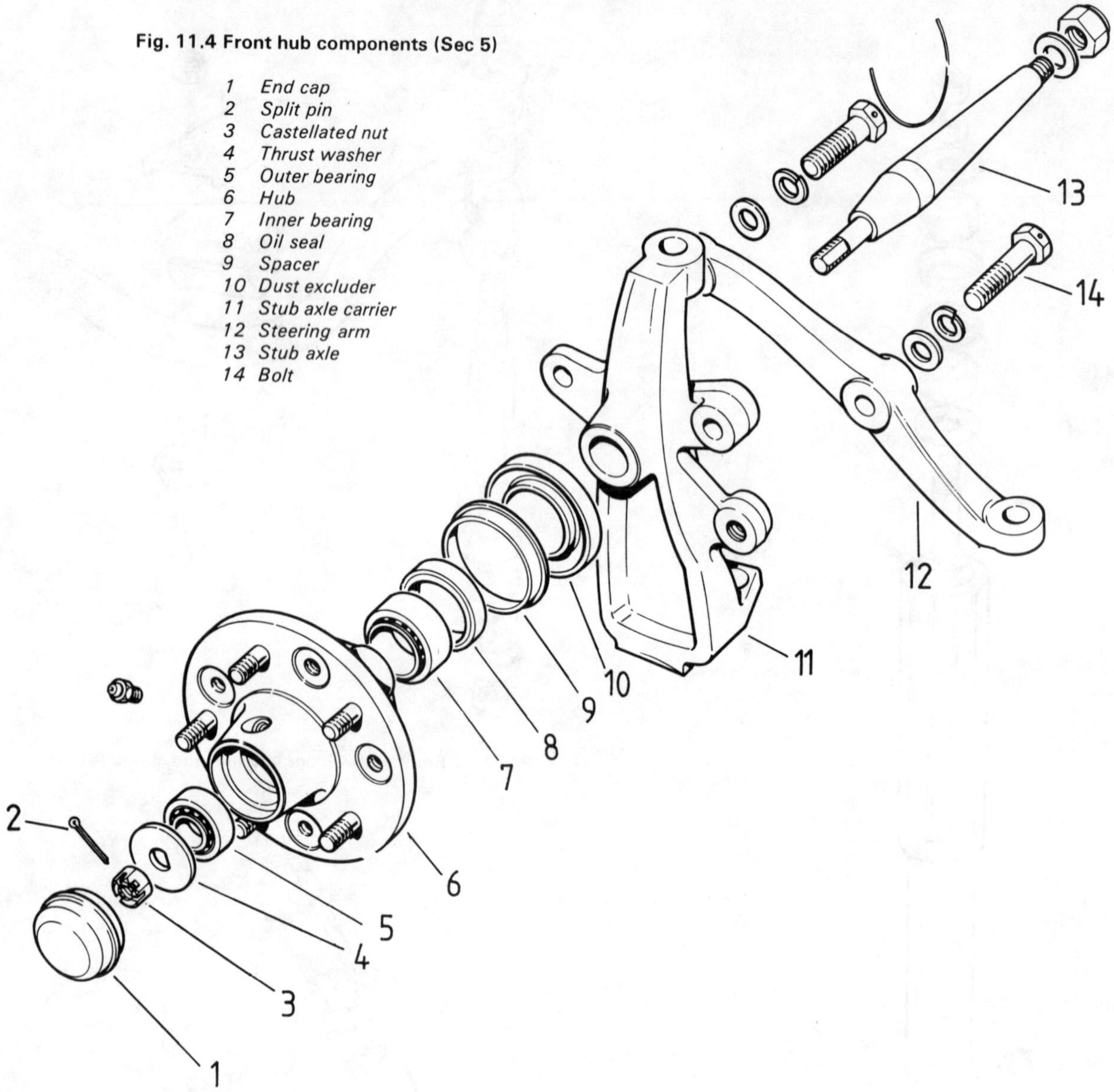

Fig. 11.4 Front hub components (Sec 5)

1 End cap
2 Split pin
3 Castellated nut
4 Thrust washer
5 Outer bearing
6 Hub
7 Inner bearing
8 Oil seal
9 Spacer
10 Dust excluder
11 Stub axle carrier
12 Steering arm
13 Stub axle
14 Bolt

Fig. 11.5 Front riding height adjustment diagram (XJ12, Double Six) (Sec 7)

A = 24⅝ in (611 mm)

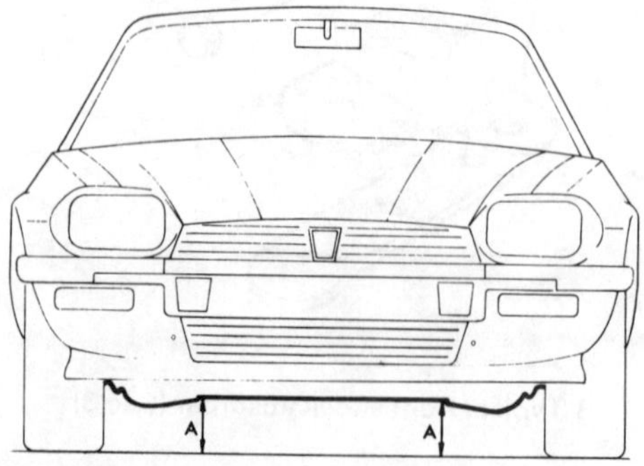

Fig. 11.6 Front riding height adjustment diagram (XJS) (Sec 7)

A = 6 in (152 mm)

1.1 Front shock absorber

5.3 Front hub nut retainer and split pin. Note grease nipple on hub

the roadwheel.

2 Working through the aperture in the disc shield, unscrew and remove the five bolts which hold the hub and brake disc together.

3 Prise off the dust cap from the end of the hub and extract the split pin from the nut retainer (photo).

4 Unscrew and remove the castellated nut and thrust washer and pull the hub assembly from the stub axle.

5 Prise out the oil seal and withdraw the inner races of the tapered roller bearings. The outer tracks can be drifted from the hub if new bearings are to be fitted.

6 If the original bearings are being refitted, clean the races and dry them.

7 Apply grease to the bearing tracks and races, install them to the hub and fit a new oil seal.

8 Refit the hub to the stub axle and screw on the castellated nut with its thrust washer finger-tight.

9 Tighten the nut until while turning the hub at the same time, its rotation is felt to be slightly restricted. Unscrew the nut between one and two flats, fit the nut retainer and insert a new split pin.

10 The correct endfloat of a front hub bearing is between 0.003 and 0.005 in (0.08 and 0.13 mm) which should ideally be checked on a dial gauge.

11 Fit the grease cap and bolt the disc to the hub, tightening to the specified torque.

12 Fit the roadwheel and lower the car to the ground.

6 Front coil spring – removal and refitting

1 A coil spring compressor will be needed for this operation. A suitable tool can be made up from a length of rod suitably threaded using nuts and large washers or crosspieces. First jack up the front of the car, support it, and remove the roadwheel.

2 With the coil spring compressed, remove the setscrews and lockwashers which secure the seat pan to the lower wishbone.

3 Slowly release the spring compressor until the tension of the coil spring is relieved. Remove the compressor, spring and seat pan. On all models, packing pieces may be found on top of the spring or in the spring pan. These are used to adjust side-to-side riding height (see next Section).

4 Refitting is a reversal of removal but align the seat pan holes with the tapped holes in the lower wishbone by using pilot studs. Withdraw these once the spring is installed.

7 Front riding height – adjustment

1 If the original roadsprings have been refitted, together with the packing pieces, the riding height should not have altered. Where a new spring has been installed, then check the front riding height in the following way.

2 Have the car filled with fuel, oil and water and the tyre pressures correct, standing on a level surface.

3 Press down on the front bumper and slowly release it, then grip the bumper, lift out and then slowly release it.

XJ12 and Double Six

4 Measure the distance (A in Fig. 11.5) between the centre of the outer headlamp and the ground on both sides of the car. The dimensions should be equal at $24\frac{5}{8}$ in (611 mm).

5 Where necessary, add or remove packing rings at the roadspring pan or crossmember. The maximum number of packing rings located in the pan is three and on the crossmember two rings. Packing rings are $\frac{1}{8}$ in (3.18 mm) thick and each one will vary the riding height by $\frac{5}{16}$ in (7.93 mm).

XJS

6 On this model, measure the distance between the lower face of the front suspension crossmember and the ground on both sides at the points indicated (A in Fig. 11.6).

7 The dimensions should be equal at 6 in (152 mm).

8 Where necessary add or remove packing rings at the spring turret, limiting their number to two.

9 The thickness and effect of the spring packing rings is as described in paragraph 5.

8 Front stub axle carrier – removal and refitting

1 Raise the front of the car by placing a jack under the lower wishbone. Remove the roadwheel.

2 Remove the brake caliper (Chapter 9).

3 Remove the hub/disc assembly (Section 5).

4 Remove the self-locking nut which secures the upper balljoint to the stub axle carrier.

5 Remove the nut which secures the lower balljoint to the lower wishbone.

6 Using a suitable extractor, separate the upper and lower balljoints from the stub axle carrier and remove the carrier.

7 The stub axle can be removed from the carrier and the disc shield unbolted and detached if necessary.

8 Refitting is a reversal of removal. Bleed the front brake hydraulic system and tighten all bolts to the specified torque.

9 Front suspension upper swivel balljoint – removal and refitting

1 The front suspension upper wishbone balljoint is a sealed unit and

if worn must be renewed as a unit.
2 To remove the balljoint, jack-up the car under the lower wishbone and remove the roadwheel.
3 Remove the bolts which secure the balljoint to the upper wishbone. Take great care to retain the packing pieces and shims and to record their locations precisely as they control the castor angle.
4 Remove the self-locking nut which secures the balljoint to the stub axle carrier. Use a suitable balljoint separator to disconnect the balljoint from the stub axle carrier.
5 During the foregoing operation, restrict the movement of the stub axle carrier by tying it with a piece of wire to prevent strain on the brake flexible hose.
6 Refitting is a reversal of removal, but make sure that the shims are returned to their original positions and that the balljoint securing bolts have their heads nearer the front of the car.

10 Front suspension lower swivel balljoint – overhaul and adjustment

1 Remove the stub axle carrier complete with balljoint as described in Section 8.
2 Remove the retaining ring and withdraw the flexible gaiter from the balljoint.
3 Extract the insert from around the taper pin.
4 Flatten the tab washers and remove the four setscrews which secure the ball pin cap to the stub axle carrier.
5 Remove the cap, shims, ball pin socket and the ball pin.
6 Renew any worn components and reassemble and re-shim in the following way.
7 The correct clearance of the ball pin in its socket is very important. Select shims which are available in two thicknesses until with the ball cap fully tightened, the ball pin can be moved stiffly by hand pressure.
8 Refit the stub axle carrier complete with the balljoint, as described in Section 8, and then grease the joint as described in Section 2.
9 Do not confuse this ball pin pre-load with removal of shims to try and compensate for wear. This must never be resorted to, always renew a worn ball pin or socket.

11 Front suspension lower wishbone – removal and refitting

1 Remove the front suspension unit as described in Section 14 or 15.
2 Using a suitable extractor, separate the tie-rod balljoint from the steering arm.
3 Unscrew the three bolts which hold the steering rack to the front crossmember.
4 Remove the roadspring as described in Section 6.
5 Unbolt the suspension upper balljoint from the wishbone levers, noting carefully which way the bolt heads are fitted (nearer rear of car) and the location of the castor control shims.
6 Unscrew the self-locking nut and using an extractor, separate the lower balljoint from the wishbone. Take off the anti-roll bar support bracket and the shock absorber lower mounting.
7 Extract the split pin from the wishbone pivot shaft nut and then drive the pivot shaft from the crossmember, recovering the plain washers.
8 Refitting is a reversal of removal. Do not fully tighten the pivot shaft nut until the weight of the car is on the roadwheels.
9 Check the front wheel alignment, castor and camber angles as described in Section 49.

12 Front suspension upper wishbone – removal, dismantling and refitting

1 Raise the car by placing a jack under the lower wishbone and remove the front roadwheel.
2 Remove the bolts from the upper wishbone arms and separate the balljoint. Note the castor control shims.
3 Tie the stub axle carrier to the suspension crossmember to prevent strain on the flexible brake hose.
4 Remove the two bolts which secure the upper wishbone pivot shaft to the crossmember. Take great care to retain and identify the locations of the shims as these control the camber angle and they

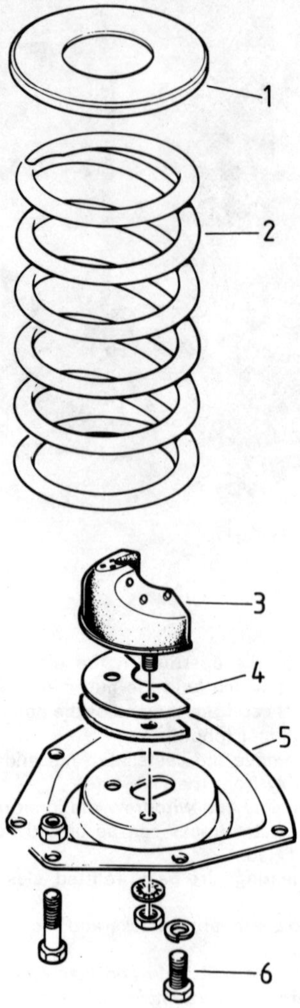

Fig. 11.7 Front road spring (Sec 6)

1 Ride height control packing piece
2 Coil spring
3 Bump stop
4 Spacers (XJS only)
5 Spring pan
6 Pan securing bolts

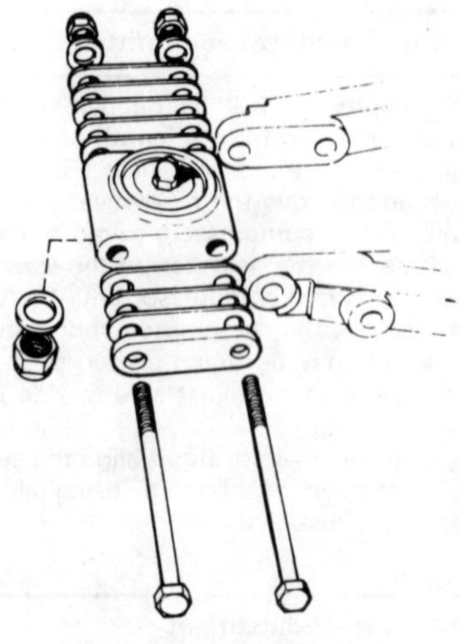

Fig. 11.8 Front suspension upper swivel balljoint and castor control shims (Sec 9)

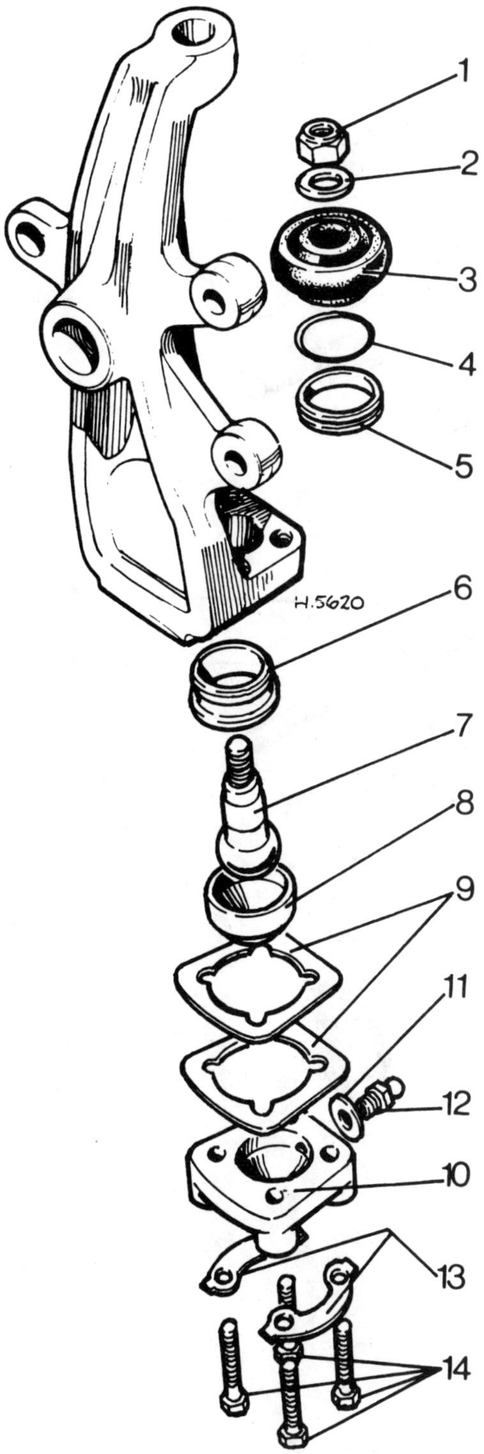

Fig. 11.9 Exploded view of a front suspension lower swivel balljoint (Sec 10)

1 Nut
2 Washer
3 Dust-excluding boot
4 Boot-retaining clip
5 Insert
6 Upper seat
7 Ballpin
8 Lower seat
9 Shims
10 Cap
11 Washer
12 Grease nipple
13 Lockplate
14 Bolts

must be returned to their original positions.

5 Withdraw the upper wishbone assembly so that the outboard ends pass either side of the shock absorber.

6 Remove the self-lockin nuts and their plain washers and withdraw the wishbone arms from the pivot shaft.

7 Release the locknuts and unscrew the rebound buffers from the wishbone.

8 The flexible bushes can be renewed after pressing them from the wishbone eyes. Use soapy water or a smear of hydraulic brake fluid to facilitate pressing in the new ones.

9 Reassembly and refitting are reversal of removal and dismantling. Make sure that the bolts which secure the balljoint to the wishbone arms have their heads towards the rear of the car.

10 Tighten all bolts to the specified torque, but do not tighten the castellated nuts which hold the wishbone arms to the pivot shaft until the weight of the car has once again been lowered onto the roadwheels.

11 Check the front steering angles on completion (see Section 49).

13 Front suspension bump and rebound stops – removal and refitting

Bump stop

1 Jack up the front of the car and remove the roadwheel.

2 Unscrew and remove the nuts from the bump stop. Withdraw the stop through the spring coils, which may require prising slightly apart.

3 On XJS models, two spacers are located under the bump stop.

Rebound stop

4 Only renew rebound stops in pairs.

5 Raise the front of the car and support the spring pan with a stand or second jack.

6 Remove the roadwheel.

7 Unscrew and remove the rebound stops from the upper wishbone.

8 Refitting is a reversal of removal.

14 Front suspension assembly (XJ12 and Double Six) – removal and refitting

1 If major operations are to be carried out to the front suspension, it may be advantageous to remove the suspension assembly complete.

2 Disconnect the battery.

3 Remove the air cleaners.

4 Working within the engine compartment, disconnect the shock absorber upper mountings.

5 With a syringe, drain the fluid from the power steering pump. Unless the fluid is absolutely clean, discard it.

6 Disconnect the hoses from the power steering pump and plug or cap the openings to prevent the entry of dirt.

7 Unscrew and remove the nuts which hold the engine front mountings to their brackets.

8 Unscrew and remove the nuts which secure the crossmember rear mountings.

9 Disconnect the links from the ends of the anti-roll bar.

10 Turn the steering wheel until the column lower universal joint pinch-bolt is accessible, then remove the bolt.

11 Turn the steering wheel until the front roadwheels are in the straight-ahead position.

12 Disconnect the wiring harness from the horns including the earth strap.

13 Remove the self-locking nuts from the pivot bolts at the crossmember front mountings. Do not attempt to drive out the pivot bolts at this stage.

14 Working within the car in the driver's footwell, slacken both pinch-bolts on the column upper universal joint. Do not turn the steering wheel from this point on.

15 Slide the steering lower universal joint off the splines of the steering gear pinion shaft.

16 Slacken the nuts on the front roadwheels.

17 An adjustable engine support crossbeam will now be required as described in Chapter 1, Section 3. Adjust the hooks until the weight of the engine is just taken.

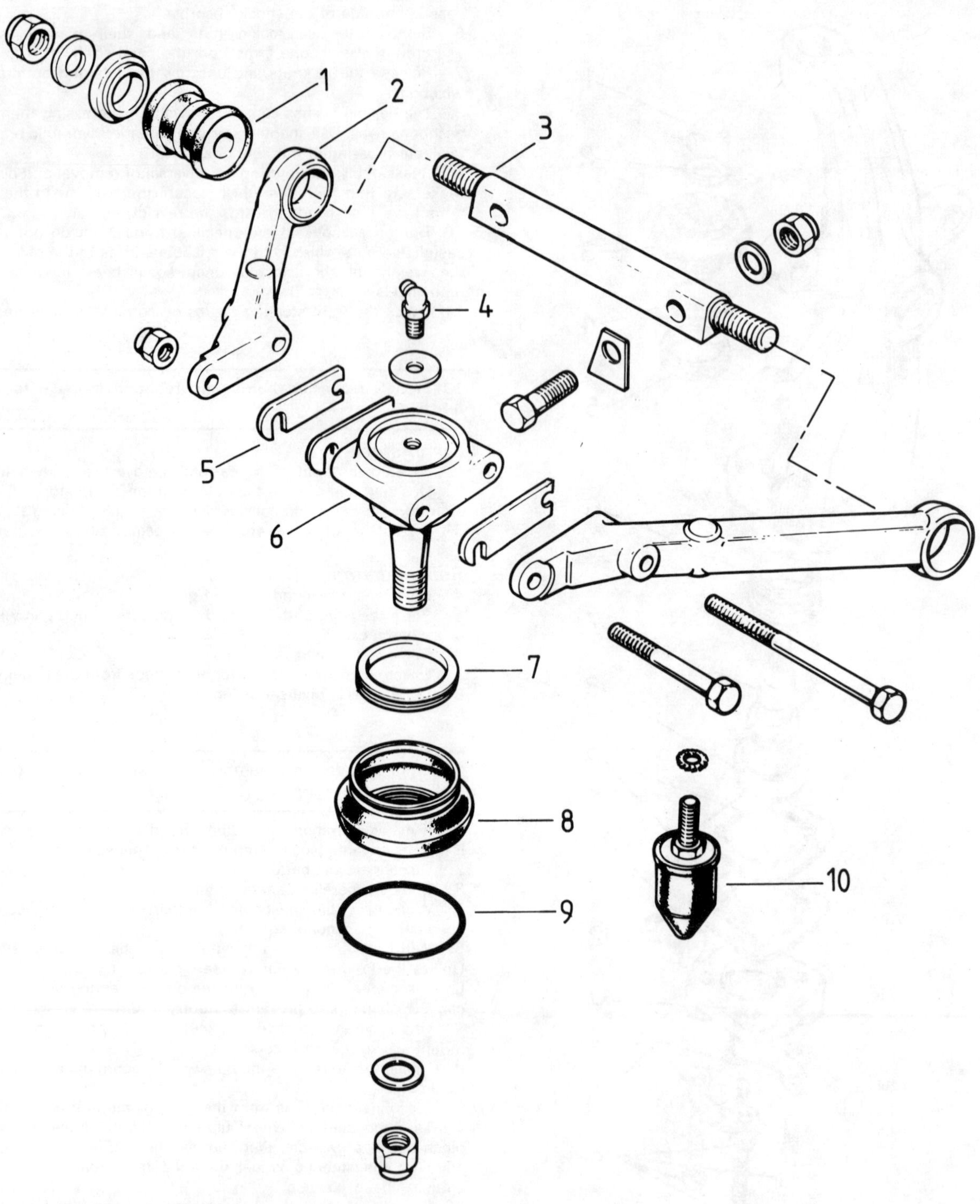

Fig. 11.10 Front suspension upper wishbone (Sec 12)

1 Flexible bush
2 Wishbone arm
3 Pivot shaft
4 Grease nipple
5 Castor control shim
6 Balljoint
7 Retaining ring
8 Dust-excluding boot
9 O-ring
10 Rebound stop

18 Set the speed selector lever to 'P' and apply the handbrake fully.
19 Place a trolley jack under the front crossmember and raise the car sufficiently high to be able to withdraw the suspension unit without fouling the underside of the car. Once this position has been reached, place stands under the front jacking points.
20 Remove the front roadwheels.
21 Disconnect the flexible hoses from the front calipers and plug or cap the opening to prevent loss of fluid.
22 With the crossmember still supported with the jack, remove the front mounting pivot bolts.
23 Lower the suspension assembly and withdraw it from under the front of the car.
24 Dismantling the suspension is carried out by following the various procedures described in the foregoing Sections.
25 Refitting is a reversal of removal, but note the following points.
26 Do not fully tighten the crossmember front or rear mounting bolts until the car has been lowered onto its wheels.
27 When reconnecting the steering column, it is important that a clearance of $\frac{3}{8}$ in (9.5 mm) exists axially in the lower universal joint. If not, move the upper joint further along the lower column to adjust the clearance.
28 Do not start the engine until the steering pump reservoir has been refilled (see Section 48).
29 Bleed the brake hydraulic system on completion.

15 Front suspension assembly (XJS) – removal and refitting

1 Refer to paragraphs 1 and 2 of Section 14.
2 The operations are very similar to those described in the preceding Section, but the following differences and suppementary work must be noted.
3 Removal of the left-hand air cleaner cover and filter element only is required.
4 Disconnect the earthing strap from the left-hand bodyframe just forward of the power steering oil cooler. Also disconnect the earthing strap from the engine sump.
5 Prise out the plastic fasteners which hold the vertical stoneguards

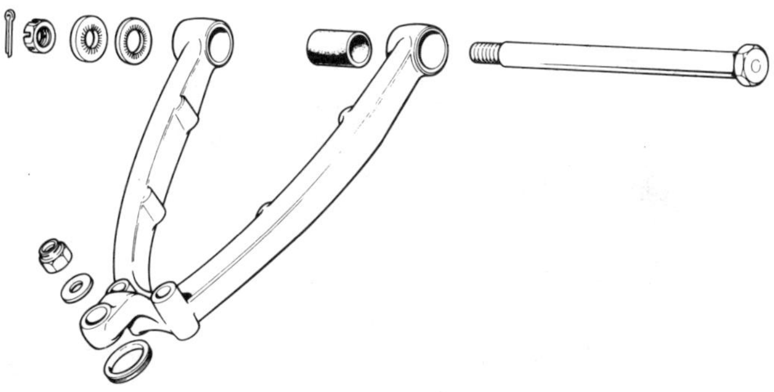

Fig. 11.11 Front suspension lower wishbone (Sec 11)

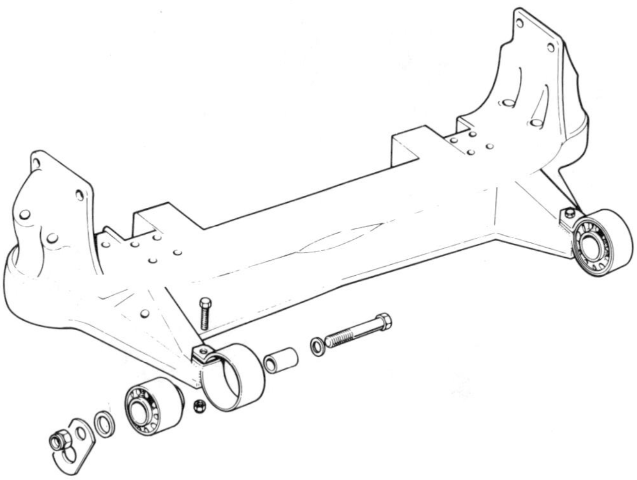

Fig. 11.12 Front crossmember (XJ12, Double Six) (Sec 14)

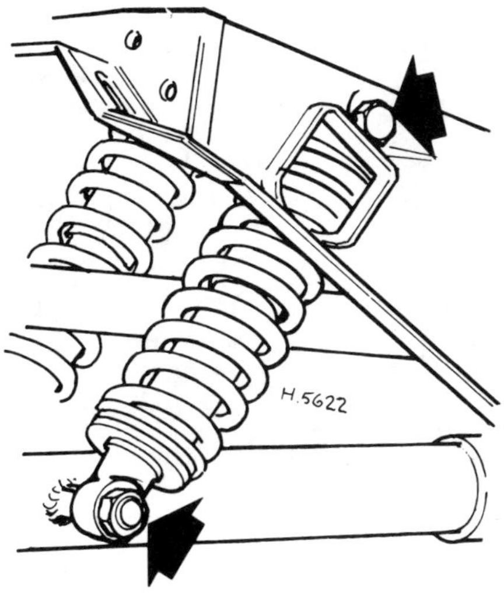

Fig. 11.13 Rear spring/shock absorber mountings (arrowed) (Sec 16)

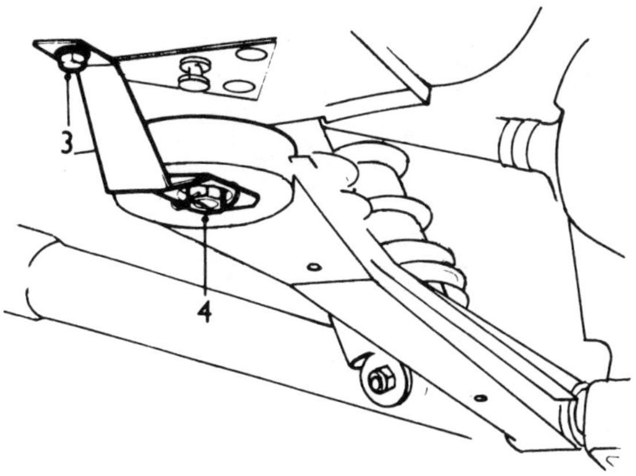

Fig. 11.14 Rear suspension radius arm safety strap (Sec 18)

3 Bolt to body floor
4 Safety strap attachment to radius arm

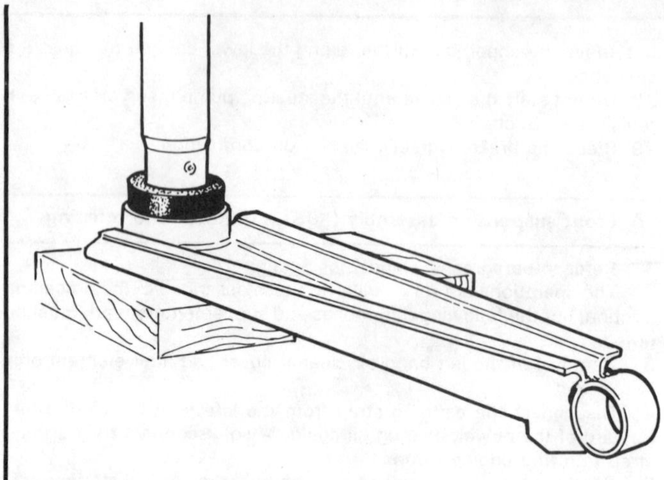

Fig. 11.15 Removing a rear suspension radius arm bush (Sec 18)

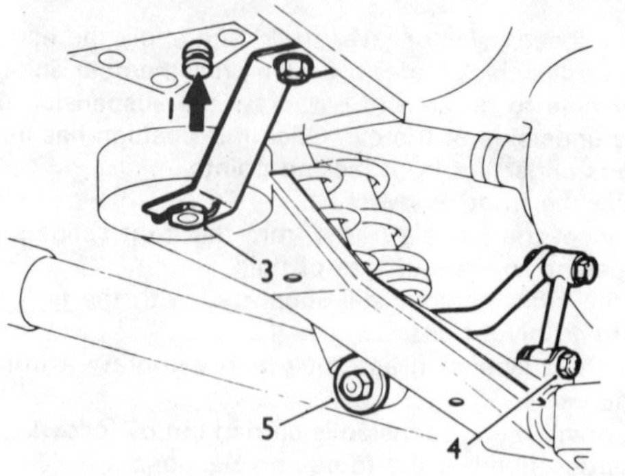

Fig. 11.16 Rear suspension radius arm showing anti-roll bar attachment on XJS models only (Sec 19)

1 Radius arm anchor point
3 Radius arm to body bolt
4 Anti-roll bar attachment
5 Spring/shock absorber lower mounting

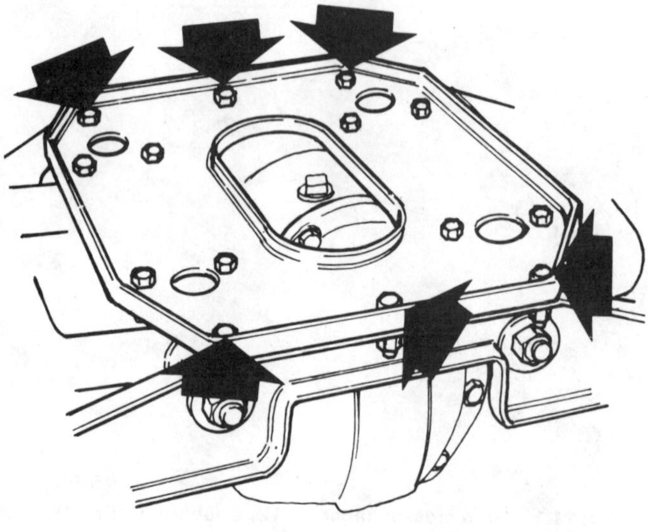

Fig. 11.17 Tie plate to crossmember securing bolts (arrowed) (Sec 20)

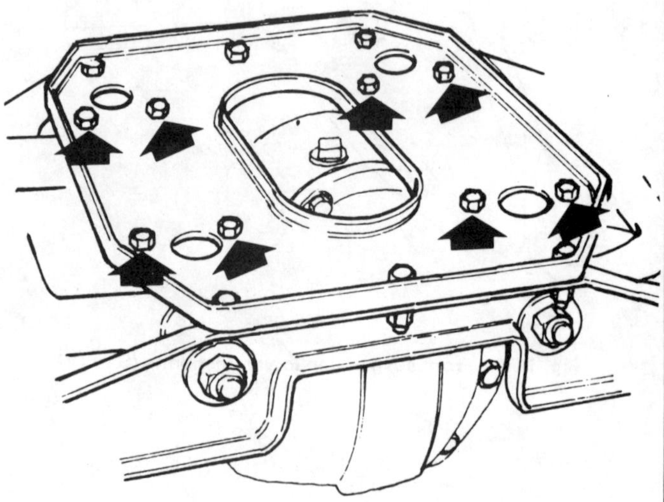

Fig. 11.18 Tie plate to inner pivot mounting bracket bolts (arrowed) (Sec 20)

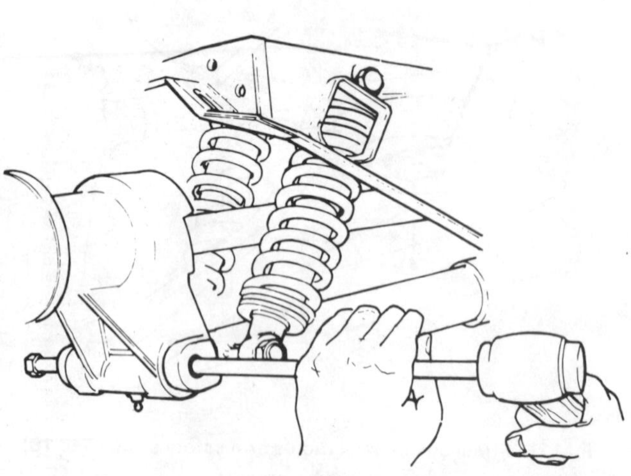

Fig. 11.19 Driving out a rear suspension wishbone outer pivot shaft (Sec 20)

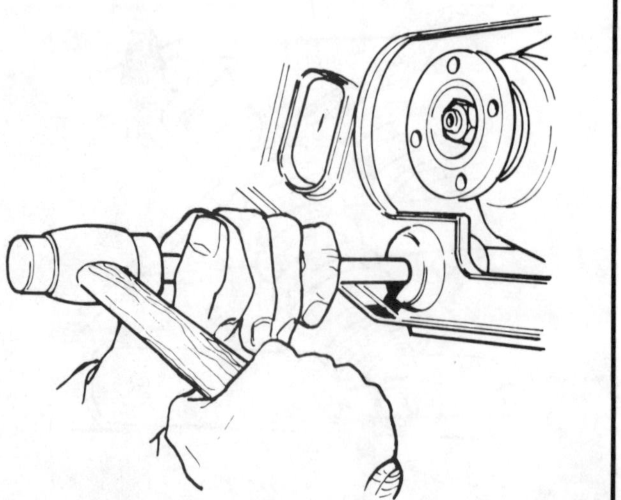

Fig. 11.20 Installing rear suspension wishbone inner pivot shaft (propeller shaft removed for clarity) (Sec 20)

within the wheel arches.
6 Remove the two screws and thirteen plastic fasteners which hold the spoiler undertray to the body and the spoiler.
7 Refitting is a reversal of removal, but before commencing the work detach the heat shield which protects the gaiter on the pinion end of the steering rack housing.
8 Refer to paragraph 27 of Section 14 and check the clearance.
9 Bleed the brakes and the power steering system.

16 Rear spring and shock absorber – removal and refitting

1 Jack up the rear of the car and support it securely on axle stands. Remove the roadwheel.
2 Remove the self-locking nut from the end of the shock absorber lower mounting pivot pin (photo).
3 Support the suspension wishbone with a jack and drive out the pivot pin.
4 Remove the spacer from the front shock absorber.
5 Disconnect the shock absorber upper mounting from the rear crossmember and withdraw the shock absorber/coil spring.
6 The coil spring must now be compressed so that the lower split type retainer can be removed and the spring removed in a downward direction.
7 Test the shock absorber as described in Section 3.
8 Renew the mounting bushes if the original ones are worn.
9 Refitting is a reversal of removal.

17 Rear hubs – removal, overhaul and refitting

1 The operations are described in Chapter 8, in conjunction with the axleshafts.

18 Rear suspension radius arm (XJ12 and Double Six) – removal and refitting

1 Jack up and support the centre of the rear suspension unit. Remove the roadwheel.
2 Cut the locking wire from the radius arm safety strap and bolt (photo).
3 Unscrew the bolt which secures the safety strap to the body floor.
4 Unscrew the radius arm securing bolt and remove the safety strap.
5 Withdraw the radius arm from the mounting post on the body.
6 Unscrew the self-locking nut which is nearest the front of the shock absorber lower pivot pin. Drive the pin far enough to clear the forward shock absorber and spacer. Extract the spacer, bend back the tabs of the lockwasher and remove the bolt which secures the radius arm to the lower wishbone mounting.
7 Remove the radius arm and examine the flexible bushes for deterioration.
8 If inspection has proved the need for renewal of the flexible bushes, make sure that the larger bush is fitted so that the two holes in it are in longtitudinal alignment with the arm. When installing the smaller bush, make sure that the metal centre sleeve projects equally on each side of the bush.
9 It is recommended that a press is used to remove and install the flexible bushes.
10 Refitting is a reversal of removal but make sure that the radius arm securing bolts are tightened to the specified torque wrench settings. Use new locking wire inserted through the hole in the bolt head and secured round the safety strap.

19 Rear suspension radius arm (XJS) – removal and refitting

1 The operations are similar to those described in the preceding Section, but the anti-roll bar link must also be disconnected from the radius arm.

20 Rear suspension wishbone (XJ12 and Double Six) – removal and refitting

1 Drain the oil from the final drive unit, remove the rear suspension assembly (Section 27) and then invert it on a bench.
2 Remove the six self-locking nuts and bolts which secure the tie plate to the crossmember.
3 Now remove the eight self-locking nuts and bolts which secure the tie plate to the wishbone inner pivot mounting brackets. Remove the tie plate.
4 Remove one of the self-locking nuts which secure the hub bearing assembly pivot shaft to the wishbone and drive out the pivot shaft.
5 Separate the hub carrier from the wishbone, noting any shims and their location so that they will be returned to their original positions.
6 The use of a rod as a dummy pivot shaft will keep the shims together. Place a piece of masking tape over each of the oil seals to prevent them being displaced.
7 Remove the self-locking nut, (nearest the front of the car), from the pivot shaft which connects the roadspring/shock absorbers to the wishbone. Tap the pivot shaft to the rear until it clears the front shock absorber and spacer. Retrieve the spacer and then move the shock absorber towards the centre of the suspension assembly.
8 Turn down the locking tab and remove the special bolt which holds the radius arm to the wishbone. Remove the radius arm.

16.2 Rear spring/shock absorber lower mounting

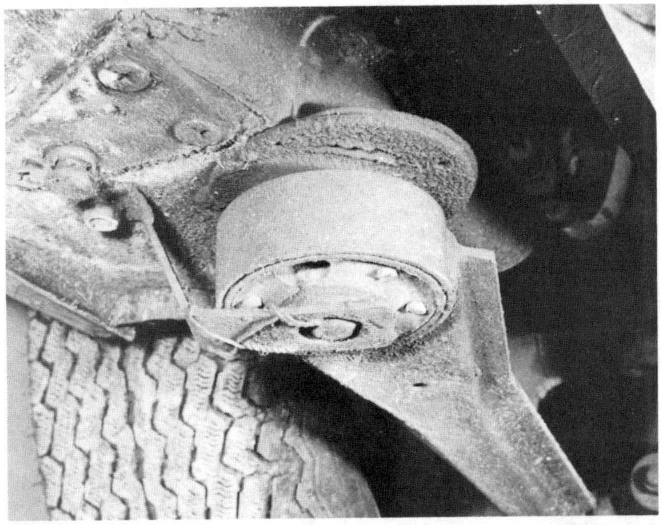

18.2 Radius arm safety strap

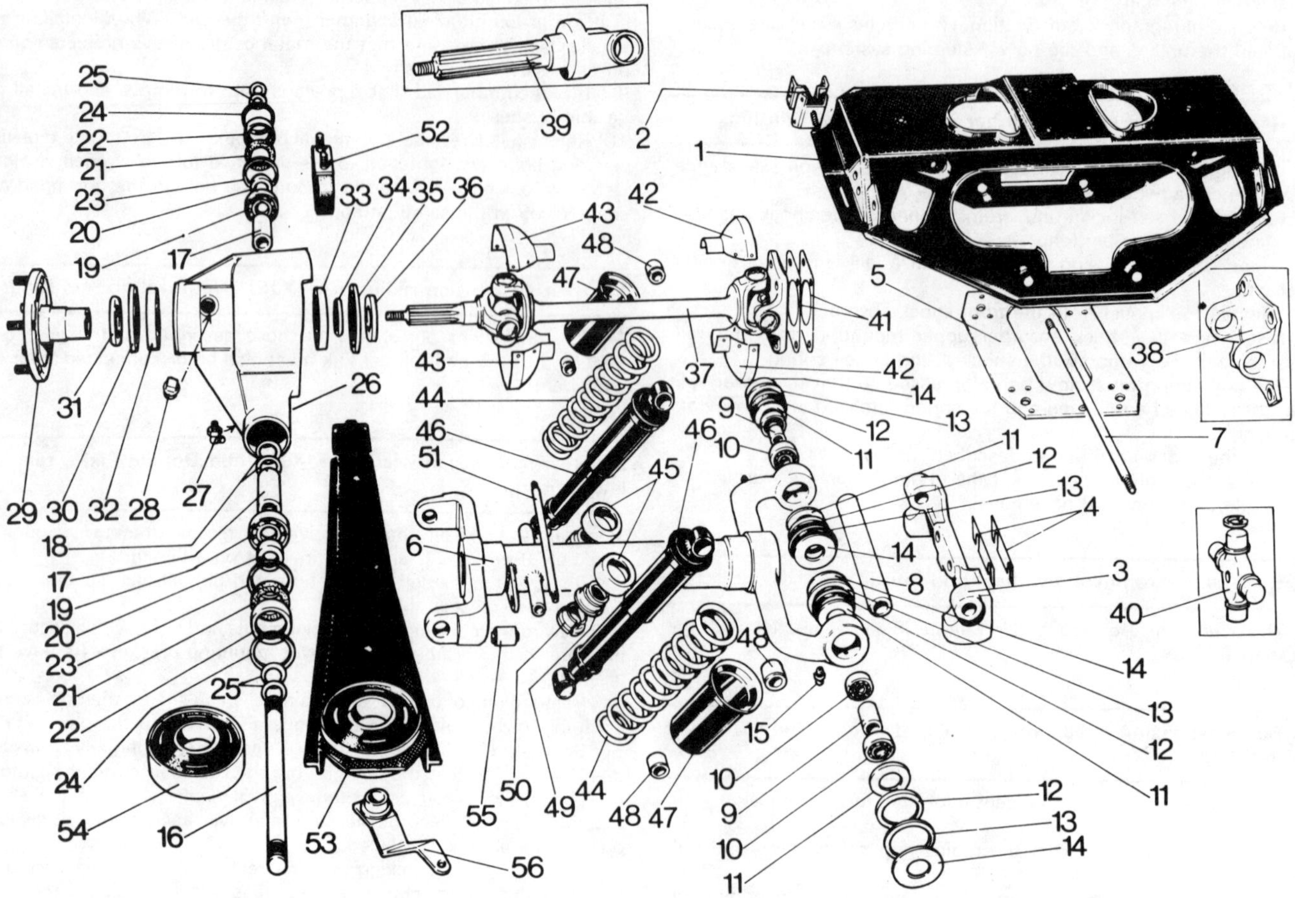

Fig. 11.21 Exploded view of the rear suspension (Sec 20)

1 Crossmember
2 Flexible mounting
3 Inner pivot mounting
4 Shims
5 Bracing plate
6 Wishbone
7 Inner pivot shaft
8 Spacer tube
9 Spacer tube
10 Needle bearing
11 Thrust washer
12 Seal
13 Retainer
14 Thrust washer
15 Grease nipple
16 Outer pivot shaft
17 Sleeve
18 Shim
19 Bearing
20 Ring
21 Oil seal
22 Oil seal retainer
23 Spacer
24 Washer
25 Shim
26 Hub carrier
27 Grease nipple
28 Grease retaining cap
29 Hub
30 Outer oil seal
31 Ring
32 Outer bearing
33 Inner bearing
34 Spacer
35 Oil seal
36 Ring
37 Driveshaft
38 Driveshaft flange
39 Splined yoke
40 Universal joint
41 Shim (camber control)
42 Joint cover (inner)
43 Joint cover (outer)
44 Coil spring
45 Packing ring
46 Shock absorber
47 Dust shield
48 Flexible bush
49 Seat
50 Retainer
51 Shock absorber lower mounting shaft
52 Bump stop
53 Radius arm
54 Flexible bush
55 Flexible bush
56 Safety strap

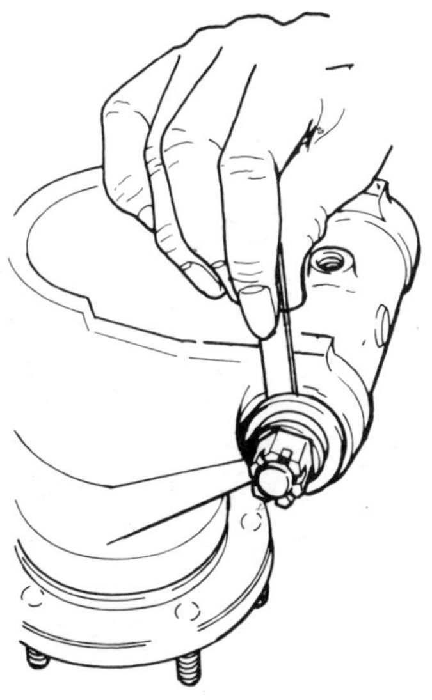

Fig. 11.22 Checking rear suspension wishbone outer pivot tapered bearing endfloat (Sec 22)

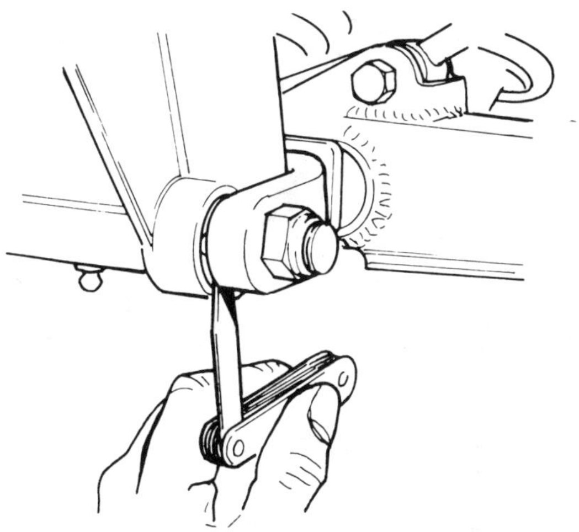

Fig. 11.23 Checking clearance between hub carrier oil seal retainer and wishbone of rear suspension (Sec 22)

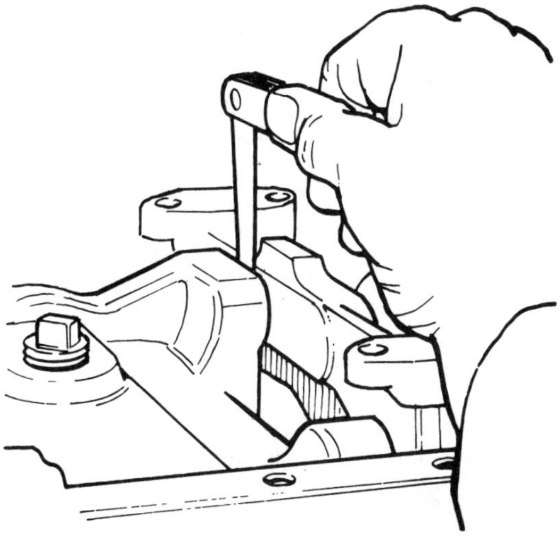

Fig. 11.24 Checking gap between rear suspension inner pivot bracket and differential casing (Sec 23)

9 Remove the pivot shaft which secures the lower ends of the roadspring/shock absorbers.
10 Remove the self-locking nut which secures the wishbone pivot shaft to the crossmember.
11 Drive the inner pivot shaft out of the wishbone and inner pivot mounting bracket.
12 Withdraw the wishbone assembly and collect the four outer thrust washers, inner thrust washers, oil seals and their retainers. Renew the oil seals if they have deteriorated.
13 Remove the two bearing tubes. There is no need to remove the spacer which is located between the inner pivot mounting bracket unless the mounting bracket is being renewed. If it must be removed, tap it out. The needle rollers can be extracted by tapping the cages out of the wishbone and then extracting the needle roller spacer.
14 If the needle rollers have been removed from the larger fork of the wishbone, press one of the roller cages into position so that the numbers on the cage face outwards. Press in the second cage. Repeat the operations on the opposite side of the wishbone.
15 Insert the bearing tubes, apply grease to the four outer thrust $\frac{1}{4}$washers, oil seals, retainers and locate them on the wishbone.
16 Offer up the wishbone to the inner pivot mounting bracket so that the radius arm mounting bracket is towards the front of the car. Align the holes and spacers. Insert a rod as a dummy shaft through each side of the crossbeam and wishbone. These rods locate the wishbone thrust washers, crossbeam and inner pivot mounting bracket and so facilitate installation of the pivot shaft proper. The dummy shaft should be fractionally smaller in diameter than the pivot shaft itself.
17 Tap the pivot shaft into position, having smeared it with grease. As it passes through the crossmember, the wishbone and the inner pivot mounting bracket, the temporary rods will be displaced from the opposite end. Keep the rods and shaft in contact at all times otherwise a spacer or thrust washer may drop out of position.
18 With the wishbone inner pivot shaft installed, tighten the two self-locking nuts to the specified torque.
19 Install the eight bolts which secure the tie plate to the inner pivot mounting bracket then refit the six bolts which secure the tie plate to the crossmember.
20 Refit the radius arm to the wishbone.
21 Remove the tape which was used to hold the oil seal tracks in position and offer up the wishbone/hub assembly.
22 Again using a rod as a dummy shaft, align the wishbone hub assembly oil seal tracks and spacers. Apply grease to the wishbone outer pivot shaft and gently tap it into position so displacing the dummy shaft.
23 Slide the pivot shaft through the wishbone and hub carrier. Using feeler blades, check the clearance between the hub carrier and the wishbone. Where necessary, install shims between the hub carrier and the wishbone to centralise the hub carrier. Tighten the nuts on the pivot shaft to the specified torque.
24 Refit the rear suspension assembly.
25 The rear suspension camber angle should be checked after a major overhaul (see Section 49).
26 Refill the final drive unit with specified oil.
27 Lubricate the wishbone grease nipples.

21 Rear suspension wishbone (XJS) – removal and refitting

1 The operations are very similar to those described in the preceding Section, except that the anti-roll bar link must also be disconnected from the radius arm.

22 Rear suspension wishbone outer pivot – dismantling, re-assembly and bearing adjustment

1 Support the hub carrier and wishbone securely.
2 Remove one of the self-locking nuts which secure the outer pivot shaft.
3 Drive out the pivot shaft and retain any shims which may be located between the hub carrier and the wishbone.
4 Separate the hub carrier and the wishbone.
5 Remove the oil seal retainer and prise out the oil seals.
6 Remove the inner races of the tapered roller bearings by tapping them out with a drift.
7 Remove the spacers and shims.
8 If new tapered roller bearings have been fitted, it will be necessary

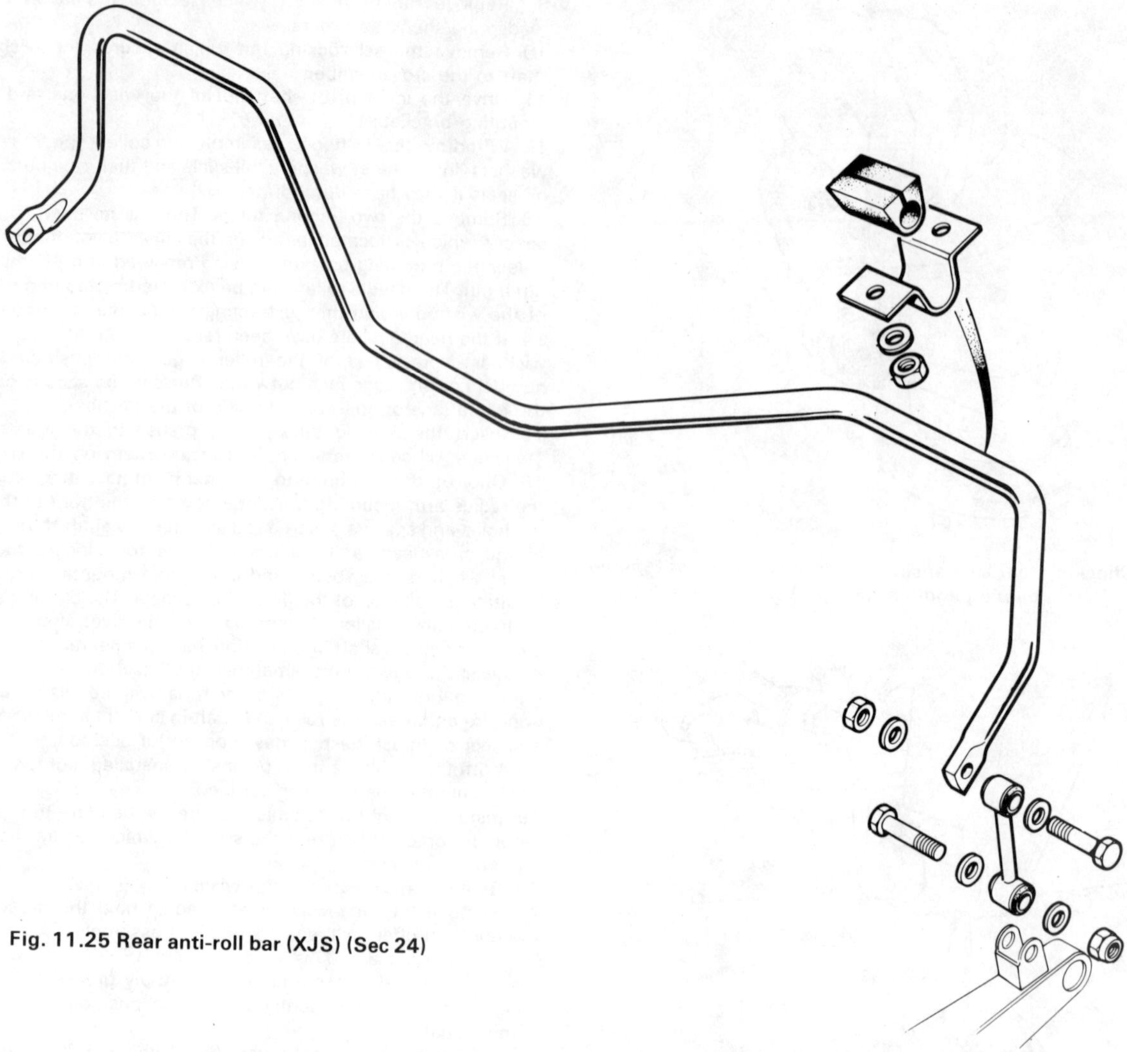

Fig. 11.25 Rear anti-roll bar (XJS) (Sec 24)

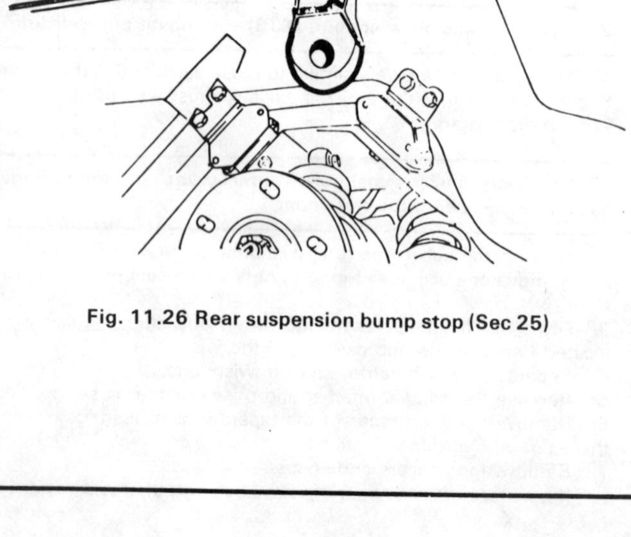

Fig. 11.26 Rear suspension bump stop (Sec 25)

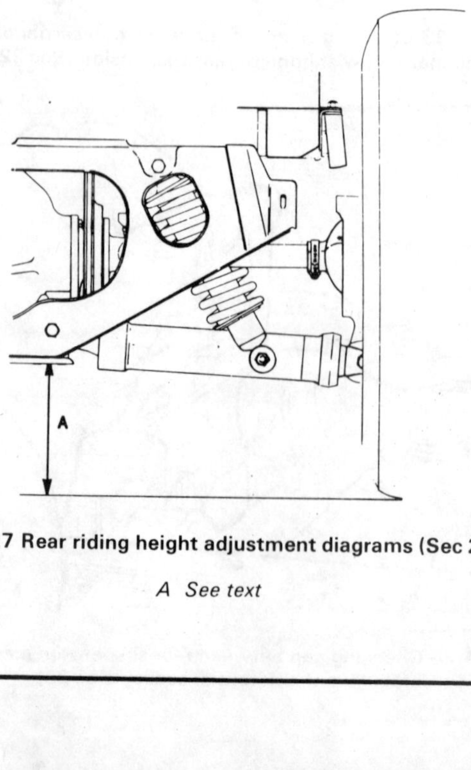

Fig. 11.27 Rear riding height adjustment diagrams (Sec 26)

A See text

to adjust them in the following way.
9 Disconnect the hub from the driveshaft as described in Chapter 8.
10 Refit the inner races for the outer pivot tapered roller bearings. Fit the spacers and a shim pack of known thickness followed by the tapered roller bearings and oil seals.
11 The bearing adjustment is controlled by shims which are located between the two pivot shaft spacer tubes.
12 To calculate the shims required to provide the specified preload of the outer pivot tapered roller bearings, drill a ho0Ole in a piece of steel plate and secure the plate in the jaws of a vice. Bolt the pivot shaft to the plate.
13 Slide an oil seal retainer onto the shaft and then install the outer pivot assembly to the shaft but without any oil seals and including an excess of shims between the spacer tubes.
14 Place an inner wishbone fork outer thrust washer onto the fulcrum shaft so that it abuts the oil seal retainer. Fill the remaining space on the shaft with washers and screw on a nut to a torque of 95 lbf ft (132 Nm).
15 Press the hub carrier assembly towards the steel support plate using a rotating motion in order to settle the tapered roller bearings. Maintain a steady hand pressure against the hub carrier and using a feeler blade, measure the clearance between the large diameter washer and the machined face of the hub carrier.
16 Subtract this measurement from the thickness of the shim pack which was included between the spacer tubes, or subtract the thickness of the shim pack from the clearance measured, whichever is the greater. The result indicates the bearing preload. The specified preload is from 0.000 to 0.002 in (0.00 to 0.05 mm) and the shim pack should be adjusted as necessary to bring the actual preload into line with that specified.
17 Refit the hub carrier to the axleshaft, install new oil seals (lips inwards) and then fit the pivot shaft into position in the hub carrier.
18 Offer up the hub carrier to the wishbone. Ease the dummy shaft through the wishbone in conjunction with the pivot shaft. Using feeler blades, measure the gap between the oil seal retainer and the wishbone.
19 Install shims as necessary to centralise the hub carrier in the wishbone fork and to prevent the ends of the fork from closing as the pivot shaft nuts are tightened to their specified torque wrench settings.
20 It will be found easier to install the wishbone if a dummy shaft is passed through the hub carrier before offering the wishbone to the carrier.
21 Refitting is otherwise a reversal of removal. Apply grease to the lubrication nipples on completion.

23 Rear suspension wishbone inner pivot mounting bracket – removal and refitting

1 Drain the oil from the final drive unit and remove the rear suspension unit as described in Section 27. Remove the tie plate as described in Section 20, paragraphs 2 and 3.
2 Remove the self-locking nut from one end of the wishbone inner pivot shaft, drive out the shaft.
3 Withdraw the wishbone fork from the pivot mounting bracket. Collect the oil seal retainers, oil seals, inner and outer thrust washers and tubes.
4 Cut the lockwire from the two setscrews which secure the inner pivot bracket to the differential unit.
5 Remove the spacer from the mounting bracket.
6 Remove the two setscrews, noting the shims located between the bracket and the differential unit.
7 Remove the wishbone inner pivot mounting bracket.
8 Refitting is a reversal of removal, but make sure that the original shims are refitted between the mounting bracket and the differential. If new components have been fitted check the clearance with feeler blades between the rear face of the bracket and the final drive housing. Add or remove shims as necessary to eliminate any clearance at this point. Pass the pivot shaft through the crossmember and the inner pivot mounting bracket.
9 Tighten the pivot bolt nut to the specified torque.
10 Refill the final drive unit.

24 Rear anti-roll bar (XJS) – removal and refitting

1 Position the car on ramps or over an inspection pit.
2 Raise the left rear of the car and support on stands.
3 Remove the left rear roadwheel.
4 Slacken the exhaust pipe clamp on the right-hand pipe just forward of the crossmember.
5 Unbolt both ends of the anti-roll bar from the links.
6 Unscrew and remove the four nuts which hold the anti-roll bar clamps to the rear seat underpan. Remove the clamps and rubber insulators.
7 Separate the exhaust pipe joint sufficiently to enable the anti-roll bar to be withdrawn through the left-hand wheel arch.
8 Refitting is a reversal of removal. Tighten nuts to the specified torque after the weight of the car has been lowered onto the roadwheels.

25 Rear suspension bump stop – renewal

1 Jack up the rear of the car and remove the roadwheel.
2 Unscrew and remove the two self-locking nuts and remove the bump stop.
3 Refit by reversing the removal operations.

26 Rear riding height – adjustment

1 Have the car filled with oil and water and fuel tanks filled. The tyre pressures must be correct with the car standing on level ground.

XJ12, Double Six

2 Measure the distance (A in Fig. 11.27) between the bottom of the rear crossmember and the ground on both sides of the car.
3 Both dimensions should be equal at between 7.20 and 7.70 in (183.0 and 195.5 mm). If they are not, check for worn mounting bushes on rear suspension components. If no fault can be found then the coil springs are weak and a new set of four must be fitted.

XJS

4 The procedure is identical to that just described for the XJ12 and Double Six models, but the measured clearance should be between 7.30 and 7.80 in (185.4 and 198.1 mm).

27 Rear suspension assembly (XJ12 and Double Six) – removal and refitting

1 If major operations are to be carried out to the rear suspension, it may be advantageous to remove the suspension assembly complete. First jack up the rear of the car and support it.
2 Remove the self-tapping screws or clamps which secure the exhaust tail pipes to the rear silencers and withdraw the pipes.
3 Release the clamps which secure the rear silencers to the intermediate pipes. Remove the rear exhaust silencers.
4 Release the clamps which secure the intermediate pipes to the front silencers. Withdraw the pipes from the suspension assembly.
5 Remove the locking wire from the radius arm safety straps and securing bolts. Remove the bolts which secure the safety strap to the body floor.
6 Remove the radius arm securing bolts and withdraw the safety straps.
7 Withdraw the radius arms from their mounting posts on the body.
8 Place a wooden block between the rear suspension tie plate and a jack, preferably of trolley type.
9 Now jack-up the rear of the car and position two chassis stands under the bodyframe members just forward of the radius arm mounting posts. Place blocks of wood between the chassis stands and the bodyframe to avoid damage.
10 Remove the rear roadwheels.
11 Disconnect the flexible brake pipe at the support bracket on the body.
12 Disconnect the handbrake cable from the caliper actuating lever which is mounted on the suspension crossbeam. Withdraw the outer cable from the trunnion on the opposite lever.
13 Remove the four bolts which secure the mounting rubbers at the front of the crossmember to the bodyframe.
14 Remove the nuts and bolts which secure the rear mounting

rubbers to the crossmember.
15 Disconnect the propeller shaft from the differential pinion flange.
16 Lower the rear suspension assembly on the jack and withdraw it from under the car.
17 Refitting is a reversal of removal, but note the following points:

(a) Renew any mounting rubbers which have deteriorated
(b) Tighten the radius arm to wishbone bolts after the weight of the car has been lowered onto the roadwheels
(c) Bleed the brake hydraulic circuit
(d) Adjust the handbrake

28 Rear suspension assembly (XJS) – removal and refitting

1 The operations are similar to those described in the preceding Section for XJ12 and Double Six models except that an additional operation must be carried out, to unbolt the anti-roll bar links from the radius arms.

29 Tie-rod outer balljoints – renewal

1 If wear is found in the tie-rod end balljoints then they must be renewed as sealed assemblies.
2 Unscrew and remove the ball pin nut and separate the balljoint from the steering arm using a suitable extractor or forked wedges.
3 Hold the tie-rod end quite still with an open-ended spanner applied to its flats and unscrew the locknut one quarter of a turn. Hold the tie-rod quite still and unscrew the tie-rod end from it. If the bellows are perforated, release their clips and withdraw them.
4 Screw on the new tie-rod end until it almost touches the locknut and then tighten the locknut, making sure that the tie-rod end is again supported in an open-ended spanner.
5 Reconnect the tie-rod end to the steering arm.
6 The front wheel alignment must be checked and adjusted, as described in Section 49.
7 It is important that the lengths of the tie-rods are equal. If for any reason thay have become unequal, set the tie-rod ends on the rods so that the distance between the centre of the tie-rod end balljoint and the face of the inner balljoint is equal to the corresponding dimension on the opposite tie-rod. Release the inner clips on the flexible bellows to measure.
8 When measuring, the front roadwheels and the steering wheel must be in the straight-ahead attitude. If there is any doubt about the steering wheel position, centre the steering rack and check the position of the steering wheel spokes.
9 To centre the steering rack, remove the grease nipple on the steering rack housing and insert a thin rod. Maintain pressure on the rod while slowly turning the steering wheel until the rod is felt to drop into an indentation on the rack. The rack is now centred. Remove the rod and screw the grease nipple back into place. If the steering wheel is not in the straight-ahead attitude, it will have to be removed and re-positioned as described in Section 32 or 33.
10 Ball pin knock which may be heard when turning right or left may be due to wear in the tie-rod inner balljoints. No adjustment can be carried out and new tie-rod/ball pin assemblies must be fitted. This work can be carried out without removing the rack from the car as described in the next Section.

30 Tie-rod inner balljoints – renewal

1 Disconnect the tie-rod outer balljoint from the steering arm.
2 Remove the bellows retaining clip from the rack housing.
3 Peel the bellows back until the inner balljoint is exposed and then flatten the tabs of the lockwasher which secures the balljoint assembly to the rack.
4 Remove the inner balljoint and tie-rod and extract the spring and spacer.
5 Remove the outer tie-rod end and then discard the worn inner balljoint/tie-rod assembly.
6 Fit the tie-rod end to the new rod/inner balljoint assembly, setting the components as described in the preceding Section.
7 Refit the inner balljoint to the rack, using a new lockwasher, and smear the joint with 2 oz (57 g) of grease.

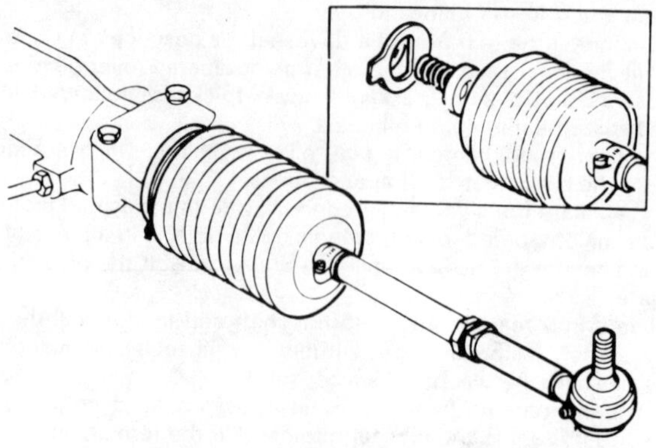

Fig. 11.28 Steering tie-rod and outer balljoint. Inset shows fixing details of inner balljoint (Sec 29)

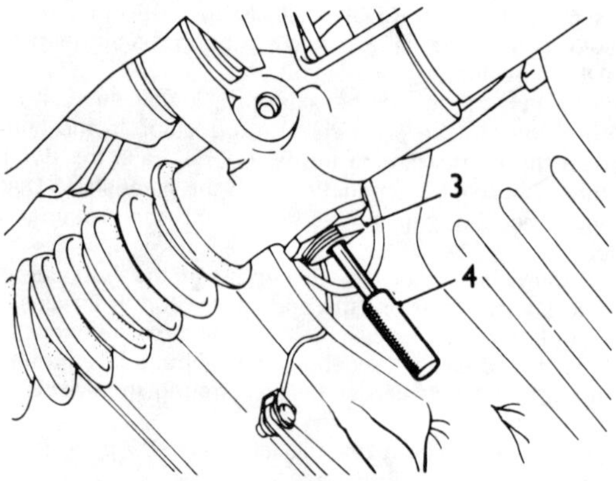

Fig. 11.29 Centering the steering rack (Sec 29)

3 Damper adjusting plug
4 Rod

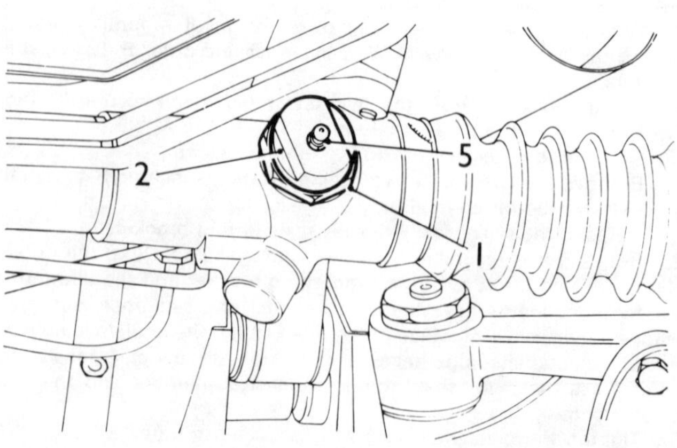

Fig. 11.30 Rack damper on steering housing (Sec 31)

1 Locknut
2 Adjuster plug
5 Grease nipple

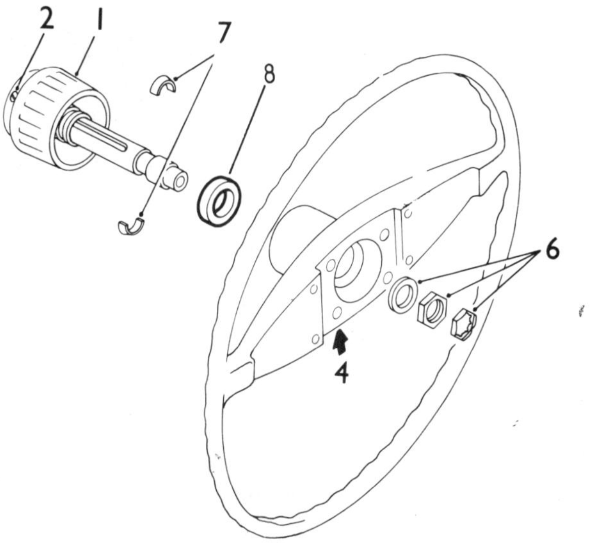

Fig. 11.31 Steering wheel details (Series 1) (Sec 32)

1 *Height adjuster*
2 *Safety screw*
4 *Steering wheel*
6 *Nut, locknut and washer*
7 *Cone halves*
8 *Impact rubber*

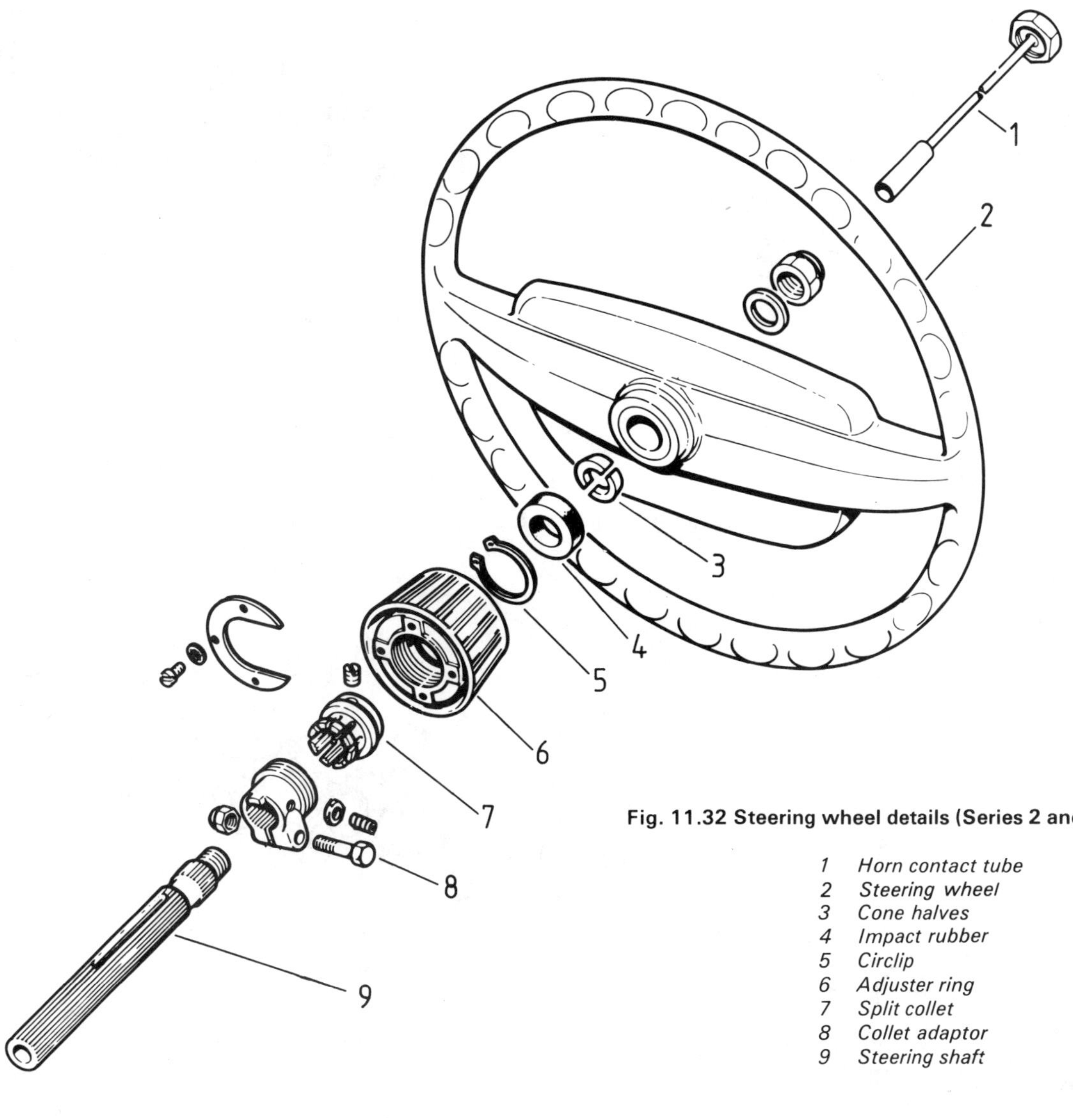

Fig. 11.32 Steering wheel details (Series 2 and XJS) (Sec 33)

1 *Horn contact tube*
2 *Steering wheel*
3 *Cone halves*
4 *Impact rubber*
5 *Circlip*
6 *Adjuster ring*
7 *Split collet*
8 *Collet adaptor*
9 *Steering shaft*

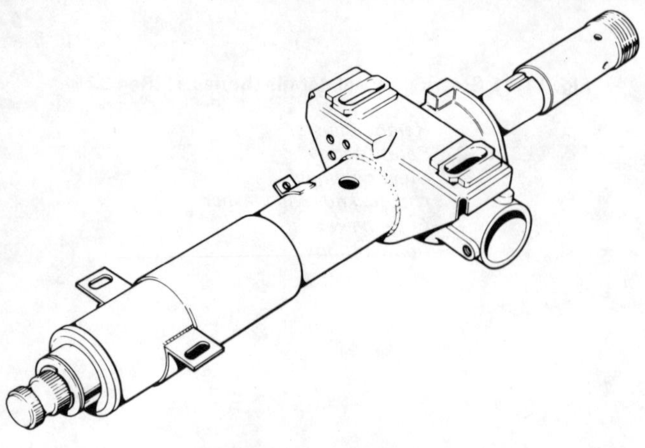

Fig. 11.33 Steering upper column (XJ12 and Double Six, Series 2 onwards) (Sec 35)

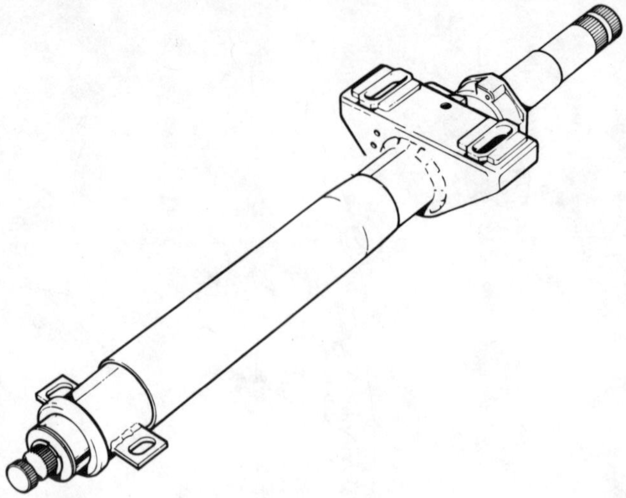

Fig. 11.34 Steering upper column (XJS) (Sec 36)

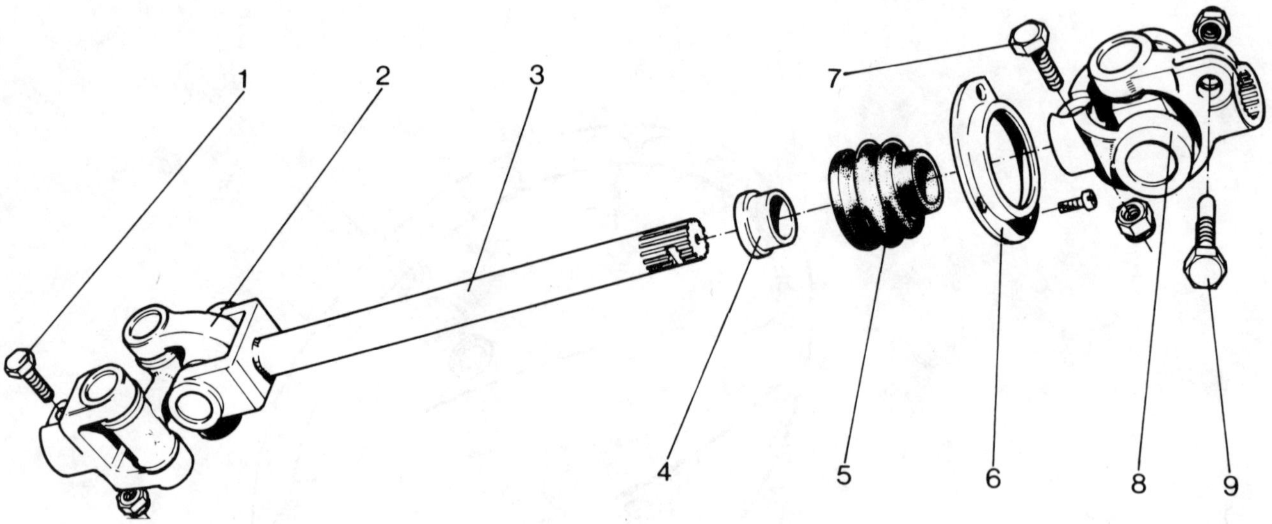

Fig. 11.35 Steering lower column (XJ12, Double Six) (Sec 37)

1 *Pinch-bolt*
2 *Bottom universal joint*
3 *Lower column*
4 *Bush*
5 *Gaiter*
6 *Retaining plate*
7 *Pinch-bolt*
8 *Top universal joint*
9 *Pinch-bolt*

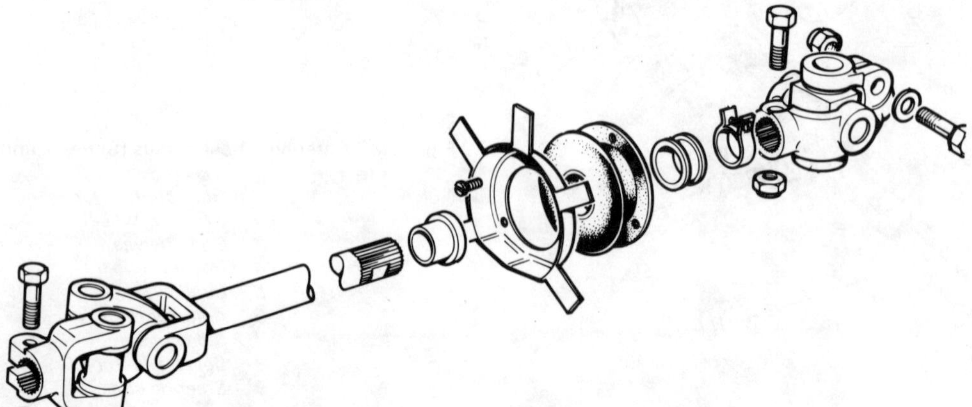

Fig. 11.36 Steering lower column (XJS) (Sec 38)

8 Refit the bellows, reconnect the tie-rod end to the steering arm and check the front wheel alignment (Section 49).

31 Steering rack – adjustment in the car

1 Should rack rattle occur when travelling over rough surfaces, the rack pad requires adjustment.
2 Release the locknut which secures the rack pad adjusting screw.
3 Screw the rack adjusting screw inwards until a stiff resistance is encountered and then release the screw one sixth of a turn.
4 Tighten the locknut.

32 Steering wheel (XJ12 and Double Six, Series 1) – removal and refitting

1 Set the front roadwheels in the straight-ahead position and mark the position of the steering wheel in relation to the column. If the steering wheel is being removed for the sole purpose of re-positioning it, then the steering rack and front roadwheels should be centred as described in Section 29. Disconnect the battery.
2 Unscrew the knurled height adjustment ring until the safety screw is exposed. Slacken the screw two turns and then unscrew the knurled adjustment ring fully.
3 Withdraw the steering wheel/upper shaft assembly.
4 If the steering wheel is to be dismantled from the shaft, first extract the four self-tapping screws from the underside of the steering wheel hub.
5 Extract the four screws which secure the horn ring to the steering wheel, detach the ring.
6 Unscrew and remove the locknut and nut from the top of the shaft. Pull off the steering wheel and retrieve the two halves of the cone, also the impact rubber where one is fitted.
7 Refitting is a reversal of removal. Make sure that the front roadwheels have not moved from the straight-ahead position and that the steering wheel marks are aligned.

33 Steering wheel (XJ12 and Double Six, Series 2 on, and XJS) – removal and refitting

1 Refer to paragraph 1 of Section 32.
2 Extract the three screws which hold the lower switch cover and detach it from the column.
3 Working from below, unscrew and remove the pinch-bolt which holds the collet adaptor to the steering column (photo).
4 Slacken the locknut of the grub screw in the collet adaptor and unscrew the grub screw two turns. On later models, a second pinch-bolt is fitted instead of the grub screw.
5 Withdraw the steering wheel complete with knurled height adjusting ring, impact rubber, collet adaptor and upper shaft (photo).
6 To remove the steering wheel from the shaft, extract the two screws from the rear face of the steering wheel boss and lift off the padded horn contact (photo).
7 Unscrew and remove the nylon nut from the top of the shaft, withdrawing the horn contact tube with it.
8 Unscrew and remove the nut which holds the steering wheel to the shaft, withdraw the wheel and retrieve the two halves of the cone.
9 Refitting is a reversal of removal, but smear all the internal friction surfaces with engine oil.
10 An alternative method of removing the steering wheel/upper shaft assembly can be carried out as follows.
11 Release the knurled steering wheel adjuster ring and pull the wheel up to its fullest extent.
12 Working from below the steering wheel, extract the three screws which hold the horseshoe-shaped retaining plate to the underside of the adjuster ring (photo).
13 Remove the plate and pull off the steering wheel with upper splined shaft.
14 The collet adaptor (some later versions incorporate two pinch-bolts) can then be removed, followed by the steering column switches and the upper cowl (photos).
15 Refitting is a reversal of removal. If the method described in paragraphs 10 to 14 was employed, make sure that the horn contact probe is central in the lower column hole when fitting the splined upper shaft.
16 Fit the column switches in conjunction with the upper cowl followed by the adaptor, pinch-bolts and horseshoe-shaped retaining plate.

34 Steering upper column (XJ12 and Double Six, Series 1) – removal and refitting

1 Disconnect the battery.
2 Remove the steering wheel, as described in Section 32.
3 Remove the three screws which secure the direction indicator switch and cowl to the outer column.
4 Disconnect the direction indicator switch leads by separating the plug and socket.
5 Remove the speedometer and the tachometer from the instrument panel, as described in Chapter 10.
6 Disconnect the horn switch lead from the contact on the steering column.
7 Disconnect the ignition switch leads at the plug and socket connector.
8 Remove the pinch-bolt which secures the upper universal joint to the steering column.
9 Remove the two nuts which secure the upper column mounting bracket to the support bracket on the body. Note the location of any packing washers under the bracket, and support the column as the bracket is released. Access for this operation is through the speedometer and tachometer apertures.
10 Remove the two nuts which secure the lower mounting bracket to the bulkhead and again note any packing washers which may be located under this bracket.
11 Withdraw the upper column from the universal joint splines. Take great care not to use force on the column or it may collapse due to shearing of the safety plastic plugs. A new column will then be required as no repair is possible.
12 Refitting is a reversal of removal but set the front roadwheels in the straight-ahead position and connect the upper column to the universal joint splines so that the pinch-bolt holes are in alignment with the column groove. Tighten the pinch-bolt to the specified torque.

35 Steering upper column (XJ12 and Double Six, Series 2 on) – removal and refitting

1 The operations are very similar to those described in the preceding Section, but additionally the under scuttle casing must be removed (see Chapter 12).
2 The electrical harness to the steering column switches is disconnected by uncoupling the three multi-pin plugs.
3 When refitting, make sure that a $\frac{3}{8}$ in (9.5 mm) clearance exists axially in the lower universal joint. If less, move the upper joint along the column to increase the clearance.
4 Once everything is refitted, check that the direction indicators self-cancel correctly. If not, remove the lower switch cover (three screws) and check that the lower dogs on the fixed section of the switch engage correctly with the cutaways on the outer (fixed) column and that a dog on the split collet enters a slot in the moveable section of the switch.
5 Turn the steering wheel until the clamp bolt of the collet adaptor is in a horizontal attitude underneath the column.
6 Remove the steering wheel again (Section 33) and turn the steering wheel to the straight-ahead position while holding the collet adaptor in its previously set position. Refit the wheel, in this attitude, to the column.

36 Steering upper column (XJS) – removal and refitting

1 Remove the instrument module as described in Chapter 10.
2 Remove the steering column lower shroud (one screw).
3 Set the front roadwheels and the steering wheel in the straight-ahead position.
4 Remove the steering wheel complete with shaft and height adjuster as described in Section 33.

33.3 Removing the collet adaptor pinch-bolt

33.5 Removing the steering wheel/upper shaft

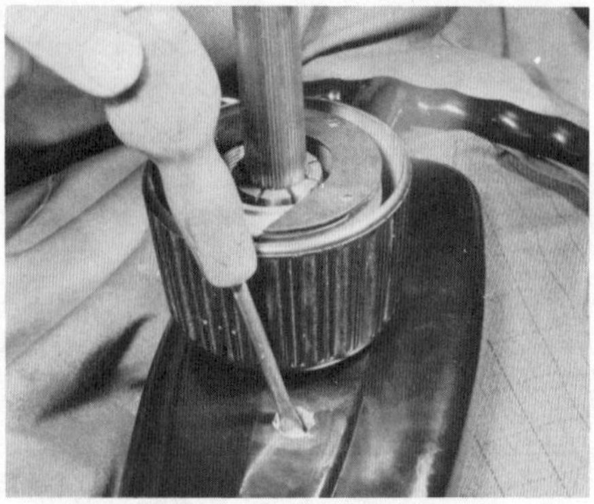

33.6 Extracting the steering wheel boss screws

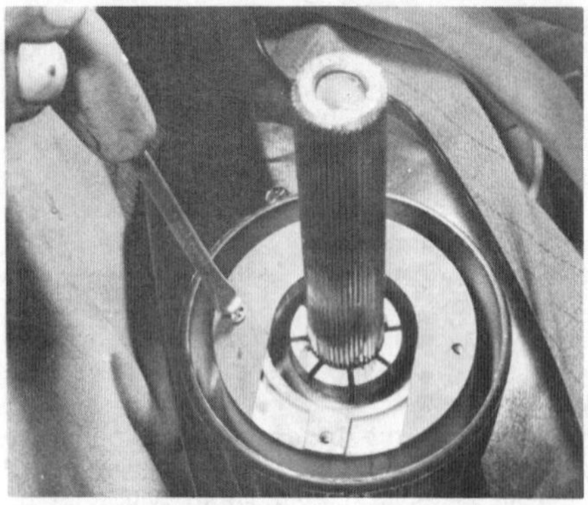

33.12 Extracting the retainer plate screws

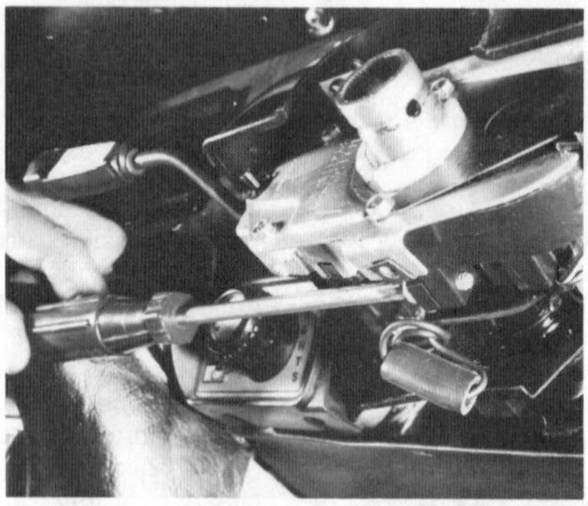

33.14A Slackening the steering column switch clamp screw

33.14B Withdrawing the steering column switches

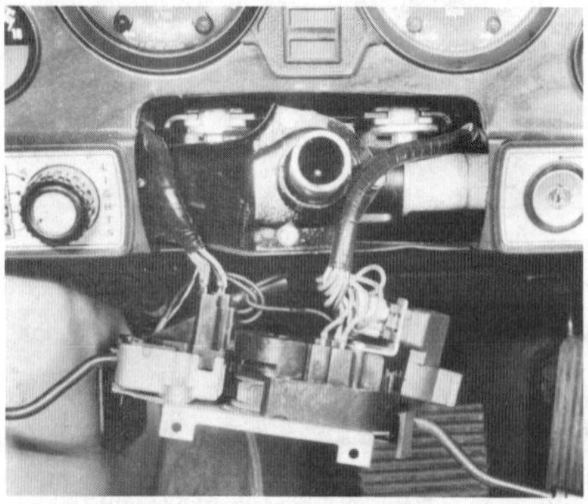

33.14C Steering column switches removed

37.1 Steering lower shaft universal joint

45.5 Steering pump mounting (lower)

5 Remove the upper and lower shrouds from the ignition switch and disconnect the switch wiring harness at the connector plug.
6 Unscrew and remove the pinch-bolt which holds the universal joint to the upper column.
7 Remove the column lower mounting bolts.
8 Disconnect the horn lead from the steering column.
9 Remove the bolts from the column upper mounting. Retrieve the distance pieces and washers.
10 Remove the column from the car.
11 Remove the switches and lock if necessary as described in Chapter 10.
12 Refitting is a reversal of removal, but screw in the mounting bolts only finger-tight until the column has been positioned centrally in its housing in the facia. Make sure that the distance pieces and washers are returned to their locations at the upper mounting and then tighten the upper and lower bolts to the specified torque.

37 Steering lower column (XJ12 and Double Six) – removal and refitting

1 Raise the front of the car and remove the pinch-bolt which secures the steering column lower universal joint to the pinion shaft on the rack housing (photo).
2 Lower the car and set the roadwheels and the steering wheel in the straight-ahead position.
3 Remove the parcels shelf and extract both pinch-bolts from the universal joint which joins the upper and lower columns.
4 Release the two mounting bolts from the bottom end of the upper column.
5 Pull the lower column from the upper universal joint.
6 Pull the lower universal joint from the steering pinion shaft and withdraw the lower column.
7 Refitting is a reversal of removal, but make sure that the steering

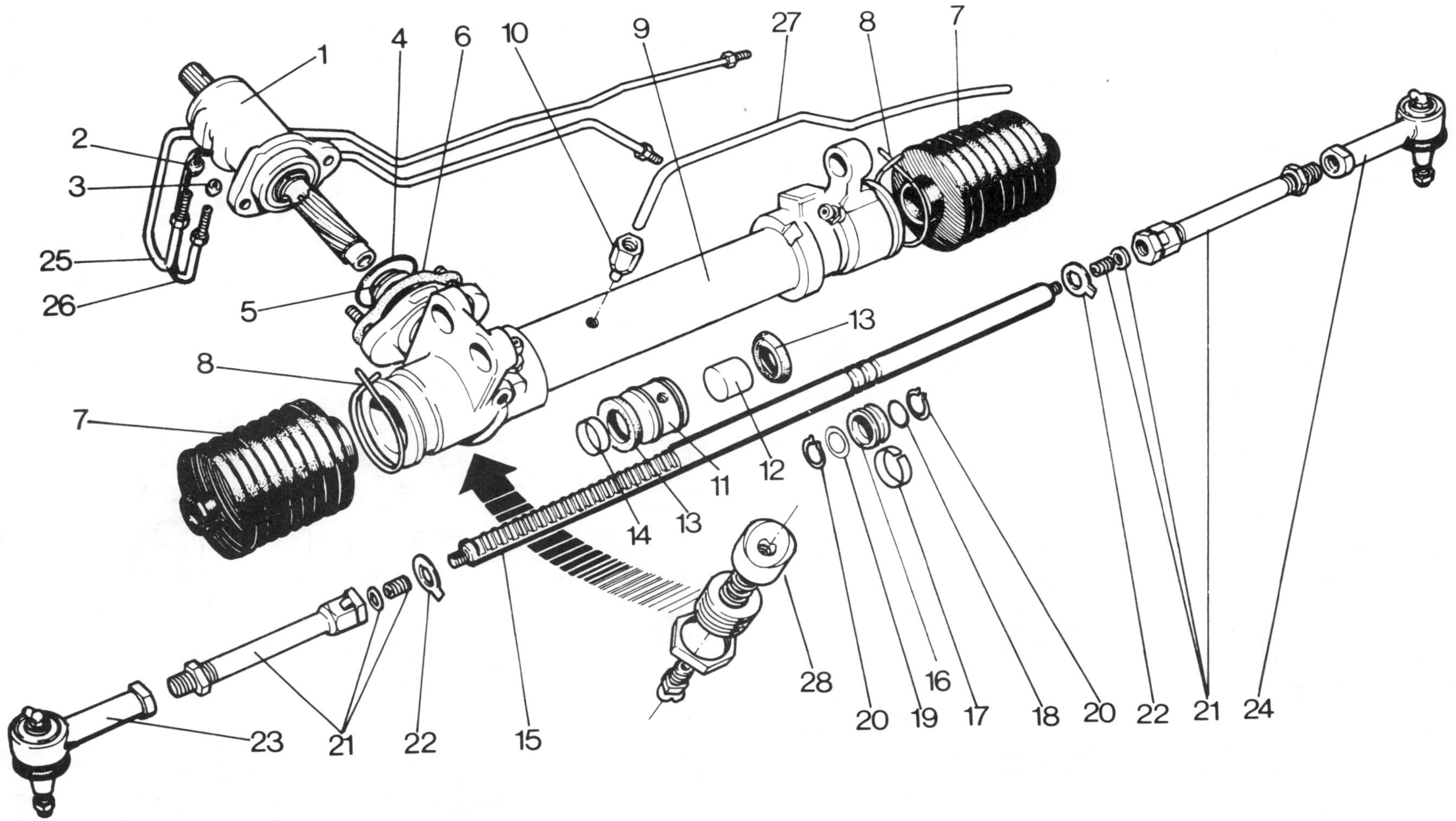

Fig. 11.37 Exploded view of steering gear (XJ12 and Double Six – typical) (Sec 41)

1 Valve and pinion assembly
2 Pipe union seat
3 Pipe union seat
4 O-ring
5 Seal
6 Gasket
7 Bellows
8 Clip
9 Rack housing
10 Adaptor
11 Seal housing
12 Bearing
13 Seal
14 Seal retainer
15 Rack
16 Piston
17 Piston ring
18 O-ring
19 Shim
20 Circlip
21 Inner balljoint assembly
22 Tab washer
23 Track rod end
24 Track rod end
25 Outlet pipe
26 Inlet pipe
27 Air transfer tube
28 Rack damper assembly

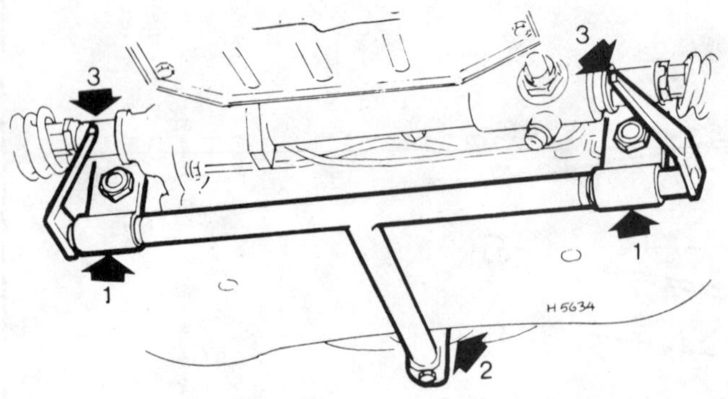

Fig. 11.38 Special tool being used to align steering gear (Sec 40)

1 Attachment brackets *3 Checking levers*
2 Sliding section

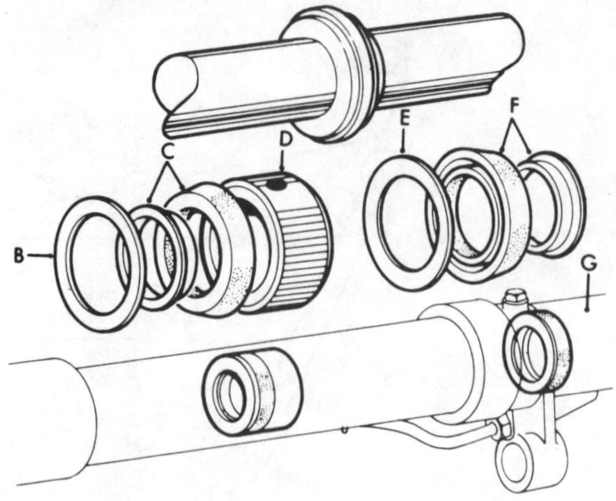

Fig. 11.39 Power steering seal arrangement (Sec 41)

For key see text

wheel and the front roadwheels are in the straight-ahead position. Make sure also that a gap of $\frac{3}{8}$ in (10.0 mm) exists between the two moving sections of the lower universal joint.

38 Steering lower column (XJS) – removal and refitting

1 Set the front roadwheels in the straight-ahead position.
2 Extract the screws which hold the right-hand heat shield adjacent to the exhaust downpipe and remove the shield.
3 Unbolt and remove the steering rack right-hand heat shield.
4 Remove the pinch-bolt which holds the lower universal joint to the pinion shaft on the rack housing.
5 Working inside the car, remove the pinch-bolts which hold the universal joint to the upper and lower columns.
6 Slide the joint from the upper column and then pull the same joint from the top of the lower column.
7 Slacken the draught-excluder clip on the lower column and working under the car, push the lower column through the bulkhead $\frac{1}{4}$until the lower universal joint disengages from the rack pinion cshaft.
8 Withdraw the lower column assembly from the draught-excluder.
9 Refitting is a reversal of removal. Make sure that the front roadwheels and the steering wheel are in the straight-ahead position before connecting the lower column joints, and adjust the position of the lower joint to provide a clearance between the moving sections of the lower joint of $\frac{3}{8}$c in (10.0 mm).

39 Steering column lock – removal and refitting

1 Refer to Chapter 10.

40 Steering gear – removal and refitting

1 Disconnect the fluid hoses from the pinion housing and cdrain the fluid into a container.
2 Plug or cap the openings to prevent the entry of dirt.
3 On right-hand drive cars only, disconnect the hose retaining clip from the rack housing.
4 Using a suitable extractor, disconnect the tie-rod ends from the steering arms.
5 Unscrew and remove the pinch-bolt which holds the lower universal joint to the steering gear pinion shaft.
6 Unscrew the three self-locking nu2ts from the steering gear mounting bolts.
7 Withdraw the steering gear downwards, retrieving the rubber bonded steel washers and shims which are located between the lugs and brackets.
8 Installation of the steering gear will require the use of a special alignment tool (JD 36) and if this cannot be borrowed, then the steering gear should be refitted and the car driven to your dealer's to have it aligned at the earliest opportunity.
9 Commence refitting by offering the steering rack to its mounting brackets.
10 Select shims so that the single lug at the end of the rack housing opposite to the pinion end is positioned midway between the lugs of the bracket on the suspension crossmember.
11 With the help of an assistant, add further shims as necessary until a gap of between 0.10 and 0.12 in (2.54 and 3.05 mm) exists between the rubber faces of the thrust washers and the inner faces of the lugs on the crossmember.
12 Check that the universal joint is engaged on the pinion shaft and tighten the steering gear mounting bolts finger-tight.
13 Pull both bellows from the rack housing having first cut the securing wire.
14 The two attachment brackets of the special alignment tool must now be located on the large hexagonal heads of the lower wishbone pivot shafts.
15 Release the locking screw and move the sliding section of the tool (2 in Fig. 11.37) until the slot registers with the weld flange at the front of the suspension member. Lock the tool in this position.
16 Lift the two checking levers (3) until contact is made with one or both rack shafts. Move the position of the steering gear if necessary until both levers make contact. Tighten the three securing bolts fully and remove the tool.
17 Reconnect the flexible bellows and fit new locking wire.
18 Reconnect the fluid lines to the steering housing, refit the upper and lower steering columns.
19 Refill the steering pump reservoir to the 'FULL' mark with clean automatic transmission fluid. Bleed the system, as described in Section 48.
20 Reconnect the tie-rod ends and check the front wheel alignment, as described in Section 49.

41 Steering gear (XJ12 and Double Six) – overhaul

1 With the steering gear removed from the car, clean away external dirt and remove the fluid pipes.
2 Mark the position of the valve/pinion housing relative to the rack housing and unbolt and remove it.
3 Cut the locking wires and fold back the flexible bellows to expose the inner balljoints.
4 Flatten the tab washers, release the locknuts and unscrew the tie-rods from the ends of the rack. Retrieve the springs and packing washers.

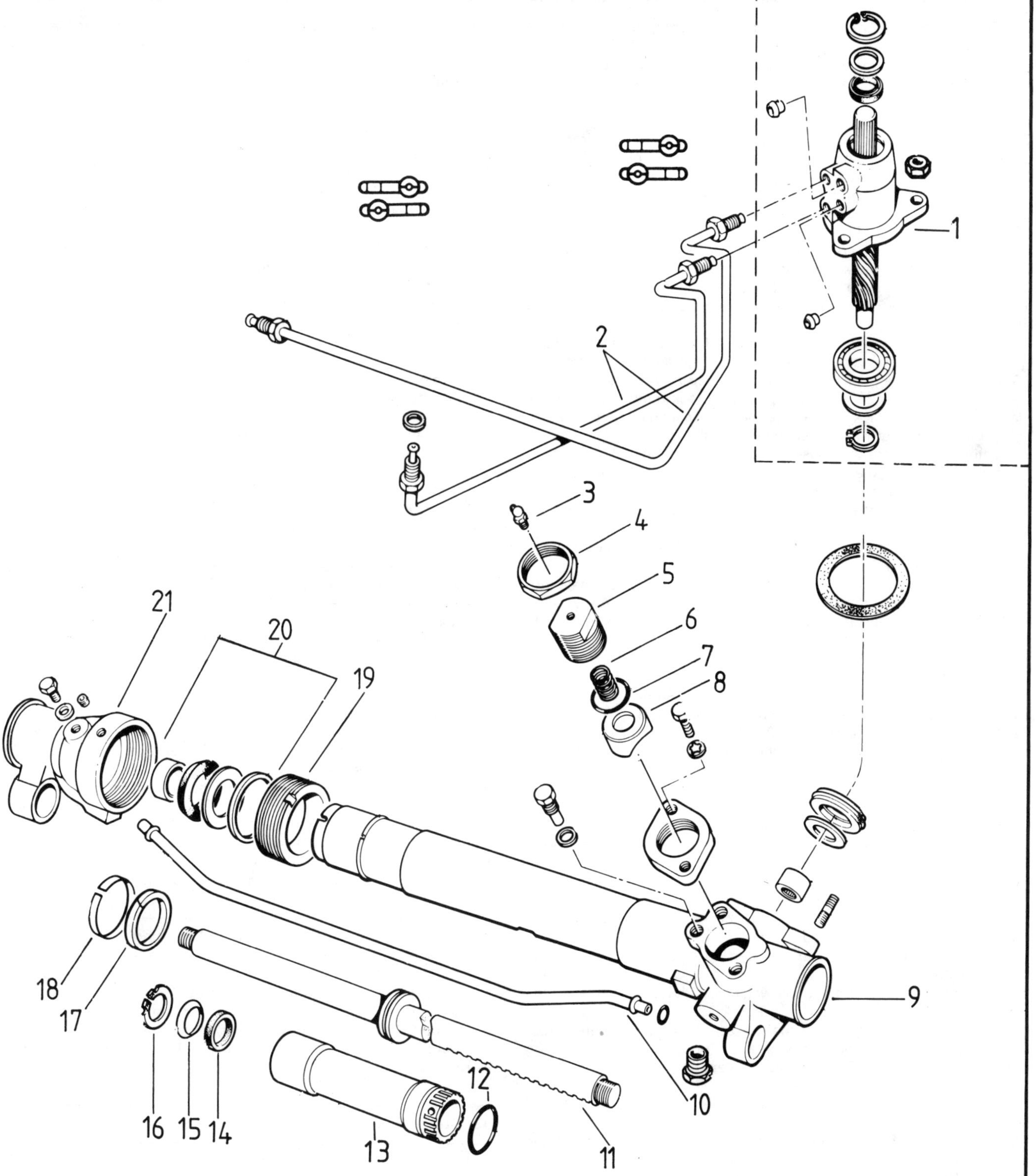

Fig. 11.40 Exploded view of steering gear (XJS – typical) (Sec 42)

1	*Pinion housing*	7	*O-ring*	12	*O-ring*	17	*Seal*
2	*Fluid pipes*	8	*Damper shoe*	13	*Inner sleeve*	18	*Clip*
3	*Grease nipple*	9	*Rack housing*	14	*Seal*	19	*Locking ring*
4	*Locknut*	10	*Air transfer pipe*	15	*Nylon washer*	20	*End cap seal assembly*
5	*Adjuster plug*	11	*Rack*	16	*Circlip*	21	*End cap*
6	*Spring*						

5 Remove the rack damper locknut and unscrew and remove the damper components.
6 Remove the air transfer pipe from both rack housing end caps.
7 With a C-spanner, unscrew the ring nut from the rack housing end cap. Remove the end cap with bush, seal, retaining washer and O-ring. Withdraw the rack and piston.
8 Remove the union adaptor and bonded seal washer from the centre of the rack housing and then extract the centre pipe fitting from the bore of the rack housing.
9 Remove the seal and washer from behind the centre fitting. Discard the seal.
10 Early models are fitted with a rack from which the piston is detachable. Such racks are identified by not having a suffix W to the code number on the rack housing. To remove the piston, extract the circlips and draw out the piston, noting any shims fitted.
11 Renew any worn or damaged components and obtain a repair kit of seals.
12 Commence reassembly by taping the rack teeth or sliding a plastic tube over them to prevent damage to the seal lips as they are installed.
13 Slide the centre pipe fitting (D in Fig. 11.39), a new seal (C) and the retaining washer (B) over the protected rack teeth and onto the plain section of the rack. Make sure that the seal lips face the centre pipe fitting. Remove the protective tape or sleeve.
14 Enter the rack into the housing so that the toothed end enters first. Align the threaded hole in the centre pipe fitting so that it registers with the hole in the rack housing.
15 Screw in the centre pipe fitting and adaptor with bonded seal washer. Tighten fully.
16 Over the plain end of the rack, fit the cap seal retaining washer (E) and then the seal (F), lips towards washer.
17 Slide the housing (G) onto the rack so that it pushes the seal into position. Secure with the ring nut.
18 Fit the air transfer pipe and the rack damper components, but do not adjust at this stage.
19 Refit the valve/pinion assembly using a new gasket.
20 Reconnect the inner balljoints to the rack using new lockwashers. Apply 2 oz (57 g) of grease to each balljoint assembly.
21 Adjust the rack damper as described in Section 31.
22 Using a grease gun apply 1 oz (28 g) of grease to the nipple on the rack housing. Too much grease will distend the flexible bellows.
23 Fit the fluid pipes.

42 Steering gear (XJS) – overhaul

1 Carry out the operations described in paragraphs 1, 3 and 4 of Section 41.
2 Remove the external fluid pipes.
3 Mark the relative position of the pinion housing to the rack housing, unscrew the nuts and remove it.
4 Discard the pinion seals in the housing recess and retrieve the metal washer.
5 Unscrew and remove the bolts which hold the rack housing to the end cap and the inner sleeve.
6 Using an Allen key, extract the socket screw from the end cap.
7 Using a C-spanner, or a hammer and a drift, unscrew the locking ring from the end cap. Remove the end cap.
8 Remove the air transfer pipe.
9 Remove the end cap O-ring seal, washer, nylon spacer, seal and seal seat.
10 Remove the bolts which hold the rack damper plate. Remove the plate, seal and spring followed by the damper.
11 Withdraw the rack from the housing.
12 Using an angled drift, drive the inner sleeve from the rack housing.
13 Extract the circlip from the end of the inner sleeve and remove the nylon washer, seal and seal seat.
14 Extract the O-ring seal from the periphery of the inner sleeve.
15 Remove the seal from the seal carrier on the rack.
16 Inspect all components for wear or damage. Obtain a seal repair kit and new gaskets.
17 Commence reassembly by lubricating the new seal for the inner sleeve.
18 Fit the seal seat, seal and nylon washer to the inner sleeve and secure with the circlip.
19 Lubricate and fit the new O-ring seal to the periphery of the inner sleeve.
20 Push the inner sleeve into the rack housing so that the notched end enters first and the hole for the locating peg is aligned with the hole in the rack end casing. Insert the locating bolt.
21 Tape over the teeth of the rack to prevent damage to the lips of the seals.
22 Fit the new nylon seal to the carrier on the rack and then push the rack into the rack housing and inner sleeve. Locate the rack centrally in the rack housing.
23 Lubricate the new seals and fit them to the rack housing end cap. These include the seal seat, seal, nylon washer, metal washer and O-ring.
24 Fit new O-rings to the air transfer pipe.
25 Fit the end cap to the end of the rack housing, making sure that the cut-out in the housing aligns with the bolt hole. Fit the bolt.
26 Fit the air transfer pipe.
27 Secure the end cap to the rack housing by screwing up the threaded sleeve. Lock the sleeve with the socket-headed screw.
28 Remove the tape from the teeth of the rack.
29 Lubricate the new seal and fit it with the metal washer and O-ring to the pinion housing.
30 Fit the pinion housing, using a new gasket and tighten the securing nuts.
31 Fit the rack damper and the fluid pipes.
32 Reconnect the inner balljoints using new lockplates. Smear each balljoint with 2 oz (57 g) of grease.
33 Adjust the damper as described in Section 31 and then inject 1 oz (28 g) of grease into the rack damper grease nipple.
34 Reconnect the bellows with wire or a clip.

43 Steering rack bellows – renewal in car

1 A split or perished bellows can be renewed without having to remove the rack assembly from the car.
2 Using a suitable extractor, separate the outer tie-rod balljoint from the steering arm.
3 Unscrew the tie-rod end locknut one quarter of a turn and then unscrew and remove the tie-rod end balljoint assembly.
4 Release the bellows clips and slide the bellows off the tie-rod.
5 If dirt has entered the split in the bellows, wipe the grease from the inner balljoints and apply 2 oz (57 g) of fresh lubricant.
6 Fit the new bellows and the clips or locking wire.
7 Screw on the tie-rod balljoint until it resumes its original position, when the locknut will only require one quarter of a turn to lock the balljoint.
8 Reconnect the balljoint to the steering arm.
9 Check the front wheel alignment as described in Section 49.

44 Steering oil cooler – removal and refitting

1 Remove the filler cap from the power steering pump reservoir and syphon out the fluid with a syringe or other suitable device.
2 Disconnect the hoses from the cooler, expect some loss of fluid.
3 Unbolt the cooler from the suspension and lift it from the car.
4 Refitting is a reversal of removal. Bleed the power steering system as described in Section 48.

45 Steering pump (XJ12 and Double Six) – removal and refitting

1 Remove the left-hand air cleaner.
2 Disconnect the hose from the outlet at the rear of the pump reservoir. Allow the fluid to drain into a suitable container and then plug the openings.
3 Disconnect the second (high pressure) hose frcom the reservoir.
4 Disconnect the pump adjusting link. Press the pump inwards, and slip the drivebelt from the pump pulley.
5 Pull the pump outwards and disconnect the bottom pivot mounting bolt (photo). Lift the pump and its mounting bracket from the engine compartment.
6 Refit the pump by reversing the removal operations. The pump drivebelt is tensioned by pulling the pump away from the engine and then tightening the adjuster link bolt. Refer to Chapter 1, Section 51.
7 Reconnect the fluid hoses, and fill the reservoir to the full mark on the dipstick with the specified fluid. Turn the pump pulley anti-

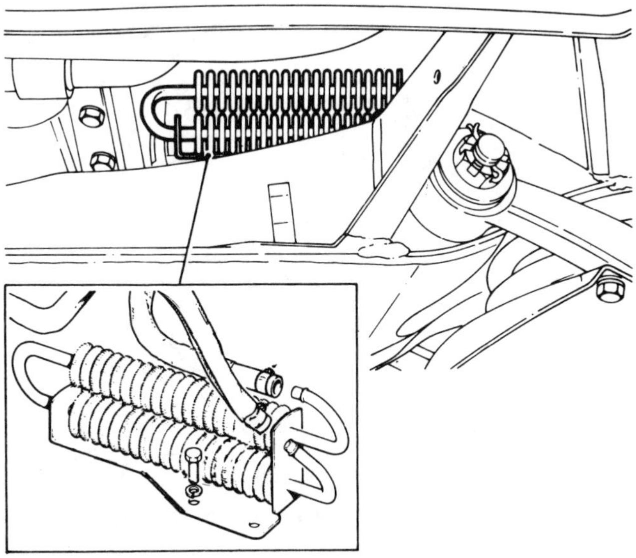

Fig. 11.41 Power steering fluid cooler (Sec 44)

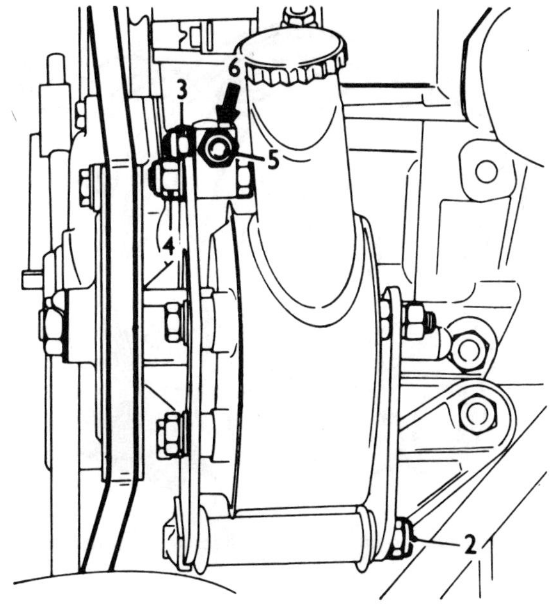

Fig. 11.42 Power steering pump mountings (XJ12, Double Six) (Sec 45)

2 Lower pivot bolt
3 Adjuster link nut
4 Trunnion block nut
5 Trunnion outer locknut
6 Trunnion inner locknut

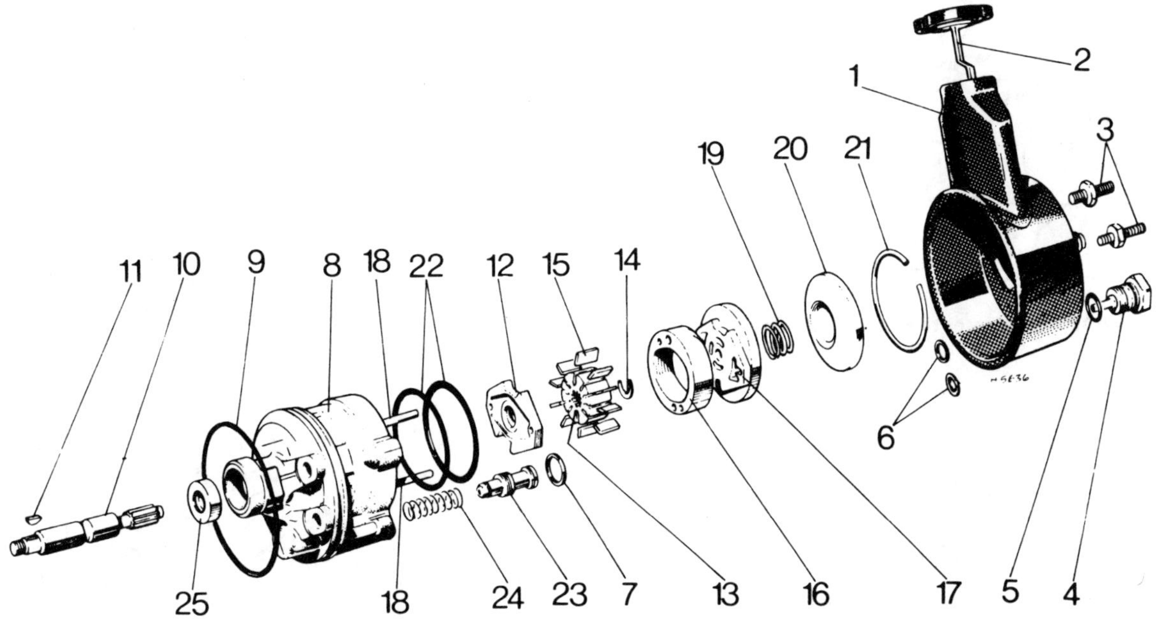

Fig. 11.43 Exploded view of the steering pump (Sec 47)

1 Reservoir
2 Dipstick
3 Stud
4 Union
5 O-ring
6 Seal
7 Seal
8 Pump body
9 O-ring
10 Shaft
11 Key
12 Thrust plate
13 Rotor
14 Clip
15 Pump vane
16 Pump ring
17 Pressure plate
18 Pin
19 Spring
20 End plate
21 Clip
22 O-ring
23 Flow control valve
24 Spring
25 Oil seal

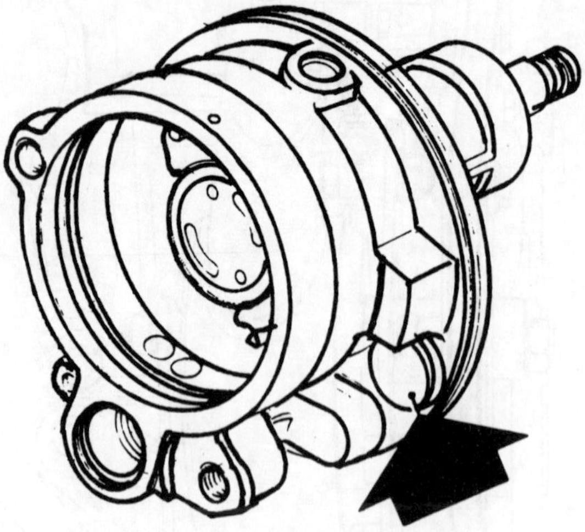

Fig. 11.44 Steering pump swarf-collecting magnet (arrowed) (Sec 47)

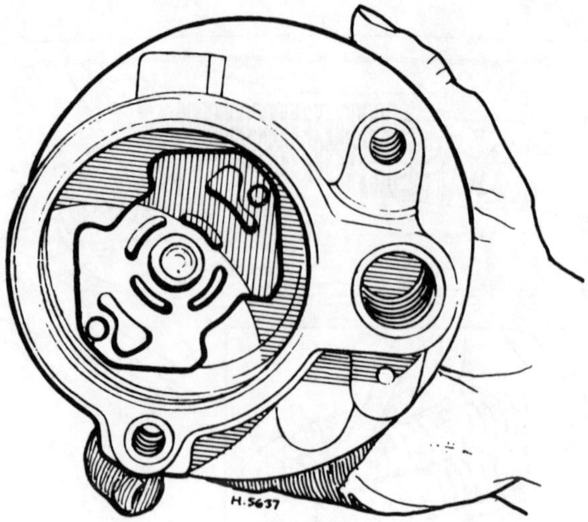

Fig. 11.45 Fitting thrust plate to steering pump (Sec 47)

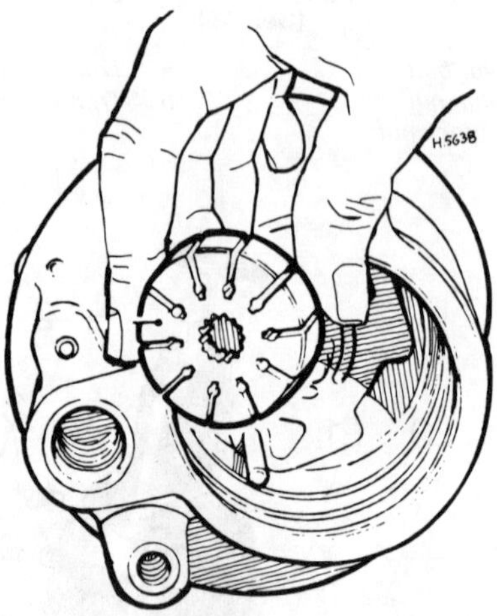

Fig. 11.46 Fitting rotor to steering pump (Sec 47)

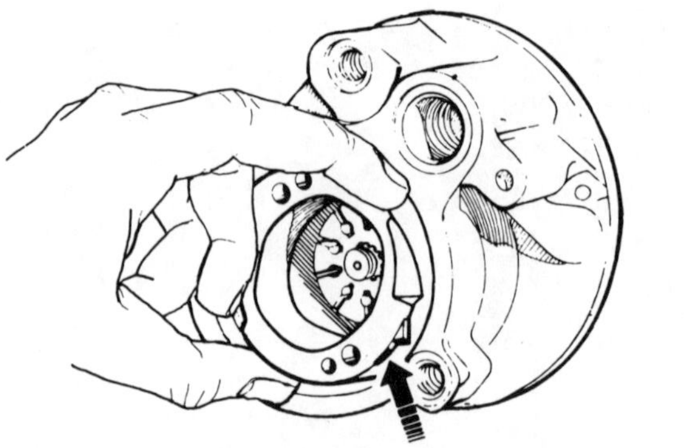

Fig. 11.47 Installing steering pump ring (arrowed) (Sec 47)

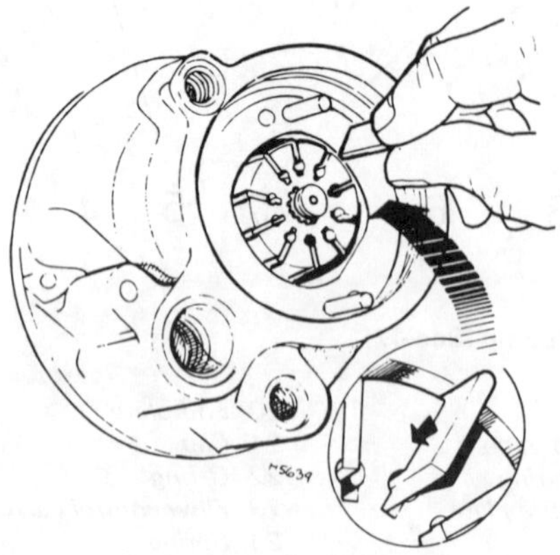

Fig. 11.48 Installing vanes to steering pump rotor plate (Sec 47)

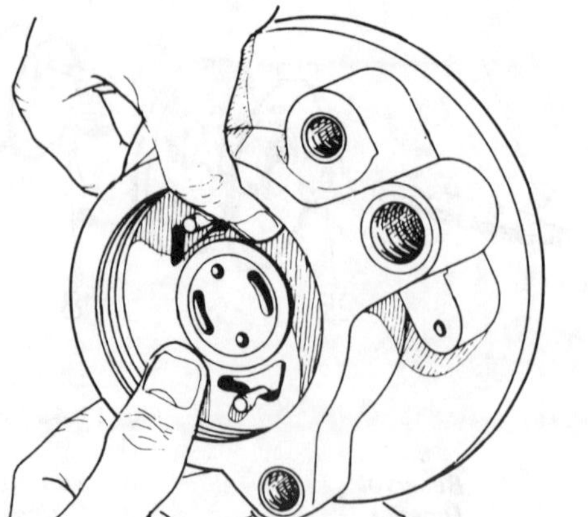

Fig. 11.49 Installing pressure plate to steering pump (Sec 47)

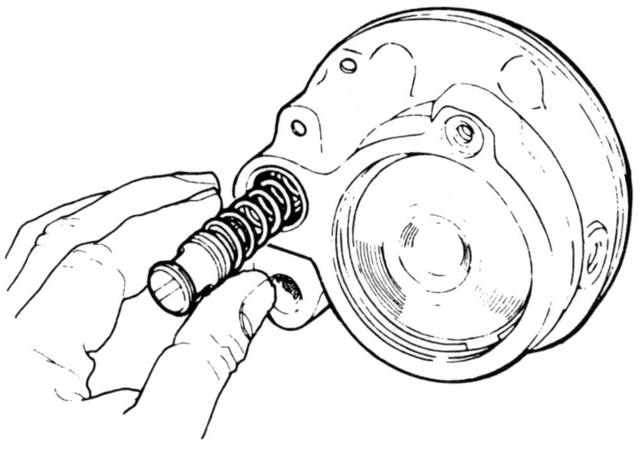

Fig. 11.50 Installing flow control valve to steering pump (Sec 47)

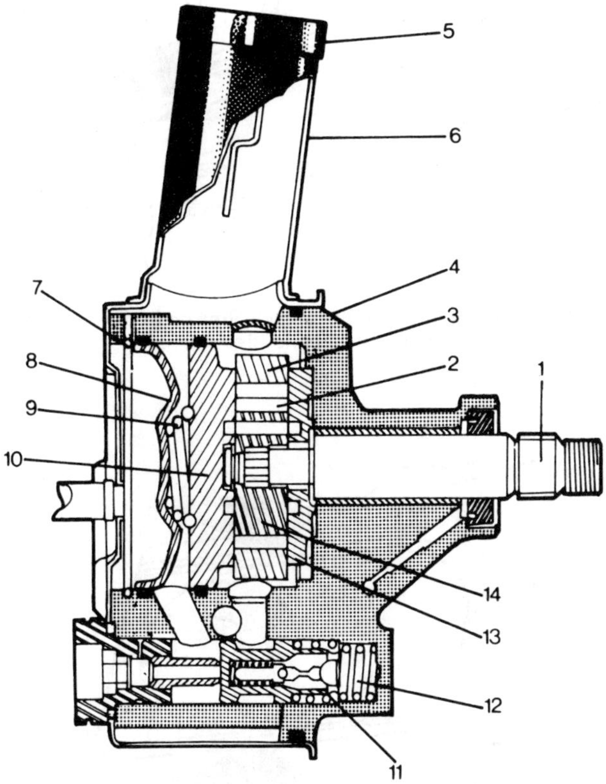

Fig. 11.51 Sectional view of power steering pump (Sec 47)

1 Driving shaft
2 Pump vane
3 Pump ring
4 Body
5 Filler cap
6 Reservoir
7 Oil seal
8 End plate
9 Spring
10 Pressure plate
11 Flow control valve
12 Spring
13 Thrust plate
14 Rotor

clockwise a few revolutions to expel any air which may be trapped in the pump.
8 Bleed the complete system, as described in Section 48.

46 Steering pump (XJS) – removal and refitting

1 Remove the cover and the element from the right-hand air cleaner.
2 Partially drain the coolant (Chapter 2) until the top coolant hose can be removed without loss of coolant.
3 Syphon the fluid from the steering pump reservoir using a syringe or other suitable device.
4 Disconnect the fluid hoses from the rear of the pump.
5 Slacken the nut which holds the drivebelt adjuster rod to the timing cover.
6 Remove the bolt which holds the adjuster rod trunnion to the pump and swing the pump clear.
7 Remove the nut from the pump lower mounting bolt, swing the pump in towards the engine and remove the drivebelt. Remove the bolt and lift the pump from the car.
8 Refitting is a reversal of removal. Tension the drivebelt as described in Chapter 1, Section 51, and bleed the system as described in Section 48.

47 Steering pump – overhaul

1 In the event of a fault occurring or wear taking place, it is recommended that a replacement pump is obtained but where it is preferred to overhaul the original unit, proceed as follows, making sure first that spare parts are available.
2 Drain the fluid from the pump and clean off all external dirt. Unbolt and remove the mounting plate.
3 Remove the nut and withdraw the pulley.
4 Secure the pump carefully in the jaws of a vice and then remove the outlet union (4) (Fig. 11.43). Extract the O-ring from the recess.
5 Remove the two mounting studs (3) and detach the reservoir from the pump body.
6 Extract the three O-rings from the recesses in the pump body.
7 Remove the endplate retaining ring by inserting a pin through the hole in the pump body and then prising out the ring with a screwdriver.
8 Remove the endplate (20), spring (19) and O-ring (22).
9 Remove the flow control valve (23) and spring (24).
10 Remove the Woodruff key (11) and gently tap the end of the shaft until the pressure plate, pump ring, rotor and thrust plate can be withdrawn as an assembly. Remove the pressure plate O-ring (22) from the pump body.
11 Separate the components taking care not to damage the pump rotor vanes.
12 Remove the clip (14), withdraw the rotor (13) and thrust plate (12). Extract the shaft oil seal (25).
13 Discard and renew all oil seals and examine components for scoring or grooves. The pump shaft and bush are supplied as a complete assembly. Check that the flow control valve slides freely in its bore, if not, renew it. On some models, a magnet is fitted to the pump body. Remove, clean and refit.
14 Commence reassembly, by smearing a new shaft seal with petroleum jelly. Install the seal to the pump body using a piece of tubing. Install the pump shaft, splined end first, from the hub end of the pump body.
15 Install the dowel pins to the pump body and then fit the thrust plate over the pins so that the face with the recesses is uppermost.
16 Fit the rotor to the splined shaft so that the countersunk side is downwards towards the thrust plate. Check that the rotor is free on the splines.
17 Fit the retaining clip to the shaft groove and then fit the pump ring to the dowel pins so that the directional arrow is uppermost.
18 Insert the vanes in the rotor slots so that the rounded end of the vane is facing outwards.
19 Apply petroleum jelly to the pressure plate O-ring and fit it into the lowest groove in the pump body. Smear the outside edge of the pressure plate with petroleum jelly and fit it to the dowel pin so that the spring circular recess is uppermost. Push the plate downwards using a piece of tubing applied to its outer edge. Do not tap the plate into position.
20 Install the endplate O-ring into its groove in the pump body, first

having applied petroleum jelly to it.
21 Fit the spring (19) into the circular groove in the pressure plate.
22 Smear the edge of the endplate with petroleum jelly and place it in position so that the retaining ring is on top. Check that the gap in the clip is not opposite the hole used for removal. Apply pressure until the retaining clip can be sprung into the groove in the body.
23 Insert the valve, spring leading, into the bore in the pump. Locate new O-ring seals in position for the reservoir retaining bolts and the outlet union.
24 Smear the large reservoir O-ring seal with petroleum jelly and insert it into its groove in the pump body.
25 Fit the reservoir retaining studs, the outlet union and O-rings.
26 Refit the Woodruff key, pulley, lockwasher and nut.
27 Refit the pump mounting plate.

48 Steering system – bleeding

1 Turn the steering to full left lock. Add fluid of the correct specification to the reservoir to bring the level to the 'COLD' mark on the dipstick.
2 Start the engine and run it at a fast idle. Recheck the fluid level and top up again if necessary to bring it to the 'COLD' mark.
3 With the engine still running, turn the steering wheel from lock to lock but do not turn the steering so far in each direction that the lock stops are contacted. As the steering is turned, keep checking the fluid level and top up as necessary.
4 Repeat the operations until all air has been bled from the system. This will be indicated by the elimination of lumpy operation when the wheel is being turned.
5 Finally set the steering in the straight-ahead position, keep the engine running for two or three more minutes and switch off the engine.
6 By this time, the temperature of the fluid should be such that the fluid level can be checked against the 'HOT' mark on the dipstick and final topping up carried out if necessary.

49 Steering angles and front wheel alignment

1 Accurate front wheel alignment is essential for good steering and slow tyre wear. Before considering the steering angle, check that the tyres are correctly inflated, that the front wheels are not buckled, the hub bearings are not worn or incorrectly adjusted and that the steering linkage is in good order, without slackness or wear at the joints.
2 Wheel alignment consists of four factors:

Camber, is the angle at which the front wheels are set from the vertical when viewed from the front of the car. Positive camber is the amount (in degrees) that the wheels are tilted outwards at the top from the vertical.

Castor is the angle between the steering axis and a vertical line when viewed from each side of the car. Positive castor is when the steering axis is inclined rearwards.

Steering axis inclination is the angle, when viewed from the front of the car, between the vertical and an imaginary line drawn between the upper and lower suspension swivels.

Toe-in is the amount by which the distance between the front inside edges of the roadwheels (measured at hub height) differs from the diametrically opposite distance measured between the rear inside edges of the front roadwheels.

3 Due to the need for very accurate measuring equipment it is not within the scope of the home mechanic to check steering angles but the method of adjusting them is described in the following paragraphs for reasons of interest.
4 Camber angle is altered by adding or removing shims at the joint of the upper wishbone pivot and the crossmember.
5 Castor angle is altered by transposing shims from one side to the other of the upper wishbone balljoint. Whenever the castor angle is altered, the front wheel alignment (toe) will need adjusting.
6 Front wheel tracking (toe) checks are best carried out with modern setting equipment but a reasonably accurate alternative and adjustment procedure may be carried out as follows:
7 Place the car on level ground with the wheels in the straight-ahead position.
8 Obtain or make a tracking gauge. One may be easily made from tubing, cranked to clear the sump and bellhousing, having an ad-

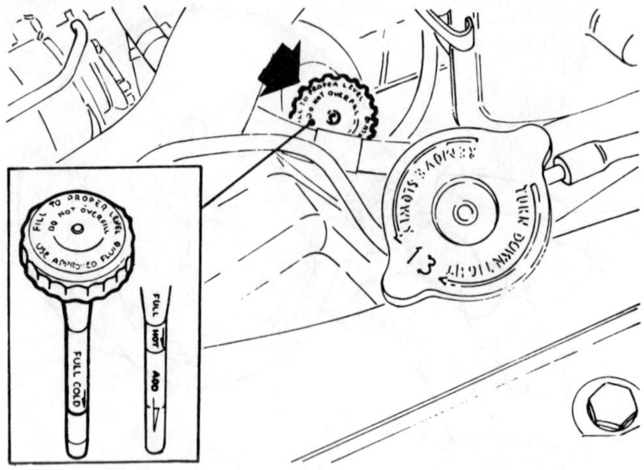

Fig. 11.52 Power steering reservoir fluid filler cap and dipstick markings (Sec 47)

Fig. 11.53 Location of camber angle shims on front suspension upper wishbone (Sec 49)

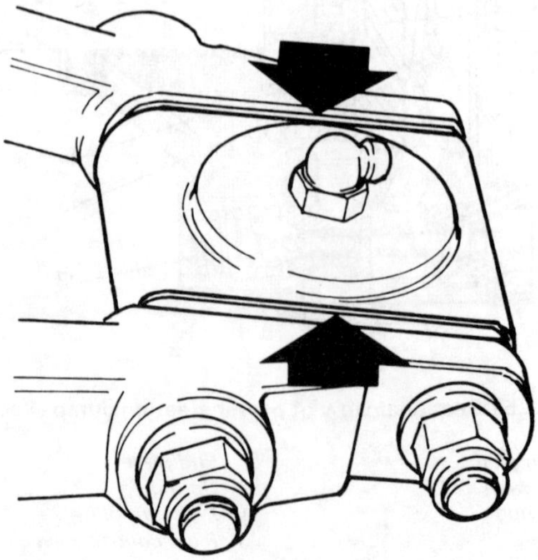
Fig. 11.54 Location of castor angle shims on front suspension upper balljoint (Sec 49)

justable nut and setscrew at one end.
9 Using the gauge, measure the distance between the two inner wheel rims at hub height at the rear of the wheels.
10 Rotate the wheels (by pushing the car forwards) through 180° (half a turn) and again using the gauge, measure the distance of hub height between the two inner wheel rims at the front of the wheels. This measurement should differ from that previously taken at the rear of the wheel and represents the correct toe-in or out, see Specifications.
11 Where the toe is found to be incorrect, slacken the locknuts on each outer track rod and rotate each track rod an equal amount until the correct toe is obtained. Tighten the locknuts, ensuring that the balljoints are held in the centre of their arc of travel during tightening.
12 It cannot be over emphasised that both during initial setting and subsequent adjustment, the effective lengths of the two track rods must be exactly equal (see Section 29).

50 Rear wheel alignment

1 The rear wheels are adjustable for camber but again due to the need for precise measuring equipment and setting links (tool No JD21) this work should be left to your Jaguar/Daimler dealer.
2 The camber angle is altered by varying the thickness of the shims which are fitted between the axleshaft inner joint flange and the brake disc.

51 Roadwheels and tyres

1 Whenever the roadwheels are removed it is a good idea to clean the insides of the wheels to remove accumulation of mud and in the case of the front ones, disc pad dust.
2 Check the condition of the wheel for rust and repaint if necessary.
3 Examine the wheel stud holes. If these are tending to become elongated or the dished recesses in which the nuts seat have worn or become overcompressed, then the wheel will have to be renewed.
4 With a roadwheel removed, pick out any embedded flints from the tread and check for splits in the sidewalls or damage to the tyre carcass generally.
5 Where the depth of tread pattern is 1 mm or less, the tyre must be renewed. On some tyres a wear indicator bar becomes visible when the tyres are ready for renewal.
6 Rotation of the roadwheels to even out wear is not recommended.
7 If the wheels have been balanced on the car then they cannot be moved round the car as the balance of wheel, tyre and hub will be upset.
8 It is recommended that wheels are re-balanced halfway through the life of the tyres to compensate for the loss of tread rubber due to wear.
9 Finally, always keep the tyres (including the spare) inflated to the recommended pressures and always replace the dust caps on the tyre valves. Tyre pressures are best checked first thing in the morning when the tyres are cold.

52 Fault diagnosis – suspension and steering

Symptom	Reason(s)
Steering feels vague, car wanders and floats at speed	Tyre pressures uneven Shock absorbers worn Spring broken Steering gear balljoints badly worn Suspension geometry incorrect Steering mechanism free play excessive Front suspension and rear axle pick-up points out of alignment
Stiff and heavy steering	Tyre pressures too low No grease in swivel joints No grease in steering and suspension balljoints Front wheel alignment incorrect Suspension geometry incorrect Steering gear incorrectly adjusted too tightly Steering column badly misaligned Loose steering pump belt
Wheel wobble and vibration	Wheel nuts loose Front wheels and tyres out of balance Steering balljoints badly worn Hub bearings badly worn Steering gear free play excessive Front springs weak or broken
Rattle on rough roads	Worn inner balljoints on ends of rack Incorrect rack pad adjustment Worn rack housing bushes
Noise from power steering pump or gear	Air in system Slack drivebelt Wear internally
Very light steering effort (lacks feel)	Steering gear valve worn or faulty (renew valve/pinion housing assembly)

Chapter 12 Bodywork

Contents

1 General description

1 The type of construction employed on all models is of the unitary method by which the body and underframe are formed as one assembly from the welding together of steel panels and sections.
2 All models are lavishly equipped, the standard depending upon the particular model concerned.
3 Air conditioning, electric door locks and electric window operation are generally standard on North American versions and optionally available on other models.
4 For purposes of operations to the bodywork, there is no difference between Jaguar XJ12 and Daimler Double Six models. For XJS versions, the different procedures are noted in the following Sections.

2 Maintenance – bodywork and underframe

1 The general condition of a car's bodywork is the thing that significantly affects it value. Maintenance is easy but needs to be regular. Neglect, particularly after minor damage, can lead quickly to further deterioration and costly repair bills. It is important also to keep watch on those parts of the car not immediately visible, for instance the underside, inside all the wheel arches and the lower part of the engine compartment.
2 The basic maintenance routine for the bodywork is washing – preferably with a lot of water, from a hose. This will remove all the loose solids which may have stuck to the car. It is important to flush these off in such a way as to prevent grit from scratching the finish. The wheel arches and underframe need washing in the same way to remove any accumulated mud which will retain moisture and tend to encourage rust. Paradoxically enough, the best time to clean the underframe and wheel arches is in wet weather when the mud is thoroughly wet and soft. In very wet weather the underframe is usually cleaned of large accumulations automatically and this is a good time for inspection.
3 Periodically, it is a good idea to have the whole of the underframe of the car steam cleaned, engine compartment included, so that a thorough inspection can be carried out to see what minor repairs and renovations are necessary. Steam cleaning is available at many garages and is necessary for removal of the accumulation of oily grime which sometimes is allowed to become thick in certain areas. If steam cleaning facilities are not available, there are one or two excellent grease solvents available which can be brush applied. The dirt can then be simply hosed off.
4 After washing paintwork, wipe off with a chamois leather to give an unspotted clear finish. A coat of clear protective wax polish will give added protection against chemical pollutants in the air. If the paintwork sheen has dulled or oxidised, use a cleaner/polisher combination to restore the brilliance of the shine. This requires a little effort, but such dulling is usually caused because regular washing has been neglected. Always check that the door and ventilator opening drain holes and pipes are completely clear so that water can be drained out. Bright work should be treated in the same way as paintwork. Windscreens and windows can be kept clear of the smeary film which often appears, by adding a little ammonia to the water. If they are scratched, a good rub with a proprietary metal polish will often clear them. Never use any form of wax or other body or chromium polish on glass.

3 Maintenance – upholstery and carpets

1 Mats and carpets should be brushed or vacuum cleaned regularly to keep them free of grit. If they are badly stained remove them from the car for scrubbing or sponging and make quite sure they are dry before refitting. Seats and interior trim panels can be kept clean by a wipe over with a damp cloth. If they do become stained (which can be more apparent on light coloured upholstery) use a little liquid detergent and a soft nail brush to scour the grime out of the grain of the material. Do not forget to keep the head lining clean in the same way as the upholstery. When using liquid cleaners inside the car do not over-wet the surfaces being cleaned. Excessive damp could get into the seams and padded interior causing stains, offensive odours or even rot. If the inside of the car gets wet accidentally it is worthwhile taking some trouble to dry it out properly, particularly where carpets are involved. *Do not leave oil or electric heaters inside the car for this purpose.*

4 Minor body damage – repair

The photographic sequences on pages 286 and 287 illustrate the operations detailed in the following sub-sections.

Repair of minor scratches in the vehicle's bodywork

If the scratch is very superficial, and does not penetrate to the metal of the bodywork, repair is very simple. Lightly rub the area of the scratch with a paintwork renovator, or a very fine cutting paste, to remove loose paint from the scratch and to clear the surrounding bodywork of wax polish. Rinse the area with clean water.

Apply touch-up paint to the scratch using a thin paint brush; continue to apply thin layers of paint until the surface of the paint in the scratch is level with the surrounding paintwork. Allow the new paint at least two weeks to harden: then blend it into the surrounding paintwork by rubbing the paintwork, in the scratch area, with a paintwork renovator or a very fine cutting paste. Finally, apply wax polish.

Where the scratch has penetrated right through to the metal of the bodywork, causing the metal to rust, a different repair technique is required. Remove any loose rust from the bottom of the scratch with a penknife, then apply rust inhibiting paint to prevent the formation of rust in the future. Using a rubber or nylon applicator fill the scratch with bodystopper paste. If required, this paste can be mixed with cellulose thinners to provide a very thin paste which is ideal for filling narrow scratches. Before the stopper-paste in the scratch hardens, wrap a piece of smooth cotton rag around the top of a finger. Dip the finger in cellulose thinners and then quickly sweep it across the surface of the stopper-paste in the scratch; this will ensure that the surface of the stopper-paste is slightly hollowed. The scratch can now be painted over as described earlier in this Section.

Repair of dents in the vehicle's bodywork

When deep denting of the vehicle's bodywork has taken place, the first task is to pull the dent out, until the affected bodywork almost attains its original shape. There is little point in trying to restore the original shape completely, as the metal in the damaged area will have stretched on impact and cannot be reshaped fully to its original contour. It is better to bring the level of the dent up to a point which is about $\frac{1}{8}$ in (3 mm) below the level of the surrounding bodywork. In cases where the dent is very shallow anyway, it is not worth trying to pull it out at all. If the underside of the dent is accessible, it can be hammered out gently from behind, using a mallet with a wooden or plastic head. Whilst doing this, hold a suitable block of wood firmly against the outside of the panel to absorb the impact from the hammer blows and thus prevent a large area of the bodywork from being 'belled-out'.

Should the dent be in a section of the bodywork which has double skin or some other factor making it inaccessible from behind, a different technique is called for. Drill several small holes through the metal inside the area – particularly in the deeper section. Then screw long self-tapping screws into the holes just sufficiently for them to gain a good purchase in the metal. Now the dent can be pulled out by pulling on the protruding heads of the screws with a pair of pliers.

The next stage of the repair is the removal of the paint from the damaged area, and from an inch or so of the surrounding 'sound' bodywork. This is accomplished most easily by using a wire brush or abrasive pad on a power drill, although it can be done just as effectively by hand using sheets of abrasive paper. To complete the preparation for filling, score the surface of the bare metal with a screwdriver or the tang of a file, or alternatively, drill small holes in the affected area. This will provide a really good 'key' for the filler paste.

To complete the repair see the Section on filling and re-spraying.

Repair of rust holes or gashes in the vehicle's bodywork

Remove all paint from the affected area and from an inch or so of the surrounding 'sound' bodywork, using an abrasive pad or a wire brush on a power drill. If these are not available a few sheets of abrasive paper will do the job just as effectively. With the paint removed you will be able to gauge the severity of the corrosion and therefore decide whether to renew the whole panel (if this is possible) or to repair the affected area. New body panels are not as expensive as most people think and it is often quicker and more satisfactory to fit a new panel than to attempt to repair large areas of corrosion.

Remove all fittings from the affected area except those which will act as a guide to the original shape of the damaged bodywork (eg headlamp shells etc). Then, using tin snips or a hacksaw blade, remove all loose metal and any other metal badly affected by corrosion. Hammer the edges of the hole inwards in order to create a slight depression for the filler paste.

Wire brush the affected area to remove the powdery rust from the surface of the remaining metal. Paint the affected area with rust inhibiting paint; if the back of the rusted area is accessible treat this also.

Before filling can take place it will be necessary to block the hole in some way. This can be achieved by the use of Zinc gauze or Aluminum tape.

Zinc gauze is probably the best material to use for a large hole. Cut a piece to the approximate size and shape of the hole to be filled, then position it in the hole so that its edges are below the level of the surrounding bodywork. It can be retained in position by several blobs of filler paste around its periphery.

Aluminum tape should be used for small or very narrow holes. Pull a piece off the roll and trim it to the approximate size and shape required, then pull off the backing paper (if used) and stick the tape over the hole; it can be overlapped if the thickness of one piece is insufficient. Burnish down the edges of the tape with the handle of a screwdriver or similar, to ensure that the tape is securely attached to the metal underneath.

Bodywork repairs – filling and re-spraying

Before using this Section, see the Sections on dent, deep scratch, rust holes and gash repairs.

Many types of bodyfiller are available, but generally speaking those proprietary kits which contain a tin of filler paste and a tube of resin hardener are best for this type of repair. A wide, flexible plastic or nylon applicator will be found invaluable for imparting a smooth and well contoured finish to the surface of the filler.

Mix up a little filler on a clean piece of card or board – measure the hardener carefully (follow the maker's instructions on the pack) otherwise the filler will set too rapidly or too slowly.

Using the applicator apply the filler paste to the prepared area; draw the applicator across the surface of the filler to achieve the correct contour and to level the filler surface. As soon as a contour that approximates the correct one is achieved, stop working the paste – if you carry on too long the paste will become sticky and begin to 'pick up' on the applicator. Continue to add thin layers of filler paste at twenty-minute intervals until the level of the filler is just proud of the surrounding bodywork.

Once the filler has hardened, excess can be removed using a metal plane or file. From then on, progressively finer grades of sandpaper should be used, starting with a 40 grade production paper and finishing with 400 grade wet-and-dry paper. Always wrap the abrasive paper around a flat rubber, cork, or wooden block – otherwise the surface of the filler will not be completely flat. During the smoothing of the filler surface the wet-and-dry paper should be periodically rinsed in water. This will ensure that a very smooth finish is imparted to the filler at the final stage.

At this stage the 'repair area' should be surrounded by a ring of bare metal, which in turn should be encircled by the finely 'feathered' edge of the good paintwork. Rinse the repair area with clean water, until all of the dust produced by the rubbing-down operation has gone.

Spray the whole repair area with a light coat of primer – this will show up any imperfections in the surface of the filler. Repair these imperfections with fresh filler paste or bodystopper, and once more smooth the surface with abrasive paper. If bodystopper is used, it can be mixed with cellulose thinners to form a really thin paste which is ideal for filling small holes. Repeat this spray and repair procedure until you are satisfied that the surface of the filler, and the feathered edge of the paintwork are perfect. Clean the repair area with clean water and allow to dry fully.

The repair area is now ready for final spraying. Paint spraying must be carried out in warm, dry, windless and dust free atmosphere. This condition can be created artificially if you have access to a large indoor working area, but if you are forced to work in the open, you will have to pick your day very carefully. If you are working indoors, dousing the floor in the work area with water will help to settle the dust which would otherwise be in the atmosphere. If the repair area is confined to one body panel, mask off the surrounding panels; this will help to minimise the effects of a slight mis-match in paint colours. Bodywork fittings (eg chrome strips, door handles etc) will also need to be masked off. Use genuine masking tape and several thicknesses of newspaper for the masking operations.

Before commencing to spray, agitate the aerosol can thoroughly, then spray a test area (an old tin, or similar) until the technique is mastered. Cover the repair area with a thick coat of primer; the thickness should be built up using several thin layers of paint rather than one thick one. Using 400 grade wet-and-dry paper, rub down the surface of the primer until it is really smooth. While doing this, the work area should be thoroughly doused with water, and the wet-and-dry paper periodically rinsed in water. Allow to dry before spraying on more paint.

Spray on the top coat, again building up the thickness by using several thin layers of paint. Start spraying in the centre of the repair area and then, using a circular motion, work outwards until the whole repair area and about 2 inches of the surrounding original paintwork is covered. Remove all masking material 10 to 15 minutes after spraying on the final coat of paint.

Allow the new paint at least two weeks to harden, then, using a paintwork renovator or a very fine cutting paste, blend the edges of the paint into the existing paintwork. Finally, apply wax polish.

5 Major body damage – repair

Where serious damage has occurred or large areas need renewal due to neglect, it means certainly that completely new sections or panels will need welding in and this is best left to professionals. If the damage is due to impact it will also be necessary to completely check the alignment of the body shell structure. Due to the principle of construction the strength and shape of the whole can be affected by damage to a part. In such instances the services of a Jaguar/Daimler agent with specialist checking jigs are essential. If a body is left misaligned it is first of all dangerous as the car will not handle properly and secondly uneven stresses will be imposed on the steering, engine and transmission, causing abnormal wear or complete failure. Tyre wear may also be excessive.

6 Maintenance – hinges and locks

1 Oil the hinges of the bonnet, boot and doors with a drop or two of light oil periodically. A good time is after the car has been washed.
2 Oil the bonnet, release the catch pivot pin and the safety catch pivot pin periodically.
3 Do not over lubricate door latches and strikers. Normally a little oil on the rotary cam spindle alone is sufficient.

7 Doors – tracing rattles and their rectification

1 Check first that the door is not loose at the hinges and that the latch is holding the door firmly in position. Check also that the door lines up with the aperture in the body.
2 If the hinges are loose or the door is out of alignment it will be necessary to reset the hinge positions, as described in Sections 25, 26 or 30.
3 If the latch is holding the door properly it should hold the door tightly when fully latched and the door should line up with the body. If it is out of alignment it needs adjustment. If loose, some part of the lock mechanism must be worn out and requires renewal.
4 Other rattles from the door would be caused by wear or looseness in the window winder, the glass channels and sill strips, or the door buttons and interior latch release mechanism.

8 Bonnet (XJ12, Double Six) – removal and refitting

1 Disconnect the battery.

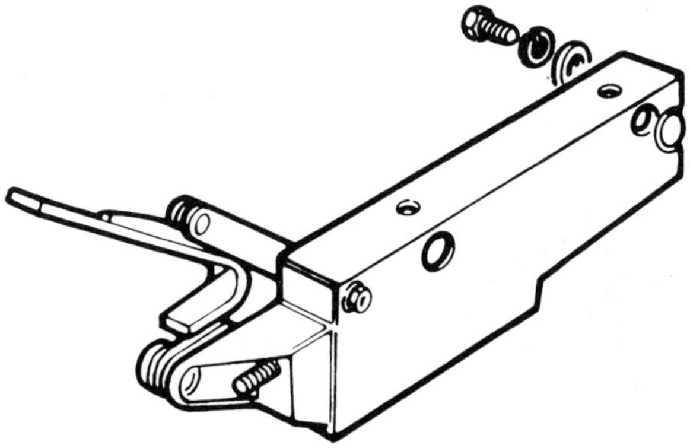

Fig. 12.1 Hinge/bumper mounting bracket (XJ12, Double Six) (Sec 10)

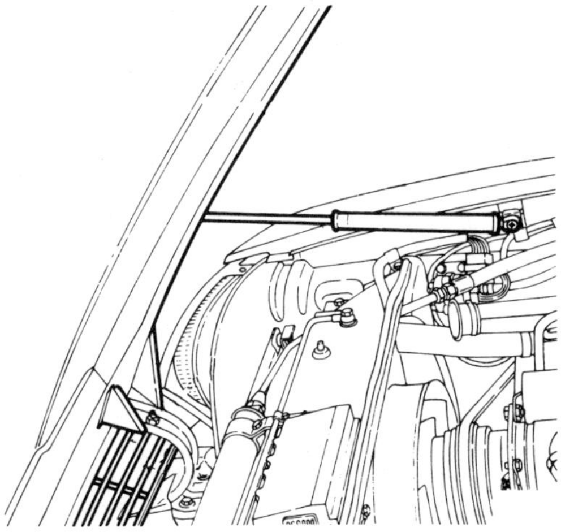

Fig. 12.2 Bonnet stay (XJS) (Sec 12)

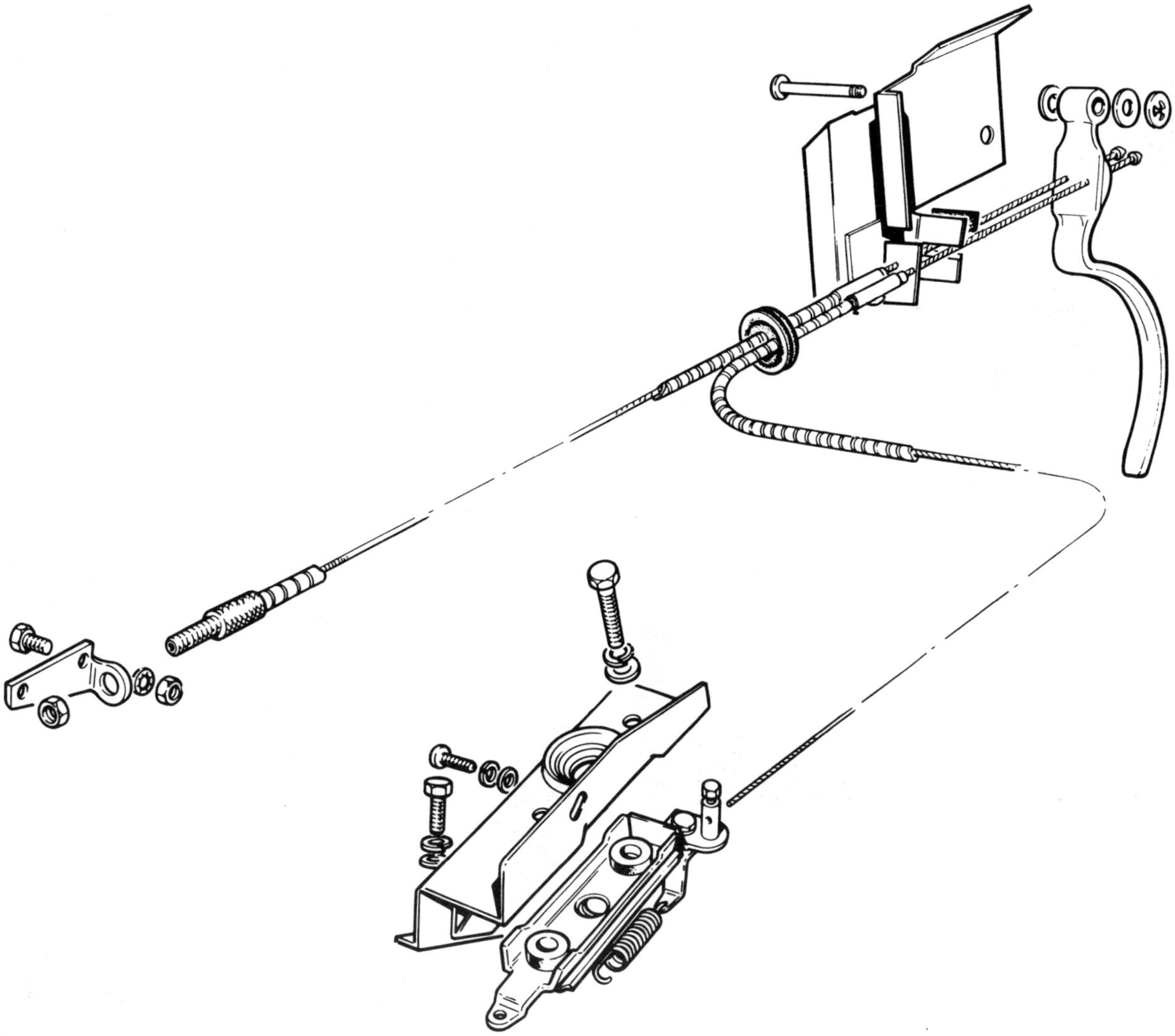

Fig. 12.3 Bonnet lock control (XJ12, Double Six) (Sec 11)

This sequence of photographs deals with the repair of the dent and paintwork damage shown in this photo. The procedure will be similar for the repair of a hole. It should be noted that the procedures given here are simplified – more explicit instructions will be found in the text

In the case of a dent the first job – after removing surrounding trim – is to hammer out the dent where access is possible. This will minimise filling. Here, the large dent having been hammered out, the damaged area is being made slightly concave

Now all paint must be removed from the damaged area, by rubbing with coarse abrasive paper. Alternatively, a wire brush or abrasive pad can be used in a power drill. Where the repair area meets good paintwork, the edge of the paintwork should be 'feathered', using a finer grade of abrasive paper

In the case of a hole caused by rusting, all damaged sheet-metal should be cut away before proceeding to this stage. Here, the damaged area is being treated with rust remover and inhibitor before being filled

Mix the body filler according to its manufacturer's instructions. In the case of corrosion damage, it will be necessary to block off any large holes before filling – this can be done with aluminium or plastic mesh, or aluminium tape. Make sure the area is absolutely clean before ...

... applying the filler. Filler should be applied with a flexible applicator, as shown, for best results; the wooden spatula being used for confined areas. Apply thin layers of filler at 20-minute intervals, until the surface of the filler is slightly proud of the surrounding bodywork

Initial shaping can be done with a Surform plane or Dreadnought file. Then, using progressively finer grades of wet-and-dry paper, wrapped around a sanding block, and copious amounts of clean water, rub down the filler until really smooth and flat. Again, feather the edges of adjoining paintwork

The whole repair area can now be sprayed or brush-painted with primer. If spraying, ensure adjoining areas are protected from over-spray. Note that at least one inch of the surrounding sound paintwork should be coated with primer. Primer has a 'thick' consistency, so will find small imperfections

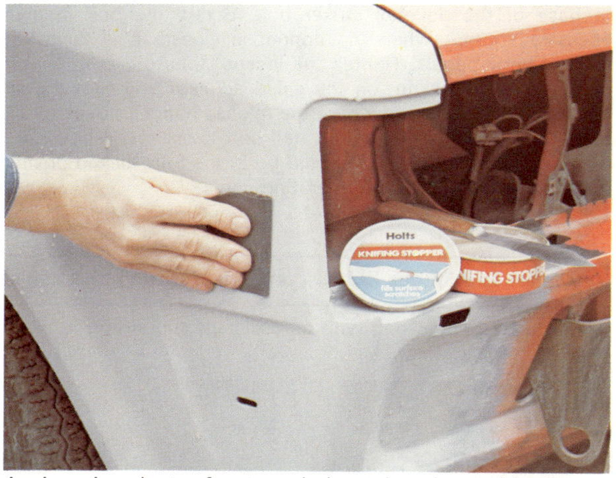

Again, using plenty of water, rub down the primer with a fine grade wet-and-dry paper (400 grade is probably best) until it is really smooth and well blended into the surrounding paintwork. Any remaining imperfections can now be filled by carefully applied knifing stopper paste

When the stopper has hardened, rub down the repair area again before applying the final coat of primer. Before rubbing down this last coat of primer, ensure the repair area is blemish-free – use more stopper if necessary. To ensure that the surface of the primer is really smooth use some finishing compound

The top coat can now be applied. When working out of doors, pick a dry, warm and wind-free day. Ensure surrounding areas are protected from over-spray. Agitate the aerosol thoroughly, then spray the centre of the repair area, working outwards with a circular motion. Apply the paint as several thin coats

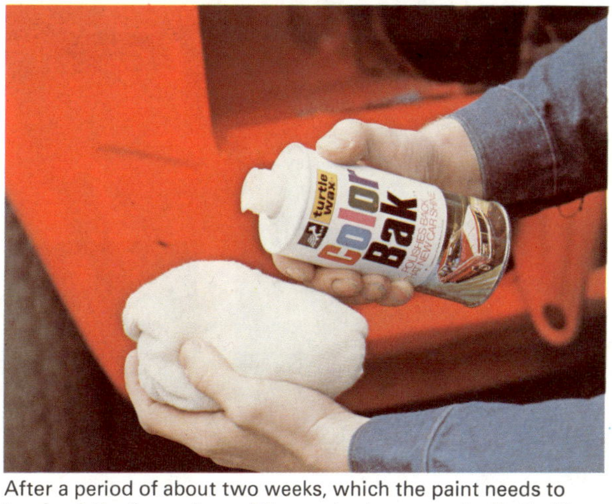

After a period of about two weeks, which the paint needs to harden fully, the surface of the repaired area can be 'cut' with a mild cutting compound prior to wax polishing. When carrying out bodywork repairs, remember that the quality of the finished job is proportional to the time and effort expended

2 Disconnect the headlamp electrical leads at their snap connectors.
3 Unbolt the end of the bonnet stay from the bonnet (photo).
4 Mark the position of the hinges on the underside of the bonnet, using a pencil or masking tape to outline them (photo).
5 Extract the bolts which hold the bonnet to the hinges and with the help of an assistant, lift the bonnet from the car.
6 Refitting is a reversal of removal.

9 Bonnet assist springs (XJ12, Double Six) – removal and refitting

1 Remove the front bumper as described in Sections 17 or 18.
2 Open the bonnet and disconnect the support stay from the bonnet. Open the bonnet to its fullest extent.
3 Using a large screwdriver as a lever, unhook the bonnet assist spring from its upper attachment point.
4 Disconnect the spring from the lower attachment and remove the spring.
5 Refit by reversing the removal operations.

10 Bonnet hinge (XJ12, Double Six) – removal and refitting

1 Remove the bonnet as described in Section 8.
2 Remove the assist spring as described in the preceding Section.
3 Remove the radiator lower grille as described in Section 20.
4 Working inside the front wheel arch, unscrew and remove the four bolts which secure the sides of the front apron panel to the body.
5 Unscrew and remove the three screws which hold the underside of the apron panel to the body and withdraw the apron panel.
6 Remove the radiator as described in Chapter 2.
7 Unbolt the hinge and bumper mounting bracket from the subframe and withdraw the hinge/bracket assembly.
8 Refitting is a reversal of removal, but on completion, seal the area where the bumper mounting bracket enters the subframe. Also seal the heads of the securing bolts. Use underseal for this.

11 Bonnet lock/cable (XJ12, Double Six) – removal, refitting and adjustment

1 Slacken the clamp nut which holds the operating cable to the bonnet lock release lever (photo).
2 Unbolt the lock from its mounting plate and slide the release lever from the cable.
3 If the control cables are to be removed, first extract the two screws which hold the longer cable adjuster bracket to the wing valance.
4 Pull the inner cable free from the lever on the catch and push it into the outer cable.
5 Remove the under scuttle casing from the driver's side (see Section 40).
6 Grip the projecting end of the inner cable at the operating lever and then withdraw the outer cable.
7 To remove the bonnet lock, unbolt it from its mounting plate.
8 The bonnet safety catch can be removed if the spring clip and clevis pin are withdrawn. Note the location of spacers and spring (photo).
9 Refitting of all components is a reversal of removal, but adjust in the following way.
10 Adjust the setting of the bonnet lock by releasing the locknut at the base of the dovetail striker bolt. Screw the bolt in or out as necessary so that when the bonnet is closed, it is flush with the adjacent body panels. Tighten the locknut (photo).
11 Slacken the locknut on the cable adjuster and turn the adjuster until the point is reached where the release handle moves to align the bonnet lock catch with the dovetail bolt lower guide hole. Once the bonnet is closed, the catch should be in the fully locked position and a little slack evident in the operating cable.

12 Bonnet and hinges (XJS) – removal, refitting and adjustment

1 Open the bonnet and with an assistant supporting it, extract the

8.3 Bonnet stay

8.4 Bonnet hinge

11.1 Bonnet lock showing cable clamp nut (arrowed)

11.8 Bonnet safety catch

11.10 Bonnet dovetail striker

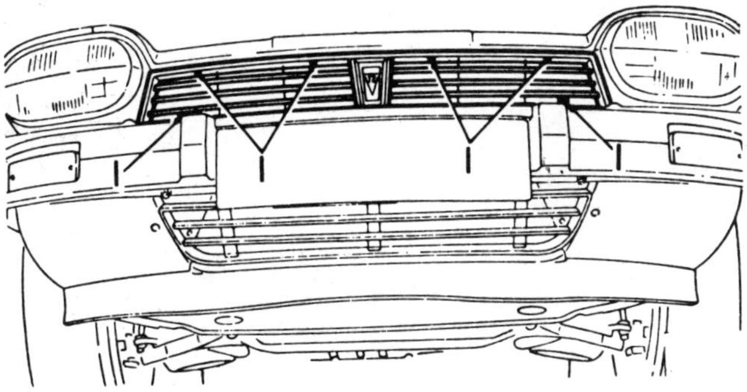

Fig. 12.4 Radiator grille (XJS) (Sec 12)

1 Securing screws

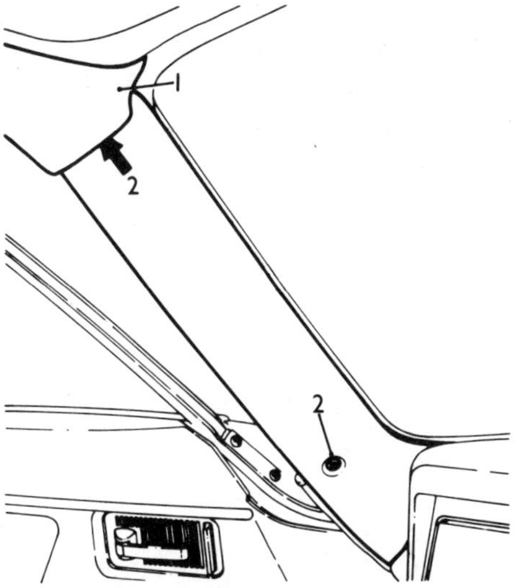

Fig. 12.5 Windscreen pillar trim (XJS) (Sec 13)

1 Crash pad *2 Securing screws*

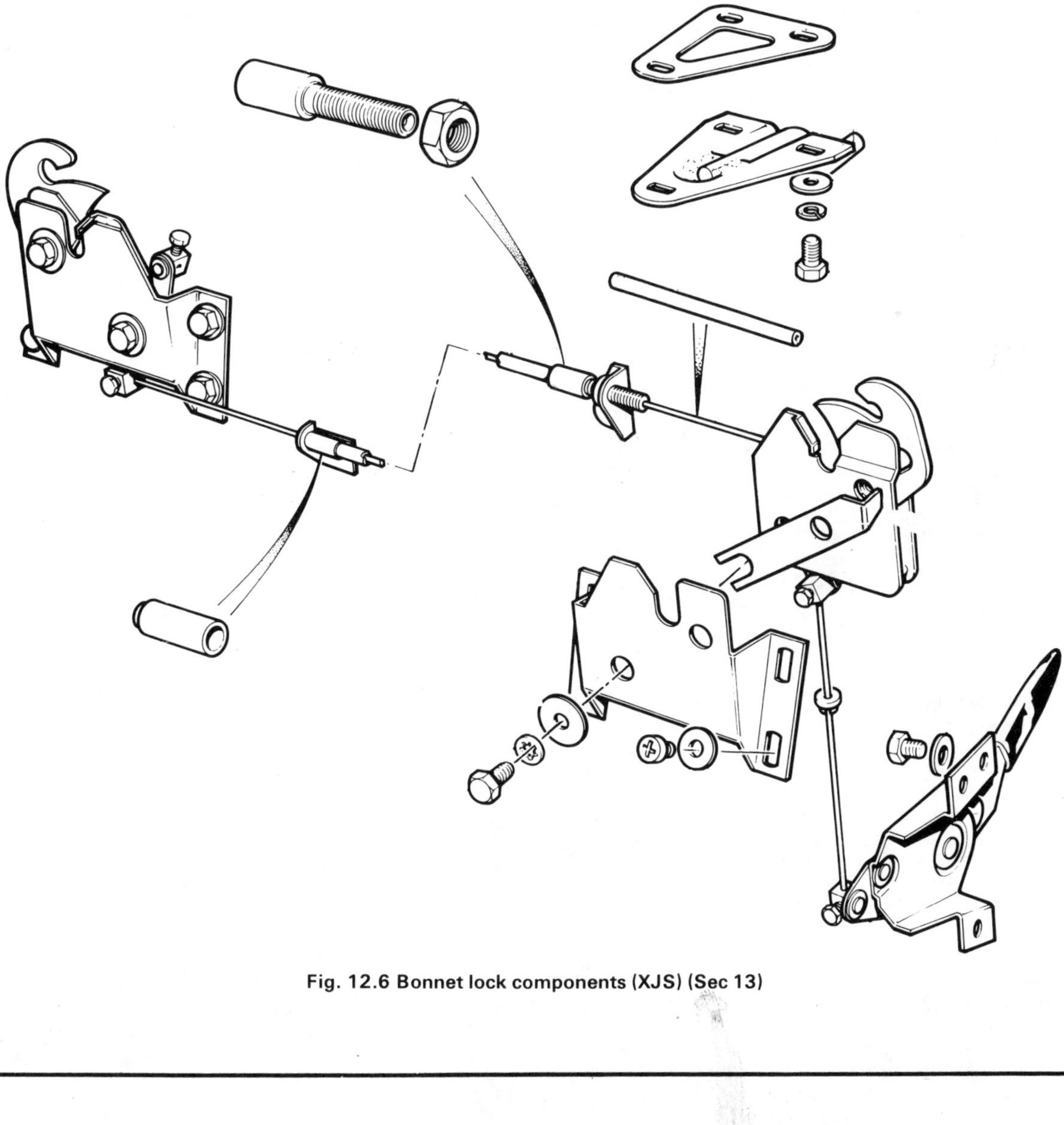

Fig. 12.6 Bonnet lock components (XJS) (Sec 13)

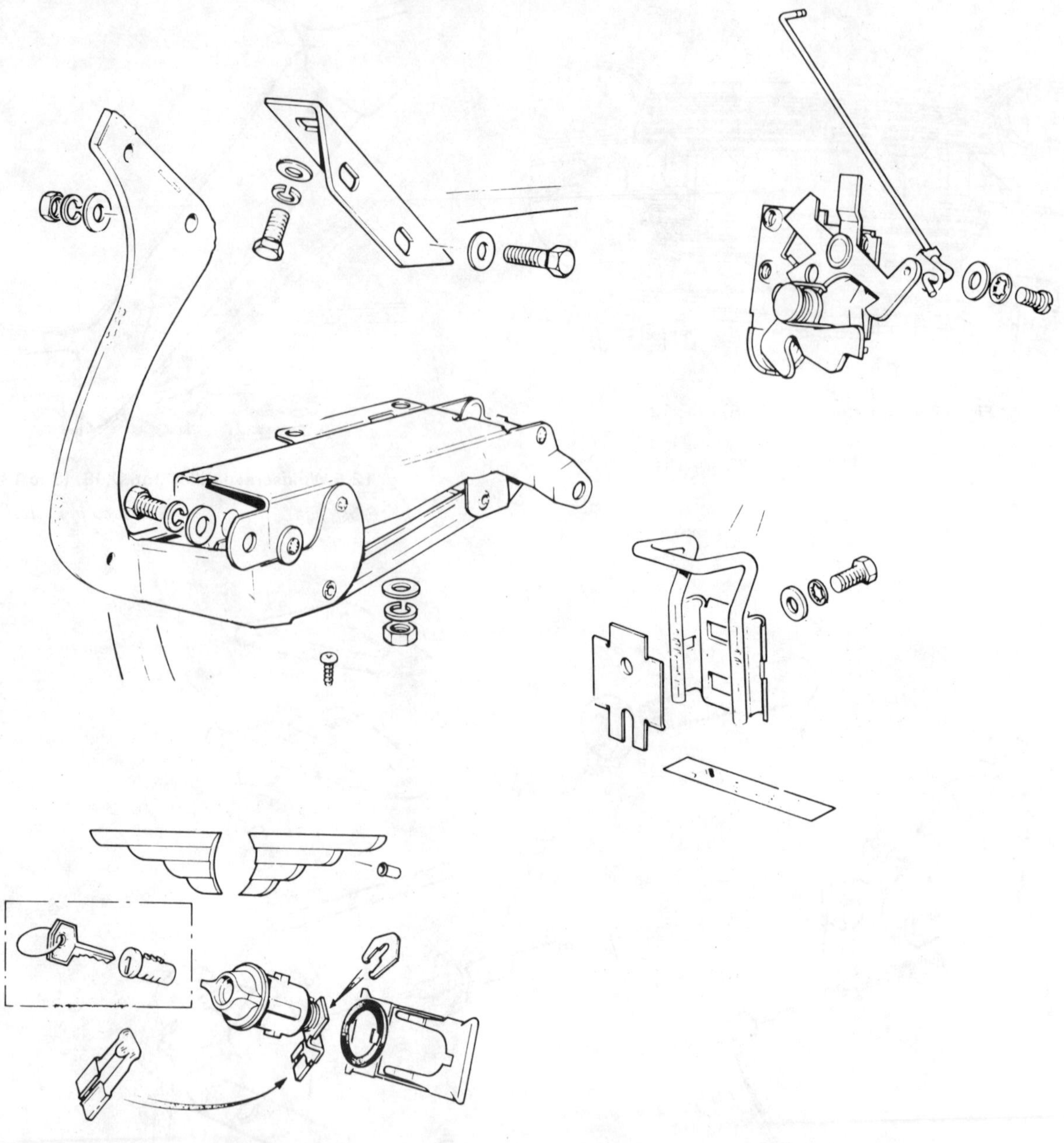

Fig. 12.7 Boot lid hinge and lock components (XJ12, Double Six) (Sec 14)

screws from both ends of the stay and remove the stay.

2 Extract the screws which hold the radiator grille to the bonnet and remove the grille.

3 Mark the position of the hinges in relation to the bonnet using a pencil or masking tape.

4 Unscrew and remove the bonnet-to-hinge bolts and with the help of an assistant, lift the bonnet from the car.

5 If the hinges must now be removed, mark their position in relation to the crossmember, extract their bolts and remove them.

6 Refitting is a reversal of removal, but do not fully tighten the bonnet-to-hinge bolts until the alignment of the bonnet has been checked.

13 Bonnet lock/cable (XJS) – removal, refitting and adjustment

1 Removal operations for the bonnet lock vary according to whether it is a left-hand or right-hand unit.

Left-hand lock removal

2 Release the control cable from the release handle and from the lock pivot.

3 Unbolt the lock from the bulkhead and remove it complete with control cable. Unbolt the lock from its mounting plate.

Right-hand lock removal

4 Extract the two screws which hold the cold start relay cover to the valance and remove the cover.

5 Unbolt the bonnet lock from the bulkhead.

6 Release the cable from the left-hand bonnet lock pivot. Remove the lock complete with cable.

7 Unbolt the lock from the backplate.

Lock trigger/release handle removal

8 Remove the side trim panel from the driver's footwell. To do this, unclip the crash roll adjacent to the pillar trim pad. Extract the screws and remove the pillar trim pad.

Fig. 12.8 Bonnet lock release handle (XJS) (Sec 13)

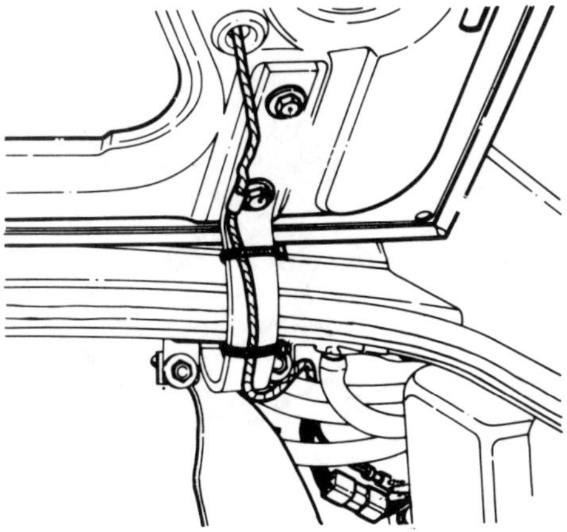

Fig. 12.9 Boot lid hinge arrangement (XJS) (Sec 15)

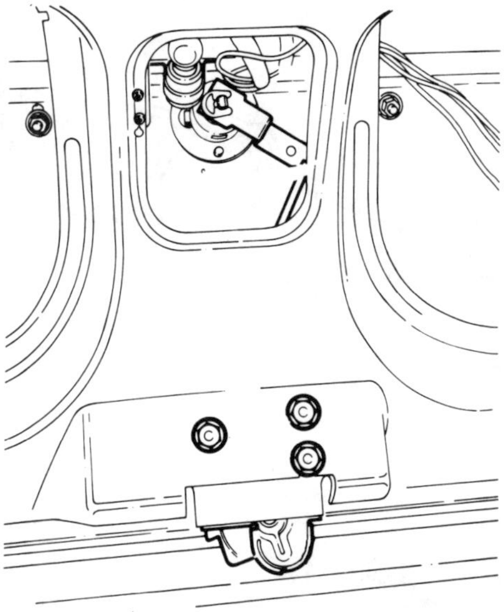

Fig. 12.10 Boot lid lock (XJS) (Sec 15)

9 Move the bonnet release handle to the 'open' position.
10 Slacken the control cable clamp screw and release the cable.
11 Move the release handle to the 'closed' position.
12 Unbolt and remove the release handle mounting bracket.

Refitting (all components)

13 Refitting all components is a reversal of removal, but the following adjustments will be required.

14 To adjust the lock, have the setscrews which hold the lock to the backplate finger-tight. Move the lock up or down within the limits of the elongated screw holes, temporarily tighten the screws and check that with the bonnet closed, the lock is securely latched and smoothly released. Re-adjust as necessary.

15 To adjust the control cable, slacken the cable clamp bolt at the left-hand bonnet lock. Eliminate slackness in the cable and then re-tighten the bolt.

14 Boot lid, hinges and lock (XJ12, Double Six) – removal and refitting

1 Disconnect the battery.

2 Detach the electric leads from the bonnet lid hinges by releasing the plastic straps. Disconnect the leads at their snap connectors.

3 Mark the position of the hinges in relation to the boot lid, using a pencil or masking tape to outline them.

4 With an assistant supporting the lid, unbolt the boot lid from the hinges and lift the lid from the car.

5 To remove the hinges, mark their relative position on the luggage boot and then unbolt and remove them. The counterbalance torsion rods will not be under tension if the hinges are removed in the fully open attitude but if preferred, the rods can be released from the hinges beforehand, using a large screwdriver or length of flat steel bar as a lever.

6 The boot lid lock can be unbolted and removed from the lid if the clip is first detached from the latch mechanism link rod.

7 If the lock striker is to be removed, first mark the projection of its legs in relation to the clamp plate to facilitate refitting.

8 Refitting of all components is a reversal of removal. Do not fully tighten the lid-to-hinge bolts until the alignment of the lid within the body aperture has been checked. The lid should close with a gentle push and release smoothly. If it does not, adjust the striker.

15 Boot lid, hinges and lock (XJS) – removal and refitting

1 The removal operations are very similar to those described in the preceding Section, but observe the following differences.

2 Peel back the carpet to gain access to the wiring harness connectors.

3 Remove the rear parcels tray shelf (see Section 44) to gain access to the hinge mounting bolts.

4 The boot lid lock handle is sited remotely from the lock and can be removed after first withdrawing the rear number plate and reversing lamp assemblies.

5 Extract the spring clip and disconnect the lock operating rod from the handle lever. Extract the handle securing screws and manoeuvre the assembly out of the aperture in the boot lid.

6 Refitting is a reversal of removal.

16 Front underrider and rear overrider (XJ12, Double Six) – removal and refitting

1 These components are simply removed from the front and rear bumpers by extracting the securing bolts.

2 If both rear overriders are being removed, note that once they are withdrawn, the bumper centre section becomes free.

3 When refitting the front underriders, make sure that their top mounting brackets are located under the rubber mounting pad.

17 Bumper blades (XJ12, Double Six) – removal and refitting

Front

1 Working within the front wheel arches, remove the bolts that hold

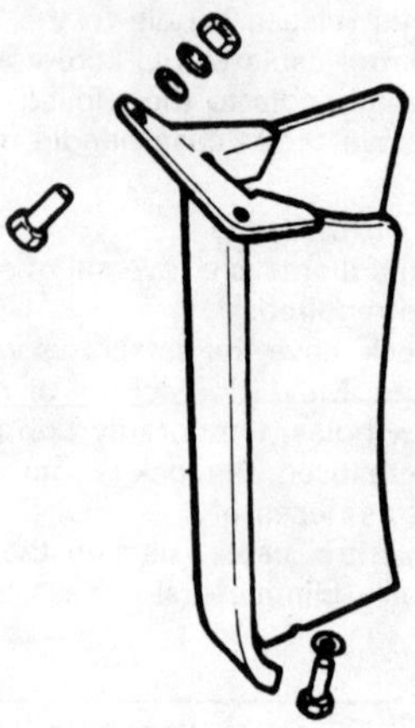

Fig. 12.11 Front underrider (XJ12, Double Six) (Sec 16)

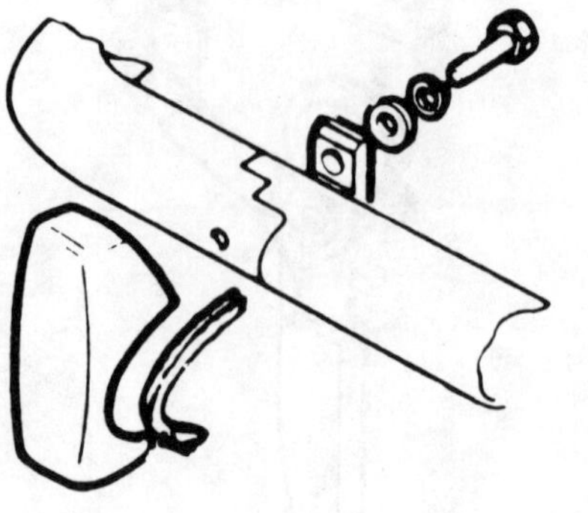

Fig. 12.12 Rear overrider (XJ12, Double Six) (Sec 16)

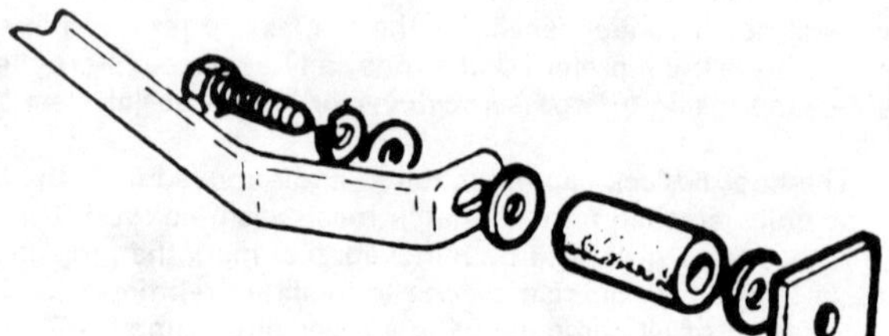

Fig. 12.13 Front bumper end fixings (XJ12, Double Six) (Sec 17)

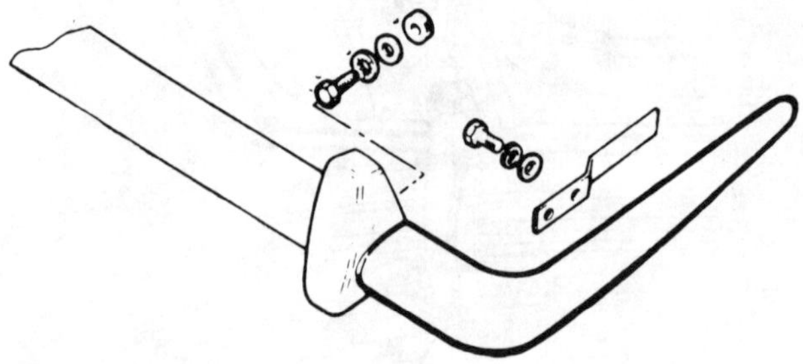

Fig. 12.14 Rear bumper end fixings (XJ12, Double Six) (Sec 17)

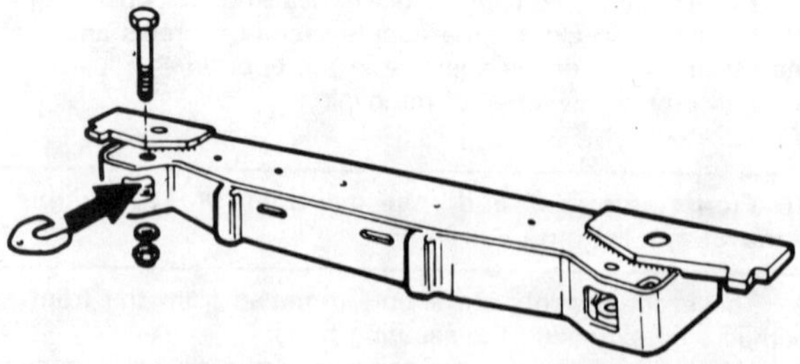

Fig. 12.15 Front bumper impact-absorbing beam (XJ12, Double Six) (Sec 18)

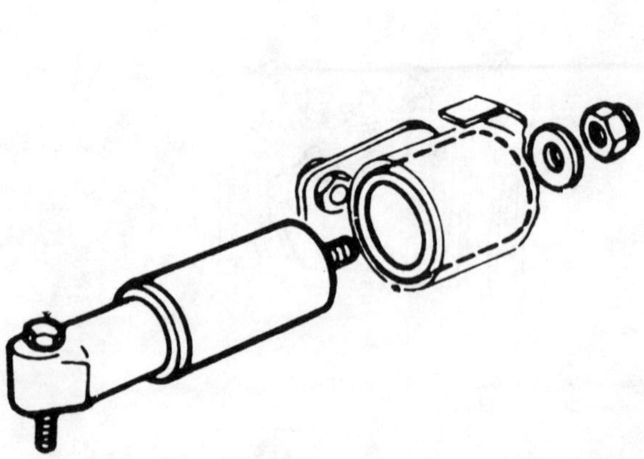

Fig. 12.16 Front bumper impact-absorbing strut (XJ12, Double Six) (Sec 18)

the sides of the bumper to the front wing support stays. Retrieve the washers, spacers and nuts.
2 Unbolt the front of the bumper from the bonnet hinge brackets (photos).
3 Extract the bolts that hold the underriders to the bonnet hinge brackets.
4 Remove the bumper from the car. Unbolt the overriders if necessary.

Rear bumper

5 Unscrew and remove the four bolts which hold the bumper to the side mounting brackets.
6 Support the bumper and unbolt it from its mountings.
7 Remove the bumper from the car.
8 On cars with this type of bumper destined for operation in North America, the side sections are separate pressings. They are held in position with nuts and bolts and incorporate a plastic beading at the joint.

Refitting (front and rear)

9 Refitting of the front and rear bumpers is a reversal of removal.

18 Bumpers (impact-absorbing type – XJ12, Double Six) – removal and refitting

1 This design of bumper is fitted to cars built to North American specification.

Front

2 Remove the bumper blade as described in Section 17.
3 Prise off the clips and remove the oval washers which hold the cover to the impact-absorbing beam. Remove the cover.
4 Unscrew and remove the self-locking nuts from the impact-absorbing beam mounting bolts. Note the location of any shims and remove the beam from the struts.
5 To remove the telescopic strut, open the bonnet and unscrew and remove the nut which holds the impact-absorbing strut to the mounting tube.
6 Using a plastic-faced hammer, tap the end of the strut stud, so driving the strut out of the mounting tube.

Rear

7 Remove the bumper blade as described in Section 17, noting particularly paragraph 8.
8 Unscrew and remove the six bolts which hold the underside of the cover to the impact-absorbing beam, release the cover clips and pull the cover from the beam.
9 Unscrew and remove the self-locking nuts from the impact-absorbing beam mounting bolts. Note the position of the shims and guide tubes and then withdraw the bolts. Lift the beam from the car.
10 Removal of the rear strut is similar to removal of the front one described above, except that the exhaust tailpipe and rear silencer will have to be removed beforehand.

Refitting (front and rear)

11 Refitting is a reversal of removal.

19 Bumpers (XJS) – removal and refitting

1 The impact-absorbing type bumper on these models can be removed in the following stages.

Front

2 Remove the six screws which hold the radiator grille and remove the grille.
3 Remove the nuts, bolts and washers which hold the centre section of the bumper blade to the impact-absorbing beam. Remove the section.
4 Remove the front flasher lamp assemblies and then extract the five screws which secure the cover to the impact-absorbing beam.
5 Disengage the cover clips and pull the cover from the beam.
6 Unbolt the impact-absorbing beam from the struts and lift the beam from the car, noting the location of the spacers.
7 The telescopic struts can be removed once the single fixing nut is unscrewed and the strut stud tapped with a plastic-faced hammer.

Rear

8 Removal is similar to that described earlier for the front assembly. Withdraw the centre section of the bumper blade, the cover from the impact-absorbing beam and then the beam itself.
9 Access to the struts can be obtained after peeling back the carpet in the luggage compartment.

Refitting (front and rear)

10 Refitting all components is a reversal of removal.

20 Radiator grille (XJ12, Double Six) – removal and refitting

1 Unscrew and remove the nuts and cross-head screws which hold the grille to the bonnet. Retrieve the washers.
2 Withdraw the grille evenly from the bonnet.
3 The lower grille can be removed if the two screws which hold the lower grille to the apron and which are located behind the spotlamps are removed.
4 The centre bar is removable independently if the two nuts which hold the upper section of the bar to the retaining plate are unscrewed, followed by the single nut which holds the lower section of the bar to the radiator grille.
5 Refitting is a reversal of removal.
6 On Series 1 models, the horn grilles are simply pulled from their locations. Do this using a piece of cord and give an even straight pull.

21 Radiator grilles and spoiler (XJS) – removal and refitting

1 The main grille can be removed from the bonnet once the securing screws have been extracted.
2 The lower grille is detachable if the screws which hold it to the wings are first extracted.
3 If the spoiler is to be removed, the front of the car should be raised or the car placed over an inspection pit.
4 Remove the two securing screws and withdraw the oil cooler grille.
5 Prise out the plastic fasteners which hold the spoiler undertray to the body and the spoiler.
6 Unscrew and remove the screws and detach the spoiler undertray.
7 Unscrew and remove the spoiler securing screws.
8 Refitting is a reversal of removal, but use new plastic fasteners on the spoiler undertray.

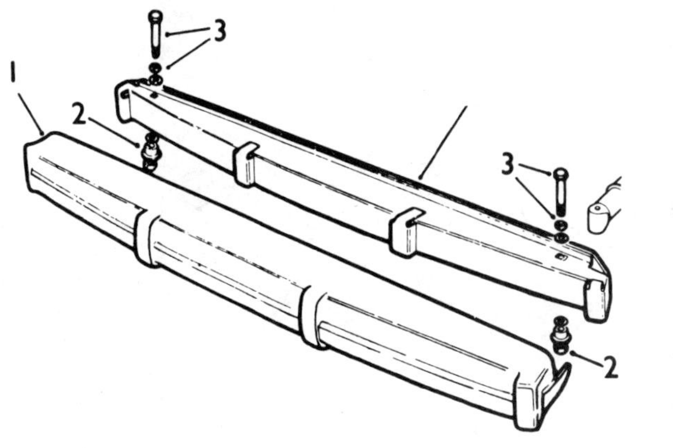

Fig. 12.17 Rear impact-absorbing bumper (XJ12, Double Six) (Sec 18)

1 Cover
2 Mounting nuts and washers
3 Mounting bolts and washers

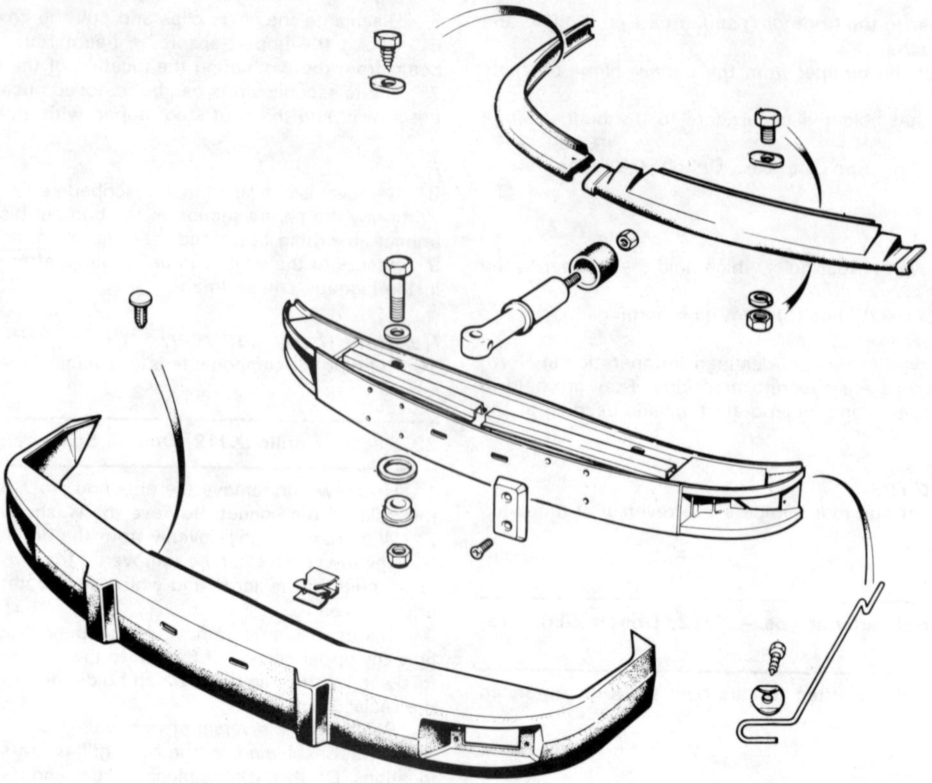

Fig. 12.18 Front bumper components (XJS) (Sec 19)

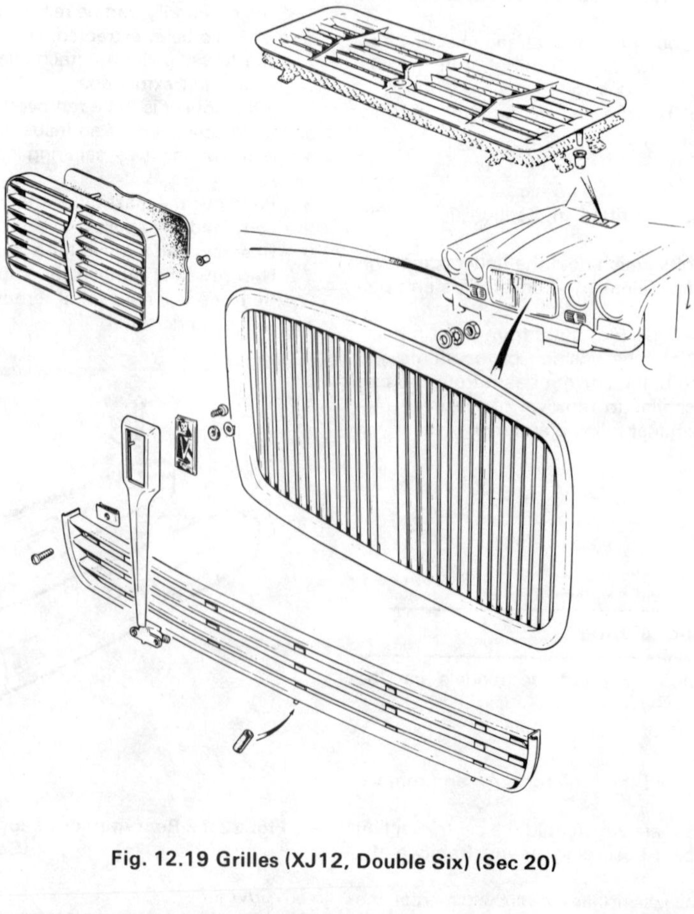

Fig. 12.19 Grilles (XJ12, Double Six) (Sec 20)

17.2A Front bumper mounting

17.2B Front bumper under-rider

22.4 Armrest screw cover plate

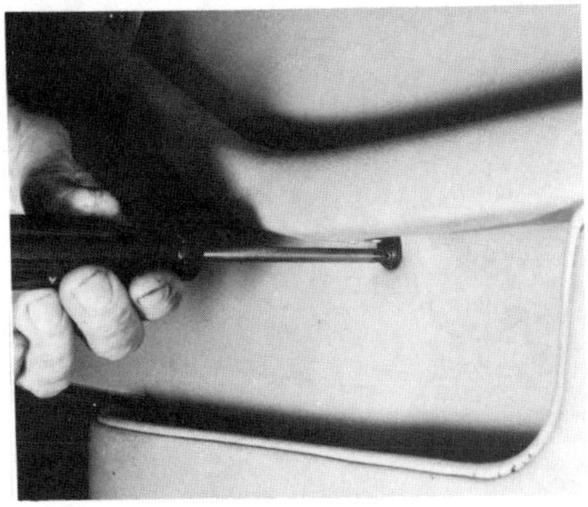

22.6A Armrest lower screw

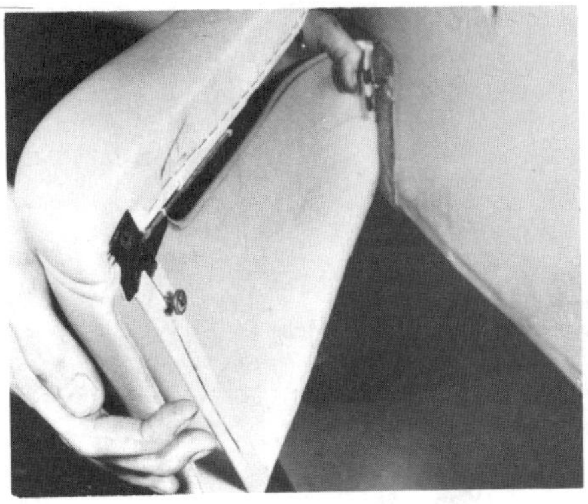

22.6B Removing door armrest

22.8 Front door inner panel

22.14 Door latch

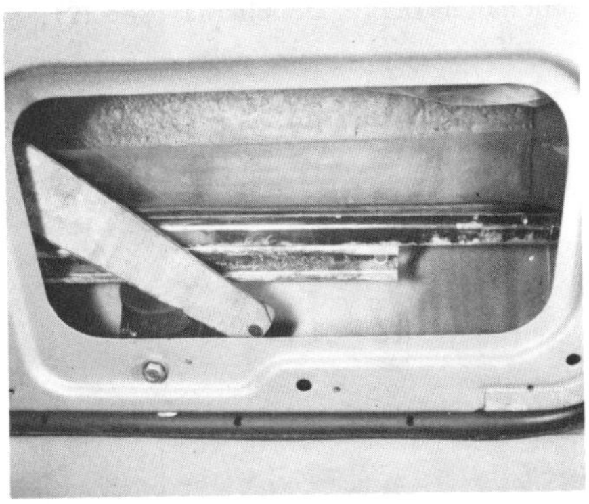

22.19 Window lift arm and guide channel

22 Front door (XJ12 and Double Six, 4-door models) – dismantling and reassembly

Series 1

1 On Series 1 models with a swivelling ventilator, remove the door capping (six screws).

2 Prise out the centre bezel from the ventilator control knob and then unscrew the bolt which is exposed. Remove the control knob.

3 Extract the securing screws and remove the crash roll and the armrest.

Series 2 onwards

4 On Series 2 and later models, pull the chrome cover from the forward end of the armrest (photo).

5 Unscrew and remove the screw which is now exposed.

6 Unscrew and remove the four screws from the underside of the armrest and remove the armrest from the door. If manually-operated window regulators are fitted, extract the single screw and pull off the handle and escutcheon (photos).

All models

7 On all models, if a remotely controlled exterior mirror is fitted, extract the screws which hold the adjuster control lever escutcheon and partially withdraw the escutcheon until the grub screw can be extracted and the escutcheon removed from the lever.

8 Insert a broad blade between the trim panel of the door and the door casing and twist the blade to release the first retaining clip. Now insert the fingers and working round the trim panel, release the remaining retaining clips. Withdraw the panel. Self-tapping screws are sometimes used at the bottom edge (photo).

9 If the door lock is to be removed, first make sure that the window is wound fully up by actuating the lift button or temporarily refitting the regulator handle.

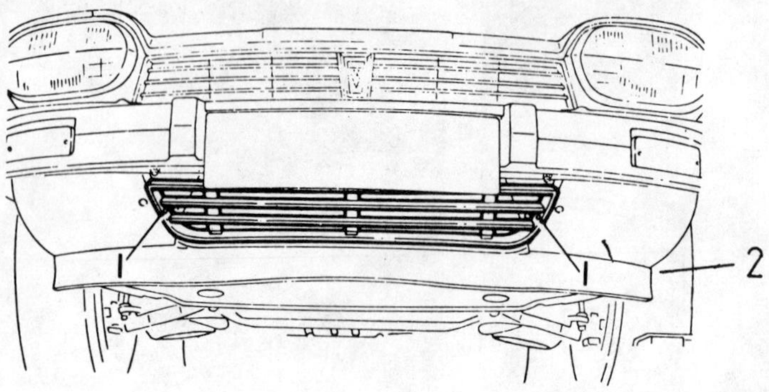

Fig. 12.20 Radiator lower grille (XJS) (Sec 21)

1 Securing screws *2 Spoiler*

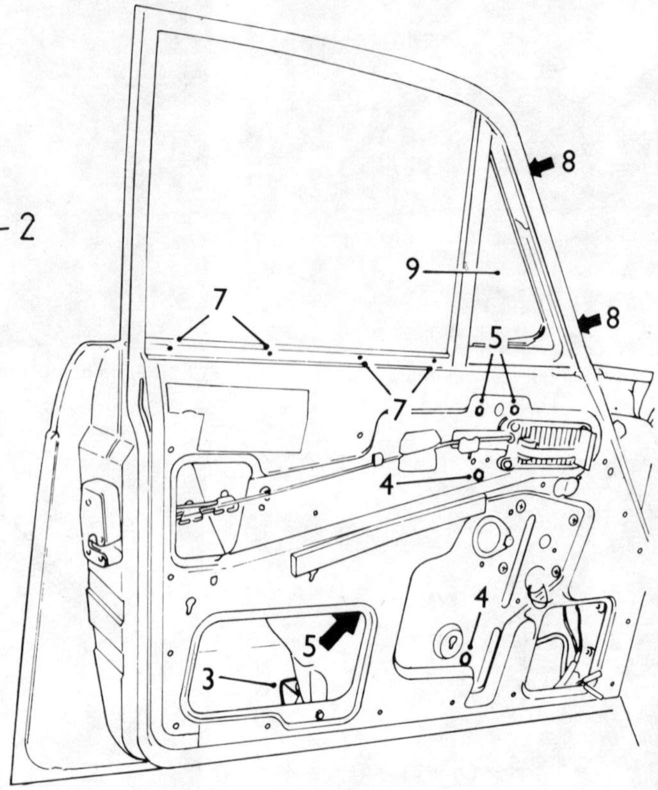

Fig. 12.21 Front door (XJ12 and Double Six, Series 1) (Sec 22)

3 Glass buffer
4 Ventilator support bolts
5 Ventilator gear fixing bolts
7 Weatherstrip screws
8 Ventilator fixing screws
9 Ventilator

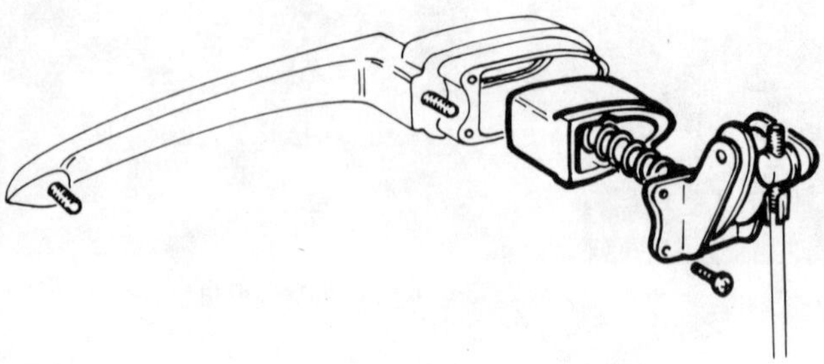

Fig. 12.22 Exterior door handle (XJ12, Double Six) (Sec 22)

Fig. 12.23 Typical XJ12, Double Six Series 1 rear door armrest (Sec 23)

2 Window lift switch

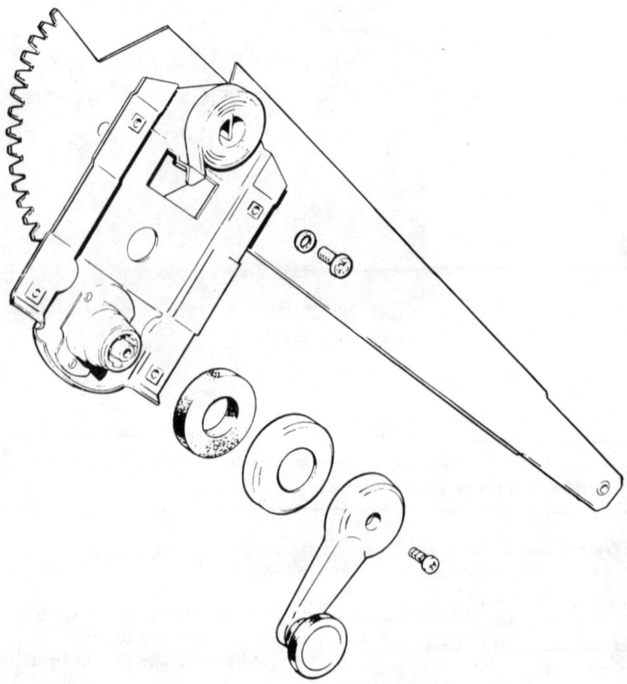

Fig 12.24 Window regulator (manually operated) (XJ12, Double Six) (Sec 22)

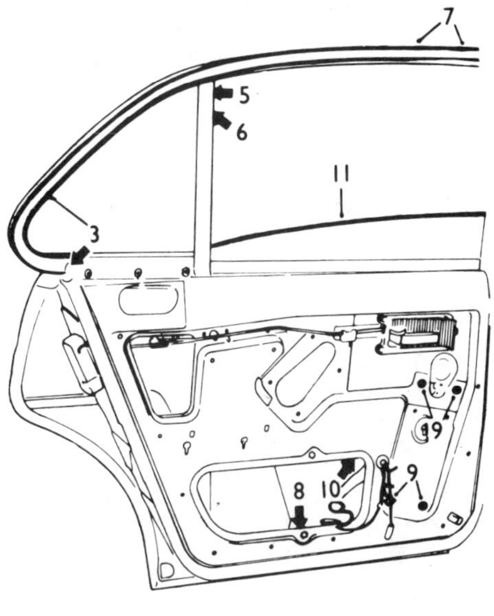

Fig. 12.25 Rear door (XJ12, Double Six) (Sec 23)

3 Chrome trim screw
5 Felt channel
6 Securing screws
7 Top frame securing screws
8 Glass buffer screw
9 Window lift fixing screws
10 Window lift arm to channel connection
11 Glass

Fig. 12.26 Rear door window regulator (manual (XJ12, Double Six) (Sec 23)

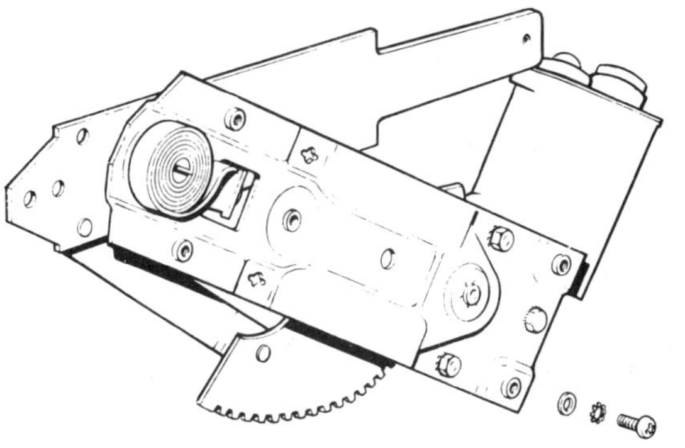

Fig. 12.27 Rear door window regulator (electric) (XJ12, Double Six) (Sec 23)

10 Release the spring clip which holds the inside handle remote control rod to the latch lever and detach the rod.
11 Detach the exterior door handle remote control rod in a similar manner. Unscrew the two nuts and remove the exterior door handle if required.
12 Detach the key lock remote control rod from the latch lever.
13 Extract the screw which holds the lower section of the window channel to the door casing.
14 Remove the screws which hold the latch assembly to the edge of the door and withdraw the assembly from the rear of the window channel (photo).
15 If the door glass is to be removed, the lock mechanism need not be removed, but on Series 1 cars the swivelling ventilator must be withdrawn in the following way. Unbolt the ventilator support leg from the door casing and then unbolt the ventilator gear mechanism from the door. Lower the main window glass to its fullest extent. Extract the weatherstrip screws and the screws which hold the ventilator to the door. Withdraw the ventilator assembly.
16 On Series 2 and later models, lower the door glass to its fullest extent and prise off the chrome beading from the base of the fixed quarterlight.
17 Remove the two bolts which hold the quarterlight support leg to the door panel and then extract the screws which hold the glass weatherstrip to the door. Remove the weatherstrip.
18 Remove the two screws which hold the quarterlight to the angular section of the door glass frame and carefully pull the quarterlight from the door.
19 Slide the door main glass forward and disengage the window lift operating arm from the guide channel (photo).
20 Withdraw the glass from the door. The guide channel and rubber seal can be detached from the glass if required, but before removing them mark their position on the glass with masking tape, or by measuring, to ensure correct reassembly.
21 Refer to Chapter 10 if the window lift motors or lock solenoids have to be removed.
22 Reassembly and refitting of all door components is a reversal of dismantling, but check the door closure and lock operation (Sections 7 and 25) before refitting the trim panel.
23 Seal the gap between the quarterlight and the chrome beading with suitable sealant.

23 Rear door (XJ12 and Double Six, 4-door models) – dismantling and reassembly

1 If the armrests incorporate the radio speakers, disconnect the battery, extract the securing screws from the lower edge of the armrest and withdraw it far enough to be able to disconnect the speaker leads.
2 Lift the armrest from the door.
3 Remove the door interior trim panel as described for the front door in the preceding Section.
4 Temporarily reconnect the battery and raise the window fully or refit the regulator handle temporarily.
5 Disconnect the remote control rods as described in the preceding Section and additionally prise the child safety link from the latch lever mechanism. Withdraw the operating link from the edge of the door.
6 To remove the main glass, prise the chrome trim free from the door glass frame and then extract the screw which holds the inner chrome trim to the door glass frame. Prise the trim free.
7 Release the rubber seal from the door glass frame.
8 Lower the glass and release the upper section of the felt channel which is fitted to the quarterlight to expose the screws. Remove the screws which hold the vertical door glass frame and then gently tap the top glass frame free. Lift the frame from the door.
9 Remove the glass buffer stop from the door panel.
10 Disengage the window lift arm from the glass guide bracket and withdraw the glass from the door.
11 Before removing the glass guide bracket and seal from the glass, mark their position with masking tape or by measuring.
12 The quarterlight can be removed independently of the main door glass. Commence by prising the chrome trim free from the quarterlight frame.
13 Prise the chrome beading from the base of the quarterlight and remove the screw from the inner chrome trim which is attached to the door glass frame. Prise off the trim.

14 Release the door seal from the quarterlight frame and extract the three screws which hold the base of the quarterlight to the door.
15 Lower the door glass to its fullest extent by temporarily reconnecting the battery and operating the control button.
16 Release the upper section of the felt channel from the quarterlight and extract the exposed screws.
17 Prise the chrome trim from the quarterlight vertical post and lift the quarterlight from the door.
18 Refitting is a reversal of removal, but check the lock adjustment as described in Section 28 before refitting the interior panel to the door.
19 Seal the gap between the base of the quarterlight and the chrome beading.

24 Door (XJ12 and Double Six, 2-door models) – dismantling and reassembly

1 The operations are similar to those described in Section 22, except that a separate quarterlight is not fitted and manually-operated windows are used on earlier models.
2 To remove the door glass, take off the trim panel and crash roll from the inside of the door. The window regulator handle will first have to be detached by extracting the screw from the chrome bezel.
3 Remove the securing screws and lift the glass bezel/guide from the front of the door.
4 Remove the securing screws from the crash roll retaining plate and withdraw the plate.
5 Prise off the glass anti-rattle pads.
6 Detach the lower portion of the polythene sheet from the door.
7 Lower the window sufficiently to gain access to the window mounting plate screws. Slacken the screws.
8 Release the two nuts which hold the window lift quadrant guide channel to the glass mounting.
9 Raise the window to its fullest extent and then remove the two screws which hold the glass to the mounting plate.
10 Remove the glass sealing rubber and carefully withdraw the glass from the door.
11 Once the glass has been withdrawn, the winder mechanism can be removed.
12 Commence by extracting the screws which hold the chrome beading and the weatherstrip to the door. Remove the weatherstrip.
13 Raise the glass carrier fully and then disengage the spring from the glass carrier plate.
14 Lower the carrier plate sufficiently to give access to the guide channel which engages with the lift motor quadrant.
15 Remove the two nuts which hold the guide channel to the glass carrier. Slide the channel from the window lift quadrant and lift the guide from the door.
16 Disengage the spring assembly and remove it.
17 Remove the nylon anti-rattle pads from the top corners of the pulley frame.
18 Move the glass carrier to give access to the four setscrews which hold the carrier plates and remove the setscrews. Remove the outer plates from the door.
19 Remove the four setscrews which hold the corners of the pulley mechanism frame to the door. Retrieve the washers which are located between the frame and the door panel.
20 Withdraw the glass carrier/pulley assembly from the door.
21 Refitting is a reversal of removal, but observe the following points.
22 When refitting the glass, have the mounting plate screws slackened and adjust the glass to obtain a $\frac{9}{32}$ in (7.0 mm) clearance between the drip rail and the glass edge. Once this clearance is obtained, fully tighten the mounting plate screws.
23 Check the door lock operation and adjust if necessary after reference to Section 28.

25 Front door (XJ12 and Double Six, 4-door models) – removal and refitting

1 Disconnect the battery and remove the door interior trim panel as described previously.
2 If speakers are fitted, remove the securing screws and pull the speakers forward until the leads can be disconnected.
3 Identify all other leads and disconnect them at their snap connectors. Withdraw the wiring loom through the hole in the leading edge of the door.
4 Support the door under its lower edge on jacks or a block in its fully open position.
5 Unscrew and remove the bolts which hold the door to the hinges. Lift the door from the car and recover the packing pieces.
6 If the hinges must be removed, jack up the front of the car and turn

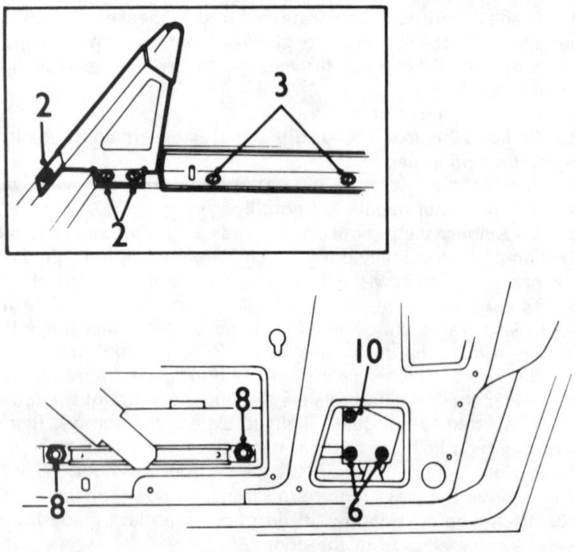

Fig. 12.28 Door components (XJ12 and Double Six, 2-door) (Sec 24)

2 Glass bezel guide screws
3 Door crash roll plate screws
6 Window mounting plate screws
8 Window lift guide channel screws
10 Screws (glass to mounting plate)

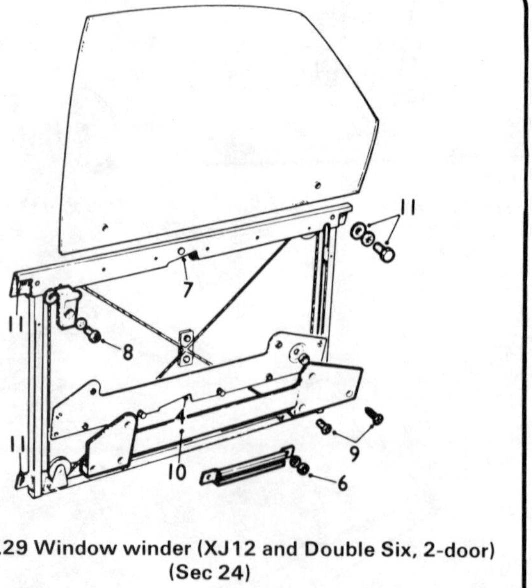

Fig. 12.29 Window winder (XJ12 and Double Six, 2-door) (Sec 24)

4 Glass carrier plate
6 Guide channel to glass carrier nuts
7 Spring to spigot fixing
8 Nylon anti-rattle pads and screws
9 Carrier plate screws
10 Carrier plate
11 Pulley pivot screws

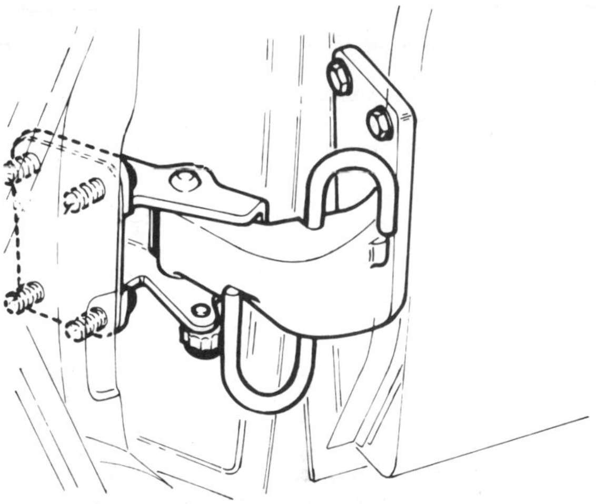

Fig. 12.30 Door hinge (XJ12, Double Six) on front doors of 4-door models and both doors on 2-door models (Sec 25)

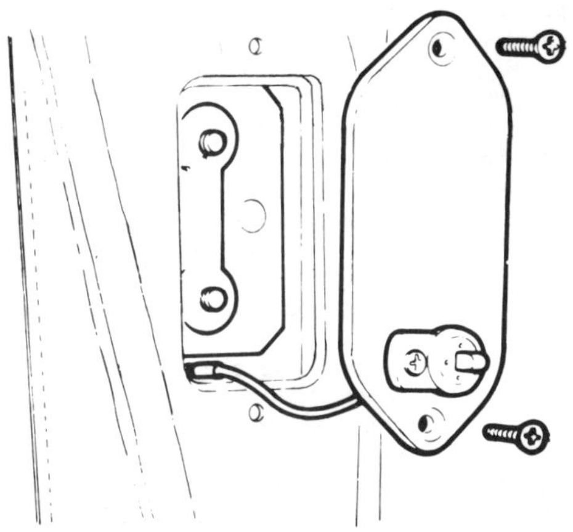

Fig. 12.31 Rear of striker plate (XJ12, Double Six) (Sec 28)

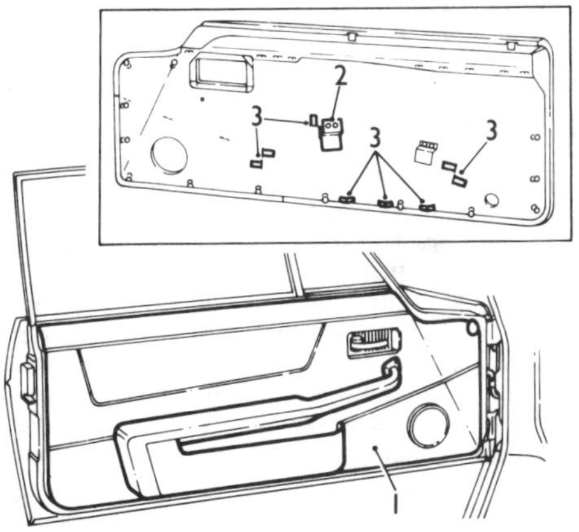

Fig. 12.32 Door trim panel (XJS) (Sec 29)

1 Trim panel
2 Retaining bracket
3 Armrest securing lugs

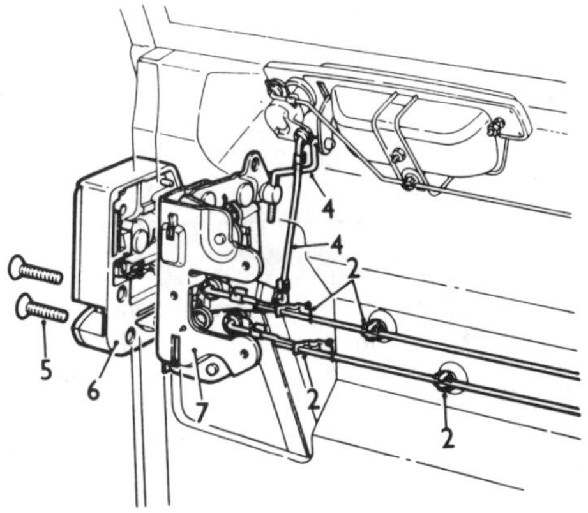

Fig. 12.33 Door lock and exterior handle operating rods (XJS) (Sec 29)

2 Lock operating rods
4 Exterior handle operating rod
5 Lock securing screws
6 Latch unit
7 Lock assembly

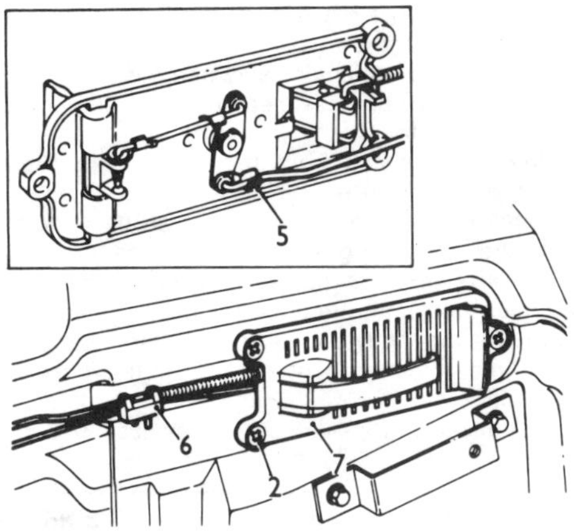

Fig. 12.34 Door lock interior handle (XJS) (Sec 29)

2 Securing screws
5 Lock control rod and clip
6 Handle control rod and plastic clip
7 Interior handle

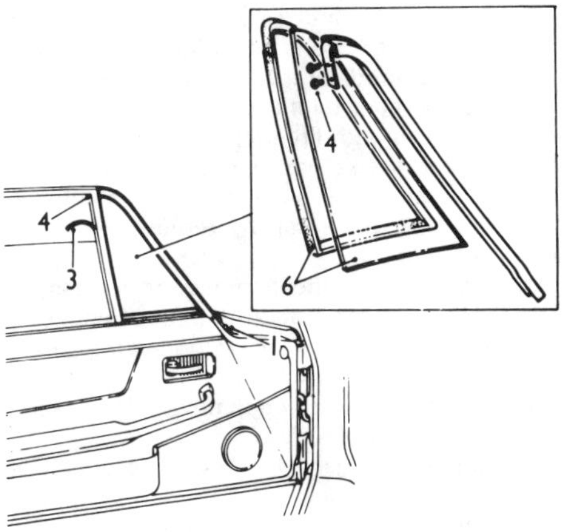

Fig. 12.35 Front fixed quarterlight (XJS) (Sec 29)

1 Quarterlight fixing screws
3 Door glass rubber
4 Quarterlight fixing screws
6 Quarterlight glass and rubber surround

the steering to full lock.

7 Working under the front wing, unbolt and remove the panel from the wheel arch. Remove the two bolts inside the wheel arch which hold the lower part of the wing to the sill.

8 Remove the two bolts located between the door hinges which hold the wing to the body pillar. Note the earth strap fitted under the top bolt.

9 Remove the bolts and washers which hold the top edge of the wing to the valance. Using a wedge, separate the lower part of the wing from the body.

10 The front door hinges can now be unbolted and removed from the body pillar.

11 To refit the hinges, reverse the removal operations. Seal the wheel arch panel with underseal on completion.

12 To refit the door, make sure that the earth strap is located behind one hinge bolt.

13 Do not fully tighten the hinge bolts until the door has been closed and has been set so that it is flush with adjacent body panels and the gap all around its edge is even. Open the door gently and fully tighten the bolts.

14 Reconnect all leads and refit the door trim panel.

15 Reconnect the battery.

26 Door (XJ12 and Double Six, 2-door models) – removal and refitting

1 The operations are identical to those described in Section 25.

27 Rear door (XJ12 and Double Six, 4-door models) – removal and refitting

1 Remove the door interior trim panel.

2 Disconnect the battery, identify the wiring inside the door and separate the leads at the snap connectors. Withdraw the wiring harness through the hole in the leading edge of the door.

3 Support the door in the fully open position on jacks or blocks padded with rag.

4 Unscrew and remove the bolts which hold the door to the hinges. Lift the door from the car.

5 If the hinges must be removed, simply unbolt them from the body pillar (photo).

6 When refitting the hinges, note the earth lead located under the hinge top bolt.

7 When refitting the door, do not fully tighten the hinge bolts until the door has been closed and adjusted to be flush with the adjacent body panels.

28 Door lock and striker (XJ12, Double Six) – adjustment

1 If the door does not open or close correctly, fails to lock when the inside handle is operated, or opens immediately the inside handle is moved, the remote control rods or their spring connections will require adjustment. Remove the door interior panel for access to the rods.

2 The door should close with little effort and close securely.

3 If necessary, release the setscrews on the striker plate and move the striker. Re-tighten the striker plate screws on completion (photo).

4 The front door striker plate can be removed completely in the following way.

5 Disconnect the battery and then remove the courtesy light switch mounting plate. Disconnect the lead at the snap connector.

6 Extract the striker plate screws and withdraw the striker assembly from the interior of the body pillar.

7 The rear door striker plate can be removed if the rear seat squab is first withdrawn (see Section 49).

8 Peel back the trim and adhesive tape which covers the striker plate access hole.

9 Unscrew and remove the striker plate screws and withdraw the striker assembly from the interior of the body pillar.

10 Refitting both striker assemblies is a reversal of removal. After adjustment, seal the edges of the striker mounting plate with suitable body sealer.

29 Door (XJS) – dismantling and reassembly

1 Release the armrest finisher from its spring clip.

2 Undo and remove the screw which holds the armrest to the door interior trim panel.

3 Release the two screws which hold the courtesy switch plate to the door. Pull the trim panel away from the striker plate.

4 Extract the screw which holds the bottom edge of the trim panel to the door.

5 Insert a broad blade between the trim panel and the door casing, twist the blade and release the first of the trim panel clips. Now use the fingers to release the remaining clips.

6 Pull the trim panel far enough from the door to be able to disconnect the radio speaker leads.

7 Extract the screws from the armrest retaining bracket and straighten the lugs if the armrest/pocket assembly is to be removed from the trim panel.

8 Disconnect the rods from the door lock interior handle.

9 Carefully move the waterproof sheeting to one side and disconnect the operating rods from the exterior door handle.

10 Extract the four screws which hold the outer lock unit to the door.

11 Remove the outer lock unit, followed by the inner unit.

12 The interior lock handle can be removed by extracting the three securing screws and disconnecting the control rods.

13 To remove the quarterlight, first withdraw the two screws which hold the bottom of the quarterlight front frame to the door casing.

14 Lower the door glass completely by operating the control button.

15 Ease the door glass rubber aside and remove the two screws which hold the quarterlight to the frame.

16 Withdraw the quarterlight.

17 To remove the main glass from the door, fully raise the window and extract the two screws which hold the window channel to the door.

18 Ease the rubber clear of the channel and then remove the channel.

19 Unbolt the glass stop from the base of the door.

20 Lower the glass, guiding it with the hand, and then tilt the glass foward so that the lift arm can be disconnected from it.

21 Holding the glass in the tilted position, lift it from the door.

22 Once the glass has been withdrawn, the door exterior handle can be removed. First detach the control rods and then unscrew the retaining nuts and withdraw the mounting plate.

23 Refitting of all components is a reversal of removal but on completion, adjust the lock and striker as described in Section 28.

30 Door (XJS) – removal and refitting

1 Open the door to the half open position and support it on jacks or blocks covered with pads of rag.

2 Remove the cover from the fuel cut-off inertia switch on the driver's door only if this door is to be removed. Release the switch from its spring clips and swing it aside.

3 Extract the two screws which hold the footwell side trim pad.

4 Remove the under scuttle casing (see Section 40).

5 Unbolt the door lock solenoid relay and ease the relay aside.

6 Disconnect the door harness electrical lead connectors, including the radio cable connector.

7 Unbolt the hinge plates from the body. With the help of an assistant, life the door from the car.

8 If the hinges must be removed, they can be unbolted from the door, but note the rubber plug on the access hole for the upper hinge.

9 Refitting is a reversal of removal, but only screw on one nut to each hinge finger-tight until the door has been closed and set so that it is flush with adjacent body panels and the gap all around its edge is of even width. Open the door gently, screw on the remaining nuts and tighten them fully.

10 Adjust the striker and lock if necessary as described in Section 28.

31 Rear quarterlight (XJ12 and Double Six, 2-door models) – removal and refitting

1 Remove the rear quarter trim casing and crash roll.

2 Extract the securing screws and remove the crash roll mounting from the quarter panel.

3 Peel away the waterproof sheeting.

4 Unbolt and remove the glass buffer from the quarter panel.

5 Lower the glass to the half open position and support it in this position.

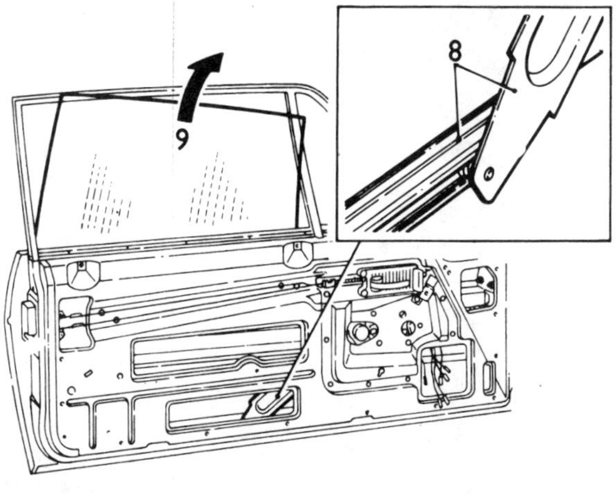

Fig. 12.36 Removing door glass (XJS) (Sec 29)

8 Window lift arm and channel *9 Direction of removal*

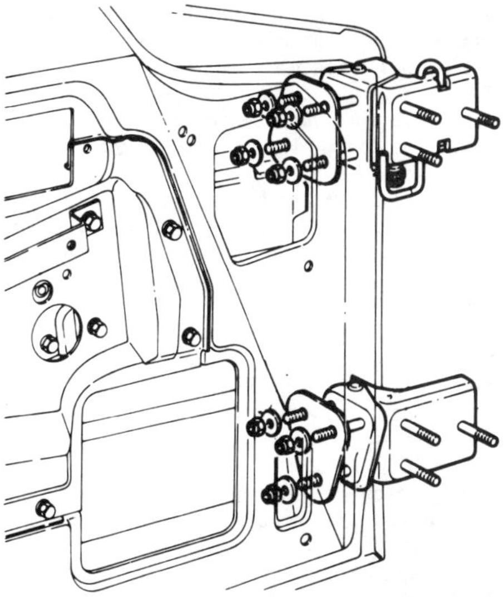

Fig. 12.37 Door hinges (XJS) (Sec 30)

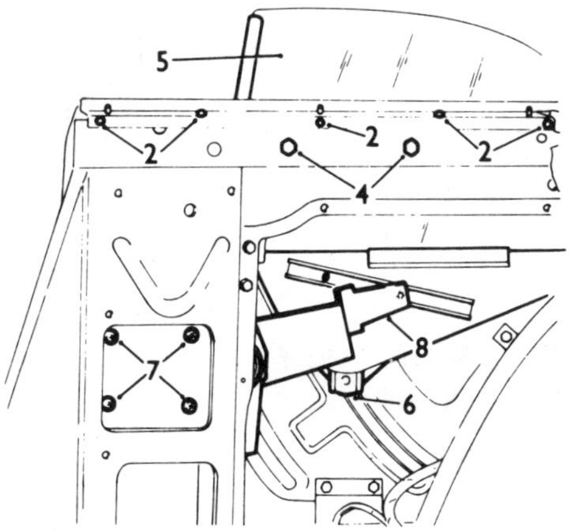

Fig. 12.38 Rear quarterlight (XJ12 and Double Six, 2-door) (Sec 31)

2 Crash roll screws
4 Glass buffer bolts
5 Glass
6 Glass supporting tool
7 Window lift motor monting screws
8 Quadrant arm

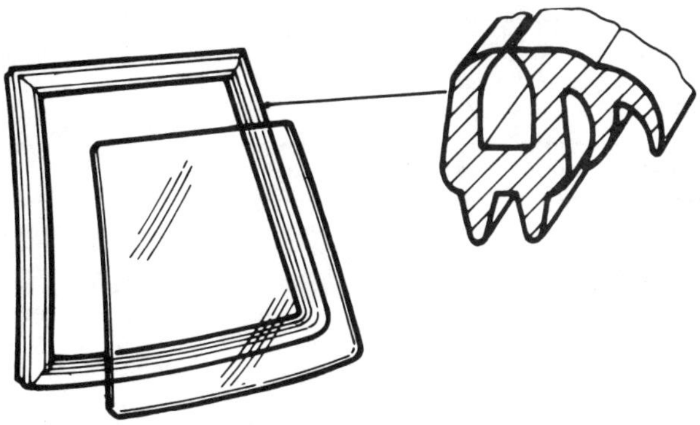

Fig. 12.39 Rear quarterlight and cross section of weatherstrip (XJS) (Sec 32)

6 Remove the four setscrews which hold the window lift motor to the quarter panel. Manoeuvre the motor to the rear of the car, disengaging the lift arm from the guide channel as it is withdrawn.
7 Manually pull the quarter glass into the fully closed position, disengage the guide rollers from the carrier plate and remove the glass.
8 The glass carrier can be removed if it is unbolted from the lower mounting bracket and from the side bracket. Extract the two screws which hold the glass carrier to the quarter panel.
9 Lower the glass carrier and disengage the upper section from the chrome beading, then remove the carrier.
10 Refitting is a reversal of removal, but apply grease to the guide channels.

32 Rear quarterlight (XJS) – removal and refitting

1 Remove the rear seat squab as described in Section 49, and the rear quarter upper and lower trim panels.
2 With an assistant pressing the glass outward, peel back the rubber weatherseal from the body at one corner until the glass can be pushed out of its frame.
3 When refitting, apply sealant into the grooves of the rubber weatherseal and use the cord method as for refitting early type windscreens (Section 33).

33 Windscreen and backlight (excluding Series 3 and XJS) – removal and refitting

1 This is a job best left to professionals but where it is decided to carry out the work yourself, proceed in the following way with the help of an assistant.
2 Where a windscreen is to be renewed then if it is due to shattering, the facia air vents should be covered before attempting removal. Adhesive sheeting is useful to stick to the outside of the glass to enable large areas of crystallised glass to be removed.
3 Where the screen is to be removed intact then an assistant will be required. First release the rubber surround from the bodywork by running a blunt, small screwdriver around and under the rubber weatherstrip both inside and outside the car. This operation will break the adhesive of the sealer originally used. Take care not to damage the paintwork or cut the rubber surround with the screwdriver. Remove the windsceen wiper arms and interior mirror and place a protective

cover on the bonnet. Remove the bright trim from the rubber surround.

4 Have your assistant push the inner lip of the rubber surround off the flange of the windscreen body aperture. Once the rubber surround starts to peel off the flange, the screen may be forced gently outwards by careful hand pressure. The second person should support and remove the screen complete with rubber weatherseal.

5 Before fitting a windscreen, ensure that the rubber surround is completely free from old sealant, glass fragments and has not hardened or cracked. Fit the rubber surround to the glass and apply a bead of suitable sealant between the glass outer edge and the rubber.

6 Cut a piece of strong cord greater in length than the periphery of the glass and insert it into the body flange locating channel of the rubber surround.

7 Apply a thin bead of sealant to the face of the rubber channel which will eventually mate with the body.

8 Offer the windscreen to the body aperture and pass the ends of the cord, previously fitted and located at bottom centre into the vehicle interior.

9 Press the windscreen into place, at the same time have an assistant pulling the cords to engage the lip of the rubber channel over the body flange.

10 Remove any excess sealant.

11 Removal and installation of the rear window glass is carried out in an identical manner, but (if fitted) disconnect the leads to the heating element in the glass.

34 Windscreen and backlight (Series 3 and XJS) – removal and refitting

1 The windscreen and rear window glass is bonded directly to the bodyshell on later models. Removal and refitting is definitely not a job for the home mechanic.

35 Interior mirror – removal and refitting

1 The interior mirror can be removed by extracting the two screws from its mounting base.

2 Alternatively, the mirror stem can be disconnected from its base by applying pressure to the stem in a forward direction. This simulates the action which would occur in the event of a collision (photo).

3 Reconnect by engaging the ball in its socket and striking the ball sharply with the hand.

36 Exterior mirror – removal and refitting

1 To remove this remotely-controlled mirror, extract the two screws which hold the control lever surround to the door interior trim panel. Partially withdraw the lever and the surround (photo).

2 Slacken the grub screw which holds the surround to the control lever. Withdraw the surround from the lever (photo).

3 Remove the two screws which hold the mirror to the door. Pull away the mirror and the mounting pad complete with adjusting cable.

4 Refitting is a reversal of removal.

37 Facia (XJS and Double Six, Series 1) – removal and refitting

Driver's side

1 Disconnect the battery.

2 Prise the radio speaker from the crash roll.

3 Extract the two screws and washer which are located in the speaker platform.

4 Extract the screws at each end of the crash roll which hold it to the screen rail.

5 Extract the screws from the centre facia panel and swing it away from the screen rail.

6 Release the two screws which hold the centre of the crash roll to the screen rail and remove the crash roll.

7 Remove the speedometer and tachometer (Chapter 10).

8 Remove the under scuttle casing (see Section 40), then grip the fresh air outlet nozzle and turn it in an anti-clockwise direction to release its bayonet fixing.

27.5 Rear door lower hinge

28.3 Door striker plate and wiring harness conduit

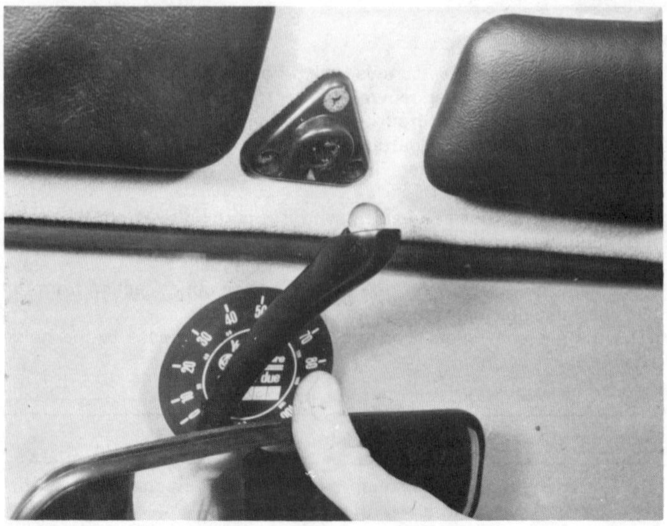

35.2 Interior mirror balljoint

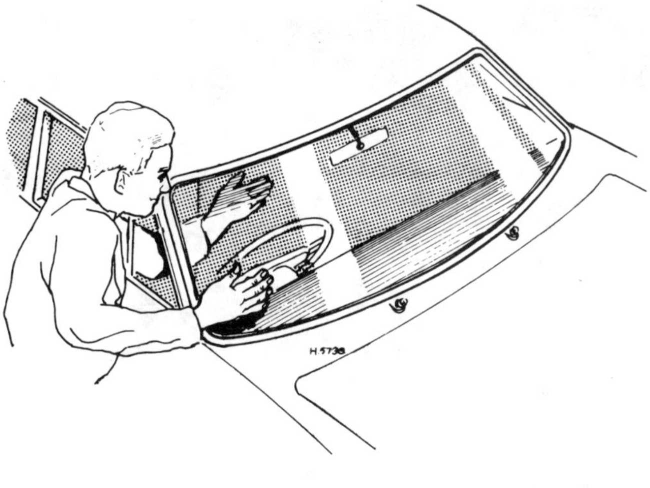

Fig. 12.40 Windscreen removal (earlier models) (Sec 33)

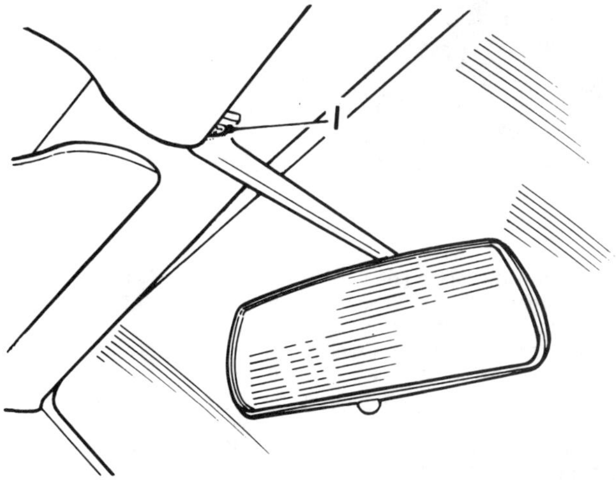

Fig. 12.41 Interior mirror (Sec 35)

1 Balljoint connection

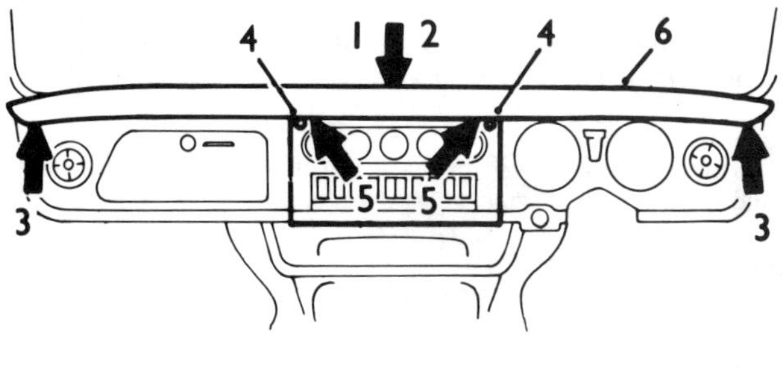

Fig. 12.42 Facia crash roll (XJ12 and Double Six, Series 1) (Sec 37)

1 Radio speaker
2 Screws in speaker recess
3 Crash roll end screws
4 Centre panel screws
5 Crash roll centre fixing screws to screen rail
6 Crash roll

9 Remove the steering wheel (see Chapter 11), then extract the three screws which hold the indicator surround and withdraw the surround from the switch. Remove the ignition switch surround.
10 Unscrew and remove the two bolts which hold the end of the facia panel to its mounting bracket. Unbolt the facia support bracket to the rear of the panel.
11 Remove the nut and washer, located adjacent to the fresh air outlet, which hold the upper part of the facia panel to the mounting bracket.
12 Withdraw the facia panel from the screen rail and disconnect the warning lamp cluster as it is withdrawn.

Passenger's side

13 Carry out the operations described in paragraphs 1 to 6 and then remove the under scuttle casing. Grip the fresh air outlet nozzle and turn it in an anti-clockwise direction to release its bayonet fixing.
14 Extract the screw which holds the facia panel support bracket to the bulkhead.
15 Remove the nut and flat washer, located adjacent to the fresh air outlet, which hold the upper part of the panel to the screen rail.
16 Unbolt the end of the panel from its mounting bracket and remove the facia panel.

Centre unit

17 With all the foregoing operations carried out, disconnect the wiring harness looms from the facia panel connecting plugs. Disconnect the harness from the facia panel mounting brackets.
18 Extract the two screws which hold the centre facia panel to its mounting bracket and then withdraw the panel.
19 Refitting of all panels is a reversal of removal.

38 Facia (XJ12 and Double Six, Series 2 on) – removal and refitting

1 Disconnect the battery.
2 Prise the air vents from the crash roll.
3 Extract the four screws which hold the front of the crash roll to the screen rail.
4 Prise the map reading lamp from the housing in the crash roll. On later cars, remove the in-car sensor (see Section 69).
5 Remove the crash roll.
6 Remove the under scuttle casing from the driver's side (see Section 40).
7 Remove the four screws which hold the facia to the screen rail.
8 Unbolt the ends of the facia from the lower mounting brackets.
9 Pull the knobs from the heater and ventilation control levers.
10 Withdraw the radio panel forward sufficently to provide access to the centre tray securing screws. Take care not to damage the fibre optic elements.
11 Remove the four screws which hold the centre shelf to the console.
12 Detach the temperature air sensor pipe from the centre tray and move the tray clear of the facia.
13 Remove the two nuts, flat washers and spring washers which hold the facia to the heater unit.
14 Release the ignition and light switch shrouds and then withdraw their mounting clamps. Detach the fibre optics from the rear of the shrouds and switches.
15 Slacken the steering column upper mounting bolts but do not remove them.
16 Remove the three screws which hold the indicator switch shroud and lift off the shroud.
17 Ease the facia panel forward until the three multi-pin connectors can be disconnected.
18 Disconnect the speedometer cable from the rear of the speedometer.
19 Lift the facia from the car, complete with air vent ducting.
20 Refitting is a reversal of removal but to facilitate the operation, slacken the four nuts which hold the demister outlets to the screen rail.

39 Facia (XJS) – removal and refitting

1 Slacken the knurled steering wheel adjuster and pull the wheel up to its fullest extent.

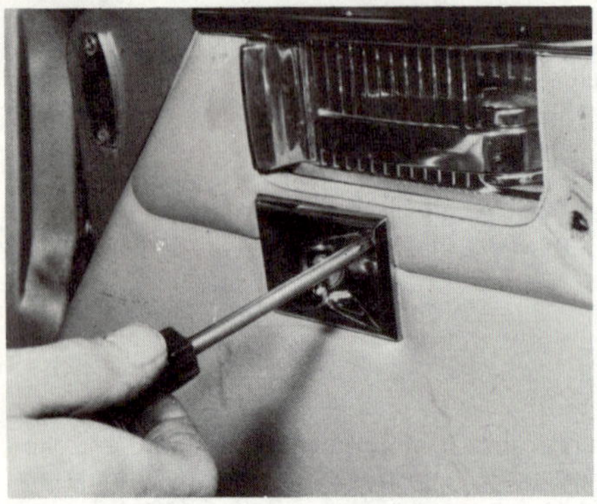

36.1 Exterior mirror control lever surround

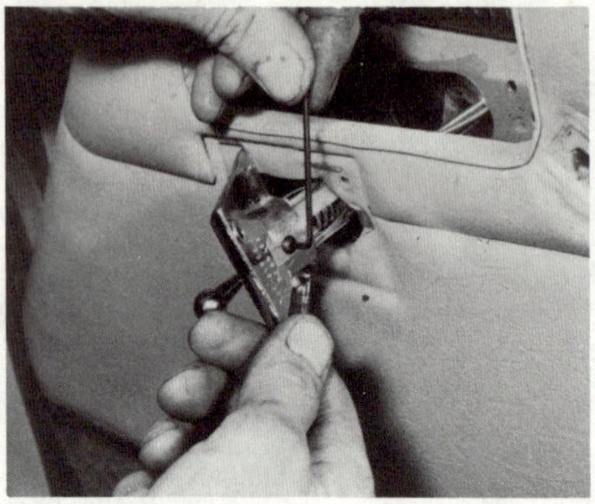

36.2 Extracting mirror control lever surround grub screw

40.2 Speedometer trip control

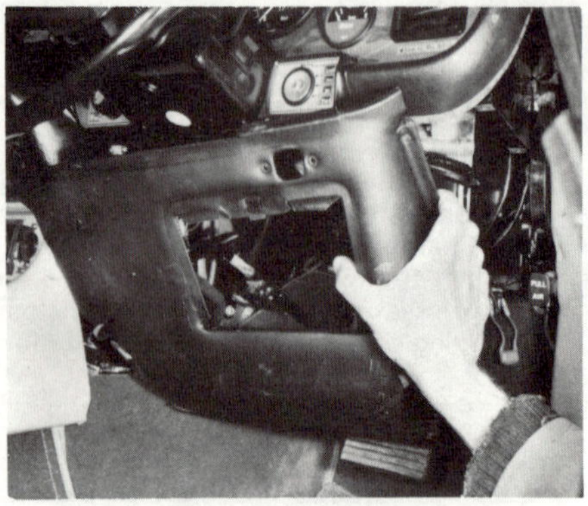

40.4A Withdrawing underscuttle casing

40.4B Rheostat switch

2 Remove the steering column shrouds.
3 Remove the pinch-bolt which holds the steering wheel/adjuster mechanism to the upper column.
4 Slacken the locknut and the Allen screw adjacent to the pinch-bolt; then withdraw the steering wheel/adjuster from the upper column.
5 Remove the trim pads from the windscreen pillars. To do this, unclip the crash roll as necessary and then extract the securing screws.
6 Remove the instrument module (refer to Chapter 10, Section 69).
7 Remove the under scuttle casing from the driver's side (see Section 40).
8 Remove the facia mounted interior/map lamp.
9 Remove the under scuttle casing from the passenger side.
10 Remove the facia switch panel (see Chapter 10, Section 42).
11 Remove the glove compartment liner. To do this, open the glovebox lid, extract the liner screws and carefully prise the liner from the facia.
12 Pull the air conditioner control knobs from their spindles.
13 Remove the radio from the centre console.
14 Extract the two screws which hold the facia and centre console to the air conditioning unit.
15 Slacken the nuts which hold the top rear part of the facia to the bulkhead.
16 Unbolt the side of the facia from the bulkhead. The bolts are accessible through the under scuttle aperture.
17 Remove the main lighting switch from its mounting.
18 Withdraw the facia from the car.
19 Refitting is a reversal of removal, but note the earth lead fitted between the left-hand facia mounting and the bulkhead.

40 Under scuttle casing – removal and refitting

XJ12, Double Six

Driver's side

1 Disconnect the battery.
2 Unscrew the locking ring which holds the speedometer trip control to the under scuttle casing. On later models, the control is held by two plastic pins which should be prised out (photo).
3 Extract the two screws which hold the under scuttle casing and quarter panel to the facia support bracket.
4 Lower the under scuttle casing far enough to give access to the rheostat. Identify and disconnect the leads from the rheostat (photos).
5 Withdraw the under scuttle casing and quarter panel.

Passenger's side

6 Open the glovebox and extract the two screws adjacent to the glovebox lid hinges. These screws hold the under scuttle casing.
7 Remove the two screws which hold the casing and quarter panel to the facia support bracket.
8 Withdraw the under scuttle casing past the fresh air outlet control in the footwell and remove it.

XJS

Driver's side

9 Extract the screws which hold the casing to the facia and the scuttle. Lower the under scuttle casing far enough to be able to disconnect the rheostat and the speedometer trip control.
10 Identify the rheostat electrical leads before pulling them from their terminals.

Passenger's side

11 Extract the under scuttle casing fixing screws and remove the casing from the facia panel.

Refitting – all models

12 Refitting is a reversal of removal according to particular model.

41 Glovebox (XJ12, Double Six) – removal and refitting

1 On series 2 and later models, remove the under scuttle casing as described in the preceding Section.
2 Extract the six screws which hold the glovebox to the facia.
3 Slacken the two screws which secure the sliding lid support arm

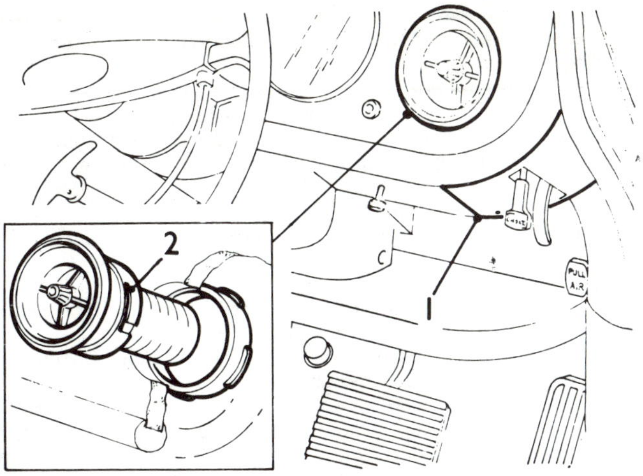

Fig. 12.43 Facia fresh air outlet (XJ12 and Double Six, Series 1)

1 *Underscuttle casing* 2 *Bayonet fixing*

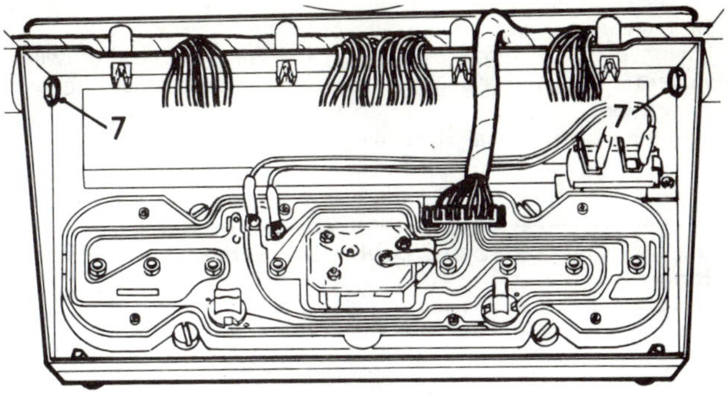

Fig. 12.44 Rear view of ventre facia panel (XJ12 and Double Six, Series 1) (Sec 37)

7 *Mounting bracket screws*

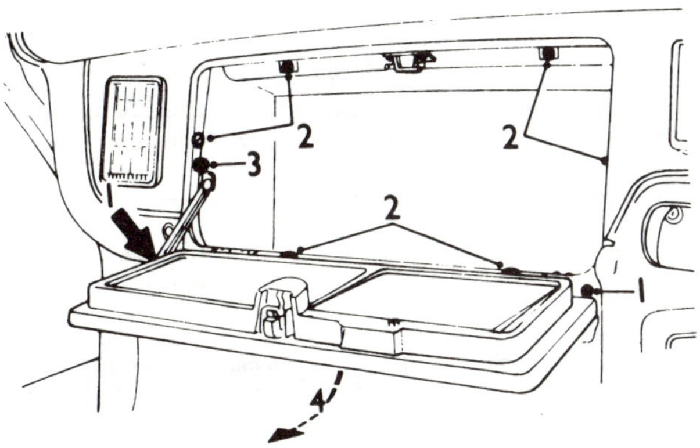

Fig. 12.45 Glovebox (XJ12, Double Six) (Sec 41)

1 *Underscuttle casing*
2 *Glovebox fixing screws*
3 *Sliding stay fixing screws*
4 *Direction of removal*

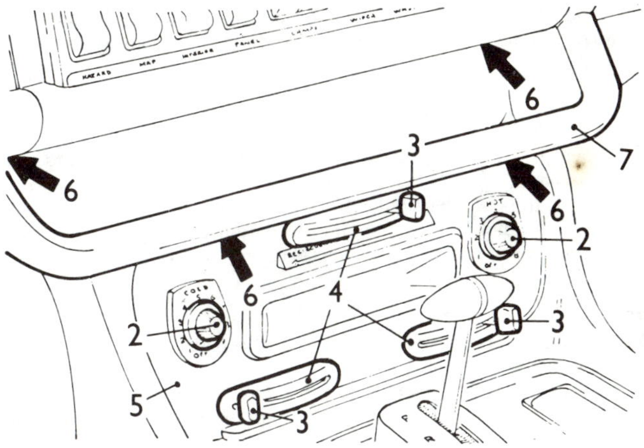

Fig. 12.46 Centre parcels tray attachment (XJ12 and Double Six, Series 1) (Sec 42)

2 *Heater knob*
3 *Vent lever knobs*
4 *Escutcheons*
5 *Panel*
6 *Parcel tray securing screws*
7 *Parcel tray*

Fig. 12.47 Rear parcels shelf (XJS) (Sec 44)

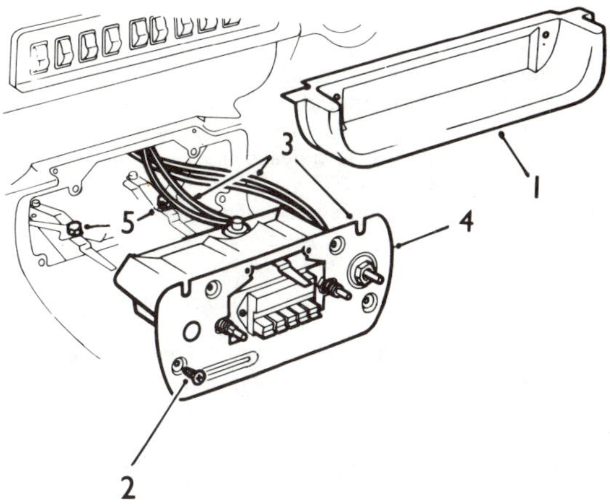

Fig. 12.48 Centre console removal (XJ12, Double Six) (Sec 45)

1 *Parcel shelf*
2 *Vent/radio control panel bracket screws*
3 *Electrical leads*
4 *Panel*
5 *Vent lever to flap link arm bolts*

to the facia.
4 Remove the glovebox by pushing it inward and withdrawing it downward through the aperture left by the removal of the under scuttle casing.
5 Refitting is a reversal of removal.

42 Parcels trays (XJ12 and Double Six, Series 1) – removal and refitting

Centre tray

1 Disconnect the battery.
2 Pull the knobs from the heater control levers.
3 Remove the plastic finishers from the fresh air ventilator control levers.
4 Prise the escutcheons from the control lever panels of the radio and ventilator fresh air outlets.
5 Pull the ventilator and radio facia panel forward to give access to the parcels tray lower mounting screws.
6 Extract the four screws which hold the centre tray to the console, withdraw the tray and identify and disconnect electrical leads as necessary.

Driver's side tray

7 Extract the three screws which hold the tray to the right-hand side of the footwell.
8 Remove the nut which holds the parcels tray to the centre console.
9 Unclip the steering column trim from the parcels tray and then release the rear of the tray from the securing clip. Remove the tray.

Passenger's side tray

10 Extract the three screws which hold the parcels tray to the left-hand side of the footwell.
11 Remove the nut which holds the tray to the centre console. Release the rear of the tray from its clip and lift the tray from the car.

All trays

12 Refitting is a reversal of removal.

43 Parcels shelves (XJ12 and Double Six, Series 2 on) – removal and refitting

Centre shelf

1 Remove the clock (see Chapter 10, Section 67).
2 Pull the knobs from the heater and ventilator control levers.
3 Pull the radio panel forward until the parcels tray securing screws are accessible. Take care not to damage the fibre optic elements.
4 Extract the four screws to release the tray and detach the temperature air sensor pipe.
5 Identify and disconnect the switch leads as necessary.

Rear parcels shelf

6 Remove the rear seat cushion and squab as described in Section 49.
7 Unscrew and remove the two bolts which hold the shelf and slide it forward to disengage it from its locating peg.

Both shelves

8 Refitting the shelves is a reversal of removal.

44 Rear parcels shelf (XJS) – removal and refitting

1 Remove the rear seat cushion and squab as described in Section 49.
2 Carefully prise the shelf from the panel.
3 Refitting is a reversal of removal.

45 Centre console (XJ12 and Double Six, Series 1) – removal and refitting

1 Refer to Section 42 and remove the centre parcels shelf.
2 Extract the screws and release the radio and ventilator control mounting bracket. Withdraw the bracket from the console and disconnect the vacuum tubes and radio leads.
3 Remove the radio from the console.
4 Unbolt the two ventilation control levers from the flap link arms.
5 Remove the nut which holds the forward section of the console to the transmission tunnel.
6 Remove the parcels shelf from the passenger side (see Section 42), followed by the one from the driver's side.
7 Extract the four screws which hold the forward side sections of the centre console to the transmission tunnel.
8 Free the trim finisher which surrounds the window operating switches and then remove the four screws which hold the switch panel to the console top finisher. Extract the screw from the rear of the top finisher, also the two screws from the front edge.
9 Raise the top finisher complete with ashtrays until the leads can be disconnected from the cigar lighter, then remove the top finisher.
10 Remove the rear ashtray mounting bracket from the console.
11 Extract the two screws which hold the rear of the console to the transmission tunnel.
12 Remove the cushions from the front seats (see Section 48).
13 Raise the rear of the console and pull it to the rear until both hoses are detached from the bulkhead ventilation outlets.
14 Withdraw the console over the speed selector control lever.
15 Refitting is a reversal of removal.

46 Centre console (XJ 12 and Double Six, Series 2 on) – removal and refitting

1 Disconnect the battery.
2 Remove the side trim casings from the centre console. To do this, extract the two screws which secure the footwell ventilation outlet grilles (photo).
3 Pull the knobs from the heater and ventilation control levers. Withdraw the control lever panel until the centre parcels shelf screws can be extracted. Take care not to damage the fibre optic elements (photos).
4 Detach the air temperature sensor pipe from the centre shelf and position the shelf away from the centre console (photos).
5 Prise the window lift switch panel from the centre console top finisher but do not disconnect the electrical leads (photo). Extract the three screws which hold the top finisher to the centre console.
6 Raise the top finisher until the leads can be disconnected from the cigar lighter and the door lock switch.
7 Pass the window switch panel assembly through the cut-out in the top finisher. Remove the finisher.
8 Remove the cushions from the front seat (see Section 48) and move the seats fully forward.
9 Remove the two screws which hold the rear window switch housing. Lift the housing and identify and disconnect the leads from the switches (photos).
10 Remove the two screws which hold the rear of the centre console to the transmission tunnel (photo).
11 Disconnect the wiring harness multi-pin plug, exposed when the rear of the console is raised, and then extract the screws which hold the wiring harness to the air duct assembly.
12 Slide the console slightly rearwards and release the wiring harness from the clips at the front end of the console.
13 Press the radio and ventilation control panel through the cut-out in the front of the console.
14 Move the console rearwards, disengaging the air duct pipes (photos).
15 Withdraw the console over the speed selector control lever.
16 Refitting is a reversal of removal. Check the operation of all switches on completion.

47 Centre console (XJS) – removal and refitting

1 Pull the knobs from the temperature and fan control levers.

46.2 Extracting a footwell vent screw

46.3A Air conditioner control knob removed

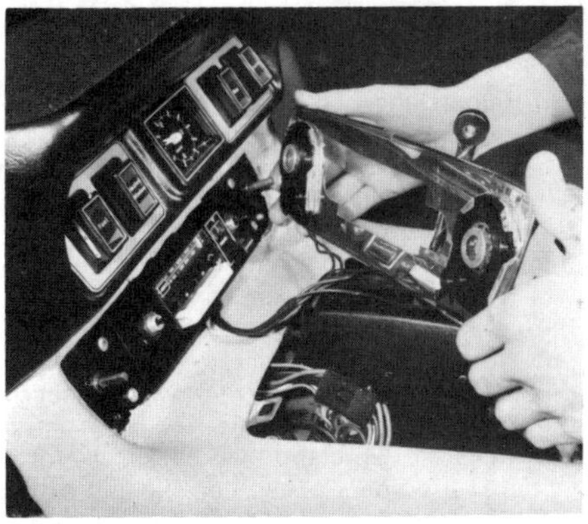

46.3B Heater/air conditioner escutcheon panel removed

46.4A Air temperature sensor pipe

46.4B Centre parcels shelf removed

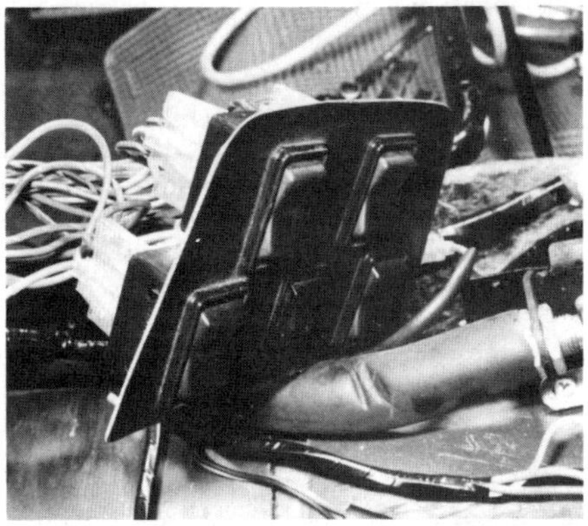

46.5 Centre console front switch panel

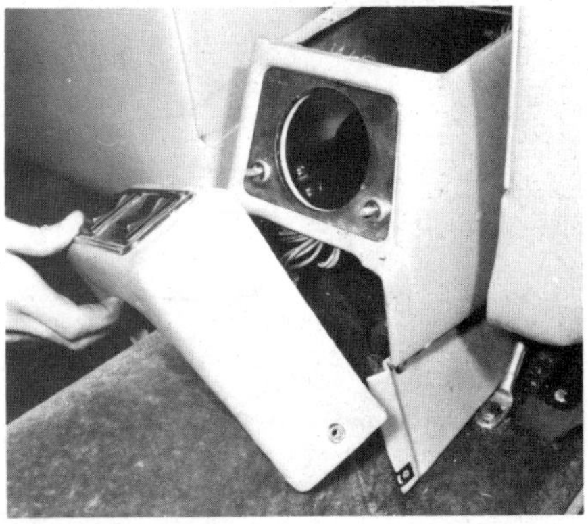

46.9A Centre console rear switch housing

46.9B Centre console rear switches removed from panel

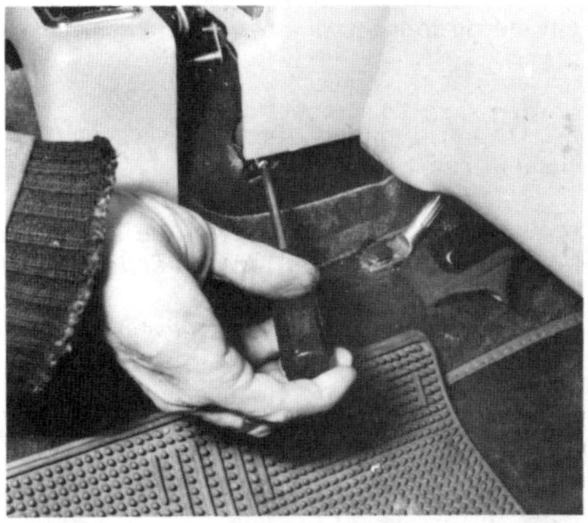

46.10 Undoing a centre console rear securing screw

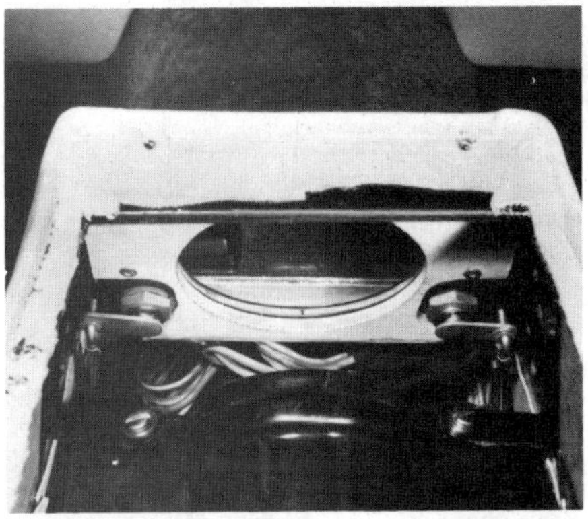

46.14A View of interior of rear end of centre console

46.14B Centre console air duct pipes

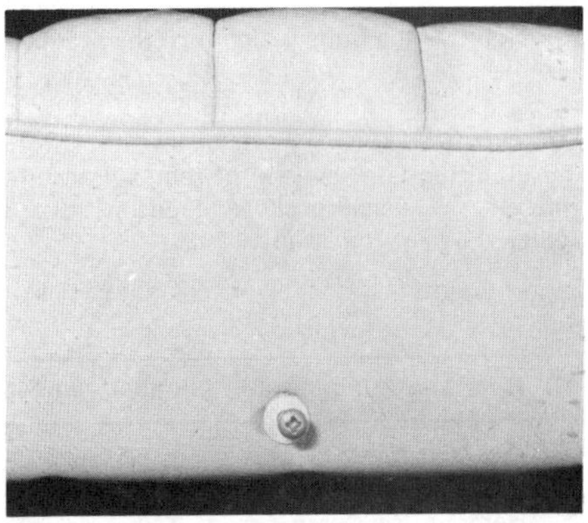

48.4 Front seat cushion screw

2 Release the two brass fasteners located below the control levers and withdraw the control panel.
3 Extract the screws which hold the side air vent grilles and panels.
4 Unscrew and remove the gear control lever knob.
5 Raise the storage compartment lid on the centre console. Extract the console centre securing screw, then remove the three screws which hold the switch panel to the console. Ease the switch panel from the console, identify the electrical leads and disconnect them, then remove the switch panel.
6 With the switch panel removed, extract the two screws which hold the front end of the console.
7 Move the seats and their backs fully forward, peel back the carpet at the rear corners of the console and extract the two screws which will be exposed.
8 Release the stoplamp failure sensor and ease it to one side.
9 Lift the centre console from the transmission tunnel.
10 Refit by reversing the removal operations. On XJ12 and Double Six models pull the armrest down before pushing the rear seat cushion into position rearwards.

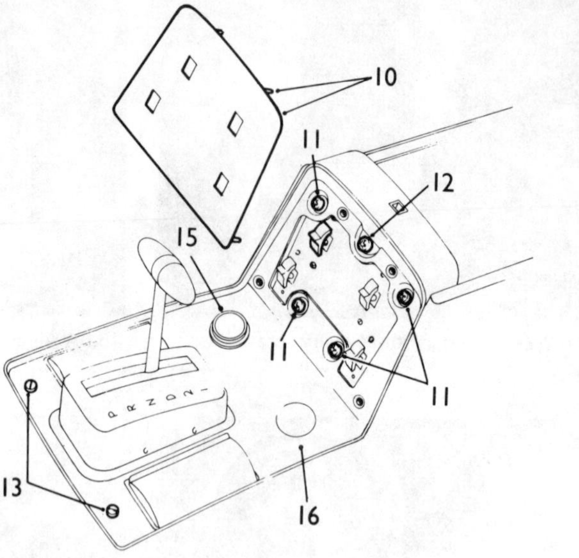

Fig. 12.49 Centre console removal (XJ12, Double Six) (Sec 45)

10 Trim finisher
11 Top finisher screws
12 Top finisher screw
13 Top finisher screws
15 Cigar lighter
16 Top finisher

48 Front seat cushions – removal and refitting

XJ12 and Double Six, Series 1

1 On North American versions, disconnect the battery.
2 Raise the front of the cushion and pull it forward (until the leads from the seat belt switches can be disconnected – North American versions).

XJ12 and Double Six, Series 2

3 On North American versions, disconnect the battery.
4 Remove the cross-headed screw which holds the front of the cushion to the bracket and then pull the bracket from the underside of the cushion (photo).
5 Move the squab to the reclining position, then lift the front of the cushion and pull it forward (until the leads from the seat belt switches can be disconnected – North American versions).

XJS

6 On these models, the front seat must be removed before the seat cushion can be detached.
7 Push the seat fully to the rear and remove the two socket-headed screws which hold the front of the seat runners to the floor.
8 Move the seat fully forward and remove the two screws from the rear of the runners.
9 Remove the seat and retrieve the spacers from under the front mountings.
10 Operate the seat adjusting lever and push the runners fully to the rear. The screws which hold the runners to the front of the seat will now be exposed and should be removed.
11 Push the runners fully forward and extract the screws which hold them to the rear of the seat.
12 Remove the runner/adjuster assembly.
13 Extract the screw which holds the rake angle adjustment lever. Lift the lever and the plastic disc from its seat. Prise the trim plate from the seat.
14 Remove the bolts which hold the seat cushion to the back rest and remove the cushion.

All models

15 Refitting is a reversal of removal according to type. On Series 2 models, the securing clip engages with the seat cross bar and goes under the seat front tube.

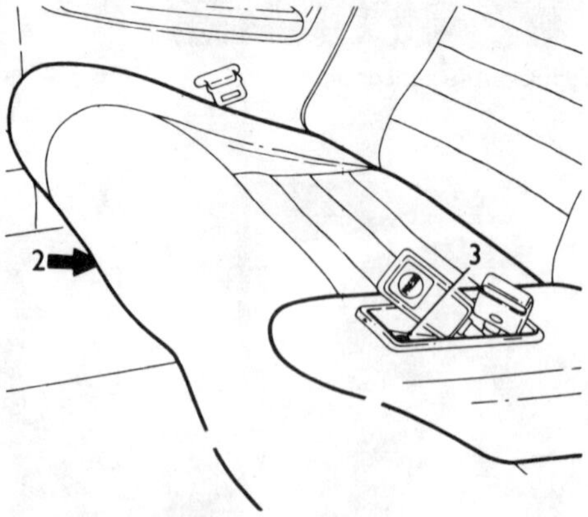

Fig. 12.50 Rear seat cushion (XJS) (Sec 49)

2 Retaining screws
3 Belt anchorage surround screw

49 Rear seat cushion and squab – removal and refitting

XJ12, Double Six

1 Move the front seats to the fully forward position.
2 Remove the screws from both sides of the transmission tunnel which hold the rear seat cushion to the seat pan crossmember. Pull the centre armrest down (photo).

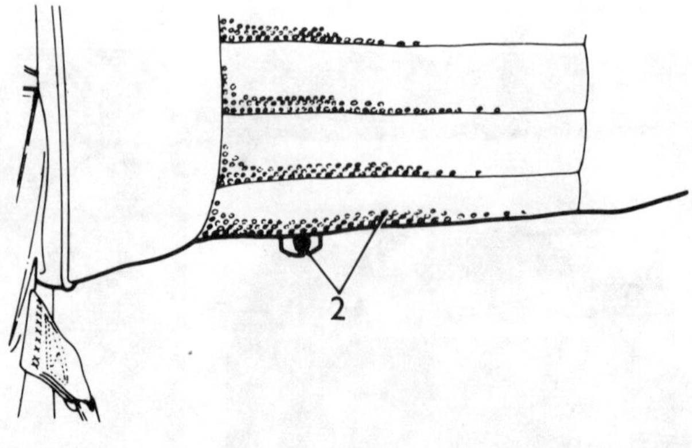

Fig. 12.51 Rear seat squab (XJS) (Sec 49)

2 Securing screw

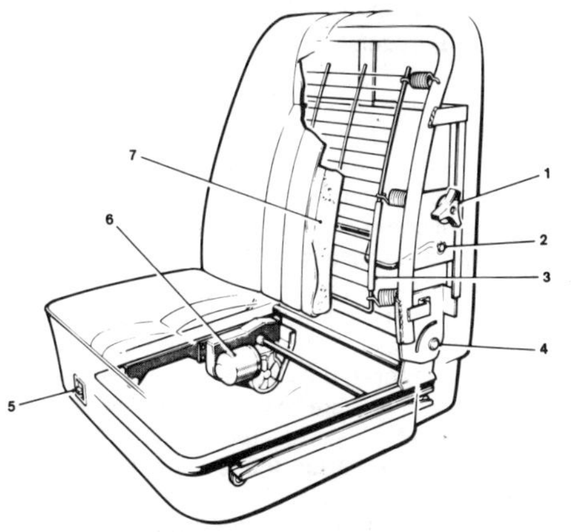

Fig. 12.52 Electrically actuated front seat (XJ12 and Double Six, Series 3) (Sec 50)

1 Adjustment knob
2 Actuating bar
3 Sprung frame
4 Hinge
5 Rise and fall switch
6 Electric motor
7 Seat squab

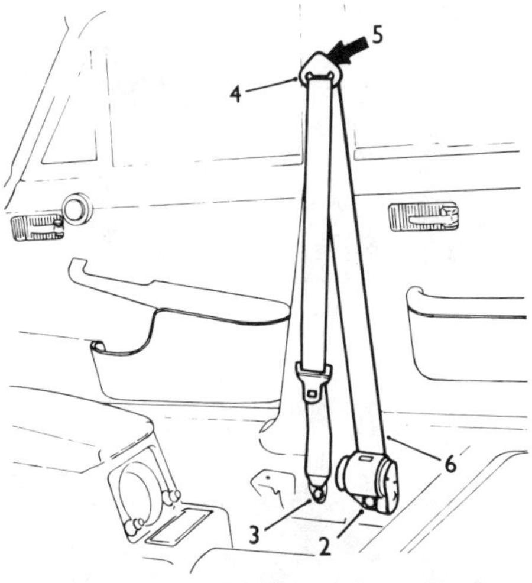

Fig. 12.53 Typical front seat belt (4-door cars) (Sec 51)

2 Reel securing bolt
3 Belt lower fixing
4 Belt upper lug outer casing
5 Upper lug securing bolt

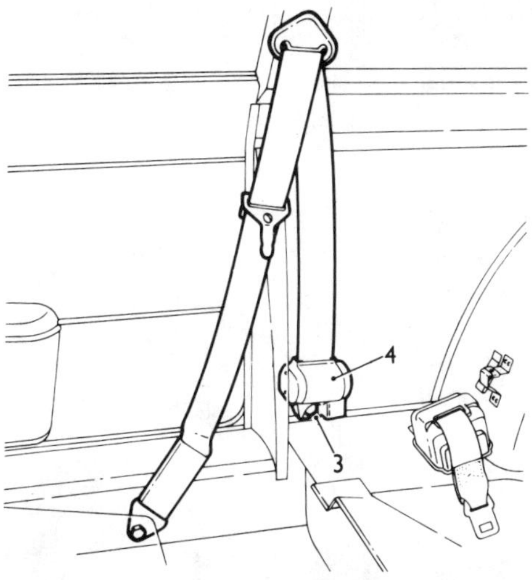

Fig. 12.54 Typical safety belt (2-door cars) (Sec 51)

3 Reel fixing bolt
4 Inertia reel

3 Draw the cushion forward and remove it.
4 Extract the two screws and washers which hold the lower section of the squab to the seat pan.
5 Push the squab upwards to disengage it from its retaining clips.
6 If required, the rear seat armrest can now be unbolted and removed from the squab frame.

XJS

7 Move both front seats and their backrests fully forward.
8 Extract the two screws below the front edge of the rear seat cushion.
9 Extract the screw which retains the safety belt anchorage surround in the centre of the rear seat cushion. Lift off the surround panel and the seat cushion.
10 The seat squab can now be removed if the screws which hold it to the seat pan are extracted.

All models

11 Refitting is a reversal of removal.

50 Front seat – electrically actuated type (XJ12 and Double Six, Series 3)

1 On these later models a lumbar support seat is standard on Double Six Vanden Plas models or as an optional extra on other models.
2 The rise and fall control of the seat is carried out by electric motor/gear mechanism.
3 When removing one of these front seats, first disconnect the battery.

51 Front seat belt and grab handle – removal, inspection and refitting

Four-door cars

1 Push the front seat fully forward.
2 Unscrew and remove the bolt which holds the lower part of the inertia reel to the sill.
3 Unscrew and remove the bolt which retains the bottom end of the belt to the body pillar. Note the sequence of fitting of spacers and washers.
4 Apply upward pressure to the casing on the belt upper attachment. Pull the casing aside and unscrew and remove the fixing bolt now exposed (photo).
5 Remove the belt assembly. Inspect for fraying or damage to the metal components. Clean the belt only with detergent and water. If the belt has been subjected to strain as the result of a collision, it should be renewed complete.
6 The grab handle which is located above the passenger door can be removed if the end covers are first prised back to expose the securing screws (photo).

Two-door cars

7 Remove the rear quarter trim casing. To do this, remove the rear seat squab as described earlier, remove the sill tread plate and pull off a few inches of draught welt from the door opening.
8 Unbolt the safety belt lower anchorage, noting the sequence of washers and spacers.
9 Unclip the plastic casing from the upper anchor plate and unbolt the plate.
10 Slide the armrest bezel forward and remove the armrest securing screw. Prise the trim casing away from the body and then slide the seat belt through the guide aperture in the casing. Remove the casing.
11 Unbolt the inertia reel belt from the body and remove the belt assembly from the car.

All cars

12 Refitting is a reversal of removal.

52 Rear seat belt – removal, inspection and refitting

Four-door cars

1 Remove the rear seat squab as described earlier in this Chapter.
2 Unbolt the safety belt from the rear of the seat pan, noting the sequence of washers and spacers.
3 Unclip the belt reel cover and withdraw it over the seat belt clip fastener.
4 Pull the belt fully out of the reel and retain it in this position.
5 Unbolt the reel from the body and remove the safety belt assembly from the car.

Two-door cars

6 Remove the rear quarter trim casing as described in Section 51.
7 Removal operations are then as described in paragraphs 2 to 5 of this Section.
8 Inspection and cleaning are as described in Section 51.

All cars

9 Refit the belts by reversing the removal operations.

53 Heater (XJ12, Double Six) – description

1 The heating system comprises the necessary intake and ducting to direct air to the windscreen, front interior and rear passenger compartment by passing the air over a matrix which is heated from the engine cooling system (photos).
2 The necessary controls are provided to regulate the air temperature and the volume and direction of flow of the air. On earlier cars, the controls are operated by vacuum from the engine. On Series 2 and later cars, the controls are of vacuum and mechanically actuated type. A vacuum tank provides a reserve to enable six operations of the controls to be carried out after the engine has been switched off (photo).
3 A two-speed booster fan is provided for use in conditions when

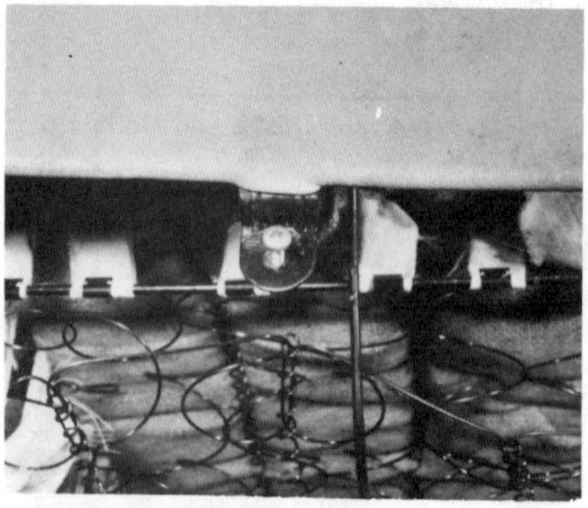

49.2 Rear seat cushion screw

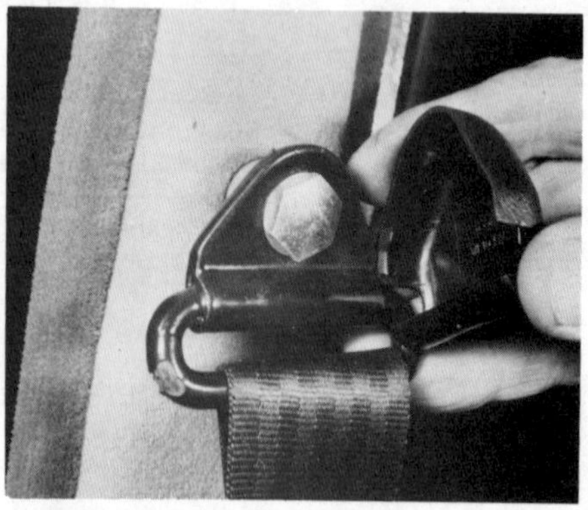

51/4 Seat belt anchor bolt cover

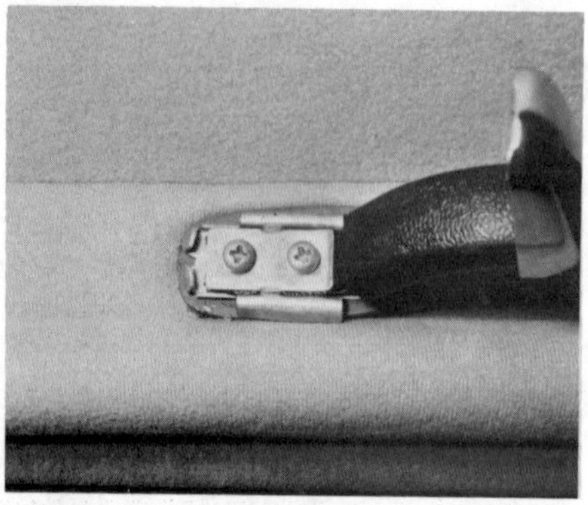

51.5 Grab handle securing screws

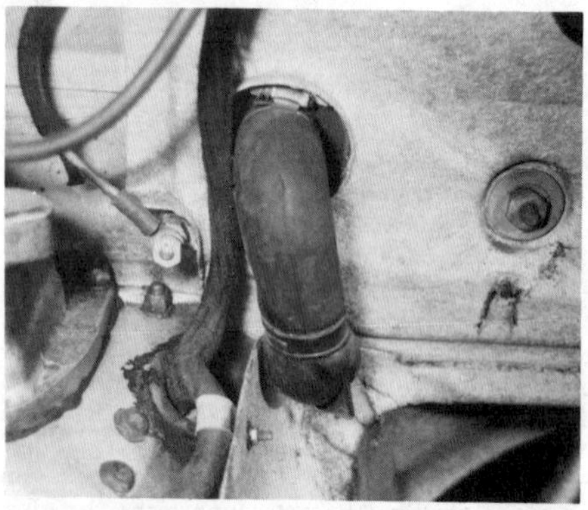

53.1A Heater plenum chamber drain pipe

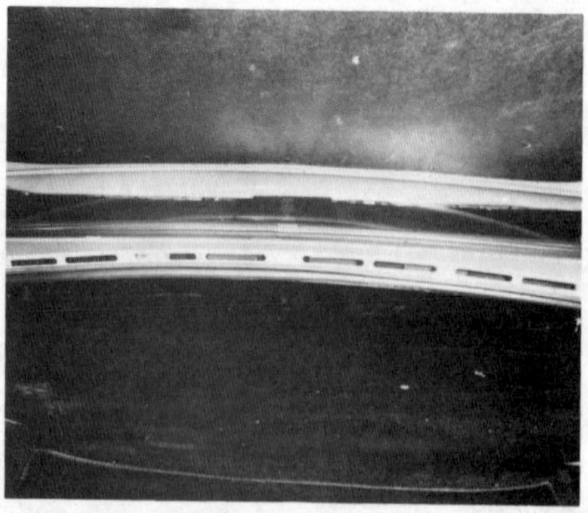

53.1B Air extraction slots at forward edge of luggage boot lid

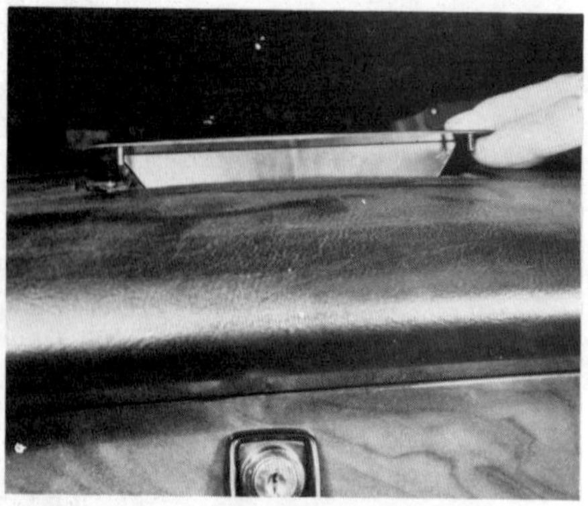

53.1C Facia crash pad demister grille

53.2 Under-wing vacuum tank

53.4 Air intake grille at base of windscreen

53.5 Headlamp fresh air intake grille

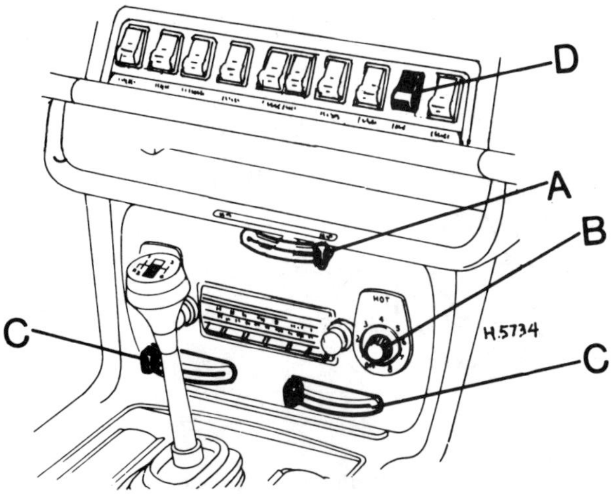

Fig. 12.55 Heater controls (XJ12, Double Six) (Sec 53)

A Fresh air
B Heat
C Air distribution
D Fan

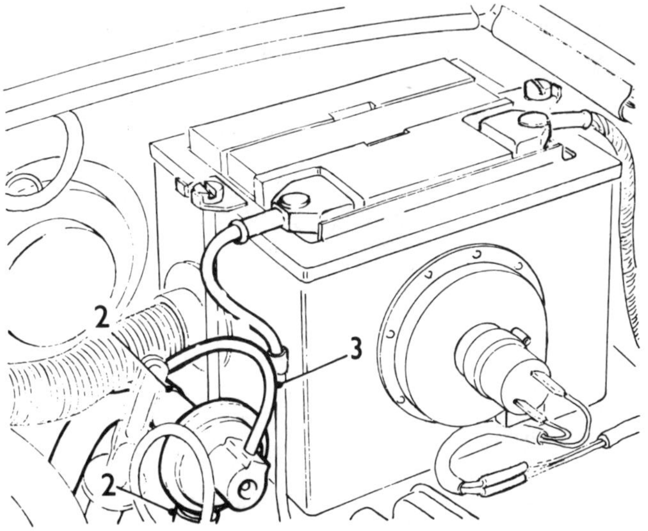

Fig. 12.56 Location of heater coolant valve (XJ12 and Double Six, Series 1) (Sec 54)

2 Coolant hoses
3 Vacuum hose

Fig. 12.57 Heater vacuum servo components (XJ12, Double Six) (Sec 54)

1 Air flap modulator
2 Actuator
3 Heat control modulator
4 Heater sensing unit
5 Water valve
6 Vacuum tank
7 Non-return valve
A To manifold
B Water inlet
C Water outlet

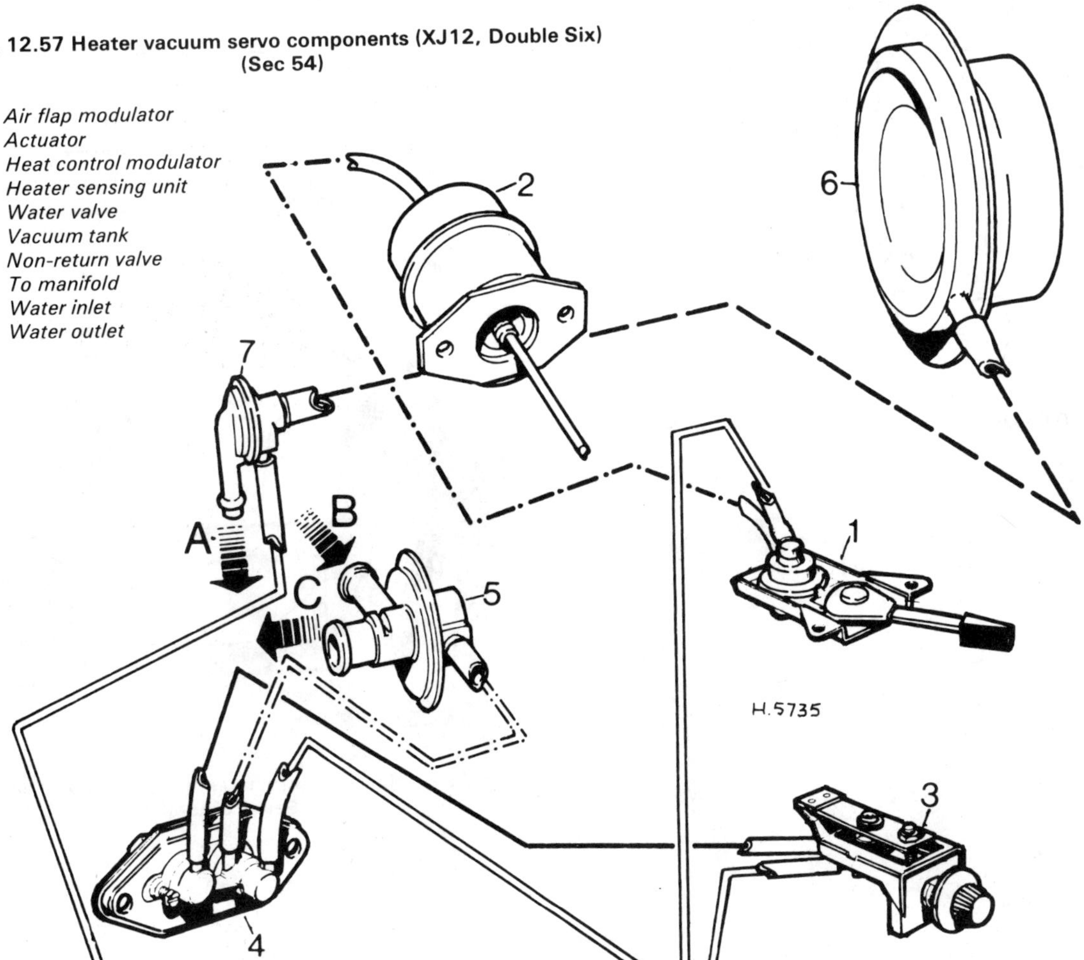

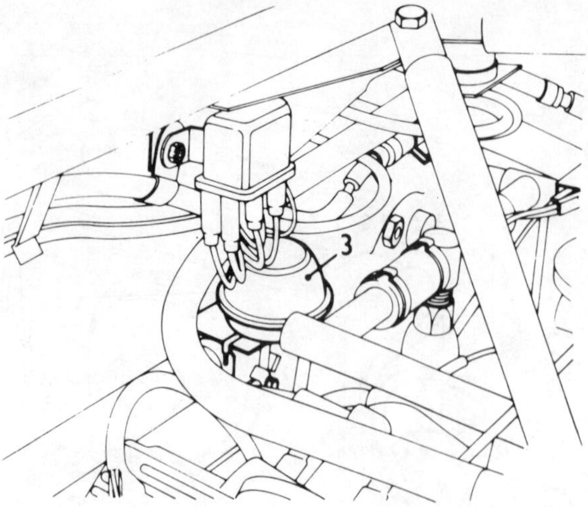

Fig. 12.58 Location of heater coolant valve (XJ12, Double Six Series 2 on) (Sec 54)

3 Coolant valve

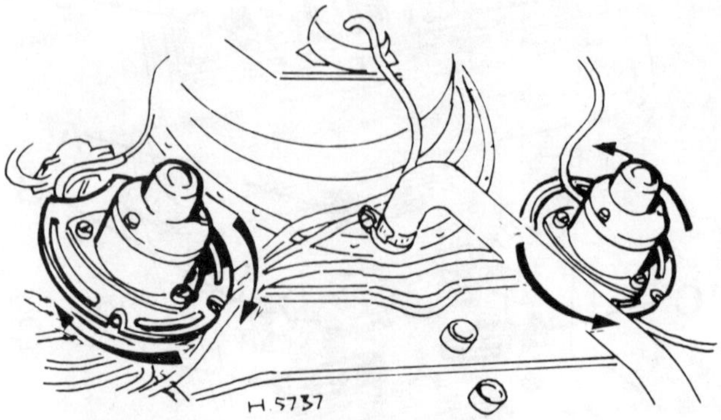

Fig. 12.59 Heater fans (earlier XJ12, Double Six). Direction of rotation is arrowed (Sec 55)

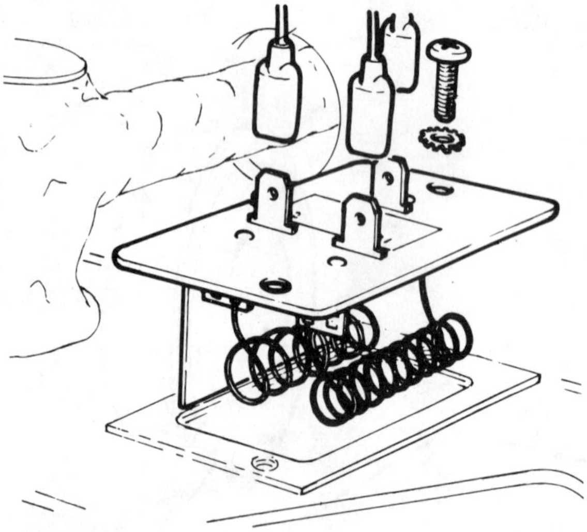

Fig. 12.60 Fan motor resistor (XJ12, Double Six, Series 1) (Sec 55)

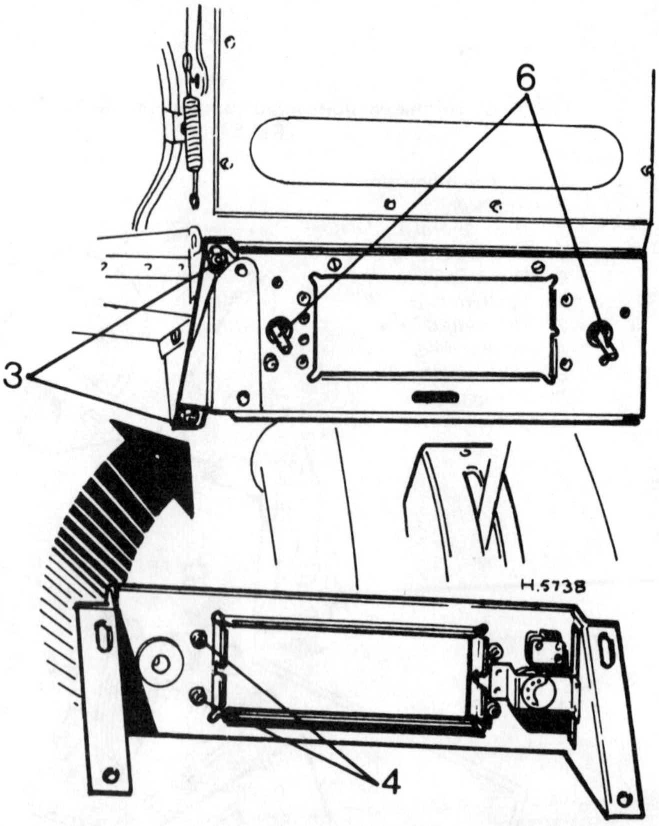

Fig. 12.61 Heater control mounting plate (XJ12 and Double Six, Series 2 on) (Sec 57)

3 Mounting plate nuts
4 Vacuum switch screws
6 Airflow and temperature control switch shafts

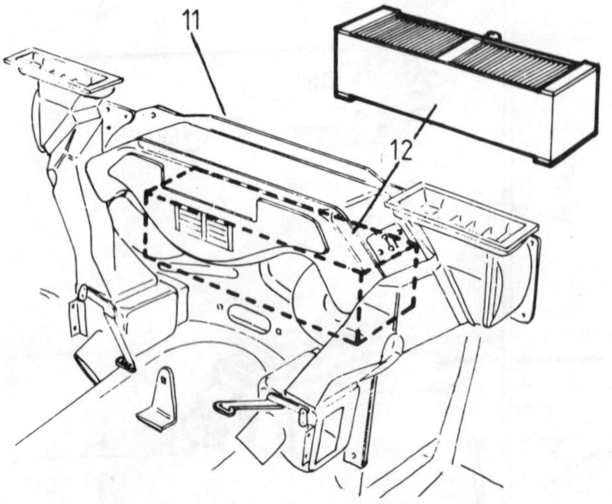

Fig. 12.62 Removal of heater matrix (XJ12, Double Six Series1) (Sec 56)

11 Plenum chamber
12 Matrix

the car is not moving forward fast enough to provide the normal ram effect.

4 An independent fresh air supply is provided from outlets on the facia panel and on later cars a further fresh air outlet at lower level is positioned for both front seat occupants. Air is drawn in through a grille at the base of the screen (photo).

5 On cars with air conditioning, when it is not operating, the fresh air supply for the interior is drawn through the grilles under the headlamp hoods (photo).

54 Heater vacuum servo system components (XJ12 and Double Six, Series 1) – removal and refitting

1 Failure of any one of the components of the vacuum control system will normally require renewal of the unit. Before taking this action however, always check the connecting hoses for security of joints and for perforation.

Flap actuator

2 This flap allows fresh air to be drawn into the heating system.

3 To remove it, prise off the air intake grille from the scuttle by inserting two small screwdrivers at opposite sides of the grille.

4 Raise the bonnet and detach the vacuum pipe from the actuator unit.

5 Remove the two nuts which are accessible from within the plenum chamber and withdraw the actuator securing bolts.

6 Disconnect the coupling rod from the flap and then remove the actuator unit.

7 Refitting is a reversal of removal but make sure that no preload is placed on the diaphragm when connecting the coupling rod to the flap. The rod length can be adjusted to avoid this situation by screwing the rod in or out

Flap control quadrant modulator

8 This is mounted centrally in the panel above the radio aperture and is a conical valve which controls the degree of vacuum which exists between the vacuum tank and the flap actuator.

9 To remove the modulator, withdraw the knobs from the three heater control levers, also the knobs from the heat control rotary modulator and the radio (and air conditioning control if fitted).

10 Insert a small screwdriver behind the lever escutcheons and lever them from the nylon bush retainers. Remove the control panel facia.

11 Extract the four screws and withdraw the heater control panel to the rear in order to gain access to the modulator securing screws.

12 Disconnect the vacuum pipes, remove the two securing screws and lift out the modulator.

13 Refitting is a reversal of removal.

Water valve servo unit

14 This is a diaphragm valve which, controlled by a combination of the vacuum tank, heat control rotary modulator and heat sensing unit, regulates the flow of water through the heater matrix.

15 To remove the unit, drain the cooling system, as described in Chapter 2.

16 Disconnect the hoses from the unit and remove it.

17 Refitting is a reversal of removal.

Heat control rotary modulator

18 This device is very similar to the flap control modulator except that it has a rotary type control knob. Refer to paragraphs 8 to 13, of this Section for removal and refitting operations.

Heat sensing unit

19 This unit is located in the air ducts below the instrument panel and is basically a valve which automatically controls the coolant flow through the water valve irrespective of the engine water pump speed.

20 Access to this component is obtained in the same way as described for the flap control modulator (paragraphs 8 to 11).

21 Disconnect the three vacuum pipes from the unit, remove the two securing screws and lift the unit away.

22 Refitting is a reversal of removal but install a new joint between the sensing unit and the duct if necessary.

55 Heater fan and resistor units (XJ12 and Double Six, Series 1) – removal and refitting

1 The twin heater booster fans are speed controlled by resistance units wired in series. In the event of wear or a fault occurring in the fan motors, they must be renewed as units.

2 To remove a fan/motor assembly, disconnect the leads from the resistance units on the engine compartment rear bulkhead.

3 Remove the motor mounting plate screws, lift the motor/fan assembly from the bulkhead, detaching the electrical leads from their clips as it is withdrawn.

4 Remove the mounting plate and impeller for fitting to the new motor. It must be noted that the units are handed for left and right-hand rotation, do not interchange them and check that the correct type has been obtained as a replacement.

5 Refitting is a reversal of removal but renew the motor mounting plate sealing gasket, if necessary, to provide a tight joint.

6 If the resistor units are to be removed, disconnect the battery and remove the facia crash roll (refer to Section 37).

7 The resistors will now be visible. Disconnect the electrical leads and extract their mounting screws.

56 Heater matrix (XJ12 and Double Six, Series 1) – removal and refitting

1 The heater matrix is located on the engine compartment rear bulkhead and it is retained in position by the compression of foam rubber pads which takes place when the heater/air duct assembly is installed.

2 Drain the cooling system (Chapter 2).

3 Disconnect the battery.

4 Disconnect the coolant hoses from the matrix.

5 Remove the radio/heater control panel.

6 Disconnect the radio and the heater control vacuum pipes, having first marked them so that they can be correctly reconnected.

7 Remove the side facia panels.

8 Remove the instrument panel.

9 Remove the centre console.

10 Remove the four nuts and detach the two struts which support the facia assembly.

11 Remove the left and right-hand air ducts (four screws).

12 Remove the plenum chamber from the bulkhead (eight screws).

13 Withdraw the heater matrix. If the matrix is leaking have it professionally repaired or renew it. If the matrix is blocked, try reverse flushing it or use proprietary cleansing compound strictly in accordance with the manufacturer's instructions.

14 Refitting is a reversal of removal, but renew the foam pads instead of refitting the original deformed ones.

57 Heater controls (XJ12 and Double Six, Series 2 on) – removal and refitting

1 Disconnect the battery and remove the centre console (Section 46).

2 Remove the two bolts which secure the control panel mounting plate to the heater.

3 Remove the three screws which secure the vacuum switches to the mounting plate. Identify the vacuum pipes and disconnect them from the switches.

4 Extract the circlip from the shaft of the temperature control switch.

5 Remove the mounting plate from its studs.

6 The micro or vacuum switches can be removed from the mounting plate after extracting the securing screws.

7 Refitting is a reversal of removal.

58 Heater temperature control cable assembly (XJ12 and Double Six, Series 2 on) – removal and refitting

1 Disconnect the battery and remove the centre console (Sec 46).

2 Remove the under scuttle casing.

3 Remove the radio/heater control mounting panel from the left-hand side of the heater.

4 Remove the four self-tapping screws which secure the air outlet duct in the right-hand footwell.
5 Remove the three self-tapping screws which secure the duct assembly in the right-hand footwell and at the rear outlet. One of these screws is located behind the control mounting panel and needs the use of a right-angled crosshead screwdriver.
6 Set the temperature control knob in the vent position, loosen the flap link operating rod locknut on the main drive wheel. Remove the nut and washer from the pivot of the main drive wheel.
7 Lift the jockey pulleys against the tension of the springs and withdraw the main drive wheel from its pivot.
8 Ease the radio/heater control panel and the right-hand footwell outlet assembly away from the heater.
9 Disconnect the control cable.
10 When refitting the cable, wind it round the main drive wheel $2\frac{1}{2}$ times. Make sure that the cable can be locked to the bollard on the wheel by the washer under the locking screw, but do not tighten it at this stage.
11 Set the temperature control at the 10 o'clock position and locate the cable round the jockey pulleys in such a way that the upper strand of the cable leaves the bollard and passes round the forward pulley. Pull the ends of the cable as far as possible horizontally and then adjust the cable until the nipples are level with each other.
12 Tighten the bollard locking screw and fit the cable end nipples into the main driving wheel, making sure that the ends of the cable do not cross.
13 Refit the radio/heater control panel and the footwell outlet assembly.
14 Keeping the cable taut, refit the main driving wheel to the pivot and screw on the nut and washer.
15 The flap linkage should be adjusted as described in the next Section.
16 Complete the refitting by reversing the rest of the removal operations.

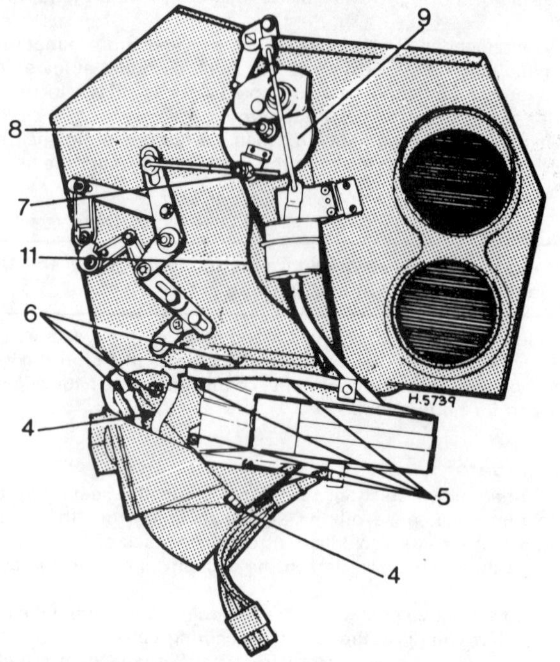

Fig. 12.63 Heater temperature control cable assembly (XJ12 and Double Six, Series 2 on) (Sec 58)

4 Control panel to heater securing unit
5 Footwell air outlet duct screws
6 Rear air outlet screws
7 Flap link rod nut
8 Drive wheel pivot nut
9 Main drive wheel
11 Temperature control cable

59 Heater flap linkage (XJ12 and Double Six, Series 2 on) – adjustment

1 Turn the temperature control knob to vent.
2 Refer to Fig. 12.64 and slacken the locking screws 'A', 'B' and 'C'.
3 Turn the lever 'R' to a fully clockwise position and hold in this position using firm finger-pressure. Tighten locking screw 'A'.
4 Press flap 'N' to a fully clockwise position and tighten locking screw 'C'.
5 Turn the temperature control knob to defrost. Using a screwdriver engaged in the slotted end of the adjusting link, push the operating flap 'Q' fully clockwise and tighten lockscrew 'B'.
6 The eccentric pivot 'T' on the upper flap actuating cam is adjustable through 180° to vary the level of face level air temperature.

60 Heater air grilles (XJ12 and Double Six, Series 2) – removal and refitting

Demister duct outlets

1 These can be removed by levering them from their surround.
2 Refit by pressing firmly into place.

Demister flap and actuator

3 Remove the crash roll from the facia (Section 38).
4 Remove the two nuts which secure the flap assembly to the screen rail.
5 Disconnect the plastic ducting and the vacuum tube and lift the flap/actuator assembly from the screen rail.
6 Refitting is a reversal of removal.

Ventilator facia outlets

7 Disconnect the battery.
8 Remove the facia (Section 38).
9 Unclip the side outlets at the rear of the facia or remove the four securing screws from the centre outlet.
10 Refitting is a reversal of removal.

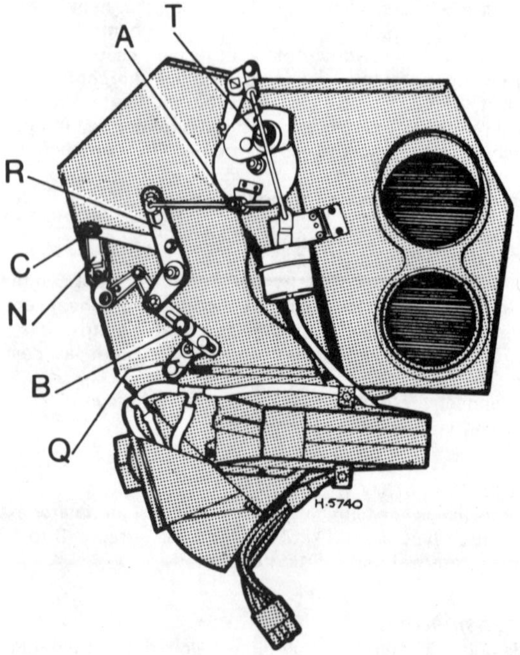

Fig. 12.64 Heater flap linkage (XJ12 and Double Six, Series 2 on) (Sec 59)

A Locking screw
B Locking screw
C Locking screw
N Lever operating flap
Q Lever operating flap
R Lever
T Eccentric pivot

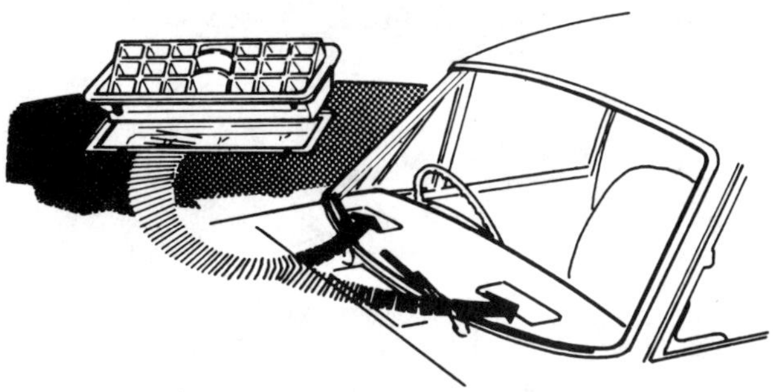

Fig. 12.65 Demister duct (XJ12 and Double Six, Series 2 on) (Sec 60)

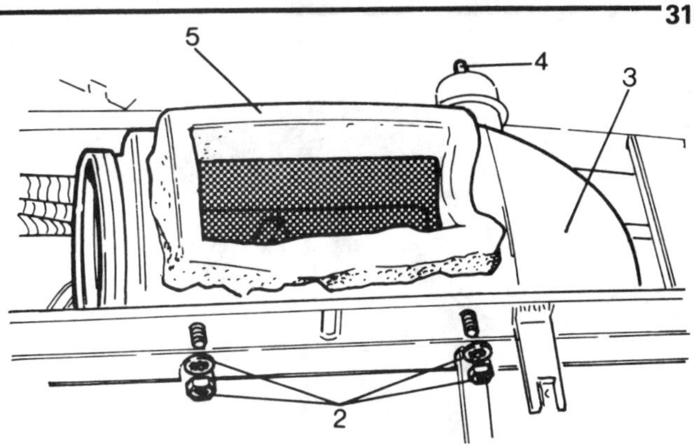

Fig. 12.66 Demister flap and actuator (XJ12 and Double Six, Series 2 on) (Sec 60)

2 · *Securing nuts to screen rail*
3 *Plastic ducting*
4 *Vacuum tube connection on actuator*
5 *Flap assembly*

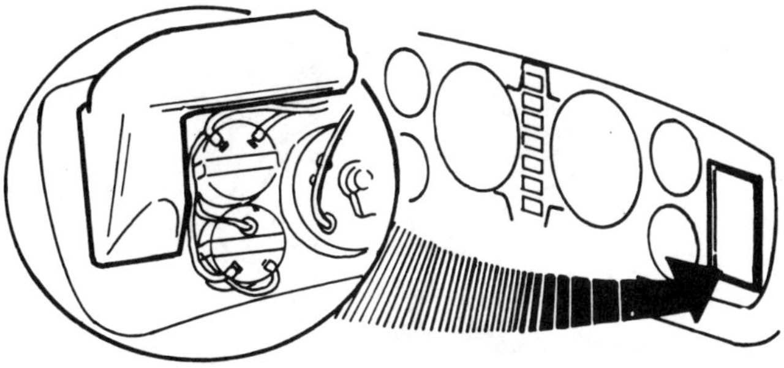

Fig. 12.67 Ventilator facia outlet (XJ12 and Double Six, Series 2 onwards (Sec 60)

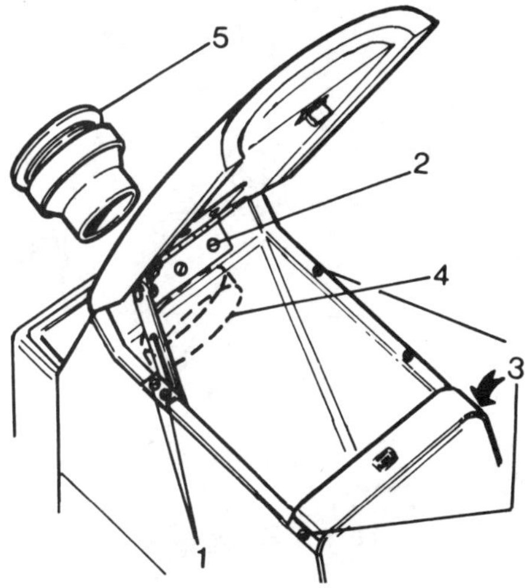

Fig. 12.68 Rear ventilator (XJ12 and Double Six, Series 2 on) (Sec 60)

1 *Lid retaining bar screws*
2 *Hinge plate screws*
3 *Liner screws*
4 *Air vent locking ring*
5 *Air vent assembly*

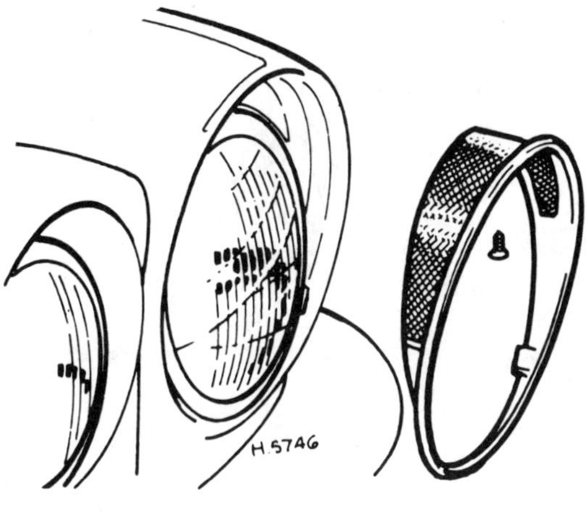

Fig. 12.69 Fresh air intake on outer headlamp (Sec 60)

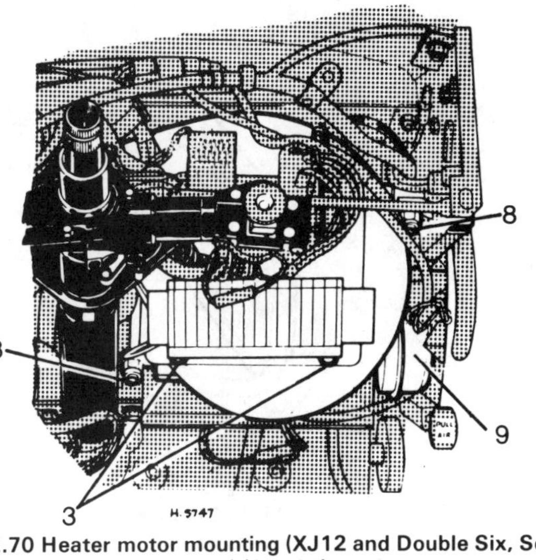

Fig. 12.70 Heater motor mounting (XJ12 and Double Six, Series 2 on) (Sec 61)

3 *Fuse block mounting nuts*
8 *Heater motor assembly mounting nuts*
9 *Vacuum actuator*

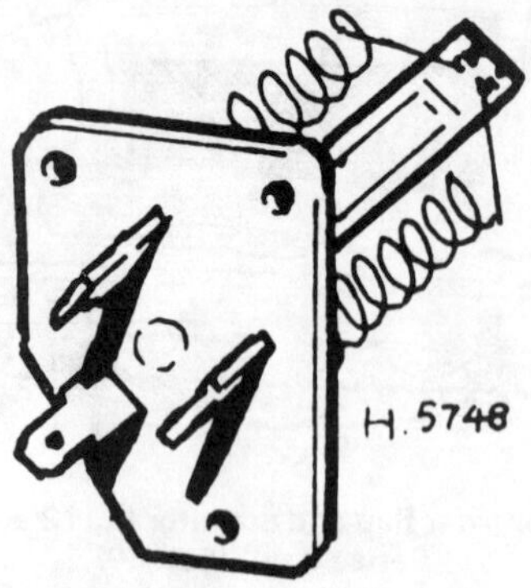

Fig. 12.71 Heater motor resistor (XJ12 and Double Six, Series 2 on) (Sec 6)

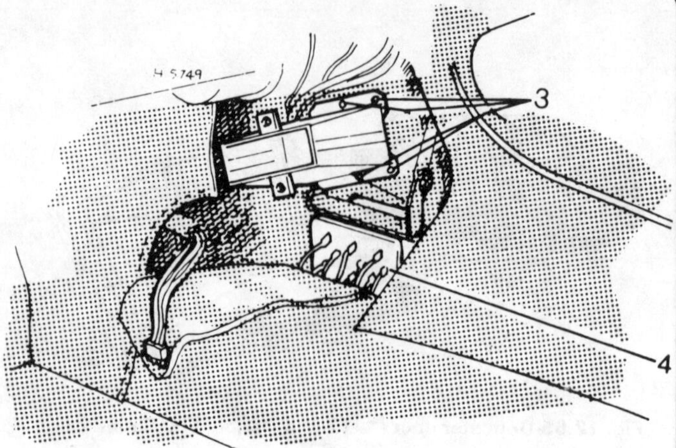

Fig. 12.72 Location of heater motor relays (XJ12 and Double Six, Series 2 on) (Sec 63)

3 Footwell air outlet *4 Heater relay*

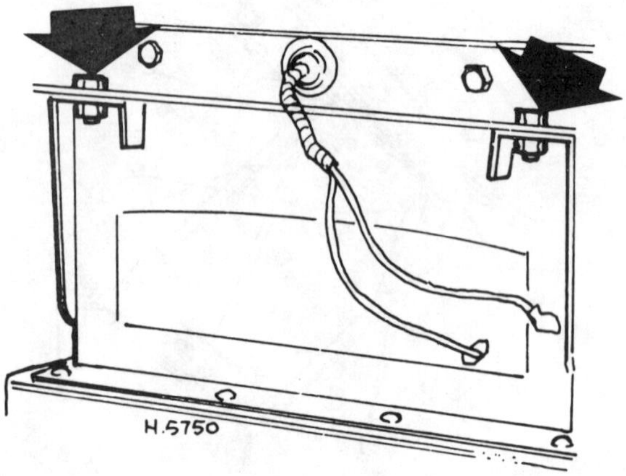

Fig. 12.73 Heater securing nuts on bulkhead (arrowed) (Sec 64)

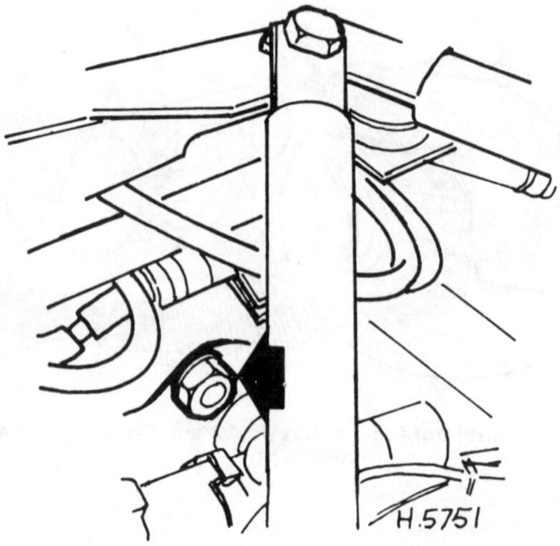

Fig. 12.74 Heater securing nuts on top rail (XJ12 and Double Six, Series 2 on) (Sec 64)

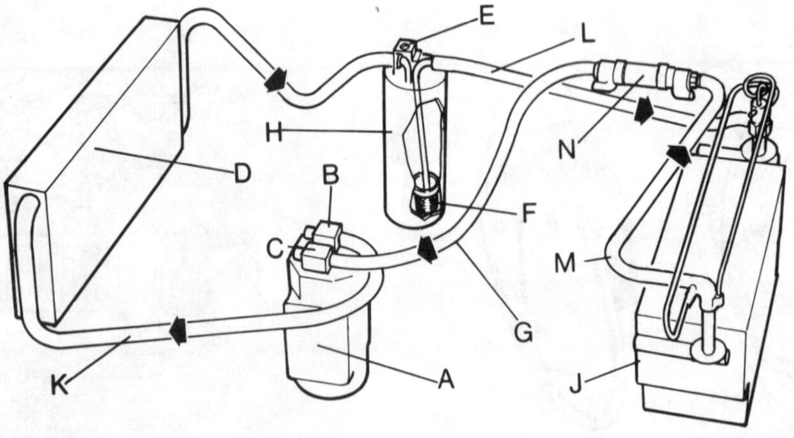

Fig. 12.75 Diagrammatic view of air conditioning system (XJ12, Double Six) (Sec 66)

A Compressor
B Discharge valve
C Suction valve
D Condensor
E Sight glass
F Bobbin
G Dessicant
H Receiver/drier
J Evaporator
K Hot vapour line
L Liquid
M Cold vapour line
N Heat exchanger (fuel)

Rear ventilator

11 Raise the console glovebox lid and extract the two screws which secure the lid retaining bar.
12 Withdraw the three screws which secure the hinge plate to the glovebox.
13 Extract the three screws which secure the glovebox liner.
14 Pass the hand under the glovebox liner and grip the bayonet type locking ring of the air vent assembly. Press in and rotate the vent anticlockwise until the locking ring releases. Withdraw the air vent assembly.

Fresh air intakes

15 To remove the grille from the scuttle just in front of the windscreen, prise it out with a sharp screwdriver.
16 Disconnect the washer tube from the washer jet.
17 To remove the intake grille located above the outer headlamp lens, withdraw the screw and lift the embellisher upwards to clear the lower retaining tags.
18 Refitting is a reversal of removal.

61 Heater motor/fan unit (XJ12 and Double Six, Series 2 on) – removal and refitting

1 Disconnect the battery.
2 Remove the under scuttle casing from the right-hand side if access to the right-hand motor is required or from the left-hand side if the left-hand motor is to be removed.
3 Remove the fusebox and move it to one side, or alternatively remove the glovebox liner, dependent upon whether the car is LHD or RHD and to which motor access is required. Inspection will enable the correct procedure to be adopted.
4 Pull the pliable air duct from the outlets at the side of the heater unit.
5 Remove the side facia panels.
6 Extract the two screws which secure the fresh air outlet control bracket.
7 Unscrew and remove the two motor mounting nuts, disconnect the vacuum tube from the actuator, disconnect the electrical leads and withdraw the motor/fan assembly.
8 Reassembly is a reversal of removal but the top air flap should be closed so that it can enter into its aperture and seal. To close the flap apply vacuum to the actuator by connecting a length of tubing between the open end of the original tubing and the actuator.

62 Heater motor resistance unit (XJ12 and Double Six, Series 2 on) – removal and refitting

Left-hand drive cars

1 Disconnect the battery and remove the facia under scuttle casing from the driver's side.
2 Remove the side panel from the centre console.
3 Mark the cables and disconnect them from the resistance unit.
4 Remove the three securing screws and withdraw the resistance unit from the heater casing.

Right-hand drive cars

5 Disconnect the battery.
6 Remove the glove compartment liner.
7 Repeat the operations described in paragraphs 3 and 4.

All cars

8 Refitting is a reversal of removal.

63 Heater motor relays (XJ12 and Double Six, Series 2 on) – removal and refitting

1 Disconnect the battery.
2 Remove the left-hand side casing from the centre console.
3 Remove the left-hand air outlet duct (four screws) from the footwell.
4 Mark the electrical leads and disconnect them.
5 Remove the securing nuts and withdraw the relay unit.
6 Refitting is a reversal of removal, but make sure that the earth lead is secured under one of the relay securing nuts.

64 Heater unit (XJ12 and Double Six, Series 2 on) – removal and refitting

1 Disconnect the battery and drain the cooling system.
2 Carry out the following operations described in other Sections of this Chapter:

Remove the facia crash roll.
Remove the facia side panel from the driver's side.
Remove the facia side panel from the passenger's side.
Remove the glove compartment liner.
Remove the centre parcels shelf.
Remove the centre console.
Remove the facia panel.

3 Disconnect the heater hoses from the nozzles on the engine compartment rear bulkhead.
4 Remove the two large nuts from the centre of the bulkhead within the engine compartment.
5 Remove the two retaining nuts from the centre of the top rail.
6 Remove the bayonet fixing type stub pipes from the sides of the heater unit.
7 Disconnect the vacuum control tubes but first mark them clearly for reconnection (photo).
8 Disconnect the multi-pin connectors at each side of the heater unit.
9 Ease the heater unit out and lift it from the car. Take care to protect the carpet against coolant which may be spilled during removal. The gearlever should be in '1' to prevent obstruction during removal of the heater.
10 Refitting is a reversal of the removal operations.

65 Heater matrix (XJ12 and Double Six, Series 2 on) – removal and refitting

1 Remove the heater unit, as described in the preceding Section.
2 Using a quick drying paint, mark the relative positions of all the heater control rods, knobs and cams.
3 Disconnect the tensioning springs from the heater matrix control flap operating arms.
4 Disconnect the operating rods.
5 Disconnect the inlet and outlet pipes from the heater casing.
6 Remove the heater matrix cover plate (six screws).

64.7 Heater vacuum control valve on engine compartment rear bulkhead

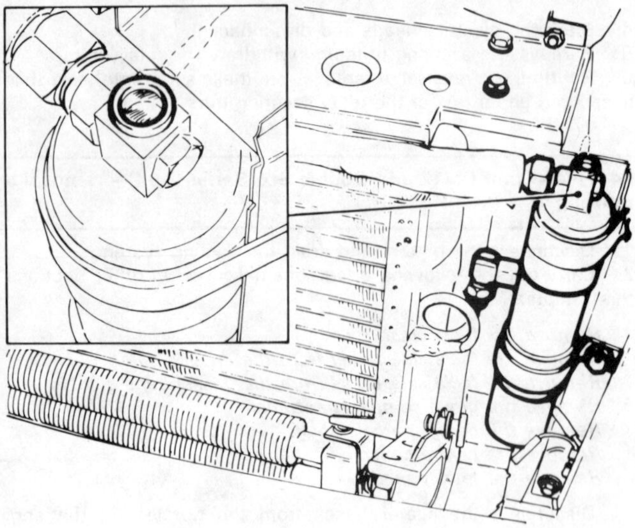

Fig. 12.76 Receiver/dryer unit (XJ12 and Double Six, Sereis 1) (Sec 67)

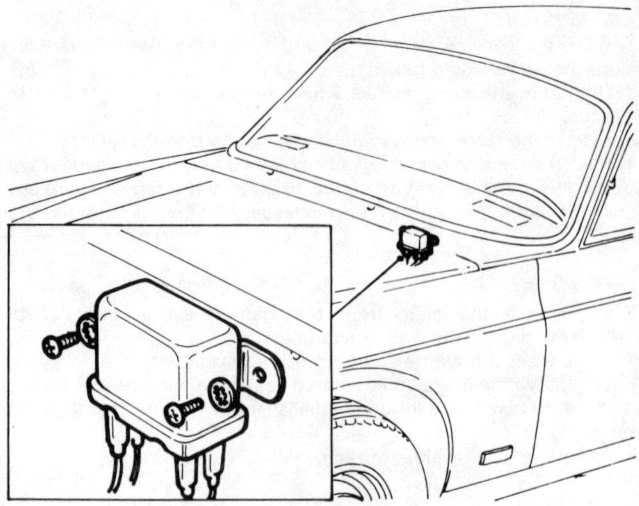

Fig. 12.77 Blower motor power relay (XJ12 and Double Six, Series 1) (Sec 67)

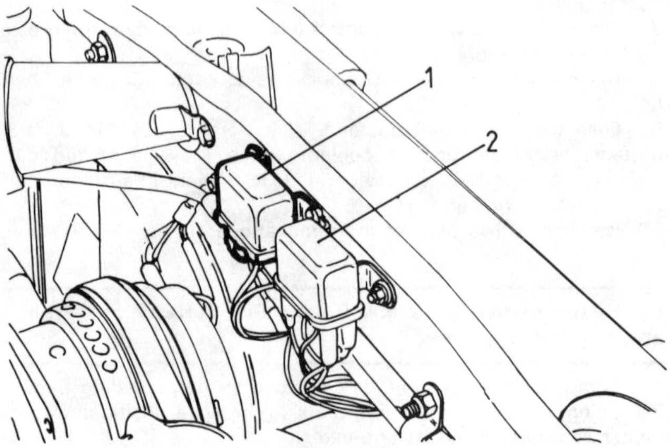

Fig. 12.78 Air conditioner main relay (XJ12 and Double Six, Series 1) (Sec 67)

1 Air conditioner relay *2 Headlamp relay*

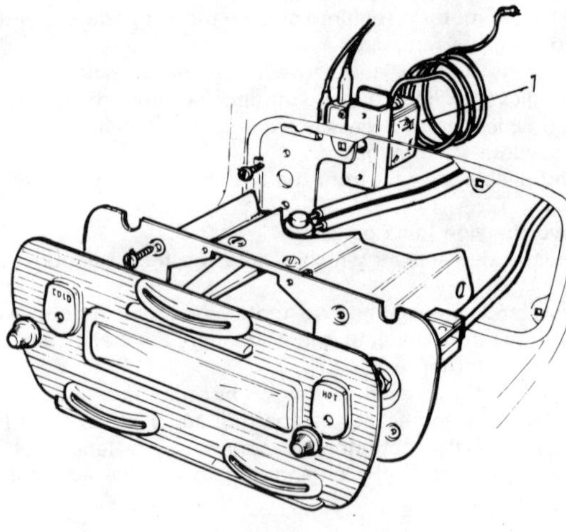

Fig. 12.79 Location of thermostat (1) (XJ12 and Double Six, Series 1) (Sec 67)

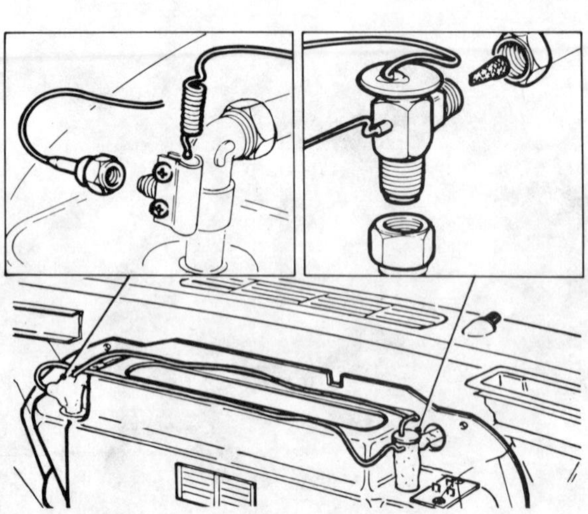

Fig. 12.80 Location of expansion valve (XJ12 and Double six, Series 1) (Sec 67)

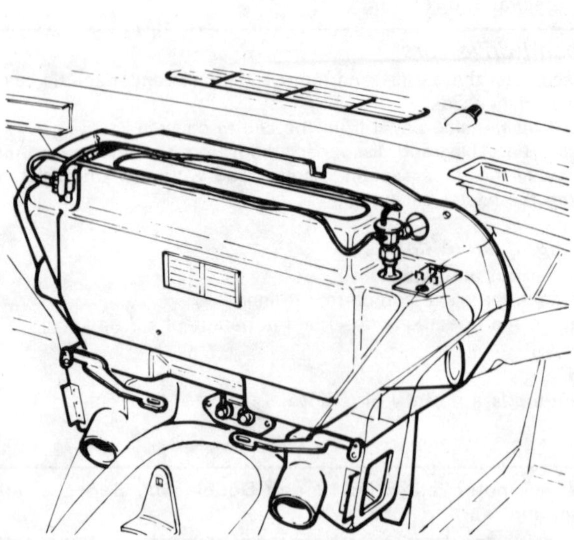

Fig. 12.81 Air conditioner (XJ12 and Double Six, Series 1) (Sec 68)

7 Remove the single screw which secures the cam and the operating arm to the footwell outlet flap shaft and remove the arm.
8 Withdraw the heater matrix from the side of the heater casing using a steady pull.
9 If the matrix has been leaking, do not waste your time trying to solder it as the heat must be localised otherwise more damage will be caused. It is better to renew the matrix on an exchange basis. If the matrix is blocked, try reverse flushing with a cold water hose. In extreme cases use a proprietary descaler and cleanser. If this fails, renew the matrix.
10 Refitting is a reversal of removal, but make sure that the shock absorbing pads are correctly positioned and that the control rods are connected with their paint marks in alignment.

66 Air conditioning system (XJ12, Double Six) – maintenance

1 This is a factory-fitted option and operations must be restricted to those described in the following Sections. On no account disconnect any part of the system as the gases and chemicals contained in the circuit can cause injury if released. If it is essential to remove one of the system components in order to gain access to other parts or assemblies always have the air conditioning system discharged and later recharged by your Jaguar/Daimler dealer or a professional refrigeration engineer.
2 Always seal pipes and components immediately the joints are disconnected in order to prevent the admission of moisture which must not be allowed to mix with, or be present in, the refrigerant, otherwise dangerous gases will be produced.
3 At the intervals specified in Routine Maintenance check the compressor drivebelt tension. This should be $\frac{1}{2}$ in (12.7 mm) total deflection at the centre of the belt.
4 Any adjustment should be carried out on the threaded adjuster rod which is accessible from under the car.
5 During the winter when the air conditioner is not normally in use, it is recommended that the system is operated for about ten minutes per week in order to maintain the components in good order.
6 If bubbles or foam appear in the sight glass (which is located adjacent to the compressor) when the system is operating, the system requires servicing by your dealer.
7 Every 12 months or before the summer have the oil level in the compressor checked by your dealer. This is a job requiring special equipment.
8 Water condensate is discharged from the air-conditioning system evaporator casing soon after the car stops and the blowers are switched off. This is a normal characterstic and a pool of water observed under cars fitted with these systems need cause no alarm.

67 Air conditioning system components (XJ12 and Double Six, Series 1) – removal and refitting

1 It is strongly recommended that the removal and refitting of any system components is left to your dealer. However, for those who feel competent to tackle the work, the system must first be discharged by your dealer before undertaking the operations marked *.
2 After the system has been discharged, disconnect the leads from the compressor as a precaution against it being operated inadvertently by engagement of its integral clutch.

Compressor and condensor**

3 Refer to Chapter 1 in connection with the removal of the engine/transmission. Always disconnect the battery.

*Receiver/dryer unit**

4 This is mounted on the left-hand side of the condensor.
5 Disconnect the pipelines from the unit and remove the mounting screws. Seal all openings immediately to avoid the admission of humid air.

Blower motor power relay

6 The location of the relay is as shown. Disconnect the battery before removing it. Remove the facia crash roll and the centre instrument panel when removing the override relay.

Main relay

7 This is located on the rear face of the radiator top rail. Disconnect the battery before removing it.

Thermostat

8 Pull the knobs from the heater/air conditioner control levers.
9 Lever the radio/heater escutcheon from its spring retainers.
10 Remove the parcels tray (four screws).
11 Unbolt and remove the air conditioner control panel and radio mounting bracket.
12 Extract the two screws which hold the temperature selector thermostatic switch.
13 Note the pattern of installation of the capillary tube and remove it from the evaporator casing. The length of tube inserted into the casing should be 4 inches (10.2 cm).
14 Disconnect cables and remove the thermostat.

Blower motor resistors

15 Refer to Section 55.

Blower motor relays

16 These are located adjacent to the power relay described in paragraph 6.

*Expansion valve**

17 Remove the facia crash roll, the facia side panel and the glovebox as described earlier in this Chapter.
18 Detach the relay which is mounted above the expansion valve.
19 Remove the sealing compound from around the valve and release the clip which holds the thermal bulb to the outlet pipe.
20 Disconnect the pipe unions and remove the valve.
21 Retrieve the gauze filter.

Blower assemblies

22 Refer to Section 55.

Refitting – all components

23 Refitting is a reversal of removal. Have the system recharged by your dealer or refrigeration engineer.

68 Air conditioning unit (XJ12 and Double Six, Series 1) – removal and refitting

1 Have the system discharged by your dealer or a refrigeration engineer.
2 Disconnect the battery.
3 Remove the front seats.
4 Remove the radio/heater control knobs and the escutcheon panel.
5 Remove the centre console.
6 Remove the parcels tray.
7 Remove the facia crash roll.
8 Remove the facia panel, instrument panel and glovebox.
9 Remove the two relays located under the crash roll. Move them to one side without disconnecting the electrical leads.
10 Release the fuse blocks from their mounting brackets and move them to one side.
11 Release the securing clips from the harness above the fuse blocks.
12 Disconnect the demister flap operating rods from the central control lever.
13 Prise out the air intake grille from the scuttle, and disconnect the control rods from the lever in the plenum chamber.
14 Disconnect all pipelines from the unit and immediately seal all openings in the pipelines and unit.
15 Extract the eight screws which hold the evaporator unit to the bulkhead. Withdraw the evaporator unit from the car.
16 Ducts may be removed if the rivets are drilled out and the sealing tape removed.
17 Refitting is a reversal of removal. Have the system recharged on completion.

69 Air conditioning system components (XJ12 and Double Six, Series 2 on) – removal and refitting

1 Refer to paragraph 1 of Section 67. If you are determined to work

on the air conditioning system, it must be discharged by your dealer or by a qualified refrigeration engineer before removing any component below marked*. Disconnect the leads from the compressor after discharging the system to prevent inadvertent operation.

Compressor and condensor**

2 Refer to Chapter 1 in connection with the removal of the engine/transmission. Always disconnect the battery.

*Receiver/drier unit**

3 The unit is located in front of the radiator top rail.
4 Disconnect the pipelines from the unit and remove the mounting screws. Seal the openings in the unit and the pipelines immediately.

Blower assembly

5 Refer to Section 61 and carry out the operations described. Additionally disconnect the electrical leads from the ambient temperature sensor.

In-car temperature sensor

6 Remove the centre parcels tray.
7 Disconnect the leads and air tube and extract the two sensor mounting screws.

Ambient temperature sensor

8 Remove the right-hand blower motor assembly (Section 61) and remove the sensor from the blower motor.

Blower motor power relay and relay box

9 Remove the left-hand front side panel from the centre console by removing the footwell air outlet grille (two screws).
10 Pull the relay directly downward from its mounting block.
11 The adjacent relay box can be unbolted and removed after extracting the connecting leads. Note the earth strap under one of the mounting nuts.
12 On later models, a four-way relay unit is fitted.

Temperature and mode selectors

13 Pull the knobs from the levers and remove the radio escutcheon panel.
14 Remove the centre console (Section 46).
15 Unbolt the selector mounting bracket from the heater/cooler unit. Identify and disconnect the vacuum pipes when removing the mode selector.
16 Disconnect the electrical leads. Note the location of the nylon limit stop and remove it from the operating shank.
17 Unbolt and remove the selector from its mounting when removing the temperature selector. Remove the switches in pairs.

Thermostat

18 Remove the right-hand front side panel from the centre console.
19 Remove the right-hand underscuttle casing.
20 Unbolt the thermostat from its bracket on the heater/cooler unit. Identify and disconnect the electrical leads.
21 Remove the thermostat by gently pulling the capillary tube.

Blower motor resistor units

22 Refer to Section 62.

Water valve temperature switch

23 Remove the under scuttle casing from the left-hand side of the car, also the glovebox liner from right-hand drive cars.
24 Identify and disconnect the electrical leads from the switch and then extract the switch mounting screws.

Water valve

25 Refer to Section 54 of this Chapter.

Expansion valve

26 Working within the engine compartment release the clip which holds the thermal bulb to the outlet pipe.
27 Disconnect the hose unions and seal the openings.
28 Remove the valve by unscrewing the union nut. Renew the mesh filter.

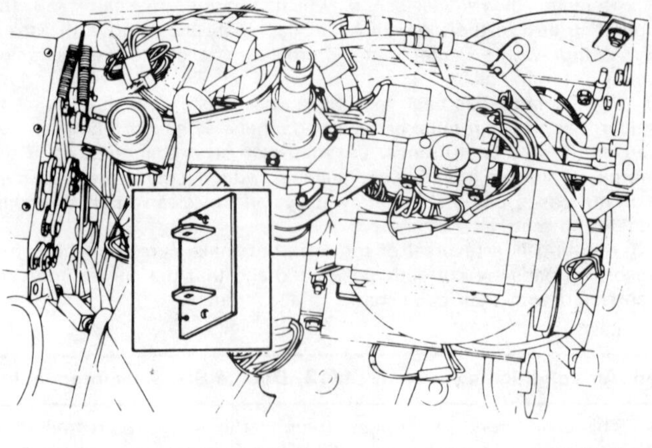

Fig. 12.82 In-car temperature sensor (XJ12 and Double Six, Series 2 on) (Sec 69)

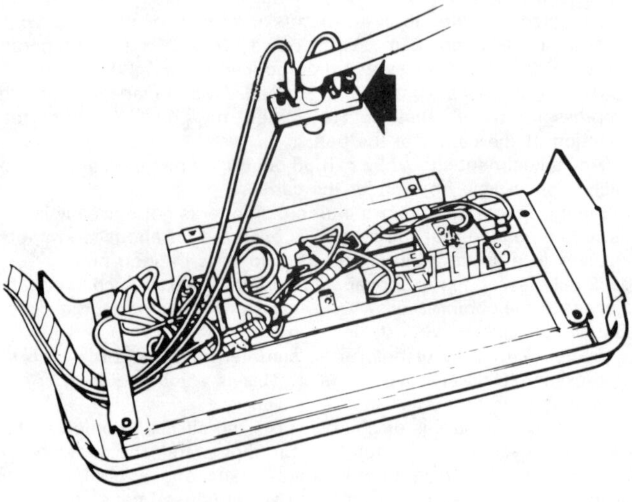

Fig. 12.83 Ambient temperature sensor (arrowed) (XJ12 and Double Six, Series 2 on) (Sec 69)

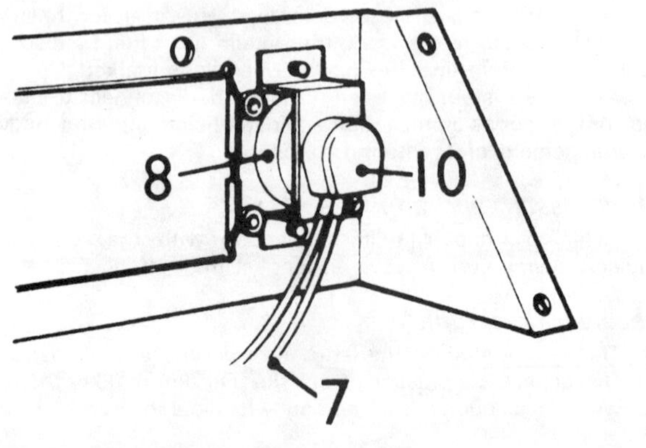

Fig. 12.84 Temperature selector (XJ12 and Double Six, Series 2 onwards) (Sec 69)

7 Leads
8 Nylon limit stop
10 Temperature selector

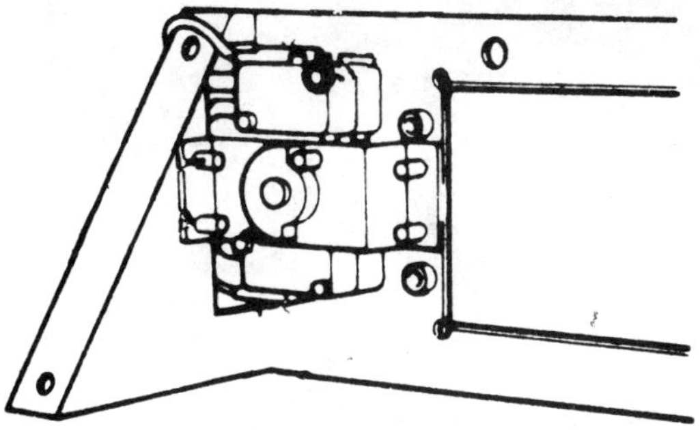

Fig. 12.85 Mode selector (XJ12 and Double Six, Series 2 on) (Sec 69)

Fig. 12.86 Water valve temperature switch (XJ12 and Double Six, Series 2 on) (Sec 69)

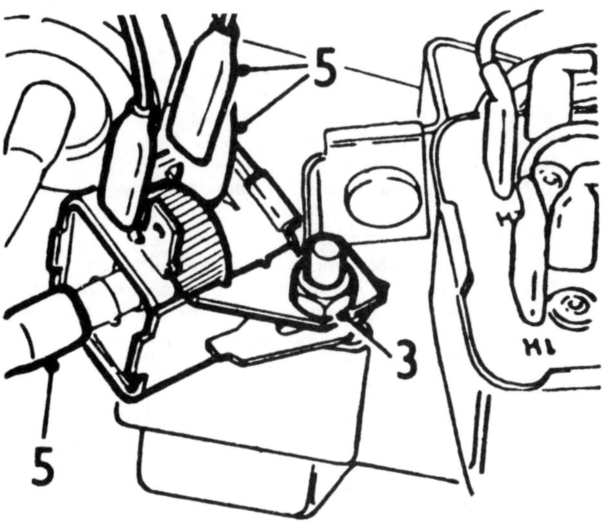

Fig. 12.87 Vacuum solenoid (XJ12 and Double Six, Series 2 on) (Sec 69)

3 Mounting nut
5 Vacuum tube
6 Electrical leads

Vacuum solenoid

29 Remove the left-hand front side panel from the centre console.
30 Unbolt the vacuum solenoid mounting bracket.
31 Identify and disconnect the electrical leads and vacuum pipes from the solenoid.

Servo and control unit

32 Remove the centre console (Section 46) and place the centre oddments tray and switch panel to one side without disconnecting the electrical leads.
33 Unbolt the control mounting bracket from the front of the heater/cooler unit and place to one side without detaching any connections.
34 Remove the footwell air inlet duct (four screws) followed by the three screws which hold the rear outlet duct and corner section of the heater/cooler unit.
35 Disconnect the two flap operating rods from their cam followers, also the wiring harness at its multi-pin socket.
36 Identify and then disconnect the vacuum pipes from the vacuum switches.
37 Remove the complete control unit and release it (two screws) from the rear outlet duct.

Amplifier unit

38 Remove the left-hand front side panel from the centre console.
39 Remove the air outlet duct (four screws).
40 Identify and disconnect the electrical leads from the relay box.
41 Unscrew and remove the nuts which hold the vacuum solenoid and relay box. Swing the relay box to one side to give access to the amplifier unit.
42 Remove the radio/air conditioner escutcheon.
43 Release the amplifier retaining clip with a flat blade and withdraw the amplifier from below the heater/cooler unit.
44 Disconnect the multi-pin plug and socket and the earth lead.
45 Refitting of all components is a reversal of removal but on completion, carry out the adjustments described in the following two Sections.

70 Air conditioner thermostat (XJ12 and Double Six, Series 2 on) – adjustment

1 Obtain access to the thermostat as described in the preceding Section.
2 Remove the clip from the rear of the thermostat and locate the adjusting screw.
3 One turn of the adjusting screw clockwise will increase the temperature by 5.4°F (3°C). The correct cut-in temperature is 35.6°F ± 1.8°F (2°C ± 1°C). The correct cut-out temperature is 33.8°F ± 1.8°F (1°C ± 1°C).

71 Air conditioner flap link (XJ12 and Double Six, Series 2 on) – adjustment

1 Before carrying out any adjustment, have the main system tension spring disconnected but the lower bypass spring connected.
2 Check that the top heater flap adjuster and bottom bypass adjustable link move freely.
3 Set the linkage in the 'FULL COLD' position by turning the servo motor clockwise. Apply slight pressure to the main link to ensure that the bottom heater flap only is closed.
4 Apply pressure to the top heater flap in a clockwise direction making sure that the flap seals. Lock the top heater flap adjuster.
5 Move the main link and check that both heater flaps close simultaneously.
6 Now move the linkage to the 'FULL HEAT' position by turning the servo motor anti-clockwise. The top heater flap should just make contact with the casing. Hold this setting, close the bottom bypass flap using the link and lock the link.
7 With the main linkage now set, rotate the main link rod to ensure that the flaps close at each end of their travel.
8 Connect the main tension spring and check that the lower bypass flap seals correctly.

72 Air conditioner (XJ12 and Double Six, Series 2 on) – removal and refitting

1 With the system discharged and the battery disconnected, drain the cooling system.
2 Remove the crash roll (Section 38).
3 Remove the under scuttle casing from the driver's side (Section 40) and the passenger's side.
4 Remove the glovebox liner and the centre parcels shelf.
5 Remove the centre console (Section 46) and the facia (Section 38).
6 Working within the engine compartment, disconnect the air conditioner hoses from the expansion valve (photo).
7 Disconnect the heater hoses from the bulkhead connectors.
8 Unscrew and remove the two large nuts located in the centre of the engine compartment rear bulkhead.
9 Remove the two retaining nuts from the centre of the top rail.
10 From the sides of the air conditioner, release the four pipe stubs which are secured by bayonet fittings.
11 Identify and disconnect the vacuum pipes.
12 Disconnect the multi-pin plugs from their sockets at each side of the unit.
13 Ease the unit forward and remove it from the car interior.
14 The evaporator can be withdrawn if the thermostat unit is first detached (two screws) and the backplate (twelve screws and two setscrews). Take care not to damage the capillary attached to the expansion valve.
15 Refit by reversing the removal operations and then have the system recharged by your dealer.

73 Air conditioning system (XJS) – maintenance

1 The air conditioning system is standard on all XJS models. It is similar to that described in Section 66, as is the maintenance procedure.
2 The unit is a combined heater/cooler assembly.

74 Air conditioning system components (XJS) – removal and refitting

1 Refer to Section 67 and observe the recommendations in paragraphs 1 and 2. System must be discharged before removal of components marked*.

Compressor and condensor**

2 Refer to Chapter 1 in connection with the removal of the engine/transmission. Note that the fuel cooler must be unbolted and swung to one side, away from the compressor. Always disconnect the battery.

*Receiver/drier unit**

3 Refer to Section 69, paragraphs 3 and 4.

Ambient temperature sensor

4 Remove the under scuttle casing from the passenger side as described in Section 40.
5 Identify the electrical leads and disconnect them from the sensor. Detach the sensor from the blower motor assembly.

In-car temperature sensor

6 Remove the facia panel as described in Section 39.
7 Remove the air tube and disconnect the electrical leads from the sensor.
8 Remove the sensor from its bracket by releasing the two plastic securing studs.

Blower motor power relay

9 Remove the left-hand front panel and air outlet grille from the centre console.
10 Disconnect the relay from its mounting block.

Temperature selector

11 Remove the centre console as described in Section 47.

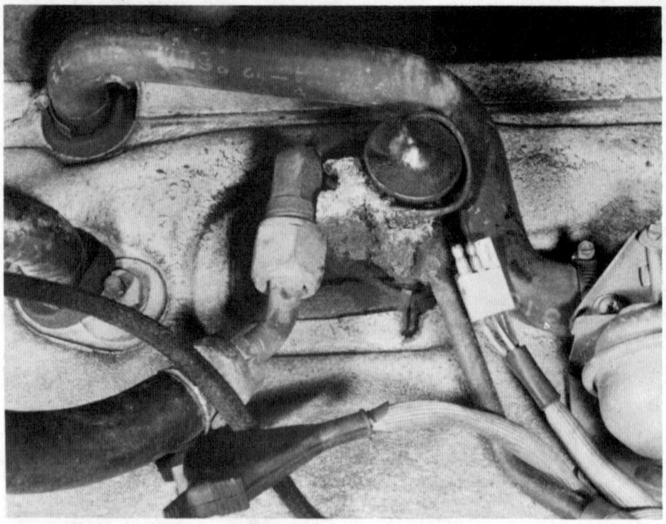

72.6 Air conditioner expansion valve on engine compartment rear bulkhead

12 Peel back the carpet from the lower end of the right-hand air conditioning assembly stay.
13 Unbolt this stay and ease it away from the switch panel on the right-hand side.
14 Remove the switch cover from the right-hand side.
15 Disconnect the vacuum pipes from the vacuum switch.
16 Disconnect the earth lead from the lower micro-switch.
17 Peel back the carpet from the lower end of the left-hand air conditioning assembly stay.
18 Unbolt this stay and ease it away from the switch panel on the left-hand side.
19 Release the panel from its mounting studs.
20 Identify the electrical leads and disconnect them at their snap connectors.
21 Unbolt the temperature selector from the switch panel.
22 Refitting is a reversal of removal.

Mode selector

23 Carry out the operations described in paragraphs 11 to 20.
24 Carefully pull the opticell fibre elements from the opticell lens hood.
25 Disconnect the mode selector electrical leads from the block connector.
26 Remove the switch panel and radio escutcheons.
27 Disconnect the electrical leads from the mode selector micro switches.
28 Note the location of the micro switches and unbolt each pair of switches. Retrieve the distance pieces.
29 Remove the vacuum switch.
30 Extract the circlip and remove the cam assembly.

Blower motor resistors

31 On left-hand drive cars, remove the under scuttle casing from the driver's side, also the front side panel from the centre console.
32 The resistor can then be removed from the heater/cooler unit.
33 On right-hand drive cars, remove the glovebox liner for access to the resistor.

Thermostat

34 The operations are as described in Section 69, paragraphs 18 to 21.

Water valve temperature switch

35 The operations are as described in Section 69, paragraphs 23 and 24.

Water valve servo unit

36 The operations are as described in Section 54, paragraphs 14 to 17.

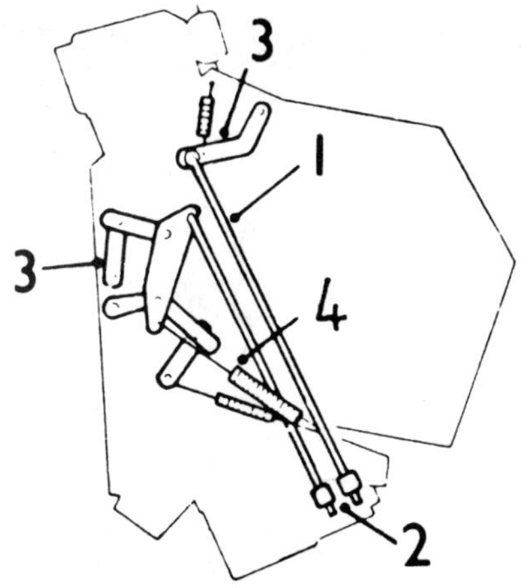

Fig. 12.88 Air conditioner flap link adjustment (XJ12 and Double Six, Series 2 on) (Sec 71)

1 Adjusting rods
2 Servo unit adjusters
3 Flap linkage
4 Tension spring

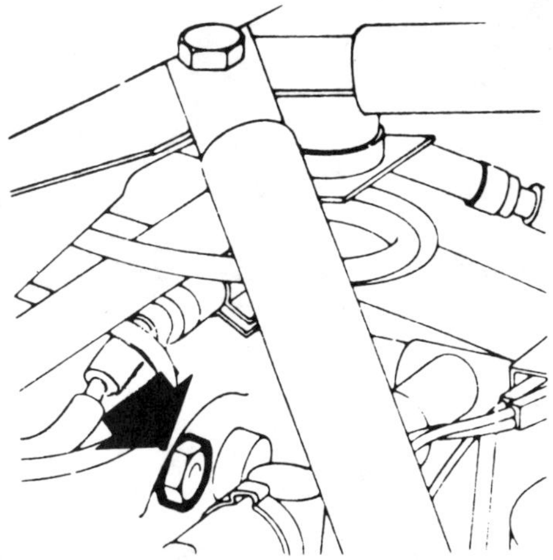

Fig. 12.89 Air conditioner mounting nut (arrowed) on engine compartment rear bulkhead (XJ12 and Double Six, Series 2 on) (Sec 72)

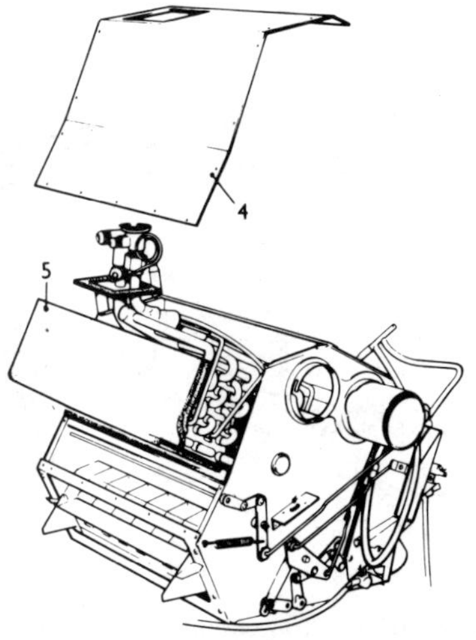

Fig. 12.90 Evaporator in air conditioner casing (XJ12 and Double Six, Series 2 on) (Sec 72)

4 Backplate
5 Evaporator

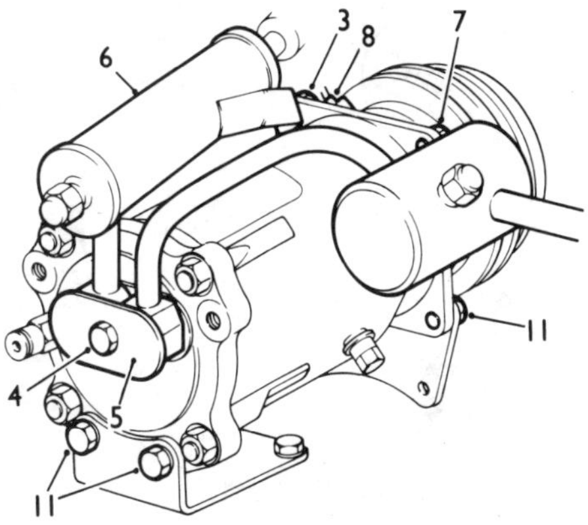

Fig. 12.91 Air conditioner compressor (XJS) (Sec 74)

3 Fuel cooler bracket
4 Valve/union assembly
5 Clamp plate
6 Fuel cooler
7 Silencer unit bracket
8 Electrical leads for operation of clutch
11 Compressor mounting bolts

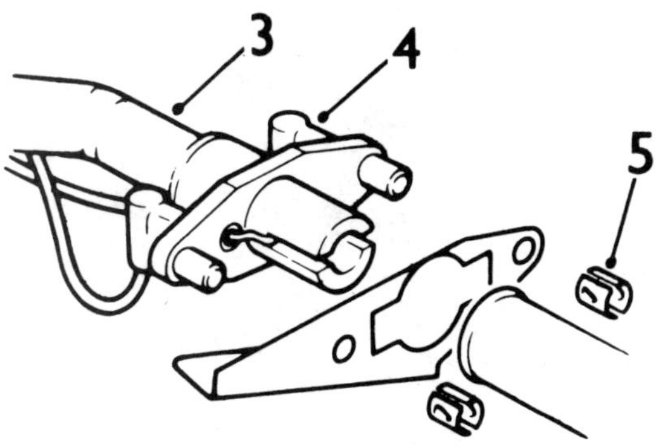

Fig. 12.92 In-car temperature sensor (XJS) (Sec 74)

3 Air tube
4 Electrical leads
5 Plastic securing studs

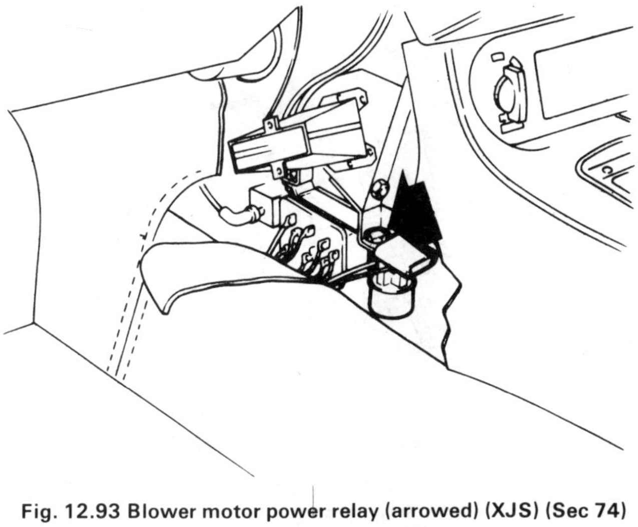

Fig. 12.93 Blower motor power relay (arrowed) (XJS) (Sec 74)

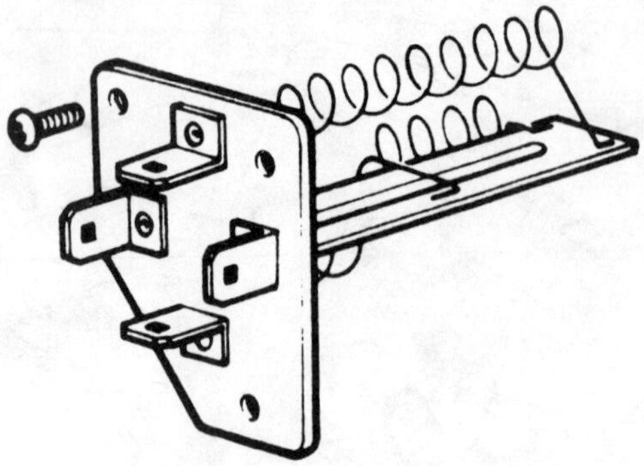

Fig. 12.94 Blower motor resistors (XJS) (Sec 74)

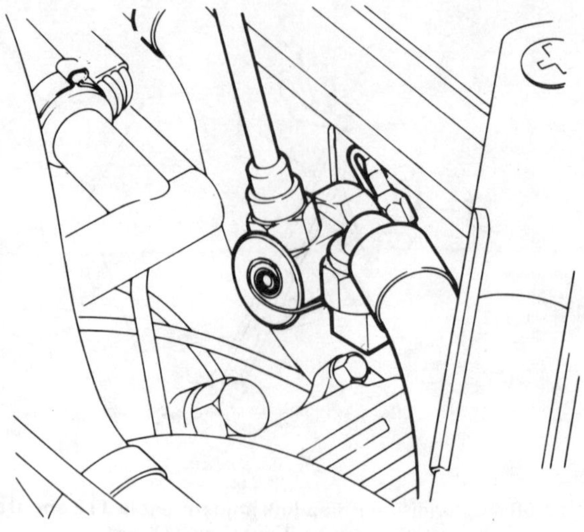

Fig. 12.95 Expansion valve (XJS) (Sec 74)

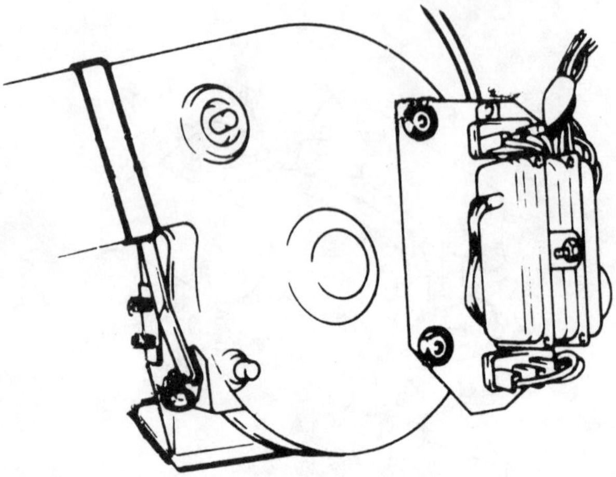

Fig. 12.96 Blower assembly (XJS) (Sec 74)

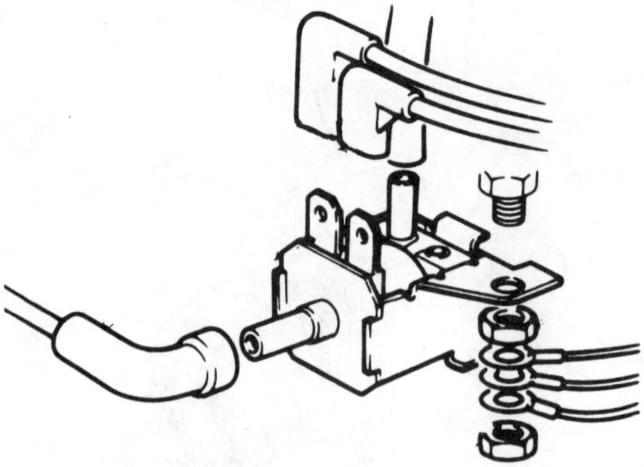

Fig. 12.97 Vacuum solenoid (XJS) (Sec 74)

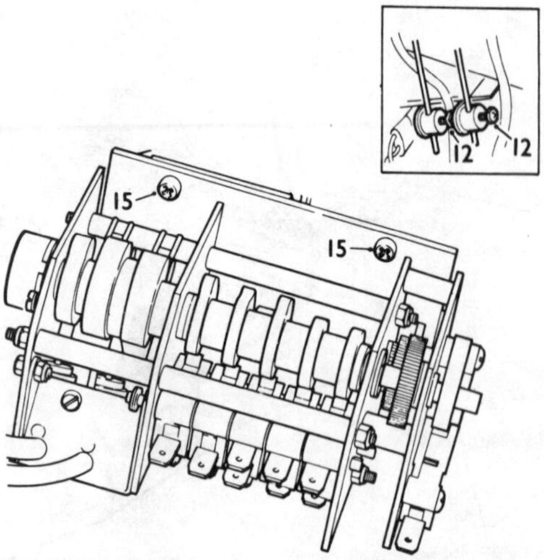

Fig. 12.98 Servo and control unit (XJS) (Sec 74)

12 Servo-controlled rods and clamps
15 Control assembly securing screws to air conditioner casing

Fig. 12.99 Location of amplifier unit (XJS) (Sec 74)

*Expansion valve**

37 Partially drain the cooling system.
38 Disconnect the hoses by releasing the unions. Plug or cap all openings immediately.
39 Disconnect the hose from the water valve and move it clear of the expansion valve.
40 Carefully remove the asbestos insulation from the capillary tube, then disconnect the capillary tube at its union.
41 Release the valve by unscrewing the union nut.
42 Release the capillary tube clamp from the valve, withdraw the valve and retrieve the gauze filter. Renew this filter.

Blower assembly (right-hand)

43 Remove the under scuttle casing and side panel from the front of the centre console.
44 On left-hand drive cars, remove the glovebox liner and unbolt the component mounting plate from the blower assembly.
45 Disconnect the in-car sensor hose from the blower duct.
46 Disconnect the flexible duct from the outlets on the side of the air conditioning unit.
47 Disconnect the blower electrical harness at the block connector.
48 Disconnect the vacuum pipe from the flap mechanism.
49 On right-hand drive cars, release the nuts on the bottom of the fuse box mounting plate, then those at the top. Move the fuse box clear of the blower.
50 Wedge open the flap in the base of the blower assembly.
51 Unbolt the blower from its mounting brackets and ease it from its location.

Blower assembly (left-hand)

52 The operations are similar to those described for a right-hand blower, but reverse the operations described for left-hand and right-hand drive cars.

Vacuum solenoid

53 The operations are similar to those described in Section 69, paragraphs 29 to 31.

Servo and control unit

54 Remove the centre console.
55 Remove the rear footwell ducting.
56 Remove the bolt that holds the support stay on the right-hand side of the air conditioner.
57 Remove the right-hand mode control switch cover and harness clip.
58 Identify and disconnect the vacuum hoses from the mode control switch also the earth lead.
59 Release the control switch panel.
60 Remove the lower bolt from the left-hand support stay.
61 Disconnect the necessary leads and move the switch panel to one side.
62 Remove the right-hand footwell outlet vent.
63 Mark the setting of the servo-controlled operating rods and slacken the clamp screws.
64 Identify and disconnect the vacuum pipes from the actuators.
65 Disconnect the electrical harness from the multi-pin connectors.
66 Unscrew the screws which hold the servo and control unit to the air conditioner and withdraw it.

Amplifier unit

67 The operations are as described in Section 69, paragraphs 38 to 44.

Refitting – all components

68 The refitting of all components is a reversal of removal. Adjust the flap link as described in Section 71.

75 Air conditioner (XJS) – removal and refitting

1 Have the system discharged by your dealer and disconnect the electrical leads from the compressor as a precaution against it being operated.
2 Disconnect the battery.
3 Drain the cooling system.
4 Remove the facia panel as described in Section 39.
5 Remove the centre console as described in Section 47.
6 Disconnect the air conditioning hoses at their connectors on the engine compartment bulkhead and expansion valve.
7 Disconnect the heater hoses at their bulkhead connectors.
8 Unscrew the air conditioner mounting nuts from the engine compartment rear bulkhead.
9 Unclip the wiring harness from the screen rail.
10 Unbolt the demist duct support rail from the body and remove it.
11 DIsconnect the flexible ducting from the stub pipes on the air conditioner.
12 Remove the rear compartment ducts.
13 Remove the air conditioner support stays.
14 Remove the cover from the automatic transmission selector quadrant.
15 Remove the bolts which hold the upper steering column to its mounting bracket and extract the support stays and earth leads.
16 Unbolt the mounting bracket from the screen rail.
17 Identify and disconnect the blower flap vacuum pipes at the tee piece.
18 Disconnect the demister duct vacuum pipe from the servo.
19 Disconnect the main panel harness electrical connectors and unclip the harness.
20 Unclip the in-car sensor from the left-hand bulkhead support.
21 Detach the switch mounting panel from the air conditioner.
22 Remove the mode selector switch protective plate, then identify and disconnect the vacuum pipes from the switch.
23 Disconnect the earth lead and motor harness multi-pin plug, then the mode selector switch leads, and withdraw the switch. Disconnect the remaining vacuum pipes from below the air conditioner.
24 At their block connectors, disconnect the in-car sensor cables.
25 Disconnect the leads from the ambient temperature sensor on the right-hand blower.
26 Disconnect the multi-pin connector for the wiper motor harness on the bulkhead.
27 Ease the drain tubes clear of their grommets in the transmission tunnel.
28 Move the main panel harness clear of the air conditioner.
29 Ease the demist duct studs from the screen rail and withdraw the demist duct.
30 Extract the screw which holds the air conditioner to the top rail and withdraw it carefully from its location.
31 The demist ducts, face level vents and brackets can now be detached if required.
32 If the heater matrix or evaporator are to be removed from the air conditioner, refer to one or both of the following Sections.
33 Refitting the air conditioner is a reversal of removal. Have the system charged on completion.

76 Heater matrix (XJS) – removal and refitting

1 With the air conditioner removed, mark the settings of all control rods and operating levers.
2 Disconnect the electrical leads from the resistor on the blower motor.
3 Disconnect the leads from the water valve temperature switch.
4 Unclip the harness and vacuum pipe.
5 Disengage the return springs from their operating levers.
6 Disconnect the operating lever from the flap hinge.
7 Release the screw which holds the operating rod (from vacuum servo to flap lever) on the matrix cover. Release the lever from the rod.
8 Extract the screws which hold the matrix cover plate to the air conditioner casing.
9 Extract the screws from the matrix pipe bracket and remove the bracket and pipe clips.
10 Pull the matrix straight out of the air conditioner unit.
11 Remove the asbestos sleeve from the top pipe, then the cover plate and the water valve temperature switch.
12 Refitting is a reversal of removal but renew the foam insulating pads if necessary.

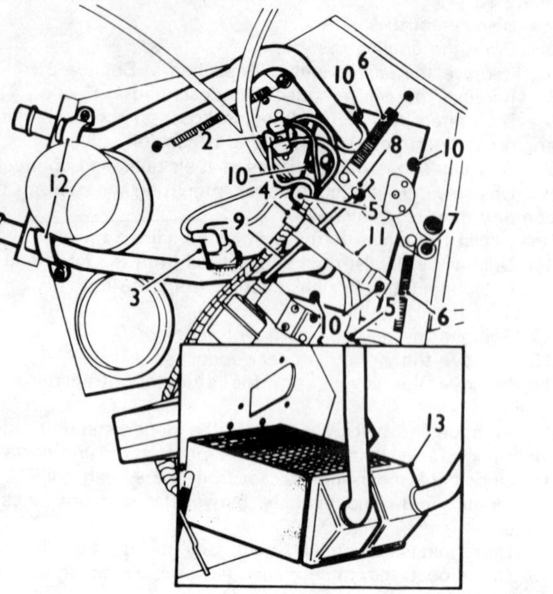

Fig. 12.100 Heater matrix withdrawn from air conditioner casing (XJS) (Sec 76)

2 *Blower motor resistance unit*
3 *Water valve temperature switch*
4 *Wiring harness clip*
5 *Vacuum pipe clips*
6 *Lever return springs*
7 *Lower flap lever screw*
8 *Vacuum servo rod screw*
9 *Vacuum servo rod*
10 *Matrix cover plate screws*
11 *Matrix pipe bracket*
12 *Matrix pipe clips*
13 *Matrix*

77 Evaporator (XJS) – removal and refitting

1 Remove the air conditioner as described in Section 75.
2 Extract the screws from the heater matrix pipe bracket.
3 Extract the screws and remove the backplate from the air conditioner. Ease the insulating pad away and withdraw the screws which hold the expansion valve mounting plate to the backplate. Ease the backplate over the expansion valve, without damaging the capillary tube.
4 Disconnect the leads from the thermostat on the side of the air conditioner.
5 Release the thermostat screws and ease the capillary tube clear of the evaporator.
6 Carefully withdraw the evaporator from the air conditioner casing.
7 Refitting is a reversal of removal but renew the foam insulating pads if necessary.

Metric conversion tables

Inches	Decimals	Millimetres
1/64	0.015625	0.3969
1/32	0.03125	0.7937
3/64	0.046875	1.1906
1/16	0.0625	1.5875
5/64	0.078125	1.9844
3/32	0.09375	2.3812
7/64	0.109375	2.7781
1/8	0.125	3.1750
9/64	0.140625	3.5719
5/32	0.15625	3.9687
11/64	0.171875	4.3656
3/16	0.1875	4.7625
13/64	0.203125	5.1594
7/32	0.21875	5.5562
15/64	0.234375	5.9531
1/4	0.25	6.3500
17/64	0.265625	6.7469
9/32	0.28125	7.1437
19/64	0.296875	7.5406
5/16	0.3125	7.9375
21/64	0.328125	8.3344
11/32	0.34375	8.7312
23/64	0.359375	9.1281
3/8	0.375	9.5250
25/64	0.390625	9.9219
13/32	0.40625	10.3187
27/64	0.421875	10.7156
7/16	0.4375	11.1125
29/64	0.453125	11.5094
15/32	0.46875	11.9062
31/64	0.484375	12.3031
1/2	0.5	12.7000
33/64	0.515625	13.0969
17/32	0.53125	13.4937
35/64	0.546875	13.8906
9/16	0.5625	14.2875
37/64	0.578125	14.6844
19/32	0.59375	15.0812
39/64	0.609375	15.4781
5/8	0.625	15.8750
41/64	0.640625	16.2719
21/32	0.65625	16.6687
43/64	0.671875	17.0656
11/16	0.6875	17.4625
45/64	0.703125	17.8594
23/32	0.71875	18.2562
47/64	0.734375	18.6531
3/4	0.75	19.0500
49/64	0.765625	19.4469
25/32	0.78125	19.8437
51/64	0.796875	20.2406
13/16	0.8125	20.6375
53/64	0.828125	21.0344
27/32	0.84375	21.4312
55/64	0.859375	21.8281
7/8	0.875	22.2250
57/64	0.890625	22.6219
29/32	0.90625	23.0187
59/64	0.921875	23.4156
15/16	0.9375	23.8125
61/64	0.953125	24.2094
31/32	0.96875	24.6062
63/64	0.984375	25.0031

Millimetres to Inches

mm	Inches
0.01	0.00039
0.02	0.00079
0.03	0.00118
0.04	0.00157
0.05	0.00197
0.06	0.00236
0.07	0.00276
0.08	0.00315
0.09	0.00354
0.1	0.00394
0.2	0.00787
0.3	0.01181
0.4	0.01575
0.5	0.01969
0.6	0.02362
0.7	0.02756
0.8	0.03150
0.9	0.03543
1	0.03937
2	0.07874
3	0.11811
4	0.15748
5	0.19685
6	0.23622
7	0.27559
8	0.31496
9	0.35433
10	0.39370
11	0.43307
12	0.47244
13	0.51181
14	0.55118
15	0.59055
16	0.62992
17	0.66929
18	0.70866
19	0.74803
20	0.78740
21	0.82677
22	0.86614
23	0.09551
24	0.94488
25	0.98425
26	1.02362
27	1.06299
28	1.10236
29	1.14173
30	1.18110
31	1.22047
32	1.25984
33	1.29921
34	1.33858
35	1.37795
36	1.41732
37	1.4567
38	1.4961
39	1.5354
40	1.5748
41	1.6142
42	1.6535
43	1.6929
44	1.7323
45	1.7717

Inches to Millimetres

Inches	mm
0.001	0.0254
0.002	0.0508
0.003	0.0762
0.004	0.1016
0.005	0.1270
0.006	0.1524
0.007	0.1778
0.008	0.2032
0.009	0.2286
0.01	0.254
0.02	0.508
0.03	0.762
0.04	1.016
0.05	1.270
0.06	1.524
0.07	1.778
0.08	2.032
0.09	2.286
0.1	2.54
0.2	5.08
0.3	7.62
0.4	10.16
0.5	12.70
0.6	15.24
0.7	17.78
0.8	20.32
0.9	22.86
1	25.4
2	50.8
3	76.2
4	101.6
5	127.0
6	152.4
7	177.8
8	203.2
9	228.6
10	254.0
11	279.4
12	304.8
13	330.2
14	355.6
15	381.0
16	406.4
17	431.8
18	457.2
19	482.6
20	508.0
21	533.4
22	558.8
23	584.2
24	609.6
25	635.0
26	660.4
27	685.8
28	711.2
29	736.6
30	762.0
31	787.4
32	812.8
33	838.2
34	863.6
35	889.0
36	914.4

Length (distance)

Unit	Multiply	=	Multiply	=
Inches (in)	X 25.4	= Millimetres (mm)	X 0.039	= Inches (in)
Feet (ft)	X 0.305	= Metres (m)	X 3.281	= Feet (ft)
Miles	X 1.609	= Kilometres (km)	X 0.621	= Miles

Volume (capacity)

Unit	Multiply	=	Multiply	=
Cubic inches (cu in; in^3)	X 16.387	= Cubic centimetres (cc; cm^3)	X 0.061	= Cubic inches (cu in; in^3)
Imperial pints (Imp pt)	X 0.568	= Litres (l)	X 1.76	= Imperial pints (Imp pt)
Imperial quarts (Imp qt)	X 1.137	= Litres (l)	X 0.88	= Imperial quarts (Imp qt)
Imperial quarts (Imp qt)	X 1.201	= US quarts (US qt)	X 0.833	= Imperial quarts (Imp qt)
US quarts (US qt)	X 0.946	= Litres (l)	X 1.057	= US quarts (US qt)
Imperial gallons (Imp gal)	X 4.546	= Litres (l)	X 0.22	= Imperial gallons (Imp gal)
Imperial gallons (Imp gal)	X 1.201	= US gallons (US gal)	X 0.833	= Imperial gallons (Imp gal)
US gallons (US gal)	X 3.785	= Litres (l)	X 0.264	= US gallons (US gal)

Mass (weight)

Unit	Multiply	=	Multiply	=
Ounces (oz)	X 28.35	= Grams (g)	X 0.035	= Ounces (oz)
Pounds (lb)	X 0.454	= Kilograms (kg)	X 2.205	= Pounds (lb)

Force

Unit	Multiply	=	Multiply	=
Ounces-force (ozf; oz)	X 0.278	= Newtons (N)	X 3.6	= Ounces-force (ozf; oz)
Pounds-force (lbf; lb)	X 4.448	= Newtons (N)	X 0.225	= Pounds-force (lbf; lb)
Newtons (N)	X 0.1	= Kilograms-force (kgf; kg)	X 9.81	= Newtons (N)

Pressure

Unit	Multiply	=	Multiply	=
Pounds-force per square inch (psi; lbf/in^2; lb/in^2)	X 0.070	= Kilograms-force per square centimetre (kgf/cm^2; kg/cm^2)	X 14.223	= Pounds-force per square inch (psi; lbf/in^2; lb/in^2)
Pounds-force per square inch (psi; lbf/in^2; lb/in^2)	X 0.068	= Atmospheres (atm)	X 14.696	= Pounds-force per square inch (psi; lbf/in^2; lb/in^2)
Pounds-force per square inch (psi; lbf/in^2; lb/in^2)	X 0.069	= Bars	X 14.5	= Pounds-force per square inch (psi; lbf/in^2; lb/in^2)
Pounds-force per square inch (psi; lbf/in^2; lb/in^2)	X 6.895	= Kilopascals (kPa)	X 0.145	= Pounds-force per square inch (psi; lbf/in^2; lb/in^2)
Kilopascals (kPa)	X 0.01	= Kilograms-force per square centimetre (kgf/cm^2; kg/cm^2)	X 98.1	= Kilopascals (kPa)

Torque (moment of force)

Unit	Multiply	=	Multiply	=
Pounds-force inches (lbf in; lb in)	X 1.152	= Kilograms-force centimetre (kgf cm; kg cm)	X 0.868	= Pounds-force inches (lbf in; lb in)
Pounds-force inches (lbf in; lb in)	X 0.113	= Newton metres (Nm)	X 8.85	= Pounds-force inches (lbf in; lb in)
Pounds-force inches (lbf in; lb in)	X 0.083	= Pounds-force feet (lbf ft; lb ft)	X 12	= Pounds-force inches (lbf in; lb in)
Pounds-force feet (lbf ft; lb ft)	X 0.138	= Kilograms-force metres (kgf m; kg m)	X 7.233	= Pounds-force feet (lbf ft; lb ft)
Pounds-force feet (lbf ft; lb ft)	X 1.356	= Newton metres (Nm)	X 0.738	= Pounds-force feet (lbf ft; lb ft)
Newton metres (Nm)	X 0.102	= Kilograms-force metres (kgf m; kg m)	X 9.804	= Newton metres (Nm)

Power

Unit	Multiply	=	Multiply	=
Horsepower (hp)	X 745.7	= Watts (W)	X 0.0013	= Horsepower (hp)

Velocity (speed)

Unit	Multiply	=	Multiply	=
Miles per hour (miles/hr; mph)	X 1.609	= Kilometres per hour (km/hr; kph)	X 0.621	= Miles per hour (miles/hr; mph)

*Fuel consumption**

Unit	Multiply	=	Multiply	=
Miles per gallon, Imperial (mpg)	X 0.354	= Kilometres per litre (km/l)	X 2.825	= Miles per gallon, Imperial (mpg)
Miles per gallon, US (mpg)	X 0.425	= Kilometres per litre (km/l)	X 2.352	= Miles per gallon, US (mpg)

Temperature

Degrees Fahrenheit (°F) $= (°C \times \frac{9}{5}) + 32$

Degrees Celsius (Degrees Centigrade; °C) $= (°F - 32) \times \frac{5}{9}$

**It is common practice to convert from miles per gallon (mpg) to litres/100 kilometres (l/100km), where mpg (Imperial) x l/100 km = 282 and mpg (US) x l/100 km = 235*

Index

C

D

E

F

G

T

V

W

Printed by
Haynes Publishing Group
Sparkford Yeovil Somerset
England